W9-ABP-908

sauces

Classical and Contemporary

Sauce Making

JAMES PETERSON

sauces

Classical and Contemporary Sauce Making

THIRD EDITION

WILEY

JOHN WILEY & SONS, INC.

Published by John Wiley & Sons, Inc., Hoboken, New Jersey
Published simultaneously in Canada

Design: BTDNYC
Composition: Jeff Baker

Library of Congress Cataloging-in-Publication Data

Peterson, James.
   Sauces : classical and contemporary sauce making / James Peterson. — 3rd ed.
      p. cm.
   Includes bibliographical references and index.
   ISBN 978-0-470-19496-6
   1. Sauces. I. Title.
   TX819.A1P47 2008
   641.8'14—dc22

                             2007046546

Printed in the United States of America
10 9 8 7 6 5 4 3 2 1

To Megan Moore

Contents

Recipe Contents

CHAPTER 6
WHITE SAUCES FOR
MEAT AND VEGETABLES

CHAPTER 7
BROWN SAUCES

CHAPTER 8
STOCK-BASED AND NON-INTEGRAL FISH SAUCES 201

CHAPTER 9
INTEGRAL MEAT SAUCES 221

CHAPTER **10**

INTEGRAL FISH AND
SHELLFISH SAUCES 287

CHAPTER **15**
BUTTER SAUCES

CHAPTER **16**
SALAD SAUCES, VINAIGRETTES, SALSAS, AND RELISHES

CHAPTER 17

PURÉES AND PURÉE-THICKENED SAUCES

CHAPTER 18

PASTA SAUCES

CHAPTER 19
ASIAN SAUCES

CHAPTER 20
DESSERT SAUCES

Acknowledgments

I'd first like to thank my editor, Pam Chirls, for continuing to be enthusiastic and committed to keeping *Sauces* up to date and always fresh. I owe many thanks to my assistant, recipe tester, and muse, Alice Piacenza. I have much admiration for the editorial team who put the new edition together, including Christine DiComo, Christina Solazzo, and Ava Wilder. The designer, Beth Tondreau, and the compositor, Jeff Baker, both did an incredible job. The copyediting was amazingly thorough because of the work of Suzanne Fass. Appreciation goes to Todd Coleman for his input on the jacket photography and for his great eye. And special thanks must go to Jeff Faust for designing the jacket and to Brent Savage who labored in Photoshop to make the chapter opening photographs look great. I must also thank my partner, Zelik Mintz, for always standing behind me and encouraging me when I become my own worst critic. Thanks must also go to my agents, Elise and Arnold Goodman, for their warmth and friendship. I'd also like to thank Sarah Leuze and Joel Hoffman for their professionalism and support.

Foreword from the First Edition

Sauces: *Classical and Contemporary Sauce Making,* faithful to its title, is a synthesis of the past and present. At nearly a century's remove, James Peterson has done for sauces that which Escoffier did for the cuisine of *La Belle Époque:* simplifying and streamlining methods and techniques and lightening the food to meet the demands of an ever more hurried society, while respecting the architecture of traditional cuisine and stressing the vital importance of fresh produce.

In his introduction to the first edition of *Le Guide Culinaire,* Escoffier wrote, "I wanted to create a tool, rather than a book . . . a constant companion, always within hand's reach . . . it is reserved especially for young people; for those who, beginning today, will be leaders in their field twenty years hence." No words could serve as a better introduction to *Sauces.*

Sauces is, above all, a manual for the professional cook and as such, it will rapidly become a classic and indispensable reference in professional kitchens. But it is much more than a manual, it is a romance as well—James Peterson's romance with the kitchen—and it is easily accessible to the home cook, to whom particular explanations and suggestions are addressed throughout. There are important sections on improvisation replete with hints and possible paths to follow, lest the reader forget that cooking is a creative art. But that creativity cannot exist in a vacuum; the cook must have a firm hold on the basic precepts of cooking before spreading his or her wings.

After a couple of decades of anarchy and chaos in the kitchen disguised as *la nouvelle cuisine,* a treatise such as *Sauces,* grounded in common sense, infuses one with renewed faith.

Richard Olney

Preface to the Third Edition

In the twenty-five-plus years since the publication of the first edition of *Sauces*, the dining public has come to expect a sauce to accompany all but the simplest dish. As this new edition of *Sauces* addresses this ever-more cosmopolitan public, it has had to take into consideration a greater variety of sauces than we would have considered possible at the time it was first published. Professional sauce making is no longer bound by the tenets of French classic cooking in either its traditional form or in the guise of *la nouvelle cuisine*, but now rests on culinary traditions from around the world. As new paradigms of sauce making are being invented and explored, the range of flavors and ingredients available to both the professional and amateur has never been more diverse.

When *Sauces* was first translated into French in 1990, the translator proposed the title *L'Art de Bien Cuisiner* (*The Art of Cooking Well*). While this translation of the title never came to pass, it referred to *Sauces* as a book about cooking with more breadth than the art of making sauces.

Sauces is, in fact, about much more than making sauces because the best sauces—what I call here integral sauces—are the direct result of a cooking process. While on the one hand we live during a period of great creativity and invention, there has never been more interest in preparing traditional and classic sauces, particularly in the realm of integral sauces. Roasting has become more popular than ever, and the need to master the jus and the gravy ever more essential. Braised dishes are also appreciated as never before, and the pleasure of sipping a natural braising liquid appeals more to our jaded palates than the most elaborate brown sauce. As readers of *Sauces* are discovering, fine sauce making does not happen in a vacuum, but depends on the proper and careful cooking of products following, for the most part, time-honored methods. These jus, essences, gravies, and braising liquids released during patient and careful cooking have come to be our favorites. It is for these reasons that this new edition contains additional material on the art of cookery, not just the preparation of a sauce outside of its context.

The third edition of *Sauces* contains recipes for such dishes as a new version of coq au vin, chicken with morels, and braised osso buco, so that it has become more of an all-around cookbook and a guidebook to sauces made *in situ*. Sauce making is in many ways the summation of the art of cooking and can only be accomplished when the techniques of cooking have themselves been at least partially mastered. I hope the new material will lead the reader to a more complete mastery of those basic techniques that constitute the art of cooking. I have also included a traditional American roast turkey with giblet gravy, an omission noticed by more than one reader of the prior editions.

The history of cooking, especially of French and Italian cooking, continues to be a source of inspiration, an inspiration reflected in this new third edition. And while many medieval and Renaissance recipes are hard to quantify, I have made an effort here to get across the flavor and character of a historical dish without assaulting modern sensibilities. Included in the new recipes are a typically seventeenth-century dish of chicken with oysters, chicken with a medieval spice mixture, and dishes that call for small amounts of sugar. These recipes support the tenets of the history section while providing dishes that are genuinely good and far more than simple curiosities.

It is the intention of this third edition of *Sauces* to make students of cooking—and of sauce making in particular—better cooks with a firmer grasp on the historical context upon which cooking techniques, both new and old, rest. In the same way that improvisation in music starts with a scale or a chord, improvisation in cooking may start with an old dish or technique. It is for this reason that these dishes and techniques are included here. As beginning cooks soon discover, the art of sauce making provides fertile ground for creativity. *Sauces* is designed to help the reader tap his or her own potential creativity and continue to make the sauce the essence of many a dish and the stamp of mastery of the careful cook.

In the first and second editions of *Sauces*, I offered many recipes for unbound sauces, broth-like sauces that float around foods rather than cling to them and mask them, allowing for sauce making with less starch and less fat. Strangely, however, there's a paucity of the traditional dishes that have a natural broth surrounding the meat or seafood. Such dishes as pot au feu and bollito misto, while eschewed in the first and second editions, are brought to light here and contribute to making *Sauces* a useful all-around cookbook.

Many of my readers lamented the exclusion of the charts from the second edition of *Sauces*. The charts have returned, so the logic of classic French sauce making is visible at a glance. While much of the nomenclature is dated, the logic and systematization of flavor remain valid. My students and readers who cling to their first editions or elaborate hand-drawn charts will, I hope, be relieved.

The third edition of *Sauces* comes with all-new photography. It was decided that the proper consistencies of sauces are very hard to convey with photography alone, so both I and my publisher have opted for photographs of finished dishes, again underlining *Sauces*'s usefulness as a general cooking text and also, I'll admit, with an eye toward seducing the reader and convincing him or her of the allure of a well-sauced, sometimes historical, dish.

While *Sauces* now contains sixty additional recipes, some readers may ask why the Asian section has not been expanded in proportion to the other sections and why many of the new techniques developed in Spain have not been incorporated. This is for two reasons. The roots of my cooking experience are in Italy and France, and since these techniques are universal, I've given them greater coverage here. I hope I have provided more insight into their execution so that any good cook will be able to apply them to any dish regardless of what ingredients are used to provide the flavor. I haven't treated much of the new Spanish cooking because of its reliance on expensive and exotic equipment, which makes it prohibitive to home cooks and, in fact, most professionals.

Sauces has been completely redesigned to make it easier to read and to use, but none of the original text has been deleted as often happens in newer editions of well-ensconced works, so that the earlier editions become collectors' items. Readers of older editions of *Sauces* will find everything here that was in those earlier works.

Preface from the First Edition

Sauce making allows the cook more freedom to work with flavors, textures, and color than any other area of cooking. A carefully constructed sauce is often prepared in several stages. Each stage has rules of its own and requires the close attention of the chef, cook, or saucier. Unlike roasts or cakes, which need only to be checked from time to time, the construction of a sauce requires constant tasting and fine tuning to balance its flavors and perfect its consistency.

A sauce is never eaten alone but exists to complement the food it is designed to accompany. Some sauces function as condiments by contrasting with foods, as mustard balances the richness of pork or the direct flavor of grilled foods. Other sauces—the natural drippings from a roast or the liquid from a stew—extend the intrinsic flavors of foods. Most sauces lie between these two poles: disparate or contrasting tastes are superimposed over a background of the food's natural flavors.

In the last twenty years, many of the techniques of sauce making have changed. Chefs are not only eager to invent new taste combinations and improve upon older methods but have set out to make sauces healthier and less rich. In the 1970s chefs in France and the United States began to eliminate flour—a standard ingredient since the eighteenth century—from their sauces and replace it with cream and butter. The latest trend is to eliminate the cream and butter and experiment with even newer methods.

Most of the training available to chefs does little to explain these newer sauce-making techniques, and the typical beginning cook is forced to learn them on the job. No amount of book learning can provide a substitute for hands-on experience, but it is helpful to understand the concepts of sauce making and to have a rudimentary knowledge of how ingredients behave and why.

Sauces presents the basic sauce-making techniques that have been used in the past and that are popular today. Because most discussions of sauce making found in textbooks or books on French cooking for the amateur contain only variations of classic sauces or a cursory treatment of contemporary methods, both approaches are discussed and analyzed herein. With a fundamental knowledge of the variety of sauce-making methods available, the chef can make his or her own decisions based on the needs of the clientele, the budget, and style of the restaurant.

Sauces is meant to encourage the chef or saucier to improvise. Basic sauce-making concepts are emphasized, and recipes that exemplify the techniques are included, but this book is not designed as a collection of sauce recipes. An attempt is made to show how liquids, flavorings, and thickeners work and to explain traditional approaches and combinations that will provide the chef with technical guidelines and underlying aesthetic principles.

Although *Sauces* can be used as a quick reference guide, a useful approach is to read it through for ideas and then to apply the ideas to the ingredients on hand, the guests, the wines, and the seasons. A basic concept is far more powerful for an improvising chef than a recipe, because concepts can be adapted to a far greater variety of ingredients and situations.

The number and kinds of sauces served during a meal must be well thought out. Sauce-making expertise is of little value if the arrangement and juxtaposition of the sauces are not carefully planned and the myriad factors inherent in the design of a meal closely considered. Every meal is an event that happens only once—a kind of reflection or distillation or a grouping of people in a particular setting.

Remember not to serve too many sauces in a single meal; one is often appropriate, and two is usually the maximum. If more than one sauce is served at the same meal, make sure that the flavors, colors, and textures of the sauces contrast while the style remains the same. The time of year and the formality of the meal will significantly affect the kinds of sauces that are best to serve.

Beginning chefs and amateur cooks sometimes include too many contrasting colors or flavors on the same plate. It is better to meld the flavors of a sauce carefully into an integral and seemingly simple whole than to cover the plate with different-flavored garnitures or more than one sauce. Usually sauces (and foods) move from light to dark and from cold to hot in the succession of courses, to avoid fatiguing the palate (or the eye). Avoid strong sauces at the beginning of the meal unless you are planning to follow through with something at least equally robust.

Sauces should be chosen according to the style and formality of a meal. An aïoli or a Mexican salsa is more likely to be served at an informal summer lunch than is a sauce poivrade, which is classic, formal, and best for fall or winter.

Sauces is organized around the principles of classic French cooking. This is not because classic French sauces are inherently better than regional sauces or sauces from other countries, but because they are based on a rigid and systematic framework that is easy to remember, build on, and refer to.

Although French cooking also has an elaborate vocabulary for discussing sauce making and general cooking techniques, much of the traditional nomenclature is confusing and contradictory. Many of the cornerstone sauces of French cooking have changed or are made in new ways. Much of this nomenclature is explained in both the text and glossary.

Despite its French orientation, the concepts and techniques explained in this book can be adapted to other cuisines. Once the saucier is familiar with basic sauce-making techniques and understands how various ingredients behave, he or she will be able to invent new combinations, devise new interpretations of classics, and more easily execute unfamiliar recipes.

A SHORT HISTORY OF SAUCE MAKING 1

Perhaps in no period in history have a nation's eating habits changed so profoundly as during the last two decades. Until twenty or thirty years ago, it seemed that the history of sauce making and cooking was complete. If asked about the future of classical cooking, a French chef would likely have replied that all the dishes had been invented by the end of the nineteenth century and that there would be no new combinations or techniques. In that era of processed and frozen foods in the United States, few would have predicted the sophistication and enthusiasm for cooking that exists today.

Why begin with a history of sauce making? A rule of cooking—and of other creative arts—is that creation must take place in the context of a tradition and set of aesthetic values. At a time when creativity and originality in cooking are considered more important than reliably executing classic dishes, one of the difficulties confronting American chefs is the lack of a rigid traditional system of cooking like the system that France adopted in the middle of the nineteenth century, which went virtually unchallenged for over a hundred years. America has a rich culinary heritage, but its cooking from many different regions has never crystallized into a national cuisine. While the limitations imposed by a rigid traditional system can be stultifying, they also provide structure. This protects the chef who is working out a combination of flavors, an innovative presentation, or a new juxtaposition of textures from eccentricity and excess.

Many chefs have been (and some still are) stifled by the dogmatism of classical French cooking. Until recently, straying from classic tradition was considered heretical and signified only ignorance or audacity on the part of the chef. Creativity was limited to interpretation within the classic structure.

As an American teaching in a French cooking school, I was particularly suspect if I deviated even slightly from classic norms. Any innovation or improvement was dismissed as an American eccentricity. My only defense was to find the idea in the literature of French cooking. By delving far enough back, it became clear that "classical" French cooking was only a stage in the evolution of cooking, rather than the culmination and assimilation of the entire history of French cooking. I also discovered that most seemingly new, even startling, combinations had been used before.

A true history of sauce making is not easy to chart. Research is limited to the written word, which until the nineteenth century described only the eating habits of the rich. Cookbooks, which have been around for thousands of years, describe an era's affinity for certain flavors and ingredients, but early cookbooks rarely give quantities. Left merely with a description of flavors and techniques, it is hard to guess how foods tasted. But a description of how flavors have been used over the centuries is often surprising—dishes that seem new or even eccentric often have a lengthy history. Veal with raspberries, roast meats with saffron and ginger, chicken with oysters—all were written about from 500 to 200 years ago.

Cookbooks also fail to describe the context of foods within a meal. Recipes are presented with little or no description of how they should be served, in what order, or with what wines. When nineteenth-century authors describe meals in a social context (Balzac and Zola are good sources), we begin to get a sense of how rich and poor ate and which foods were reserved for special occasions.

ANCIENT GREEK COOKING

Some historians have theorized that the Greek dietetic system, which was closely linked with Greek medicine, had a powerful influence on both Western European and Middle Eastern cuisine. Unfortunately, no complete copies of Greek cookbooks survive. Much of what we know of Greek gastronomy is found in the writings of Archestrate, which focus on the origin of the products—giving recommendations on how to purchase various foods, especially fish—rather than the techniques used in their preparation. The cooking techniques that are mentioned are simple and direct—usually frying or roasting. (Archestrate's most famous recipe recommends that a hare be roasted rare and simply sprinkled with salt.) Cheese and oil are often used in sauces and are sometimes flavored with cumin. One fish recipe warns against preparation by a Sicilian or an Italian, who will "ruin it with too much cheese, vinegar, and asafetida-infused brine."

ANCIENT ROMAN COOKING

Much of our knowledge of Roman cooking comes from Marcus Gavius Apicius, who lived in the first century A.D. Many of the ingredients used in Apicius's recipes are seen again in medieval European cooking. Although reproductions of his manuscripts have been available in Europe since the Middle Ages, it is difficult to know whether the style of medieval European cooking was a direct result of his influence or the natural outcome of preparing food in a particular cultural and geographical climate.

Although many of the ingredients in Apicius's text are familiar and sometimes even appetizing to the modern reader, we have little idea how they tasted because of the almost universal use of *garum*. Garum, a liquid mixture based on fish entrails, was used abundantly in Roman cooking, not only alone as a sauce but in combination with other ingredients such as leeks, onions, a wide variety of spices, wine, honey, and olive oil. Apparently it was not a haphazard conglomeration of ingredients: A note in Apicius's *De re coquinaria* describes a remedy for garum that has taken on an unpleasant odor or too salty a taste, implying that there were criteria for garum. We can only guess how it tasted; the closest modern equivalents are probably the fermented fish sauces used in Southeast Asian cooking (*nampla* in Thailand, *nuoc mam* in Vietnam, *patis* in the Philippines).

Most Roman sauces, in addition to garum, called for honey as well as a variety of spices and herbs. Many of these are still used today but are more common in Asian cooking than in European cuisines: cumin, coriander leaves (cilantro), lovage, asafetida (a stinky spice that turns surprisingly mild when cooked, popular in Indian cooking), rue, dill, bay (laurel) berries, and caraway. Wine and vinegar were often used in Roman cooking, but the wines that were served—and probably used in cooking—were often flavored with spices and combined with honey. The Roman predilection for adding honey to wine probably indicates that naturally fermented sweet wines were not common. There are, however, references to a sweet wine made with raisins (*passo*). Sauces were sometimes colored with wine that had been cooked down (*defritum*) to an intense inky color.

Many Roman recipes tell the reader to "bind" the sauce, often without saying what to use. Some recipes mention starch. Others suggest whole eggs.

Below are several sauces translated from Apicius's *De re coquinaria* (via the French translation by Jacques André; bracketed additions are mine).

Cumin Sauce for Oysters. [Crushed] pepper, [chopped] lovage, parsley, dried mint, malobathre [cassia leaves, related to but not to be confused with cinnamon, which at the time was worth more than its weight in gold], a little more [sic] cumin, honey, vinegar, and garum.

Sauce for Gourds. Grind together pepper, cumin, and rue. Cover the mixture of spices with vinegar, garum, and a small amount of oil. Cook the sliced gourds in the sauce. Bind the sauce with starch, and sprinkle with pepper.

Celery Purée. Boil the celery in water containing bicarbonate of soda [technique sometimes used today to keep vegetables green]. Drain and chop finely. With a mortar and pestle, grind together pepper, lovage, oregano, onion. Moisten the mixture with wine, garum, and oil. Cook the spice mixture in a pot, and add the chopped celery.

Sauce for Cardoons. Grind together fresh rue, mint, coriander, and fennel. Add pepper, lovage, honey, garum, and oil.

COOKING IN THE MIDDLE AGES

There is very little literature describing the cuisine of Europe—indeed, there was very little literature of any sort—between the fall of Rome and the late Middle Ages. Most historians agree that the cooking of Europe was influenced by the Saracens, whose cuisine was in turn influenced by the ancient Greeks. The limited number of cookery books of medieval Europe reflects the influence of Middle Eastern ingredients, often originating in India, and the acquired tastes of the returning Crusaders.

Many Crusaders to the Middle East in the eleventh, twelfth, and thirteenth centuries found the lifestyle there more inviting and never returned to Europe. Those who did return brought back ingredients never before tasted in Europe, including sugar (in cane form), almonds, pistachios, pomegranates, citrus fruits, and spinach. Spices had been used in Western Europe since Roman times, but their variety was limited, and they were served only in noble and royal circles. As the Crusaders returned, the use of spices became more common, as they not only provided flavor but probably masked the taste of tainted meat.

Verjuice (the unsweetened juice of unripe grapes and sometimes crab apples) and vinegar are most often called for when a liquid is needed. In later manuscripts, influenced by Middle Eastern cooking, orange and lemon juice were sometimes used.

Verjuice and vinegar are distinctly sour ingredients, and the Saracens and Western Europeans juxtaposed them with sweeteners. Honey and dried fruits were used initially but were partially replaced with sugar, which remained quite rare and was treated as a spice. The medieval *brouet* (a kind of liquid stew) was sometimes sweetened with dates, raisins, or sugar.

The modern system of preparing stocks had not yet appeared, but beef bouillon and the cooking liquids of both meats and fish were bound with bread, almonds, and egg yolks to convert them into sauces.

Almost every medieval recipe includes spices, such as saffron, ginger, nutmeg, cloves, cinnamon, cardamom, and long pepper. Rarely was the flavor or nuance of one spice emphasized in contrast with a dish. Instead, most dishes contain three or more spices with seemingly little attention to their relationship. Medieval texts (Taillevent's *Le Viandier* and *Le Ménagier de Paris*) are filled with recipes for soups and ragoûts in which the element being prepared—liver, meat, fish—is puréed and used to bind the liquid.

When bread or almonds were used to bind sauces, they were pounded together at the beginning and moistened with verjuice, vinegar, wine, almond milk, and sometimes cow's milk. When used, egg yolks were beaten and added at the end, just as they are today. In some recipes, liver (it is often not clear what kind) is used to thicken the sauce.

Although we do not know what the exact textures of sauces were like in medieval cooking, the eating habits of the times would have made it difficult if not impossible to appreciate a delicately balanced sauce. Most foods were served on thick slices of bread (trenchers) instead of plates and eaten with the fingers instead of with forks. If a sauce were too thin, it would have been absorbed by the bread. More than likely, sauces were thickened so they would cling to the foods and stay on top of the trenchers. Later, as plates came into more widespread use, it became possible to make thinner, more delicately thickened and flavored sauces that would not disappear into the bread. Two recipes from Taillevent's *Le Viandier* follow.

Brouet de Canelle. Cook a chicken in water and wine or other liquid. Remove it from the liquid, and cut it into quarters. Cook the quarters in fat. Cook unpeeled almonds and cinnamon in beef broth. Grind them and strain them with beef bouillon, and moisten the chicken pieces with this liquid. Add verjuice, ginger, cloves, grains of paradise [*Aframomum melegueta*]. The sauce should be well bound.

Brouet Gorgié. Cut the chicken or meat being prepared into pieces. Cook the pieces in lard with finely chopped parsley and onions. Take livers, lightly toasted bread, wine, and beef broth, and boil everything together [the text is not clear whether these are boiled with the meat or separately]. Simmer the mixture until it thickens, and flavor with ginger, cloves, and saffron. Add verjuice.

⬤━ SPICE MIXTURE

Here is a spice mixture written about in the middle of the sixteenth century. Long pepper, grains of paradise, and galangal are sold online. Galangal can be found in shops that sell Thai ingredients.

YIELD: ½ CUP (125 MILLILITERS)

powdered ginger	3 tablespoons	45 milliliters
freshly ground black pepper	2 teaspoons	10 milliliters
grated nutmeg	1 tablespoon	15 milliliters
grains of paradise, ground in a coffee grinder	1 tablespoon	15 milliliters
ground cinnamon	1 tablespoon	15 milliliters
long pepper, ground in a coffee grinder	1 tablespoon	15 milliliters
ground cloves	2 teaspoons	10 milliliters
powdered galangal (also called *laos*)	1 tablespoon	15 milliliters

Stir together all the ingredients and store in a tightly sealed container in the freezer. Use to dust chicken and seafood to lend a medieval flavor.

Adapting Medieval Recipes

Adapting historical recipes to modern tastes is an exciting means of designing new dishes that are still grounded in culinary tradition. The flavors, textures, and colors inherent in an old recipe can be adapted to modern tastes without losing sight of the original recipe. References to the aesthetic of the original can be made without compromising the dish's flavor or appeal.

One can only guess at the intensity and balance of the flavors. Most authors assume that the spices were used in large quantities. Some have also assumed that spices were used carelessly because many spices were used in one preparation. Whether or not these assumptions are true is irrelevant to the modern cook, who is free to adapt historical recipes to today's tastes. Obviously the quantities of spices used can be adjusted to taste, and a variety of spices in the same dish—as Indian curries prove—does not necessarily imply a careless hodgepodge of flavors.

The choice of liaison requires liberty on the part of the chef. Although bread is an interesting liaison (see "Bread," page 134), a bread-thickened sauce may not be appealing in a contemporary dish. Binding sauces with nut butters, however, is both authentic and satisfying.

When experimenting with an unknown dish in which a variety of flavors meld—such as a medieval recipe containing three or more spices—infuse the spices individually in small amounts of liquid, such as stock or cream, and then gradually combine the liquids until the flavors of the spices are in balance.

GOLD-PLATED CHICKEN WITH GINGER, SAFFRON, AND ALMONDS

This modern adaptation is not based on any particular recipe but is taken from several recipes in Taillevent's *Viandier* (fourteenth- and fifteenth-century manuscripts). Ginger, saffron, and mint are the principal flavorings; ginger and saffron were the spices most often called for in medieval recipes, and mint was one of the most commonly used herbs. The sauce is bound with almond butter, a typical medieval liaison (bread can also be used). Green-colored marzipan almonds and pomegranate seeds are used as the garniture. The almonds are a reference to the medieval cook's tendency to fashion one food from another to surprise and titillate the diner. They are sweet (and surprisingly good with the sauce), recalling the inclination to juxtapose the savory with the sweet in the medieval meal. The gold plating is extravagant and can be eliminated (or silver leaf can be substituted), but it is taken from an authentic recipe. Gold and silver foil are still used in Indian cooking to decorate desserts. Medieval diners were fond of bright colors, hence the gold, the pomegranate seeds, the saffron, and the colored almonds.

The chicken is prepared like a fricassée, but the recipe could be adapted to a sauté model as well.

YIELD: 4 SERVINGS

chicken, quartered, 1	3 pounds	1.4 kilograms
salt and pepper	to taste	to taste
butter or lard	2 ounces	60 grams
onion, chopped	1 medium	1 medium
white chicken stock	2 cups	500 milliliters
almond paste	2 ounces	55 grams
green food coloring or chlorophyll	several drops	several drops
pomegranate	1	1
saffron threads	1 pinch	1 pinch
hot water	1 tablespoon	15 milliliters
finely grated fresh ginger	2 teaspoons	10 milliliters
mint leaves	1 small bunch	1 small bunch
almond butter (page 415)	2 tablespoons	30 milliliters
egg yolk	1	1
gold or silver leaf	4 sheets	4 sheets

1. Season the chicken pieces with salt and pepper. In a 4-quart (4 liter) straight-sided sauté pan, gently cook the seasoned chicken pieces, skin side down, in the butter. After about 10 minutes, turn and cook the flesh side. Avoid browning the chicken or burning the butter. Remove the chicken.

2. Add the chopped onions to the butter in the pan and sweat, without browning, until they are translucent.

3. Add the chicken stock to the pan. Arrange the chicken pieces in the liquid and cover.

4. Cook the chicken in a 350°F (175°C) oven or over low heat on the stove for 15 to 20 minutes.

5. While the chicken is cooking, work the almond paste with the food coloring until it is bright green. Shape the colored paste into 12 almonds and set aside.

6. Remove and reserve the seeds from the pomegranate. Discard the flesh.

7. Soak the saffron threads in the hot water for at least 20 minutes.

8. Transfer the chicken to a plate and keep it warm. Add the grated ginger to the liquid in the pan and let it infuse for 5 minutes.

9. Strain the sauce into a 2-quart (2 liter) saucepan and reduce it to ¾ cup (185 milliliters). Skim carefully.

10. Gradually add the saffron, tasting so that its flavor becomes apparent but does not overpower the flavor of the ginger. Add the mint.

11. Whisk in the almond butter until the sauce has the desired consistency. Add salt and pepper to taste.

12. Beat the egg yolk with a large pinch of salt to make an egg wash.

13. Brush the top of the chicken pieces with the egg wash.

14. Apply the gold or silver leaf by holding the sheet about ½ inch (1 cm) from the surface of the chicken and systematically blowing on the back of the gold leaf through a 5-inch-long (12.5 cm) plastic straw.

15. Serve the chicken surrounded with the sauce, the pomegranate seeds, and the green almonds.

RENAISSANCE COOKING: THE SIXTEENTH CENTURY

Surprisingly little has been written about cooking in the sixteenth century. In France one important book was published, a translation of Bartolomeo Platina's *De Honeste voluptate.* Whereas most other books were based on earlier works and were medieval in character, Platina gives us a deeper understanding of both the cooking and the priorities of Renaissance Italy and France. During the Renaissance and for several centuries thereafter, culinary methods were closely linked to health and medicine. Much of Platina's writing was influenced by medieval medicine, which itself was based on Greek medicine with its elaborate system of humors and emphasis on the use of diet to balance the basic "personalities": sanguine, phlegmatic, choleric, and melancholic. The ingredient that appears in greater quantities in sixteenth-century recipes is sugar. Although by no means inexpensive, refining methods made it more accessible than it had been during the Middle Ages. Coupled with intense interest in gardening and cultivation, this resulted in new methods of preserving fruit, including jellies and jams as they are known today. Previously, fruits were preserved by drying or by storage in vinegar and honey.

LEEKS WITH ALMOND MILK, CINNAMON, AND ROSES

Almond milk, extracted from almonds using hot water, was popular in medieval and Renaissance cooking as a substitute for dairy products. It can still be used today for its flavor and for vegan cooking. The rosewater is typical of the Renaissance; it and attar of roses are obtainable at Indian groceries.

YIELD: 6 SIDE-DISH SERVINGS

whole almonds	1 cup	150 grams
sliced almonds	1 small handful	1 small handful
hot water	2 cups	500 milliliters
rosewater	1 teaspoon	5 milliliters
or	or	or
attar of roses	1 drop	1 drop
ground cinnamon	1 small pinch	1 small pinch
heavy cream	½ cup	125 milliliters
sugar	1 teaspoon	5 milliliters
leeks, greens removed, whites split lengthwise, rinsed	6 medium	6 medium
salt and pepper	to taste	to taste

1. Preheat the oven to 350°F (175°C). Separately toast the whole almonds and sliced almonds in the oven for 15 minutes. Let cool. Set aside the sliced almonds. Grind the whole almonds in a food processor for 1 minute and put in a pot with the hot water. Bring to a simmer and let steep for 15 minutes. Work through a fine-mesh strainer. Reserve the liquid and discard the almonds or grind them further with a mortar and pestle to use as a sauce thickener.
2. Add the rosewater, cinnamon, cream, and sugar to the almond milk. Adjust the seasonings.
3. Spread the leeks in an oval baking dish just large enough to hold them and pour over the almond milk. Bake until tender, about 35 minutes. Sprinkle over the sliced almonds and serve.

THE SEVENTEENTH CENTURY

In the seventeenth century, French cooking began to distinguish itself from that of the rest of Europe; a new aesthetic developed with criteria that are much the same as those of today.

Particularly important to sauce making was the notion that food should taste of itself. Spices that disguised natural flavors were gradually abandoned. Sauces began to concentrate and emphasize the flavor of a particular dish rather than accent or distort it. Barbara Wheaton, in her book *Savoring the Past*, discusses how cooking over the centuries has gravitated from one pole to another on an aesthetic spectrum:

> Cooks and diners have long argued over whether the best cooking makes food "taste of itself" or transmutes ingredients into something new and unrecognizable. To satisfy its advocates, food that tastes of itself should be locally produced and in season, served at the peak of its natural ripeness; in contrast, transmuted food is a compound of the rare, exotic, and the difficult, made from ingredients belonging to other places and seasons and produced by techniques that require special skills or equipment. From the sixteenth century onward, both points of view have had persuasive supporters; they are the extremes to which the pendulum swings. In the late sixteenth century, the early eighteenth century, and the nineteenth century the transmutationists usually prevailed; at other times the purists have had the upper hand. At present two parts of our society are pursuing separate paths: traditionalist cooks and diners interested in fine cooking emphasize recognizable ingredients; food technologists and the mass market are more interested in the final combination of flavors. Ironically, today the simpler ingredients are likely to be more expensive. Most of us would not recognize many of the ingredients prominent in processed foods. How many of us can differentiate, with eye, nose, or palate, among hydrolyzed vegetable protein, guar gum, and BHA? Food technologists claim that they can synthesize the flavors of our familiar foods, transmuting, for example, textured soy protein into bacon. Analogously, the chefs and confectioners who served the sixteenth-century diner contrived to astonish him by clever deceptions. The plates of sugar "fish" at the reception for Elizabeth of Austria exemplify this point of view. Then, as now, the willing suspension of disbelief on the part of the diner is essential.

The most obvious manifestation of this shift from one end of the aesthetic spectrum to the other was the complete abandonment of certain medieval spices (ginger, saffron, galangal, and others) and a moderate use of modern spices, especially pepper, which were less likely to distort the intrinsic flavor of foods.

As spices were less used, chefs relied more on indigenous herbs and vegetables to supply aromatic interest to their sauces and stews. Although medieval cooks used some herbs (especially mint, parsley, and hyssop), many of the herbs we use today (including tarragon, chervil, basil, and thyme) did not enter into the culinary mainstream until the seventeenth century.

Although onions were often called for in medieval recipes, aromatic ingredients such as shallots, carrots, and celery were little mentioned until the seventeenth century. Wild mushrooms and truffles, so prized in later centuries, were first used in seventeenth-century recipes. Savory ingredients such as anchovies, capers, and cornichons (sour gherkins) also gradually made their way into French cooking and sauce making.

Another noticeable difference between cooking texts of the Middle Ages and those of the seventeenth century is the substitution of butter for lard. In Taillevent's *Viandier*, lard is the fat most often used for the preparation of the flavor base, usually sweated onions. In the seventeenth century, butter is used not only to brown and sweat ingredients but also as a component in sauces. The principal liquid flavorings used in medieval sauces, vinegar and verjuice, are extremely acidic. Remnants of these sauces can be seen in simple green sauces flavored with herbs, especially mint and sorrel (see Chapter 16, "Salad Sauces, Vinaigrettes, Salsas, and Relishes," page 423). These plain vinegar-based sauces are still sometimes served with cold roasts. Although vinegar and other acidic liquids continued to be used, their acidity was attenuated by combining them with oil (somewhat equivalent to modern cold and hot vinaigrette), coulis (like a modern sauce Robert), and butter.

The following recipe, from *L'Art de bien traiter* by L.S.R. (1674), is for a butter-bound white sauce similar to a beurre blanc. It also contains capers, anchovies, oranges, and lemons, all of which are typical seventeenth-century ingredients. The recipe, which was originally designed to be served with pike, is a fairly exact translation of the original and suggests that all the ingredients be put in the pan at the beginning. A more reliable approach would be to make an infusion with all the ingredients except the butter and then whisk in the butter in the same way as when preparing a beurre blanc.

> In a saucepan combine fresh butter, 1 or 2 spoonfuls of court-bouillon, a pinch of salt and white pepper, capers, several slices of lemon or orange, nutmeg (optional), and one anchovy (desalted and chopped). Stir the sauce with a wooden or silver spoon [over the heat] until the sauce binds and thickens. Serve the sauce immediately so that it does not turn into oil, which is most undesirable and disgusting in a bound sauce.

Medieval sauces would have contained more acidic ingredients and some additional spices, but no butter, making them very strong. This implies that the medieval concept of a sauce was similar to the modern view of condiments such as mustard. The idea of a suave, delicate sauce that gently supported the flavor of a dish had not yet come into being.

Medieval and Roman sauces often contained both sweet and sour ingredients, varying combinations of verjuice and vinegar with honey, dried fruits, cooked wine must (*raisiné*), and later, sugar. Although some of these sweet-and-sour combinations still exist—gastrique, red-currant jam in a sauce grand-veneur, mint jelly for roast lamb, duck with orange sauce—their use declined rapidly in the seventeenth century.

The basic mixtures that function as cornerstones in French cooking—the bouillons, stuffings, and liaisons—were first categorized at this time. What later became a cohesive cooking system—expanded in the eighteenth and nineteenth centuries—and still forms the basis for French cooking today, started in the seventeenth century.

One of the most important innovations was the introduction of roux (*farine frite*). Before then, toasted bread was the thickener most often used in sauce making. Although bread has certain advantages (a less floury taste), roux provides a smoother-textured sauce and became the thickener of choice well into the twentieth century. When first used, roux was an integral step in the preparation of a coulis, the concentrated veal or beef essences that were critical to seventeenth- and eighteenth-century French cooking. The meat was cooked with bouillon and aromatic vegetables until it "attached" to the bottom of the pot and began to caramelize. (The term *pincer* was later used in French cookbooks to describe this process.) Flour was then added to the caramelized juices and cooked until it took on a toasty smell or turned a reddish color (probably the origin of the term *roux*). This method of thickening is still used for making stews and gravies, but in classic sauces, roux is prepared separately and measured before being combined with stock. The older method, *pincer*, is rarely used because it is very difficult to cook both the meat and the vegetables properly in one vessel: The former burns or the latter remain raw. (In the early twentieth century, Escoffier warned against it and instead recommended careful sweating of the aromatic vegetables and separate browning or searing of meats on the stove or in the oven.)

In the seventeenth century, a system of preparing intensely flavored liquid bases from enormous quantities of meat was used. A *jus* was prepared by browning large pieces of meat, poking the meat with a knife, and then putting it in a press to extract the juice. A *restaurant* was prepared by putting meat in a well-sealed bottle and gently cooking until the meats released their natural juices; no liquid was used. Brown sauces were relatively simple and were mostly based on *coulis*. The coulis was the basis for brown sauces well into the nineteenth century, when it was replaced by sauce espagnole and classic demi-glace. Coulis was prepared by moistening a variety of meats (mutton was often used, along with beef, veal, and chicken) with an already rich bouillon.

Although a version of roux was introduced during the seventeenth century, other liaisons were also used. Puréed almonds, used since medieval times, were often added to thicken coulis. La Varenne's *Cuisinier françois* listed several liaisons, including almonds (combined with bouillon, breadcrumbs, and egg yolks, the mixture flavored with lemon juice, onions, mushrooms, and cloves); mushrooms were puréed with almonds, onions, parsley, breadcrumbs, egg yolks, and capers, the mixture then worked through a drum sieve and saved until needed as a thickener; roux was made with lard, onions were added after cooking the flour, and the mixture was seasoned with bouillon, mushrooms, and vinegar—a kind of primitive velouté that was kept on "hot ashes" to be quickly accessible as a thickener; truffles were puréed along with flour, onions, and mushrooms and used to thicken ragoûts.

Some of the sauces that eventually made their way into the classic French repertoire first appear in seventeenth-century cookbooks. Seventeenth-century *sauce poivrade* has a distinctly medieval character: It was made with onions or scallions, vinegar, lemon and lime zests, and pepper. No coulis, stock, or butter was used to attenuate the acidity of the vinegar. A modern Sauce Poivrade (page 188) is made with concentrated stock and no lemon or orange. La Varenne's green sauce (*sauce verte*), made from chard and vinegar, also has a distinctly medieval character: No oil, butter, or stock was used and the sauce was thickened with toasted bread.

CHICKEN WITH CAPERS AND OYSTERS

Seventeenth-century cooks, or at least those who wrote about cooking, were excessively fond of capers—capers show up in the most unlikely places—and had nothing against pairing fowl and seafood. This dish is particularly good with oysters from northern climes, especially Belons.

YIELD: 4 MAIN-COURSE SERVINGS

chicken, quartered, 1	4 pounds	2 kilograms
butter	1½ ounces	45 grams
chicken broth	2 cups	500 milliliters
heavy cream	½ cup	125 milliliters
capers, drained	2 tablespoons	30 milliliters
finely chopped chives (optional)	1 tablespoon	15 milliliters
oysters, shucked, patted with a kitchen towel to eliminate grit	12	12
salt and pepper	to taste	to taste

1. Cook the chicken over medium heat in butter, about 5 minutes on each side. Discard the fat and add the chicken broth. Simmer, covered, until the chicken bounces back to the touch, about 10 minutes.

2. Take the chicken out of the pan and boil down the stewing liquid to about ½ cup (125 milliliters). Whisk in the cream and simmer until the sauce has the consistency you like.

3. Add the capers, chives, if using, and oysters and heat just enough to see the oysters curl a little. Season with salt and pepper.

4. Spoon the oysters, capers, and sauce over the pieces of chicken. See the photograph in the color plates.

THE EIGHTEENTH CENTURY

The eighteenth century brought about greater systemization of the basic components—coulis, jus, and bouillons—introduced during the seventeenth century. This made it easier for professional cooks to work in different kitchens and produce consistent results. Once this system was mastered, individual recipes were easy to remember and integrate into a cook's repertoire.

Although many of the sauce recipes found in seventeenth-century cookbooks were little-changed versions of medieval recipes, by the eighteenth century, few of these sauces remained in the literature. Most were replaced by versions containing coulis, butter, and the contemporary flavors such as anchovies, capers, and cornichons (sour gherkins).

Cookbooks before the eighteenth century were written primarily for royalty and the aristocracy; they were likely written for the masters of the households rather than the cooks, who were usually illiterate. The eighteenth century saw the first cookbook for the middle class, Menon's *La Cuisinière bourgeoise*, which is filled with accessible and delicious recipes.

Many new sauces were introduced in the eighteenth century. Until then, sauces were usually one of two types. The first were made by slightly modifying a basic coulis, but it was essentially the coulis that gave the character to the sauce. This is by no means a criticism—sauces made from rich coulis are still the best brown sauces—but this approach is distinctly different from a later approach, popular in the nineteenth and twentieth centuries, which placed more emphasis on the final flavoring of the sauce than the coulis or demi-glace base. The second category of sauces, usually based on vinegar, verjuice, or citrus juices flavored with herbs and sometimes spices, was more medieval in character. As sauce making progressed during the eighteenth century, these two sauce styles began to merge. Coulis was added to an acidic sauce base (for example, sauce Robert); oil or butter was added to acidic sauce bases for a softer-flavored sauce with more finesse (for example, vinaigrette, beurre blanc); egg yolks, although used since the Middle Ages as sauce thickeners, were used (or at least described) more carefully; and the first versions of the modern hollandaise began to evolve.

In classic French cooking, roasts are served in their natural, unthickened juices (*jus de rôti*). In eighteenth-century cooking, chefs were far more likely to convert the natural juices from the roasts into an array of flavored sauces.

Oranges, chopped shallots, truffles, anchovies, garlic, foie gras, and herbs were all used to give roasting juices a variety of flavors.

Roux became the liaison of choice. Early versions of velouté (*coulis bourgeois*) appeared and were made in much the modern way: preliminary cooking of roux, addition of bouillon flavored with wine, parsley, bay leaf, mushrooms. The only spices used were cloves and nutmeg in moderation. Flour was used in roux (now prepared with butter instead of lard), and for beurre manié. During the eighteenth century, many classic sauces—espagnole, béchamel, italienne—were developed. Although these sauces have changed over the last 200 years, the ingredients used still sound appealing and appropriate.

CHICKEN WITH ANCHOVIES, OLIVES, CAPERS, AND ORANGE JUICE

This chicken comes from a book by the late-seventeenth- and early-eighteenth-century writer Massailot. This combination of olives, capers, and orange juice was very popular at the time. This recipe is completely authentic except for finishing the sauce with butter.

YIELD: 4 MAIN-COURSE SERVINGS

chicken, quartered, 1	4 pounds	2 kilograms
salt and pepper	to taste	to taste
olive oil	2 teaspoons	10 milliliters
chicken broth	2 cups	500 milliliters
dry white wine	½ cup	125 milliliters
pitted olives	½ cup	125 milliliters
capers, drained	1 tablespoon	15 milliliters
anchovy fillets, rinsed	12	12
minced chives	1 tablespoon	15 milliliters
finely chopped parsley	1 tablespoon	15 milliliters
juice of 1 orange		
butter	2 ounces	60 grams

1. Season the chicken with salt and pepper and brown it in a sauté pan in olive oil for about 5 minutes on each side over high heat.
2. Take the chicken out of the pan, discard the fat, put the chicken back in and pour over the chicken broth and white wine. Simmer the chicken, covered, for about 10 minutes, until firm to the touch.
3. Take the chicken out of the broth and simmer the broth down to a syrupy glaze. Add the olives, capers, anchovy fillets, chopped herbs, and the orange juice and stir gently to heat through all the ingredients.
4. Whisk in the butter. Season to taste with salt and pepper. Spoon the sauce over the chicken.

THE NINETEENTH CENTURY

Before the nineteenth century, the greatest cooking in France was done in private homes and palaces for the wealthiest classes. When the French Revolution brought the fall of the aristocracy, a large number of talented chefs found themselves out of work. At the same time, a newly assertive middle class was eager to establish itself and emulate the fallen aristocracy. French cooking moved out of the home and into the restaurant, where the elaborate creations of the chefs were suddenly accessible to anyone who could afford them. An insecure bourgeoisie, eager to compete for social status, brought about an almost obsessive interest in cuisine and gastronomy. The great chefs were treated like stars. Whereas many of the basic preparations of the eighteenth century and before (including béchamel, Mornay, and soubise) were named for members of the nobility, many of the dishes and sauces invented in the nineteenth century were named for professional chefs (Duglére, Véron). During the first half of the nineteenth century, a clear break occurred between what is now called *cuisine à l'ancienne* and the contemporary cooking of the time, which is now called *la cuisine classique.*

Early-nineteenth-century cookbooks used dishes and techniques popular in the late eighteenth century, but new ingredients and sauces also appeared. In eighteenth-century texts, sauce espagnole was given the same attention as other sauces, but by the early nineteenth century, it began to take on special importance. Velouté (also called *coulis blanc*) first appeared, as did the first versions of tomato sauce, hollandaise sauce (made with hard-boiled egg yolks), and ketchup (spelled *ket-chop* and made with mushrooms and anchovies). An early version of mayonnaise—a kind of vinaigrette with herbs but no egg yolks—also appeared. Antonin Carême is usually considered the father of classic French cooking. Carême was the most prolific food writer of the nineteenth century (perhaps of all time), but more important, he systematized the fundamental *sauces mères* (mother sauces) and derivative sauces of classic French cooking. Although most of the so-called *grandes sauces* had been in use long before Carême, he was the first to state clearly that the four basic sauces—espagnole, velouté, allemande, and béchamel—were the basis for an infinite variety of *petite sauces.* Before Carême, even the so-called petite sauces were prepared by moistening additional meat (usually ham and veal) with various stocks, jus, and coulis, which made each sauce time consuming to prepare. Carême emphasized the importance of reducing the mother sauces so that only the basic flavors (he used an assortment of fumets and essences) had to be added to prepare last-minute derivative sauces. In addition to his descriptions of the classic mother sauces with their modern names, Carême also described many of the classic derivative sauces that are still used today. The first modern description of mayonnaise (spelled *magnonaise*), made with raw egg yolks, olive oil, and aspic, was also recorded.

Carême enabled chefs working throughout the nineteenth century to invent derivative sauces using his foundation as a base. Many sauces invented by the famous Parisian chefs of the time were the same sauces with a single ingredient changed or added.

The first cookbooks with regional recipes were published in the nineteenth century. Parisians had never tasted Provençal cooking until one of the first restaurants of the century (Les Trois Frères Provençaux) began serving it. Later books on regional cooking, with their simple but judiciously prepared recipes, were a welcome relief from the baroque constructions of late-nineteenth-century classic cooking. They often emphasized the quality and origin of ingredients, with dishes prepared in simple, direct ways that enhanced their flavor.

THE TWENTIETH CENTURY

As the nineteenth century drew to a close, the innovations of chefs building on the foundations established by Carême were recorded by Auguste Escoffier in *Le Guide Culinaire*. *Le Guide Culinaire* standardized the cooking of the nineteenth century and for many still remains the ultimate authority on classical French cooking. As complicated as some of the recipes appear to the modern reader, Escoffier clearly pointed out that his recipes were a simplification of late-nineteenth-century cooking. He specifically mentioned eliminating the plinth (*socle*), the base that was widely used for the elaborate presentations of the late nineteenth century.

Escoffier continued to simplify sauce-making methods by eliminating many of the essences and fumets used by Carême and by affirming the importance of four mother sauces—espagnole, velouté, béchamel, and tomato (an addition since Carême)—and to a lesser degree, hollandaise and mayonnaise. His recipes were concise and easy to follow.

Escoffier used the recipes in *Le Guide Culinaire* to standardize the cooking at the Ritz hotels in England and on the continent—one striking difference between the cooking of the late nineteenth and early twentieth centuries and the approach to food today. At the turn of the century, typical wealthy diners in a Ritz hotel would insist on consistency in a particular dish whether they were in Nice or London. Today, sophisticated diners would be more reassured by the appearance of regional dishes using local ingredients than by a menu that seems to exist independently of the location.

Although less widely read than Escoffier, Edouard Nignon, an early-twentieth-century restaurateur, wrote several important books that discuss sauce making. His sauce recipes are particularly interesting because the brown sauces contained no flour; instead of basing his brown sauces on espagnole and demi-glace in the tradition of Carême and Escoffier, his sauces were prepared with concentrated veal stock (*blond de veau*), with veal glace and concentrated veal and beef stock (*jus brun*). These methods, while resembling eighteenth-century methods, were precursors of those now used in contemporary French restaurants.

One of the most admired French chefs of the twentieth century is Ferdinand Point, who owned a restaurant in Vienne (near Lyons) in the late 1940s and early 1950s. He started one of the trends of what is now called *nouvelle cuisine* by developing and enhancing the cuisine of his region. Regional cuisine, for years considered the domain of women cooks, has been gradually adopted by professional chefs (both men and women) and prepared with the same technical expertise that had been reserved for classic French cooking. Ferdinand Point was one of the first to pay homage to the cuisine of his region and was an inspiration to many of his apprentices, who later became the influential chefs of the 1960s and 1970s.

The term *nouvelle cuisine* was first used in the late 1960s (so-called nouvelle cuisine had already appeared several times over past centuries). Initially, and perhaps most important, the development of a "new" cooking gave chefs permission to invent. This concept may be difficult for an American chef to understand, because unless European-trained, an American chef has no rigid system from which to break away. But in France the precepts and techniques of classical cooking were questioned, and many of the old dishes were lightened and simplified or completely abandoned.

Of the technical innovations of the 1960s and 1970s, none were more profound or long-lasting than those in the area of sauce making. Chefs began to eliminate flour from their sauces (used in one way or another since the Middle Ages) and to thicken their sauces with cream, butter, and egg yolks. Sauces were served in smaller quantities and were usually lighter textured.

Some chefs and authors question the value of eliminating flour from sauces. Preparing flourless sauces takes skill and experience; many of the sauces used by our current nouvelle cuisine chefs are overly rich and overly reduced. Although many chefs and writers claimed that the new sauces were lighter than the older flour-thickened versions, the reverse is actually true. Some chefs, in an effort to eliminate flour, thickened their sauces almost entirely with cream and butter; the result was far from light. Often the decision to use flour as a thickener is a question of style. In the rarefied atmosphere of a Michelin three-star restaurant, a flour-thickened sauce, unless prepared in the careful tradition of Escoffier and the nineteenth century, may seem incongruous. On the other hand, a regional dish such as a coq au vin or one of the many varieties of country-style stews is best served with its own cooking liquid lightly thickened with flour, preferably added at the beginning, during the browning of the meat.

One of the most innovative chefs of the 1970s was Michel Guérard, whose book *La Grande cuisine minceur* contained recipes for sauces made almost entirely without cream, butter, or egg yolks. He was one of the first to suggest serving dishes surrounded by full-flavored aromatic broths with no liaison. He introduced yogurt and fresh cheese as liaisons and developed a method for using a light sabayon to thicken savory sauces.

Both French and American chefs have borrowed largely from ethnic and regional cuisines to devise new techniques and flavor combinations for sauce making. American chefs are finally beginning to use regional American cooking as a source of inspiration and exciting sauce ideas. Jeremiah Tower, in his book *New American Classics,* has integrated the satisfying, rough-hewn cuisine of California and the American Southwest with the sophistication and technique of traditional French cooking. French chefs are experimenting with the traditional dishes of the provinces instead of automatically following the precepts of a classic cuisine. French chefs working both in France and the United States have looked to the cuisine of India and their own medieval past, and after centuries of neglect, they are beginning to experiment with spices in sauce making. In the history of cooking and sauce making, there have been periods of both innovation and stagnation. Vincent de la Chapelle wrote during the first half of the eighteenth century that if a nobleman served the same dishes at his table that had been popular twenty years before, his guests would leave dissatisfied. The same is true today—food is fashionable, and the public has grown fickle and eager for innovation. The American public has become almost fanatically health conscious and concerned with diet—a trend reminiscent of the sixteenth century—so that the pleasures of the table are rarely appreciated at face value. Even though this concern with health sometimes detracts from the pleasure of a good meal, it has forced Americans to be conscious of the foods they eat and more open to experimenting with new dishes. Unfortunately, this obsession with diet and health is often misguided. Perhaps it is the loss of good culinary instinct that causes the salubrity of natural products to be doubted while completely artificial foods go unquestioned. Americans blithely drink diet soda filled with artificial flavors and sweeteners yet paste warning labels on bottles of wine; they decry the dangers of eating butter and claim that margarine, a completely manufactured artificial product, is better for you. Are we so out of touch with our senses, our intuition, and our cultural heritage that we cannot eat well without consulting medical journals and diet books? We can only hope that the precepts of good cooking and innate good taste lead us to a cuisine that is naturally satisfying and healthy, so that we can eat, not self-consciously, but with gusto and spontaneity.

EQUIPMENT 2

Much of the equipment essential for sauce making will probably already be on hand in a well-equipped home or restaurant kitchen. But read this section carefully. Some of the equipment—especially fine-mesh sieves, drum sieves, and saucepans with sloping sides—is specialized for sauce making and may need to be added to a collection of kitchen equipment.

COOKWARE

There seems to be no perfect material for constructing pots and pans. Copper is heavy and needs to be retinned, stainless steel is expensive and a poor conductor of heat, aluminum stains certain sauces; the list of disadvantages goes on. The best pots and pans (and the most expensive) combine materials to make the optimum use of each.

Whatever the material, the most important consideration in selecting pots, saucepans, and sauté pans is that they be thick. If not, they will heat unevenly, and the bottoms will burn or scald and possibly warp.

Materials

Aluminum

Despite some recent controversy over whether it contributes to the development of Alzheimer's disease, aluminum has become popular in professional kitchens because it is inexpensive. Good-quality heavy-gauge aluminum conducts heat fairly well, so it can be used for roasting pans, sauté pans, and, to a limited degree, saucepans. It is especially practical for large stockpots, which would be prohibitively expensive in copper or stainless steel.

Aluminum is only a moderately efficient conductor of heat. Large sauté pans and roasting pans tend to warp, because the center expands before the outside does. This problem occurs less often if a flat-top stove is used, rather than burners that concentrate the heat in one area of the pan. Aluminum pans also tend to stick, so they should be avoided when sautéing fish or fragile meats.

Aluminum saucepans can discolor white sauces and especially sauces containing egg yolks. Any kitchen should have at least a couple of lined copper or copper-bottomed stainless-steel saucepans for emulsified egg sauces.

Several types of aluminum cookware are available. The most important factor is to choose as heavy a gauge as possible. Most aluminum has a plain, shiny surface. One brand, Calphalon, uses a special treatment that renders the aluminum inert, preventing it from reacting with foods. It is attractive but quite expensive. It also has the disadvantage of being almost black on the inside, making it difficult to see the condition of any caramelized juices before deglazing.

Copper

Because it is an excellent heat conductor, copper has long been the material of choice for professional cookware. When made of heavy-gauge copper, saucepans and sauté pans distribute heat evenly, decreasing the risk of burning pan drippings or scalding sauces. Because of its conductivity, copper is also less likely to warp.

Copper pots and pans, however, are expensive, and they must be tinned on a regular basis so that the copper does not come directly in contact with foods.

Restaurants that cannot dispense with their copper pots for days at a time are often tempted to let this task slide, using pots and pans with copper exposed. This practice is especially dangerous for sauces, which can absorb toxic doses of copper if allowed to sit in untinned copper. Recently, professional-quality copper pots and pans that are lined with longer-lasting, relatively inert metals such as nickel have appeared on the market. They are only slightly more expensive than the tinned versions and will last for many years before needing a new lining.

Copper should also be polished each time it is washed. Although tarnish does not affect the efficiency of copper cookware, a kitchen filled with tarnished pots somehow looks sloppy and amiss. One of the advantages of copper is the gleaming professional look it gives to a restaurant kitchen.

When purchasing copper cookware, be sure to select pots and pans with iron rather than brass handles. Because iron is a poor conductor of heat, the handles will not get hot so quickly.

Earthenware

Although many home cooks could never do without earthenware for slow-cooking stews and braises, it is rarely practical in a professional kitchen, where it is unlikely to survive the frenzied pace. It is often used, however, for dishes such as gratins, which are served in the same dish in which they are baked.

Enameled Cast Iron

Although enameled cast iron is impractical for saucepans and sauté pans for several reasons (it rusts easily, may discolor some foods, and is very heavy), it is excellent for braising because it conducts heat slowly and evenly. If in good condition, the enameled surface is also nonreactive, unlike plain cast iron, which will rust if not kept perfectly dry and oiled. Enameled cast-iron pots are also available in a variety of sizes and shapes, including oval, which makes them convenient for braising when a close-fitting vessel is important.

Enameled cast iron is not suitable for roasting pans or sauté pans because the juices from meats and fish do not adhere to it, making the separation of the juices from the fat before deglazing difficult.

Over the years, enameled cast-iron cookware can become chipped, so that sections of the iron start showing through. If this happens, it is essential to scrub the pots thoroughly so that bits of food do not collect in the exposed areas and cause food poisoning.

Nonstick Surfaces

Nonstick cookware is excellent for quickly sautéing meats and fish when a minimum of fat or oil needs to be used. Nonstick pans, however, are not good for making integral sauces, which involve deglazing; none of the meat or fish juices will adhere to the surface.

Stainless Steel

The advantage of stainless-steel cookware is that it is almost completely inert; it will not rust, tarnish, or react with foods. Its disadvantages are that it is a relatively poor conductor of heat and it is expensive.

The best stainless-steel pots and pans have a thick disk of copper in the base of the pan that helps conduct heat and prevent scalding. Well-made copper-bottomed stainless-steel pots and pans are a good choice for a professional kitchen.

Types of Cookware

Bain-Maries and Inserts

Traditional bain-marie pans are used to keep sauces warm during a restaurant service. They have a tall, cylindrical shape with a handle near the top and are designed to be set in a pan of hot water.

Some version of a bain-marie is essential for sauces that are made in advance. Unfortunately, tinned-copper bain-marie pans are expensive, and aluminum reacts with too many sauces. Stainless-steel bain-marie pans are difficult to find.

Good substitutes for bain-marie pans are the stainless-steel cylindrical inserts used in steam tables. When new they tend to be expensive, but they can often be found in good condition secondhand. They can also be filled with hot water and used to hold whisks, tasting spoons, and ladles during the restaurant service.

Casseroles

In American usage a casserole is a heavy pot with relatively low sides (but not as low as a sauté pan) that is usually used for stewing and braising. This may confuse cooks accustomed to French terms; in French, *casserole* simply means "saucepan," and the term *cocotte* is used to describe the American casserole.

Casseroles are either round or oval. For stews the shape is of little importance, but for braising larger pieces of meat, where the casserole must fit the dimensions of the meat as closely as possible, an oval casserole is indispensable.

Purists insist that the best material for slow, even cooking is earthenware—and that the best method is to bury the earthenware casserole (in one of its many regional shapes and carefully sealed with flour-and-water luting paste) under the ashes in the hearth. The purpose of these conditions is to protect braising meats from sudden increases in temperature, which might cloud the braising liquid. Professional chefs are rarely willing to sacrifice efficiency to cook in this way and usually substitute heavy copper or enameled iron casseroles with tight-fitting lids.

Most casseroles have rounded lids that cause condensed moisture to drip down the sides of the pan rather than over the meat. When using casseroles it is often helpful to put the lid on upside down so the condensation bastes the meat.

Until the twentieth century, copper *braisières* with sunken lids were made in France in a variety of shapes and sizes so the perfect size for a particular piece of meat was always on hand. The sunken lids were designed to hold coals, surrounding the braise evenly with heat. Today there is a type of oval casserole with a recessed cover called a *doufeu*. Instead of filling the cover with coals (although this is possible), water is used. The water protects the braise from overheating and causes moisture inside the pot to drip back down and baste the meat. The water also allows the cook to check the temperature of the pot without opening it: If the water on top approaches boiling, the oven needs to be turned down.

Gratin Dishes and Baking Dishes

Because food is often served in gratin dishes, the dishes need to be both efficient and attractive. Most gratin dishes are made of porcelain or stoneware that gives the finished dish a comforting, rustic look and also retains heat well. Some restaurants use tinned-copper gratin dishes when serving more elaborate classic gratins such as crayfish or lobster.

Gratin dishes traditionally have an oval shape, but in the United States, individual enameled iron or porcelain gratin dishes are sometimes round with small wing handles on each side.

Lids

Most pots and saucepans are available with their own exactly fitting lid, but in a busy professional kitchen, there is rarely time to rummage through the lids to find the right size. In older kitchens a series of copper lids with iron handles were always on hand, but these have become almost as expensive as good saucepans. Today's cooks will often haphazardly grab a lid—even if it is too large—and turn it upside down over the pot. If the lid is rounded on top, it will stay in place even if too large.

The most practical lids for the professional kitchen are inexpensive aluminum with rounded tops (the lid does not come in contact with the food).

Roasting Pans

It is imperative that roasting pans be made of heavy-gauge metal with a clear shiny surface. If the roasting pan is too thin, it will heat unevenly and the juices from the roast will burn. Aluminum or tinned copper make the best roasting pans because they enable the condition of the meat drippings to be seen. Dark metals, such as cast iron or treated aluminum, although suitable conductors of heat, make it difficult to see whether the drippings are burning. Enameled iron should be avoided because the drippings tend to float into the fat, making it difficult to separate them to prepare a jus.

Many cooks make the mistake of using a roasting pan that is too large, so that the meat drippings burn. A well-equipped kitchen should have several sizes. Since it is sometimes difficult to find roasting pans in a variety of shapes and sizes—most are square—heavy-bottomed sauté pans or oval casseroles can be substituted.

Saucepans, Sloping-Sided

A surprisingly large number of professional kitchens do not have a single saucepan with sloping sides (*sauteuse évasée*). They are essential for making hot emulsified sauces, where constant beating is necessary to emulsify and incorporate air. The bottom corners of a regular saucepan are too sharply angled to allow access with a whisk, therefore egg yolk sauces curdle.

Sloping-sided saucepans must be made with heavy copper or copper-bottomed stainless steel. Each saucepan's characteristics will take a little getting used to when making emulsified sauces; a heavy-bottomed pan retains a lot of heat and will continue to cook for a short while after being removed from the heat.

Saucepans, Straight-Sided

These saucepans (*casseroles* in French) should be made of heavy copper, aluminum, or copper-bottomed stainless steel with iron or hollow handles. A professional kitchen should have a good collection of different sizes. The size of the saucepan should match the flame under it: If the flame wraps around its sides during reduction, browning and discoloration of the sauce may result.

Sauté Pans, Sloping-Sided

These frying pans (*poêles*) are made from a variety of materials. In France they are usually treated iron, which when seasoned and properly used develops a nonstick surface. In the United States, they are often aluminum. There are advantages and disadvantages to both types. The French type has the advantage of not sticking, which makes it excellent for quick sautés of vegetables, fish, and breaded foods. Its disadvantage is that it cannot be deglazed; if it is, the carefully seasoned nonstick surface will be destroyed, at least temporarily. In restaurants where fish is prepared on a regular basis, oval sauté pans come in handy.

Aluminum sauté pans are used for sautéing because they can be deglazed. They are also inexpensive—an important advantage in restaurants that serve many sautéed foods with made-to-order sauces, making it necessary to have dozens of pans on hand.

Sauté Pans, Straight-Sided

Many cooks, including professionals, confuse straight-sided sauté pans (*plats à sauter* or *rondeaux*) with sloping-sided sauté pans—what Americans call frying pans, and the French, *poêles*. The difference is important. A straight-sided sauté pan is excellent for making integral sauces, because meats, vegetables, and other ingredients can be browned in the pan and the sauce made in the same pan used for sautéing. This is difficult in a pan with sloping sides where a sauce can scald or burn during reduction.

Straight-sided sauté pans should be constructed of heavy-gauge copper, aluminum, or copper-bottomed stainless steel. Most straight-sided sauté pans have a long iron handle on one side, which makes it easy to move them around on the stove. In some instances, however, it is useful to finish cooking certain dishes in the oven, and a sauté pan with two small handles (*rondeau*) is more useful. These pans can also double as roasting pans.

Steamers

The most useful steamer—a *couscoussière*—has a large pot with a colander-like insert that fits tightly inside, on top. It is excellent for quick steaming of fish, meats, and vegetables because any aromatic liquid can be boiled in the bottom pot and used to scent the foods steaming in the basket.

Stockpots

In professional kitchens where stocks are prepared on a regular basis, it may be necessary to have a collection of large pots for stocks in various stages of preparation and reduction. The most important consideration in choosing a stockpot is that it must have a heavy bottom; since the sides do not come in contact with the heat, they are of little importance. Make sure that stockpots have handles riveted onto both sides.

Some stockpots have taps on the bottom to facilitate draining—an especially useful feature when preparing large quantities, which are cumbersome to move.

A variety of smaller pots is also necessary in kitchens where reduced stocks and glaces are prepared regularly. A pot that is only a third full of liquid is difficult to skim and degrease; the liquid should be transferred to a smaller pot.

KITCHEN TOOLS AND UTENSILS

Chinois

Two types of chinois, sometimes called china caps, are essential in the professional kitchen. The first type, a coarse chinois, has a conical shape with a sturdy stainless-steel or tinned handle. The wall of the cone is made from a heavy sheet of stainless steel, aluminum, or tinned steel that is perforated with small holes. A coarse chinois will stand up to wear and tear that would quickly damage a fine chinois. Although a coarse chinois will not eliminate small particles from liquids, stocks containing bones or liquids containing sharp objects (such as lobster or crab shells) that would damage a fine chinois must be strained first through a coarse chinois.

A fine chinois is essential for straining sauces and stocks. Most have a fine-meshed conical screen made of stainless or tinned steel, held in place around a sturdy circular frame. They are expensive and must be treated carefully to help them last. When buying a fine chinois, inspect it carefully for small holes or spaces in the mesh—one small hole will defeat its purpose. When using a fine chinois to strain sauces, always use a small ladle and a gentle up-and-down motion to get the liquid to drain through. Never use a spoon and never use pressure. Do not throw a fine chinois into a sink with dirty dishes, where it might be damaged.

Drum Sieves

Drum sieves are necessary for straining relatively stiff mixtures, such as vegetable purées, that would damage a chinois. Drum sieves consist of a sheet of mesh screen held in place by a circular wooden or metal frame. A professional kitchen should have a sturdy metal-framed drum sieve for straining hard or coarse purées and a fine-meshed nylon sieve for finishing purées that require a very fine consistency.

When straining mixtures through a drum sieve, place it on a flat surface rather than over a bowl (unless the mixture is very liquid). This makes it easier to hold the sieve in place while applying pressure from the top. Mixtures are traditionally forced through sieves with a wooden pestle-like implement called a *champignon* (because of its mushroom-like shape). A plastic pastry scraper or even the bottom of a small stainless-steel bowl will also work well.

When selecting a drum sieve, try to find one with a removable frame that allows for the replacement of the screen, usually the first part to wear out.

Fat Separators

Very few of the gadgets that accumulate on the shelves of home kitchens make it into a professional setting; professionals prefer proven traditional equipment and techniques. A glass or plastic fat separator may become one of the few exceptions. It consists of a pitcher with a tubular spout attached to the bottom. When roasting juices or other liquids that need to be degreased are placed in the fat separator, the fat floats to the top. The liquid is then poured off from the bottom.

Food Mills

These devices are useful for straining purées or thick sauces such as tomato or tomatillo. They are available in different sizes. The smaller sizes are not of much use in a professional kitchen, because it is just as easy to work a small amount of the mixture through a cheap medium-mesh strainer. A large food mill, however, is almost indispensable for straining large amounts of tomato coulis and purée-thickened mixtures. Food mills come with several perforated metal plates that can be switched depending on the desired consistency of the mixture.

Ladles

Ladles are constantly used in professional kitchens for skimming stocks, straining liquids, and saucing foods on the plate. There should be a variety of sizes, always within easy reach.

Today most ladles are made of stainless steel, which will not tarnish or rust and is easy to clean. Select ladles with handles that are almost perpendicular to the surface of the bowl, which facilitates skimming stocks and removing fats from roasting juices. The best ladles are constructed of a single piece of stainless steel, rather than a separate bowl and handle that have been welded or riveted together. Ladles that have been welded together are more difficult to clean because food residue accumulates in the joint.

Larding Needles

Two types of larding needles are used to insert strips of fatback into large pieces of meat to keep them moist during braising. The larger of the two, a *lardoire*, consists of a hollow tube that is open on one side and has a sharp pointed tip and a handle. The strip of fat is put into the tube, and the larding needle is pushed through the meat so that the fat is left running through. The second type of larding needle, an *aiguille à piquer*, is used for larding the surface of meats. It resembles a small knitting needle and has a clamp on the back end to hold the strip of fat. The needle is used to "sew" the strips through the meat's surface.

Mandolines

This indispensable kitchen tool is used for quickly julienning and slicing an array of vegetables. Until recently, the large French stainless-steel mandoline was the only type found in professional kitchens, where it has been used since the nineteenth century.

A mandoline-style vegetable slicer, the Benriner cutter from Japan, has appeared in recent years. It has a razor-sharp blade that will slice vegetables from ¼ inch (5 mm) thick to almost paper thin. It works especially well for truffles (much better than the expensive Italian truffle slicer) and for extremely fine juliennes.

Measuring Cups and Spoons

These utensils are rarely used in professional kitchens, where most sauces are made by eye. In instances where careful measurement is necessary—such as for roux or when standardizing recipes for food costing—a kitchen scale is more reliable and easier to use.

Because they are made of glass, graduated glass pitchers, whether or not they are used for measuring, are useful for degreasing roasting juices.

Mortars and Pestles

Although often thought of as an anachronism, a good mortar and pestle are necessary for grinding certain ingredients when the action of a food processor either is too brutal or will not crush the ingredients in the way necessary to release their flavor.

Mortars and pestles are probably not used more often because they are difficult to find and good ones can be very expensive. The best are relatively large and made of a solid chunk of marble. Marble has the advantage of being very heavy, so that the mortar does not move around during grinding, and it does not absorb odors.

A good second choice is a heavy glazed-porcelain mortar with an unglazed inner surface that acts as an abrasive and helps along the grinding. Because even porcelain mortars and pestles are expensive, cooks often buy them too small, which makes them very difficult to use. Shops selling Southeast Asian ingredients sometimes sell relatively inexpensive but efficient stone mortars and pestles from Thailand. A *suribachi*, a wide Japanese mortar with flaring sides and ribbed interior, is especially efficient for grinding sesame seeds. It is often used in Japanese cooking.

Strainers

A selection of cheap, dime-store-variety strainers is useful for quick and easy straining of purées and fruit coulis, for getting the peels out of a small amount of tomato coulis, and for other coarse straining.

Truffle Slicers

These elegant little gadgets slice or shave white truffles at the table. In the kitchen a Japanese mandoline does a more efficient job, but for the dining room, an Italian truffle slicer is far more presentable.

Whisks

The best whisks for sauce making are made entirely of stainless steel and have an elongated shape and a large number of fine wires. Balloon whisks are designed for beating air into mixtures and are less convenient for stirring and reaching into the corners of a saucepan.

Many professionals leave a small whisk in a sauce or in an insert on the side so they can quickly give the sauce a stir every few minutes if necessary. A sauce whisk is best held like a pencil and rotated in a circular or figure-eight motion.

Wooden Spoons and Spatulas

Although a whisk is usually used in professional kitchens to stir sauces, wooden spoons and spatulas are indispensable for stirring egg yolk–thickened sauces, for which it is essential to reach into the corners of the saucepan. A whisk will also generate too much hard-to-remove froth on the surface of some egg yolk–thickened sauces. For some sauces (such as crème anglaise), a wooden spatula is essential for verifying the sauce's consistency.

Wooden spoons are also useful for stirring sauces that have not yet been strained and contain chunks of food such as vegetables, bones, and crustacean shells, which would get caught in the wires of a whisk.

Never leave a wooden spoon or spatula sitting in a sauce, or the flavor of the wood may affect the sauce's flavor. It is also impossible (and unsanitary) to taste a sauce from a wooden spoon—the wooden flavor is too pronounced.

MACHINES

Blenders

Always buy the simplest blender available. Small home-kitchen types with an array of buttons for every conceivable consistency of liquid are usually less powerful and reliable than a simple type with a heavy base and only two speeds, slow or fast. Waring manufactures both types.

Waring also manufactures a heavy-duty one-gallon-capacity blender for commercial use, but it is unlikely that many restaurants will prepare sauces in such huge quantities. Soups are another matter, and a heavy-duty blender can of course be used for both.

Observe two precautions when using blenders for hot liquids: Always start the blender on slow speed, and wrap a kitchen towel tightly around the lid of the container. Hot liquids expand quickly in the blender and can shoot out the top and make a nasty spill. Never fill a blender more than half full with hot liquids. When using a blender for sauces containing a large proportion of cream, remember that the sauce must be 120°F (50°C) or more or the cream will turn into butter.

When combining a stiff mixture (such as blanched watercress leaves) with a liquid (such as stock or cream) in a blender, it is always best to add the stiff mixture first and then slowly pour the liquid component through the opening in the center of the lid while the blender is on. If the liquid is added too quickly, the stiff mixture may escape the blender blades and remain in large pieces.

Electric Mixers

Electric mixers are essential for preparing compound butters—especially crustacean butters—for which long working of the ingredients is necessary. Large Hobart mixers or the smaller KitchenAids are the most reliable and useful on today's market. They come equipped with a flat paddle blade that is used for working stiff ingredients such as cold butter or very stiff purées. The whisk attachment can be used to whip butters and beat cream and egg whites.

A colander and sieve attachment is also available for straining stiff purées and fish or meat mousselines. It consists of a flat perforated disk and a series of rotating blades that force mixtures through the disk's holes. If stiff purées such as chestnut or bean are made on a regular basis, the attachment may be worth the investment.

Food Processors

A food processor is especially useful for preparing stiff purées that would be too much of a burden for a blender. It is often used for stiff mixtures and purées that were traditionally prepared with a mortar and pestle or by laborious working through a drum sieve.

It is better not to use a food processor for starchy purées such as those made with potatoes or celeriac, which will quickly become gluey if overworked. In some instances, especially for vegetable and fruit purées and coulis, it is useful to purée the mixture in a food processor before forcing it through a drum sieve.

SERVING UTENSILS

Plates

A collection of different-size plates is essential in a serious restaurant, where foods are served with a variety of sauces with different colors and textures, in different quantities.

Plates must have a distinct rim, which prevents the sauce from running up onto the plate's border. The depth of the inner section of the plate will depend on the style of sauce and presentation. Obviously, more of a light, thin-textured, broth-like sauce will be served than an intensely concentrated brown sauce. For light-style sauces, a relatively deep well is appropriate. For denser sauces served in smaller amounts, the plate's inner well should be smaller, or the sauce will spread too thinly and congeal.

Sauce Spoons

These spoons are a recent innovation that allow the diner to sip a thin sauce from the bottom of the plate without having to resort to dipping chunks of bread in it, which dulls the sauce's flavor and adds unwanted bulk to the meal. Sauce spoons are oval shaped and are almost perfectly flat so they can be easily slid against the bottom of the plate.

Wide Bowls

Unbound sauces are often too pale and too liquid to be served on regular plates. Many chefs are presenting dishes in wide soup bowls, from which the sauce can be sipped with a spoon.

INGREDIENTS 3

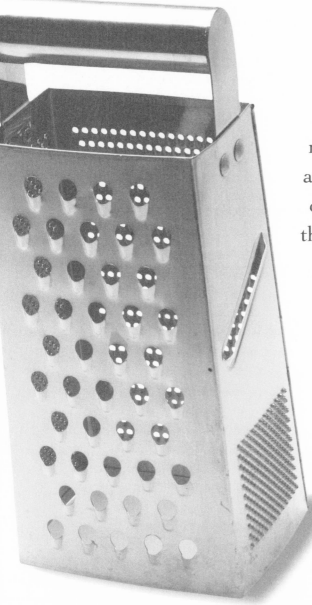

Because sauces are often more intensely flavored than the foods they accompany, they must be prepared with the best available ingredients. The foods described below comprise both the liquid medium for a sauce— ingredients such as dairy products and wine—and flavorings, such as herbs, spices, anchovies, and vinegar. Some of these ingredients also function as sauce thickeners.

ASIAN SAUCES, CONDIMENTS, AND OTHER INGREDIENTS

Bonito

A fish closely related to tuna, bonito is dried and smoked and sold in hard banana-like chunks called *katsuo-bushi*. In the best kitchens, katsuo-bushi is shaved into flakes almost immediately before being used, but more commonly bonito is sold already shaved in flakes called *hana-katsuo* or *kezuri-bushi*. Bonito flakes are infused in hot water that has already been infused with a strip of konbu to make the broth called dashi (see page 520), which is almost universal in Japanese cooking.

Chile Oil

Because commercially available chile oils are often of questionable quality, most serious cooks of Chinese foods make their own (see page 431). Chile oil is made by infusing dried chiles or chile flakes, and sometimes other aromatic ingredients such as ginger, in vegetable oil (usually peanut oil) combined with dark Asian sesame oil. It is used for flavoring dipping sauces or to give heat and flavor to stir-fries. If you must buy it, Aji Oil, packed by Kadoya; Sesame Chile Oil, packed by Iwai; and Japanese Food Corporation's Sesame Chile Oil are the best brands.

Chinese Chile Paste

Bottled Chinese chile paste provides a convenient method of quickly incorporating heat and flavor into last-minute sauces and stir-fries. Chinese chile paste also has a particular flavor of its own because it has been fermented. Lan Chi Brand is excellent and easy to find in Chinese groceries.

Coconut Milk

This is almost essential for making Southeast Asian curries and curries from Southern India, where it is used in much the same way Western cooks would use cream.

Many cooks who think that coconut milk is the liquid trapped inside a fresh coconut are surprised to discover that coconut milk is made by soaking the ground or grated pulp in hot water and then squeezing out the liquid (method follows). Coconut cream is the rich, congealed coconut fat that floats to the top of both homemade and good canned coconut milk. The cream should be added along with the milk. Fortunately, excellent coconut milk (Thai brands are best) is available, inexpensively, in cans. Avoid coconut milk containing sugar or stabilizers (even the best brands, however, contain sodium benzoate as a preservative), which are designed for making piña coladas.

To make about 2 cups (500 milliliters) of fresh coconut milk, shake the coconut to hear whether there's liquid sloshing around inside. If there's no liquid, the coconut may have been punctured and may have turned rancid inside. Use a hammer and a screwdriver to puncture holes in two of the coconut "eyes" (the dark oval spots near the top). Drain out the liquid, which is perfectly drinkable but too thin to use in a sauce. Bake the coconut in a 375°F (190°C) oven for 20 minutes to get the pulp to separate from the shell. Wrap the coconut in a towel and hit it with a hammer to crack it open. Pull out the pulp. Peel the thin dark peel off the sections of pulp with a vegetable peeler. Grind the pulp in a food processor for about 1 minute or grate it with a hand grater.

Put the grated pulp in a mixing bowl and add 1 cup (250 milliliters) of boiling water. Let the mixture sit for 10 minutes and then strain through a medium-mesh strainer over another bowl, reserving the liquid. Wrap the drained pulp in a kitchen towel and wring out any remaining liquid over the bowl. Put the wrung-out pulp in the original mixing bowl and add another cup of boiling water. Repeat the straining and wringing process.

Fresh coconut milk and opened canned coconut milk can be kept in the refrigerator for 1 week or frozen for several months.

Fermented Black Beans

These salted and partially dried beans look like dark raisins but have an intense salty flavor that makes them particularly delicious in Chinese stir-fries and sauces. Black beans are often used in conjunction with dried chiles (or chile paste), garlic, ginger, and sesame oil. Purists argue about whether black beans should be rinsed, but if they're not rinsed, fewer should be used or they'll make the sauce too salty. When buying fermented black beans, look for brands that have been flavored with ginger but not with Chinese five-spices. Yang Jiang brand, which comes in a cardboard container, is one of the best and is easy to find.

Fish Sauce

This bottled sauce is as fundamental to Southeast Asian cooking as soy sauce is to the cuisine of China. Fish sauce is made by allowing anchovies, other small fish, and occasionally squid to ferment in barrels for months at a time. The liquid released becomes fish sauce. Just as olive oil comes in different grades and potencies, so too does fish sauce (although the best quality will cost only a dollar or two more than the cheapest). Fish sauce keeps for at least a year in the refrigerator, although it may grow dark.

Although much of the best fish sauce is from Vietnam, Thai brands are easier to find and are perfectly suitable. Golden Boy Brand, Three Crabs Brand, and Flying Lion Brand are all excellent. Tiparos Brand is also good and widely available.

Ghee

See "Dairy Products," page 45.

Hoisin Sauce

This popular Chinese sauce is rather sweet and has a jam-like consistency. Hoisin sauce, like so many Asian sauces and condiments, is based on fermented soy beans. It is best known, combined with sesame oil, as an accompaniment to Peking duck. Used alone, hoisin sauce is overly sweet and thick, but it can be used in combination with other Chinese sauce ingredients (rice vinegar, soy sauce, sesame oil, and so on) to provide a note of sweetness or as a glaze for grilled meats. Small amounts of these mixtures are also welcome additions to simple stir-fries. Koon Chun Sauce Factory is considered one of the best brands of hoisin sauce and is available in Chinese groceries. Bruce Cost (in *Asian Ingredients*) also recommends Ma Ling Brand from China.

Kafeer Lime

See "Herbs," page 54.

Kinome Leaves

See "Herbs," page 54.

Kochujang

This Korean red chile paste, made from red chiles, Korean soy bean paste (*twoenjang*), and rice flour, is used as a spicy flavoring in Korean sauces, soups, and stews. It's almost essential in some recipes for contributing a characteristically Korean flavor. Sak-Dong Brand "Hot Pepper Paste" is excellent (see also "Chinese Chile Paste," page 34).

Legumes

In India, peas, beans, and lentils are all called *dal*. Almost any dried pea, lentil, or bean can be ground into a purée and used as a sauce thickener. Indian cooks also use certain varieties of beans as spices. Tiny black gram beans are a common ingredient in Northern India, where they are used to make rich and luxurious dishes containing plenty of ghee. In Southern India, black gram beans are split and hulled into the white and quick-cooking version called *urad dal*. Urad dal is used in very small quantities as a spice (often in conjunction with brown mustard seeds) in vegetarian dishes. It is also ground and combined with other spices and dried legumes to make Sambaar Powder (page 552), a Southern Indian spice mixture.

Two other legumes, *moong dal* and *channa dal*, are also used to make sambaar powder, along with various spices. Anyone who has grown their own bean sprouts has seen whole mung beans (dark green and cylindrical). But what is referred to as moong dal in Indian groceries is usually the yellow hulled and split version (ideal for use as a thickener). Channa dal are yellow split peas similar to, but not the same as, our supermarket yellow split peas. In addition to being cooked up in soups and in flavorful porridge-like dals, channa dal and moong dal are ground and used as thickeners.

Lemongrass

See "Herbs," page 55.

Mirin

A very sweet, sake-like cooking wine, mirin is often used in Japanese sauces. It provides the perfect balance to the smokiness of dashi and to the saltiness of soy sauce. Mirin is found in small bottles in Japanese specialty stores. It's inexpensive and keeps indefinitely in the refrigerator. Kikkoman brand is excellent and available almost everywhere.

Miso

This is the best known of fermented soy bean pastes (China and Korea have an assortment of their own), probably because of the popularity of Japanese cooking but also because miso is relatively delicate. There are subtle differences between every brand of miso, so it's worth experimenting with a few to find out which work best in particular sauces. The most commonly found miso in the United States is *shinshu-miso*, which has a pale tan color, is relatively inexpensive, and makes a good all-purpose miso. *Shiro miso*, which contains a large proportion of rice, is very pale yellow and relatively sweet and is excellent in delicate sauces such as cold dipping sauces or salad sauces. It can also be combined with stronger red miso to balance the shiro miso's sweetness and the red miso's saltiness. Of the darker, more savory misos, *inaka miso*, or "red" miso, and *hatcho miso* (the more expensive of the two) are the best for full-flavored broth-like sauces. Most brands of miso are of consistently good quality. Yamabuki brand is excellent (see also "Twoenjang," page 40, and "Soy Bean Pastes," page 38).

Oyster Sauce

Often used as a condiment and flavoring to give a sea-like note to Chinese sauces and stir-fries, oyster sauce, however, has none of the delicacy of fresh oysters. Sa Cheng "Oyster Flavored Sauce" is one of the best and is easy to find in a Chinese grocery, but Barbara Tropp (in *The Modern Art of Chinese Cooking*) recommends oyster sauce from Hop Sing Lung Oyster Sauce Company.

Rice Wine

See "Wine," page 80.

Salam Leaves

See "Herbs," page 57.

Seaweed

There are many kinds of seaweed (also somewhat euphemistically called "sea greens" or "sea vegetables"), but only one, *konbu*, is used with any regularity for sauce making.

Konbu is a dried seaweed sold in 18-inch to 3-foot-long (45 to 90 cm) strips that have been folded over themselves for easy packaging. The best konbu comes from the northern Japanese island of Hokkaido and is usually covered with a white, delicate, salt-like dust. Along with dried bonito, konbu is the basis for the basic broth dashi, common to most Japanese broth-like sauces.

Sesame Oil

See "Oils," page 42.

Sesame Paste

The better-known version of sesame paste, tahini, sold in Middle Eastern groceries, is made from raw sesame seeds and has a rather delicate flavor. In Asian cooking, it is preferable to use sesame paste made from toasted seeds. Toasting and grinding sesame seeds is not terribly difficult (see page 65), but Chinese sesame paste (on some bottles called "sesame butter") is made from roasted seeds and makes a good substitute for homemade.

Sesame Seeds

See "Nuts and Seeds," page 65.

Shiso Leaves

See "Herbs," page 57.

Shrimp Paste

A popular condiment in Southeast Asian cooking, shrimp paste, made by fermenting shrimp in the sun, has a strong fishy smell that takes some getting used to. But when used discreetly it gives an essential depth of flavor to Southeast Asian sauces and stews. If used in the way most recipes recommend (by cooking in oil before liquid is added), its odor is overwhelming. An alternative is to wrap the shrimp paste in aluminum foil and then toast it in a skillet and let it cool before it is used, or simply to stir small amounts directly into sauces and stews. Trachang brand from Thailand is excellent.

Soy Bean Pastes

The most familiar of all soy bean pastes is the Japanese version, miso, but Korea has its own version (*twoenjang*), and China has its sauce-like *jiang*. Soy bean pastes are all fermented but are combined with differing amounts of various grains, spices, and salt. The beans themselves may be left whole, chunky, or ground to a smooth paste. Any of these versions can be added to Asian sauces (Japanese or Korean broth-like sauces or sauces based on Chinese stir-fries) to give the sauces a distinctive and easily recognized regional or national character. Most fermented soy beans and pastes are first combined with a small amount of liquid (such as dashi or broth) and worked to a smooth paste before being combined with the rest of the ingredients (see also "Miso," page 37, and "Twoenjang," page 40).

Soy Sauce

There are so many varieties of soy sauce that it can be difficult deciding which is best for incorporating into sauces and other dishes. After a little experimentation, a particular soy sauce may emerge as a favorite, but when working with soy sauce for the first time there are a few things to look out for. Most important, avoid cheap synthetic supermarket brands (such as La Choy or Chun King brands) and look for an authentic sauce that has been naturally brewed (most of the best brands say so on the label). In any case, naturally brewed soy sauces will mention only water, soy beans, wheat, salt, and occasionally sodium benzoate, a preservative. Authentic soy sauce is made by fermenting roasted soy beans with wheat for at least four months and up to two years.

It's also important to distinguish between Japanese and Chinese soy sauces. Japanese soy sauces are less salty than Chinese versions, and, although Chinese cooking purists would disagree, Kikkoman soy sauce, made in the United States, has a pleasant clean flavor that makes it useful in both Japanese and Chinese dishes. Japanese soy sauce comes in both dark and light (light in color, not "light" as in light-tasting or low-calorie), with the light soy sauce containing more salt. Light soy sauce is mostly used in sauces where the deep color of dark soy sauce would discolor the dish in an unpleasant way. To experiment with authentic Chinese soy sauce, start out with Pear River Bridge and Koon Chun brands, keeping in mind that they're more salty than Kikkoman.

Indonesia has its own soy sauces, called *kecap* and pronounced like "ketchup." *Kecap asin* is dark and salty, whereas *kecap manis*, also dark, is very sweet. ABC brand from Jakarta and Conimex brand from Holland are both excellent.

Tamarind (Tamarindo)

Tamarind in the husk looks vaguely like a withered and dried brown fava bean. The husk is removed to reveal a series of beans (again like fava beans) surrounded with a sticky brown pulp. The pulp, not the beans, is used in Southeast Asian cooking to give sourness to sauces, soups, and stews.

Extracting tamarind pulp from fresh tamarind pods can be a nuisance, and since fresh tamarind isn't always available, it's fortunate that packages of tamarind paste (which looks like brown tar) are inexpensive and easy to find in Asian markets (or by mail order) and keeps for months in the refrigerator. To make tamarind extract, dissolve a walnut-size chunk of tamarind paste by working it around with a wooden spoon in ½ cup (125 milliliters) of boiling water and strain it through a fine-mesh strainer. Lime or lemon juice can be used as a substitute for tamarind.

Twoenjang

The Korean equivalent of miso, twoenjang, has a distinctive (and stronger) flavor, essential in a number of Korean sauces. Miso can be used as a substitute, but there's always the risk that the sauces will end up tasting too much like Japanese sauces. An excellent brand, available in the United States, has no English on the label except for the weight (1.05 pounds/475 grams) and the distributor, Pulmuwon U.S.A., Inc. (see also "Soy Bean Pastes," page 38, and "Miso," page 37).

CONDIMENTS

Mustard

Mustard is commercially available in three forms: dried, powdered mustard; crushed mustard macerated in some kind of flavorful liquid; and whole-grain mustard. Variations in the mustard's flavor are then controlled by changing the liquid used to macerate the mustard seeds or by adding herbs or other flavors at the end. Whole-grain mustard is easy to prepare and adapt to whim and imagination.

RED WINE MUSTARD

YIELD: 2 CUPS (500 MILLILITERS)

black mustard seeds	4 ounces	125 grams
distinctly flavored red wine	¾ cup	185 milliliters
red wine vinegar	¾ cup	185 milliliters
shallot, finely chopped	1	1
salt	1 teaspoon	5 milliliters
freshly ground black pepper	to taste	to taste
chopped herbs (thyme, marjoram, tarragon)	to taste	to taste

1. Combine all ingredients in a bowl, cover with plastic wrap, and refrigerate overnight.
2. Purée the mixture in a blender until it attains the desired thickness and texture.
3. Store refrigerated in a jar with a tight-fitting lid. (This mustard sometimes tastes bitter when first made, but the bitterness disappears after a few hours.)

Oils

Because they are derived from a variety of natural sources — grains, seeds, nuts, and fruits — oils offer a wide range of flavors, which the cook uses in many different ways. Oils are used for sautéing and deep-frying and are the predominant ingredient in mayonnaises, vinaigrettes, flavored oils, and even some hot emulsified egg sauces.

Oils vary widely in quality and cost, and the cook must use them judiciously so as not to waste an expensive oil needlessly or spoil a dish using a cheap one. Delicately flavored oils, for example, should not be used for sautéing, as the high heat would destroy their flavor.

The most common problem with oil is rancidity. A surprising number of cooks are so accustomed to using rancid oil that they no longer recognize it; it tastes and smells like stale nuts. A good-quality oil should be either completely tasteless (when used to sauté or to dilute the flavor of more assertive oils in sauces) or have the clear taste of the plant from which it is derived. Oils are best stored well covered in a cool place or in the refrigerator. Nut oils are particularly susceptible to rancidity and should be used within a couple of months of opening the container.

Because oils contain no protein or other emulsifiers, as do butter, egg yolks, and cream, they are usually not added directly to a sauce unless some kind of emulsifier is used with them (see Chapter 16, "Salad Sauces, Vinaigrettes, Salsas, and Relishes," page 423).

Grapeseed Oil

Grapeseed oil is the latest discovery by chefs in France and is beginning to become known in the United States. It is used for browning meats and fish because of its high smoking temperature and can be used to dilute the flavor of olive or nut oils because it is almost tasteless.

Nut Oils

Walnut and hazelnut oils have long been used in French regional cooking; in some regions they were once the only oils available. Since World War II, with improvement in the transporting of foods, home cooks often use olive or even neutral-tasting peanut oil (peanuts are actually legumes, like beans and peas) in place of these distinctively flavored nut oils.

Nut oils are mainly used for making vinaigrettes that are excellent with assertive or bitter greens, fennel, and artichokes. Most chefs combine nut oils with either olive oil or a tasteless vegetable oil such as *huile d'arachide* (specially processed peanut oil). Some chefs have also begun using nut oils to flavor mayonnaise.

The different brands of nut oils vary greatly. Some are more complex and deeply flavored than others; taste and smell them carefully before settling on a particular brand. Nut oils are the most perishable of all oils and should be kept in the refrigerator and used within a month or two after they are opened.

Nut oils made from roasted nuts have a deeper color and fuller flavor than oils made from raw nuts. Roasted nut oils are less perishable and keep their flavor for several months in the refrigerator (see Sources, "Nut oils," page 588).

Olive Oil

Of all the oils, olive oil is the most versatile and essential for sauce making and general cooking. It is available in different grades that are based on how the oil is extracted from the olive and the amount of oleic acid it contains. Oleic acid gives olive oil a harsh, biting feel in the mouth. The best-quality olive oil, extra-virgin (*vierge extra* in French, *extra vergine* in Italian), contains 1 percent or less of oleic acid and usually has the words "first cold pressed" or "*première pression à froid*" on the label. This implies that cold pressure alone, rather than heat or chemicals, has been used to extract the oil from the olives. Extra-virgin olive oil is a completely natural product of often startling delicacy and complexity, which is influenced by climate, soil, the age of the trees, the vintage, and other factors. There are no reliable rules as to which oils — Italian, Spanish, French, Greek — are the best; like wine, each oil needs to be judged on its own particular merits.

One consistent difference between French and Italian olive oils is that Italian oil is usually green and the French is golden brown. This is because the French use ripe olives; the Italians, green. Again, one is not consistently better than the other, but some chefs find that the green oil gives a peculiar color to mayonnaise.

Although there are several grades of olive oil, the only other grade seen on the American market is designated "pure." Pure olive oil is allowed to contain up to 4 percent oleic acid, can come from second or later pressings, and need not be cold pressed. It is useful for sautéing and deep-frying, when the delicacy of extra-virgin olive oil would be destroyed. Pure olive oil is considerably less expensive. Many professional chefs keep both oils in the kitchen: extra-virgin for sauces and flavorings, and pure for sautéing, deep-frying, and to use in conjunction with extra-virgin to soften its flavor in certain sauces.

Sesame Oil

This intensely flavored, deep brown oil is used sparingly in many Asian sauces and, nowadays, in Western-style sauces as well. Use only dark sesame oil, made from roasted seeds, and preferably a brand from Japan. Avoid pale and clear sesame oil sold in health food stores (it has little flavor). Maruhon Brand is excellent.

Vegetable Oils

Although raw cold-pressed oils made from grains can be found in health food stores, the tasteless commercial variety is most useful to the saucier. In addition to their use for browning meats and fish (they smoke at a very high temperature), these oils are sometimes used by sauciers in conjunction with olive oil or a flavorful nut oil for vinaigrettes and mayonnaises.

In France an inexpensive, commercially available peanut oil (*huile d'arachide*) is used whenever a tasteless oil is needed. In the United States, the situation is somewhat more difficult because many of the widely available brands of peanut oil, corn oil, vegetable oil, and safflower oil have a peculiar and unpleasant taste. When heated, these oils often smell like fish. Relatively tasteless and odorless brands of these oils can be found (Hollywood brand safflower oil is one), but a little searching and comparative tasting may be needed. It is also possible to buy French *huile d'arachide*, but it is almost as expensive as olive oil. A good-quality pure olive oil will often work better than vegetable oils when a relatively tasteless oil is needed.

Use vegetable oils sparingly in mayonnaises and vinaigrettes; they not only can adversely affect the taste but will often leave an unpleasant greasy feeling in the mouth.

Verjuice

Verjuice is the juice of underripe grapes. It was widely used as a sauce flavoring and condiment in medieval and Renaissance French and Italian cooking. Very acidic, its function in a sauce is somewhat like that of vinegar or lemon juice but not exactly like either one. It is the latest darling of French chefs and is beginning to show up in sauces, usually for fish. It seems to go particularly well with fennel and coriander seeds. Try experimenting with verjuice as a replacement for lemon juice in fish sauces.

Verjuice is still somewhat difficult to find in the United States, so unless there is a vineyard within easy access, it may be necessary to make do with substitutes. Some chefs substitute Pineau des Charentes, an aperitif from the Cognac region that contains incompletely fermented wine (the fermentation is stopped by adding Cognac). It has the flavor of unfermented grapes but none of the acidity characteristic of authentic verjuice.

Vinegar

Vinegar is an indispensable ingredient for sauce making. A few drops added to a sauce along with the final seasoning will awaken the flavor of the sauce without making it overwhelmingly acidic. Vinegar can also be used in surprisingly large amounts for stewing and braising meats—the result is full-flavored and mild. It is also, of course, a primary ingredient in vinaigrette.

Many types of vinegar are available, and, as with most ingredients, the way to determine which is best is to taste and compare them. Essentially, vinegar consists of a mixture of acetic acid and water; additional flavor components derived from the source of the vinegar (such as wine, cider, beer) and developed during aging give the vinegar its finesse and make it useful in the kitchen.

Most commercial vinegars range in strength from 5 to 7 percent acetic acid. European vinegars usually contain a higher percentage of acetic acid than American vinegars. Wine vinegar is the type most often used for sauce making. Distilled white vinegar should be avoided, as it contains none of the by-products that soften the flavor of vinegar and make it palatable.

Select a wine vinegar that has a high acid content but is not harsh. Most commercially available wine vinegar is made from low-quality wine and has little character. Sherry vinegar and French Champagne vinegar are exceptions. Sherry vinegar has a rich, complex flavor and full acidity that make it excellent for finishing brown sauces. Champagne vinegar is much less complex in flavor than sherry vinegar but has a clean, sharp taste that makes it useful in preparations where sherry vinegar would be too assertive, such as beurre blanc and sauce béarnaise.

Authentic balsamic vinegar is a specialty of Modena, Italy. It is one of the most expensive of all foods. Waverly Root describes how it is made in *The Food of Italy:*

> A line of 12 kegs is standing on some sort of platform . . . . The first keg in the row contains newly made herb-flavored wine vinegar. Its qualities are still a mystery. It is too young to have developed its own character. It will reach full potentiality after a journey from barrel to barrel, during which it will enter into different blends and absorb other perfumes. This is the process into which the vinegar in the other casks has already entered. As you move along the row, each barrel is richer than its predecessor; the last is the acme of what this cellar has so far been able to produce. It may have had a long life—in some of Modena's cellars you can find kegs containing vinegar 50, 60, or even 70 years old. It was started with the encouragement of a vinegar mother at least ten years old, in a keg of red oak, and in the course of years has been transferred from one keg to another—of oak, of chestnut, of mulberry and of juniper wood. Each of these added new fragrances to the liquid. This is traditional too, but nowadays it is also obligatory; the law stipulates that only casks made of these woods can be used for *aceto balsamico.* At the end of several years of blending, of moving, and of aging, the vinegar is a dense dark brown, almost black, with a pleasing characteristic aromatic odor, and a taste that is a mixture of tart and sweet. Acidity is not less than 6 percent, alcoholic content is not more than 1.5 percent.

Most of the so-called balsamic vinegar used by home cooks and in restaurant kitchens is factory made. Even these mass-produced substitutes have an appealing sweetness and complexity that makes them useful for sauce making. They are, however, only pale reminders of the real thing—at one-fiftieth the price. In Asia, vinegars are hardly ever made from grapes but instead from grains such as rice, wheat, millet, and sorghum. The mildest of these vinegars (useful to provide a simple acidity) is Japanese rice vinegar, which has been diluted down to a manageable 4.3 percent acetic acid (Marukan brand is good). Chinese rice vinegars are far more flavorful and are better in dishes with stronger, more competitive flavors (Narcissus brand or Swatow brand are best). The most flavorful Chinese vinegar is black vinegar, made mostly of fermented wheat but also other grains and aged in much the same way as balsamic vinegar. One brand (Gold Plum Chinkiang Vinegar) seems to have it hands-down over all the others.

Vinegar can also be used in the kitchen for storing herbs, particularly tarragon, whose flavor is far less altered by vinegar than by drying. There are many types of herb vinegars on the market, but the herb flavor in these vinegars is often not assertive enough to make them useful for sauce making. If you have a garden, or fresh herbs are available, it is more practical to prepare these vinegars yourself. An assortment of full-flavored herb vinegars will enable you to adjust the sauce's final flavor without having to chop the herb, add it to the sauce, give it time to infuse, and perhaps strain it out.

Much attention has been given to fruit-flavored vinegars in recent years. These vinegars were popular in the eighteenth century, then almost forgotten for 200 years. It is best to prepare these vinegars yourself by steeping a particular fruit in wine vinegar for a week or two and then straining the mixture through a chinois or a fine-meshed drum sieve. Commercially available fruit vinegars seem to contain cooked or concentrated fruits that give them an excessively sweet, candy-like flavor. (For a discussion of herb-infused vinegars for vinaigrette, see page 434).

DAIRY PRODUCTS

Butter

The subtle flavor and satiny texture of butter make it one of the most important ingredients in sauce making. It can contribute its own nuances to a sauce while gently amplifying and bringing into perspective the sauce's primary flavors. Butter, if used in moderation, can be added to a sauce or flavor base without diluting the sauce's flavor or distorting its character.

Any wholesome salt-free butter can be used in sauce making with good if not excellent results, but some butters have different flavors and behave differently. As you use one particular type of butter, its behavior will become familiar and you can more closely predict how it will act in specific preparations.

French butter tastes and behaves differently from American butter. French butter is made from *crème fraîche*—cream that has thickened as a result of natural fermentation caused by the bacteria that are present in milk. When cream that has been fermented in this way is churned into butter, the butter will have a complex, slightly nutty taste. Butter made from fresh cream or from cream that has been pasteurized soon after being separated from the milk will have a milder flavor than butter made from crème fraîche.

Chefs are often confused by discussions of *wet* and *dry* butters. Sometimes these terms refer to the actual water content, which can vary from 15 to 25 percent. Moisture content is important in sauce making because it helps determine how much butter will be needed to give the desired consistency to a liquid. If the butter has a high water content, more will be required to thicken a sauce. The terms "wet" and "dry" also refer to the types of fat that constitute the butter. Wet butter will leave an oily film on the hands, whereas a dry butter will leave the hands relatively dry. This difference is caused by the differing proportions of naturally hydrogenated fats contained in each. Dry butters (which contain more hydrogenated fats) will work more effectively as liaisons in sauce making.

Because the flavor of milk, and hence butter, depends on an almost infinite variety of conditions, butter can be an extremely individual product. Butter is also affected by the species of cows and their grazing conditions. Cows that feed in fresh pastures will produce fuller-tasting milk than cows fed on hay. Traditional farm butter may taste different from one farm to the next.

Unfortunately, as methods of mass production take over farming and dairies become larger and larger, the cream from different farms is blended and the individuality of each is lost. (This is roughly the equivalent of blending all the wines of the Médoc to produce a consistent-tasting red Bordeaux.) Although commercially available sweet butter is a sound product, it has no individuality.

In France a traditional farmhouse butter has an even greater potential for developing individual nuances because of the microbial action that is allowed to take place before the butter is churned. Strains of bacteria differ from region to region and even from farm to farm (farmhouse cheeses represent a remnant of the individuality once typical of butter). Each batch of butter results from the activity of an individual ecosystem on the components in the cream. Each of these bacterial "societies" leaves traces of flavor components in the butter, giving the butter its character.

In mass-produced French-style butter, the cream is pasteurized *before* it is allowed to thicken. It is then inoculated with laboratory-cultured bacteria to give it the gentle acidic tang to which the French have grown accustomed. These bacteria contribute to the cream's—and ultimately, the butter's—complexity, but because the butter is always prepared from the same bacterial strain, individuality is lost.

If only mass-produced butter is available, you might want to experiment with French brands. In large American cities, French butters can often be found for almost the same price as domestic brands. In some states, where the sale of raw milk products such as cream and butter is legal, you may find experimenting with making your own butter worthwhile.

Butter, once considered a wholesome, nutritious food, has suffered in recent years as more has been learned about the role of cholesterol and saturated fats in heart disease. Although these discoveries are relatively recent, French chefs and writers have long been conscious of how to use butter so that it can be easily digested. Because butter is a natural emulsion containing fat, water, and a complex collection of proteins, it must be handled carefully so that this emulsion stays intact. Once butter has been melted, the water and proteins separate from the fats. The fats alone are what constitute clarified butter, which has long been considered indigestible, while whole butter has been thought of as one of the most digestible of foods. Recent medical evidence has shown that the nonfat components of butter may play a role in the healthy metabolism of cholesterol. In other words, a beurre blanc may be healthier than a beurre noisette because the butter's emulsion is intact and all its components are present. In any case, it is hard to imagine that a synthetic, hydrogenated compound such as margarine could be less harmful than a simple, natural product such as butter.

Cheese

Three families of cheese are used in sauce making: fresh cheeses, dry cheeses, and blue cheeses.

Fresh Cheese

Fresh cheese (*fromage blanc*) is manufactured in two ways. One method relies on rennet to coagulate the milk, whereas the other uses a lactic acid–producing bacterial culture. Fresh cheese is difficult to obtain in the United States, and when available is often too old to be used in sauce making. The best fresh cheese for sauce making is made with bacterial cultures rather than rennet. It is not difficult to make, but check your local health regulations before serving a homemade version to the public.

Fresh cheese is sometimes used as a thickener for low-fat white sauces. Because it often has a rough texture in the mouth, it is best combined with at least a small amount of heavy cream or crème fraîche.

Dry Cheeses

Although Parmesan and Gruyère are the cheeses most often used for making traditional cheese sauces, almost any well-aged, dry, honest cheese will do. If a cheese has too high a moisture content or is insufficiently aged, it will lack flavor and make the sauce stringy. It may even ruin the sauce by bunching up into a solid mass.

Always try to use authentic cheeses rather than substitutes. There are several unpleasant-smelling cheeses on the market that are called Parmesan; they have nothing in common with the real thing. Buy only Italian Parmesan cheese labeled Parmigiano-Reggiano. Never buy grated Parmesan.

Swiss cheese is a generic term that denotes a certain style but in no way guarantees the quality or flavor of the cheese. Authentic Emmentaler cheese is sometimes labeled "Imported from Switzerland." Although this is an honest cheese, it is unsuitable for sauce making because it contains too much moisture and will turn stringy. Gruyère and Fribourg have less moisture and are excellent in sauces. The French often use Comté instead of Gruyère in sauce making.

American and British recipes often call for Cheddar cheese. Authentic, well-aged Cheddar from England as well as American Cheddar-style cheese can be excellent in sauces. Unfortunately, Americans (unlike the English, who leave theirs alone) have the habit of coloring Cheddar-style cheeses with orange dye. The best English Cheddars come in fat cylinders (about 12 inches high and 12 inches in diameter/30 × 30 cm) called truckles. There are several Cheddar-style cheeses made in the United States—Vermont produces some especially tasty versions—which, when well aged and left undyed, are excellent in sauces.

Blue Cheeses

These cheeses are excellent for giving a complex yet forthright flavor to sauces. In addition to their popularity in the United States as salad ingredients, blue cheeses are especially good in sauces served with egg dishes such as soufflés.

Unfortunately, many cooks do not realize that there are many types of blue cheese; some are almost unbelievably delicious, whereas others border on being inedible. It is always worth the extra few dollars to buy the best available.

The best-known blue cheese is Roquefort. Authentic Roquefort comes from a closely delineated area in France and is made entirely of sheep's milk. When sufficiently aged (unfortunately, it is often eaten too young), it is one of the world's finest cheeses.

Although France produces over thirty varieties of blue cheese, some are more distinctive than others and make more interesting sauces. Apart from Roquefort, Fourme d'Ambert, Bleu d'Auvergne, and Bleu de Bresse are especially good.

Two deservedly famous blue cheeses—Stilton and Gorgonzola—can also be used to give their own character to sauces. Danish blue and industrial blue cheeses manufactured in the United States are not recommended.

Cream

Heavy cream is indispensable for most contemporary white sauces. It is especially valuable because it is an extremely stable emulsion that can be boiled and reduced to almost any consistency.

Unlike milk, which must be stabilized with emulsifiers such as flour or egg yolks, heavy cream will not break unless it is boiled without stirring or is overreduced. Heavy cream contains about 58 percent water, from 35 to 37 percent fat, 3 percent carbohydrates, and a small percentage of ash and various minerals. Sometimes cooks are tempted to substitute milk or half-and-half for heavy cream. Because these contain less fat and a higher percentage of protein, they are more susceptible to curdling when exposed to heat or other ingredients. When light cream is needed, it is better to use a mixture of water and heavy cream, which is more stable.

In Europe, thick versions of heavy cream, such as crème fraîche and mascarpone, are used for sauce making. Although these creams are thick, one should not assume that they have a higher fat content. In unpasteurized cream, the thickening is caused by lactic acid–producing bacteria that naturally occur in milk. In pasteurized cream, a laboratory-bred culture is added after pasteurization.

Ghee

A favorite cooking fat and flavoring in India, ghee is essentially clarified butter (but instead of simply melting the butter, skimming off the froth, and ladling off the pure fat, ghee is made by gently cooking the butter until the milk solids caramelize slightly and give the butter a characteristic butterscotch flavor). The process is identical to making Beurre Noisette (page 412) without the added lemon.

Sour Cream

Manufactured sour cream is prepared by mixing milk fat and skim milk with nonfat solids and other ingredients. The mixture is then pasteurized, inoculated with lactic acid–producing bacteria, and allowed to set.

Because of the texture, many beginning cooks assume that sour cream is as rich as heavy cream and can be used in the same way. Sour cream contains less butterfat (about 18 percent) than heavy cream (35 percent) and is a much less stable emulsion. For this reason sour cream cannot be reduced or even boiled, or it will curdle. A large number of recipes (of mostly Eastern European origin) finish stews and sauces with sour cream (such as beef Stroganoff). When finishing a sauce with sour cream, make sure the sauce base is overly thick before adding the sour cream, which will thin it. A too-thick sauce can easily be thinned, but once the sour cream has been added, no further reduction is possible.

Yogurt

Yogurt is manufactured by inoculating whole or skim milk with a culture containing two types of bacteria, *Lactobacillus bulgaricus* and *Streptococcus thermophilus*. The ratio between the two organisms has much to do with the flavor of the yogurt. When *L. bulgaricus* dominates, the yogurt will have more acidity and tang. A greater percentage of *S. thermophilus*, on the other hand, will give the yogurt a deeper flavor with more finesse. In food establishments where yogurt is used on a regular basis, it may be worth obtaining cultures of both microorganisms so that the flavor of the yogurt used in sauce making can be closely controlled.

Some sauces (primarily fish sauces) benefit from the acidity of a tangy yogurt, whereas a less acidic yogurt is useful for lightening mayonnaises, emulsified egg yolk sauces, and similar preparations (see Chapter 5, "Liaisons: An Overview," page 109).

Yogurt is often used as a liquid ingredient in Indian curries (stews), where it provides texture and lends an acidic tang. It is best used in curries that contain thickeners such as cooked lentils, which prevent the yogurt from curdling.

HERBS

Although there is no clear botanical distinction between herbs and spices, in culinary usage spices are usually roots, seeds, berries, bark, and fruits, whereas herbs are leaves or flowers. The aromatic vegetables, such as garlic and shallots, comprise a third group of flavorings.

An experienced saucier uses herbs at several stages of the sauce-making process. The decision as to when to use a particular herb depends on the herb's flavor and its reaction to heat. Some herbs are used to contribute to the background flavor of a sauce, whereas others are added at the last minute to add finesse and freshness or a character of their own. The saucier must decide how the herb's flavor will function in the sauce.

Some herbs, such as thyme and bay leaf, release their flavor slowly into the surrounding liquid. When added discreetly at the beginning of the sauce's preparation, their flavor is subtle enough to blend with the sauce's savory constituents, giving the sauce complexity without distracting from its primary flavor. Used in this way, herbs meld with the other ingredients in the sauce so their presence, though not immediately recognizable, gives a sauce mystery and depth of flavor. Thyme can also become the sauce's predominant flavor. When thyme is used in this way, it is usually chopped and added near the end of the sauce's preparation. The sauce's other components then function as background elements to reflect, heighten, and relieve the primary flavor of thyme.

Certain herbs, primarily parsley, chervil, and chives (three of the four herbs that constitute *fines herbes*), can be finely chopped and added to give the sauce finesse and freshness. The flavor of these herbs dissipates quickly, so they should be chopped and added during the last few minutes of cooking to give the sauce freshness and vitality without altering its predominant flavor.

Some sauces are constructed with the flavor of a specific herb in mind. The chef may even decide to name the sauce after the herb being used—for example, chicken with tarragon sauce, grilled saddle of lamb with basil sauce. When herbs are used in this way, they are added near the end or at several stages during cooking so that their flavor is kept intact. Certain herbs release their flavor immediately when added to hot liquids and thus should always be added near the end of the sauce's preparation. For instance, the flavor of fresh basil is volatile and will cook out of a sauce within a few minutes.

>*Small Bouquet Garni.* Tie in a bundle with kitchen twine, or in a sachet if using dried thyme: 1 bay leaf, 3 sprigs parsley, 1 sprig thyme (or ½ teaspoon/3 milliliters dried leaves).

>*Medium Bouquet Garni.* Tie in a bundle with kitchen twine, or in a sachet if using dried thyme: 1½ bay leaves, 6 sprigs parsley, 2 sprigs thyme (or ¾ teaspoon/4 milliliters dried leaves).

>*Large Bouquet Garni.* Tie in a bundle with kitchen twine, or in a sachet if using dried thyme: 2 bay leaves, ½ bunch parsley (about 15 sprigs), 5 sprigs thyme (or 1 teaspoon/5 milliliters dried leaves).

Dried Versus Fresh Herbs

Some dried herbs retain their flavor better than others. Thyme, marjoram, oregano, lavender, savory, and rosemary can be dried without altering or seriously attenuating their flavor. It is always preferable, however, to start with the fresh herb and dry it on the branches. Bottles of dried thyme or savory leaves never have the same flavor as leaves that have been dried and left on the branches.

The flavor of some herbs is either lost or irreversibly distorted once dried. Basil, chervil, tarragon, parsley, and chives do not dry well and should not be used. If confronted with an abundance of fresh tarragon, it is better to pack it tightly in jars with white wine vinegar than to dry it. In this way its flavor stays intact almost indefinitely. The flavors of basil, chervil, chives, and parsley, however, are unpleasantly altered when they are stored in vinegar.

Chopping Herbs

Many chefs and amateur cooks, in an attempt to be well prepared, chop their herbs in advance and have them on hand in little bowls to be used as last-minute flavorings. Some chopped herbs immediately begin to lose flavor, or worse, their flavor is unpleasantly changed.

When chopping herbs, make sure they are perfectly dry. If an herb is chopped while wet, the flavors dissipate into the surrounding liquid. The chopped herb will also form clumps and become impossible to chop finely and evenly. Many cooks wring chopped parsley out in a towel after it is chopped to eliminate excess moisture and make the parsley easy to sprinkle in sauces or over foods. Such parsley may be easier to handle, but most of its flavor and finesse will be lost.

Always use an extremely sharp knife. If herbs are chopped with a dull knife, they are crushed, prematurely releasing most of their flavor into the surrounding air or into the cutting board.

Certain herbs, such as basil and tarragon, almost immediately turn black when chopped. The best way to prevent this discoloration is to protect the herb from oxygen by first coating the leaves with a thin layer of olive oil or by chopping the herbs with a small chunk of butter. In either case, chop the herbs as close to the last minute as possible.

Fines Herbes

The term *fines herbes* refers to a mixture of four herbs: tarragon, chervil, parsley, and chives. Of the four, tarragon is by far the most assertive and will overwhelm the mixture unless a very small amount is used. Because fines herbes are primarily used in sauce making to wake up a sauce and give it finesse (not to impart the character of any particular herb), many chefs leave the tarragon out of the mixture entirely. Fines herbes without tarragon are especially useful for sauces that taste flat because of long cooking and reduction.

Types of Herbs

Basil

Basil's vibrant sunny smell and bright flavor make it a natural component of intense, full-flavored sauces. It is not a subtle herb, but works beautifully with other assertively flavored ingredients, such as saffron, garlic, and olive oil. It is irresistible when used in Mediterranean fish sauces.

Basil works best when added to a sauce at the very end of the sauce's cooking. Its flavor is so volatile that it will rapidly dissipate if cooked for more than a few minutes. Like tarragon, basil will quickly turn black when chopped, so it is best to dribble a little extra-virgin olive oil over the leaves before beginning.

Basil does not dry well but can be frozen if chopped finely with olive oil and stored in tightly sealed plastic containers.

Bay Leaf

One of the basic components of a bouquet garni, bay leaf, if cooked for an hour or more, lends a gentle complexity to stews and to red wine and game sauces. The amount to use must be gauged carefully, or the flavor either will be too dominating or will disappear altogether. Dried bay leaf is acceptable, but the leaves should be broken in two and sniffed to ensure they are not stale. California bay leaves have an aggressive eucalyptus flavor and should not be used.

Chervil

Chervil, one of the most delicate of all herbs, has only recently become widely available in the United States. Most Americans had seen only the dried, bottled variety and were no doubt mystified as to what use something so flavorless and odorless could have in the kitchen. Fresh chervil has a delicate anise flavor, vaguely reminiscent of tarragon but far more subtle and fleeting.

Because of its delicacy, chervil should be used only in the last few minutes of cooking. If added sooner, its flavor will be entirely lost. It is one of the four herbs in the classic mixture fines herbes. Some recipes (chicken chasseur comes to mind) use chervil in combination with tarragon, which is a far more assertive herb. The flavor of the chervil is completely lost in these mixtures.

Chives

Chopped chives can be used near the end of cooking to impart their delicate, onion-like flavor to a sauce. When cooked for only a minute or two, their flavor melds with the other components and gives the sauce renewed vitality. Unlike onions or shallots, chives are never overly assertive.

Be careful when chopping chives. Hold a small bunch firmly between the thumb and first three fingers of the left hand (or right hand if you are left-handed), and carefully chop with a very sharp knife. If chives are chopped haphazardly, the pieces will be uneven and the excitement of seeing the tiny cubes in the sauce will be lost. Chives should always be chopped finely. Longish pieces of chives floating in a sauce may be appealing to the eye, but they are unpleasant in the mouth and will release their flavor suddenly and aggressively rather than gently caressing the sauce's basic flavors.

Cilantro

The leaves of the plant that produces the spice coriander are known as cilantro. Freshly chopped cilantro leaves have a natural affinity for tomatoes, garlic, and hot peppers. The flavor is especially delicious in Mexican salsas and Indian curries.

This herb is also discussed in conjunction with coriander in the "Spices" section, page 69.

Curry Leaves

These leaves look somewhat like bay leaves but have a milder and distinctly different flavor and are used in larger amounts. Curry leaves are widely used in

India (especially Southern India) as a flavoring for vegetarian bean and lentil dishes. Curry leaves can be found dried, frozen, and occasionally fresh in Indian groceries.

Dill

The flavor of dill is so distinctive that it doesn't meld well with other herbs. It is delicious with seafood such as scallops and salmon and works particularly well with sauces containing cream, which attenuates its dominating character. Some chefs confuse it with fennel—it looks vaguely like fennel greens—but the taste is entirely different.

Hyssop

The subtle piney flavor of hyssop makes it useful in much the same way as thyme or savory: It can be used in a bouquet garni, finely chopped and used on grilled meats, or infused in broth-style brown sauces or meat jellies. It was often called for in medieval recipes. Hyssop can be difficult to find, but most herb suppliers would probably grow it on request. It is also easy to grow in a home or restaurant garden.

Kafeer Lime

Kafeer lime rind, leaves, and juice are all used in Southeast Asian cooking. Kafeer lime (*Citrus hystix*) is closely related to our common lime (*Citrus aurantifolia*), but the flavor of kafeer lime is more subtle and more lemony. Kafeer lime leaves are simmered whole in Southeast Asian sauces and stews in much the same way as bay leaves enter into their Western equivalents.

Kafeer lime rind, sold frozen in Asian markets, is usually ground to a paste as a component of Thai curries (pages 534 to 538) and kafeer lime juice (difficult to find) is used to provide acidity. The zest of the common lime can be used as a substitute for kafeer lime leaves and rind, and regular lime juice can be used to provide acidic tang.

Kafeer leaves are sold fresh or frozen in Asian markets. Both the leaves and rind will keep frozen for several months.

Kinome Leaves

These mildly spicy mint-like leaves come from the prickly ash tree. They are in season in the spring and are a popular garniture for Japanese dishes. Shiso leaves (see page 57), sprigs of watercress, or other baby leaves make a good substitute. The pods of the prickly ash are ground into sansho pepper, which is unlike white or black pepper and is often sprinkled on grilled foods in Japanese cooking.

Lavender

There are several varieties of lavender, but the most aromatic, and the best for cooking, is French lavender, *Lavandula spica*. Chefs rarely use lavender as the only herb in a dish, and they may use it unknowingly in French *herbes de Provence* mixtures, of which it is a component. When used instead of thyme or marjoram, lavender gives foods a distinctive aromatic flavor. It is wonderful with garlic; the two can be crushed together to a paste in a mortar and sprinkled over sautéed mushrooms or zucchini about a minute before they are removed from the heat — the flavor is irresistible. Lavender can be hard to find in food stores, but it is sometimes sold in shops that supply herbal remedies. It is also easy to grow.

Lemongrass

Lemongrass comes in stalks about 18 inches (45 cm) long that look a bit like elongated miniature ears of corn. Often the tough outermost sheath is peeled off and discarded and only the relatively soft white root end is used, usually thinly sliced. Traditionally, sliced lemongrass is infused in Southeast Asian sauces, stews, and soups or ground up with other ingredients in Thai curries. Western chefs have caught on to lemongrass and are now beginning to infuse it in delicate broth-like sauces.

Because lemongrass has the flavor of lemon without the acidity, a finely julienned zest of one lemon, boiled for a minute in water to eliminate its bitterness, can be used to replace a 3-inch (8 cm) section of lemongrass stalk. Lemongrass can be kept several months, tightly wrapped, in the freezer.

Lemon Thyme

Although lemon thyme looks similar to regular thyme, its flavor is distinctly different. It has a delicate, lemony flavor that makes it delightful in fish sauces and delicate court-bouillons served *à la nage*. It should not be thought of as a replacement for regular thyme, however, because it does not meld with other flavors in the same way. Lemon thyme should be used only where its flavor needs to stand out.

Lovage

Because lovage leaves have a domineering, celery-like flavor, they should be used in long-cooked preparations (stews, poached meats, and the like), where their taste will eventually meld with the other ingredients.

Marjoram

Although its flavor is completely different, marjoram is sometimes confused or used interchangeably with oregano, its botanical cousin. Fresh marjoram has an unmistakable aroma and flavor all its own. It is difficult to imagine a food that would not be complemented by fresh chopped marjoram (dried will do in a pinch), but it seems to work best with Mediterranean foods and flavors. It is excellent with grilled meats and fish and all sorts of vegetables, especially tomatoes, mushrooms, and squash. It can be used to enhance fish stews and soups by including it in the bouquet garni along with fresh thyme.

Mint

Often called for in medieval French recipes, today mint is used only occasionally in French and Italian cooking. It is more popular with Americans and the English, who never eliminated it from their repertoire of culinary herbs. There are many varieties—best known are spearmint and peppermint—with a wide spectrum of flavors. Mint is an excellent flavoring in salad vinaigrettes, where it is best ground with a pinch of coarse salt using a mortar and pestle and then combined just before serving with lemon juice and oil. It is also excellent for scenting heavy cream served as a sauce for cucumbers and figs.

Oregano

Oregano is one herb that becomes fuller flavored and improved when it is dried. There is considerable confusion as to the flavor of oregano, which seems to be influenced by the climate where it is grown. The fresh cultivated oregano available in the United States is surprisingly delicate. It is lovely with grilled rabbit.

Parsley

In the United States, parsley is cut into sprigs and used as a garniture that is pushed to the side of the plate, uneaten. Its value as one of the most versatile and useful herbs for sauce making is usually ignored. Plus it is almost always available.

Freshly chopped parsley can be added to a sauce during the last minute of cooking to contribute freshness and flavor without taking over. In larger amounts, it can be used as a primary flavor. Parsley should never be kept for more than an hour after it has been chopped; its fresh, pungent vitality rapidly dissipates. Stale parsley has a sour, grassy smell and taste and should be thrown out.

Flat parsley is usually more flavorful and pungent than curly parsley, but freshness is a more important factor than variety.

Rosemary

Although rosemary occasionally makes its way into a bouquet garni in Italian and southern French stews, it is best when used sparingly to scent grilled and roasted meats. It can be used in a marinade so that its flavor will be softened by the time it is captured in the roast's natural jus. If used carelessly or in excess, rosemary easily dominates the surrounding flavors. Because the flavor of rosemary is an oil, it dissolves quickly in fats, and it will become overly strong in stews or roasts if the cooking liquid or jus is inadequately degreased.

The most subtle use of rosemary is to throw a handful of the twigs on the hot coals near the end of grilling. The smoke lightly scents the grilled foods. If an integral sauce is being prepared to accompany the grilled food, the now-delicate perfume of the rosemary can be worked into the surrounding liquid.

Sage

When fresh (be careful with dried—it sometimes smells and tastes like dust), sage is wonderfully aromatic but can be frightfully strong. It is usually too aggressive to be used as a flavor finish for sauces but can be used for scenting roasts (veal and pork) or grilled meats and poultry, where its flavor will be more subtle in the finished jus.

Salad Burnet

This attractive perennial is rarely used in sauce making. It is used only in conjunction with other herbs to provide color and to soften the flavor of green sauces. It has a slightly bitter, cucumber-like taste that makes it better suited for tossing in a salad than for making sauces.

Salam Leaves

These leaves look somewhat like bay leaves and are used in much the same way by Indonesian cooks. Salam leaves should be used sparingly (again, in the same amounts as bay leaves) and can be simmered in stews or added to the water used for making rice. Bay leaves can be used as a substitute but they won't lend a characteristic Indonesian flavor in the same way as salam leaves.

Savory

Two types of savory are used—summer (*Satureia hortensis*) and winter (*Satureia montana*). Both have a pungent yet malleable perfume reminiscent of thyme, which they sometimes replace in a bouquet garni. Winter savory seems to be the more useful of the two in sauces because its flavor is more subtle and melds more easily with other ingredients.

Shiso Leaves

These gently spicy heart-shaped leaves are a popular garniture for Japanese dishes. Both red and green shiso appear in markets, but green shiso has the best flavor and can usually be found, year-round, in Japanese groceries. Sprigs of watercress, mint, or other small fresh leaves can be used as a substitute.

Sorrel

Sorrel has a faint perfume but an intense, sour flavor. It is best used in fish sauces, where its sharp tang is a welcome alternative to the ubiquitous lemon wedge. Sorrel should be used in sauces containing at least a small amount of cream, which softens its acidity.

Sorrel can either be stewed and puréed or sliced raw into a chiffonade before being added to a sauce. When used as a purée, it not only contributes flavor but helps bind the sauce and give it texture. The disadvantage to sorrel purée is its sullen grayish hue; to the uninitiated it may seem overcooked.

Raw sorrel chiffonade can be added to a sauce near the end of cooking. It cooks and loses its texture almost immediately. Sorrel chiffonade is best used in individual made-to-order sauces. If added to larger quantities of sauce, it invariably becomes a hopelessly tangled clump at the bottom of the pot or bain-marie.

Tarragon

Tarragon is an assertive, full-flavored herb with an intense anise-like flavor. Unlike chervil and parsley, which willingly sacrifice their individuality to the whole, tarragon retains its character and always makes its presence felt. For this reason, it is always used as either the focal point or as a sharp accent to a sauce's flavors. Despite its lack of subtlety, tarragon is a beautiful accent to the flavor of chicken, veal, and crustaceans such as lobster and crayfish.

Tarragon is usually added near the end of sauce preparation, as the flavor is only weakened by lengthy cooking.

Tarragon turns black when exposed to air and thus should be chopped with a small chunk of butter to protect it from air. Tarragon does not dry well; drying not only attenuates but distorts its flavor. If fresh tarragon is not available, tarragon in vinegar is an excellent substitute.

Thyme

Thyme is one of the most subtle and versatile herbs used in sauce making. The saucier can control the directness of its flavor by using it at different stages during a sauce's preparation. Thyme added at earlier stages (such as in a bouquet garni in a stock) will meld into the background flavors of the sauce. When used in this way, it not only contributes its own subtle flavor but tends to unify the sometimes disparate flavors of vegetables, wine, meat, or fish. Owing to these characteristics, thyme is one of the three components of a traditional bouquet garni (the others are bay leaf and parsley).

If the saucier wants the flavor of thyme to be more predominant and more direct, thyme can be added at a later stage. Typically, thyme used in this way is sweated along with mirepoix vegetables, which are in turn moistened with wine, stock, or other flavored liquids to give the sauce its final character (as in sauce bordelaise and sauce bretonne). A sprig of thyme can also be added to sauces in the later stages of reduction to impart freshness and to offset the loss of flavor and ensuing flatness caused by long reduction.

If the saucier wants to capture the direct flavor of thyme and bring it into the foreground, thyme can be finely chopped and added during the last few minutes of cooking.

Verbena

This herb, *Verbena officinalis*, also known as vervain, is most often used in sooth-ing herbal teas or in combination with other herbs for making liqueurs. It is only occasionally used in cooking, where it is infused in milk for crème anglaise or in light broths to accompany chicken or fish.

MUSHROOMS AND TRUFFLES

Mushrooms

Until twenty years ago, most Americans were suspicious of anything other than the standard white mushroom, *Agaricus bisporus*, found on supermarket shelves. Today, wild mushrooms have become a virtual craze, with new varieties con-stantly appearing in fancy food markets. Cultivation of different varieties of mushrooms has also become a viable industry, so that many of the mushrooms habitually called "wild" are actually commercially grown in a way similar to *Agaricus bisporus*.

Most sauce recipes calling for mushrooms, duxelles, or mushroom cooking liquid will be raised to new heights by substituting wild or nonstandard culti-vated varieties.

Many cooks are confused by conflicting recommendations in food books about whether or not to wash mushrooms. If the mushrooms are clean or if bits of sand and soil can easily be brushed free, it is best to avoid washing them. Mushrooms absorb water very quickly, which dilutes their flavor and makes them soggy. This is especially a problem if the mushrooms are to be sautéed. If it is necessary to wash the mushrooms, rinse them under rapidly running cold water rather than letting the mushrooms soak in a bowl or sink. Immediately place the mushrooms on a dry towel to absorb the water from their surface as quickly as possible.

Mushrooms that have dried slightly are preferable to those that are soggy or have a moldy smell. Never store mushrooms in plastic bags or plastic con-tainers. They are best kept loose in paper bags or even spread out on baking sheets covered with dry towels, exposed to air.

When mushrooms are being incorporated into a sauce, they often benefit from being first sautéed in hot fat or oil, which lightly caramelizes their juices and concentrates their flavor. Most mushrooms have a high water content and must be sautéed over a high flame. One mistake that beginning cooks often make when sautéing mushrooms is to heat the pan and add the mushrooms all at once. This inevitably cools the pan and causes the mushrooms to steam, re-lease liquid, and finish by stewing in their own juices. It is better to add the mushrooms in three or four stages, allowing each batch to heat up before adding more. Some mushrooms contain so much water that they should be allowed to dry in the open air for several days before sautéing.

The quality of dried mushrooms varies considerably. Morels take best to the drying process, followed by *Boletus edulis*, called *cèpes* by the French, and *porcini* by the Italians.

Boletes

Although the English name for this family of mushrooms is boletes, American chefs usually call them by their French name, *cèpes*, or the Italian, *porcini*. There are several varieties of edible boletes, but the best and deservedly most famous is the *Boletus edulis*. Boletes come in all sizes, from small, with 2-inch (5 cm) caps, to quite large, with caps over a foot (30 cm) in diameter. Boletes have the classic *Alice in Wonderland* mushroom shape.

Boletes are sometimes infested with insects, especially in the stems, so check them carefully either by slitting the stem in half lengthwise or by peeling off a patch of the outer skin. It is best to select boletes that have dried out slightly. Avoid boletes that are wet or soggy. Boletes can be grilled, sautéed, or baked and served either alone or as a garniture for other dishes. Much of the excitement in eating boletes comes from their thick and meaty texture, so do not slice them too fine (at least when cooked—raw in salads is something else).

If you want to incorporate the flavor of boletes into a sauce, it is best to either grill or sauté them before their flavor is infused into a sauce. Their character is better brought out when they are sautéed in olive oil or goose fat or when they are brushed with either of these during grilling. Their flavor stands well alone, but some chefs like to sprinkle them with a mixture of parsley and garlic or shallots near the end of sautéing or grilling.

While dried boletes (usually labeled "dried porcini") have little of the plump meaty texture of fresh boletes, good-quality dried porcini have a delicious and intense flavor that makes them excellent in sauces, especially pasta sauces. When buying dried boletes, look for large slices with the classic shape of the mushroom cross section. Avoid bags of broken up little pieces. Dried porcini should be quickly rinsed and soaked for about 30 minutes in barely enough warm water to cover before the mushrooms are incorporated into a sauce. The soaking liquid should be saved and also added to the sauce by pouring gently so any grit is left behind in the bowl.

Chanterelles

Chanterelles (*Cantharellus cibarius*) are often called *girolles* in French. These golden horn-shaped mushrooms range from 2 to 3 inches (5 to 8 cm) long and 1 to 2 inches (2.5 to 5 cm) wide. They have become very popular in the United States, probably because they are pretty, plentiful, and easy to cook. They are also easy for the amateur mushroom hunter to recognize. Unlike some mushroom varieties, they do not release a large amount of water during cooking, so they are often sautéed in olive oil, butter, or goose fat and sprinkled with herbs, garlic, and other flavorings near the end of cooking.

Horns of Plenty

The French name for these mushrooms (species name, *Craterellus cornucopioides*) is *trompettes de la mort*—trumpets of death—because of their shape and black color. Fortunately, they are delicious, and their jet-black color is striking on the plate.

Morels

Morels (*Morchella esculenta*) are found in the spring, from March to May. They have a distinctive shape—a kind of sponge-like cone that makes them difficult to confuse with most other varieties. Their flavor, which varies considerably depending on where they were harvested, is often extremely delicate but, once brought out with careful cooking, is complex and irresistible. Their flavor is best brought out by sautéing in foie gras fat or goose fat or by gentle stewing with Madeira. They make magnificent duxelles and can be used in any sauce recipe that calls for mushrooms. Chopped morels first simmered in Madeira make an excellent flavoring for mayonnaise.

Top-quality dried morels are imported from France and India. The French variety tends to be larger and more regularly shaped, with a more intense flavor, but the Indian type is perfectly acceptable. Morels are dried over wood fires, which gives them a smoky flavor that some connoisseurs find domineering but that complements their flavor without distorting it.

Dried morels should be quickly rinsed under cold running water to eliminate sand and other particles. After they have been rinsed, put them in a bowl and sprinkle them with Madeira (unless they are to be used raw, in which case use water or Madeira that has been simmered to eliminate the alcohol). They usually require about 20 to 30 minutes to soften and absorb the surrounding liquid. Be sure to save any liquid left in the bottom of the bowl as an additional flavoring for sauces.

Gyromitra mushrooms, sometimes called "false morels" or "brain mushrooms," are sometimes sold as morels. They are less flavorful and have gnarled and irregular caps. Although they are an acceptable mushroom for cooking, they should cost half the price of morels.

Truffles

Considering the lavish praise that they have received over the centuries, it is a bit sad that many American cooks and chefs have never worked with or even seen a truffle. Those who have had the opportunity to use truffles in the kitchen have often had to resort to canned or preserved versions and are left wondering how something with so little flavor could become so renowned.

The most famous and aromatic truffles, winter truffles, are in season for only about four months, from November to March. The less-flavorful but not-to-be-ignored summer truffle (*Tuber aestivum*) is in season, as the name implies, during the summer and is occasionally available frozen at other times of the year. If you want truffles at any other time, you will have to use truffles that have been preserved in some way. Although there are several excellent methods for preserving truffles, the flavor of preserved truffles will never match that of fresh truffles served in season.

Truffles *are* expensive. If you have never cooked with them and are planning to do so, be prepared to be extravagant. When truffles are used sparingly, their effect is lost—to some it may even be undetectable. The best way to offset the price of truffles is to serve them only when they are in season—perhaps only a night or two a year—but generously.

Nineteenth- and early-twentieth-century French recipes constantly call for truffles. Most classically trained French chefs of those times thought of truffles as do most Americans think of tomatoes—as a year-round staple—although truffles have little flavor for eight months out of the year. Contemporary chefs are adopting the older, more wholesome approach of always using the best of what is in season.

According to Waverly Root, there are forty-two varieties of truffle, but only a few types have enough flavor or become available often enough to be important to the saucier. The most famous are the French black *truffe du Périgord* (*Tuber melanosporum*) and the white truffle (*Tuber magnatum*).

Italian white truffles are harvested starting in November and usually show up in the United States two or three weeks before the black French variety. The flavor and odor of truffles is almost impossible to describe, but those who have made an attempt usually agree that the white Italian variety has a pungent, garlic-like aroma. The Italians almost always use white truffles raw, often shaved over fresh pasta or into a risotto, but I have had success cooking them with chicken (sliding the sliced truffles under the skin, wrapping the whole bird in aluminum foil, and baking, then unwrapping at the table).

Black truffles start appearing in the United States in December, a fortunate time of year, because some of the expense can be justified for holiday feasting. The aroma and flavor of black truffles is more subtle and complex than that of the Italian white type and can elude the cook who has had little experience dealing with truffles.

Buying Truffles

A fresh truffle, either white or black, should be firm to the touch and fill a room with its aroma almost immediately once the container is opened. If the scent is barely detectable, the truffles are probably stale or of inferior quality.

The best preserved truffles, by far, are frozen, but these are sometimes hard to find and must be obtained from a reliable source that has frozen them soon after they have been harvested. Preserved truffles in jars and cans can also be found at most fancy food shops. The best-quality black truffles usually come in jars rather than cans and are often labeled "*première cuisson*" and either "*surchoix*" or "*1er choix.*" Première cuisson indicates that the truffles have been cooked only once during the preservation process. Inferior brands of canned truffles have been cooked twice and, as expensive as they are, have little flavor. Surchoix guarantees that the truffles are of a certain size and have a regular shape; 1er choix truffles are also an excellent quality, but they are likely to be slightly smaller and a bit more irregular than those labeled "surchoix."

Truffle peelings and chunks of summer truffles, *Tuber aestivum,* are commercially available and are far less expensive than genuine French black truffles, *Tuber melanosporum.* Unfortunately, they have almost no flavor, and using them in sauces has no purpose other than deceiving the unwary diner.

One commercial product that can be extremely useful in sauces is black truffle juice. It is not actually the juice of the truffle but the cooking liquid from the preserving process. This "juice" can be used to give sauces a subtle hint of truffle (perhaps even unrecognizable, but giving the sauce a mysterious complexity). It works especially well in cold sauces such as mayonnaise- and vinaigrette-based sauces. Brands of truffle juice vary considerably in quality; some have little flavor and are too salty, so a bit of comparative tasting is worthwhile.

Storing Fresh Truffles

Fresh truffles should be used as quickly as possible but can be kept for a week to ten days in tightly sealed jars. Most marketers of truffles recommend keeping them embedded in a jar of raw rice. This does no harm to the truffle but not much good either. The rice keeps the truffles dry but does nothing to seal their perfume, and the rice itself gains nothing in the process; when cooked, any truffle aroma it may have absorbed is lost.

Because the aroma of truffles clings to foods containing fats, such as eggs, butter, and cream, it makes more sense to store truffles in a jar with butter or with whole eggs (in their shells). Butter that has been stored with truffles can then be used to finish sauces. The aroma of truffles penetrates eggshells and perfumes the egg inside. The eggs can then be used for omelettes or the yolks used for egg-based emulsified sauces.

Preserving Truffles

If black truffles are needed out of season, their flavor is best preserved by wrapping them tightly in plastic wrap, sealing them again in plastic bags, and then freezing them in a cold freezer, preferably a deep-freeze. In this way they are never cooked, as with some other methods. Unfortunately, this method will not work for white truffles, which must be used fresh.

In southwestern France, black truffles are often placed in jars and covered with goose fat, which preserves them for 2 to 3 months. For longer storage they are placed in Mason jars and sprinkled with a little salt and Cognac. The jars are then sealed and placed in a boiling water bath for 20 to 30 minutes, long enough to sterilize the truffles.

Chopping and Slicing Truffles

Truffles are more easily sliced if the peels, which are somewhat hard, are first removed with a paring knife. The peelings can then be chopped and used as a decorative finish for sauces or omelettes. Either chopped or sliced truffles can be used in sauces—sliced truffles usually have a more impressive effect. The best method for slicing truffles is to use a Japanese mandoline (see page 29), which can cut them paper thin. An Italian truffle slicer can also be used—especially if the slicing is being done at the table—but it will not slice as thinly as a Japanese mandoline.

Using Truffles in Sauce Making

The flavor and aroma of truffles are extremely volatile and will be attenuated or completely lost if the truffles are cooked uncovered for long periods. Consequently, most recipes recommend infusing chopped or sliced truffles in a sauce in a covered saucepan during the last 10 minutes of cooking.

What chefs often ignore when cooking with truffles is that the aroma is far easier to infuse in fat than in liquids such as stock or fortified wines. The flavor of fortified wines such as Madeira works well with truffles but does little to draw the truffle flavor into the sauce. If a truffle sauce contains fat such as butter, cream, or egg yolks, the best way to flavor the sauce is to infuse the chopped or sliced raw truffles with the butter, cream, or egg yolks for an hour or two before making the sauce.

For butter-enriched sauces, such as Sauce Périgourdine (page 192), store the butter overnight with the truffles and infuse the sliced truffles in the sauce *after* finishing the sauce with the butter. The flavor of the truffles will permeate a sauce containing butter far more completely than it will a flavor base containing no fat.

When finishing sauces with cream, cover the sliced or chopped raw truffles with the heavy cream before using it in the sauce. If the cream is to be reduced, reduce it first, add the truffles, cover the pan, and let the truffles infuse for 20 to 30 minutes before finishing the sauce with the reduced cream.

Truffles work extremely well in emulsified egg yolk–based sauces that have been finished with butter (the béarnaise family). It is best to prepare these sauces 1 or 2 hours in advance and keep them covered before they are served to allow their flavor to infuse into the sauce.

NUTS AND SEEDS

Almonds

Slivered almonds add a much-needed crunch to stir-fries and curries. In medieval cooking, almond milk (extracted by soaking the ground almonds in water) was called for in sauce making almost as much as cow's milk. Almond butter is used as a thickener in Indian cooking, although nowadays it has largely been replaced by cashews, which are less expensive. Bitter almonds, which are much more intensely flavored than regular almonds, are used in the proportion of one bitter almond to one hundred sweet almonds. This mixture is often used as a flavoring for marzipan or in other sweets where an intense almond flavor is desirable.

Bitter almonds cannot be sold in the United States because of their high natural cyanide content. Regular almonds can be toasted to enhance their flavor, and almond extract can be used (very sparingly) to emulate the flavor of bitter almonds (see also page 481).

Cashews

In addition to their role in Chinese stir-fries, Thai curries (in the finished dishes, not as the paste), and in other Asian dishes, cashews are ground into cashew butter that is then used as a thickener and flavoring in Indian curries.

Kemiri Nuts

Indonesian cooks grind these plump round nuts (they look a lot like macadamia nuts) into a paste, usually with other ingredients such as chiles and ginger, and use the paste as a sauce thickener. Kemiri nuts contain a mild toxin, which is destroyed when the nuts are heated, so raw kemiri nuts should never be nibbled on as a snack.

Macadamia Nuts

Macadamia nuts are sometimes used as a substitute for kemiri nuts, but they don't have the same distinct flavor that gives Indonesian sauces their authentic character.

Peanuts

Ground into peanut butter, peanuts are used throughout the world (in Africa, Asia, and South America) as a thickener and flavoring in sauces and stews. They are delicious when combined with coconut milk, tomatoes, cilantro, and curries.

Sesame Seeds

Both white and black sesame seeds are used in Japanese cooking. White sesame seeds, by far the more popular of the two, are lightly toasted and used as a garniture or ground into a coarse flaky paste with a traditional Japanese mortar and pestle called a *suribachi*. A suribachi has grooves along the inside of the mortar that make it perfect for grinding small seeds. Lacking a suribachi, you can grind toasted sesame seeds in a coffee grinder. It is difficult, however, to grind sesame seeds with a regular mortar and pestle because the mortar has smooth sides. Freshly made sesame seed paste is used as a thickener and flavoring in dipping sauces and salad sauces. Commercially made sesame paste (sold in groceries that carry Middle Eastern ingredients) is not an adequate substitute for freshly ground seeds.

Black sesame seeds are less often used than white but can be ground in the same way into a somewhat stronger paste or sprinkled over pale foods for a bit of drama.

PORK PRODUCTS

Raw pork and various cured pork products such as ham, pancetta, and bacon are often used to contribute savor to a sauce's flavor base. Because some of these products have a delicate flavor whereas others are smoked or cured with strong spices, the saucier should know how to select them.

Bacon

In the United States, bacon is smoked pork breast. It should not be used as an all-purpose component of a flavor base or to contribute savor and natural gelatin to a braise because of its strong smoky taste. It can, however, be used as a substitute for salt pork and cut into small strips (lardoons) and used as a garniture for a variety of dishes. The lardoons should be blanched for 10 minutes in boiling water to eliminate some of the smoky taste.

Fatback

Another version of pork breast, fatback, has no lean and consists entirely of fat. Used primarily as a source of fat in charcuterie, it is also used to lard large pieces of meat for braising or the individual pieces of meat in a stew. Sheets of fatback called "bards" are also wrapped around roasts or braises to prevent the meat from drying out while cooking.

Ham

In sauce making, ham is used primarily to contribute savor and depth of flavor. In eighteenth-century French recipes for braises, a slice of ham was used to line the bottom of the pot. Before liquid was added to the braise, the pot was gently heated until the juices released by the ham caramelized on the bottom of the pot. By the nineteenth century, this method had been streamlined by including the ham in the mirepoix, which in turn was sweated or caramelized before moistening.

Although it is possible to use uncooked pork leg, called fresh ham, there are less-expensive sources of raw pork meat. Most ham has been cured in one of a variety of ways and is available either raw or cooked.

The most versatile ham for sauce making is an unsmoked, raw, salt-cured prosciutto such as Parma ham from Italy or Bayonne ham or *jambon d'Auvergne* from France. Until recently these hams were unavailable in the United States. Because they are very expensive, it is best to trim off little pieces from the bone after the slices have been served in the restaurant and save them for sauces.

Many of the raw cured hams available in the United States, such as Smith-field and Westphalian, are delicious in their own right but have been smoked and—in the case of Smithfield ham—heavily encrusted with spices. When used sparingly, pieces of these hams can add distinction and a delicate smoky taste to red wine sauces. But use them carefully; their flavor is dominating. These hams are also very salty and should be used only in tiny amounts for heavily reduced sauces.

Commercially produced cooked hams—especially the canned variety—have no place in sauce making. They are either too aggressive or have no flavor at all. There do exist good-quality cooked hams—from York, England, and a few from New England—but these are best eaten for what they are. They are usually smoked and would overwhelm a sauce.

Pancetta

Like bacon, pancetta is pork breast, but it has been rolled rather than left in slabs. Because it is not smoked and probably because pigs are slaughtered at an older age in Italy, it has a deep pork flavor that makes it excellent for sauce making. When rolled and cut into strips, it can be used in stews and braises in the same way as lean salt pork.

Pork Rinds

The rinds from unsalted fatback, unsmoked bacon, and fresh or unsmoked ham can be saved and used to provide natural gelatin to brown stocks, stews, and braised dishes.

SPICES

Spices were the main flavoring used in medieval European cooking until the seventeenth century, when they were largely replaced by herbs. They have always been important in Middle Eastern and Indian cooking but only relatively recently have been rediscovered in European-style cooking. Contemporary chefs are experimenting more and more with delicate infusions of spices in both white and brown sauces.

Allspice

The small dried berries known as allspice have a smell and flavor very similar to cloves but somewhat more complex. In European cooking, allspice is most often used in combination with other spices, such as ginger, nutmeg, and curry mixtures. It is also used in marinades, sometimes with juniper berries.

Aniseed

See "Fennel Seeds," page 70.

Asafetida

Usually sold as a powder (although Julie Sahni, in her excellent book *Classic Indian Vegetarian and Grain Cooking,* recommends buying it in the purer lump form and grinding it as needed), asafetida is used by vegetarian cooks as a replacement for onion. Asafetida does have a peculiar pungent odor when heated, only vaguely reminiscent of onions. Asafetida is one of the flavorings in Sambaar Powder (page 552).

Cardamom

One of the principal ingredients in curry, cardamom has an intense piney aroma and flavor. It is sold in small green pods that must be peeled before they are used, in tiny granules (the shelled pods), and in powdered form. The best way to get the little black seeds out of the green pods is to crack open the pods by rocking over them with a heavy-bottomed pot and then pulling away the shells.

Cardamom has long been used in curry powders and more recently infused in combination with other spices such as coriander in brown and white sauces. It can also be infused in crème anglaise and used in dessert sauces.

Indian cooks also use black cardamom, which has black instead of green pods and is much larger. It has a much gentler and more subtle flavor than the green variety and is one of the spices used in preparing Garam Masala (pages 550 and 551). The seeds are taken out of the pod in the same way as for green cardamom.

Cayenne Pepper and Ground Chiles

Cayenne pepper is made by grinding cayenne chiles, hot little red chiles grown in such disparate locations as Louisiana, Asia, and Africa. Excellent for adding zest to sauces where large amounts of black or white pepper would be inappropriate, cayenne works especially well with sauces containing tomatoes, sweet peppers, and cilantro. It can also be used in almost imperceptible amounts to wake up the flavor of fish sauces. Sauces can be given subtle nuances by replacing ground cayenne pepper with chile powders made by grinding other dried chiles such as anchos, guajillos, mulatos, or pasillas in a food processor or blender and then working the mixture through a strainer (see also "Chiles," page 82).

Cinnamon

In contemporary Western cooking, cinnamon is used almost exclusively to accompany sweets. Cinnamon was used in medieval cooking, often in conjunction with ginger, saffron, and cloves, for both meat and fish sauces. Vestiges of these flavor combinations can still be found in English and eastern European recipes (for example, mincemeat pie). Cinnamon is also an important ingredient in Indian curries, where it is often combined with other "sweet" spices such as cloves and cardamom.

The ground or whole cinnamon sold on supermarket spice shelves in the United States is actually cassia. Cassia comes in many different grades and may come from China, Indonesia, or recently, from Vietnam. In supermarkets, cinnamon is sold ground or in hard tightly wound woody sticks; specialty spice shops and Asian groceries sometimes sell Chinese or Indonesian cinnamon in chunks. Like cassia, true cinnamon comes in tightly wound sticks, but cinnamon sticks are softer and easier to break. True cinnamon is from Ceylon and has a less aggressive, more subtle flavor than cassia.

Cinnamon leaves (actually cassia leaves) are sometimes gently cooked in oil and used in Indian curries in much the same way that bay leaves are used in Western-style red wine and meat stews.

Cloves

The most common use of cloves in European cooking is in meat broths, when a clove is stuck into an onion. By the time the sauce is reduced and used in sauce making, the clove flavor is almost imperceptible. Ground cloves were often used in medieval cooking along with saffron, ginger, and cinnamon.

Cloves are also a common ingredient in Indian cooking, where they are used (often in conjunction with cinnamon or cardamom) to flavor rice and meats. They are added to classic Indian spice mixtures including Garam Masala (pages 550 and 551).

Coriander

The leaves, seeds, and roots of the coriander plant all have different flavors and uses. Coriander seeds are small and round with a thin husk; they vaguely resemble white peppercorns. They are only rarely called for in classic French cooking (in salade grecque, for example), but have recently become a favorite of chefs in both Europe and the United States, who have been experimenting with them in both meat and fish sauces. Their flavor merges amazingly well with fennel. Coriander seeds are also used as an ingredient in Indian curries, to which they add an aromatic, almost floral, aroma and soften the more aggressive flavors of other curry spices. Coriander seeds can be roasted in a hot oven for 5 minutes or gently tossed in a hot skillet on top of the stove until they release their aroma. Coriander seeds are also easy to grind in a blender or coffee grinder, and the ground mixture can be gently toasted in a dry sauté pan on the stove.

Indian cooks sometimes work ground coriander to a paste with a little water and then cook the paste on top of the stove.

Coriander leaves (called "cilantro" or "Chinese parsley") have a distinctly different flavor from that of the seeds and are used in Mexican, Chinese, Thai, and Indian cooking. Coriander (cilantro) roots, seeds, and stems all enter into Thai curries (see pages 534 to 538).

Cumin

Available in small, slightly curved seeds (the same shape as fennel seeds) or in powder form, cumin has a distinctive flavor that can easily overwhelm the flavor of a sauce, especially when used alone. Cumin is rarely used in French cooking but is commonly used in India, the Middle East, and Mexico. In India, cumin is roasted, ground, and sprinkled over appetizers and salads as well as used often in spice mixtures. Black cumin, which has little resemblance to the familiar common variety (called "white" cumin in India), can sometimes be found in Indian groceries. Black cumin seeds are smaller than regular cumin seeds and have a pungent pine-like aroma and taste. Black cumin seeds are usually used whole.

Curry Powder

Most Western chefs treat curry powder as a single spice. In fact, it is a mixture of up to twenty different spices and can be made differently, depending on how it is to be served. In India, it would be unthinkable to resort to a commercial curry powder for cooking instead of working with the individual flavors.

For Western chefs eager to expand their vocabulary of flavors, blending curries is an educational project. Grind each of the spices separately in a coffee grinder and combine them a bit at a time. A good method for tasting curries is to infuse each separate spice into a small amount of stock or heavy cream and then combine the liquids; it is difficult to taste the powdered spices alone.

Most recipes for Indian curries suggest roasting some of the spices to bring out their flavor before they are ground. In classic French cooking, curry powder is cooked in a small amount of butter for a minute or two before it is added to a sauce.

Fennel Seeds

Fennel seeds are often used in Mediterranean cooking to impart an anise-like note to fish stews and soups. They are also sometimes used in marinades for grilled meats and fish. Fennel seeds are stronger than fresh fennel, so they should be used carefully. In sauce making it is often preferable to use fresh fennel (infused in a court-bouillon, chopped in a marinade, dried and smoked on the grill) or a small amount of fennel liqueur such as Pernod or Ricard. Fennel has a marvelous affinity for other Mediterranean flavors, such as tomatoes, garlic, olives, basil, and fresh seafood. Fennel seeds are also used, whole or ground, in Indian spice mixtures and curries.

Fenugreek Seeds and Leaves

Ground or whole, fenugreek seeds are rarely used alone. They are primarily a component in curry powders. Ground fenugreek seems to harmonize the flavor of the other spices. Fenugreek has a vaguely maple-like taste and is in fact used as a flavoring in artificial maple syrup. Fenugreek leaves are sometimes used in Indian cooking, primarily as a flavoring for starchy vegetables such as potatoes.

Galangal

Similar in appearance to ginger, galangal is most often used in Indonesian and Thai cooking as a flavoring for soups, curries, and sauces. It has a distinct and exotic pine-resin flavor. Galangal has not been used in European cooking since medieval times. The best place to find galangal is in Thai or Indonesian specialty food stores, where it is called *kha* or *laos*. Galangal can sometimes be found fresh but is usually sold frozen, either whole or in slices. Dried and powdered galangal is also available, but it is much less aromatic than fresh or frozen.

Ginger

Until recently, ginger had been almost completely ignored in European cooking since the Middle Ages. In Asian cooking it is used almost as universally as onions and garlic in the West. In Indian cooking it enters into an almost ubiquitous flavor base in the same way that carrots, onions, and celery compose French mirepoix. European and American chefs have finally begun to experiment with ginger in sauce making. It is an excellent flavoring for crème anglaise but also works well in savory sauces. Medieval sauce recipes are a good source of ideas for how to combine ginger with other spices. It works especially well with saffron and fennel, but medieval recipes also use it with cinnamon, cloves, mace, and others.

Ginger is available candied, powdered, and fresh. Although powdered ginger is a suitable substitute, fresh ginger is widely available in the United States.

Horseradish

Grated horseradish root gives an exciting, dissonant note to a variety of sauces. It is marvelous in sauce suédoise (mayonnaise with apples and horseradish), and it works beautifully with mustard. It can also be used with dill.

Juniper Berries

Because juniper is the principal flavoring in gin, most people are familiar with its smell and flavor. It has a piney aroma and in European cooking is usually used with full-flavored meats, especially game. Juniper berries are most often used in marinades, but they can be finely ground and sprinkled into sauces as needed. They can be used in sauces along with marc or grappa to impart a distinct gamy flavor.

Mace

The outer lace-like coating of the nutmeg, mace is close to nutmeg in flavor. In French cooking its use is restricted to sauce béchamel, gratins, and cheese soufflés. Mace is often encountered in Northern Indian cooking. Mace is stronger and more pungent than nutmeg, with a slightly different flavor.

Mustard Seeds

Rarely used whole in European cooking, mustard seeds are popular in Indian cooking. Indian mustard seeds are dark brown (they are often called "black" or "brown" interchangeably) and in Southern Indian cooking are often cooked whole in hot oil for a few seconds until they pop and spatter. Brown mustard seeds are also used as a pickling spice and in some parts of India they are ground into a paste. Indian mustard paste has little resemblance to Western bottled mustards.

Nutmeg

Although often used in spice mixtures such as *quatre épices* (French four-spice mixture; opposite), nutmeg is very domineering and should be used in only minute quantities. It is available whole (a small grater is used) or powdered. In sauce making, nutmeg is most often used in white sauces, especially traditional flour-thickened white sauces containing cheese. Nutmeg is also used in Northern Indian cooking.

Paprika

A member of the same genus of peppers (*Capsicum*) that provides cayenne and fresh peppers, paprika is made by finely grinding sweet red peppers. In Hungary and Spain, there are different versions, some as hot as cayenne pepper, but in the United States, most paprika is so mild that it has almost no taste at all. Good-quality fresh paprika has a distinctive flavor that makes it useful in fish stews and the traditional Hungarian goulash. Before buying paprika, always smell it: It should have a fresh, pungent aroma.

Pepper

Pepper, *Piper nigrum,* is unrelated to *Capsicum* peppers, which include sweet bell and hot peppers. It is the most useful and indispensable of all the spices. Black, white, and green peppercorns are all berries of the same plant picked at different degrees of maturity.

Peppercorns that have been allowed to fully mature are black. They come in various sizes, the largest being the most aromatic and expensive. Malabar peppercorns, and the even larger Tellicherry peppercorns from India, are considered the best.

White peppercorns are actually black peppercorns that have been allowed to mature even further, then soaked in water until the black outer husk can be removed. Some chefs put both black and white peppercorns together in a pepper mill. Freshly ground white pepper is especially useful for white sauces in which black flecks would be distracting.

Pepper should always be ground as it is needed, never in advance. The flavor of pepper is aromatic and volatile, so pepper should be added or infused into sauces only at the last minute. Pepper added to stocks or sauces too early loses its aromatic, piney scent and leaves an unpleasant harsh quality that is hard to eliminate.

Green peppercorns first appeared in the late 1960s and quickly became one of the new food products to be adopted by *nouvelle cuisine* chefs. Green peppercorns are picked before the berries are completely mature. They have a fresh, pungent, pine-like aroma and are sold dried or packed in brine. Dried green peppercorns can be ground like black or white peppercorns or reconstituted in water. Green peppercorns soaked in brine should be crushed with the side of a knife before being added to sauces; biting into a whole peppercorn can be a bit overwhelming to the diner. Green peppercorns in brine or vinegar should be used within a few weeks of opening, or they will take on an unpleasant gray color that stains sauces. They also lose some of their aroma.

Pink peppercorns are not related to black, white, or green peppercorns but come from a common shrub, *Schinus terebinthifolius*. All the rage in the early 1980s, pink peppercorns inspired some debate as to their toxicity, but nevertheless, enforcement of the ban seems to be lax, and they still appear on menus. They are less intense than green peppercorns, so they can be presented and eaten whole.

QUATRE ÉPICES

One of the few spice mixtures used regularly by the French, *quatre épices* ("four-spice mixture") is rarely used in sauce making but mostly for forcemeats and terrine and sausage fillings. A typical mixture follows.

YIELD: 6 TABLESPOONS (90 MILLILITERS)

powdered cloves	1 teaspoon	5 milliliters
powdered ginger	1 tablespoon	15 milliliters
powdered nutmeg	1 tablespoon	15 milliliters
ground white pepper	¼ cup	60 milliliters

Stir together all the ingredients and store in a tightly sealed container.

Saffron

Taken from the flowers of the autumn crocus, saffron is expensive, but fortunately a little goes a long way. Saffron has been used in Italian and French regional cooking for centuries but has been ignored in French classical cooking since the Middle Ages. In the last twenty years, it has become more and more popular, especially in Mediterranean-style fish dishes. It has a natural affinity for Mediterranean flavors, such as tomatoes, basil, and fennel. Saffron is also used in Indian cooking in a number of curries and even desserts.

Saffron was used almost universally in medieval European cooking in conjunction with other spices such as ginger, cinnamon, and cloves.

Saffron is available in little threads (the whole dried stigma) or in a powder. Most chefs prefer the threads, which can be decorative when left in the sauce. Saffron threads should be soaked for 20 minutes in 1 tablespoon (15 milliliters) of warm water before they are incorporated with the water into the sauce.

Star Anise

Actually the dried fruit of a variety of magnolia, star anise contains small seeds that have a pungent anise flavor. The ground seeds, known as *ba jiao*, have long been used in Chinese cooking (most often as an ingredient in Chinese five-spice mixture) and in Malaysian curry mixtures. Star anise has recently been discovered by French chefs, who have been experimenting with infusing it in meat broths and natural aspics.

Szechuan Peppercorns

These berry-like peppercorns bear little resemblance to black pepper. They are brown rather than black and have a pleasant spicy and pine-like aroma. Unlike black peppercorns, Szechuan peppercorns should be roasted before they are used to bring out their perfume. They can be ground over foods in the same way as black pepper, or they can be infused in oil destined for stir-frying, used for Chinese smoking, and added to a variety of Chinese sauces.

Turmeric

A root with a distinctive, pungent flavor, turmeric is unfortunately difficult to find except in powdered form, which usually has little if any flavor. It is used primarily as an inexpensive coloring (often to mimic the costly saffron) and as a component of curries, chutneys, and commercial mustard. Turmeric is handy to have around for coloring curries that standard spice mixtures may have turned a dull gray or brown.

SPIRITS

Spirits are prepared by distilling fermented liquids to concentrate the alcohol and some of the flavor components. They are often used to flavor and give complexity to sauces. Spirits usually contain both volatile and nonvolatile components. Volatile components are those that come off the still during distillation and develop to some degree while the spirit is aging. These components cook off rapidly when spirits are heated. Nonvolatile components comprise mostly wood extracts that work their way into the spirit during aging. These tend to remain during cooking and may even be concentrated.

Spirits are used in different stages in sauce making. They are often added as the first deglazing liquid in long-cooked stews such as boeuf bourguignon, lobster or squid à l'américaine, octopus daube, and coq au vin, where their flavor contributes complexity to the sauce. They can also be used at almost the very end to heighten the flavor of brown sauces; it is essential that they be cooked for at least 20 to 30 seconds to evaporate their alcohol.

Brandy

Applied loosely, the term *brandy* describes distilled wine made from any fruit, coming from any part of the world. More typically, the term describes distilled grape wine (see "Fruit Brandies," page 76, for a discussion of other types).

The best brandy for use in sauce making is one of the less-expensive Cognacs or Armagnacs. Both of these brandies are natural, pot-distilled products that contain the natural flavors useful for sauce making. The best method for choosing a Cognac or Armagnac for the kitchen is by systematically smelling and tasting the less-expensive brands and types. When selecting a Cognac or Armagnac for the kitchen, look for a full, fruity flavor with a background of oak (the oak will be more predominant in Armagnac than in Cognac). Do not judge the quality of the brandy by the subtlety or finesse of the bouquet. These traits, although important to the brandy drinker, will be lost once the brandy is heated. Fullness, roundness, fruit, and purity of flavor are much more important in the kitchen.

Many chefs and restaurateurs substitute a generic brandy chosen blindly off the shelf or recommended by the liquor wholesaler. Such brandies often have meaningless designations such as "Fine French Brandy" or "Napoleon Brandy." These brandies may be half the price of an expensive Cognac or Armagnac but usually have little flavor. What flavor they do have is harsh and biting.

When preparing sauces with brandy, the brandy should be added near the end of the cooking. If it is added too early, practically all its flavor will be lost. If, however, it is added at the *very* end, alcohol will remain in the sauce.

Although traditional sauces seem to use brandy infrequently, it can be used to shape the final flavor of brown sauces and to wake up and add subtlety to brown sauces and red wine sauces.

Fruit Brandies

Fruit brandies are of two types: fruit-flavored grape brandy and genuine fruit brandy made by distilling fruit wines. Fruit-flavored grape brandies are usually made by adding a concentrated fruit flavoring to the brandy. The result is syrupy and often sickeningly sweet.

Genuine fruit brandies are clear and perfectly dry. They do not have the characteristic amber hue of grape brandies because they have not been aged in oak casks. In France, Germany, and Switzerland, there are hundreds of varieties of these brandies (called *eaux-de-vie*). Fruit brandies are useful in sauce making when they are used to underline the character of a fruit-based or fruit-flavored sauce; for example, the sauce for a roast duck with cherries can be finished with kirsch (cherry brandy), or a roast or braise garnished with plums could be finished with mirabelle (plum brandy).

Practically all the flavor contained in fruit brandies is volatile, so it is especially important to use fruit brandies in the very last stages of a sauce's preparation. A few drops of the brandy should be added to the sauce at the end, and the sauce should then be removed immediately from the heat.

Marc and Grappa

Marc and grappa are the French and Italian names for the same thing: brandy distilled from the grape pomace—the pits, stems, and skins that remain after the juice has been run off for wine making. Carefully taste marc or grappa before using it in sauce making, as the quality varies enormously from raw, clear brandy served in the villages near the distillery to deep-colored, long-aged products from famous vineyards. All genuine marc or grappa has a characteristic earthy flavor that makes it useful and interesting in sauces. Recently, the term *grappa* is used in Italy to describe brandy made from wine rather than pits and stems. Such "grappa" has more of the fruity flavor of eaux-de-vie such as framboise or kirsch than it does traditional grappa. It is often possible to substitute marc or grappa in a recipe that calls for Cognac, Armagnac, or brandy to give a more rustic, regional flavor to the finished sauce. Marc and grappa are splendid in game sauces and with chocolate.

Rum, Vodka, and Gin

Occasionally a recipe will call for one of these spirits. Vodka is useless in sauce making because it is a completely neutral-tasting product. Gin is sometimes useful to reinforce the flavor of juniper in certain game sauces. Rum is useful in dessert sauces but must be chosen correctly. Most rum found in the United States comes from Puerto Rico and is distilled in column stills, so that it has little of the flavor that has made rum a popular flavoring in desserts and dessert sauces. Martinique rum is the best for cooking because it is pot-stilled and full flavored. The color of rum has little to do with its depth of flavor.

Whiskey

Whiskey is made by fermenting grain that has first been treated with malt enzymes to convert the starch into sugar. The fermented mash is then distilled. The types of grain used, the method of distillation, and the aging process determine the type of whiskey. Scotch whiskey and Irish and bourbon whiskeys can all be used to give their characteristic nuances to a sauce. Although recipes that use whiskey are far less common than those that call for Cognac (probably because whiskey is not made in France), whiskey can be used as a substitute for Cognac. The result is different but can be very satisfying.

Whiskeys are often blended with neutral spirits to make them more palatable for drinking. The most flavorful whiskeys, which are best for sauce making, are unblended, pot-stilled products. When selecting whiskey for the kitchen, be sure to use a pot-stilled type rather than one that has been blended with neutral spirits. Malt whiskey, for example, is preferable to blended Scotch whisky, which is usually only 40 to 50 percent pot-stilled—the rest is neutral and contributes no flavor. When using bourbon whiskey, select one labeled "straight bourbon" rather than blended whiskey, which contains a high percentage of neutral spirits. Canadian whiskey is blended and too light for sauce making.

WINE

It is hard to imagine food without wine, not only as an integral component of the cooking process itself but also as the perfect accompanying beverage. Because of wine's variety and complex flavor, it never becomes tiresome or rote. It not only accents food at the table but enhances and brings out the natural flavor of meats, fish, and vegetables.

Many cooks assume that wine chosen for drinking is also the best for cooking. Because wine is radically transformed by heat and other aspects of the cooking process, the criteria for selecting cooking wines depend on the type of wine and the preparations in which it is to be used. The finesse and complexity of great wines is destroyed by heat, which makes their use in the kitchen impractical. Meat jellies, which are sometimes finished with fine wines, are an exception to this axiom because the wine never comes in contact with heat.

Champagne

The term *Champagne* has been misused for so many years that many chefs assume that it refers to any sparkling wine. Authentic Champagne comes from a closely delineated region of northern France whose soil imparts a characteristic steely/chalky flavor to the wine. Still Champagne is converted to the sparkling variety using an involved traditional process (*méthode champenoise*).

Those who write recipes using Champagne often naively assume that the flavor and elegance of Champagne are somehow going to work their way into a cooked preparation. Cooking will immediately destroy the natural carbonation that has required so much time and expense, and it will destroy much of the natural finesse of the wine as well. Many chefs, when confronted with one of these recipes, are horrified at the idea of opening an expensive bottle of Champagne and will substitute a less-expensive sparkling wine. This makes no sense, because the bubbles will be lost and only the basic flavors of the wine will remain. It is far more logical to substitute a still Champagne (Coteaux Champenois), which will have the same basic flavors as sparkling Champagne minus the yeastiness and some complexity. Although these wines are never cheap, they are usually half the price of the sparkling variety.

Recipes that call for Champagne should be examined closely to determine why. Champagne (both the sparkling and still varieties) contains a great deal of natural acid, which makes it delightful to drink but troublesome to cook with. In some sauces acidity is desirable (beurre blanc), and a still Champagne would work well. If the recipe calls for long or radical reduction of the wine, most of the subtlety will be lost, so that using even a still Champagne would be a needless expense. In this case it would be practical to substitute a less-expensive wine with a similar structure (dry, high acidity) such as Muscadet or a French Sauvignon Blanc.

When a preparation calls for very gentle cooking or no cooking at all—dessert sabayons, cold fruit sauces, for example—the added expense of Champagne may be justified.

Madeira

Although Madeira is no longer the popular drink it was in the eighteenth and nineteenth centuries, it makes an excellent cooking wine. It has a distinctive, nutty flavor that blends well in brown sauces and natural meat jellies, giving them both complexity and finesse. Genuine Madeira is produced on the island of Madeira, but as with port there are imitations made in other places. None of these has the depth of flavor and balance of genuine Madeira, so they are best avoided or at least carefully tasted before being added to the saucepan.

There are several types of Madeira. Sercial is completely dry, and, because of its acidity and complete lack of sugar, is little used in the kitchen. Verdelho is sweeter and softer than sercial, which makes it useful for sauce making. Bual and malmsey are the richest and sweetest types of Madeira. They can be used in sauces calling for Madeira—they are often the best—but use them carefully, because they are often extremely sweet.

Because Madeira is not a popular beverage in the United States, it is not easy to find a wide selection of varieties. The most common variety found in America is a medium-sweet blend called Rainwater. It has a good balance of complexity, sweetness, and acidity, making it a good standby for sauce making. It is also easy to find.

Port

Port is often used to impart a subtle, caramel-like sweetness to sauces. Genuine port comes from Portugal. Wine makers in other countries have attempted to make port-like wines, some of which are very good, but unless you are certain of the quality, it is best to use a genuine Portuguese port. There are many inexpensive imitations of port on the market, which at best will contribute nothing to a sauce. At worst, they will give the sauce a coarse, cloying sweetness.

Port comes in several varieties, but all port is made by adding alcohol or brandy to the must before fermentation is completed. This stops the fermentation prematurely and leaves natural grape sugar in the wine. Basically, there are four kinds of port. Vintage port is made from grapes of a single year and is left for a relatively short time in wood before being bottled. It is allowed to mature at least ten to fifteen years in the bottle and is the most expensive of the four types. Late-bottle vintage port (wood port) is left longer in wood than vintage port, so that it matures more quickly. It is lighter in style and less expensive than vintage port. Tawny port is traditionally manufactured by blending ports from different vintages and allowing them to age for many years in oak, which causes the color to turn from deep red to a characteristic brick-like hue. Some less-expensive tawny ports are simple blends of red and white port. Ruby port is a young, blended port. It is the lightest and least expensive of the port types.

Because of the price of good port, ruby port is used most often in the kitchen. Select a port with a deep red color, full flavor, and a complex caramel or butterscotch background in the mouth. Some brands of ruby port are so light (visible in the glass) and at the same time so sweet that they will impart little to the sauce. It is often practical to use a slightly more expensive brand of port with more flavor, body, and color than an inexpensive brand. Less of the better port will be needed to give the necessary complexity and sweetness to the sauce.

Red Wine

The behavior of red wine in cooking is complex. When cooked with foods that contain protein, such as fish or meat, the tannins and pigments contained in the wine combine with the proteins that are released during cooking. This removes much of the color, acidity, and any astringency due to the tannins. The process is essentially one of clarification. If the wine used is extremely tannic (young and astringent in the mouth), the pigments may separate completely during cooking, so that specks of pigment will be visible in the sauce.

If red wine is reduced either alone or with flavor components such as onions or garlic, which contain no protein, the result will be entirely different from when the wine is cooked with meat, fish, or stock. Red wine reduced in the absence of protein is liable to be extremely acidic and astringent because the acids and tannins will not have been "clarified" by the protein. A red wine sauce prepared by first combining the wine with a meat stock and then carefully reducing the mixture (skimming, not allowing the sauce to boil) will be entirely different from a sauce prepared with red wine that has been reduced alone and then combined with reduced stock.

Lightly colored, fruity wines, such as Beaujolais or California Gamay, should not be used for sauce making. The delicate fruitiness that makes these wines charming to drink will be lost. The lightness of these wines will result in a pallid-appearing, acidic-tasting sauce.

The best red wines for sauce making are deeply colored, low-acid wines. Wines from hot climates or those made from early-ripening grapes, such as Merlot, which are often considered too "soft" or "flabby" by wine connoisseurs, are the best red wines for sauce making. Choose red wines with several years of bottle age, so that the flavors are well developed and most of the tannins have fallen out. A certain amount of "oakiness" is also welcome in a red wine sauce. California Zinfandel and Merlot work especially well, as do Spanish wines such as Rioja. Some Algerian red wines, if available, are excellent because of their low acidity and low price.

It is sometimes possible to find red wines that have passed their peak and are no longer agreeable to drink. The volatile acids contained in these wines will be attenuated by cooking (if not eliminated entirely).

Rice Wine

Japanese rice wine, *sake,* is the best known of Asian rice wines and is often added to mixtures of dashi, mirin, soy sauce, and sometimes miso to flavor broth-like Japanese sauces. Unless the sake is being cooked, it's a good idea to simmer it for a minute in a saucepan to burn off the alcohol. Sake imparts freshness to sauces and functions in much the same way as white wine, except that it doesn't have the acidity of white wine.

Chinese Shaoxing wine is made with rice but using a different process from that used for making sake. Shaoxing wine is fairly alcoholic with a deep amber color that makes it more like sherry than sake or white wine. Sherry can be used as a substitute in recipes calling for Chinese rice wine.

Sherry

Although sherry was often served with the consommé at elaborate dinners at the turn of the twentieth century, there are relatively few sauces that call for it. It can be used for sauce making in the same way as Madeira, but unlike some styles of Madeira, authentic sherry is almost never naturally sweet. Authentic Spanish sherry is available in several different styles. Amontillado, which is aged longer than other types and has a full-bodied, nutty flavor, is best for sauce making. Sherry can be used as a substitute for Shaoxing rice wine in Chinese cooking.

White Wine

When selecting a white wine for the kitchen, remember that the alcohol will evaporate when exposed to heat. What will remain is the basic fruit flavor of the grape and the nonvolatile acids contained in the wine. If the wine is reduced, the tartaric, malic, and other nonvolatile acids in the wine will be concentrated.

In some cases this concentrated acidity is useful. A fairly acidic wine should always be used in the preliminary reduction for a beurre blanc (Muscadet is traditional). Because beurre blanc contains such a high proportion of butter, the nervous tang of a wine's natural acids is necessary to the character and flavor of the finished sauce. French white wines, especially Sauvignon Blanc or Muscadet, are best for beurre-blanc-based sauces or other sauces in which a large proportion of cream or butter is used to finish the sauce.

For integral sauces, which are the result of the reduction of a cooking liquid (for example, chicken or fish cooked in white wine), a less acidic wine should be used. California white wines generally have less acidity than their French counterparts and work especially well in these types of preparations. Sauvignon Blanc is especially good because of its clean, vibrant flavor. California Chardonnay will also work, although it is more expensive and many of the subtleties of the grape will be lost in cooking.

OTHER INGREDIENTS

Anchovies

The quality of anchovies varies greatly, so experiment with different styles and brands. Anchovies packed in salt are preferable to canned anchovies packed in oil because it is easier to remove the salt. The flavor of inferior packing oil is also avoided. Because salt-packed anchovies are sometimes hard to find, it may be necessary to use canned anchovies packed in oil. The Italian brands packed in extra-virgin olive oil seem to be the best.

Salted anchovies should be cleaned and soaked in cold water (see directions below). Canned anchovies may also be soaked for 5 minutes to rid them of some of their salt and oil, but this is somewhat a matter of taste. If confronted with a large can of salted anchovies (the smallest can of the best brand, Agostino Recca—Acciughe Salate, weighs 1 pound 5 ounces/600 grams), you can preserve them in extra-virgin olive oil in mason jars. Run cold water over the anchovies in the can and gently separate them. Soak them in cold water for 20 minutes, changing the water several times. Gently pull the fillets away from the backbone (these come packed as whole fish, not fillets), starting from the head and working down toward the tail. Pack the fillets in jars and add enough extra-virgin olive oil to completely cover by at least 1 inch (2.5 cm). Store in a cool place or in the refrigerator for up to several months. Unlike anchovies out of a jar or can, which may benefit from a 5-minute soaking in cold water, these anchovies don't need to be soaked again before they are used.

Chiles

Sometimes erroneously called "peppers" (chiles have no relation to peppercorns), chiles come in many shapes, sizes, colors, and, most important, flavors. They also come fresh, dried, smoked, ground, and occasionally canned. Because of their diversity, chiles can be used in sauces to add not only heat but an array of subtle flavors, variously described as smoky, leathery, fruity, and earthy.

Fresh chiles can be used in sauces in much the same way as other aromatic vegetables such as onions (gently sweated in fat before liquid is added, or roasted, peeled, and finely chopped in salsas). They can also be directly infused in liquids such as meat broths, tomato broth, or cream.

Because dried chiles often have a more complex flavor than fresh chiles, they are especially delicious in sauces. Typically, dried chiles are lightly roasted (often by just tossing them in a hot skillet) and then soaked before they are chopped and infused in liquids to make sauces.

DRIED CHILE CREAM SAUCE

This is the simplest of all chile sauces, and it allows the flavor of the chiles to come through unaltered by other ingredients such as onions or garlic (or in the case of mole, chocolate) that usually enter into classic Mexican chile sauces. Not only are these sauces delicious, but because each chile will give its own identity to the sauce, they provide an excellent training ground for cooks wanting to familiarize themselves with the nuances of individual dried chiles. This sauce requires little reduction because, surprisingly, the chiles act as thickeners.

YIELD: 1 CUP (250 MILLILITERS), ENOUGH FOR 4 MAIN-COURSE SERVINGS

large dried chiles such as anchos, guajillos, mulatos, pasillas, pasillas de Oaxaca, or chihuacle negros	2	2
heavy cream	1 cup	250 milliliters
salt	to taste	to taste
cayenne pepper (optional)	to taste	to taste

1. Cut the stems off the chiles, cut the chiles in half lengthwise, and shake out their seeds. Toss the chiles in a hot skillet for a minute or two until they smell fragrant. Put them in a bowl and add enough boiling water to barely cover. Soak the chiles for about 30 minutes, until they feel soft and leathery. Drain and discard the soaking liquid. Chop the chiles very fine, until

they have a paste-like consistency, and combine them with the cream in a small saucepan.

2. Bring the cream to a slow simmer over medium heat, while whisking. Take the pan off the stove and let it sit for 5 minutes to give the flavor of the chiles time to infuse. Put the pan back on medium heat and simmer, while whisking, for 30 seconds to 2 minutes, until the sauce has the consistency you like. Season to taste with salt and cayenne.

Chocolate

Many beginning cooks and chefs do not realize that the flavor and quality of chocolate desserts is determined almost entirely by the chocolate itself. Many factors influence the quality of chocolate, not the least of which is the origin of the beans. The laws governing the production of chocolate in the United States are much less strict than those in Europe, where the quality is closely controlled. So when making high-quality chocolate dessert sauces, always use European chocolate; France, Switzerland, and Belgium all have excellent brands.

Most chocolate sauces call for bittersweet or semisweet chocolate. One is not necessarily more bitter than the other—the names simply differ, according to brand. Chocolate labeled bittersweet or semisweet contains two major components, cocoa solids and cocoa butter. The cocoa solids are responsible for the color, bitterness, and depth of flavor of chocolate, whereas the cocoa butter gives it finesse and a smooth texture. In Europe the manufacturer is required to put the percentage of cocoa solids on the label. This percentage is a fairly reliable indicator of the depth of flavor of the chocolate. Bittersweet chocolate will have anywhere from 35 to 55 percent cocoa solids and approximately 15 percent cocoa butter, with the rest sugar. The best method for determining the quality of a brand of chocolate is simply to taste.

Milk chocolate, less commonly used in sauce making than bittersweet or semisweet, contains added milk solids that give it a paler color and a less direct flavor. Unsweetened, bitter, or baking chocolate is more often used by American cooks than by Europeans, so it is sometimes difficult to find good-quality European brands of bitter chocolate. When it is available, it is excellent for sauce making: The sweetness of the sauces can be completely controlled by the chef, and less chocolate is needed, making it more economical.

White chocolate contains no cocoa solids; it is simply a mixture of cocoa butter, milk solids, and sugar. In fact, in the United States, it cannot be legally called chocolate. Because of the milk solids it contains, it is very sensitive to temperature and should never be heated to higher than 120°F (50°C).

Foie Gras

Foie gras is the liver taken from a specially fattened goose or duck. Geese and ducks that are raised for their livers are not allowed to move during the last months of their lives. This lack of movement, and a diet rich in starch, causes fats and glycogen (a compound chemically similar to starch) to build up in the liver, causing it to expand to five times its normal size. In France the animals are force fed, but in the United States, foie gras is now being produced with an especially ravenous species of duck that needs no inducement to overeat.

Foie gras has long been a luxury staple in French cooking. Most typically, it is lightly seasoned, rolled into cylinders, and gently baked in terrines. When the terrines have cooled, they are covered with melted lard and kept in a cool place until needed. Serving hot foie gras has recently become popular in both Europe and the United States.

When a small amount of puréed foie gras is whisked into cooking liquids or stocks, it provides a rich creamy texture and a full, complex flavor to the finished sauce.

If you are using whole raw livers, for terrines or other foie gras preparations, the veins running along the inside of each lobe should first be removed with a small paring knife. Bits and pieces that are left over from this process can be puréed by gently pressing them through a fine-mesh drum sieve and saved for use in sauces.

If adding puréed foie gras to a hot cooking liquid or flavor base, first combine the foie gras with an equal quantity of butter. Otherwise, the foie gras may coagulate slightly on contact with the hot liquid, and the resulting sauce will have a grainy texture. Once the foie gras has been added to the sauce, the mixture should not be allowed to boil.

Different types of foie gras behave differently, depending on the water content of the livers. Because American foie gras tends to contain a larger amount of water than French varieties do, it is better to use foie gras that has been precooked so that any excess liquid has been released. Goose or duck foie gras work equally well in sauce making, but duck foie gras is usually fuller flavored and less subtle.

When raw foie gras is cooked, either when being baked in a terrine, sautéed, roasted, or poached, it renders a deeply flavored yellow fat. If the fat has not been exposed to too high a temperature, it can be saved for other uses. Because of its intense full flavor, a small amount can be used to give character to a sauce. When using foie gras fat, remember that it cannot be stirred directly into a sauce unless the sauce is already emulsified (or the fat would just melt and float to the top). Whisk the fat (melted or not) only into sauces that have been finished with cream, butter, egg yolks, or some other stable emulsion such as vegetable purée.

The flavor of foie gras fat can also be introduced into a sauce by using it to gently sweat preliminary flavor components, such as onions, mirepoix, or bits of meat, before they are moistened with liquid.

Marrow

Beef marrow is sometimes used in sauce making, especially for traditional Sauce Bordelaise (page 179). Even though it is delicious, it has become less popular in recent years because it is practically pure fat. Some wholesalers sell perfect cylinders of marrow already removed from the bone; if these are unavailable, marrow bones cut into 2-inch (5 cm) lengths should be ordered. Usually the marrow can be removed from the bone by pressing firmly on one end with both thumbs. When this method does not work, the bone should be set end up on a butcher block and cracked with a cleaver in two places.

Once the marrow has been removed from the bones, it should be soaked overnight in heavily salted ice water. The salt draws out the blood, which turns an unsightly gray when cooked.

Marrow added to sauces as a garniture should be added just long enough before serving to heat it through; any longer and it will melt to nothing.

STOCKS, GLACES, AND ESSENCES

4

A *stock* is a flavorful extract made by cooking meat, fish, or vegetables in water or broth. The purpose of stocks in sauce making is to supply or augment the nutritive and savory components that are released by meats and fish during cooking. *Glaces* are stocks that have been slowly cooked down (reduced) to a thick syrup. These are convenient to have on hand in professional kitchens because they keep well and can be added to sauces at the last minute to give a richer flavor, a deeper color, and a smoother texture. Some chefs rely almost entirely on meat glace (*glace de viande*) for preparing brown sauces (see Chapter 7, "Brown Sauces," page 157).

Classic *demi-glace* is a stock that has been reduced and bound with starch until it has the consistency of a very light syrup or glace. Classic demi-glace is the basis for classic brown sauces. Natural demi-glace, also called *coulis*, is thickened by reduction or continual remoistening with additional meat; no starch is used in its preparation.

The term *jus* traditionally describes the light, natural liquid derived from the drippings of a roast. Because a natural jus is perhaps the most satisfying and flavorful of all sauces, chefs use a variety of techniques to simulate the flavor of a natural jus, using meat trimmings and bones. To prepare a stock with some of the full, natural flavor of a jus, meat trimmings are usually browned and cooked for a short time with a previously made full-flavored stock.

Essences are extracts made from vegetables, meats, or seafood and are used as last-minute flavorings for sauces. In classic sauce making, essences are usually used as a final flavoring for more complex stock-based sauces. In most of these situations, essences can be dispensed with and the ingredient itself simply infused in the sauce and strained out at the last minute.

STOCKS

Stocks were originally invented to facilitate kitchen organization and to augment integral sauces. *Integral sauces* are those prepared directly from the juices that are released by meats and fish during cooking. There are two major difficulties in preparing sauces with only the natural savory elements released in cooking. First, meats and fish rarely supply enough of their own flavorful elements to make enough savory sauce to go around. Second, in a restaurant setting, it is difficult and impractical to prepare an integral sauce for each dish. Because of these problems, chefs developed stocks, which can be made from less-expensive cuts of meat, inexpensive meat trimmings, and bones.

The obvious method for supplying additional savory meat juices or drippings is to prepare extra meat; for example, roast two turkeys to make enough full-flavored gravy for one. This was common in French cooking until the eighteenth century: Extra jus was prepared by roasting meat and squeezing out the juices in a press.

The first stocks were simple broths, by-products of poached meat and fish dishes. Before the method of preparing stocks was refined and systematized, meat was often braised or roasted with a thick slice of ham or veal to give extra body to the sauce.

The challenge to the chef is to get the maximum flavor into a stock with a minimum of expense. A stock made with a large proportion of meat that is then carefully reduced to a light glace will have a magnificent flavor but will be too expensive for most restaurants. For this reason, many chefs have replaced much of the meat in older stock recipes with bones. Although bones can supply gelatin and a minimal amount of savor to a stock, a stock made with bones will never have the depth and flavor of one made with meat.

Much of the expense of using meat in a stock can be defrayed by saving the cooked meat for another use, either to serve in the restaurant or to the staff. Boiled beef can, for instance, be made into excellent salads (with capers, pickles, vinaigrette), into a *salade bouchère* (made with diced boiled beef, hard-boiled eggs, potatoes, tomatoes, and chopped parsley), and into ravioli filling (seasoned, chopped with a little beef marrow). It can also be reheated in tomato sauce or cooked in a *miroton* (baked into a kind of gratin with stewed onions, breadcrumbs, and a little vinegar) with potatoes (*hachis Parmentier*—the meat is minced, covered with mashed potatoes, and baked).

Traditional stock recipes are divided into white and brown. White stocks are usually prepared by first blanching meat and bones and then moistening them with cold water. Brown stocks are prepared by first browning the meats or bones, either in the oven or on top of the stove. Most of the recipes in this book that use stock call for brown stocks, mainly because they have a richer, more complex flavor.

Improving a Stock's Flavor

Prepare Double and Triple Stocks

Stocks can always be improved by using an already prepared stock to moisten meats for a new batch. When the moistening liquid for a stock is an already prepared stock, the result is called a double stock. If a double stock is in turn used to moisten more meat, the result is a triple stock. The elaborate stocks of the eighteenth and nineteenth centuries were made using this method of continuous remoistening with progressively richer and richer stock to prepare coulis and essences.

Making double and triple stocks is expensive. Most methods for making stock are designed to imitate double and triple stocks without the expense. If, however, the chef can defray the cost of the ingredients so that double and triple stocks made with meat can be used for sauce making, the resulting sauces will have an inimitable depth, complexity, and savor.

Caramelize the Ingredients

Stocks can be given heightened color and flavor by first caramelizing the meat juices on the bottom of the pan before the final moistening with water or stock. Precooking the ingredients in this way will also result in a clearer stock. For a detailed description of this method, see "Jus" and "Essences" later in this chapter.

Add Gelatinous Cuts

Some recipes call for the addition of a veal foot (split and blanched, starting in cold water) or strips of pork rind to stocks. These ingredients contribute gelatin and give the stock a smoother, richer texture.

Balance the Ingredients

The final decision as to how stocks will be prepared depends on the kitchen's cooking style and budget. The chef will have to rely on experience and expertise to balance the components in the stock to derive the best flavor from the ingredients.

If a stock is to be radically reduced for sauce making or if double or triple stocks are being prepared, the chef must determine whether additional vegetables and a second or third bouquet garni are needed. If too many vegetables are added to the preliminary stock or if additional vegetables are added at each stage in the preparation of a double or triple stock, the natural sugars in the vegetables may become too concentrated, and the stock will be too sweet. You may find that, as the stock nears completion, one of the vegetables or one of the herbs in the bouquet garni is too assertive; decrease the amount of that ingredient the next time you make the stock.

If a finished stock tastes flat, its flavor can be improved by adding a fresh bouquet garni and some freshly sweated mirepoix vegetables. Whether or not this is necessary depends on how the stock will be used.

Dos and Don'ts

1. Always moisten stock with *cold* liquid. If hot water is added to meat, it causes the meat to release soluble proteins (albumin) quickly into the surrounding liquid. These proteins immediately coagulate into very fine particles and cloud the stock. When cold liquid is used and slowly heated, the proteins contained in the meat (or fish) coagulate in larger clumps and float to the top, where they can be skimmed. When adding liquid to an already simmering stock to compensate for evaporation, make sure it is cold.

2. Never allow a stock to boil. As meat and bones cook, they release proteins and fats into the surrounding liquid. Stock should be heated slowly to only a simmer. At a slow simmer, these components appear as scum on top of the stock and can be skimmed. If the stock is boiling, these substances are churned back into the stock and become emulsified. The resulting stock is cloudy and has a dull, muddy, greasy flavor, which will only worsen if the stock is reduced (or bound) for a sauce. When the stock comes to a simmer, skim it every 5 to 10 minutes for the first hour with a ladle to prevent fat and scum from working their way back into the stock. As the stock cooks, it needs to be skimmed only every 30 minutes to an hour. Keep the ladle in a container of cold water next to the pot so it is convenient for skimming and so that it does not become caked with fat and scum.

3. Do not use too much liquid. The higher the proportion of solid ingredients to liquid, the more flavorful the stock will be. Many beginning cooks completely cover the solid ingredients with liquid at the beginning of cooking. Because the solid ingredients in a stock settle during cooking, the cook often finds that he or she has added more liquid than necessary and the resulting stock is thin. It is best to use only enough liquid or stock to come three-quarters of the way to the top of the ingredients. The only exceptions to this rule are stocks with extremely long cooking times, where any excess liquid will evaporate anyway.

4. Do not move the contents of the stock during cooking and straining. As stock cooks, albumin and other solids settle along the bottom and sides of the pot. If the stock is disturbed, these solids will break up and cloud the stock. When straining the finished stock, do not press on the ingredients in the strainer; allow enough time for the liquid to drain naturally.

5. Do not overreduce. Stocks are often reduced to concentrate their flavor and to give them an appetizing, light, syrupy texture. Although reduction is an almost essential technique for converting stocks into sauces, much of the delicacy and flavor of meats is lost if reduced for too long. Many of the flavors contained in stock are aromatic and evaporate when simmered over a prolonged period, leaving a flat taste. Highly reduced stocks often contain a large concentration of gelatin, which gives them a sticky feeling and texture in the mouth.

   It is preferable to prepare a double or triple stock rather than to try to reduce a stock to intensify its flavor. The expense will be the same per given quantity of finished stock.

6. Do not add the liaison until all the fat and scum have been carefully skimmed. Traditional recipes often suggest adding a thickener, such as roux, cornstarch, or arrowroot, to stock to thicken it lightly and give it texture. Once starch is added to a stock, any fat emulsified in the liquid will be held in solution by the starch and will become difficult to skim.

7. Store stocks carefully. Warm stock is a perfect medium for bacteria (beef broth was originally used to line Petri dishes in laboratories). Avoid keeping stocks between 40° and 140°F (4° and 60°C) for long periods. The danger of spoilage increases in hot weather and when larger amounts of stock are being prepared. A quart or two (1 to 2 liters) of stock can be allowed to cool at room temperature before it is refrigerated with little danger of spoilage. Larger amounts of stock are best cooled by floating a container (make sure the bottom is well scrubbed) of ice in the stock to chill it before refrigerating. Large amounts of stock may require several batches of ice.

BROWN CHICKEN STOCK

Brown chicken stock is especially useful in kitchens where it is not practical to prepare meat glaces and beef stocks regularly. If the kitchen does not generate enough chicken carcasses for the stock, most wholesale butchers will deliver chicken carcasses at a nominal cost. Stewing hens can also be added to the stock for a fuller flavor, but this of course increases the stock's cost.

Brown chicken stock can be used for deglazing sauté pans and roasting pans and as a base for more concentrated, specialized stocks, such as game or pigeon. It is good to have brown chicken stock on hand to use as a thinner for sauces that may have become too reduced.

YIELD: 8 QUARTS (8 LITERS)

chicken carcasses or stewing hens	12 pounds	6 kilograms
onions, 2 medium	1 pound	500 grams
carrots, 2 medium	8 ounces	250 grams
celery, 1 stalk	3 ounces	100 grams
cold water	9 quarts	9 liters
bouquet garni (1 bay leaf, 1 large bunch fresh thyme, 1 handful tarragon stems, 1 bunch parsley, preferably with roots)	1	1

1. Preheat the oven to 400°F (200°C).
2. Thoroughly rinse the chicken carcasses with cold water. Give them a sniff to make sure they are fresh. Drain them well. Trim any excess fat off the carcasses. Cut off the tail, which is attached to the back. (If using stewing hens, check the inside of the cavity and pull out any unhatched eggs. Rinse the cavity thoroughly and remove any clumps of fat. Cut the hens into ten pieces: four pieces of breast, two drumsticks, two pieces of back, and two thighs.) Break the chicken carcasses up with a cleaver.
3. Spread the broken-up chicken parts and carcasses over the bottom of a large roasting pan. Make sure the chicken covers the pan in a single layer. (If the chicken is heaped up in the pan, it will not brown. Conversely, if sections of the roasting pan remain exposed, the juices are liable to burn.) Slide the roasting pan into the hot oven.
4. Coarsely chop the onions, carrots, and celery (it is not necessary to peel these—just make sure they are rinsed well).
5. Check the chicken after about 20 minutes. It should be golden brown on top. Stir it around with a wooden spoon, add the chopped vegetables, and continue roasting.
6. After 45 minutes to 1 hour of roasting, when the pieces of chicken are completely browned and any juices have caramelized on the bottom of the roasting pan, remove the pan from the oven and place it on top of the stove.
7. If there is a large amount of rendered chicken fat in the bottom of the roasting pan, it can be ladled off at this point. Add 1 quart (1 liter) of the cold water to the roasting pan and place on the stove over a high flame.

Scrape the bottom of the roasting pan with a wooden spoon to dissolve the caramelized juices.

8. Carefully transfer the browned chicken parts to a 25-quart (22 liter) stock-pot, along with the water containing the deglazed juices. Add the remaining cold water to the pot. The water should cover the chicken carcasses only about three-quarters of the way up. The chicken carcasses will sink down in the pot during cooking. If they are completely covered with water at the beginning, the stock will be too thin.

9. Gently bring the stock to a slow simmer. Do not let it boil. Skim the stock regularly with a ladle to remove fat and scum. After about 40 minutes, most of the excess fat should be gone, and the bouquet garni can be added to the pot. Push it down into the pot with the back of a ladle so it does not keep floating to the top.

10. Cook the stock for a total of 3 hours. Do not cover the pot at any point.

11. Strain the finished stock first through a coarse chinois and then through a fine chinois. Do not press on the pieces of carcass while they are draining, or the stock may cloud. Let the stock cool at room temperature and then in an ice bath before refrigerating.

12. After the stock has completely cooled, any remaining fat will have congealed on its surface and should be carefully scraped off with a metal spoon. Brown chicken stock will keep for 3 to 4 days in the refrigerator. If it needs to be kept longer, it can be brought to a simmer for 10 minutes, skimmed, and quickly cooled. It will last for another 3 to 4 days.

Red Wine Chicken Stock

Prepare the Brown Chicken Stock (above) but replace the water with red wine. Simmer in the same way.

WHITE CHICKEN STOCK

Although white chicken stock is less flavorful than brown chicken stock, it is useful for sauces where a pure white appearance is important and as a poaching liquid for white stews (*blanquettes*).

Because the chicken carcasses are not browned in the oven before being moistened, it is important that they be well trimmed of fat before being put into the stockpot. White chicken stock will render more fat than brown once it is simmering in the pot, so be especially careful to keep the stock from boiling, and be sure to skim frequently.

If white chicken stock is prepared with only carcasses—without stewing hens—it will be cloudy unless the carcasses are thoroughly sweated before the water is added. Clouding is not a problem if the stock is to be used in an opaque sauce containing cream, but if the clarity of the stock is important, be sure to include the stewing hen, as in the recipe that follows.

YIELD: 8 QUARTS (8 LITERS)

chicken carcasses	8 pounds	4 kilograms
stewing hen, 1	4 pounds	2 kilograms
onions, 2 medium	1 pound	500 grams
carrots, 2 medium	8 ounces	250 grams
celery, 1 stalk	3 ounces	100 grams
bouquet garni (1 bay leaf, 1 large bunch fresh thyme, 1 handful tarragon stems, 1 bunch parsley, preferably with roots)	1	1
cold water	8 quarts	8 liters

1. Smell the carcasses to make sure they are fresh. Rinse and drain them well in a colander. Carefully trim the carcasses of excess fat. Cut off any tails left attached to the backs. Coarsely chop the carcasses with a cleaver.
2. Pull any unhatched eggs from inside the stewing hen (these would cloud the stock). Cut the stewing hen into 10 pieces.
3. Coarsely chop the onions, carrots, and celery.
4. Place the chopped vegetables and the bouquet garni in a 20-quart (18 liter) stockpot and cover them with the chicken carcasses and pieces of hen. Add enough water to come three-quarters of the way up the carcasses. (The meat and bones will settle as the stock cooks.)
5. Slowly bring the stock to a simmer (this should take about 40 minutes). Carefully skim with a ladle any fat and scum that float to the top of the pot. (Because the bones and meat for white stock have not been browned first in the oven, there will be more fat and scum than for a brown stock.) Continue slowly simmering the stock for 3 hours.
6. White chicken stock should be strained and cooled in the same way as brown chicken stock.

BROWN BEEF STOCK

Brown beef stock can be prepared in two ways. The first and simplest method, given here, consists of browning and cooking beef for 5 to 6 hours. A second method, designed to extract the maximum gelatin from the bones, consists of separating the meat and the bones and making a preliminary stock by cooking the bones for 12 to 24 hours (see Brown Beef-Bone Stock for Meat Glace, page 96). This bone stock is used to moisten the meat, which is then cooked for 5 to 6 hours. In the following recipe, the bones and meat are browned on the stove. It is also possible to combine the meat and vegetables and brown everything together in the oven. When using the oven, be sure to turn the ingredients from time to time to ensure that they are thoroughly and evenly browned.

beef shanks, cut into 1½-inch-thick (4 cm) rounds	12 pounds	6 kilograms
pure olive oil or vegetable oil	9 tablespoons	135 milliliters
onions, 2 medium	1 pound	500 grams
carrots, 2 medium	8 ounces	250 grams
celery, 1 stalk	3 ounces	100 grams
garlic head, cut crosswise in half	1	1
cold water or stock	1 cup	250 milliliters
blanched pork rinds (optional)	1 pound	500 grams
cold water	9 quarts	9 liters
large bouquet garni (page 51)	1	1

1. If you wish to save the marrow from the beef shank bones, remove it by gently pressing on the narrow end of the bone with both thumbs. Usually the marrow will slide out in an even cylinder. If you cannot get it out using this method, cut the meat away from the bone and crack the bone on two sides with a cleaver. Pull the bone away to free the marrow. The marrow can be saved in the refrigerator in a bucket of heavily salted water (which also removes streaks of blood) or frozen until needed for pâtés, ravioli filling, garniture, and the like. If you have no need for the marrow, it can be left in the bones, but skim the stock carefully because the marrow will render extra fat. If there are large clumps of fat surrounding the meat, trim them away. Carefully pat the rounds of shank with towels until they are completely dry (otherwise, they will not brown properly).
2. Heat ½ cup (125 milliliters) of the oil in the bottom of a heavy pot or roasting pan. Gently brown the shank rounds in the hot oil. Avoid putting the pieces of shank in the oil all at once; this lowers the temperature of the oil and will make it more difficult to brown the meat.
3. While the meat is browning, coarsely chop the onions (see Note), carrots, and celery. The vegetables need not be peeled if they are thoroughly washed.
4. After the meat has been browned on both sides, remove it and pour off the cooked oil. Carefully examine the pot to make sure that the caramelized juices on the bottom have not burned. If they have, do not bother deglazing the pan.
5. Add the remaining tablespoon (15 milliliters) of fresh oil to the bottom of the pot (or to a fresh pot if the bottom of the pot has burned) and gently brown the chopped vegetables and garlic. After these are evenly browned, deglaze the pan with the cup of water or stock, and transfer both the meat

and vegetables, as well as the deglazing liquid, to a 25-quart (22 liter) stockpot. Over high heat, completely reduce the water or stock until it caramelizes on the bottom of the pot. This step causes the meat to release its juices so that they can be caramelized on the bottom of the pot before water is added, giving the stock a deeper color and flavor. Be very attentive at this stage, to prevent the juices from overreducing and burning.

6. If using the blanched pork rinds, add them to the meat and vegetables, cover with the cold water, and gently bring to a simmer. Add the bouquet garni. Be sure to secure it under one of the shank rounds so that it does not float to the top and interfere with skimming. Slowly simmer the stock for 5 to 6 hours, skimming every 10 to 15 minutes for the first hour.

7. Gently strain the stock through a chinois. Do not push on the pieces of meat to force out the liquid or the stock may cloud.

8. Brown beef stock can be cooled and stored in the same way as brown chicken stock.

Note: In professional kitchens where a flat-top stove is used, onions are often cut in half crosswise, and the exposed surfaces are burned by turning them faced down on the stove surface. Onions blackened in this way contribute color to brown stocks. If the meat and vegetables have been adequately browned, this method should not be necessary.

BROWN BEEF-BONE STOCK FOR MEAT GLACE
Glace de Viande

YIELD: 10 QUARTS (10 LITERS)

beef knuckle bones	12 pounds	6 kilograms
onions, quartered, 2 large	1½ pounds	750 grams
carrots, quartered, 2 medium	8 ounces	250 grams
celery, 1 stalk	3 ounces	100 grams
garlic head, cut crosswise in half	1	1
cold water	10 quarts	10 liters
large bouquet garni (page 51)	1	1

1. Preheat the oven to 450°F (230°C).
2. Smell the bones to make sure they are fresh. Thoroughly rinse them in cold water, drain, and place them in a heavy-bottomed roasting pan that is just large enough to fit them in a single layer. Place in the preheated oven.
3. Check the bones after 20 minutes. When the tops begin to brown, turn them over with tongs. Add the onions, carrots, celery, and garlic to the roasting pan. (Some chefs like to blacken halved onions on top of the stove

to give a deeper color to the stock. Since this stock will be highly reduced to make meat glace, this step should not be necessary.) Continue roasting and turning the bones from time to time until they are evenly browned. The whole process should take from 45 minutes to 1 hour.

4. Remove the roasting pan from the oven and transfer the bones and vegetables to a 25-quart (22 liter) stockpot. Because the bones are heavy and unwieldy, it is best to remove them from the pan with a pair of large tongs rather than trying to lift the whole roasting pan.

5. Pour off any fat remaining in the roasting pan. Check the bottom of the pan to make sure the drippings from the bones have not burned. If they are intact, place the pan on top of the stove and deglaze it with 1 to 2 cups (250 to 500 milliliters) of the cold water. Scrape the drippings over the heat with a wooden spoon.

6. Pour the deglazing liquid from the roasting pan over the bones. Cover the bones with the remaining cold water and slowly bring the stock to a simmer. Wedge the bouquet garni under the bones so it does not float to the top of the pot and interfere with skimming. Simmer the stock for 10 to 12 hours. Add cold water every few hours to replace what is lost via evaporation.

7. Strain and store beef-bone stock in the same way as brown chicken stock and brown beef stock.

OXTAIL-RED WINE STOCK

Sauces that call for red wine are typically made by reducing the wine and then adding meat glace or demi-glace. The mixture is then reduced to the right consistency and finished with butter. The problem with this method is that the tannins and acid in the wine are concentrated in a way that makes the sauce harsh. That can be alleviated somewhat by reducing the wine simultaneously with the demi-glace, whose proteins clarify out some of the tannins. The best method of all is to make a red wine stock by moistening meat or bones with red wine, cooking the stock in the usual way, and reducing it to a sauce-like consistency before finishing with butter. This method is also useful when making braised dishes that call for red wine—coq au vin, for example—for which the braising time is relatively short, too short to soften the tannins in the wine.

YIELD: 2 QUARTS (2 LITERS)

oxtails or beef knuckle bones	7 pounds	3.25 kilograms
carrots, cut into 1-inch (2.5 cm) sections	3	3
onion, quartered	1 large	1 large
garlic head, cut crosswise in half	1	1
medium bouquet garni (page 51)	1	1
full-bodied red wine	5 (750-milliliter) bottles	5 (750-milliliter) bottles

1. Preheat the oven to 450°F (230°C).

2. Spread the oxtails in a roasting pan with the carrots, onion, and garlic in one layer and roast, turning from time to time, until well browned, about 1 hour.

3. Put the bouquet garni in a 15-quart (14 liter) stockpot and cover with the oxtails and vegetables. Pour off any fat remaining in the roasting pan. Deglaze the roasting pan with 1 to 2 cups (250 to 500 milliliters) of the red wine and pour over the oxtails. Add the remaining red wine.

4. Gently simmer for 5 hours, adding water as needed to keep the oxtails covered; skim off any fat and froth.

5. Strain into a clean pot and reduce by half. Cool and store in the same way as brown chicken stock.

VEAL STOCK

Veal stock is an excellent base for both white and brown sauces because it has a deep, subtle flavor that makes it especially adaptable to a variety of preparations. Veal stock—both white and brown—was the basic stock used in professional kitchens during the nineteenth and into the twentieth centuries. Because of its expense, it has largely been replaced with beef stock, chicken stock, or stocks made with veal bones alone.

The ingredients below can be used for either white or brown veal stock; the initial procedure is for white stock, with the variation for brown stock following. The stock uses a portion of veal shank. If preparing white veal stock with bones alone, the bones should first be blanched—placed in a pot of cold water and brought to a simmer—then drained and rinsed before being used in the final stock. If this step is ignored, the stock will be cloudy and gray. When meat is used, it clarifies the stock, making blanching unnecessary. If using only bones, increase the quantity of veal knucklebones to 5 pounds (2.5 kilograms).

YIELD: 5 QUARTS (5 LITERS)

veal knucklebones	3 pounds	1.5 kilograms
veal shanks	2 pounds	1 kilogram
onions, peeled and halved	2 medium	2 medium
carrots, halved	2 medium	2 medium
celery, 1 stalk	3 ounces	100 grams
large bouquet garni (page 51)	1	1
cold water	5 quarts	5 liters

1. Put the bones in a pot with enough cold water to cover and bring to a simmer. Boil the bones for about 5 minutes and drain in a colander. Rinse them thoroughly with cold water.

2. Place all the ingredients except the water in a 15-quart (14 liter) stockpot. Make sure the vegetables and the bouquet garni are secured beneath bones or meat so they do not float to the top and interfere with skimming.

3. Cover the ingredients with the cold water. Add enough water to come about 4 inches (10 cm) above the top of the meat and bones.

4. Bring the stock slowly to a simmer (this should take at least 45 minutes). Skim off any froth, fat, and scum that float to the surface. Cook the stock at a very low simmer for 6 hours more, skimming every 30 minutes.

5. Carefully strain the stock, first through a coarse chinois and then through a fine chinois. If a perfectly clear stock is needed, it can be strained a third time through cheesecloth.

Brown Veal Stock

Roast all the ingredients for white veal stock, except the bouquet garni and water, in a 400°F (200°C) oven. Turn the meat, bones, and vegetables from time to time until they are evenly browned. Avoid burning any of the ingredients or letting the juices burn on the bottom of the roasting pan. Transfer the ingredients to a stockpot and add the bouquet garni. Deglaze the roasting pan with water. When all the juices have dissolved, add the deglazing liquid to the ingredients in the stockpot. Moisten, cook, and strain the stock as for white veal stock.

MODERN VEAL DEMI-GLACE

Not many cooks use veal to make stock anymore because of the cost, and veal bones simply don't provide the savor of a stock made with meat. One approach is to use veal breast, which is the least expensive cut of veal, and serve the veal for dinner with mustard and some little pickles or a homemade tomato sauce. If you decide not to serve the meat, simmer for 12 hours instead of 5 to extract a maximum of savor and gelatin.

YIELD: ABOUT 1 QUART (1 LITER)

breast of veal	15 pounds	7 kilograms
carrots, cut into 1-inch (2.5 cm) sections	4	4
onions, quartered	2	2
medium bouquet garni (page 51)	1	1
cold water	12 quarts	12 liters

1. Preheat the oven to 450°F (230°C). Trim away any obvious pieces of fat from the breast and slice between the ribs.

2. Put the cut-up breast in a roasting pan with the vegetables and roast, turning from time to time, until well browned, about 1 hour.

3. Transfer the meat and vegetables to a 15-quart (14 liter) pot and nestle in the bouquet garni. Pour off any fat remaining in the roasting pan. Deglaze the roasting pan with 1 to 2 cups (250 to 500 milliliters) of water and pour over the meat and vegetables. Add enough water to come about 4 inches (10 cm) above the top of the meat and vegetables. Simmer gently for 5 hours, skimming off any froth, fat, and scum that float to the surface. Strain into a clean pot.
4. Reduce down to about 1 quart (1 liter), skimming regularly, until the stock has a lightly syrupy consistency.

CHICKEN DEMI-GLACE

Chicken demi-glace takes less time to prepare than beef or veal demi-glace, and often has a better flavor.

YIELD: 1 QUART (1 LITER)

brown chicken stock (page 91)	8 quarts	8 liters

Reduce the stockdown to 1 quart (1 liter), skimming regularly, until a lightly syrupy consistency.

FISH STOCK

Fish stock is normally prepared with bones and trimmings of lean, flat fish such as sole and flounder. Oily varieties of fish, such as salmon and mackerel, should be avoided except when preparing red wine sauces. In areas where fresh fish is abundant (an increasingly rare occurrence), fish stock can be made with fresh whole fish rather than bones. Whether fish or fish bones are being used, it is essential that they be impeccably fresh and that the fish stock be prepared within an hour or two from the time the fish is filleted. If the bones have a fishy or strong iodine smell, throw them out.

Since the publication of the second edition of *Sauces,* high-quality demi-glace and *glace de viande* has become available commercially and can be found in most gourmet stores or high-end supermarkets. These can be diluted with hot water—the amount needed depends on the brand and particular glaze—to the consistency of demi-glace and used in the recipes given here. Another trick: To give these glazes a homemade flavor, add them to stocks at the very beginning of reduction to increase the yield of demi-glace by as much as three times.

Fish skeletons should be thoroughly gutted (fishmongers do not bother gutting fish for fillets), and the gills should be removed. The bones should be well rinsed to remove any traces of blood, which would discolor the stock. Never add the skin from fillets to a fish stock—it will turn gray. The vegetables used for the stock, as well as the bouquet garni, can be varied depending on the final use of the stock. Fennel branches add a lightness and freshness and are too often ignored in recipes for fish stock.

If impeccably fresh ingredients are not available, it is often better to substitute court-bouillon or the cooking liquid from mussels or clams in sauces that call for fish stock. Remember that fish stock and fish sauces should smell and taste of the sea and should not be fishy.

YIELD: 3 QUARTS (3 LITERS)

assorted fish or fish bones	5 pounds	2.5 kilograms
onion, 1 medium	8 ounces	250 grams
carrot, 1 medium	4 ounces	125 grams
celery, ½ stalk	2 ounces	50 grams
leeks, green parts only	1 bunch	1 bunch
butter	1 ounce	30 grams
fennel branches	4 ounces	125 grams
garlic head, cut crosswise in half	1	1
cold water	3 quarts	3 liters
dry white wine	2 cups	500 milliliters
bouquet garni (1 bay leaf, 1 small bunch fresh thyme, 1 small bunch tarragon branches), 1 bunch parsley, preferably with roots	1	1

1. Carefully smell and examine the fish or fish bones, checking for freshness. Remove the gills and pull out any roe or viscera from inside. There is often a vein containing blood running along the spinal column where the ribs join. This should be scraped with the tip of a paring knife so the blood can be washed away during rinsing. Cut the fish into 1-inch (2.5 cm) sections. If bones are being used, snap them over themselves so each skeleton is broken in two or three places. Rinse inside the cavity of whole fish. If bones are being used, rinse them thoroughly under cold running water for 10 to 15 minutes and transfer to a colander to drain.

2. Peel and roughly dice the onion, carrot, and celery into ¼-inch (5 mm) cubes (they are cut small to cook quickly). Cut the leek greens into 1-inch (2.5 cm) lengths.

3. Melt the butter in an 8-quart (8 liter) pot. Sweat the diced vegetables, leek greens, fennel, and garlic in the butter for 5 minutes, and then add the bones or fish. Stir the ingredients over medium heat for about 5 minutes more, until the bones turn white and start to smell appetizing.

4. Add enough water to come three-quarters up the sides of the pot. Pour in the wine. Gently bring the stock to a simmer.

5. When the stock simmers, carefully skim off any fat and scum that float to the top. Add the bouquet garni. Continue gently simmering the stock for 40 minutes.

6. Strain the stock through a fine chinois and let it cool in a plastic or stainless-steel container. If a perfectly clear fish stock is required, leave the stock undisturbed for an hour or two, then carefully draw the stock off the top with a ladle. The particles of fish, which are harmless, will have settled to the bottom. The remaining cloudy stock is perfectly acceptable and can be used for sauce finished with cream or for poaching liquid. Fish stock should be used the same day it is made.

Note: The recipe for fish stock given here differs somewhat from the classic version. A classic fish stock contains no carrots, celery, or fennel and the bones are not cooked before water is added.

VEGETABLE STOCK
Court-Bouillon or Nage

Vegetable stock can be used to impart a lightness and a delicate aromatic flavor to sauces. In traditional cooking it was primarily used as a poaching liquid for fish and sometimes calves' brains. Contemporary chefs are using it more frequently in sauce making because of its delicacy, freshness, and ease of preparation. Vegetable stock can also be used instead of water for steaming fish, meats, or vegetables. It is often an excellent substitute for fish stock when good-quality fresh fish or fish bones are unavailable.

Although the terms *court-bouillon* and *nage* are often used interchangeably, court-bouillon describes a broth from which the vegetables have been strained, whereas a nage is used for serving fish and shellfish *à la nage* —a style of presentation in which the fish is served surrounded by the poaching liquid containing the vegetables cut into decorative shapes.

The technique for preparing court-bouillon depends on whether the chef wants the vegetables to release all their flavor into the surrounding liquid or prefers them to retain some of their flavor and texture (as in the preparation *à la nage*). To get the vegetables to release the most flavor into the surrounding liquid, they are best sweated in a small amount of butter before being moistened. They should then be cooked in water alone for at least 15 minutes before any wine or vinegar is added—the acidity in both these liquids prevents the vegetables from cooking completely. When preparing a nage, where the vegetables will be served as an accompaniment, bring the wine and water to a simmer and slide in the chopped and sliced vegetables. There are no hard and fast rules for which and how many vegetables should go into the stock. This decision depends largely on the final use of the stock. It is practically impossible to add too many onions, leek greens, or fennel branches, whereas too many carrots can make the stock too sweet, especially if it is going to be reduced for a sauce. The following recipe suggests the usual bouquet garni ingredients, but these too can be altered to give the stock a personal or regional character.

Full-flavored herbs, such as oregano, marjoram, or lavender, should generally be avoided except under special circumstances, for example, for grilled fish surrounded by a court-bouillon-based sauce or for steamed crustaceans. Although traditional recipes call for a standard combination of vegetables to arrive at an anonymously flavored vegetable stock, contemporary chefs often prepare court-bouillon using only one or two vegetables to give a sauce a particular, subtle flavor. Court-bouillon made with leeks or fennel alone will give a delicate yet pronounced character to a sauce. Salt should be added to a vegetable stock only if the stock is to be used as is, without reduction.

This recipe emphasizes the flavor of the broth rather than the integrity of the vegetables. If using vegetable stock as an accompaniment to fish or meats cooked *à la nage,* the vegetables should be cut carefully and evenly. Vegetable stock is best used the day it is made.

YIELD: 3 QUARTS (3 LITERS)

red or yellow onions, 2 large	1½ pounds	750 grams
carrots, 2 medium	8 ounces	250 grams
celery, 1 stalk	3 ounces	100 grams
garlic cloves, peeled	4	4
fennel branches	4 ounces	125 grams
olive oil	2 tablespoons	30 milliliters
or	*or*	*or*
butter	1 ounce	30 grams
large bouquet garni (page 51)	1	1
cold water	3 quarts	3 liters
dry white wine	2 cups	500 milliliters
good-quality white wine vinegar	½ cup	125 milliliters

1. Coarsely peel and dice the onions, carrots, and celery.
2. In an 8-quart (8 liter) pot, sweat the diced vegetables, garlic, and fennel in the olive oil for about 10 minutes. Do not allow them to brown.
3. Add the bouquet garni and the cold water and bring to a simmer. Simmer gently for 10 minutes.
4. Add the white wine and vinegar and continue simmering for 15 to 20 minutes more.
5. Let the court-bouillon cool before straining out the vegetables.

GLACES

MEAT GLACE
Glace de Viande

Meat glace takes from 8 to 12 hours to prepare from already made stock. If it is difficult to work in a single stretch, the glace can be reduced for a couple of hours, allowed to cool, and then continued the next day. It is best to begin reduction of the bone stock in a wide-mouthed pot to encourage evaporation and rapid reduction. As the stock reduces, it should be transferred into clean pots of decreasing size. Usually three pots are required to reduce 10 quarts (10 liters) of stock.

Meat glaces can be prepared from any kind of stock, but the technique works best for stocks that already contain a fair amount of gelatin. For this reason, meat glace is most often prepared with a stock made from beef knuckle bones, which release a large amount of gelatin into the surrounding liquid (Brown Beef-Bone Stock for Meat Glace, page 96). Stocks containing little gelatin require too much reduction to become glaces, and by the time the reduction is complete, much of their savor has been compromised.

YIELD: 1 QUART (1 LITER)

brown beef-bone stock	10 quarts	10 liters

1. Transfer the beef-bone stock into a wide-mouthed 12-quart (12 liter) stockpot. If the stock is cold and jelled, use a ladle. (Do not try to pour jelled stock from one pot into another—it will bounce out onto the floor.) Gently bring the stock to a simmer over a 40-minute period.
2. Keep a ladle in a container of cold water next to the pot during reduction. (The water rinses the ladle after each use and prevents it from becoming caked with scum and gelatin.) Skim the stock every 10 to 15 minutes during the first 2 hours of reduction. After this, occasional skimming should suffice.
3. When the stock has reduced by half (after 3 to 4 hours), strain it through a chinois lined with three thicknesses of cheesecloth into a 5-quart (5 liter) pot. (When using cheesecloth, rinse it thoroughly in cold water to eliminate any chemicals adhering to the cloth.)
4. Continue simmering. As the glace becomes increasingly concentrated, transfer it to a 2-quart (2 liter) pot and use a smaller ladle for skimming.
5. The glace is ready when it has the consistency of honey and leaves a thick coating on the back of the ladle. The stock should have reduced to one-tenth of its original volume (for example, 10 quarts/10 liters of stock should yield 1 quart/1 liter of glace). Strain the glace through a fine chinois

into a nonaluminum container with a tight-fitting lid. Do not use cheese-cloth, as it will clog.

6. After the meat glace cools, it should have the texture of hard rubber. It can be kept in the refrigerator for a month or longer.

Fish Glace (Glace de Poisson)

Fish glace is prepared in the same way as meat glace except that fish stock is used instead of meat stock. Fish glace has a strong, fishy taste that it can impart to sauces if used in more than tiny amounts. It is better to substitute reduced mussel or clam cooking liquid or reduced court-bouillon. If concentrated fish stock is required, prepare a double fish stock by moistening fish or fish bones with a previously made fish stock.

JUS

Long, slow cooking is not always the best way to prepare a stock or jus with the flavor of a specific meat. Although slow simmering will extract much of the gelatin and nutritive elements from meat and bones, much of the character, individuality, and freshness of the meat will be lost. Many chefs mistakenly assume that the best method of extracting and intensifying the character of a particular meat such as game, duck, pigeon, or lamb is through long cooking and subsequent reduction. Actually, the best method for extracting the natural flavor from meats is to brown them in a heavy-bottomed pot or saucepan with a small proportion of mirepoix vegetables until their juices are released and caramelize on the bottom of the pot. This process of caramelization is essential to extracting and amplifying the natural savors and should be repeated several times by deglazing the pan with a small amount of stock or wine. These successive deglazings create steam that further cooks the meat and causes it to release juices, which can again be caramelized on the bottom of the pot.

After several deglazings, the meat and bone trimmings should have released most of their savor, which will in turn have caramelized on the bottom of the pot. At this point, any fat will have separated and can be easily removed. The caramelized trimmings should then be moistened with water or stock and cooked only long enough to dissolve the juices that have already been released. If the trimmings are moistened with a full-bodied stock, the jus should not require any reduction. If a thicker texture is desired, it is better to add meat glace to the jus rather than reducing it.

In the recipe that follows, a small amount of jus is prepared in a pot. To master the technique of caramelizing the meat trimmings in stages, it is easier to see and control the process in a pot on top of the stove. For larger quantities, however, it is often easier to brown the ingredients in a roasting pan in the oven.

⌐•● MEAT JUS

YIELD: 1 CUP (250 MILLILITERS)

meat trimmings or carcasses	1 pound	500 grams
onion, 1 small	3 ounces	100 grams
carrot, 1 small	3 ounces	100 grams
pure olive oil	2 tablespoons	30 milliliters
freshly chopped thyme leaves	1 pinch	1 pinch
white wine	½ cup	125 milliliters
brown chicken stock (page 91), brown beef stock (page 94), or water	3 cups	750 milliliters

1. Remove as much fat as possible from the meat trimmings. Chop the meat trimmings or carcasses into small pieces, ¼- to ½-inch (5 millimeter to 1 cm) cubes.
2. Peel and dice the vegetables into ¼-inch (5 mm) cubes.
3. Heat the olive oil in a 4-quart (4 liter) heavy-bottomed pot or saucepan. Add the chopped meat trimmings and vegetables.
4. Brown the meat trimmings and vegetables over medium heat for 10 to 20 minutes. (If the pot is too crowded for the meat and vegetables to brown, do not worry—the juices are the concern here, and they will brown on the bottom of the pot.) As the mixture of meat and vegetables browns, keep checking the bottom of the pot to see whether the juices are beginning to adhere and caramelize. There may be an initial stage when the trimmings have released juices that have not yet browned.
5. When the juices have browned (the fat will also separate out at this point), add the thyme leaves. Stir for a minute or two, then add the white wine. Scrape the bottom of the pot with a wooden spoon so that the caramelized juices dissolve in the wine. Continue cooking until the juices caramelize a second time.
6. Add 1½ cups (375 milliliters) of stock to the pot, scrape the juices, and let the stock reduce until the juices caramelize a third time. If there is a large amount of fat, carefully drain it off.
7. Turn down the heat and add the rest of the stock to the pot. Gently bring the stock to a simmer and cook the mixture for 15 minutes. Skim off any scum or fat that floats to the surface.
8. Strain the mixture through a fine chinois.

ESSENCES

Contemporary chefs use essences, sometimes tightly bound with butter or oil, as light-bodied sauces.

Before the twentieth century, cookbooks made frequent reference to essences, especially essences of specific game birds. Most cooks assume that the best way to extract the essence of flavor from a pigeon carcass, for example, is to roast it with a little mirepoix (correct) and then simply simmer it for a couple of hours (incorrect). Truth be told, long simmering does little to extract the essential flavor of a carcass or meat trimmings; it will, however, produce a stock that is always useful in the kitchen as a base for essences. In short, if you're making a pigeon essence and you're fortunate enough to roast pigeons on a regular basis, proceed as follows: Brown broken-up carcasses in a pot with onion and carrot. Add a bouquet garni and just enough broth to cover. Simmer for 2 hours and strain. This is the stock. Take another batch of carcasses, brown them thoroughly with onion, carrot, and perhaps a little thyme, and deglaze the pan with the stock you made. Scrape up the caramelized juices and stir the carcasses around in the stock over the heat for about 5 minutes. Strain; *this* is the essence. Use the barely cooked carcasses to make stock for the next batch. By using this method—this quick deglazing with very little cooking—you capture the essence of a thing. The stock provides body and a backdrop, but it's the final 5 minutes that capture the essence.

Mushroom Essence

Mushroom essence is made by reducing mushroom cooking liquid to one-fourth its original volume. Mushroom cooking liquid is prepared by cooking mushrooms for 15 minutes in a covered pot with an equal weight of water (for example, 1 pound/500 grams of mushrooms to 2 cups/500 milliliters water). Although most recipes calling for mushroom essence assume that ordinary cultivated mushrooms are used, the essence is far better when prepared from wild types such as morels, cèpes, or chanterelles.

JAPANESE-STYLE MUSHROOM SAUCE

This sauce is broth-like and should surround the food it sauces, such as fish or chicken, in a wide bowl. Substitute whatever mushrooms are available.

YIELD: ENOUGH FOR 6 SERVINGS

dashi (page 520)	2 cups	500 milliliters
mirin	1 tablespoon	15 milliliters
soy sauce	1 tablespoon	15 milliliters
dried porcini mushrooms, soaked until soft in just enough water to cover	½ cup	125 milliliters
dried morel mushrooms, soaked until soft in just enough water to cover	½ cup	125 milliliters
dried shiitake mushrooms, soaked overnight in enough water to cover, stems removed	8	8

1. Bring the dashi to a simmer and add the mirin and soy sauce.
2. Slice the mushrooms and add them to the simmering dashi. Add the mushroom soaking liquid to the dashi, leaving any grit behind in the bowls.
3. Simmer the mushrooms for 10 minutes. Serve the "sauce" over and around chicken or fish.

Truffle Essence

Older recipes for classic sauces often call for truffle essence. Truffle essence is prepared by infusing sliced truffles in a small proportion of brown stock in a covered saucepan. Today, truffles are so scarce that it is unlikely that a restaurant would make truffle essence to have on hand to use in sauces. It is more likely that sliced truffles would be infused in the sauce itself or that the sauce would be finished with truffle butter or commercially available truffle juice.

Vegetable Essences

Almost any vegetable can be chopped and cooked in a small amount of stock, water, or wine. The method is almost the same as preparing a court-bouillon except that the flavor of one vegetable is accentuated, rather than a combination. These flavorful essences can then be served as accompaniments to delicately flavored foods such as fish or can be combined with other ingredients for more complex sauces.

5

LIAISONS: AN OVERVIEW

A *liaison* is an ingredient used to thicken liquids, transforming the liquids into sauces. Until recently it was often consistency alone that distinguished a sauce from a broth; poaching liquids, stocks, and other flavorful liquids became sauces as soon as they were thickened, usually with starch. Today, the difference between a sauce and a broth is less clear, especially in contemporary kitchens, where unbound but intensely flavored liquids are served with meats, fish, and vegetables. Sauces are distinguished from broths and soups not only because they are thicker but because they are more intensely flavored. Liaisons were used in ancient and medieval cooking as thickeners so that the sauces would cling to the foods they accompanied, making the food easier to eat with the fingers. These liaison-thickened sauces were further developed in the seventeenth century as an economical alternative to earlier sauces, which were essentially concentrated extracts made with enormous quantities of meat. For centuries since, sauces have been thickened not only to help them cling to food but to give them the look of highly concentrated and flavorful meat juices or cooking liquids.

Nowadays, chefs and diners have become skeptical of sauces that are thickened only to give them a richer appearance. Today's diner is more impressed by a light-appearing sauce than one that is thick or seems overly rich. Modern sauces are often less thick or have been thickened by reduction alone.

HOW LIAISONS THICKEN

Liaisons usually cause thickening by dispersing solids or insoluble liquids in a water-based medium; on a molecular level, these fine components prevent the water from moving freely and thus increase the sauce's viscosity.

Starch thickens sauces because its large molecules (made up of bush-like rows of sugar molecules) unravel in the liquid medium and bond into larger groupings with the water molecules. The efficiency of a particular starch as a thickener depends on the shape and size of its molecules and how they disperse in the liquid medium.

Whereas the viscosity of starch-thickened sauces can be attributed to solids suspended in a liquid (the scientific term for this kind of system is *sol*), emulsified sauces consist of two mutually insoluble liquids—usually fat and water—suspended one within the other. Emulsions rely on various additional ingredients to prevent the tiny particles from running into one another, joining up into larger particles, and eventually separating into two distinct layers—the usual course of events when combining water and oil alone.

Emulsifiers usually work in one of two ways. In the first, the emulsifier is made up of long molecules that float between the microscopic globules of fat (or water, depending on what is suspended in what), preventing the globules from touching one another; the stability of butter sauces containing flour is an example of this. In the second system, the emulsifier molecules are asymmetrical: Half of the molecule is soluble in fat, the other half in water. The result is that half of the molecule embeds itself in the suspended globule while the other half protrudes into the liquid medium. The protruding ends of these molecules prevent the globules from touching and forming larger aggregates. Egg yolks emulsify in this way.

Vegetable and fruit purées can also be used as thickeners and function in different ways depending on how they are used. Some vegetable purées contain sufficient starch so that they behave like purified starches such as flour or cornstarch, but most purées contain insoluble components that give most purée-thickened sauces a relatively rough texture and mat appearance. They also contribute flavor, whereas plain starch does not (at least not an agreeable one). Some purées, such as those made with tomato or green vegetables, contain so little starch that they thicken a sauce simply by adding a large bulk of fine solid particles to a liquid medium. Sauces thickened with these purées alone will separate into liquid and solid when left to sit unless another liaison is used along with the purée. Vegetable purées are also used as emulsifiers in vinaigrettes, where they prevent the vinegar (or other acid) and the oil from coalescing (joining up into larger globules).

Sauces can be thickened by suspending solids in liquids (such as starch- and vegetable purée–thickened sauces), liquids in liquids (emulsions, such as hollandaise and mayonnaise), and, in some cases, air in liquids (foams, such as sabayons and hollandaise). A well-made sauce béarnaise is both a foam and an emulsion: Minute fat globules and microscopic bubbles of air are surrounded by a liquid medium.

GELATIN

As meats and fish cook, they release juices that contain gelatin, a water-soluble protein. Depending on the cooking method, these juices end up in the roasting pan or the sauté pan, or, in the case of poaching and braising, they are released into the surrounding liquid. When the gelatin is sufficiently concentrated, it gives the cooking liquid a natural, lightly syrupy consistency.

The natural gelatinous consistency that is so appealing in sauces and braising liquids can be achieved in several ways. The most obvious and expensive is to continually reuse meat or fish stocks as moisteners for more meat or fish until the gelatin (and flavor) is so concentrated that the stock has a natural consistency of its own. The resulting liquid is a natural, unthickened demi-glace. Home cooks and professionals have long added strips of pork skin, veal feet, veal knuckles, or chicken or turkey wing tips to stews and stocks to contribute additional natural gelatin. Restaurant chefs often combine these methods with careful reduction to eliminate liquid and concentrate the natural gelatin. In a restaurant setting, natural gelatin is most often added to sauces at the last minute in the form of meat glace (*glace de viande*) or fish glace (*glace de poisson*). These glaces not only give a finished sauce the natural texture that results from careful reduction but also provide a complex flavor backdrop to offset more assertive components, such as wine or herbs, that are added to give the sauce its final character.

In the last twenty years, sauces made by natural reduction and concentration of meat and fish flavors have gradually replaced the more traditional flour-thickened sauces. Although these sauces are almost always better than a carelessly made roux-based sauce, there are disadvantages to relying on reduction alone to give a sauce a syrupy or "sauce-like" consistency. If a sauce has been overly reduced, it will feel gluey in the mouth; it will also quickly congeal on hot plates. Stocks and sauces that have been overly reduced often have a flat, cooked taste that must be offset with more assertive flavors. For this reason, natural gelatin alone is rarely relied on to thicken a sauce. Sauces containing a high concentration of natural gelatin are often finished with butter, which attenuates the gelatin's stickiness.

BRAISED LAMB SHANKS WITH SHALLOTS

Lamb shanks contain a large amount of natural gelatin that gives body to the braising liquid. The braising liquid becomes the only sauce. Aromatic vegetables such as garlic cloves, carrots, or turnips can be used in this recipe instead of shallots.

YIELD: 8 SERVINGS

lamb shanks	8	8
salt and pepper	to taste	to taste
olive oil	¼ cup	60 milliliters
water or clear stock	as needed	as needed
medium bouquet garni (page 51)	1	1
shallots, peeled	24	24

1. Preheat the oven to 300°F (150°C). Trim the excess fat from the lamb shanks. Season the shanks with salt and pepper. Gently brown them in the olive oil in a heavy-bottomed pot that just holds them in a single layer. Add 1 cup (250 milliliters) of water or stock, and boil it down until only fat is left in the bottom of the pan.
2. Add enough water or stock to the pan so that it comes halfway up the sides of the shanks. Add the bouquet garni and cover the pan. Bring the liquid to a slow simmer on top of the stove.
3. Place the shanks in the oven for 90 minutes to 2 hours, or until the meat is easily pulled away from the bone. Check periodically to make sure the braising liquid is not boiling.
4. Transfer the shanks to a plate and strain the braising liquid. Raise the oven temperature to 350°F (175°C).
5. Bring the braising liquid to a slow simmer in a saucepan, and with a ladle skim off any fat that floats to the surface.
6. Put the shanks into a clean sauté pan, pour over the strained braising liquid, add the shallots, and return them to the oven. Baste the shanks and shallots with the braising liquid until the liquid takes on a lightly syrupy consistency and glazes the shanks.

7. When the shanks are ready to serve, heat them in the braising liquid. Serve the shanks surrounded with the shallots and napped with the braising liquid, which should have a lightly syrupy consistency. See the photograph in the color plates

STARCHES

Starches derived from roots and grains are among the oldest and most versatile thickeners for sauces. They are inexpensive and efficient in small amounts, so that they can be used without imparting a flavor of their own.

Starches must be combined with liquid and heated almost to boiling to be effective. Some starches are purer than others. Cornstarch, arrowroot, and potato starch are almost pure starches and produce shiny sauces, whereas flour contains protein, which gives flour-thickened sauces a slightly matte appearance.

Flour

In Western cooking, flour has long been the most popular sauce thickener. Although flour has largely been replaced in recent years by other thickeners, it is still the appropriate choice for many country-style and regional dishes. Chefs are also learning to use flour in limited amounts in conjunction with other thickeners.

One precaution to take when using flour for sauce making is to always make sure that liquids to be thickened have been thoroughly degreased before the flour is incorporated. Flour binds with fat and holds it in suspension throughout the liquid, making it difficult to skim. The result is a greasy, indigestible sauce with a muddy texture and flavor.

Roux

The most common method for thickening liquids with flour is to prepare a roux by cooking the flour with an equal volume of butter. This attenuates the flavor of the flour and eliminates lumps. Hot liquids are then added to the cooked roux, and the mixture is brought to a simmer until it thickens. Because flour contains proteins and other compounds that impart flavor, sauces thickened with roux are usually skimmed for at least 30 minutes once they have been brought to a simmer to eliminate impurities.

Although stock that is used for sauce making should be carefully skimmed and degreased *before* it is combined with roux, further skimming is necessary once the roux has been added, to eliminate the butter and to remove impurities in the flour.

One excellent method for using flour is to cut the amount called for in classic sauces by half and then reduce the thickened sauce carefully to the desired thickness. This method allows more time for skimming and degreasing and will attenuate any floury taste.

In classic French cooking, both white and brown roux are prepared. White roux is used for white sauces; brown roux, for espagnole, the traditional base for the classic brown sauces. To prepare brown roux, the flour is either cooked for 15 to 20 minutes in clarified butter or browned first in the oven and cooked with butter in the same way as white roux. Brown roux is rarely seen in modern restaurant kitchens.

To prepare roux, use a whisk to stir together equal volumes of butter and flour in a saucepan over medium heat. Bring the liquid to be thickened (such as stock or milk) to a simmer in another pot. Cook the roux for about 5 minutes, until it has a pleasant toasty smell, and then remove the saucepan from the heat for a minute to let the roux cool. Return the pan to the heat and pour in the hot liquid while whisking. Continue whisking until the sauce comes to a simmer. Turn down the heat and slowly simmer the sauce (such as béchamel or velouté) for 30 minutes. Skim any froth and impurities from the sauce's surface with a ladle. (It is also possible to thicken liquids with roux by simply adding the cold liquid to the hot roux, thus saving time and a pot. When using this method, however, be careful to whisk thoroughly to prevent lumps.)

Beurre Manié

Like roux, beurre manié contains equal parts by volume of butter and flour. It differs from roux, however, in that it is not cooked and is usually added at the end of a sauce's cooking rather than at the beginning. It is most often used to thicken stews at the end of cooking when the braising liquid is too thin.

To prepare beurre manié, simply work together equal parts by volume of flour and butter with the back of a dinner fork until they form a smooth paste. To thicken a liquid, simply whisk in the beurre manié a bit at a time, and wait for the liquid to come to a simmer (the thickening effect does not occur and cannot be gauged until the mixture comes to a simmer). Continue in this way until the liquid has the right thickness. Unlike roux, beurre manié should not be cooked any longer once the mixture thickens or the sauce will develop a strong floury taste. One of the peculiarities of flour is that it develops a strong floury taste after 2 minutes of cooking that begins to disappear as the cooking progresses, usually after 30 minutes.

Flouring Ingredients for a Stew

In home-style and country cooking, stew meat is often floured (in French, *singer*) before it is browned in hot fat. This is an excellent technique because the flour is thoroughly browned, eliminating any starchy flavor; moreover, the browning of the meat is made easier because the flour helps form a crust. The total amount of flour added to the stew is relatively small so that, if necessary, the cook can add more thickener (beurre manié) or reduce the stewing liquid at the end of cooking.

Some cooks add flour to stews by cooking it in the pan along with chopped aromatic vegetables after the meat has been removed. This method is effective as long as the caramelized meat juices on the bottom of the pan are not allowed to burn and too much flour is not used. Be sure to discard any burned fat and replace it with fresh butter or olive oil before stirring in the flour.

Gravy

A gravy is a jus (the natural juices from a roast) that has been thickened with flour. Depending on the amount of cooking liquid remaining in the roasting pan, gravies can be prepared using one of two similar techniques. If a small amount of jus remains in the pan, it should be boiled down on top of the stove until it caramelizes; all but a tablespoon or two (15 to 30 milliliters) of fat should be removed and discarded. The flour is then added and cooked for 2 or 3 minutes in the roasting pan on top of the stove; the mixture is then moistened with stock, water, or other liquids. If a large amount of roasting jus remains in the pan, it should be transferred to a saucepan or glass container and the fat skimmed off with a ladle. A roux is then prepared in the roasting pan with a little of the fat or some fresh butter. The jus is then returned to the roasting pan and whisked until smooth and thickened.

Because flour used as a last-minute thickener for gravies has little time to cook, an alternative is to use a previously thickened velouté- or espagnole-style flour-thickened sauce instead of plain stock to deglaze the pan; the roux is then omitted.

Other Starches

In the first edition of *Le Guide Culinaire,* published at the turn of the twentieth century, Escoffier predicted that the traditional roux-thickened sauces would be replaced with sauces thickened with purer forms of starch such as arrowroot, potato starch, and cornstarch. Using these starches would eliminate the need for the careful skimming necessary to rid flour-thickened sauces of impurities. He was correct in predicting the demise of flour-thickened sauces but incorrect in assuming that other starches would be used to fill the gap.

Perhaps the glossy look of sauces thickened with these pure forms of starch explains why Western chefs and diners have never grown accustomed to cornstarch- or arrowroot-thickened sauces. The look of these sauces is almost too perfect, like costume jewelry that glitters just a bit too garishly.

Almost any thickener has drawbacks that can be lessened by using the thickener in tandem with other methods or ingredients. A small amount of starch added to an already well-reduced stock or cooking liquid will hardly be noticed.

One method that is occasionally used in contemporary kitchens is to prepare a basic brown stock, reducing and degreasing it to concentrate flavor and eliminate impurities, and then thickening the entire stock with arrowroot. This lightly thickened brown sauce base—a kind of arrowroot espagnole—is then used as a base for made-to-order derivative sauces. When preparing a base in this way, starch must be used judiciously: There is nothing more irksome than a deeply colored, glistening sauce with no taste.

Purified starches should be worked to a thin paste with cold water before being added to hot liquids. If added directly, they will form insoluble lumps that must be strained out. Purified starches are approximately twice as efficient as flour is in thickening.

Arrowroot

Although not as easy to find as cornstarch, arrowroot is the best of the purified starches for thickening sauces because it remains stable even after prolonged exposure to heat. It is used in the same way as cornstarch.

Cornstarch

Of the purified starches, cornstarch is the most familiar. It should be used only as a last-minute thickener for sauces and cooking liquids that are being served immediately. When it is cooked for long periods it begins to break down and lose its thickening power.

Potato Starch

Although potato starch was one of the first starches to be used in French cooking, it has never been popular as a sauce thickener in the United States. It is used in the same way that cornstarch and arrowroot are. Like cornstarch, it tends to break down after prolonged exposure to heat.

EGG YOLKS

Because they thicken sauces in several ways, egg yolks are versatile liaisons. They provide the base for emulsified sauces, such as mayonnaise and hollandaise, and are used in conjunction with cream to finish the cooking liquid of poached meats and fish. They not only form emulsions of fat and liquids but also combine with air so they can be used for sabayon sauces. They are also used to give richness and texture to crème anglaise.

Egg yolks contain several emulsifiers—among them, cholesterol and lecithin—which account for their versatility. Many scientific studies have been done to explain the behavior of egg yolks, but a few tips and precautions are especially useful to the saucier. Sauces containing egg yolks should not be allowed to boil unless they contain flour, which stabilizes them. Sauce allemande and pastry cream are examples of sauces with flour that are boiled after the yolks are added. Egg yolks are also stabilized to some degree by sugar and acids such as lemon and vinegar, but not so much that the yolks can be boiled without curdling.

When combining egg yolks with hot liquids, be sure to whisk some of the hot liquid into the yolks before returning the mixture to the saucepan. If the yolks are added directly to a hot liquid, they are liable to coagulate as soon as they come in contact with the heat. Never cook sauces containing egg yolks in aluminum pots, or the sauces will turn gray.

Finishing Poaching Liquids: Egg Yolk and Cream Liaisons

Egg yolks are rarely used alone as a thickener for sauces but are usually combined with cream and added to a liquid that has already been lightly thickened with flour. Blanquette de veau, a white veal stew finished with cream and egg yolks, one of the cornerstones of French home cooking, illustrates the use of egg yolks as a final liaison for poached meats. The pieces of veal are poached in water or white veal stock along with aromatic vegetables and a bouquet garni. When the veal is tender, the liquid is strained, thickened into a classic velouté with flour—about 3½ ounces (100 grams) roux to 1 quart (1 liter) poaching liquid—and then finished with the cream and egg yolk liaison. Recipes vary, but an egg yolk liaison is usually made by combining each yolk with 3 to 4 tablespoons (45 to 60 milliliters) heavy cream and then using 3 to 4 egg yolks' worth of this mixture to thicken 1 quart (1 liter) of velouté. After the liaison has been added to the velouté, the sauce is gently stirred until it naps the back of a spoon. The stability of the egg yolks will depend on the proportion of flour in the velouté, but most recipes do not risk curdling and warn against letting the sauce boil.

A mixture of egg yolks and cream is also used to finish a traditional chicken fricassée and for fish cooked *en sauce* (see Chapter 10, "Integral Fish and Shellfish Sauces," page 287). Contemporary chefs sometimes use cream and egg yolks as the only finish for flourless sauces, creating a kind of savory crème anglaise (see Chapter 6, "White Sauces for Meat and Vegetables," page 137).

See also Chapter 13, "Hot Emulsified Egg Yolk Sauces," page 375, and Chapter 14, "Mayonnaise-Based Sauces," page 391, for additional information on egg yolks as liaisons.

CREAM

Heavy cream has long been used to finish cooking liquids and sauces, but only in recent years has reduced cream largely replaced roux as a thickener, becoming an almost universal base for white sauces. Because of its richness, chefs are beginning to use cream more judiciously, and many of the reduced cream–thickened sauces of the last two decades are being abandoned for lighter versions, in which only enough cream is used to contribute a smooth texture.

Heavy cream can be used to finish a sauce, to give it a smooth texture and a more subtle flavor, but it becomes effective as a thickener per se only when it is reduced. Heavy cream or crème fraîche can be reduced and used in two ways. They can be reduced alone and used as needed as thickeners for last-minute sauces, or the cream can be combined with the sauce base or cooking liquid and the two reduced together. The second method is best used for sauces made in advance. One of the most commonly used methods is to finish pan sauces with cream (opposite).

Whichever method is used, several precautions should be followed when reducing cream. Always reduce cream in a saucepan three or four times its volume; if cream is allowed to boil for even a few seconds, it will boil over. Although it is not necessary to stir or whisk simmering cream continually, give the cream a quick whisking at least every 2 minutes while it is reducing. Cream that is allowed to sit unheeded over even a low flame will become granular and may break.

Always use a saucepan with a large enough diameter to accommodate a medium to high flame. If the pan is too small, the flame will wrap around the outside of it and cause the cream to brown along the pan's inside, discoloring the finished sauce. This is less of a problem on an electric range.

Never cook cream covered. Water will condense on a lid or covering and drip down into the cream, causing it to become granular and eventually to break.

When using reduced cream as a thickener for wine sauces, be sure to reduce the wine thoroughly before adding the cream. Not only can the raw wine's acidity cause the cream to break but an unpleasant flavor of uncooked wine will remain in the sauce.

The degree that heavy cream should be reduced can vary, from one-third to two-thirds its original volume, depending on its butterfat content and the desired thickness of the finished sauce. In other words, if 1½ cups (375 milliliters) of heavy cream were added to ½ cup (125 milliliters) of flavor base, the mixture could be reduced to ½ cup (125 milliliters) for a very thick sauce or to 1 cup (250 milliliters) for a lighter sauce.

When used alone, reduced cream is very rich and sometimes has a slightly chalky texture in the mouth. Thus it is rarely used as the only thickener for sauces but is usually used in conjunction with butter, egg yolks, or flour. Butter is often used to finish reduced cream sauces to give them an appealing sheen and a smoother texture; it of course does nothing to attenuate the sauce's richness. Some chefs use roux as a preliminary thickener for the sauce base or add beurre manié at the end so that the sauce requires less reduction and is hence less rich (and expensive). Using flour to augment the thickening power of cream is almost the same as preparing a classic sauce suprême, except the approach is reversed.

Double Cream

European recipes often call for double cream, or *crème double*. Double cream has an especially high butterfat content and is particularly useful as a sauce thickener because it requires less reduction. It is not marketed in the United States but can be prepared using homemade crème fraîche. To prepare double cream, line a large strainer with a wet napkin or a triple layer of cheesecloth, fill it with crème fraîche, tie it at the top, and suspend it overnight in the refrigerator. The whey drains from the cream, leaving the remaining cream with a higher butterfat content. The approximate butterfat content of the finished cream can be calculated by measuring the amount of liquid (whey) that drained off the cream. For example, if 1 quart (1 liter) of cream released 2 cups (500 milliliters) of whey—that is, half its volume—then the butterfat content can be doubled, to 70 percent, given that heavy cream is 35 percent butterfat.

⬤━ PAN SAUCES FINISHED WITH CREAM

Heavy cream is a handy thickener for both brown and white pan sauces that are made to order. Most sauces that are finished with cream also include a small amount of butter to smooth the texture and give the sauce an appealing sheen.

YIELD: ½ CUP (125 MILLILITERS)

wine, fortified wine, or cider	¼ to ½ cup	60 to 125 milliliters
stock	½ cup	125 milliliters
or	or	or
meat glace (page 104)	1 tablespoon	15 milliliters
heavy cream or crème fraîche	6 tablespoons	90 milliliters
butter	1 ounce	30 grams
salt and white pepper	to taste	to taste

1. Remove the meat or fish from the sauté pan as soon as it is cooked, or finish cooking it in the oven while making the sauce. Throw away any fat in the bottom of the pan.
2. Deglaze the pan with the wine and reduce it until only 2 tablespoons (30 milliliters) remain.
3. Add the stock and reduce it until only about 6 tablespoons (90 milliliters) remain in the pan (or simply add the meat glace).
4. Add the cream and reduce it until the sauce has the desired consistency.
5. Swirl in the butter and season to taste with salt and pepper. If the sauce contains unsightly specks, it can be strained through a fine chinois.

Note: In a restaurant setting, where sauces are made to order in small quantities, it is best to prereduce certain ingredients, such as the stock, the cream, and sometimes even the deglazing liquid. This, of course, saves time but also improves the flavor of the sauce by avoiding long reduction in the sauté pan. The character of a well-made pan sauce is imparted by the caramelized juices that adhere to the bottom of the pan after sautéing meats or fish. This flavor is lost if it is cooked for more than a minute or two while the sauce is being reduced. Ideally, liquids used for making the sauce should remain in the pan only long enough to dissolve the caramelized juices.

WHITE WINE SAUCE WITH THREE LIAISONS

YIELD: APPROXIMATELY 3 CUPS (750 MILLILITERS)

white wine	1 cup	250 milliliters
shallots, minced	2	2
heavy cream or crème fraîche	1 quart	1 liter
flour	2 tablespoons	30 milliliters
butter	5 ounces	150 grams
lemon juice	to taste	to taste
salt and pepper	to taste	to taste

1. Combine the white wine and shallots in a 2-quart (2 liter) saucepan and reduce the mixture by three-fourths.
2. Add the cream to the reduced white wine–shallot base and bring the mixture to a simmer.
3. Work together the flour and 1 ounce (30 grams) of the butter to make a beurre manié; whisk it into the cream sauce. Continue reducing the cream mixture until it has the desired consistency.
4. Cut the remaining butter (4 ounces/120 grams) into chunks and whisk into the sauce.
5. Add lemon juice to taste. Adjust the seasoning. If desired, thin the sauce with cream or water. (Do not ever thin a finished sauce with raw wine.)

BUTTER

Butter has long been used in classic French cooking to finish sauces thickened with flour and for certain simple pan-deglazed sauces. In recent years it has become popular as a liaison for flourless sauces and in fact has become the thickener of choice for made-to-order brown sauces.

When butter is whisked into a hot liquid, it forms an emulsion, similar to the action of egg yolks. The milk solids and proteins contained in the butter act as emulsifiers that keep microscopic globules of fat in suspension and give butter sauces their characteristic sheen and consistency. Because the milk solids contained in the butter are what maintain the emulsion, sauces and cooking liquids cannot be thickened with clarified butter. In fact, cold butter, itself an emulsion, is preferable to warm butter that may have begun to turn oily.

Emulsions based on butter alone are less stable than reduced-cream sauces, egg yolk sauces, or sauces that contain flour. Until recently butter was almost always used in conjunction with other thickeners. Even today, many emulsified butter sauces are made to order only so they do not sit around and break.

Enriching Sauces with Butter (Monter au Beurre)

Finishing sauces with butter has become one of the most important and widely used techniques in contemporary sauce making. The technique consists of swirling chunks of cold butter into a hot flavor base, usually just before serving. Essentially the technique is the same as that used for making beurre blanc or other emulsified butter sauces except that today the technique is most often used for last-minute made-to-order sauces.

Certain precautions should always be followed when using butter as a thickener. If too large or too small a proportion of butter is used for a given amount of liquid, the sauce will break. The proportion of butter used to thicken a given amount of liquid can vary from about 20 percent butter to almost ten times as much butter as flavor base (for example, Beurre Blanc, page 410). If too small a proportion of butter is used, it tends to separate and float to the surface of the sauce unless the sauce is already an emulsion based on cream or egg yolks, or it contains flour. Large proportions of butter are used to finish intensely flavored liquids—beurre blanc is an example—but if too much butter is used the taste of the flavor base is lost, the sauce takes on a thick, waxy appearance, and it may break.

Most chefs finish made-to-order sauces by eye and can quickly judge the correct amount of butter to add based on the sauce's look and flavor. Even though many well-reduced flavor bases do not require a liaison because of the natural gelatin they contain, butter is often added to soften the sauce's flavor and also to eliminate the sticky consistency of highly reduced meat and fish sauces. When using butter to finish a flavor base, it is better to risk overreducing the flavor base before adding the butter; a butter sauce can easily be thinned, but thickening a sauce containing butter would require reduction, and boiling a butter-enriched sauce for any length of time will cause it to break and become oily.

As a general rule, a made-to-order butter sauce should contain about one-third butter. In other words, 4 ounces (125 grams) of butter should be used to finish 1 cup (250 milliliters) of liquid sauce base. These proportions will vary widely, depending on the thickness of the sauce base, the intensity of its flavor, the water content of the butter, and the desired consistency of the finished sauce.

Because of the richness of butter-enriched sauces, many chefs are starting to use butter in combination with vegetable purées. Tomato and mushroom purées work especially well as a preliminary thickener for brown sauces. Much less butter is then required to give subtlety and a brilliant shine to the sauce.

BUTTER-THICKENED MADE-TO-ORDER RED WINE SAUCE

YIELD: ENOUGH SAUCE TO ACCOMPANY 2 SERVINGS OF MEAT

steak, lamb chops, pork chops, or the like	2 servings	2 servings
vegetable oil or rendered fat (for sautéing)	as needed	as needed
red wine	½ cup	125 milliliters
brown stock	½ cup	125 milliliters
or	or	or
meat glace (page 104)	1 tablespoon	15 milliliters
butter, cut into cubes	1½ ounces	45 grams
salt and pepper	to taste	to taste

1. Sauté the meat in the oil or fat in a heavy-bottomed sauté pan. When the meat is done, transfer it to a plate and discard the burned fat in the sauté pan.
2. Pour the red wine into the sauté pan and reduce it by half.
3. Add the brown stock and reduce until only 6 tablespoons (90 milliliters) remain (or simply stir in the meat glace).
4. Whisk in the butter and bring the sauce to a simmer for about 10 seconds.
5. If desired, adjust the thickness of the sauce by thinning with stock or thickening with more butter. Adjust the seasonings.

GIBLETS AND FOIE GRAS

Americans have long been familiar with the traditional giblet gravy served with the holiday turkey. Most home cooks precook the gizzards, liver, and heart by simmering them in water. The giblet broth is then used along with the roasting juices to make the gravy; the giblets are chopped and added to the gravy at the end. Giblets cooked and chopped in this way, while contributing texture and contrast, do not actually thicken.

The French—both professionals and home cooks—have long used raw giblets, often in conjunction with blood, to finish sauces. Giblets used in this way thicken the sauce; contribute a full, often gamy, flavor; and give the sauce a characteristic muddy appearance, sometimes unappealing to the uninitiated but delicious once tasted.

The most straightforward technique is to finely chop the raw giblets (liver, gizzard, heart, and lungs) of a bird to be roasted or braised with about half their weight in butter (the butter prevents the mixture from clumping when it is combined with the sauce). Appropriate herbs, a few drops of marc or Cognac, port, or crushed juniper berries can also be added to the giblet mixture to enhance its flavor. The roasting or braising juices are then prepared in the usual way and finished with the chopped giblet-butter mixture.

In restaurant settings, the technique can also be used for made-to-order pan sauces.

SAUTÉED PIGEON BREASTS WITH GIBLET SAUCE

It is best to obtain pigeons that have been eviscerated but contain all the giblets—heart, liver, gizzard, and lungs. If these are unavailable, the pigeon livers can be used alone. This dish is particularly good with fresh boiled and buttered fava beans.

YIELD: 4 SERVINGS

pigeons	4	4
onion, chopped	3 ounces	100 grams
carrot, chopped	3 ounces	100 grams
garlic cloves, peeled	2	2
oil	as needed	as needed
brown chicken or other stock	2 cups	500 milliliters
small bouquet garni (page 51)	1	1
butter	3 ounces	90 grams
juniper berries, crushed and chopped	5	5
marc or grappa	1 tablespoon	15 milliliters
salt and pepper	to taste	to taste
wine vinegar	to taste	to taste

1. Remove the giblets from the pigeons and set them aside. Carefully remove the pigeon breasts (with skin attached) and the thighs from the carcasses. Coarsely chop the pigeon carcasses.
2. Brown the chopped carcasses in a pan with the onion, carrot, and garlic, in a very small amount of oil.
3. Deglaze the pan with ½ cup (125 milliliters) of stock; reduce it rapidly until it forms a glace and caramelizes. Add the rest of the stock and the bouquet garni and simmer for 20 minutes. Strain this base and reserve.

4. Combine the butter, the giblets, the juniper berries, and the marc. Purée them to a paste in a food processor. Cover this mixture with plastic wrap and keep refrigerated until needed.

5. When ready to serve, sauté the pigeon breasts and thighs in a small amount of oil. Transfer them to a plate, discard the fat in the pan, and deglaze the pan with the pigeon stock.

6. Finish the sauce with about 1 tablespoon (15 milliliters) of the giblet mixture per serving.

7. Adjust the seasonings and add vinegar, drop by drop, to taste.

8. Nap or surround the sautéed breasts and thighs with the sauce. If you like, slice the breasts lengthwise and arrange them over a vegetable such as fava beans. See the photograph in the color plates.

Foie Gras

Foie gras can be used in the same way as giblets: combined with one-third to one-half its weight in butter and whisked into sauces at the end. The finished sauce is smoother and paler, with a more delicate flavor. Foie gras can be used for finishing roasting and braising juices and pan juices and even as a finishing touch in Red Wine Beef Stew (page 262).

ROAST CHICKEN WITH GARLIC AND FOIE GRAS

The roasting method used here is the same as for Oven-Roasted Chicken (page 230), except that garlic cloves replace the standard aromatic vegetables and the finished roasting juices are flavored and thickened with garlic purée and foie gras.

When using foie gras as a thickener, it is better to use foie gras that has been cooked first, so that excess water is released in advance.

YIELD: 4 SERVINGS

roasting chicken, 1	4 pounds	2 kilograms
garlic heads, broken into cloves, unpeeled	2	2
foie gras mousse or bloc	2 ounces	50 grams
butter	1 ounce	30 grams
brown chicken stock (page 91)	1 cup	250 milliliters
salt and pepper	to taste	to taste

1. Surround the chicken with the garlic cloves and roast it. If the garlic cloves or roasting juices start to burn on the bottom of the pan, add a few tablespoons of water or stock every few minutes during the roasting.

2. Purée the foie gras with the butter in a food processor. If your food

processor cannot handle such a small quantity, work the butter and foie gras together in a bowl with a wooden spoon and then force it through a drum sieve.

3. Remove the chicken from the roasting pan. Deglaze the pan, which still contains the garlic cloves, with the stock. Strain the roasting juices, skimming off excess fat.

4. Force the garlic cloves through a coarse chinois or drum sieve.

5. Whisk half the foie gras mixture and half the garlic purée into the roasting juices.

6. Adjust the texture and flavor of the finished sauce by adding more garlic purée and foie gras mixture as needed. Adjust the seasonings as desired.

Note: In restaurants or in fast-paced situations, it is sometimes impractical to prepare the garlic purée along with the chicken jus as described here. The garlic purée may be prepared in advance and used as needed (see Baked Garlic Purée, page 467).

ROAST TURKEY WITH JUS, GRAVY, OR GIBLET GRAVY

A gravy is made by thickening juices from a roast with flour. Making a generous amount of well-flavored turkey jus or gravy involves a paradox; if the turkey is properly cooked or if it is stuffed, it will release little in the way of juices. When overcooked, as most turkeys are, it will provide plenty of juices for your gravy. If the turkey has released an abundance of juices—a couple of cups (500 milliliters) or more—serving the jus is a simple matter of skimming off the fat and serving the juices as they are, as a "jus." To convert them to gravy, make a roux and add the juices to that. To make giblet gravy, roast the giblets in the pan along with the turkey, chop them fine, and add them to the gravy.

If you've cooked your turkey just right, you won't see much in the bottom of the pan and what there is won't have a whole lot of flavor. To get the most flavor out of a small amount of juices, boil down the juices until they caramelize on the bottom of the pan, pour out the fat (or leave a few tablespoons in the pan if you're making a roux), and deglaze the pan with water or broth. Use only as much broth as you need to serve the guests at hand—about 3 tablespoons (45 milliliters) per person—because the more broth you add, the less flavorful the juice will be. If you're a fanatic, you can bring up the flavor of the jus by adding a little broth at a time and caramelizing after each addition. To stretch a small amount of jus without diluting its flavor, consider swirling in ½ ounce (15 grams) of butter per serving.

roast turkey, giblets roasted in the pan with the turkey	1	1
flour (for gravy)	3 tablespoons	45 milliliters
turkey or chicken broth or water (as needed if there are insufficient juices)	2 cups	500 milliliters
cold butter, sliced (optional)	3 ounces	90 grams
salt and pepper	to taste	to taste

1. Transfer the turkey to a platter and pour any juices that have accumulated in the cavity into the roasting pan.
2. Chop the giblets until quite fine but not into a purée.
3. If the pan is swimming in juices, pour all the juices into a glass pitcher and skim off and discard the fat with a ladle. If you're making gravy, put 3 tablespoons (45 milliliters) of the fat back in the roasting pan.
4. If there are less than 2 cups (500 milliliters) of juices in the roasting pan, put the pan on the stove over high heat. Move the pan around every couple of minutes so it's heated evenly. Continue in this way until a brown crust forms on the bottom of the pan and the only liquid in the pan is a layer of shiny liquid fat. Pour out the fat; if you're making gravy, leave 3 tablespoons (45 milliliters) of the fat in the pan.
5. If you're making gravy, add 3 tablespoons (45 milliliters) of flour to the fat in the pan and stir over medium heat until it smells toasty, about 3 minutes. Whether making a jus or gravy, add the broth and bring to a simmer. Scrape the bottom of the pan with a wooden spoon to dissolve the juices. Stir in the giblets. Whisk in the butter, if using. Season with salt and pepper.

VIETNAMESE-STYLE GIBLET SAUCE

This sauce is an example of how giblets can be used in sauces to provide flavor and texture. In most versions of this sauce, pork liver is used, but here we use chicken livers or duck livers. This recipe is inspired by one in Andrea Nguyen's book *Into the Vietnamese Kitchen*.

chicken livers	3	3
or	*or*	*or*
duck livers	2	2
salt and pepper	to taste	to taste
vegetable oil	2 tablespoons	30 milliliters
garlic cloves, minced	2	2
thai bird chiles, stemmed, seeded, minced	2	2

water	1 cup	250 milliliters
hoisin sauce	¼ cup	60 milliliters
fish sauce	1 tablespoon	15 milliliters
tomato paste	1 tablespoon	15 milliliters
cornstarch	2 teaspoons	10 milliliters
roasted peanuts, chopped	2 tablespoons	30 milliliters

1. Season the livers with salt and pepper and sauté them, over high heat, in vegetable oil until well browned on all sides and until they feel firm to the touch. Pat dry on paper towels and discard the burned oil.
2. Add the garlic and chiles to the still-hot pan and stir them around until they release their aroma. Pour in the water, the hoisin sauce, fish sauce, and tomato paste and bring to a simmer.
3. Chop the livers and add them to the sauce.
4. Work the cornstarch to a paste with 1 tablespoon (15 milliliters) water and add the mixture to the sauce. Work the sauce through a strainer.
5. Add the peanuts to the finished sauce.

ROAST AND BRAISED HARE

Many people think that a hare is just a giant rabbit, but in fact the meat is completely different and deep red, while rabbit meat is white. The saddle of the hare—the backbone and loin section—must be roasted rare, while the legs, ribs, head, and any giblets can be braised and used for making a sauce. Here we use vinegar and pepper and end up with a flavor much like a classic Poivrade (page 188) but with the deep gamy flavor of hare.

The legs of a hare are tough and have to be braised. In this way they release their flavor into the sauce, which can then be used on the saddle.

YIELD: 2 SERVINGS

hare, dressed	1	1
butter (for the giblet butter)	1 to 2 ounces	30 to 60 grams
carrot, diced	1	1
onion, minced	1 small	1 small
red wine	1 cup	250 milliliters
sherry vinegar	1 cup	250 milliliters
chicken or veal broth	2 cups	500 milliliters
meat glace (page 104; optional)	2 tablespoons	30 milliliters
small bouquet garni (page 51)	1	1
butter (for browning the saddle)	1 ounce	30 grams
heavy cream	½ cup	125 milliliters
truffle, peeled, peelings chopped, peeled part cut into julienne (optional)	1	1
salt and pepper	to taste	to taste

1. Preheat the oven to 400°F (200°C). Break down the hare into the saddle, two hind legs with thighs, the rib cage, two forelegs, and the head, split in two. Purée the giblets in a miniature food processor or chop them fine and work them through a strainer. Work in the same volume of butter.

2. Hack up the forelegs and rib cage with a cleaver and put these parts in the oven with the head, thighs, and the vegetables. Turn the parts occasionally and continue to roast until everything is well browned. Transfer to a small pot, deglaze the roasting pan with the wine, and pour over the wine, vinegar, broth, and meat glace, if using, and nestle in the bouquet garni. Simmer for 3 hours and strain the braising liquid. Discard the vegetables, head, hind legs, forelegs, rib cage, and the bouquet garni. Reserve the thighs. Reduce the broth slightly and skim off any scum or fat.

3. Preheat the oven again to 400°F (200°C). Put the two thighs in a clean pan just large enough to hold them and slide them into the oven. Baste the thighs with the braising liquid until it becomes syrupy and they're coated with a shiny glaze.

4. Brown the saddle in butter on top of the stove and slide it into the oven. Cook rare, to about 120°F (50°C) in the center.

5. Finish the braising liquid with the cream and truffles, if using, and the giblet butter. Season generously with salt and pepper

6. Slice the saddle lengthwise into strips—don't forget to turn it over and carve the tenderloins—and serve the strips with one of the thighs. Spoon over the sauce.

BLOOD

Blood has long been used in European cooking to finish sauces for braised or roasted game, poultry, or rabbit. A sauce finished with blood has a characteristic matte appearance; it will look vaguely like chocolate sauce. Blood not only deepens a sauce's flavor but also acts as a thickener.

Whereas European recipes often substitute pork blood for the blood of the animal being cooked, fresh pork blood is not easy to obtain in the United States, so it is necessary to use live or at least recently killed game or poultry. (In some states, serving foods cooked with blood is illegal, so be sure to check with local health authorities before serving a blood-based sauce to the public.) Many American cities have live-poultry markets that kill birds to order and are willing to save the blood. Be sure to bring a jar containing a tablespoon (15 milliliters) of Cognac and a few drops of wine vinegar as a receptacle for the blood. The Cognac and vinegar will prevent the blood from coagulating. Be sure to strain the blood to eliminate feathers, animal hairs, and other debris. Remember also to wait at least 24 hours before cooking freshly killed animals or they will be tough.

When finishing a sauce with blood, the blood must never be allowed to boil; the hot sauce should be whisked into the blood and the mixture returned to the saucepan, not the other way around.

CIVET DE LAPIN
Braised Rabbit Stew

A *civet* is a stew that has been finished at the last minute with blood. In this recipe, large rabbits are first carefully larded and then braised. The braising liquid is used to heat the rabbit pieces and is then finished to order with the reserved blood. Large rabbits (5 pounds/2.25 kilograms after cleaning) are best for braising.

YIELD: 8 SERVINGS

large rabbits	2	2
cognac	1 tablespoon	15 milliliters
wine vinegar	1 teaspoon	5 milliliters
fatback	14 ounces	400 grams
garlic cloves, peeled	2	2
parsley	½ bunch	½ bunch
lard (optional)	¼ cup	50 grams
onion, coarsely chopped	1 medium	1 medium
carrot, coarsely chopped	1 medium	1 medium
garlic cloves, unpeeled	2	2
brown veal or chicken stock	1 quart	1 liter
medium bouquet garni (page 51)	1	1

1. Have the rabbits killed and the blood saved in a jar containing the Cognac and wine vinegar.
2. Cut 12 ounces (350 grams) of the fatback into strips about 6 × ⅜ × ⅜ inches (15 cm × 5 mm × 5 mm). Finely chop the peeled garlic and parsley and toss with the strips of fatback (lardoons). Let this mixture sit for several hours or overnight.
3. Remove the thighs and the saddles from the rabbits. The saddles should be cut away from the front quarters so that three ribs remain attached to each side of the saddle. Remove the forelegs and cut the rib cages into three sections. Cut the heads in half. The saddles can be halved crosswise or boned.
4. Thoroughly lard the saddles and thighs.
5. Preheat the oven to 350°F (175°C). Cube and render the remaining 2 ounces (50 grams) of fatback in a heavy-bottomed rondeau (or use already rendered lard). Brown the pieces of rabbit, including the forelegs, heads, and rib cages. Add the chopped onion and carrot and unpeeled garlic cloves midway through the browning.

6. When the rabbit is thoroughly browned, pour off any excess fat and add enough stock to come two-thirds of the way up the sides of the rabbit. Add the bouquet garni. Bring the stock to a slow simmer on the stove.

7. Remove from the heat and cover the rondeau with aluminum foil and a tight-fitting lid. Braise the rabbit in the oven until the pieces are easily pierced with a skewer, usually in 1½ to 2 hours. Check from time to time to make sure the braising liquid is not boiling.

8. Remove the rabbit thighs and saddles and keep covered on a plate. Leave the oven on. Strain the braising liquid into a saucepan; discard the bones, vegetables, and bouquet garni. (The forelegs can be eaten by the kitchen staff but should not be served.)

9. Bring the braising liquid to a slow simmer and skim off any fat or froth that floats to the surface. Simmer and skim for at least 30 minutes.

10. Place the rabbit thighs and saddles in a clean rondeau and add the braising liquid. Put the rondeau, uncovered, in the oven. Baste the rabbit with the braising liquid for 30 to 45 minutes, until the rabbit looks shiny and glazed.

11. Strain the braising liquid and reserve. Keep the rabbit pieces covered until needed.

12. Place the appropriate number of rabbit pieces per order in a saucepan with sloping sides or in a straight-sided sauté pan with a tight-fitting lid. Add about ¼ cup (60 milliliters) of braising liquid per order, cover the pan, and gently heat for 15 minutes.

13. Just before serving, put 1 tablespoon (15 milliliters) of blood per order in a stainless-steel bowl. Whisk in the hot braising liquid. Transfer the rabbit pieces to serving plates and return the braising liquid to the saucepan or sauté pan.

14. Gently heat the sauce while whisking until it thickens. Serve over the rabbit.

Note: Although this sauce is almost unbelievably rich and deeply flavored, many chefs like to add a few drops of vinegar and a tiny bit of Cognac to bring its flavors into focus. Parsley, finely chopped at the last minute, will also enhance the sauce, giving it a note of freshness. The civet can be garnished with mushrooms, pearl onions, or glazed root vegetables.

Finishing Sauces with Giblets and Blood

Many roasts, especially poultry and game, are often finished with a mixture of chopped giblets and blood, rather than either alone. In the case of wild game, the blood, liver, lungs, and heart are combined with a little Cognac and vinegar. The mixture is then chopped together and used to finish the braising or roasting juices.

Blood and giblets are also used to finish a special type of roast, called a *salmis*. To prepare a bird *en salmis*, the bird is first partially roasted, and the meat and giblets are removed from the carcass. The partially cooked giblets are then finely chopped and seasoned, the carcass is pressed in a duck press, and the resulting jus thickened with the chopped giblets. The meat is then gently stewed in the finished sauce. In France, salmis are prepared with special ducks and sometimes pigeons that have been strangled so that their blood remains in the meat. Since these are unavailable in the United States, the process can be circumvented by saving the blood when the animal is killed and adding it to the chopped giblets just before finishing the sauce.

SAUCE ROUENNAISE I

Nineteenth-century food writers simplified sauce rouennaise by defining it as derived from a red wine sauce base — Sauce Bordelaise (page 171) finished with puréed livers. Named for the Norman city Rouen, it is unlikely that sauce rouennaise has its roots in Bordeaux.

A more elaborate and probably more authentic version (except for the foie gras, which can be omitted anyway) can be prepared with duck stock, duck blood and liver, and foie gras.

YIELD: 1½ CUPS (375 MILLILITERS)

red wine	½ cup	125 milliliters
small bouquet garni (page 51)	1	1
brown duck stock	1 cup	250 milliliters
duck liver (not foie gras)	1	1
foie gras	1 ounce	25 grams
butter	1 ounce	30 grams
heavy cream or crème fraîche	¼ cup	60 milliliters
duck blood	¼ cup	60 milliliters
cognac	few drops	few drops
wine vinegar	few drops	few drops
salt and pepper	to taste	to taste

1. Reduce the red wine by half in a saucepan with the bouquet garni.
2. Add the duck stock and reduce the mixture again by half. Skim off any froth that floats to the surface.
3. Purée the duck liver, foie gras, and butter in a food processor. Keep the mixture covered with plastic wrap until needed.
4. Add the cream to the reduced red wine–stock mixture. Bring to a simmer for 1 minute.
5. Off the heat, whisk the liver mixture into the reduced stock mixture.

6. Whisk the hot sauce into the blood in a stainless-steel bowl. Return the sauce to the saucepan.

7. Add a few drops of Cognac and vinegar to the sauce. The sauce can be thinned if necessary by adding stock or cream. Adjust the seasonings as desired.

YOGURT AND FRESH CHEESE

Both yogurt and fresh cheese (*fromage blanc*) can be used to finish and thicken sauces. In European cooking they are mainly used as dietetic substitutes for heavy cream or butter.

Because yogurt and fresh cheese contain lactic acid, which is responsible for their tangy flavor, they must be used in small quantities or in combination with cream or butter, which attenuates their acidity.

The best yogurt for sauce making is the thick Middle Eastern type called *leben*. Because it is so thick, a relatively small amount is needed to thicken a sauce. If leben yogurt is unavailable, lighter plain yogurt can be thickened by draining overnight in a colander lined with several layers of cheesecloth.

Fresh cheese is widely available in France, where it is flavored in a variety of ways and used as a snack or breakfast food in the same way yogurt is eaten in the United States. The closest equivalent available in the United States is ricotta, which is far too rough-textured for use in sauce making. Most fresh cheese is made with skim milk and contains very little fat, but there are richer varieties available made from whole milk or even cream. Although fresh cheese contains less lactic acid than yogurt (some of the acid is drained off in the whey or, if the cheese is made with rennet, it never develops in the first place), it still must be used sparingly or it will give the sauce a rough, chalky texture.

Fresh cheese should be used as soon after it is made as possible. As it sits, the curd becomes coarser and the texture rougher. Although fresh cheese is available in fancy food shops, it is rarely as fresh as it should be for sauce making and is rarely consistent. If fresh cheese is used on a regular basis, a bit of experimentation with in-house fabrication might be worthwhile (see "Fresh Cheese," page 47).

Finishing Sauces with Yogurt

Yogurt is an excellent thickener for fish sauces, which benefit from its natural acidity. It is best used with a small amount of heavy cream (not crème fraîche, which will make the sauce even more acidic), which smoothes out the sauce's texture. Yogurt can partially replace the cream or butter used to finish braised fish sauces, such as that used in Fillets of Sole Bercy and its variations (page 296). The exact amount of yogurt to use depends on the desired consistency of the finished sauce.

YOGURT-FINISHED FISH SAUCE

YIELD: 1½ CUPS (375 MILLILITERS)

heavy cream	¼ cup	60 milliliters
sauce base (see Note)	1 cup	250 milliliters
leben yogurt or drained yogurt	2 to 6 tablespoons	30 to 90 milliliters
salt and pepper	to taste	to taste

1. Add the cream to the sauce base and bring the mixture to a simmer.
2. Whisk the hot sauce mixture into the yogurt in a saucepan, preferably one with sloping sides.
3. Gently heat the sauce but do not allow it to boil.
4. Adjust the seasonings.

Note: The sauce base may be braising liquid, poaching liquid (nage), court-bouillon, fish stock, white wine sauce base, or other appropriate fish sauce bases.

Finishing Sauces with Fresh Cheese

Fresh cheese can be used to thicken sauces traditionally finished with heavy cream or crème fraîche. It is used in the same way as yogurt, but since it contains less acid, it is more appropriate than yogurt for meat sauces. The amount of fresh cheese needed to thicken a given amount of liquid will vary according to the style and freshness of the cheese. Because fresh cheese sometimes has a grainy texture, finish these sauces in a blender to smooth them.

VEAL BLANQUETTE WITH FRESH CHEESE

Traditional blanquette is prepared by poaching veal in stock or water (see "Integral Sauces Derived from Poached Meats" page 235), reducing and thickening the poaching liquid with roux, and finishing the sauce with a final cream and egg yolk liaison. Richer, more contemporary versions leave out the roux, reduce the poaching liquid more radically, and finish it with the egg yolk–cream liaison or heavy cream alone. Blanquette poaching liquid, with or without the roux, can also be finished with fresh cheese and heavy cream.

YIELD: 1½ CUPS (375 MILLILITERS)

veal poaching liquid	1 cup	250 milliliters
heavy cream or crème fraîche	2 tablespoons	30 milliliters
fresh cheese (see page 47)	¼ cup	60 grams
salt and pepper	to taste	to taste

1. Bring the poaching liquid to a simmer and add the cream.
2. Place the fresh cheese in a blender. While blending at medium speed, pour in the hot poaching liquid.
3. Adjust the seasonings as desired.

WINE LEES

French chefs occasionally refer to using the sediment at the bottom of the oak casks used to age wine as a thickener for red wine sauces. Reliable recipes are difficult to track down, but for someone living in a vineyard area, it would be a worthwhile experiment to whisk a few tablespoons of these "lees" into an unbound brown sauce or red wine sauce base. Lees from Pinot Noir would be best in keeping with the Burgundian tradition.

CORAL

Coral is actually the ovary, often containing eggs (roe), of female shellfish. A variety of shellfish corals can be used as last-minute flavorful sauce thickeners. Sea urchin roe and scallop coral are among the most popular. To use either of these, purée them in a food processor with half as much butter, and then work the mixture through a drum sieve. The mixture can then be whisked into a sauce as a final flavorful finish. Lobster coral is excellent for finishing crustacean sauces (see "Special Flavors and Finishes for Fish Sauces," page 386).

BREAD

Before the development of roux in the seventeenth century, bread was an almost universal thickener for sauces and cooking liquids. It is still used today as a thickener for a rather bland béchamel-like sauce that the English like to serve with game. It is also used in thick and strongly flavored sauces, such as the Spanish romesco, sauce rouille, and in some versions of the French garlic mayonnaise aïoli, where it attenuates the flavor, gives the sauce body, and makes the sauce less rich, so it can be eaten in larger amounts.

The majority of medieval sauces were thickened with bread that was lightly toasted in front of the fire. The technique is still a valid one for making rustic, rough-hewn sauces without resorting to flour, with its predictable, sometimes monotonous consistency. Bread, especially when it has been toasted, gives a satisfying nutty flavor to sauces. Bread-thickened sauces have a comforting homey flavor and texture. Many Mediterranean sauces that today contain puréed potatoes were originally made with breadcrumbs.

Most medieval sauce recipes contain a combination of several spices. However, some of the simpler recipes found in fourteenth-century French cookbooks closely resemble regional sauces still found in Mediterranean cooking. The main difference seems to be that medieval cooks had a liking for acidic ingredients, either vinegar or verjuice.

Some recipes from Taillevent's *Viandier*, written in the late fourteenth century, also follow. None of the recipes contains quantities, so we can only guess whether the sauces had a pomade-like texture similar to a modern romesco or were thinner and used to nap meats and fish.

SAUCE ROUILLE

Traditionally, sauce rouille is served as an accompaniment to Provençal fish soups, including bouillabaisse. It can be whisked into the soup just before serving or presented at the table in a mortar. It is also delicious served on slices of toasted French bread.

YIELD: 1 CUP (250 MILLILITERS)

sweet red pepper, grilled, peeled, and chopped	½	½
garlic cloves, coarsely chopped	3	3
cayenne pepper	½ teaspoon	2 milliliters
powdered saffron	1 small pinch	1 small pinch
slightly stale white bread, crusts removed	2 slices	2 slices
fish or chicken stock	¼ cup	60 milliliters
extra-virgin olive oil	½ cup	125 milliliters
salt	to taste	to taste

1. Work the chopped red pepper, garlic, cayenne, and saffron into a paste with a mortar and pestle.
2. Soak the bread in the stock. Combine the moistened bread and the paste with the mortar and pestle. Work the mixture until it is smooth.
3. Slowly add the extra-virgin olive oil in the same way as when preparing mayonnaise. Adjust the seasoning with salt.

Raw Sauces (Saulces non Boullues)

Saulce aulx Blans. Work together garlic and bread. Thin the mixture with verjuice.

Saulce aulx Camelins. Grind cinnamon and bread with a mortar and pestle. Thin the mixture with vinegar.

Saulce Verte. Grind together bread, parsley, and ginger with a mortar and pestle. Thin the mixture with vinegar and verjuice.

Cooked Sauces (Saulces Boullues)

Poivre Jaunet. Grind together ginger, saffron, and lightly toasted bread (*pain hallé*). Thin the mixture with vinegar, and boil.

Poivre Noir. Grind together ginger and dark toasted bread with a mortar and pestle. Thin the mixture with vinegar and verjuice, and boil.

WHITE SAUCES FOR MEAT AND VEGETABLES

Traditional white sauces are prepared with milk or white stock, thickened with white roux and finished with cream, egg yolks, or butter. In today's kitchens, sauce béchamel—essentially milk thickened with roux— is often replaced with reduced cream. Sauce velouté is identical to sauce béchamel except that the milk is replaced with white stock. When sauce velouté is enriched with cream, it becomes a sauce suprême; when finished with egg yolks, it becomes a sauce allemande. Today, velouté sauces are often replaced with butter-enriched sauces or reduced-cream sauces, which contain no roux.

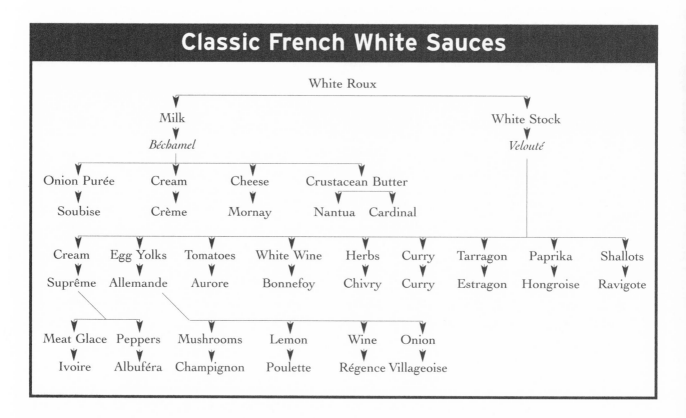

Classic French White Sauces

White Roux
→ Milk → *Béchamel* → White Stock → *Velouté*

From Béchamel:
Onion Purée → Soubise
Cream → Crème
Cheese → Mornay
Crustacean Butter → Nantua / Cardinal

Cream → Suprême
Egg Yolks → Allemande
Tomatoes → Aurore
White Wine → Bonnefoy
Herbs → Chivry
Curry → Curry
Tarragon → Estragon
Paprika → Hongroise
Shallots → Ravigote

Meat Glace → Ivoire
Peppers → Albuféra
Mushrooms → Champignon
Lemon → Poulette
Wine → Régence
Onion → Villageoise

SAUCE BÉCHAMEL

Until twenty years ago, sauce béchamel was a mainstay in both professional and home kitchens. In the last two decades, however, the reaction agains flour-thickened sauces has been so vehement that this one-time cornerstone of classic French cooking has been almost completely abandoned. In many instances, it has been replaced with sauces based on reduced cream. While these modern cream-based versions have their merits, the straightforward appearance and flavor of a béchamel-covered gratin will often satisfy a deeper need than a refined and intricate cream sauce.

One of the best uses for sauce béchamel is in a gratin. It is prepared by blanching or sweating the vegetables, spreading them in a flat, usually oval baking dish, pouring over a layer of béchamel, sprinkling them with grated cheese or breadcrumbs, and baking until a flavorful, lightly browned crust forms on the surface. Some chefs have replaced the béchamel in vegetable gratins with heavy cream or crème fraîche. For gratins of starchy foods such as pasta or potatoes, cream is a welcome replacement. Many vegetable gratins, however, become too rich when the béchamel is replaced with cream. Béchamel will also allow the brown crust, so characteristic of gratins, to form on its surface, whereas cream will overreduce and get oily.

Like recipes for practically any sauce, béchamel recipes have changed dramatically over the centuries. Early recipes have little relation to modern versions and were based on velouté sauces to which heavy cream was added (now called sauce suprême).

The simplest and most modern version of sauce béchamel prescribes thickening milk with white roux and cooking the mixture long enough to eliminate the flour taste. Some recipes suggest onion (either first sweated in butter and then sprinkled with flour to become an integral part of the roux or left whole or in large pieces, poked with a clove, and simmered with the milk), a piece of bay leaf, and a tiny pinch of nutmeg. Nineteenth-century recipes often begin by sweating mirepoix, ham, and veal as components of the roux before moistening with milk or a mixture of milk and stock.

Whether to prepare the simplest form of béchamel (given below) or to give it complexity and additional flavor with ham, veal, mirepoix, onion, or other aromatics depends largely on common sense. Béchamel used for a gratin of leeks hardly needs to be flavored with onions, but a few trimmings from a cured ham cooked with the roux will work beautifully. Much of the appeal of sauce béchamel comes, paradoxically, from its *lack* of flavor, and, like a rest in music or a simple expanse on a canvas, it provides a backdrop for the flavor and texture of the other ingredients.

SAUCE BÉCHAMEL

The amount of roux per given amount of milk depends on the use of the sauce. Thick versions, used as the base thickener in traditional soufflé recipes, often call for as much as 8 ounces (250 grams) of roux per quart (liter) of milk, whereas béchamel-based soups use approximately 2 ounces (60 grams) per quart (liter) of milk. The following recipe produces a medium-thick sauce, appropriate for vegetable gratins.

YIELD: 1 QUART (1 LITER)

milk	1 quart	1 liter
butter	2 ounces	60 grams
flour	¼ cup	60 milliliters
seasonings (for example, salt, pepper, nutmeg)	to taste	to taste

1. Bring the milk to a simmer in a 2-quart (2 liter) saucepan. Whisk it from time to time to prevent a skin from forming on its surface (see Note).
2. In a second 2-quart (2 liter) saucepan, gently melt the butter and add the flour. Stir the butter and flour over medium heat for about 2 minutes, until the flour has a pleasant, toasty smell. Remove from the heat for about 30 seconds to cool slightly.

3. Whisk the simmering milk into the roux. Return the sauce to the stove and bring it back to a simmer while whisking.

4. Once the sauce has returned to a slow simmer, turn down the heat and move the saucepan so that only one side is over the flame. (This will cause a skin to form on only one side of the sauce's surface, making it easy to skim.) Cook the sauce gently for 30 minutes to 1 hour, skimming off the skin that forms on its surface. It is a good idea also to occasionally rub around the bottom and corners of the saucepan with a wooden spoon to prevent the sauce from scalding.

5. When the starchy taste has been cooked out of the sauce, it can be seasoned and strained, depending on its final use. Béchamel should be stirred while it is cooling to prevent a skin from forming on its surface. Putting the pan over a tray of ice will, of course, speed cooling.

Note: Some chefs do not first bring the milk to a simmer and instead pour cold milk, all at once, over the roux. This method saves time—and a pot—but be sure to whisk the sauce vigorously to prevent lumps and skin from forming.

Derivatives of Béchamel Sauce

Three traditional derivatives of sauce béchamel are sauce Mornay, which contains cheese; sauce soubise, which contains blanched and puréed onions; and sauce crème, traditional cream sauce, made by finishing sauce béchamel with heavy cream. All of these sauces are excellent for gratins. Sauce Nantua (crayfish sauce) is also a derivative of béchamel, but today it is usually prepared using a base of cream (page 334).

Sauce Mornay

Sauce Mornay is usually used as the base for cheese soufflés or for gratins. When it is used for gratins, additional cheese and sometimes breadcrumbs and butter are added to its surface to encourage the formation of a crust. Sauce Mornay is made by adding grated cheese to sauce béchamel. Be sure to choose a full-flavored, well-aged cheese for this sauce. If the cheese is too young, the sauce will not only lack flavor but will be stringy.

Classic recipes use half grated Gruyère and half grated Parmesan (at least three-year-old Parmigiano-Reggiano), but the sauce can be made with other well-aged, honest cheese. English farmhouse Cheddar and Vermont Cheddar (not the commercial kind that has been dyed orange) both work well. Blue cheeses can also be incorporated into Mornay sauces, but be sure to taste and select them carefully to avoid some of the poor-quality versions that have a coarse, sour-milk smell and flavor. Select genuine Roquefort, Stilton, Gorgonzola, Fourme d'Ambert, or Bleu d'Auvergne.

To prepare sauce Mornay, add approximately 4 ounces (115 to 125 grams) of cheese per quart (liter) of béchamel. Stir the sauce just long enough for the cheese to melt; overcooking the cheese can cause it to turn stringy. Some recipes call for finishing Mornay with egg yolks (about 2 per quart/liter of sauce). This is useful if the sauce is being used as a base for cheese soufflé, but otherwise the yolks contribute little to the sauce except unnecessary richness.

Sauce Soubise I

Sauce soubise is prepared by combining onion purée with sauce béchamel. Modern versions sometimes replace the béchamel with cream, but when the sauce is being used for gratinéed dishes—the most famous is veal Orloff, a veal chop covered with a layer of duxelles, napped with soubise, then Mornay, and gratinéed under the broiler—the béchamel is essential; a cream-based soubise would break.

Traditional recipes for sauce soubise call for blanching sliced onions before sweating them in butter and combining them with the béchamel, but for a fuller-bodied sauce, this step can be eliminated. The key is not to allow the onions to brown. Sweat 1 pound (500 grams) of sliced white onions (blanched or not) until they are soft, and combine them with 2 cups (500 milliliters) of sauce béchamel. Cover the sauce and cook it slowly, either in the oven or on top of the stove, for approximately 30 minutes. Purée in a blender and strain through a fine chinois. (For a flourless version, see Stewed Onion Purée, page 472).

Sauce Crème (Cream Sauce)

Traditional cream sauce is prepared by finishing 1 quart (1 liter) of béchamel with 7 fluid ounces (200 milliliters) of heavy cream or crème fraîche, reducing the mixture down to three-quarters its original volume, and then adding 5 fluid ounces (150 milliliters) more of heavy cream to enrich it and provide the correct consistency. The sauce is then seasoned and finished with the juice of half a lemon. In most modern kitchens, unless the surface of the sauce needs to be glazed under the broiler, cream sauce is usually replaced with lightly reduced cream.

SAUCE VELOUTÉ

In classical cooking, most white sauces are based on sauce velouté, which is white stock that has been thickened with white roux. This basic sauce is then flavored and used as the foundation for a myriad of derivative sauces. The two most important derivatives of basic velouté are sauce allemande (literally, "German sauce") and sauce suprême. Sauce allemande is prepared by finishing sauce velouté with egg yolks and mushroom cooking liquid. Sauce suprême is prepared by finishing a velouté with mushroom cooking liquid, heavy cream, and butter. Sauce allemande and sauce suprême are themselves usually flavored to make additional derivative sauces.

SAUCE VELOUTÉ

YIELD: 1 QUART (1 LITER)

white stock (veal, chicken, or other)	5 cups	1.2 liters
butter	2 ounces	60 grams
flour	¼ cup	60 milliliters

1. Bring the stock to a simmer in a 2-quart (2 liter) saucepan. Whisk it from time to time to prevent a skin from forming on its surface.
2. In a second 2-quart (2 liter) saucepan, gently melt the butter and add the flour. Stir the butter and flour over medium heat for about 2 minutes, until the flour has a pleasant, toasty smell. Remove from the heat for about 30 seconds to cool slightly.
3. Whisk the simmering stock into the roux. Return the sauce to the stove and bring it back to a simmer while whisking.
4. Once the sauce has returned to a slow simmer, turn down the heat and move the saucepan so that only one side is over the flame. (This will cause a skin to form on only one side of the sauce's surface, making it easier to skim.) Cook the sauce gently for 1 hour while skimming off the skin that forms on its surface. It is also a good idea to occasionally rub around the bottom and corners of the saucepan with a wooden spoon to prevent the sauce from scalding.
5. Strain the velouté through a fine chinois and stir it until it cools, to prevent a skin from forming on its surface.

Primary Derivatives of Sauce Velouté

Sauce Suprême

Combine 1 quart (1 liter) of sauce velouté with 1 quart (1 liter) of white veal, chicken, or other white stock; 1 cup (250 milliliters) of mushroom cooking liquid; and 1 cup (250 milliliters) of heavy cream or crème fraîche. Reduce the mixture by two-thirds until only 1 quart (1 liter) is left. Be sure to skim off any scum or fat that forms on the surface during reduction. Finish the sauce by swirling in ½ cup (125 milliliters) of heavy cream and 3 ounces (90 grams) of butter. Yield: 1 quart (1 liter).

Sauce Allemande

Whisk together 5 egg yolks, 2 cups (500 milliliters) of white veal, chicken, or other white stock, 1 cup (250 milliliters) of mushroom cooking liquid; and 1 tablespoon (15 milliliters) of lemon juice. Whisk this mixture into 1 quart (1 liter) of hot sauce velouté and return the sauce to a saucepan. Reduce the sauce by about one-third, until approximately 1 quart (1 liter) remains. Whisk 4 ounces (125 grams) of cold butter into the sauce. Yield: 1 quart (1 liter).

Notice that this sauce is reduced *after* the addition of egg yolks. Sauces containing egg yolks can be boiled, provided they contain a fairly large amount of flour, which stabilizes them (pastry cream is another example of this principle). When translating traditional sauce recipes containing flour into flourless versions, the egg yolks should be added only at the end; the sauce should not be allowed to boil.

Modern Techniques for Velouté Sauces

In today's kitchens, traditional veloutés, sauce allemande, sauce suprême, and their derivatives have been largely replaced by reduced stocks finished with heavy cream, butter, and occasionally egg yolks. The flavors used in these modern-style sauces often rely on the same ingredients as the classic French derivative sauces, but because no flour is used, the sauces are left comparatively thin or are reduced to the appropriate consistency.

BUTTER-ENRICHED WHITE SAUCES

These sauces are prepared by finishing reduced white stock, sometimes combined with aromatic ingredients such as wine or herbs, with butter. They have a more intense flavor and an even more velvety texture than traditional flour-thickened veloutés. They are, however, extremely rich and require extremely concentrated stock.

The stock used should be approximately six times as concentrated as a simple stock. The concentrated stock can be prepared by reducing simple stock down to one-sixth its original volume, by making fresh stock with an already prepared stock (six times), or by using a combination of both methods—for example, reducing double stock by two-thirds. The amount of butter needed to give the sauce the desired consistency depends on the water content of the butter; the lower the water content, the less butter is needed to thicken the concentrated stock. French butter, because of its low water content, works especially well in butter-enriched sauces.

When preparing butter-enriched sauces, the stock should be reduced until it has the consistency desired for the finished sauce. Once the butter is added, the sauce will be somewhat thick and can be thinned by adding additional stock, which is preferable to thickening the stock once the butter has been added.

Because this sauce is somewhat unstable, it should not be kept hot for more than an hour or two before serving. For this reason, the following recipe produces only 2 cups (500 milliliters).

| concentrated white stock | 2 cups | 500 milliliters |
| butter | 7 ounces | 200 grams |

1. Melt the stock in a 1-quart (1 liter) saucepan. Reduce it if necessary, until it has a lightly syrupy consistency.
2. Cut the butter into chunks and whisk it into the hot stock.
3. Bring the sauce quickly to a boil; allow it to boil for only about 5 seconds — any longer may cause it to break. This short boil gives the sauce an agreeable sheen. If a more opaque, matte look is wanted, do not allow the sauce to boil at all. The sauce can be kept warm for an hour or two in the saucepan in a pot of hot water. Check the temperature of the sauce and whisk it lightly every 20 minutes to prevent it from breaking.

WHITE SAUCES BASED ON REDUCED CREAM

In the last two decades, sauces thickened with reduced cream have become almost universal and in most cases have completely replaced roux-thickened white sauces. Because they are given body by reduction instead of with roux, they are usually more intensely flavored than their roux-thickened predecessors. The main disadvantages to using reduced-cream-thickened sauces are the large amount of stock required and the time needed to reduce them to give them body and full flavor. Despite their light appearance, these sauces have an extremely high fat content — more than roux-thickened versions.

One error beginning sauciers sometimes make is trying to make cream-finished sauces too thick. If a reduced cream sauce is boiled down until it is as thick as a traditional flour-thickened sauce, the resulting sauce is heavy and cloyingly rich, and much of the intense flavor of the meat stock will be lost. One method of avoiding this is to serve meats in deep plates or shallow bowls and to think of the sauce as more of a creamy broth than as a sauce that must adhere to the surface of the meat.

When reduced cream is combined with concentrated stock, the resulting sauce is roughly analogous to a traditional sauce suprême. The only differences are that roux-thickened stock (sauce velouté) is replaced with concentrated, unbound stock, and a higher proportion of cream is used.

Different brands of heavy cream contain varying amounts of butterfat and will hence thicken to a different consistency at different stages of reduction. Generally, heavy cream reduced by one-third will have a light consistency, about the same as a beurre blanc. Cream reduced beyond this point thickens quickly. When reduced to between 55 and 60 percent of its original volume, it has the texture of a classic white sauce such as sauce béchamel. When reduced by half (50 percent), it becomes thick and gloppy. Reduced beyond this point, it is liable to break.

Concentrated (reduced) stock is often used for making flourless sauces, not only because of its intense flavor but because it contains natural gelatin, which, along with the reduced cream, contributes to the texture of the finished sauce. The amount of reduction needed to concentrate the flavor of a stock depends on the stock's quality, but reduction by three-fourths (four parts stock reduced to one part) is usually best.

YIELD: 1 QUART (1 LITER)

heavy cream	1 quart	1 liter
concentrated white stock (see Note)	2½ cups	625 milliliters
salt and pepper	to taste	to taste

1. Reduce the cream in a 4-quart (4 liter) saucepan over medium to high heat until it starts to thicken. (The saucepan should be especially large to prevent the cream from boiling over.) If the cream threatens to boil over, whisk it or reduce the heat. In any case, the cream should be whisked for a few seconds every minute or so to prevent it from breaking or becoming grainy.
2. Heat the reduced stock in a 2-quart (2 liter) saucepan.
3. Whisk the reduced cream into the reduced stock. The sauce will have a light texture. The consistency can be adjusted by reducing if the sauce is too thin or by adding cream or stock if it is too thick.
4. Adjust the seasonings and strain the sauce through a fine chinois.

Note: To concentrate the white stock, reduce 2½ quarts (2.5 liters) of stock to 2½ cups (625 milliliters).

EGG YOLK-THICKENED WHITE SAUCES

A traditional sauce allemande is prepared by finishing a sauce velouté with egg yolks. Egg yolks can also be used to thicken reduced stocks for lighter-textured modern sauces. One method of using egg yolks as thickeners is discussed in Chapter 13, "Hot Emulsified Egg Yolk Sauces," page 375. The other method is given below. Remember that egg yolk–thickened sauces must never be allowed to boil unless they contain a relatively large amount of flour.

YIELD: 1 QUART (1 LITER)

full-flavored white stock	3 cups	750 milliliters
egg yolks	10	10
butter	4 ounces	125 grams
salt and white pepper	to taste	to taste

1. Bring the stock to a simmer in a 2-quart (2 liter) saucepan. Be sure to skim off any scum or froth that floats to the surface.

2. Whisk the egg yolks for about a minute in a 2-quart (2 liter) mixing bowl, until they turn from orange to pale yellow. (This preliminary whisking helps stabilize them so they do not curdle when the stock is added.)

3. Pour half of the hot stock over the egg yolks, whisking quickly until thoroughly combined. Remove the saucepan containing the remaining half of the hot stock from the stove. Return the egg yolk–stock mixture to the saucepan containing the rest of the stock.

4. Heat the sauce over a medium flame and stir gently with a wooden spatula, being especially careful to reach into the corners of the saucepan to prevent the egg yolks from overheating and congealing. Continue stirring until the sauce begins to thicken. Egg yolk–thickened sauces do not thicken as dramatically as starch-thickened sauces do. The best way to check the sauce's consistency is to lift the wooden spatula out of the sauce, hold it sideways, and draw a horizontal line with the tip of a finger. If the sauce clinging to the spatula runs together, immediately obscuring the line, the sauce is not ready. If the line remains, the sauce should be removed immediately from the heat.

5. Whisk in the butter. Continue stirring the sauce after removing it from the heat to keep it from setting and also to prevent a skin from forming on its surface.

6. Adjust the seasonings and strain the sauce through a fine chinois.

Other Derivatives of Sauce Velouté

Nowadays, the traditional velouté-based sauces are prepared using an array of alternative methods. The following recipes describe the traditional methods using sauce velouté as a base, as well as using reduced stock enriched with butter. Although sauces containing cream are more akin to sauce suprême and its derivatives, versions finished with reduced cream are also described.

Sauce Aurore (Tomato-Flavored Velouté)

This sauce works well with veal, chicken, or eggs. Veloutés based on veal, chicken, fish, or other white stocks can all be used. Traditional sauce Aurore is always strained so that it is pale pink (*aurore* means "dawn") and perfectly smooth. Some chefs like to finish the sauce with small cubes of chopped tomato for contrast of both color and texture, although purists would argue that it is then no longer a sauce Aurore. One or two teaspoons (5 to 10 milliliters) of wine vinegar will enhance all versions of this sauce.

Classic Method. Combine 3 cups (750 milliliters) of sauce velouté with 1 cup (250 milliliters) of tomato purée. Adjust the sauce's consistency by reducing it (to thicken) or by adding a small amount of stock (to thin). Complete the sauce by whisking in 4 ounces (125 grams) of butter. Adjust the seasonings. Yield: 1 quart (1 liter).

Butter-Enriched Method. Combine 1 cup (250 milliliters) of concentrated (four to six times) stock with ¼ cup (60 milliliters) of tomato coulis that has been cooked down until it is completely dry. Reduce the mixture slightly if necessary to give it a lightly syrupy consistency. Whisk in 4 ounces (125 grams) of butter and adjust the seasonings. Yield: 1.5 cups (350 milliliters).

Reduced-Cream Method. Combine 1 cup (250 milliliters) of reduced-cream white sauce with ¼ cup (60 milliliters) of cooked tomato coulis. Adjust the consistency by further reducing the sauce (to thicken) or adding stock or heavy cream (to thin). Finish the sauce with 1½ ounces (45 grams) of butter to give it a smooth texture.

Sauce Bonnefoy (White Wine Bordelaise)

This sauce is similar to an early-nineteenth-century version of a sauce bordelaise made with garlic, tarragon, and Sauternes.

Classic Method. Combine 2 cups (500 milliliters) of white wine with ¼ cup (60 milliliters) of finely chopped shallots, 1 teaspoon (5 milliliters) of cracked pepper, 1 sprig of fresh thyme, and 1 small bay leaf. Reduce the mixture until only ½ cup (125 milliliters) remains. Add 1 cup (250 milliliters) of full-flavored sauce velouté to the reduction and simmer slowly for 15 minutes, skimming off any scum that floats to the surface. Strain the sauce through a fine chinois and stir in 1 tablespoon (15 milliliters) of chopped tarragon and 1 to 2 teaspoons (5 to 10 milliliters) of lemon juice to bring out the sauce's flavor. Yield: 1.5 cups (375 milliliters).

Butter-Enriched Method. Prepare and reduce the white wine infusion as described for the classic method. Add 2 cups (500 milliliters) of concentrated (three to four times) white stock and reduce the mixture until it has the consistency desired for the finished sauce. Whisk in approximately 4 ounces (125 grams) of butter. Taste the sauce before adding all the butter to avoid adding too much and obscuring the flavor of the sauce. Finish with 1 tablespoon (15 milliliters) of blanched tarragon leaves, chopped or left whole. Yield: 2 cups (500 milliliters).

Reduced-Cream Method. Prepare and reduce the white wine infusion as described for the classic method. Add 1 cup (250 milliliters) of reduced-cream white sauce to the infusion. Reduce the sauce slightly if necessary. Finish the sauce with 1 ounce (30 grams) of butter and 1 tablespoon (15 milliliters) of blanched tarragon leaves, chopped or left whole. Adjust the seasonings. Yield: 2 cups (500 milliliters).

Sauce Chivry (Herb Sauce)

Traditionally, sauce Chivry is made by first preparing an infusion of herbs and white wine and then straining it through a kitchen towel before combining it with the other ingredients. An easier method is to combine all the ingredients and strain the sauce at the end. Strictly speaking, sauce Chivry should always be prepared with the herbs listed, but the methods presented here can be used for sauces based on other herbs.

Classic Method. Bring ½ cup (125 milliliters) of white wine to a simmer and simmer long enough to cook off the alcohol. While the wine is still hot, add 1 teaspoon (5 milliliters) each of chervil, parsley, tarragon, chives, and salad burnet (if available). Cover the pan and let the mixture infuse for approximately 5 minutes. Add this infusion to 3 cups (750 milliliters) of sauce velouté and finish the sauce by whisking in 4 ounces (125 grams) of Chivry Butter (page 416). Strain the sauce through a fine chinois. Yield: 1 quart (1 liter).

Butter-Enriched Method. When sauce Chivry is prepared following the classic method given above, a flavored velouté is finished with Chivry butter (herb butter). The only difference when preparing a strictly butter-enriched version is that the flour-thickened velouté is replaced with concentrated white stock and a higher proportion of butter is used. Prepare the infusion as described for the classic method. To ½ cup (125 milliliters) of infusion, add 1 cup (250 milliliters) of concentrated (four times) white stock. Reduce the mixture until 1 cup (250 milliliters) remains, and whisk in 4 ounces (125 grams) of Chivry Butter (page 416). Yield: 1½ cups (375 milliliters).

Reduced-Cream Method. Prepare the herb infusion as described for the classic method and combine it with 1 cup (250 milliliters) of reduced-cream white sauce. Reduce the sauce if it seems too thin. Finish it with 1 ounce (30 grams) of butter. If it seems too thick, it can be thinned at the end with a little stock or cream. Yield: 1½ cups (375 milliliters).

Curry Sauce

There are many methods for preparing curry sauce, some of which use completely different sauce bases, such as hollandaise, mayonnaise, and sabayon. The traditional white sauce version of curry sauce is prepared using a mixture of sauce velouté and coconut milk (see page 34).

Commercial curry powders vary enormously in hotness and flavor. It is also possible to prepare your own curry, balancing the spices according to taste (see Basic Curry Powder, page 552). When preparing butter-enriched or reduced-cream versions of curry sauce, freshly prepared coconut milk can be reduced and added, or coconut can be infused directly into the sauce. Almost any curry sauce is enhanced by adding 1 tablespoon (15 milliliters) of chopped fresh cilantro per 1 cup (250 milliliters) of sauce at the end.

Classic Method. Finely chop 1 medium onion and sweat it in butter, being careful not to let it color. Sprinkle the onion with 2 tablespoons (30 milliliters) of curry powder and sweat the mixture for a minute or two more, to bring out the flavor of the curry. Add 2 cups (500 milliliters) of canned or homemade coconut milk (see page 34) and 2 cups (500 milliliters) of sauce velouté to the onion-curry mixture, and let the sauce simmer for 15 minutes. Skim off any scum that floats to the top of the sauce. Finish the sauce with ½ cup (125 milliliters) of heavy cream and the juice of half a lemon. Yield: 1 quart (1 liter).

Butter-Enriched Method. Prepare the mixture of onion and curry as described for the classic method. Add 2 cups (500 milliliters) of concentrated white stock and 4 ounces (125 grams) of chopped coconut to the mixture. Simmer the sauce for 10 to 15 minutes. Strain out the coconut. Reduce the mixture slightly if necessary to give it the desired final consistency. Finish the sauce with 5 ounces (150 grams) of butter and 2 teaspoons (10 milliliters) of lemon juice. Yield: 2 cups (500 milliliters).

Reduced-Cream Method. Prepare the mixture of onion and curry as described for the classic method. Add 2 cups (500 milliliters) of reduced-cream white sauce and 4 ounces (125 grams) of chopped coconut. Gently simmer the sauce for 15 minutes to infuse the coconut before straining it through a fine chinois. Yield: 2 cups (500 milliliters).

Sauce Estragon (Tarragon Sauce)

Older recipes for this sauce suggest blanching tarragon leaves, working them to a paste with a mortar and pestle, and then combining them with sauce velouté. An easier method is to infuse a small bunch of tarragon, stems and all, in the velouté or concentrated stock, and then strain the sauce before finishing it with tarragon butter. The methods described below can also be used to prepare sauces flavored with other herbs.

Classic Method. Blanch 2 tablespoons (30 milliliters) of fresh tarragon leaves in simmering water for 5 seconds. Quickly rinse them and dry them on a towel. Crush the leaves in a mortar and gradually add ¼ cup (60 milliliters) of sauce velouté to form a paste. Add the paste to 1 quart (1 liter) of hot velouté, strain the sauce, and finish with 1 tablespoon (15 milliliters) of freshly chopped tarragon. Yield: 1 quart (1 liter).

Butter-Enriched Method. Combine 2 cups (500 milliliters) of concentrated white stock with 1 bunch of tarragon and bring the mixture to a simmer. Reduce if necessary until it is lightly syrupy. Turn off the heat and cover the pan. Let the tarragon infuse in the stock for 10 minutes. Strain the sauce and finish it with 4 ounces (125 grams) of Tarragon Butter (page 419) and 5 ounces (150 grams) of plain butter. Adjust the seasonings. Yield: 2 cups (500 milliliters).

Reduced-Cream Method. Chop 1 small bunch of tarragon and infuse it in 2 cups (500 milliliters) of reduced-cream white sauce for 10 minutes. Strain the sauce through a fine chinois and finish it with 4 ounces (125 grams) of Tarragon Butter (page 419). It may be necessary to thin the finished sauce slightly by adding white stock. Yield: 2½ cups (625 milliliters).

Sauce Hongroise (Paprika Sauce)

Most commercially available paprika has a stale, dusty taste and contributes little flavor to a sauce. Consequently, it makes better culinary sense to prepare a Sauce Albuféra (page 154), which is finished with Sweet Red Pepper Butter (page 418). The following recipes can be used if good-quality paprika is available. They are also excellent models for other spice-flavored sauces.

Classic Method. Finely chop 1 large onion and sweat it in butter without letting it brown. When the onion is completely cooked, sprinkle over 2 tablespoons (30 milliliters) of paprika. Add 1 quart (1 liter) of sauce velouté to the mixture and gently simmer the sauce for 10 to 15 minutes. Thin the sauce to the desired consistency with white stock, milk, heavy cream, or a mixture. Strain the sauce through a fine chinois and finish it by whisking in 4 ounces (125 grams) of butter. Yield: 1 quart (1 liter).

Butter-Enriched Method. Sweat 1 medium onion in butter and add 2 tablespoons (30 milliliters) of paprika. Add 2 cups (500 milliliters) of reduced white stock to the paprika-onion mixture and reduce slightly until the stock is lightly syrupy. Add ½ cup (125 milliliters) of heavy cream, reduce again to the same syrupy consistency, and finish the sauce with 10 ounces (300 grams) of butter or Paprika Butter (page 418). Yield: 2 cups (500 milliliters).

Reduced-Cream Method. Sweat 1 medium onion in butter and add 2 tablespoons (30 milliliters) of paprika. Add 2 cups (500 milliliters) of reduced-cream white sauce and simmer the mixture for 10 minutes. Strain the sauce and finish with 2 ounces (60 grams) of butter or Paprika Butter (page 418). Yield: 2 cups (500 milliliters).

Sauce Ravigote (Shallot and Herb Sauce)

Older recipes for this sauce (those by Escoffier and others) flavor it by finishing it with shallot butter. A simpler method is to infuse chopped shallots in the white wine and vinegar reduction before adding the sauce velouté or concentrated white stock. A butter-enriched method for making this sauce is not given below because it would be virtually identical to a beurre blanc.

Classic Method. Combine ½ cup (125 milliliters) of white wine vinegar with ½ cup (125 milliliters) of white wine and reduce the mixture by half. Add 3 cups (750 milliliters) of sauce velouté to the reduction and bring the mixture to a simmer. Remove the sauce from the heat and finish it with 3 ounces (75 grams) of shallot butter. This sauce will probably need to be thinned with stock, heavy cream, or milk. Yield: 1 quart (1 liter).

Reduced-Cream Method. Infuse ¼ cup (60 grams) of finely chopped shallots in a mixture of ½ cup (125 milliliters) of white wine and ½ cup (125 milliliters) of white wine vinegar. Reduce the mixture by three-quarters. Add 2 cups (500 milliliters) of reduced-cream white sauce to the infusion, reduce if necessary, and finish the sauce with 3 ounces (90 grams) of butter or shallot butter. Adjust the seasonings. Straining is optional. Yield: 2½ cups (500 milliliters).

Derivatives of Sauce Allemande

These sauces are based on a traditional sauce allemande (sauce velouté thickened at the end with egg yolks). They can be adapted to flourless sauce-making techniques by thickening the flavor base with egg yolks, reduced cream, or butter. When egg yolks are the only thickener used, 8 to 10 yolks per quart (liter) of liquid should be used, depending on the desired thickness of the sauce.

When thickening liquids with egg yolks, remember that they must not boil. Bring the liquid to be thickened to a simmer on top of the stove and whisk the egg yolks together in a bowl. Pour half of the simmering liquid over the yolks while whisking. Return the mixture to the pot containing the rest of the simmering liquid. Turn the flame down quite low and stir the sauce with a wooden spoon or spatula. Be sure to reach into the corners of the saucepan, where the sauce is most likely to congeal. Keep checking the thickness of the sauce by lifting the wooden spatula out of the sauce, holding it so the flat side is facing sideways, and making a horizontal line with the tip of a finger. When the line remains—that is, when the sauce does not run over and obscure it—the sauce is thick enough and should be removed from the heat.

Classic sauce allemande is finished with about 10 percent its volume of butter. When the allemande is being used as a base for derivative sauces, the butter should be added to the derivative sauce at the end. Butter is also recommended for flourless versions, which otherwise taste too eggy.

Sauce Poulette (Mushroom and Lemon Sauce)

Sauce poulette is best prepared with either fresh or dried wild mushrooms, but be forewarned that wild mushrooms, especially dried ones, will often discolor the sauce. It goes particularly well with hot vegetables and seafood.

Classic Method. Reduce 1½ cups (375 milliliters) of mushroom cooking liquid by two-thirds and add it to 3 cups (750 milliliters) of sauce allemande (without the butter). Reduce the sauce if necessary until it has the appropriate thickness. Finish with 3 ounces (90 grams) of butter, 2 teaspoons (10 milliliters) of lemon juice, and 2 tablespoons (30 milliliters) of chopped parsley. Yield: 1 quart (1 liter).

Modern Method. Combine 1½ cups (375 milliliters) of mushroom cooking liquid with 1½ cups (375 milliliters) of concentrated white stock. Reduce this mixture slightly if necessary to concentrate the flavor of the mushrooms. Combine the mushroom-stock mixture with 10 to 12 egg yolks, as described for egg yolk–thickened white sauce (page 145), and gently cook until the sauce thickens. Finish the sauce with 3 ounces (90 grams) of butter, 2 teaspoons (10 milliliters) of lemon juice, and 2 tablespoons (30 milliliters) of finely chopped parsley. Yield: 1 quart (1 liter).

Tarragon Sauce

Although there is no classic version of this sauce, an allemande-based tarragon sauce could be prepared by swirling tarragon butter and lemon juice into a sauce allemande. This tarragon sauce should not be confused with a classic sauce estragon that is based on sauce velouté.

Modern Method. Thicken 2 cups (500 milliliters) of full-flavored white chicken stock with 6 egg yolks, as described for Egg Yolk–Thickened White Sauces (page 145), and gently cook until the sauce thickens. Finish the sauce with 3 ounces (75 grams) of Tarragon Butter (page 419) and 2 teaspoons (10 milliliters) of lemon juice. Blanched tarragon leaves can be added as a garniture and for additional flavor. Yield: 3 cups (750 milliliters).

Sauce Régence Blanche (Rhine Wine, Mushroom, and Truffle Sauce)

Classic Method. Combine 1 cup (250 milliliters) of Rhine wine, 1 cup (250 milliliters) of mushroom cooking liquid, and 2 ounces (60 grams) of chopped black truffles or truffle peelings. Reduce the mixture by half and add 3 cups (750 milliliters) of sauce allemande (without the butter). Strain the sauce through cheesecloth or a fine chinois. Finish the sauce with 2 tablespoons (30 milliliters) of truffle essence (or juice) and 4 ounces (125 grams) of Truffle Butter (page 419). Yield: 1 quart (1 liter).

Modern Method. Combine the Rhine wine, mushroom cooking liquid, and the chopped black truffles as described for the classic method, and reduce the mixture by half. Add 2 cups (500 milliliters) of concentrated white stock to the mixture and reduce slightly if necessary to concentrate its flavors. Thicken the sauce with 8 egg yolks. Finish with 2 ounces (60 grams) of Truffle Butter (page 419). Yield: 3 cups (750 milliliters).

Sauce Villageoise (Mushroom and Onion Sauce)

This sauce can be prepared by adding mushroom cooking liquid to white stock as suggested in the classic method below, or sliced mushrooms can be infused directly in the stock before it is finished with velouté, butter, or reduced cream. Either traditional béchamel-based soubise or the Stewed Onion Purée (page 472) can be used to finish any of the versions.

Because the sauce is traditionally finished with egg yolks, it is included as a derivative of sauce allemande.

Classic Method. Add ½ cup (125 milliliters) of white veal stock and ½ cup (125 milliliters) of mushroom cooking liquid to 3 cups (750 milliliters) of sauce velouté. Reduce the sauce down to 3 cups (750 milliliters) and strain it through a fine chinois. Add 1 cup (250 milliliters) of Sauce Soubise I (page 141), and finish the sauce with 4 egg yolks and 4 ounces (125 grams) of butter. The sauce may need to be thinned with stock or heavy cream. Yield: 1 quart (1 liter).

Butter-Enriched Method. Combine 1 cup (250 milliliters) of mushroom cooking liquid with 2 cups (500 milliliters) of concentrated white stock, and reduce the mixture until it has the desired consistency of the finished sauce. Add 1 cup (250 milliliters) of Sauce Soubise I (page 141), and finish the sauce with 8 ounces (250 grams) of butter. Yield: 3 cups (750 milliliters).

Reduced-Cream Method. Combine 1 cup (250 milliliters) of mushroom cooking liquid with 2 cups (500 milliliters) of reduced-cream white sauce. Reduce the mixture until it has the desired final consistency; add 1 cup (250 milliliters) of Sauce Soubise I (page 141). Thin the sauce with stock or reduce it slightly if necessary to adjust its consistency, and finish with 1½ ounces (45 grams) of butter. Yield: 3 cups (750 milliliters).

Derivatives of Sauce Suprême

Sauce suprême is a sauce velouté that has been enriched with heavy cream or crème fraîche. In classical sauce making, it can be finished with additional ingredients to produce derivative sauces. The modern equivalents of classic suprême-based sauces are based on reduced white stock and reduced cream.

Sauce Albuféra (Red Pepper Sauce)

Classic Method. To 3 cups (750 milliliters) of sauce suprême, add ½ cup (125 milliliters) of meat glace. When the glace has completely dissolved, finish the sauce by whisking in 2 ounces (50 grams) of Sweet Red Pepper Butter (page 418). Yield: 1 quart (1 liter).

Butter-Enriched Method. Peel 1 large sweet red pepper by burning off the skin on a grill, in the flame of a gas stove, or under a broiler. Remove the seeds from the pepper, coarsely chop the pulp, and put it into a saucepan with 2 cups (500 milliliters) of concentrated white stock. Slowly simmer the chopped red pepper in the stock for 10 minutes. Add ½ cup (125 milliliters) of heavy cream to the mixture and reduce the mixture if necessary to the desired consistency. Finish the sauce with 8 ounces (250 grams) of butter. Season the sauce and strain it through a fine chinois. A small pinch of cayenne pepper or a few drops of hot pepper sauce will help wake up the flavor of this sauce. Some chefs prefer making this sauce with Sweet Red Pepper Purée (page 418), which gives it more color and a more assertive taste. Yield: 3 cups (750 milliliters).

Reduced-Cream Method. Prepare the infusion of white stock and sweet red pepper as described for the butter-enriched method. Add 2 cups (500 milliliters) of reduced cream to the infusion, reduce if necessary, and finish the sauce with 2 ounces (60 grams) of butter or Sweet Red Pepper Butter (page 418). Yield: 3 cups (750 milliliters).

Sauce Ivoire (Ivory Sauce)

This sauce is given an ivory color by adding 3 tablespoons (45 milliliters) of meat glace to 1 quart (1 liter) of sauce suprême.

IMPROVISING WHITE SAUCES

In real-life situations, a saucier is likely to use a combination of methods to prepare a particular sauce rather than adhering rigidly to one technique at a time. The methods presented in this chapter represent extremes within a range of possibilities. Each technique has its advantages and disadvantages and must often be adapted to a particular situation. Butter-enriched white sauces are delicious but require an enormous amount of stock because the stock must be reduced four to six times for it to have the natural consistency that these sauces require. This time-consuming reduction is often impractical in all but the most expensive restaurants. Reduced-cream sauces are also delicious, but they are extremely rich and, like butter-enriched sauces, require large amounts of reduced stock. Classic versions are less expensive to prepare but will often taste flat to diners accustomed to flourless sauces.

Some chefs prepare butter-enriched and reduced-cream sauces with stock that has been only partially reduced (for example, by half instead of by four or even more) and then thickened with arrowroot before it is finished with cream and butter. Excellent sauces can also be prepared by making traditional roux-thickened stocks with half as much roux as the classic recipes stipulate and then reducing them to the necessary consistency before using them in sauces finished with cream, butter, or egg yolks. The resulting sauce will have a smoother texture and a lighter consistency than its traditional counterpart but will not be as rich as a completely flourless sauce.

Light-textured flourless sauces can also be left thinner than the classic versions. Although these sauces will appear lighter, they will have a more intense flavor than the classic versions, will be less expensive to prepare because less reduction is required, and will be less rich.

To improvise a new sauce or to improve one that is already familiar, gather together the necessary ingredients—reduced stocks, meat glace, cream, butter, the necessary aromatics (such as chopped herbs, wild mushrooms), any wines that might work, vinegars, spirits, and the like. Once you decide on the basic flavor of the sauce, the first step is to decide how to extract and accent this flavor. Three methods can be used: (1) the ingredients can be infused in an appropriate liquid such as wine or stock, (2) they can be worked with butter to prepare a compound butter that is whisked into the sauce at the end, or (3) they can be puréed and used both as thickeners and flavorings for the sauce. The next step is to decide on the final consistency of the sauce and determine how the sauce will be thickened—with reduced cream, starch, egg yolks, butter, or a combination.

Once you have an idea of what the consistency of the finished sauce should be, prepare your flavor base, reduce it if it needs to be more intense, and start working with the liaisons. Cream is the easiest to experiment with because it can be reduced; remember, when working with butter or egg yolks, that once they are added, you will not be able to reduce the sauce. When the basic sauce is complete—that is, has attained the desired consistency—start tasting and thinking about how to enhance its flavor. This is the most creative part of the sauce-making process. You can experiment with adding herbs, spices, chiles, compound butters, or spirits to impart different nuances. The last step is to bring the flavors into focus with vinegar, lemon juice, salt, and pepper.

7
BROWN SAUCES

The methods used to make brown sauces have been evolving for centuries, and chefs still battle over ingredients for stock and which thickeners, if any, should be used. Brown sauce methods were standardized by Escoffier in 1902 and remained almost unchanged until the 1960s, when chefs began to eliminate flour-thickened demi-glace and to thicken their sauces with butter. In the last ten years, more and more chefs have been experimenting with using no thickener at all, serving meats with flavorful bouillon instead. Until the seventeenth century, most brown sauces for meat were derived from the natural cooking juices of roasted and braised meats.

In the homes of the wealthy, these natural integral sauces were often supplemented by adding a large slice of veal or ham to the bottom of the pot if the meat was braised (braised dishes were much more popular than they are now). The resulting enriched braising liquid had a deep, full flavor and a natural, lightly syrupy consistency. Roast meats were sometimes wrapped with fat and a layer of matignon containing ham and aromatic vegetables before being put on the spit.

In large kitchens, this method of preparing an individual integral sauce for each dish was inconvenient and difficult to organize. In the seventeenth century, a system was developed for streamlining the preparation of many sauces. Instead of adding additional meat to each preparation, the extra meat was poached, and the resulting broth was then used to moisten a particular preparation. In wealthy homes, these broths were enriched several times by using a previously made broth to moisten more meat. In France, each stage of the preparation had a name of its own. A simple brown stock was called an *estouffade*. When an estouffade was in turn used to moisten more meat, the resulting liquid was called a *fond de braisage* ("braising stock"). When the fond de braisage was used to moisten the last batch of meat, the result was a *coulis*. Over the course of the eighteenth century and into the nineteenth, the system of preparing stocks, glaces, demi-glaces, and essences was perfected and systematized. The most basic brown sauces, or mother sauces, were prepared and used as the basis for a wide variety of derivative sauces.

After the method of making stocks was perfected, it became possible to make meat sauces independent of a particular preparation. When the chef or saucier had at hand the necessary stocks and glaces, he could quickly manipulate their character and produce an almost infinite number of sauce preparations. These sauces are traditionally called petite sauces, derivative sauces, or compound sauces. Once the basic sauces were standardized at the beginning of the nineteenth century (credit is usually given to Carême), chefs went about inventing new compound sauces. A "new" sauce would often consist of a slight variation of an already known sauce—maybe onions would replace shallots, or vice versa—and be given a new, dramatic name.

By the end of the nineteenth century, although chefs did not always agree on the exact method of their preparation, these derivative sauces had become familiar classics. The recipes for these classic sauces were standardized in Escoffier's *Le Guide Culinaire* in 1902.

DEMI-GLACE AND COULIS

Demi-glace (half-glace) is brown stock that has been thickened with roux and reduced until it has the consistency of a light syrup. By the beginning of the twentieth century, demi-glace had become the standard sauce base (mother sauce) in professional kitchens and replaced many of the elaborate preparations that had been used up to that time.

A *coulis* (a natural demi-glace without roux or any other thickener) is prepared by poaching meat in stock and then using the resulting broth to remoisten more meat. The process is repeated until a natural, lightly syrupy liquid is obtained. This method requires about four batches of meat. The resulting coulis was the basis for brown sauces into the seventeenth and eighteenth centuries, when it was replaced with the more economical roux-thickened demi-glace. Although a stock with the consistency of coulis can be prepared by reducing brown stock to one-fourth or one-fifth its original volume, concentrated stock prepared by reduction is not as flavorful as a coulis prepared by successive moistenings, because much of the aromatic flavors are lost during long cooking.

Needless to say, coulis is extremely expensive to prepare, especially if the traditional meats (veal and beef) are used in the beginning broth and again for the second and third moistenings. The need for an economical sauce base led chefs to use thickeners, usually roux (see page 113) to give the basic mother sauces the necessary light syrupy consistency without using as much meat. Escoffier's 1902 demi-glace, although a far cry from the extravagant preparations of the eighteenth and nineteenth centuries, requires more expense and labor than most modern chefs and restaurants can afford.

ESCOFFIER'S DEMI-GLACE AND SAUCE ESPAGNOLE

Escoffier's demi-glace is prepared by reducing the sauce espagnole, given in the following recipe, to a lightly syrupy consistency. Escoffier described demi-glace as sauce espagnole "taken to the extreme limit of perfection." Sauce espagnole is simply reduced brown stock containing roux and fresh tomatoes or tomato purée. The tomatoes give a deeper color to the sauce. Because tomatoes are not always desirable in a brown sauce, they are listed below as optional.

Notice that 12 quarts (12 liters) of brown stock are used to prepare 5 quarts (5 liters) of demi-glace (a reduction of about two-thirds). This recipe uses approximately 4½ ounces (150 grams) of roux per quart (liter) of finished sauce, which sounds like a very large amount of roux. But much of the roux is eliminated by long slow cooking and continuous skimming.

YIELD: 5 QUARTS (5 LITERS)

butter	11 ounces	330 grams
flour	1 cup plus 6 tablespoons	340 milliliters
brown stock (see Note)	12 quarts	12 liters
lean, unsalted pork breast or blanched bacon	5 ounces	150 grams
carrots	8 ounces	250 grams
onions	5 ounces	150 grams
thyme	1 small bunch	1 small bunch
bay leaves	2	2
white wine	6 tablespoons	90 milliliters
tomato purée (optional)	1 quart	1 liter
or	or	or
fresh tomatoes (optional)	2 pounds	1 kilogram

1. Prepare a brown roux with the butter and flour (see "Roux," page 113).
2. Bring 8 quarts (8 liters) of the brown stock to a simmer. Whisk the brown roux into the stock. Make sure the roux is slightly warm before adding it to the stock; otherwise it will poach before it has a chance to dissolve into the stock and may form lumps.
3. Place the pot of hot stock containing the roux on the stove so that the flame is to one side of the bottom of the pot. (This causes the stock to simmer on one side only. The scum that floats to the top of the pot will therefore be forced to one side and will be easier to skim.) If a flat-top range is used, wedge a spoon or wooden spatula under one side of the pot so there is more heat on one side. Skim the stock regularly. Be sure to keep the stock from boiling.
4. Chop the pork breast, carrots, and onions into ¼-inch (5 mm) cubes. Gently sweat the pork cubes in a sauté pan until they start to render fat. Add the vegetable cubes, the thyme, and the bay leaves to the pork. Gently cook until the vegetables soften. Pour off the excess fat, deglaze the pan with the white wine, and reduce the wine by half.
5. Add the vegetable-pork mixture to the simmering stock. Continue to skim the stock to eliminate any fat released by the mixture.
6. After about 1 hour of simmering the stock with the aromatic vegetables and pork, strain the mixture into a new pot and add 2 quarts (2 liters) more of brown stock. Simmer for 2 hours more while skimming. (At this point, the stock may be strained and allowed to cool, so the process can be finished the next day, if desired.)
7. Add the final 2 quarts (2 liters) of brown stock and, if desired, the tomato purée or the chopped fresh tomatoes to the sauce. Simmer the sauce for 1 hour more, being careful to skim.
8. Strain the sauce through a coarse chinois lined with two thicknesses of cheesecloth.

Note: The brown stock for this sauce should be made with equal parts of veal and beef shanks. (Use the recipe for Brown Beef Stock on page 94, replacing half of the beef shanks with veal shanks.)

Alternative Liaisons for Demi-Glace

Many chefs do not like the texture and floury taste that roux gives to sauces. Because flour is an impure form of starch (it contains a fairly high percentage of protein), it must be simmered in the stock and carefully skimmed for several hours to eliminate insoluble components that could cloud the finished demi-glace. It also has a distinct smell and taste that only long cooking can eliminate. Because roux contains butter, it is also necessary to cook it long enough in the stock to release the butter, so it can be skimmed from the surface of the stock.

For these reasons, other types of starch, such as arrowroot, cornstarch, or potato starch, can also be used to bind stocks and give them a demi-glace consistency. Because these are purer forms of starch, they can be added nearer the end of cooking. If too much of any of these starches is used, the sauce may develop an unnatural, glossy sheen and an unpleasant, slippery texture. Cornstarch also has the disadvantage of breaking down after long cooking.

Modern Demi-Glace and Meat Glace (Glace de Viande)

To make modern demi-glace, simply take good gelatinous stock and reduce it to about a fifth of its original volume; to make meat glace (*glace de viande*), reduce the stock to a tenth or even a twentieth its original volume.

MODERN METHODS FOR MAKING BROWN SAUCES

The long-evolved method of making sauces with demi-glace is easy to abuse. The time and money required to prepare classic demi-glace (to say nothing of coulis) can be daunting, and many chefs have not resisted the temptation to use the stockpot indiscriminately for kitchen refuse, including poorly defatted meat trimmings, stale carcasses, and vegetable ends. Indeed, many chefs have gradually replaced the meat in their stocks with bones.

Although bones can contribute body and natural gelatin to a stock and the resulting sauce, they do not supply the necessary savor to a demi-glace thickened with roux. Remember that roux was originally added to stocks as an economy measure; roux-thickened meat stocks were seen as a compromise and replacement for the natural coulis of the seventeenth and eighteenth centuries. To make stock with bones and then thicken it with roux is thus a double economy with far from satisfying results. This method has caused chefs to react,

What Is "Natural" Demi-Glace?

Escoffier's demi-glace, which required a frightful amount of meat, was thickened with flour (roux) so that it didn't have to be reduced so much to get it to have the right consistency. Essentially the roux was used as a way to cut costs and end up with more demi-glace with less reduction. The demi-glace recipes given here are all for "natural" demi-glace, which is to say demi-glace that has thickened naturally by concentrating the gelatin in the stock by extreme reduction. While these demi-glace recipes will make sauces as good as any anywhere, they're frightfully expensive. To obtain more demi-glace from one of these recipes, the stock can be thickened with roux. Keep in mind that 1 tablespoon (15 milliliters) of flour thickens 2 cups (500 milliliters) of liquid, so if you wanted a demi-glace recipe to provide you with 2 quarts/2 liters (instead of 1 quart/1 liter of unthickened demi-glace), whisk in a roux made with ¼ cup (60 milliliters) of flour and 2 ounces (60 grams) of butter at the beginning of reduction.

often unjustifiably, against demi-glace and sauce espagnole, usually because they have never tasted a correctly made version of either one.

It is perhaps in part because of these abuses that modern chefs have reacted against the use of starches as liaisons in sauces. Butter- and cream-thickened sauces, or sauces with no thickener at all, have become de rigueur. Today most chefs prefer brown sauces prepared with meat glace (*glace de viande*) or very light, unbound sauces. Both of these methods are economy measures; most meat glace is prepared with bones, but sauces made with carefully made meat glace are far superior to those made with carelessly or cheaply made demi-glace. Although unbound sauces can be made from intensely flavored coulis, they are usually made from a light broth or jus.

When *Sauces* was first published in 1991, there were no substitutes for demi-glace or meat glace made "in house" or at home. Since then, More Than Gourmet, an Ohio company (see "Sources," page 592) has begun production of demi-glace, meat glace, and an assortment of "jus" and reduced stocks. These products are especially useful for home cooks and small restaurants where the long cooking needed for traditional sauce bases is impractical.

Preparing Brown Sauces with Meat Glace

Classic brown sauces are made by first preparing a basic flavor element. Usually some type of wine is used to extract the flavor of a particular ingredient, such as onions, shallots, mirepoix, herbs, or mushrooms. Once this flavor element is ready, demi-glace is then added to give the sauce body, a meaty flavor, and a lightly syrupy consistency. The sauce is then usually reduced to thicken it slightly. After straining, butter, compound butters, essences, mustard, herbs, truffles, ham, or other ingredients are then added to give the sauce its final character.

Sauces prepared with meat glace instead of demi-glace are approached somewhat differently. The preliminary flavor base is prepared in the same way, but instead of adding demi-glace to the base, a proportionately smaller amount of meat glace is added. Because meat glace is highly reduced (by ten), the resulting mixture is extremely thick and syrupy. The chef will often thin the mixture by adding a small amount of stock or appropriately flavored liquid (wines or liquors can be used in small amounts, depending on the type of sauce). The sauce is then finished by swirling in butter or by adding heavy cream. If cream is used, the sauce is then reduced to the desired consistency. Sauces finished with either cream or butter require a higher proportion of flavor base, because both cream and butter greatly soften the taste of the sauce.

Sauces prepared with meat glace are thickened with a relatively large proportion of butter or cream. Using butter or cream as a thickener gives the resulting sauce a velvety texture and a delicate flavor. The disadvantage to these sauces is that they are extremely rich.

For many years, the basic stocks used to prepare brown sauces have been based on veal and beef. This is partly because these meats were abundant (at least for the wealthy) when brown sauces were first being invented. These meats, especially veal, are relatively neutral in flavor and thus will not overwhelm a sauce's flavor. Unfortunately, their cost has become prohibitive, necessitating a variety of compromises: the use of roux- and starch-thickened mother sauces, stocks prepared from bones alone, and the exclusive use of meat glace for preparing brown sauces.

Other meats, especially pork and turkey, can be used to prepare brown stocks that are much less expensive than versions made with beef and veal. A brown stock made with pork shoulder or shanks and turkey wings will cost one-fourth as much as a stock made with beef and veal. Because these stocks are cooked for long periods and carefully skimmed, the character of the meats is softened and blended into the whole.

Although natural coulis made from meat will never be inexpensive, coulis made with pork and turkey is a viable possibility.

ALTERNATIVE COULIS

This coulis has a fairly neutral taste because it is concentrated by reduction, which makes it an excellent backdrop for brown sauces. A more savory version can be prepared by repeating the recipe four times, omitting the vegetables for the last two, and moistening the meat with the stock from the previous batch. This may sound extravagant, but the cost is actually the same because the yield is four times greater.

YIELD: 5 QUARTS (5 LITERS)

onions, 6 medium	3 pounds	1.4 kilograms
carrots, 6 medium	1½ pounds	750 grams
celery, 3 stalks	9 ounces	250 grams
turkey wings	20 pounds	9 kilograms
pork shoulder	20 pounds	9 kilograms
large bouquet garni (page 51)	1	1

1. Preheat the oven to 400°F (200°C). Rinse the onions, carrots, and celery well. It is not necessary to peel them. Trim any large chunks of fat off the pork shoulder and cut the pork into 2-inch (5 cm) cubes.
2. Roast the turkey wings with half the vegetables in the oven until they are well browned, 45 minutes to 1 hour.
3. Roast the pork cubes with the remaining vegetables in a separate roasting pan until they are well browned, 45 minutes to 1 hour.

4. Combine the vegetables, bouquet garni, turkey wings, and pork cubes in a 40-quart (36 liter) stockpot. Deglaze the roasting pans with water and pour this liquid into the stockpot. Add enough cold water to the stockpot to cover the meat.

5. Slowly bring the stock to a simmer. Skim off any froth and fat that floats to the top. Allow the coulis stock to simmer slowly for 5 to 6 hours.

6. Strain the coulis stock through a coarse chinois into a 20-quart (18 liter) stockpot.

7. Reduce the stock by half while skimming carefully. Strain it through a fine chinois into a 12-quart (12 liter) pot. Reduce again by half.

Brown Sauces Without Liaisons

Most liaisons add little if any flavor to a finished brown sauce, affecting only its consistency and appearance. Until very recently, diners have always expected sauces to have a certain consistency, an ability to cling to meats or other foods. The flavor of a thick, deeply colored sauce is often a disappointment if too much thickener has been used or if the sauce has been overly reduced. Chefs often compromise the flavor of a sauce in an attempt to make the sauce thicker.

Chefs are, however, beginning to serve light, flavorful broths and natural jus instead of artificially thickened sauces. Sophisticated diners are no longer impressed by thick, clinging sauces and usually prefer a light, natural broth to the same broth bound with too much butter or flour.

When serving light, unthickened sauces, the choice of china and silverware is important. Be sure to use fairly deep plates or even wide, flat bowls so the sauce is contained and does not run up on the rim of the dish. Spoons—either very flat sauce spoons or European-style oval soup spoons—should be included at each setting.

Classic brown sauces can be prepared in a modern light style simply by using flavorful stock where demi-glace or meat glace would normally be used.

Some of the sauces described in this chapter are rarely served today but are included as sources of ideas and as examples of sauce-making technique. The recipes include classic methods using coulis or demi-glace and modern methods that use meat glace or leave the sauce unbound. The recipes using meat glace are all finished with butter. Some chefs prefer to finish these brown sauces with cream. When using cream, replace the butter with three times its amount of heavy cream, and reduce the sauce as desired to the appropriate consistency.

NAMING BROWN SAUCES

Most derivative brown sauces were "invented" in the nineteenth century and compiled by Escoffier in his famous *Le Guide Culinaire* at the beginning of the twentieth century. Whereas today chefs tend to give sauces descriptive names (such as red wine duck sauce or shallot butter sauce), nineteenth-century chefs named their sauces more whimsically.

When preparing a variation on a classic sauce, the chef may decide to retain the original classic name or give the sauce an entirely new name. In the United States, where the dining public is less familiar with traditional sauce names, chefs usually dispense with classic French names entirely and name the sauce descriptively for what it contains.

It is sometimes difficult to determine when a traditional French sauce, modified by an individual chef's whim and style, steps out of the classic definition and becomes another sauce entirely. To the conservative, the slightest alteration in the sauce's flavor or texture means that the sauce can no longer be called by its classic name, whereas others will allow for more flexibility.

In much the same way as the classical musician shapes the rhythm and dynamics of a piece of music within the bounds of the written score, making each rendition an individual creation, the chef can create and improvise flavors within the context of a classic recipe. The chef can also choose to step out of the boundaries of a classic recipe and use it as a reference point, in the same way the jazz musician continually improvises but returns to his theme.

In America, where the name of a classic French sauce is less likely to conjure up associations and expectations, the acceptable boundaries of the sauce's definition are less important than in France. But the way a sauce is named will still influence how it will be experienced by the diner. When the chef has worked out a variation, he may decide to alert the diner to what might otherwise go unnoticed, or he may prefer understatement and surprise. Understatement can, of course, be taken too far. To make a chicken chasseur with boletus mushrooms sautéed in goose fat and deglazed with Sauternes will produce a dish so different from the classic that naming it for the classic may confuse the diner.

When a chef decides how to name a sauce, he or she should consider the intended dining audience. There is usually no point in using an obscure classic sauce name for a dining public unlikely to have ever heard it—to whom it is meaningless. Perhaps it is in reaction to snobbishness and pseudosophistication that both French and American chefs have taken to naming their dishes in a clear, descriptive way. This is certainly a healthy trend, but there may be times when a little mystery and even obscurity will intrigue the diner and set his or her appetite on edge. Much of the decision on how to name a classic sauce variation will depend on the attitude of the dining public. An audience eager to learn and experiment may well be intrigued by a little uncertainty, whereas a group of diners that views eating as a backdrop for another event or as a simple biological need will want no surprises.

INTEGRAL VERSUS STOCK-BASED BROWN SAUCES

The brown sauces presented in this chapter are based on stocks and are prepared independently of a specific dish such as roasted, braised, or sautéed meats. In modern kitchens, integral sauces made from the juices released during the cooking of meats have largely replaced sauces made from stock alone.

In a professional kitchen, the saucier will combine methods, using both stock-based brown sauce and integral sauce techniques. For example, the chef may sauté a steak and deglaze the pan with a premade sauce bordelaise base, or the drippings from a roast chicken may be incorporated into a tarragon sauce (see Chapter 9, "Integral Meat Sauces," page 221).

WHITE WINE–BASED DERIVATIVE BROWN SAUCES

Sauce Chasseur (Mushroom Sauce for Chicken)

Because sauce chasseur is most often used for chicken sautés, it is best prepared in the pan used to brown the chicken, so the caramelized juices from the chicken contribute their flavor to the sauce.

Classic Method. Sauté 3 ounces (75 grams) of sliced mushrooms in butter until they start to brown lightly. Sprinkle the mushrooms with 1 heaping tablespoon (20 milliliters) of finely chopped shallots about 2 minutes before they are done. When the mushrooms are lightly browned and no liquid remains in the bottom of the sauté pan, pour off any cooked butter and deglaze the pan with 6 tablespoons (90 milliliters) of white wine and 2 tablespoons (30 milliliters) of Cognac. Quickly reduce the wine-Cognac mixture by half. Add 6 tablespoons (90 milliliters) of tomato sauce (optional) and 6 tablespoons (90 milliliters) of coulis or demi-glace. (If the tomato sauce is omitted, use ¾ cup/185 milliliters of demi-glace.) Bring the sauce to a simmer and skim off any fat or scum that floats to the top. Whisk in 1½ ounces (45 grams) of butter. Finish the sauce with 1 teaspoon (5 milliliters) of chopped chervil and 1 teaspoon (5 milliliters) of chopped tarragon. Yield: 1 cup (250 milliliters).

Meat-Glace Method. Prepare the flavor base used in the classic method (that is, sauté the mushrooms, add the shallots, deglaze with Cognac and white wine, and reduce by half). Dissolve 3 tablespoons (45 milliliters) of meat glace in the flavor base. Thin the mixture to a light syrup by adding from

½ to ¾ cup (125 to 185 milliliters) of concentrated brown chicken stock. The base should have approximately the same consistency as the finished sauce. If you add too much stock and the base seems too thin, reduce it for a minute or two to bring it to the right consistency. It is preferable that the base be slightly thick rather than too thin; the sauce can be easily thinned at the end but cannot be reduced after the butter has been added.

Once the mixture has the right consistency, whisk in 1½ ounces (45 grams) of cold butter and add 1 tablespoon (15 milliliters) of chopped chervil and 2 teaspoons (10 milliliters) of chopped tarragon. Bring the sauce to a simmer for about 20 seconds to give it sheen. Adjust the seasonings and correct the consistency by adding a small amount of chicken stock if necessary. Yield: 1 cup (250 milliliters).

Unthickened Method. Sauce chasseur can be presented as a light, almost fat-free broth by replacing the demi-glace called for in the classic version with a well-reduced flavorful stock or jus and omitting the butter. Yield: 1 cup (250 milliliters).

Alternatives and Variations. Because sauce chasseur is used almost exclusively for chicken, it should expand the flavors of the chicken and bring them into focus. For this reason, it is better to use reduced brown chicken stock rather than demi-glace or coulis based on other meats. If practical, the mushrooms should be sautéed in the pan used to brown the chicken (be careful not to burn the caramelized juices).

A large number of sauce chasseur variations are possible. Practically any variety of edible wild mushroom can replace the cultivated mushrooms, and olive oil or goose fat can replace the butter used for sautéing the sliced mushrooms. As the mushrooms are sautéed, they can be sprinkled with fresh chopped thyme, chopped hyssop leaves, marjoram, lavender, or winter savory (eliminating the tarragon added at the end). A white wine with a distinct character, such as Sauternes, or one with a lightly madeirized character, can be used to give the sauce individuality and distinction. The Cognac can be replaced with marc, grappa, Armagnac, or a local brandy (if making the sauce in California, a good pot-stilled brandy will give the sauce a bit of regional character). The herbs used at the end can be replaced (the tarragon *should* be replaced if any of the strong Provençal herbs mentioned above are used—the flavors clash).

If a special brandy or wine is used in the sauce, herbs should be chosen and used carefully, so the nuances imparted by the wine or brandy are not lost. It would be best to finish the sauce with fines herbes without tarragon, or with any of the three individual herbs (chives, parsley, chervil).

Derivative Brown Sauces

WHITE WINE

Mushrooms Shallots Cognac Chervil Tarragon	Shallots Vinegar Cayenne	Tarragon	Fines Herbes	Mirepoix Ham Mushroom Essence	Mirepoix Rhine Wine Truffles	Mirepoix Meat Trimmings	Shallots Onions Tomato Purée Ham Garlic Horseradish	Shallots Mushroom Essence Tomato Purée Duxelles	Onions Mustard	Mushroom Julienne Ham Truffles
↓	↓	↓	→	→	→	→	→	→	→	→
Chasseur	Diable	Estragon	Fines Herbes	Godart	Régence	Salmis	Hussarde	Duxelles	Robert → Gherkins → Charcutière	Zingara B

RED WINE

Shallots Peppercorns Thyme Bay Leaf Lemon Juice (Marrow)	Shallots Parsely Thyme Bay Leaf Mushrooms (Beurre Manié)
↓	→
Bordelaise → Duck Livers → Rouennaise	Meurette

FORTIFIED WINES

Madeira	Port → Porto
Madère → Truffles → Financière	

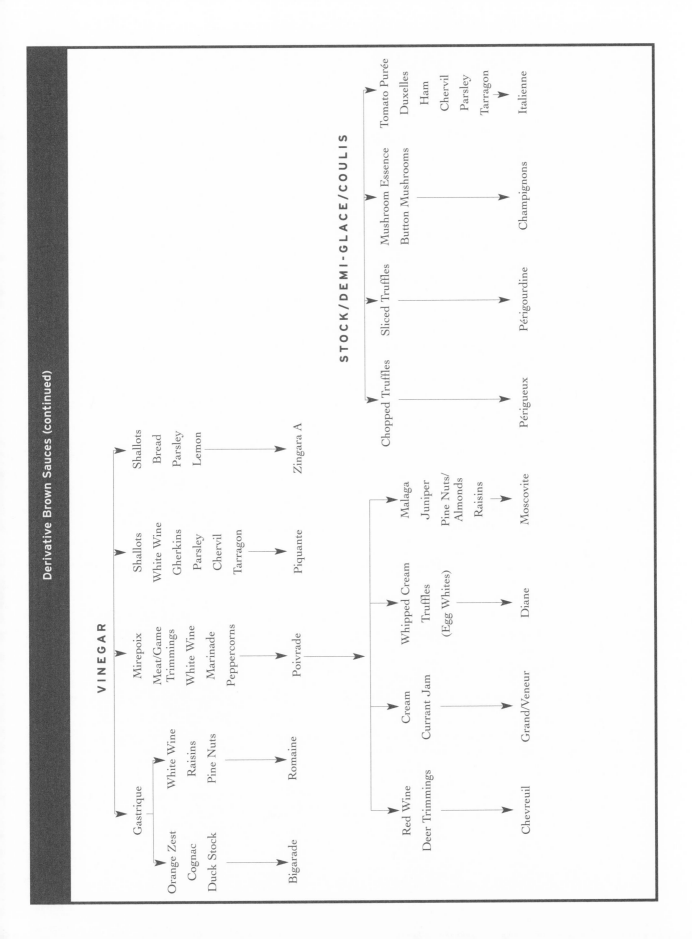

VINEGAR

Gastrique

Orange Zest
Cognac
Duck Stock
→ Bigarade

White Wine
Raisins
Pine Nuts
→ Romaine

Mirepoix
Meat/Game Trimmings
White Wine
Marinade
Peppercorns
→ Poivrade

Red Wine
Deer Trimmings
→ Chevreuil

Cream
Currant Jam
→ Grand/Veneur

Whipped Cream
Truffles
(Egg Whites)
→ Diane

Malaga
Juniper
Pine Nuts/
Almonds
Raisins
→ Moscovite

Shallots
White Wine
Gherkins
Parsley
Chervil
Tarragon
→ Piquante

Shallots
Bread
Parsley
Lemon
→ Zingara A

STOCK/DEMI-GLACE/COULIS

Chopped Truffles
→ Périgueux

Sliced Truffles
→ Périgourdine

Mushroom Essence
Button Mushrooms
→ Champignons

Tomato Purée
Duxelles
Ham
Chervil
Parsley
Tarragon
→ Italienne

Sauce Diable

This sauce is best served with grilled chicken or other poultry. Its flavor should be straightforward and fairly acidic to balance the grilled flavor. Some traditional recipes use only white wine, whereas others insist on vinegar. The following recipes use a combination. The sauce is finished with cayenne pepper and should be quite spicy.

Classic Method. Finely chop 3 shallots (2 ounces/60 grams) and combine them with 5 fluid ounces (150 milliliters) of white wine and 5 fluid ounces (150 milliliters) of white wine vinegar. Reduce the mixture by two-thirds, until about 6 tablespoons (90 milliliters) of flavor base remain. Add 7 fluid ounces (200 milliliters) of demi-glace or coulis, and reduce slightly until the sauce has a very lightly syrupy consistency. Add cayenne to taste. Yield: 1 cup (250 milliliters).

Meat-Glace Method. Prepare the same flavor base as described for the classic method. There should be approximately 5 tablespoons (75 milliliters) of flavor base remaining after reduction. Add 2 tablespoons (30 milliliters) of meat glace to the reduction. Adjust the consistency of the mixture by either thinning with stock or reducing slightly. Whisk 1 ounce (30 grams) of butter into the sauce. Season to taste with cayenne. Yield: ½ cup (125 milliliters).

Unthickened Method. Replace the demi-glace or coulis called for in the classic recipe with a full-flavored brown chicken stock or jus. Taste the sauce before adding all the stock or jus so as not to completely muffle the taste of the flavor base. The flavor of the finished sauce can be enhanced with freshly chopped thyme, savory, or marjoram. Yield: 1 cup (250 milliliters).

Alternatives and Variations. Although purists would insist that it is no longer a sauce diable, the sauce will have a more complex flavor if the shallots are gently caramelized in a small amount of butter before being moistened with the white wine and vinegar. This will also give a darker, richer color to the sauce.

If the sauce diable is being used for grilled poultry such as chicken, pigeon, or pheasant, some of the trimmings, such as the wing tips or necks, can be caramelized with the shallots before being moistened with the vinegar and white wine. It is also possible to impart some of the grilled flavor to the sauce by lightly grilling the trimmings before adding them to the sauce. The flavor of all three versions of the sauce is enhanced by finishing the sauce with 1 tablespoon (15 milliliters) of chopped chives.

Sauce Estragon (Tarragon Sauce)

This sauce is best served with veal or chicken.

Classic Method. Bring ¾ cup (185 milliliters) of white wine to a simmer. Let it simmer just long enough to evaporate the alcohol, then add a handful—about 4 teaspoons (20 milliliters)—of coarsely chopped tarragon stems. Cover the pan and let the stems infuse in the hot wine for 10 to 15 minutes. Add 1 cup (250 milliliters) of demi-glace or coulis to the infusion, and reduce the mixture by one-third. Strain through a fine chinois. Finish the sauce with 2 teaspoons (10 milliliters) of tarragon leaves that have been chopped at the last minute. Yield: 1 cup (250 milliliters).

Meat-Glace Method. Prepare the tarragon infusion as described for the classic method. Add 3 tablespoons (45 milliliters) of meat glace to the infusion, and reduce slightly until the mixture has a lightly syrupy consistency. Strain the mixture and whisk in 1½ ounces (45 grams) of butter or Tarragon Butter (page 419). Finish with 2 teaspoons (10 milliliters) of freshly chopped tarragon leaves. Yield: 1 cup (250 milliliters).

Unthickened Method. Prepare the infusion as described for the classic method but replace the demi-glace with jus or stock. This mixture will be considerably more acidic than the same sauce made with coulis or demi-glace. In some cases, this acidity is desirable, and the mixture can be left as is. Otherwise, additional stock or jus can be added to taste. Decorate the sauce with whole blanched tarragon leaves. Yield: 1 cup (250 milliliters).

Alternatives and Variations. This sauce can be used as a model for almost any herb sauce: a preliminary infusion in white wine; reduction with demi-glace, coulis, or meat glace; and a final finishing with the chopped herb leaves. The method without thickener can also be used as a model.

Sauce Fines Herbes

Most recipes for this sauce contain the traditional fines herbes mixture: equal parts chervil, tarragon, parsley, and chives. Of these four herbs, tarragon is by far the most assertive. The sauce will be better balanced if the amount of tarragon is reduced by three-fourths or even eliminated. The technique and quantities are identical to those used for sauce estragon (above) except that tarragon is replaced by the fines herbes mixture.

Sauce Godart (Prosciutto and Mushroom Sauce)

Classic Method. Prepare 2 ounces (50 grams) of finely chopped mirepoix, which should consist of one-quarter unsmoked cured ham, such as prosciutto. Combine the mirepoix with 7 fluid ounces (200 milliliters) Champagne or white wine. Reduce the mixture by half. Add 6 tablespoons (90 milliliters) of mushroom cooking liquid and reduce the mixture again by half. Add 2 cups (500 milliliters) of demi-glace or coulis. Simmer the sauce gently for 10 minutes, skimming any froth that floats to the surface. Strain through a chinois. Put the strained sauce in a clean saucepan and reduce it by one-third. Strain through a fine chinois. Yield: 2 cups (500 milliliters).

Meat-Glace Method. Prepare the white wine–mirepoix mixture and reduce it by half as described for the classic method. Add 6 tablespoons (90 milliliters) of mushroom essence and reduce the mixture again by half. About 6 tablespoons (90 milliliters) of liquid should remain. Dissolve 3 tablespoons (45 milliliters) of meat glace in the hot flavor base. Check the consistency of the base: It should be lightly syrupy. If it is too thin, reduce it or add a bit more meat glace. If it is too thick, thin it with stock. Whisk in 1½ ounces (45 grams) of butter. Strain the sauce through a fine chinois. Yield: ¾ cup (185 milliliters).

Unthickened Method. Prepare the white wine–mirepoix mixture as described for the classic method. Replace the coulis or demi-glace with the same amount of jus or stock. Mushrooms can be poached directly in the broth if mushroom cooking liquid is not on hand. Yield: 1 cup (250 milliliters).

Alternatives and Variations. Champagne is not necessary for this sauce, but be careful to select a fairly austere white wine with relatively high acidity (such as Coteaux Champenois, Muscadet, French Chablis, or Sancerre). If the ham used in the mirepoix is too salty, the slices should be soaked in cold water. The flavor of the sauce can be made more assertive by sweating the ham and mirepoix in ½ ounce (15 grams) of butter until they lightly caramelize, before moistening with the wine.

Much of the character of this sauce comes from the mushroom cooking liquid, so avoid trying to alter it by finishing the sauce with strongly flavored ingredients. The sauce will be greatly enhanced by using wild mushrooms. Wild or cultivated mushrooms, whole, chopped, or cut into julienne, make an attractive garniture for the finished sauce.

Sauce Hussarde (Prosciutto-Scented Horseradish Sauce)

This sauce traditionally accompanies grilled red meats.

Classic Method. Gently sweat 1 finely chopped shallot (1 ounce/25 grams) and 1 finely chopped medium onion (6 ounces/150 grams) in ½ ounce (15 grams) of butter until they are translucent but not browned. Add 7 fluid ounces (200 milliliters) of white wine to the onion-shallot mixture and reduce by half. Add 7 fluid ounces (200 milliliters) of demi-glace, 1 tablespoon (15 milliliters) of tomato purée, 6 tablespoons (90 milliliters) of white veal or chicken stock, 1 ounce (25 grams) of chopped cured ham (such as prosciutto), ½ clove of garlic (crushed), and 1 small bouquet garni (page 51). Slowly simmer the mixture for 30 minutes. Strain the sauce through a fine chinois. Finish the sauce with 1 ounce (25 grams) of ham cut into brunoise, 1 teaspoon (5 milliliters) of freshly grated horseradish, and 1 tablespoon (15 milliliters) of finely chopped parsley. Yield: 2 cups (500 milliliters).

Meat-Glace Method. Prepare the shallot-onion–white wine reduction as described for the classic method, which should produce about 5 tablespoons (75 milliliters) of flavor base. Add 3 tablespoons (45 milliliters) of meat glace to the reduction, along with 1 tablespoon (15 milliliters) of tomato coulis, 1 ounce (25 grams) of chopped unsmoked raw ham, ½ clove of garlic (crushed), and 1 small bouquet garni (page 51). Simmer the sauce for 30 minutes. Strain the sauce and finish it with the ham, horseradish, and parsley as described for the classic method. Thin if necessary with stock. Whisk in 1½ ounces (45 grams) of butter. Yield: 1 cup (250 milliliters).

Unthickened Method. Like many of the derivative brown sauces, unthickened sauce hussarde can be presented as a bouillon or consommé underneath the meat. When presenting the sauce in this way, the horseradish should be julienned instead of grated and should be allowed to infuse in the bouillon for about 15 minutes. The ham should be carefully cut into brunoise and lightly poached; otherwise it may cloud the bouillon. If the sauce has been carefully skimmed and strained, it will have the clarity of a consommé without needing clarification with egg whites. Yield: 1 cup (250 milliliters).

Alternatives and Variations. The classic recipe for sauce hussarde is based on an infusion of shallots and onions in white wine. The flavor of these ingredients can be intensified by lightly caramelizing them in a small amount of butter and with a pinch of sugar before moistening them with the white wine. This method will also give a deeper color to the sauce. If the sauce is being presented unbound, in a bowl, the butter should be carefully skimmed off after the liquid has been moistened with stock.

Sauce Régence (Rhine Wine and Truffle Sauce)

Rhine wine is traditionally called for in the flavor base for this sauce. The term "Rhine wine" encompasses a variety of wines that include dry, Alsatian-style Rieslings and Sylvaners as well as German Rheingau, Rheinhessen, or Rheinpfalz wines, which usually contain some residual sugar. A light sweetness in the sauce works well with the truffles, so if you want to be traditional, a German Spätlese or Auslese Riesling would work best. These wines also have an intense varietal character that is more likely to hold up after the addition of the other ingredients. Late-harvest California Rieslings can also be used.

Classic Method. Prepare 2 ounces (50 grams) of mirepoix and gently cook it in butter until it softens. Moisten with 5 fluid ounces (150 milliliters) of Rhine wine. Reduce the mixture by half, and add 1 tablespoon (15 milliliters) of chopped truffle peelings or ¼ cup (60 milliliters) of truffle essence. Add 1¾ cups (450 milliliters) of demi-glace to the infusion, and bring the sauce to a simmer. Skim off any scum that floats to the top and strain through a fine chinois. Yield: 2 cups (500 milliliters).

Meat-Glace Method. Prepare the mirepoix–Rhine wine infusion as described for the classic method. Add the truffle peelings or essence, and replace the demi-glace with ¼ cup (60 milliliters) of meat glace. Adjust the consistency to a light syrup by reducing slightly or by thinning with stock. Finish the sauce with 2 ounces (60 grams) of butter or Truffle Butter (page 419) before straining. Yield: 1 cup (250 milliliters).

Unthickened Method. Gently simmer 5 fluid ounces (150 milliliters) of Rhine wine with an equal amount of full-flavored stock or jus until the mixture reduces by half. Finish the sauce with truffle essence or simply add fresh julienned or sliced truffles. Cover the sauce and cook the truffles for 5 to 10 minutes. Serve immediately in deep plates or bowls. Yield: 1 cup (250 milliliters).

Alternatives and Variations. Traditional recipes stipulate straining out the chopped truffle peelings used to flavor the sauce. Truffles have become such a rarity, and most diners are so unaccustomed to seeing truffles on their plates, that the sauce will probably be more appreciated if they are retained. In fact, the sauce can be made more dramatic by adding thinly sliced black truffles to it at the end.

To impart a more intense truffle flavor, the sauce can be finished with Truffle Butter (page 419).

Sauce Robert (White Wine–Mustard Sauce)

This brightly flavored sauce is excellent with grilled meats and pork dishes. Use a fairly acidic white wine — Muscadet and French versions of Sauvignon Blanc both work well.

Classic Method. Sweat 1 medium chopped onion (6 ounces/150 grams) in ½ ounce (15 grams) of butter until translucent. Add 7 fluid ounces (200 milliliters) of white wine and reduce by two-thirds. Moisten the onion–white wine infusion with 1¼ cups (300 milliliters) of demi-glace. Cook the sauce for 10 minutes to infuse the flavor of the onions thoroughly. The sauce may either be strained or the onions may be retained. Finish the sauce with a pinch of sugar (to bring out the flavor of the onions) and 1 tablespoon (15 milliliters) of Dijon mustard. Do not allow the sauce to come to a boil after adding the mustard. Yield: 1½ cups (375 milliliters).

Meat-Glace Method. Sweat the onion and add the wine as described for the classic method but reduce by only half. Add 3 tablespoons (45 milliliters) of meat glace to the infusion in place of demi-glace. Adjust the consistency of the sauce, add the mustard and sugar, and finish with 1½ ounces (45 grams) of butter. Yield: 1 cup (250 milliliters).

Unthickened Method. Sauce Robert works particularly well when no flour or butter is used. The acidic mustard flavor works especially well with grilled meats and pork. Prepare sauce Robert in the same way as for the classic method, but replace the demi-glace with unthickened full-flavored stock or jus (pork jus is especially good). An unthickened, almost medieval version can also be prepared with no stock at all, but it is too sharp and acidic for most modern tastes. Yield: 2 cups (500 milliliters).

Alternatives and Variations. Sauce Robert is traditionally finished with Dijon mustard. Other mustards, such as whole-grain Meaux-style or homemade mustard, can be used instead to give the sauce a personal touch. Herb-flavored mustards can also be used, but if you want the flavor of a particular herb, it is usually better to finish the sauce with an unflavored mustard and add the chopped fresh herb separately.

Sauce Charcutière (White Wine and Gherkin Sauce)

To 2 cups (500 milliliters) of sauce Robert, add 2 ounces (50 grams) of sour gherkins (cornichons), cut into julienne.

Sauce Duxelles (Chopped Mushroom Sauce)

This sauce is based on duxelles, a standard mushroom preparation used in classic French cooking. Duxelles is prepared by slowly cooking chopped mushrooms in butter until all their moisture has evaporated. It is best when prepared with wild mushrooms (cèpe stems are magnificent) but is most often made with cultivated mushrooms. To prepare 1 cup (250 milliliters) duxelles, finely chop 1 pound (500 grams) of mushrooms or mushroom stems and 3 shallots. Sweat the shallots for 5 minutes in 1 ounce (30 grams) of butter and add the mushrooms. Sprinkle the mushrooms with the juice of half a lemon, to prevent the duxelles from turning black, and gently cook the mushrooms until no moisture is left in the bottom of the pan. Keep them covered in a bowl until needed.

Classic Method. Combine 1 tablespoon (15 milliliters) of finely chopped shallots with 6 tablespoons (90 milliliters) of white wine and 6 tablespoons (90 milliliters) of mushroom cooking liquid. Add 1 cup (250 milliliters) of demi-glace or coulis, ¼ cup (60 milliliters) of tomato purée, and 2 tablespoons (30 milliliters) of fine, dry duxelles to the sauce. Simmer the sauce for 5 minutes, and finish it with 2 teaspoons (10 milliliters) of finely chopped parsley. Yield: 2 cups (500 milliliters).

Meat-Glace Method. Use the same ingredients and procedure as for the classic method but replace the demi-glace with ¼ cup (60 milliliters) of meat glace. Finish the sauce with 1½ ounces (45 grams) of butter. Yield: 1½ cups (375 milliliters).

Unthickened Method. Duxelles will usually disperse when mixed with a full-bodied broth, creating a sauce that looks somewhat like mushroom soup. It is better to cut the mushrooms into julienne and add them directly to the broth. This method is even more impressive if a combination of different-colored wild mushrooms is used, such as black trumpets, white oyster mushrooms, chanterelles, and the like. To prepare an unthickened version, follow the directions for the classic method but replace the duxelles with julienned mushrooms and the demi-glace or coulis with a lighter stock or jus. Yield: 2 cups (500 milliliters).

Sauce Salmis

This excellent sauce is usually made to accompany game and small birds, but the same method can be used for almost any kind of meat. Because the trimmings from the game enter into the preparation, the sauce has much of the wholesomeness and character of an integral sauce or natural jus. Whatever kind of trimmings you use, be sure that all skin and fat are removed. If they are left on, they may make the sauce greasy.

Classic Method. Sweat 3 ounces (75 grams) of mirepoix in butter until it starts to soften. Break up 1 pound (500 grams) of game meat or fowl trimmings into ½-inch (1 cm) pieces with a cleaver or heavy knife and add them to the hot mirepoix. When the trimmings begin to brown, add 5 fluid ounces (150 milliliters) of white wine and reduce by two-thirds. Add 1¾ cups (450 milliliters) of demi-glace. Cook the sauce for about 45 minutes to extract the flavor from the trimmings and mirepoix. Strain the sauce, first through a coarse chinois and then through a fine chinois. Add 7 fluid ounces (200 milliliters) of appropriate-flavored stock to the strained sauce. Reduce if necessary to thicken. Finish the sauce by whisking in 2 ounces (60 grams) of butter. Adjust the seasoning. Yield: 2½ cups (625 milliliters).

Meat-Glace Method. Sweat the mirepoix and add the trimmings as described for the classic method. Gently cook the mirepoix with the trimmings until the juices on the bottom of the pan begin to caramelize. Add 6 tablespoons (90 milliliters) of white wine to the pan and continue reducing until all the liquid evaporates, leaving a brown layer of caramelized juices on the bottom of the pan. (The steam generated by the reducing wine causes the trimmings to release their juices, which should then caramelize on the bottom of the pan.) When the wine has been completely reduced, add ½ cup (125 milliliters) of brown beef or chicken stock, and again reduce until no liquid remains, gently scraping the bottom of the pot with a wooden spoon or spatula while the stock is reducing, so that the caramelized juices dissolve. When the stock has reduced and formed a thick caramelized glaze on the bottom of the pot, add 6 tablespoons (90 milliliters) of white wine and cook it just long enough to scrape up and dissolve the caramelized juices. Add 1¾ cups (450 milliliters) of brown beef or chicken stock (or game stock if available), and simmer the mixture for 45 minutes. Strain the sauce into a clean saucepan through a coarse chinois. Stir enough meat glace into the sauce to give it the consistency of a light syrup and to reinforce its color—usually about ¼ cup (60 milliliters) of meat glace is needed. Whisk 2 ounces (60 grams) of butter into the sauce. Strain through a fine chinois. Yield: 2 cups (500 milliliters).

Sauce Zingara B

Sauce Zingara has such a convoluted history and so many variations that, by the time the classic sauces were categorized at the end of the nineteenth century, two types of it—imaginatively named Zingara A and Zingara B—had to be listed. Zingara A is one of the few sauces in the classic repertoire that is thickened with breadcrumbs, a technique used since the Middle Ages. Because it is based on vinegar, its recipe is included in the section on vinegar-based derivative brown sauces (see page 191). Zingara B is white wine based and finished with an elaborate garniture of ham, mushrooms, and truffles.

Zingara B—Classic Method. Prepare 2 ounces (50 grams) of julienned mushrooms. Simmer the julienne for 5 minutes in 5 fluid ounces (150 milliliters) of white wine. Strain the wine and save the mushroom julienne to add to the sauce at the end. Return the white wine to the saucepan and reduce it by half. Add 7 fluid ounces (200 milliliters) of demi-glace or coulis, 1 cup (250 milliliters) of tomato sauce, and ¼ cup (60 milliliters) of white chicken or veal stock. Gently simmer and skim the sauce for 5 or 10 minutes, until it has a lightly syrupy consistency. Strain the sauce through a fine chinois, and finish it with the julienned mushrooms as well as 2 tablespoons (30 milliliters) of raw cured ham cut into fine julienne and 1 tablespoon (15 milliliters) of black truffles also cut into julienne. Yield: 2½ cups (625 milliliters).

Zingara B—Meat-Glace Method. Prepare the sauce exactly as for the classic method, but replace the demi-glace with 3 tablespoons (45 milliliters) of meat glace. Finish the sauce by whisking in 2 ounces (60 grams) of butter just before adding the julienned mushrooms, ham, and truffles. Yield: 2 cups (500 milliliters).

Zingara B—Unthickened Method. Prepare the sauce as for the classic method, but substitute a lighter stock for the demi-glace or coulis. Yield: 2½ cups (625 milliliters).

RED WINE–BASED DERIVATIVE BROWN SAUCES

Red wines used for sauce making must be chosen carefully (see "Red Wine," page 79). A red wine sauce will always be improved if the wine is cooked with meat trimmings or stock rather than being reduced by itself or with aromatic vegetables alone; the proteins in the meat or stock help eliminate undesirable tannin from the wine. Most classic recipes take this into consideration and call for reducing the red wine a second time with demi-glace or meat stock.

Do not make meat glace–based sauces by simply reducing red wine, adding the glace, and finishing with butter. The resulting sauce will be sour or even bitter because of the concentration of the wine's tannin and acids during reduction. Keep meat trimmings and stock on hand when preparing these sauces.

When preparing red wine sauces, it is best that the red wine be cooked for at least 30 minutes with stock or meat trimmings or that red wine stock made with beef or chicken (pages 97 and 93) be used instead of the usual red wine reduction combined with meat glace. This is especially important in unthickened sauces because butter, which would help attenuate the wine's acidity, is not used. If the resulting sauce is nonetheless sharp or even astringent, you will have to relent and swirl in a little butter or lightly thicken the sauce with a vegetable purée, such as mushroom, lentil, or tomato. If neither stock nor meat trimmings is available, excellent red wine sauces can be prepared using a base of mirepoix with unsmoked raw ham (see Meurette Sauce, page 181).

Sauce Bordelaise

In the first half of the nineteenth century, recipes for sauce bordelaise called for white wine. A similar sauce, Sauce Bonnefoy (page 147), is still made with white wine.

Classic Method. Combine 1¼ cups (300 milliliters) of red wine with 2 tablespoons (30 milliliters) of finely chopped shallots, 1 teaspoon (5 milliliters) of crushed black pepper, a sprig of fresh thyme, and half a bay leaf. Reduce the mixture by three-fourths. Add 6 tablespoons (90 milliliters) of demiglace or coulis to the reduction. Gently simmer the sauce for 15 minutes, being sure to skim off any scum that floats to the surface. Strain the sauce through a fine chinois into a clean saucepan. Adjust the consistency of the sauce by stirring in 1 tablespoon (15 milliliters) of meat glace. Add 1 teaspoon (5 milliliters) of lemon juice and 2 ounces (60 grams) of beef marrow cut into dice or rounds or butter cut into cubes. Adjust the seasonings. Yield: 1 cup (250 milliliters).

Meat-Glace Method. A good-tasting sauce bordelaise is difficult to make using meat glace as the only form of meat protein; meat stock, meat trimmings, or both are essential. Sweat 5 ounces (150 grams) of beef or veal trimmings with 2 tablespoons (30 milliliters) of finely chopped shallots in ½ ounce (15 grams) of butter. When the meat trimmings and shallots begin to brown lightly, pour 6 tablespoons (90 milliliters) of red wine into the pan. Reduce the red wine until it evaporates completely, but do not let the bottom of the pan burn. Add 6 tablespoons (90 milliliters) of brown beef or chicken stock, and again reduce until the stock evaporates and lightly caramelizes on the bottom of the saucepan. Add 1¼ cups (300 milliliters) of red wine, 6 tablespoons (90 milliliters) of brown beef or chicken stock, half a bay leaf, a sprig of fresh thyme, and 1 teaspoon (5 milliliters) of freshly crushed black pepper.

Gently simmer the mixture for 15 to 20 minutes. Strain through a fine chinois into a clean saucepan. Dissolve 2 tablespoons (30 milliliters) of meat glace into the hot sauce to give it a thicker, lightly syrupy consistency. Finish with 1 teaspoon (5 milliliters) of lemon juice and 2 ounces (50 grams) of beef marrow cut into dice or rounds, or 1½ ounces (45 grams) of butter. Yield: 1½ cups (375 milliliters). See the photograph in the color plates.

Unthickened Method. Sauce bordelaise can be presented under meats in deep plates or wide plate-like soup bowls. To prepare an unthickened version, follow the procedure given for the meat-glace method but omit the meat glace and butter. Yield: 2 cups (500 milliliters).

Alternatives and Variations. Purists would argue that a sauce without marrow cannot be called a bordelaise, but the sauce is perfectly good tasting without it. Finely chopped parsley or chervil added along with the butter to finish the sauce will give it a freshness that is otherwise missing, and the green flecks against the deep red background are pleasing to the eye. A teaspoon (5 milliliters) of Cognac or Armagnac added just long enough before the end to cook off the alcohol will give the sauce a bit more depth and mystery, as will a drop or two of Kirsch. The finished sauce can be made less rich by adding 2 tablespoons (30 milliliters) of tomato coulis, which acts as a thickener, and by cutting the butter in half.

BORDELAISE SAUCE MADE WITH RED WINE STOCK

This classic sauce, once made with white wine, is made in a classic kitchen by adding demi-glace or meat glace to a red wine reduction and finishing the sauce with cubes of beef marrow. The marrow can be replaced with a swirl of butter. The red wine is best reduced along with the demi-glace or meat glace so the proteins take out some of the tannin. Best of all is a bordelaise sauce made with Oxtail–Red Wine Stock (page 97). As for all brown sauces, the thickness of the sauce is largely a matter of taste. If red wine stock is used, very little reduction will be required to cook off the acid and tannin in the wine and the sauce can be left almost broth-like, served around a good steak in a soup plate, or it can be reduced and thickened with butter.

YIELD: 1 CUP (250 MILLILITERS), ABOUT 6 SERVINGS

oxtail-red wine stock	2 cups	500 milliliters
or	or	or
red wine	1 cup	250 milliliters
and	and	and
veal, beef, or chicken demi-glace	¾ cup	185 milliliters
or	or	or
meat glace (page 104)	¼ cup	60 milliliters
minced shallots (about 1 shallot)	2 tablespoons	30 milliliters

black pepper, crushed	1 teaspoon	5 milliliters
fresh or dried thyme	1 sprig	1 sprig
or	or	or
dried thyme leaves	1 pinch	1 pinch
imported bay leaf	½ leaf	½ leaf
red wine vinegar, to taste	2 teaspoons	10 milliliters
cognac	2 teaspoons	10 milliliters
beef marrow cubes or cold butter	1½ ounces	45 grams
salt	to taste	to taste

1. Combine the red wine stock, or the red wine and the demi-glace or meat glace, with the shallots, pepper, thyme, and bay leaf and simmer gently until reduced by slightly more than half or until the sauce has a lightly syrupy consistency. Strain into a clean saucepan.
2. Whisk in the vinegar and Cognac, simmer for 30 seconds, and whisk in the marrow. Season to taste with salt.

MEURETTE SAUCE
Burgundian Red Wine Sauce

The classic version of this sauce contains no meat stock, so that it can be quickly prepared by home cooks. Meurette sauce is popular in Burgundy, where it is served over poached eggs, but it is a versatile sauce that can also be used over meat or even fish. This sauce is made by sweating aromatic vegetables (mirepoix) with ham (unsmoked prosciutto) and then moistening with red wine. It can be improved by sweating fresh meat trimmings with the ham-mirepoix base and by using some concentrated stock along with the red wine. Add a bouquet garni and 3 cups (750 milliliters) of red wine, and gently simmer the mixture for 30 minutes.

The sauce base can be reduced to a very small amount and the sauce finished with butter alone or the base can be reduced less dramatically and the sauce then finished with beurre manié (butter and flour paste).

YIELD: 1 CUP (250 MILLILITERS), ABOUT 6 SERVINGS

onion, peeled, minced	1 small	1 small
carrot, minced	1 medium	1 medium
celery, minced	½ stalk	½ stalk
garlic cloves, crushed	2	2
prosciutto, chopped (see Note)	3 tablespoons	45 milliliters
meat trimmings, diced (optional)	1 cup	250 milliliters
butter (for the mirepoix)	1 ounce	30 grams
meat glace (page 104; optional)	2 tablespoons	30 milliliters

red wine	3 cups	750 milliliters
medium bouquet garni (page 51)	1	1
cold butter	3 ounces	90 grams
or	or	or
butter	1 ounce	30 grams
worked to a paste (beurre manié) with		
flour	2 tablespoons	30 milliliters
red wine vinegar	2 teaspoons	10 milliliters
salt and pepper	to taste	to taste

1. Cook the vegetables, prosciutto, and meat trimmings (if using) in butter in a saucepan over medium heat until well browned and any juices released by the meat have caramelized on the bottom of the pan. Stir in the meat glace, if using, and stir over medium heat for about 2 minutes to caramelize the glaze slightly.

2. Pour over the red wine and add the bouquet garni. Simmer gently for 30 minutes. Strain into a clean saucepan and simmer down to ½ cup (125 milliliters) if you're using butter alone or ¾ cup (185 milliliters) if you're using flour.

3. Whisk in the butter or beurre manié and bring back to a simmer for just a second. Whisk in the vinegar and season to taste with salt and pepper. See the photograph in the color plates.

Note: When buying prosciutto for sauce making, ask for the ends. Often they are available for very little cost.

Classic Method. Gently sweat 2 tablespoons (30 milliliters) each finely chopped onion and carrot, 1 tablespoon (15 milliliters) of finely chopped celery, 2 crushed garlic cloves, and 2 tablespoons (30 milliliters) of chopped unsmoked raw ham in 1 ounce (30 grams) of butter. Gently cook the mixture for 15 to 20 minutes, until the ingredients and the bottom of the pan are lightly browned. Add 3 cups (750 milliliters) of red wine and a bouquet garni, and gently simmer the mixture for 30 minutes. Strain the sauce through a fine chinois. About 1½ cups (375 milliliters) of sauce base should remain. Thicken the sauce base with 2 tablespoons (30 grams) of beurre manié. Yield: 1½ cups (375 milliliters).

Meat-Glace Method. The beurre manié can be eliminated from the sauce by reducing the red wine infusion by two-thirds instead of half and then finishing the sauce with butter only. Adding 1 to 2 tablespoons (15 to 30 milliliters) of meat glace or reduced stock will give the sauce more body and complexity. Yield: 1½ cups (375 milliliters).

Unthickened Method. Meurette sauce can be prepared with no thickener in the same way as Sauce Bordelaise (page 180).

Alternatives and Variations. If wild mushrooms are available, by all means use them. They can be infused in the simmering red wine for 5 to 10 minutes, removed, and added whole to the sauce at the end, or they can be simply sautéed, sprinkled with herbs and chopped shallots, and used as a garniture.

Sauce Rouennaise II

This sauce is prepared by thickening Sauce Bordelaise, page 179 (without the marrow), with a purée of raw duck livers. Purée 1 duck liver with an equal volume of butter in a food processor for about 3 minutes. Force this mixture through a drum sieve. Gently whisk the purée into 1 cup (250 milliliters) of hot sauce bordelaise. Be careful to not let the sauce boil once the liver has been added, or it will break and turn grainy. If using meat glace–based bordelaise, replace the butter called for with the liver-butter purée. Yield: 1 cup (250 milliliters). (For a different, and perhaps more authentic, version of sauce rouennaise that is thickened with blood and liver, see page 131.)

DERIVATIVE BROWN SAUCES BASED ON FORTIFIED WINES

Most fortified wines used in sauce making have a large amount of residual sugar that remains in the wine after fermentation. Whereas red wines will become acidic if overly reduced, fortified wines, if used carelessly, are liable to make a sauce too sweet. Because different styles and brands of Madeira and port have different amounts of natural sugar, do not blindly follow a recipe for these sauces, because each wine will behave slightly differently.

Sauce Madère (Madeira Sauce)

Classic Method. Combine 2 cups (500 milliliters) of demi-glace with ¼ cup (60 milliliters) of Madeira. Gently reduce the mixture back down to 2 cups (500 milliliters). Skim off any froth or scum that floats to the surface. Yield: 2 cups (500 milliliters).

Meat-Glace Method. Reduce 1 cup (250 milliliters) of Madeira by half. Add 3 tablespoons (45 milliliters) of meat glace to the reduction, and finish with 2 ounces (60 grams) of butter. Adjust the seasonings. Yield: 1 cup (250 milliliters).

Unthickened Method. Reduce ½ cup (125 milliliters) of Madeira by half. Add ¾ cup (185 milliliters) of concentrated (four times) brown stock to the reduction. Reduce or thin the sauce as necessary to adjust its consistency. Yield: 1 cup (250 milliliters).

Alternatives and Variations. Adding 2 tablespoons (30 milliliters) of reduced mushroom essence to 1 cup (250 milliliters) of sauce will greatly improve meat glace–based Madeira sauce; or wild or cultivated mushroom stems can be simmered for 5 minutes in the Madeira.

Sauce Porto (Port Sauce)

The methods for making port sauce are the same as for Madeira sauce except that the Madeira is replaced with a full-bodied port.

Port and Mushroom Sauce

This unbound sauce is similar to a Sauce Duxelles (page 176) except that port is used in the sauce base and the mushrooms are cut into julienne. Reduce ½ cup (125 milliliters) of port by half. Add 1 cup (250 milliliters) of concentrated (four times) brown stock and 2 ounces (50 grams) of mushrooms cut into julienne. Reduce or thin the sauce as necessary to adjust its consistency. Finish with 1 tablespoon (15 milliliters) of chopped parsley. Adding 1 to 2 teaspoons (5 to 10 milliliters) of balsamic vinegar to the sauce at the end will bring up the flavor of the mushrooms. Yield: 1 cup (250 milliliters).

Sauce Financière

This sauce is prepared by flavoring Madeira sauce with truffles. Classic recipes reduce the Madeira sauce by one-tenth and then add enough truffle essence to return the sauce to its original volume. In this way, the truffle essence is never cooked in the sauce, which would cause much of its aroma to evaporate.

An alternative to using truffle essence is to finish the sauce with butter that has been stored with fresh truffles (see "Storing Fresh Truffles," page 63). The sauce can also be finished with chopped truffle peelings or truffle slices.

VINEGAR-BASED DERIVATIVE BROWN SAUCES

There are two kinds of vinegar-based classic brown sauces. The first includes sweet-and-sour sauces, such as the sauce used for duck à l'orange. These sauces are usually prepared with a mixture of vinegar and caramelized sugar called a *gastrique*. The second type of vinegar-based classic brown sauce is the Poivrade family (page 187). These sauces, which are traditionally used for red meats and game, are prepared by cooking mirepoix vegetables and meat trimmings with vinegar and the marinade used for the meat.

Sweet-and-Sour Sauces

A *gastrique* is prepared with approximately one part sugar to two parts wine vinegar. Usually about 2 tablespoons (30 milliliters) of gastrique are used per quart (liter) of sauce, but the amount may vary depending on the type of sauce and the strength of the vinegar.

Heat ½ cup (100 grams) of granulated sugar in a heavy-bottomed saucepan or in a copper *poêlon*, used specifically for making caramel. When the sugar has melted and turned a pale brown, pour ½ cup (125 milliliters) of wine vinegar into the saucepan to dissolve the caramel and stop the cooking. Stand back in case the mixture spatters. Heat and stir the gastrique to make sure the caramelized sugar is completely dissolved in the vinegar. Even though this may seem like a large amount of gastrique, it is hard to prepare in smaller amounts. In any case, it will keep for several weeks in the refrigerator.

Most classic recipes for gastrique suggest caramelizing the sugar by moistening it with the wine vinegar. Because of the high heat required to caramelize sugar, little if any vinegar remains in the gastrique when this method is used.

To use the gastrique in a sauce, pour small amounts into the sauce, not the other way around. Be careful to taste as you go; gastrique is powerful, and a few drops too many can spoil a sauce.

In classic French cooking, gastrique is used only in sweet-and-sour sauces or sauces containing fruit. When used discreetly, gastrique can enhance the flavor of other brown sauces as well (see "Using Gastrique," page 197).

Sauce Bigarade (Orange Sauce for Duck)

Sauce bigarade is named after the bitter Seville oranges that were first used to flavor duck à l'orange. Most recipes for sauce bigarade are integral sauces prepared from the braising liquid or pan drippings from a roasted duck. The sauce can also be prepared from reduced duck stock, gastrique, and orange zests.

Prepare a concentrated duck stock either without liaison by reducing the stock to a lightly syrupy consistency or adding meat glace, or by binding the partially reduced stock with a starch liaison such as roux, cornstarch, or arrowroot.

Reduce the juice of 4 oranges (1¼ cups/300 milliliters) by half. Add 1 cup (250 milliliters) of the concentrated duck stock and reduce the sauce until it has a lightly syrupy consistency. Add 4 teaspoons (20 milliliters) of gastrique to the sauce. Add the gastrique gradually, while tasting, to avoid adding too much.

Strain the sauce through a fine chinois. Finish the sauce with 2 ounces (60 grams) of butter and 1½ teaspoons (8 milliliters) of julienned and blanched orange zest. The flavor of the sauce can be improved by adding 1 to 2 teaspoons (5 to 10 milliliters) of Cognac. Yield: 2 cups (500 milliliters).

Unthickened Method. A deeply flavored yet light duck broth can be prepared by lightly browning duck trimmings with aromatic vegetables and then moistening them with a previously made duck, chicken, or veal stock and simmering the broth for 20 minutes. This method combines the advantages of long-simmered and short-simmered stocks: long-simmered stocks provide body, whereas short-simmered ones provide flavor, character, and vitality. The finished duck broth should then be infused with the orange zest for 5 to 10 minutes and flavored with gastrique.

Sauce Romaine (Raisin and Pine Nut Sauce for Game)

This gastrique-based sauce is finished with both white and dark raisins and toasted pine nuts. Traditionally it is served with game. Although this delicious sauce is undeservedly ignored today, it is an excellent model for fruit-flavored brown sauces.

Classic Method. Add 1 tablespoon (15 milliliters) of gastrique to 1¼ cups (300 milliliters) of demi-glace and 5 fluid ounces (150 milliliters) of game stock. Reduce the sauce by one-fourth and strain it through a fine chinois. Finish with 1 tablespoon (15 milliliters) of dark raisins (plumped) and 1 tablespoon (15 milliliters) of white raisins (plumped). (Soak each type of raisin in 1 tablespoon (15 milliliters) of warm water for 20 minutes to plump and soften them before adding to the sauce.) Lightly toast 1 tablespoon (15 milliliters) of pine nuts in the oven and add them to the sauce. Yield: 1½ cups (375 milliliters).

Meat-Glace Method. Soak 2 tablespoons (30 milliliters) each white and dark raisins in ¼ cup (60 milliliters) of port. Heat the mixture on the stove for 5 minutes to soften the raisins — do not let it boil. Add 5 fluid ounces (150 milliliters) of game or other brown stock to the port-raisin base. Instead of adding demi-glace, add ¼ cup (60 milliliters) of meat glace and 2 teaspoons (10 milliliters) of gastrique to the mixture. Reduce the sauce slightly, until it has a lightly syrupy consistency. Finish it by whisking in 2 ounces (60 grams) of butter and 2 tablespoons (30 milliliters) of toasted pine nuts. Yield: 1 cup (250 milliliters).

Unthickened Method. Soak 2 tablespoons (30 milliliters) each of white and dark raisins in ¼ cup (60 milliliters) of port. Heat the mixture on the stove for 5 minutes to soften the raisins—do not let it boil. Add ¼ cup (60 milliliters) of concentrated brown stock to the port-raisin base. Flavor the sauce with 2 teaspoons (10 milliliters) of gastrique, and finish with 2 tablespoons (30 milliliters) of toasted pine nuts. Yield: 1 cup (250 milliliters).

Barbecue Sauces

Sauces basted on meats and fish during barbecuing are unique because they end up being scented with smoke. By stoking the fire with wood chips or sawdust, there is a constant source of smoke to flavor whatever is under the lid of the grill.

SWEET-AND-SOUR SAUCE FOR RIBS OR BRISKET

The basic flavors, sugar and vinegar, give this sauce a sweet and sour tang, while beer provides flavor and moisture.

YIELD: ENOUGH FOR 4 STRIPS OF RIBS OR 1 BRISKET

onion, minced	1 medium	1 medium
garlic cloves, minced	3	3
chipotle chiles, reconstituted dried or rinsed canned, chopped fine	2	2
cider vinegar	1 cup	250 milliliters
sugar	½ cup	100 grams
beer, 2 bottles	3 cups	750 milliliters
white wine	1 cup	250 milliliters
minced cilantro	2 tablespoons	60 milliliters

Combine all the ingredients in a saucepan and simmer gently for about 10 minutes to dissolve the sugar and cook the alcohol off the wine and beer. Use the mixture to brush on barbecuing ribs or brisket.

The Poivrade Family of Sauces

These deeply flavored sauces are prepared by moistening caramelized mirepoix with vinegar and the marinade used for red meats and game. The marinade itself is prepared with herbs, mirepoix vegetables, and white wine. Traditional recipes then moisten this intensely flavored infusion with demi-glace. The sauces are then flavored by infusing cracked black pepper 10 minutes before the sauce is strained. Pepper should never be cooked for more than 10 minutes in the sauce or its delicate, pine-like perfume will be lost—only a grating harshness will remain.

Nowadays many chefs feel that strong marinades distort the natural flavor of meats. For this reason, you may wish to prepare the marinade simply to use in the sauce. If you do not have marinade on hand, replace the amount called for in the recipe with white wine.

Marinade for Poivrade Sauces

Finely slice 1 small onion (3 ounces/100 grams), half a medium carrot (3 ounces/100 grams), and 1 shallot (1 ounce/25 grams). Crush and peel a clove of garlic. Cover the aromatic vegetables with 3 cups (750 milliliters) of white wine and 1 cup (250 milliliters) of white wine vinegar. Add 1 small handful of parsley stems, 2 or 3 sprigs of fresh thyme, half a bay leaf, and 1 crushed clove to the mixture. If the meat is to be marinated, add ½ cup (125 milliliters) of extra-virgin olive oil. Store the marinade in a plastic or stainless-steel container (not aluminum, which will react with the acidity in the wine and vinegar) overnight in the refrigerator. Yield: 1 quart (1 liter).

Sauce Poivrade (Pepper-Flavored Game Sauce)

Classic Method. Coarsely chop 1 small onion (3 ounces/100 grams) and half a medium carrot (3 ounces/100 grams); you can also strain out the vegetables in the marinade and use those. Brown the vegetables in 1½ ounces (45 grams) of butter with 1 pound (500 grams) of trimmings from red meat or game. As the meat begins to brown, add 3 sprigs of fresh thyme, half a bay leaf, and 1 small handful of parsley stems. Cook the mixture for several minutes more. When the vegetables and meat trimmings are well browned, tilt the pan and drain off the butter.

Moisten the browned trimmings and vegetables with 5 fluid ounces (150 milliliters) of white wine vinegar and 6 tablespoons (90 milliliters) of white wine. Reduce the liquids until they evaporate completely, leaving a caramelized glaze on the bottom of the pan.

Add 2 cups (500 milliliters) of demi-glace, concentrated brown stock, or coulis; 1 quart (1 liter) of brown game, beef, or chicken stock; and 2 cups (500 milliliters) of the strained marinade or white wine. Bring the liquids slowly to a simmer and skim off any froth or scum that floats to the top. Cover the pot and cook over a very low flame for 3 hours.

Skim off any fat or scum that has floated to the top of the sauce during simmering. Crush 10 whole peppercorns and add them to the hot sauce. Let them infuse for 10 minutes and then strain the mixture through a fine chinois into a fresh saucepan.

Add ½ cup (125 milliliters) of strained marinade and ½ cup (125 milliliters) of brown beef, game, or chicken stock to the strained sauce. Gently bring the sauce back to a simmer. Skim the sauce and reduce it until it has a lightly syrupy consistency. Strain through a chinois and finish with 2 ounces (60 grams) of butter. Yield: approximately 2 cups (500 milliliters).

Meat-Glace Method. Follow the steps for the classic method, but replace the demi-glace with an appropriately flavored brown stock. During the last stage, when the sauce has been strained into a clean saucepan, dissolve 5 tablespoons (75 milliliters) of meat glace in the reducing sauce. Finish the sauce with slightly more butter than is called for in the classic method (3 ounces/90 grams). Yield: 2 cups (500 milliliters).

Unthickened Method. Prepare the sauce base in the same way as for the classic method: Brown the trimmings with the aromatic vegetables, deglaze with the vinegar and white wine, and reduce the liquids completely until they form a glaze on the bottom of the pan. Add 1 cup (250 milliliters) of full-flavored brown stock to the pan and reduce a second time, until the liquids evaporate and caramelize on the bottom.

Moisten the mixture with 2 cups (500 milliliters) more stock and 1 cup (250 milliliters) of marinade. Gently simmer the sauce for 30 minutes, skimming off any froth that floats to the surface. Add 10 crushed peppercorns to the sauce, and let them infuse for 10 minutes. Strain through cheesecloth. Yield: 2 cups (500 milliliters).

Alternatives and Variations. If the sauce poivrade is being served with game, a teaspoon or two (5 to 10 milliliters) of good marc added near the end will give the sauce a pleasant gamy flavor. Adding 10 crushed juniper berries at the same time as the peppercorns or 1 teaspoon (5 milliliters) of good gin will also contribute gamy nuances to the sauce. (Purists may argue that such a sauce is now a Moscovite, page 90, without the raisins.)

Sauce Chevreuil (Red Wine Sauce for Game)

Sauce chevreuil (literally "deer sauce") is almost identical to sauce poivrade except that ½ cup (125 milliliters) of red wine replaces the marinade or white wine during the final reduction. Classic recipes also suggest adding ham to the mirepoix and meat trimmings during caramelization of the flavor base.

Sauce Grand-Veneur (Cream-Finished Sauce Poivrade)

Sauce grand-veneur is a poivrade finished with cream and lightly sweetened with red currant jelly. It is delicious when served with game. To 2 cups (500 milliliters) of sauce poivrade that has not been finished with butter, add 1 tablespoon (15 milliliters) of red currant jelly and ½ cup (125 milliliters) of heavy cream. If necessary, the sauce can be lightly reduced. Yield: 2½ cups (625 milliliters).

Sauce Diane (Whipped Cream and Truffle–Finished Game Sauce)

Sauce Diane is simply a sauce poivrade that is folded with whipped cream just before serving. It has a light, airy texture along with incredible depth of flavor. Classic authors call for truffle slices cut into crescent shapes (use a small cookie cutter) and cubes of hard-boiled egg white to be added at the end. The sauce is improved by eliminating the egg white. It is not essential to finish the sauce with truffles, though when used they will add a whole new dimension to the sauce. Cutting them into crescent shapes is a nineteenth-century affectation, and their flavor will certainly not suffer if they are julienned, sliced, or chopped. It is also possible to impart the flavor of truffles by whisking Truffle Butter (page 419) into the sauce before folding in the whipped cream, or by storing the sliced truffles overnight in the refrigerator in the cream to be whipped.

Combine 5 fluid ounces (150 milliliters) of sauce poivrade (either classic or meat glace based) with ¼ cup (60 milliliters) of heavy cream that has been beaten until medium-stiff. Do not overbeat the cream, or it will leave tiny globules of fat on the surface of the finished sauce. Finish the sauce with 1 tablespoon (15 milliliters) of chopped truffles. Yield: 1 cup (250 milliliters).

Make sure that the sauce poivrade is well reduced and quite thick before folding it with the whipped cream. Otherwise, the mixture will separate into a layer of runny sauce covered with a layer of whipped cream. Do not try to serve this sauce too hot, or the whipped cream will fall and the sauce will turn runny.

Sauce Moscovite (Juniper-Infused Sauce Poivrade)

This obscure poivrade-based sauce is flavored with juniper berries and Malaga, a fortified wine that is difficult to obtain in the United States. Other fortified wines, such as Madeira or port, can also be used. Juniper berries are excellent for reinforcing, even mimicking, the flavor of game. In classic recipes the sauce is finished with white raisins and toasted almonds or pine nuts.

Add ½ cup (125 milliliters) of Malaga wine and 10 crushed juniper berries to 2 cups (500 milliliters) of sauce poivrade. Gently simmer the sauce for 15 to 20 minutes to reduce the wine and infuse the juniper. Strain through a fine chinois. Add 1 ounce (25 grams) of white raisins and 1 ounce (25 grams) of toasted almonds or pine nuts. Yield: 2 cups (500 milliliters).

Other Vinegar-Based Sauces

Sauce Piquante

Sauce piquante is most often used for grilled meats or pork. Sauces for grilled meats and pork (such as Robert and charcutière) should always be fairly acidic, to cut through the richness of pork and the assertive, smoky flavor of barbecued and grilled meats. When preparing these sauces with meat glace, be careful not to use too much butter in the end, or the sauce will be too rich and its directness will be lost.

Classic Method. Combine 5 fluid ounces (150 milliliters) of white wine and 5 fluid ounces (150 milliliters) of white wine vinegar with 2 tablespoons (30 milliliters) of finely chopped shallots. Reduce the mixture by half, and add 1¼ cups (300 milliliters) of demi-glace. Simmer for 10 minutes more, being careful to skim off any scum that floats to the surface. Remove the saucepan from the heat and add 1 tablespoon (15 milliliters) of sliced cornichons (sour gherkins) and 1 teaspoon (5 milliliters) each of chopped parsley, chervil, and tarragon. Yield: 2 cups (500 milliliters).

Meat-Glace Method. Follow the procedure for the classic method, but add 3 tablespoons (45 milliliters) of meat glace to the white wine–vinegar reduction instead of the demi-glace. Finish with the chopped herbs and 1 ounce (30 grams) of butter. Yield: 2 cups (500 milliliters).

Unthickened Method. Combine the white wine, vinegar, and shallots as for the classic method, but reduce the infusion by three-quarters instead of by half. Add 1¼ cups (300 milliliters) of full-bodied brown stock to the reduction, and simmer the mixture slowly for 20 minutes. Strain through a fine chinois. Yield: 1 cup (250 milliliters).

Sauce Zingara A

There are two types of sauce Zingara. Zingara A, based on a very acidic reduction of vinegar and shallots, is one of the few breadcrumb-thickened sauces that survive in the classic repertoire. (Zingara B, page 178, is based on white wine).

Combine ½ cup (125 milliliters) of white wine vinegar with 1 tablespoon (15 milliliters) of finely chopped shallots. Infuse the flavor of the shallots in the vinegar by reducing by half. While the vinegar is reducing, gently cook 3 ounces (75 grams) of breadcrumbs in 2 ounces (60 grams) of butter. Cook the breadcrumbs until they begin to smell toasty, but do not let them brown. Add ¾ cup (185 milliliters) of brown chicken or beef stock to the vinegar reduction, and add the breadcrumbs. Simmer the sauce for 5 to 10 minutes. Finish the sauce with 1 tablespoon (15 milliliters) of finely chopped parsley. (Some recipes suggest finishing the sauce with lemon juice, but taste the sauce first: It is probably already acidic enough.) Yield: 1 cup (250 milliliters).

DERIVATIVE BROWN SAUCES WITHOUT WINE OR VINEGAR

Most derivative brown sauces are prepared by infusing flavorful ingredients, such as mirepoix, shallots, ham, or onions, in wine or vinegar. For delicately flavored sauces, the acidity of wine and vinegar can be troublesome. This is especially true of sauces containing truffles or mushrooms. And sauces that contain other acidic ingredients, such as tomatoes or sorrel, do not usually benefit from the additional acid derived from wine and vinegar.

Sauce Périgueux and Sauce Périgourdine

Both of these sauces are traditionally prepared by adding truffle essence to demi-glace. The only difference between the two is that Périgueux sauce is finished with chopped truffles whereas périgourdine sauce is finished with truffles turned in miniature olive shapes or with whole truffle slices. If you are using whole truffles, it is certainly far more dramatic to slice them than it is to chop them. If you have a Japanese mandoline (see page 29), a single truffle will supply fifty to sixty slices. Both of these sauces will benefit by finishing with Truffle Butter (page 419).

Truffle Essence (page 108) is used in these sauces to reinforce the flavor of the truffles. If none is available, it can be replaced with a full-bodied brown stock.

Classic Method. Bring 1½ cups (375 milliliters) of demi-glace or coulis to a slow simmer. Skim off any froth that rises to the surface. Add 5 tablespoons (75 milliliters) of truffle essence and 2 ounces (50 grams) of either chopped or sliced truffles. Remove the saucepan from the stove and cover with a tight-fitting lid, allowing the truffles to infuse into the sauce for at least 15 minutes. Yield: 2 cups (500 milliliters).

Meat-Glace Method. Bring 5 tablespoons (75 milliliters) of appropriately flavored brown stock (that is, beef stock for beef, duck stock for duck, and so forth) to a slow simmer. Skim off any froth that rises to the top, and add 5 tablespoons (75 milliliters) of truffle essence and 3 tablespoons (45 milliliters) of meat glace. As soon as the meat glace dissolves in the hot stock, whisk in 2 ounces (50 grams) of butter or Truffle Butter (page 419), and add 2 ounces (50 grams) of chopped or sliced truffles. Cover the saucepan and put the sauce back on the stove just long enough for it to come to a simmer and give it sheen. Cover the sauce and remove the pan from direct heat (the sauce should not boil). Let the truffles infuse for at least 10 minutes in the covered saucepan before serving. Yield: 1 cup (250 milliliters).

Unthickened Method. A consommé-like version of sauce périgourdine looks striking when served on a deep white plate or wide bowl. The easiest way to prepare an unbound version is to simply infuse truffle slices in a deeply flavored beef or appropriately flavored clear brown stock for 10 minutes over low heat.

TOURNEDOS ROSSINI
Filets of Beef with Sauce Périgueux

A *tournedo* is a perfect center-cut filet mignon from the tenderloin. Tournedos should always have the chain muscle that runs along one side of the filet removed. The classic "Rossini" garniture consists of a slice of terrine of foie gras and sauce Périgueux, made with chopped and sliced truffles.

YIELD: 4 MAIN-COURSE SERVINGS

center-cut filets mignons, chain muscle removed, 6 ounces (175 grams) each	4	4
salt and pepper	to taste	to taste
clarified butter or vegetable oil	2 tablespoons	30 milliliters
foie gras terrine slices, 2 ounces (60 grams) each, warmed in a low oven	4	4
sauce périgueux	¾ cup	185 milliliters

1. Season the tournedos and allow them to come to room temperature.
2. In a 2-quart (2 liter) straight-sided sauté pan, sauté the tournedos in the clarified butter on both sides to the desired doneness, preferably rare. Pat off the cooking fat with paper towels and place on heated plates.
3. Place a slice of warm foie gras on each tournedo. Pour the sauce over and serve. See the photograph in the color plates.

Sauce aux Champignons (Mushroom Sauce)

Mushroom sauce is simply a combination of reduced mushroom essence and demi-glace or meat glace and butter.

Classic Method. Reduce 5 fluid ounces (150 milliliters) of Mushroom Essence (page 107) in half. Add 1¾ cups (450 milliliters) of demi-glace to the reduction. Bring the mixture to a simmer and skim off any froth that rises to the surface. Strain through a fine chinois and whisk in 1 ounce (30 grams) of butter. Finish with 2 ounces (60 grams) of button mushrooms that have been simmered in a covered saucepan in ¼ cup (60 milliliters) of water or light stock. The cooking liquid from the mushrooms can be used to supply or augment the mushroom essence. Yield: 2 cups (500 milliliters).

Meat-Glace Method. Add ¼ cup (60 milliliters) of meat glace to 5 fluid ounces (150 milliliters) of Mushroom Essence (page 107). Gently simmer the mixture long enough for the meat glace to dissolve. Finish with 2 ounces (60 grams) of butter and 1 ounce (30 grams) of cooked button mushrooms. Yield: 1 cup (250 milliliters).

Unthickened Method. Full-flavored brown stock can be infused with mushrooms by bringing equal parts mushrooms and stock by weight to a simmer and letting the mixture infuse for 10 minutes in a covered pot. That is, use ½ pound (250 grams) of mushrooms per cup (250 milliliters) of stock.

Alternatives and Variations. This sauce can be used as a model for sauces based on a wide variety of wild mushrooms. The mushrooms are first cooked in a small amount of water or stock, which then becomes the basis for the sauce. The cooked mushrooms are reserved and then added at the end. Although the foregoing recipes call for whole button mushrooms, leaving the mushrooms whole is impractical with large wild mushrooms such as *Boletus edulis* (cèpes). It is, of course, acceptable to slice or cube the mushrooms.

The flavor of mushrooms can be made more assertive by first sautéing them in hot olive oil, goose fat, or butter until they brown. Some recipes call for sprinkling the mushrooms with chopped shallots, chopped garlic, or persillade.

Sauce Italienne

This sauce is almost identical to Sauce Duxelles (page 176) except that traditionally sauce italienne contains ham.

Classic Method. Add 5 tablespoons (75 milliliters) of tomato purée to 1½ cups (375 milliliters) of demi-glace. Simmer the sauce gently for 10 minutes. Skim off any scum or froth that floats to the surface. Add 2 tablespoons (30 milliliters) of duxelles and 2 ounces (50 grams) of ham cut into small cubes (brunoise). Finish the sauce with 1 teaspoon (5 milliliters) each of chopped parsley, chervil, and tarragon. Yield: 2 cups (500 milliliters).

Meat-Glace Method. Combine 5 fluid ounces (150 milliliters) of brown chicken or beef stock with ¼ cup (60 milliliters) of tomato purée. Dissolve ¼ cup (60 milliliters) of meat glace into the mixture. Finish the sauce with 1 tablespoon (15 milliliters) duxelles, 1 ounce (25 grams) of ham cut into

Using Meat Trimmings to Improve Brown Sauces

Virtually all brown sauces are based on reduced broth that provides a meaty flavor and sauce-like consistency from the gelatin in the reduced stock. But many of meat's most direct and vital flavors are cooked off during the long simmering of the stock. To restore these flavors, follow the same principles as when making a jus—augment the meat flavors with caramelized meat juices. For example, if you're making a filet with a bordelaise sauce and the sauce calls for meat glace, try cooking some meat trimmings in a little butter with a little onion until the trimmings brown. Add some stock or sauce, 1 cup (250 milliliters) or so, and boil it down until it caramelizes on the bottom of the pan. Deglaze with another cup of stock and repeat as many times as you wish or can afford. Add the final deglazing to your sauce and reduce to the desired consistency before adding any enrichment such as butter.

cubes, 1 ounce (30 grams) of butter, and 1 teaspoon (5 milliliters) each of chopped parsley, chervil, and tarragon. Yield: 1½ cups (375 milliliters).

Unthickened Method. Sauce italienne can be reinterpreted by finishing a full-flavored brown stock with cubes of fresh tomatoes, a mushroom julienne or tiny chanterelles, and the cubes of ham and herbs called for in the classic sauce.

TIPS ON IMPROVING THE FLAVOR OF BROWN SAUCES

Using Meat Trimmings

Restaurant cooks often develop the habit of tossing meat trimmings indiscriminately into the always-simmering stockpot. If the fat has been carefully removed, these trimmings will help enrich the stock, but much of their flavor will be lost after the long simmering and reduction that stock often undergoes.

In a well-organized kitchen, these meat trimmings can be put to better use. A brown sauce will always be improved if meat is sweated and caramelized along with the aromatic vegetables used to prepare the flavor base. Early French recipes almost invariably called for lining the bottom of the pot with a slice of ham or veal as a preliminary step in sauce preparation.

Cured unsmoked ham will also contribute enormously to the flavor and complexity of a sauce. Cut the ham into cubes and sweat it along with the aromatic vegetables used to make the flavor base.

Successive Caramelization

The majority of classic brown sauce recipes combine raw or gently sweated aromatic vegetables with wine or stock before adding demi-glace. The flavor of these sauces can be greatly improved if the aromatic vegetables are cooked long enough with meat trimmings or ham so that their juices fall to the bottom of the saucepan and lightly caramelize. This process can be repeated by moistening the ingredients with stock or wine and reducing the liquid until it forms a glace and caramelizes a second or third time on the bottom of the pot. When the vegetables and meats used for the sauce base have been caramelized in this way, they are then ready for the final moistening with coulis, demi-glace, or stock. After the final moistening, the glazed vegetables and meat trimmings should not be simmered for more than 45 minutes, or the deep, meaty flavor brought out by successive caramelization will be lost. In classic French sauce making, this technique is called *faire tomber à glace*—literally, "to cause to fall to a glaze."

This procedure is time consuming because the pot has to be closely watched so the juices do not overreduce and burn, but the technique will give a fresh jus-like character to the sauce.

Increasing Acidity

Long-simmered brown sauces, even when carefully prepared with the best ingredients, often taste flat, usually because during the long reduction, the volatile flavor components in the meats, herbs, and vegetables have been cooked off. A small amount of good-quality wine vinegar (anywhere from a few drops to a few teaspoons per cup of sauce) added to the sauce near the end will awaken the flavor.

Reducing Acidity

Even experienced professional chefs are perplexed about correcting a sauce that has become too acidic as a result of using a poorly chosen wine for cooking or because of the reduction of acidic ingredients such as tomatoes. The obvious solution is to add sugar. Some sauces, such as long-simmered tomato sauces, benefit from a little sugar, which when used carefully will compensate for the lack of natural sugar that would have been present if the tomatoes were ripe.

In brown sauces, sugar rarely melds successfully with the other flavors and often tastes out of place even when used discreetly. For this reason, chefs usually prefer to introduce sweetness into a sauce by adding a small amount of fortified wine such as port or Madeira.

Although sweetness seems the obvious counterbalance to excess acidity in a sauce, there are instances when a particular kind of tartness refuses to be attenuated or balanced by sweetness alone. Although it sounds like a contradiction, a sauce's tartness is often softened and brought into perspective by adding vinegar. The best method for dealing with stubborn, excess acidity is to work with the sauce before the addition of butter so that, if necessary, its consistency can be adjusted by reduction. Add a small amount of port and reduce the sauce slightly to evaporate the alcohol. Keep doing this bit by bit until the sweetness begins to be barely perceptible. Then add a small amount of wine vinegar—just enough so that you can no longer taste the sweetness of the port. Add a bit more port, then a bit more vinegar. Keep repeating this process, going back and forth between port and vinegar, until the sauce's acidity is in balance with the other flavors.

Adding Cognac, Armagnac, or Kirsch

A teaspoon or two (5 to 10 milliliters) of Cognac or Armagnac added to 1 cup (250 milliliters) of sauce at the very end of cooking will give complexity and depth to a sauce's flavor. Once the Cognac or Armagnac has been added, a sauce should be held at a simmer for 10 to 15 seconds to evaporate the alcohol.

Kirsch is particularly useful for bringing out the natural fruitiness of red wine– and fortified wine–based sauces. Use only a few drops at a time, tasting all the while. Be careful in your choice of kirsch (see "Fruit Brandies," page 76).

Using Gastrique

The use of gastrique has traditionally been limited to specific sweet-and-sour sauces, which nowadays are most often served with duck. The delicate balance of bitterness, tartness, and sweetness characteristic of a carefully prepared gastrique will often enhance a variety of other brown sauces as well.

Finishing with Fresh Herbs

As noted previously, sauces that have been greatly reduced or cooked for long periods will often end up tasting flat. A small bouquet garni containing a sprig of thyme, a piece of bay leaf, and a small bunch of parsley can be simmered with the reduced stock for about an hour before the stock is strained and added to the sauce's flavor base. The aromatic flavor of the herbs will help restore the stock's flavor.

A quick way of refreshing the flavor of almost any sauce is to finish it with freshly chopped parsley, chervil, or chives. None of these herbs will overpower the sauce, either when used alone or in a fines herbes mixture without tarragon.

IMPROVISING BROWN SAUCES

When preparing a classic French sauce, the skillful saucier constantly adjusts the sauce's flavor, consistency, and color. Several brown sauce methods have been presented in this chapter, including classic demi-glace, natural coulis, meat glace, and unbound versions. Experienced sauciers rarely adhere to one method alone when constructing a sauce and will usually prepare a sauce using a combination of methods, sometimes inventing and improvising as they go along.

As an example, consider a sauce hussarde. The flavor base is prepared by gently sweating onions and shallots in butter and then adding white wine, which is reduced by half. If, at this point, the chef has on hand a full-flavored brown stock but no demi-glace, he or she could add flour to the sweating onion-shallot mixture to ensure that the sauce quickly develops a lightly thickened consistency. If the chef wants to avoid flour, and if time and budget permit, he or she may decide to reduce the brown stock until it has the consistency of a natural coulis. Or he or she might decide, after adding the stock, to thicken the sauce with a little cornstarch or arrowroot, combined first with cold water. If demiglace is on hand, the chef may decide to combine techniques and use demi-glace along with a full-flavored brown stock or jus and then adjust the consistency of the sauce with meat glace. He or she may then decide to finish the sauce with butter or cream. Or the chef may decide to keep the sauce unbound except for a small amount of butter added at the end. The saucier's ability to shift among techniques and methods allows the creation of the best possible sauce, given the limits of time, cost, and clientele.

When the chef wants to design a sauce to accompany meats, he or she must first decide whether the purpose of the sauce is to concentrate and extend the natural flavors of the meat or whether the sauce is to function as a condiment or accent. If the sauce's role is to concentrate or extend the inherent flavors of

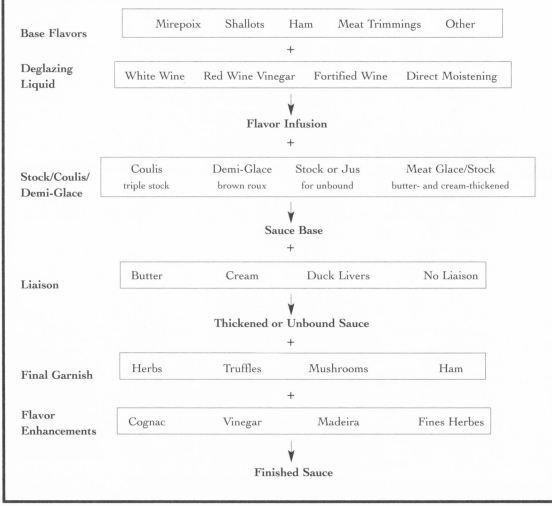

Preparing Stock-Based Brown Sauces

The stages used to prepare a classic French sauce or a modern variation can be traced in this chart. Moving down from the top of this chart, one or more ingredients can be chosen from each box for either a classic or improvised sauce, for a total of 5,120 sauce possibilities.

Base Flavors | Mirepoix   Shallots   Ham   Meat Trimmings   Other

+

Deglazing Liquid | White Wine   Red Wine Vinegar   Fortified Wine   Direct Moistening

↓

Flavor Infusion

+

Stock/Coulis/ Demi-Glace | Coulis *(triple stock)*   Demi-Glace *(brown roux)*   Stock or Jus *(for unbound)*   Meat Glace/Stock *(butter- and cream-thickened)*

↓

Sauce Base

+

Liaison | Butter   Cream   Duck Livers   No Liaison

↓

Thickened or Unbound Sauce

+

Final Garnish | Herbs   Truffles   Mushrooms   Ham

+

Flavor Enhancements | Cognac   Vinegar   Madeira   Fines Herbes

↓

Finished Sauce

the meat, the chef should combine classic brown sauce techniques with integral sauce methods (see Chapter 9, "Integral Meat Sauces," page 221) and should take care that flavor elements used to finish the sauce do not mask the meat's natural flavors. If, however, the primary function of the sauce is to accent and juxtapose with the flavors of the meat, then all the saucier must consider is how the sauce will be presented (which will help decide its texture) and what its flavor will be. As the sauce hussarde example illustrates, a sauce's consistency can be manipulated by shifting among several techniques.

Whereas the methods for constructing a sauce can be categorized and illustrated using classic French sauces as examples, the final choice of how to flavor a sauce will depend on whim, setting, availability of ingredients, and a variety of circumstances. The ethnic or regional character of the food will usually provide a set of ingredients for the saucier to use as a source of flavor ideas.

For example, in a restaurant serving Mexican food, the chef may decide to use a purée of tomatillos instead of tomato purée, or to sweat garlic and hot peppers instead of shallots for the flavor base. Instead of using parsley and chervil to finish the sauce, he or she may choose cilantro. In a restaurant serving Thai

Troubleshooting Brown Sauces

Problem	Probable Cause	Solution
Too thin; watery consistency and flavor	Stock too thin Insufficient reduction	Check stock method Reduce to correct consistency before finishing sauce
Too thick; sticky when tasted	Overly reduced Too much meat glace added	Thin with stock or wine if appropriate
Pale color	Vegetables and meats for stock insufficiently browned	Add vegetables caramelized with stock to sauce
Flat taste	Long cooking or reduction Lack of acidity	Add vinegar Add freshly chopped parsley, chives, or chervil Add fortified wines, gastrique
Greasy or oily texture and appearance	Stock was allowed to boil and was inadequately skimmed	Try slow simmering and skimming first Reduce sauce until it breaks and fat separates
Too sweet	Too many vegetables used to prepare stock Too much fortified wine Excessive reduction	Add small amount vinegar and Cognac
Too salty	Overly reduced stock (this is more common with stocks made with meat only)	Lengthen with butter, cream, or light stock; serve as sauce with thinner consistency
Too acidic	Improperly chosen cooking wine Wine reduced without stock or trimmings Too much vinegar added	Balance with fortified wine and vinegar

food, the saucier might replace the vinegar called for in a flavor base with an infusion of lemongrass and then finish the sauce with coconut milk instead of butter.

Sometimes the chef will want to design a sauce around a special ingredient, perhaps a newly found, locally grown herb, a basket of fresh morels, or a particularly fat and stinky truffle. The emphasis is then on how best to extract and concentrate the ingredient's individual flavor. In a sense, the meat then becomes the backdrop for the sauce.

Because of their potential for subtlety, brown sauces are usually enhanced when served with wine. At times a chef will need to design sauces around a menu highlighting a special bottle or type of wine. This task is often very difficult. Many chefs mistakenly assume that the sauce should share as many flavors with the wine as possible, whereas, in fact, a wine's nuances are better showcased when they contrast gently with but are not overpowered by the flavors of food. Considering the origin of the wine will be helpful in deciding on appropriate flavors for the sauce.

TIPS FOR THE RESTAURANT CHEF

Brown sauces were originally designed to streamline the organization of professional kitchens. A modern kitchen, where stocks and glaces are made as part of the daily routine, will always have on hand the necessary bases for preparing classic and improvised sauces. Because the sauce bases are prepared in advance, the cooks are freed from last-minute reductions and can put together complicated, time-consuming sauces in a matter of minutes.

The advantages of having standard sauce bases on hand in the professional kitchen are obvious. Unfortunately, the long-simmered stocks and glaces of the classic French kitchen can sometimes detract from the character and individuality of different types of dishes. It is perhaps for this reason that home-cooked meals are often satisfying in a way that restaurant meals are not. Consequently, many contemporary chefs have at least partially abandoned many of the traditional techniques used in classic sauce making and kitchen organization and are instead preparing integral sauces to order, keeping little in reserve beyond some freshly made stocks.

Some restaurants may use only chicken stock as an all-purpose moistening and deglazing liquid for made-to-order sauces. It can be prepared in various versions—reduced, as a twice-moistened jus, and so on. Preparing meat glace is time consuming, but once the glace is finished, it is easy to store and always useful for last-minute sauces. Coulis, even the alternative version described at the beginning of this chapter, is expensive and time consuming to make, but any restaurant willing to invest in it will be able to prepare magnificent sauces.

STOCK-BASED AND NONINTEGRAL FISH SAUCES

The best fish sauces are integral sauces prepared using the methods in Chapter 10, when a sauce is made at the same time or immediately after the fish is cooked. In many restaurant or catering situations, however, it is impractical to prepare a sauce at the last minute. Over the centuries, chefs have designed sauce-making methods to deal with the constraints imposed when limited personnel are available to prepare dishes for a large number of people. In these settings, a batch of sauce is prepared in advance and ladled out over or around the cooked fish as it is needed.

In classic French cooking, fish sauces usually capture the flavor of the fish itself. The development of fish stock was the natural outcome of preparing integral-like sauces in advance. In one sense, stock-based sauces for fish are integral sauces made ahead of time with fish heads and bones.

For hundreds of years, and until the last two or three decades, fish velouté has been the basis for the majority of stock-based fish sauces. Fish velouté is fish stock thickened with roux, then flavored with a variety of infusions, herbs, compound butters, cream, and wines, to produce the whole range of classic derivative fish sauces.

Starting in the 1950s and 1960s, roux-thickened sauces were gradually eliminated, the idea being that flour makes a sauce needlessly rich and detracts from its finesse and clear flavor. (Actually, the sauces that replaced the old flour-thickened sauces are far richer.) Traditional fish velouté was replaced with sauces based on reduced fish stock (fish glace, or *glace de poisson*) and reduced cream, butter, or a combination of both. Egg yolk–thickened hollandaise-type sauces containing reduced fish stock, sabayon sauces, sauces thickened with vegetable purées, and allemande-type sauces (thickened with egg yolk like a crème anglaise but containing no flour) are other attempts to eliminate flour from the kitchen.

Most of the sauce-making methods that were developed to replace the classic roux-thickened sauce techniques were designed to duplicate the thick consistency of the classic sauces. For this reason, many of these sauces can be extremely heavy and rich—most of the cream and butter is used not to improve the flavor of the sauce but to give it a supposedly appropriate texture and consistency.

Today, many of the butter- and cream-thickened sauces popular in the 1960s and 1970s have given way to lighter, broth-like versions. These light but intensely flavored sauces were made possible by two innovations in the dining room: deep plates with rims (*assiettes creuses*) that will hold a sauce almost like a soup, and the sauce spoon (*cuillère à sauce*), which enables the diner to sip the sauce without having to rely on the sauce clinging to the fish to get it from plate to mouth. Instead of serving the fish coated with a sauce, it is surrounded with the sauce, like a fish stew or even soup.

CLASSIC FRENCH FISH SAUCES

Although today's chefs have abandoned many of these classic sauces, the sauces still provide valuable models and flavor combinations. Most of these sauces begin with an infusion of flavor components, such as white wine, shallots, various herbs, and mushroom essence. Fish velouté is added to the infusion, and the sauce is then enriched with any number of elements, such as egg yolks, cream, butter, compound butters, and crustacean butters.

Classic French Fish Sauces

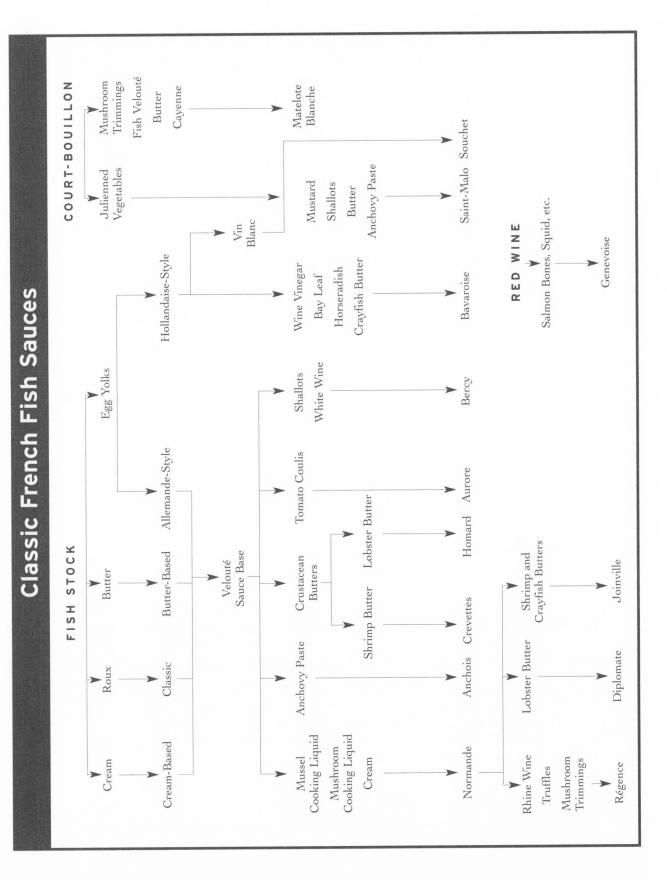

In flourless versions of these classics, the fish velouté is replaced with a much smaller quantity of fish glace; the sauce is then finished with many of the same enriching ingredients as the original versions.

Contemporary broth-textured versions of classic fish sauces use a small amount of freshly prepared fish stock or may even replace the fish stock with a light vegetable stock (court-bouillon). At no point is the fish stock (if it is used) or the finished sauce reduced, the feeling being that reduced fish stock and fish sauces develop a strong, flat, fishy flavor. Contemporary fish sauces often include acidic elements, such as vinegar, lemon or lime juice, or verjuice, which give them a brighter, more assertive flavor than their classic counterparts. Contemporary sauces and contemporary interpretations of classic sauces need to be more intensely flavored than the traditional versions because, in most cases, less of the sauce is served: 2 to 3 tablespoons (30 to 45 milliliters) is typical.

FISH VELOUTÉ

YIELD: 1 QUART (1 LITER)

fresh fish stock	1½ quarts	1.5 liters
butter	1 ounce	30 grams
flour	3 tablespoons	45 milliliters

1. Bring the fish stock to a simmer in a 2-quart (2 liter) saucepan. Skim off any froth that floats to the surface.
2. Prepare a white roux with the butter and flour; cook it in a heavy-bottomed 2-quart (2 liter) saucepan over low heat for 5 to 10 minutes.
3. Remove the roux from the heat and pour in the simmering fish stock. Whisk the mixture to dissolve the roux.
4. Place the mixture on top of the stove and allow it to come to a slow simmer. Make sure that the saucepan is placed slightly to one side of the flame; this encourages a film to form to one side of the sauce, where it can be more easily skimmed.
5. Skim the velouté for approximately 30 minutes until it has reduced down to 1 quart (1 liter). Strain through a fine chinois. Stir the velouté while it is cooling to prevent a skin from forming on its surface.

Sauce Normande

Sauce normande is one of the most important of the classic fish sauces because it is relatively neutral but full flavored, making it good in itself as well as adaptable to variation. The classic version uses mussel cooking liquid, but other shellfish cooking liquids, such as those from clams or cockles, can be used with excellent results.

Because sauce normande contains so many of the elements of modern fish sauces, it is useful to examine the sauce in detail, with an eye to possible variations and modifications.

●━━● CLASSIC SAUCE NORMANDE

A classic sauce normande is based on fish velouté to which mushroom cooking liquid, mussel cooking liquid, and additional fish stock are added, giving the sauce deeper flavor and a more complex character. The sauce is finished with heavy cream (in the manner of a Sauce Suprême, page 142), lemon juice, and egg yolks (in the manner of a Sauce Allemande, page 142). Classic recipes call for reducing the sauce after the addition of the egg yolks (the idea being that the egg yolks are stabilized by the flour) but this is risky, as the yolks often curdle. A more reliable system is to complete reduction before adding the egg yolks and then gently cook the sauce—without boiling—just long enough for the egg yolks to contribute their characteristic satiny texture to the sauce.

YIELD: 1 QUART (1 LITER)

fish velouté	3 cups	750 milliliters
mushroom cooking liquid	½ cup	125 milliliters
mussel cooking liquid	½ cup	125 milliliters
fresh fish stock	1 cup	250 milliliters
heavy cream	1½ cups	375 milliliters
egg yolks	5	5
lemon juice	2 tablespoons	30 milliliters
butter	4 ounces	125 grams
salt and pepper	to taste	to taste

1. Combine the fish velouté, mushroom cooking liquid, mussel cooking liquid, fish stock, and cream in a 2-quart (2 liter) saucepan and bring the mixture to a simmer.
2. Reduce the sauce by about one-third over medium to high heat, or until the sauce takes on the desired consistency.
3. Whisk 1 cup (250 milliliters) of the hot sauce into the egg yolks in a small mixing bowl. Stir this mixture into the rest of the sauce off the heat. Heat the sauce over low to medium heat, while stirring, until it thickens slightly and becomes satiny. Do not allow it to boil.
4. Stir the lemon juice and butter into the sauce and strain through a fine chinois. Season to taste with salt and pepper.

Contemporary Variations of Sauce Normande

Although classic sauce normande is rarely prepared in restaurants today, many contemporary fish sauces contain similar elements. Modern fish sauces contain no flour and rarely use three rich liaisons—cream, butter, and egg yolks.

Some contemporary normande-style sauces contain only a few of the traditional flavor elements. Mussel or clam cooking liquid finished with a small amount of heavy cream is in itself an excellent sauce, as is mushroom cooking liquid, especially if made with morels or other wild mushrooms.

When preparing a contemporary sauce normande, it is important to decide how the completed dish will be presented. If a thick sauce is needed to coat the fish or the fish fillets, the basic flavor elements (fish stock, mussel cooking liquid, and mushroom cooking liquid) will have to be reduced until they are almost dry, and a relatively large amount of cream, butter, or some combination will be required to give the sauce the necessary consistency. A fish sauce made in this way will have a smoother, more unctuous consistency than a traditional sauce normande but will be extremely rich because its consistency is derived almost entirely from fats. A less dense sauce will require far less cream or butter and very little, if any, reduction.

CREAM-BASED SAUCE NORMANDE

The cream-based model for sauce normande is analogous to the contemporary Sauce Suprême (page 142).

YIELD: 1 QUART (1 LITER)

fresh fish stock	2 cups	500 milliliters
mushroom cooking liquid	1 cup	250 milliliters
mussel or clam cooking liquid	1 cup	250 milliliters
heavy cream	1 quart	1 liter
butter	4 ounces	125 grams
salt and pepper	to taste	to taste

1. Combine the fish stock, mushroom cooking liquid, and mussel cooking liquid in a 4-quart (4 liter) saucepan and reduce the mixture until only 1 cup (250 milliliters) remains. (Be careful to keep the flames from wrapping around the sides of the saucepan or the insides of the saucepan will turn dark brown and will discolor the sauce when the cream is added.)
2. Add the cream to the reduction and boil it over medium heat, while whisking, until the sauce has the desired consistency.
3. Swirl in the butter and adjust the seasonings. (Salt is rarely needed because of the intense saltiness of the mussel or clam cooking liquid.)

BUTTER-BASED SAUCE NORMANDE

In this sauce model, the flavor elements are reduced in the same way as for a reduced-cream version, until they are almost dry. The reduction is then converted into a sauce by whisking in a large amount of butter. The sauce is analogous to a Beurre Blanc (page 410) in which reduced fish stock, mushroom cooking liquid, and mussel or clam cooking liquid replace the white wine–shallot reduction.

YIELD: 1 QUART (1 LITER)

fresh fish stock	2 cups	500 milliliters
mussel or clam cooking liquid	1 cup	250 milliliters
mushroom cooking liquid	1 cup	250 milliliters
heavy cream	1 cup	250 milliliters
cold butter	1 pound	500 grams
salt and pepper	to taste	to taste

1. Combine the fish stock, the mussel cooking liquid, and the mushroom cooking liquid in a 4-quart (4 liter) saucepan and reduce them until only 1 cup (250 milliliters) remains.
2. Add the cream and reduce until the mixture thickens slightly.
3. Cut the butter into large cubes and add one-fourth of it to the hot reduction. Whisk rapidly over medium to high heat until the butter dissolves, add another fourth of the butter, and whisk; continue in this way until all the butter has been added. Adjust the seasonings.

EGG YOLK-BASED SAUCE NORMANDE

Egg yolk–thickened fish sauces can be approached in two ways. The first, analogous to a traditional Sauce Allemande (page 142) or a Crème Anglaise (page 560), is cooked gently on the stove until it thickens. It is never allowed to boil. Sauces thickened in this way have the advantage over cream- and butter-thickened sauces of not requiring reduction of the fish stock and mussel or clam cooking liquid. Consequently, they retain more of their vitality and freshness. The thickness of the sauce can be adjusted by varying the number of egg yolks used, from 8 to 16 yolks per quart (liter) of liquid. Most egg yolk–thickened sauces are finished with butter (about one-tenth by volume). Remember, when using egg yolks, avoid cooking them in aluminum pots.

The second method of thickening with egg yolks involves reducing the flavor elements, whisking them with egg yolks to form a Sabayon (page 564), and then finishing the sauce with varying amounts of whole or clarified butter, in the style of a Sauce Hollandaise (page 381) or sabayon. This method is used for a traditional Sauce Vin Blanc (page 211).

Method 1: Allemande Style

YIELD: 5 CUPS (1.2 LITERS)

fresh fish stock	2 cups	500 milliliters
mussel or clam cooking liquid	1 cup	250 milliliters
mushroom cooking liquid	1 cup	250 milliliters
heavy cream	½ cup	125 milliliters
egg yolks	8	8
butter	4 ounces	125 grams
salt and pepper	to taste	to taste

1. Combine the fish stock, mussel cooking liquid, mushroom cooking liquid, and cream in a 4-quart (4 liter) saucepan. Bring the mixture to a simmer.
2. Whisk the egg yolks until they are smooth and slightly pale.
3. Whisk half of the simmering fish liquid into the egg yolks. Remove the remaining fish liquid from the heat. Whisk the egg yolk mixture into the hot fish liquid.
4. Stir the sauce with a wooden spatula or spoon over low to medium heat until it thickens (a line drawn along the back of the spoon or spatula will remain).
5. Remove the sauce from the heat and continue to stir for a minute or two to cook it slightly and prevent the egg yolks from curdling.
6. Whisk in the butter and adjust the seasonings.

Method 2: Hollandaise Style

YIELD: 2 CUPS (500 MILLILITERS)

fresh fish stock	2 cups	500 milliliters
mussel or clam cooking liquid	1 cup	250 milliliters
mushroom cooking liquid	½ cup	125 milliliters
egg yolks	4	4
solid, melted, or clarified butter	8 ounces	250 grams
salt and pepper	to taste	to taste

1. Combine the fish stock, mussel cooking liquid, and mushroom cooking liquid in a 4-quart (4 liter) saucepan and reduce the mixture until only 6 tablespoons (90 milliliters) remain. Allow the reduction to cool slightly.
2. Whisk the reduction into the egg yolks in a 4-quart (4 liter) saucepan with sloping sides (*sauteuse*). Whisk the mixture over medium heat until it thickens and you can see the bottom of the pan while whisking.
3. Remove the mixture from the heat and whisk for a few seconds more to cool it slightly, so the yolks do not curdle.
4. Whisk in the butter and adjust the seasonings.

COMBINING METHODS

Each of the methods for flavoring and thickening fish sauces has certain disadvantages. Cream and butter sauces are rich and expensive to prepare, egg yolk–thickened sauces sometimes have an eggy taste or a chalky texture, and flour-thickened sauces often taste starchy.

Preparing a successful fish sauce sometimes requires using several techniques. One method is to prepare a very light, classic velouté with one-quarter as much roux as the classic recipe calls for, carefully reducing the velouté by half (skimming carefully and removing any skin that forms on its surface), and then finishing this lightly prethickened base with cream, butter, egg yolks, or a combination of the three.

Derivatives of Fish Velouté and Sauce Normande

Many of the classic fish sauces are based on either fish velouté or sauce normande. Most of these variations are prepared by making an infusion of basic flavors, adding fish velouté or sauce normande as a sauce base and thickener, sometimes reducing the mixture (unless a flourless egg yolk–thickened version is used), and then enriching it with cream, butter, or both. The sauces are usually finished with additional flavorings, such as tomatoes, anchovy butter, herbs, crustacean butter, and the like.

Sauce Anchois (Anchovy Sauce)

Sauce anchois is prepared by adding Anchovy Butter (page 416) to sauce normande and then finishing the sauce with diced anchovy fillets. The anchovy butter should be added to taste, but the usual parameter is one part anchovy butter to nine parts sauce normande and one-half part diced anchovies. If available, use anchovies packed in salt, rather than canned anchovies: Salted anchovies have a better flavor, and it is easier to remove the salt. Soak salted anchovies for 30 minutes in cold water. Remove the two fillets from the backbone and dry them on paper towels. If using canned anchovies, soak the fillets for 5 minutes in cold water and pat them dry on paper towels to remove excess salt and oil.

Sauce Aurore for Fish

Sauce Aurore is usually known as a white sauce for meats, prepared by adding tomato purée to a Sauce Velouté (page 142). A version for fish can be prepared by adding tomato purée to a traditional fish velouté or to any of the versions of sauce normande. A traditional sauce Aurore for fish is made by adding one part tomato purée to three parts fish velouté, reducing if necessary, and then finishing the sauce with butter (one part butter to nine parts sauce).

Flourless variations of sauce Aurore can be prepared by adding tomato purée in the same proportions to the egg yolk–based, cream-based, or butter-based sauces described above.

When ripe summer tomatoes are available, they can be peeled, seeded, chopped, lightly stewed, and added to the Aurore without straining.

Sauce Bercy

This version of sauce Bercy contains similar ingredients to the integral version described in Chapter 10 (see page 296), but is based on fish velouté and made ahead of time.

To prepare the traditional version, add 1 cup (250 milliliters) of white wine and 1 cup (250 milliliters) of fish stock to 2 chopped shallots that have been sweated in butter. Reduce the mixture to 1½ cups (375 milliliters). Add 3 cups (750 milliliters) of fish velouté; finish the sauce with 4 ounces (125 grams) of butter and 1 tablespoon (15 milliliters) of chopped parsley, whisked in off the heat. Yield: 1 quart (1 liter).

Today, a Bercy-type sauce is best prepared by reducing the shallot–white wine–fish stock base more radically and then finishing the sauce with cream or butter, using the same proportions and methods as for a cream- or butter-based sauce normande.

Sauce Matelote Blanche (White Matelote Sauce)

This sauce is prepared by combining reduced court-bouillon with fish velouté and then flavoring the mixture with mushroom trimmings. It is in some ways a precursor of contemporary sauces because of its use of court-bouillon. Many contemporary chefs replace fish stock entirely with court-bouillon.

Add 1 ounce (30 grams) of mushroom trimmings to 1½ cups (375 milliliters) of court-bouillon. Reduce the mixture until ½ cup (125 milliliters) remains. To prepare the traditional version, add 3 cups (750 milliliters) of fish velouté and finish with 5 ounces (150 grams) of butter; season with cayenne pepper. Yield: 1 quart (1 liter).

Flourless versions of this sauce can be prepared by thickening the reduction with cream, butter, or egg yolks using the same proportions as the models presented on pages 206 to 208.

Sauce Régence for Fish

A classic sauce Régence is prepared by adding reduced Rhine wine and fish stock to a sauce normande and infusing the sauce with mushrooms and truffles. Combine 1 cup (250 milliliters) of Alsatian Riesling with 1 cup (250 milliliters) of fish stock. Add 1 ounce (25 grams) of truffle peelings and sliced mushrooms or mushroom stems and reduce the mixture by half. Add 3 cups (750 milliliters) of sauce normande to the reduction. Strain and complete the sauce with chopped truffles, Truffle Butter (page 419), or thin slices of fresh truffle. Yield: 1 quart (1 liter).

Hollandaise-Style Fish Sauces

Sauce Vin Blanc (White Wine Fish Sauce)

Classic white wine fish sauce is prepared using one of two methods, both of which use egg yolks. The first method is based on a sabayon prepared with reduced fish stock and egg yolks, then finished with butter in the same way as a sauce hollandaise. The second method consists of finishing fish velouté with egg yolks and butter as in preparing a sauce allemande.

Hollandaise Method. Reduce 1 cup (250 milliliters) of fish stock (which includes the white wine) by two-thirds. Let the reduction cool and combine it with 5 egg yolks. Whisk the mixture over the heat until it becomes airy and thickens. Finish it with butter in the same way as preparing sauce hollandaise. Classic recipes call for almost 4 ounces (125 grams) of butter per egg yolk, but the sauce can be made lighter by using half as much. Yield: 2 to 3½ cups (500 to 875 milliliters), depending on the amount of butter used.

Allemande Method. Finish 3 cups (750 milliliters) of fish velouté with 4 egg yolks and 4 ounces (125 grams) of butter, or prepare a flourless version by finishing 3 cups (750 milliliters) of fish stock with 8 egg yolks and 4 ounces (125 grams) of butter. The sauce should first be thickened with the egg yolks, with the butter whisked in at the end. Remember, do not let the sauce boil. Yield: 3½ cups (875 milliliters).

Sauce Saint-Malo

This sauce is prepared by finishing a sauce vin blanc with mustard, shallot butter, and anchovy butter or paste. Finish 2 cups (500 milliliters) of sauce vin blanc (hollandaise method) with 2 teaspoons (10 milliliters) of mustard, 1½ ounces (50 grams) of shallot butter, and 1 teaspoon (5 milliliters) of anchovy paste. Yield: 2¼ cups (560 milliliters).

Sauce Souchet

This little-known sauce contains several interesting touches that are useful in contemporary sauce making. A court-bouillon is prepared with a julienne of vegetables; the julienne is then reserved to garnish the fish while the court-bouillon is bound with a sauce vin blanc (hollandaise method) made in advance.

Julienne 1 medium carrot, 1 medium celeriac, and 1 leek. Sweat the julienne for 10 minutes in butter and then pour in 1 cup (250 milliliters) of water or fish stock. Simmer slowly until the vegetables are cooked. Strain out the vegetables and save them to garnish the fish. The cooking liquid can then be used for poaching the fish or directly for making the sauce. Thicken the liquid by whisking in enough sauce vin blanc (hollandaise method) to achieve the desired consistency. Yield: 1 to 2 cups (250 to 500 milliliters), depending on the amount of sauce vin blanc used.

Fish Sauces Flavored with Crustacean and Coral Butters

Crustacean butters are often used to finish fish sauces to give them additional complexity and an appealing red or orange hue. Many of the classic fish sauces that are finished with crustacean butter have a similar taste because it is hard to distinguish among the different crustacean butters. To capture the full complexity of a crustacean's flavor, it is essential to start with the whole living animal (see Chapter 11, "Crustacean Sauces," page 325). The sauces listed below should be thought of as fish sauces nuanced with crustacean butters rather than the full-flavored crustacean sauces that can be found in Chapter 11.

Sauce Bavaroise (Bavarian Sauce)

Combine 1 cup (250 milliliters) of white wine vinegar, 1 bay leaf, 1 sprig of thyme, 1 sprig of parsley, 5 black peppercorns, and 1 tablespoon (15 milliliters) of grated horseradish and reduce by half. Combine the reduction with 4 egg yolks, whisk it over heat until it becomes thick and airy, and then add 1 cup (250 milliliters) of clarified butter. (Clarified butter is essential to make the sauce thick because the sabayon is very light.) Strain the sauce and finish it with 2 ounces (50 grams) of crayfish butter and 2 tablespoons (30 milliliters) of whipped cream. The sauce can also be finished with crayfish tails cut into cubes. Yield: 2 cups (500 milliliters).

Sauce Crevettes (Shrimp Sauce)

This sauce is prepared by finishing fish velouté or sauce béchamel with two types of crustacean butters: the bright red crustacean butter made with crustacean shells, and shrimp butter made with whole shrimp. Both of these butters are described in Chapter 11, "Crustacean Sauces," page 325.

Either traditional fish velouté or flourless versions can be used for the sauce base. If using traditional fish velouté, add ½ cup (125 milliliters) of heavy cream to 2 cups (500 milliliters) of the velouté before adding the butters.

Whisk ½ ounce (15 grams) of red crustacean butter and 1½ ounces (45 grams) of shrimp butter into 2 cups (500 milliliters) of fish velouté. Strain through a fine chinois. Sprinkle in a small amount of cayenne pepper and adjust the seasonings. The sauce can be garnished with cooked shrimp cut into cubes. Yield: 2 cups (500 milliliters).

Sauce Diplomate

Add 1½ ounces (45 grams) of lobster butter to 2 cups (500 milliliters) of sauce normande. Finish the sauce with 1 tablespoon (15 milliliters) of cubed truffles and 1 tablespoon (15 milliliters) of cubed lobster tail. Yield: 2 cups (500 milliliters).

Sauce Homard (Lobster Sauce)

This sauce is identical to a sauce crevettes except that the shrimp butter is replaced with lobster butter. Yield: 2 cups (500 milliliters).

Sauce Joinville

This sauce is identical to a sauce diplomate except that, instead of lobster butter, 1½ tablespoons (25 grams) each of shrimp and crayfish butters are used for every 2 cups (500 milliliters) of sauce normande. Yield: 2 cups (500 milliliters).

⊶ SEA URCHIN SAUCE

Sea urchin butter (equal parts roe and butter) can be used to give a delicate, sea-like flavor to a variety of sauce bases, or the sea urchin roe can be left in chunks and gently infused alone into the sauce base. The following sauce combines the roe with egg yolks and cream and has a very light, soup-like consistency. If a thicker sauce is needed, the shellfish cooking liquid should be reduced with half the cream before the egg yolk–roe mixture is incorporated. Sea urchin sauces are best served with delicate fish dishes such as poached sole, turbot, or other flat fish.

YIELD: 2 CUPS (500 MILLILITERS)

court-bouillon	½ cup	125 milliliters
mussel or clam cooking liquid	½ cup	125 milliliters
heavy cream	¾ cup	185 milliliters
roe from 12 sea urchins		
egg yolks	3	3
finely chopped chives	1 tablespoon	15 milliliters

1. Bring the court-bouillon, mussel cooking liquid, and half the cream to a simmer in a 2-quart (2 liter) saucepan.
2. Remove the roe from the sea urchins and work it through a fine-mesh drum sieve. Combine the strained roe with the egg yolks and the remaining cream.
3. Whisk half of the simmering court-bouillon mixture into the roe–egg yolk–cream mixture. Return to the saucepan.
4. Gently heat the sauce over medium heat until thickened; do not let it boil.
5. Finish the sauce with the chopped chives (or other herbs).

Sauces Using Scallop Coral

Because most American scallops are marketed without the roe, there is little opportunity to use it in sauce making. If fresh scallops with the roe are available, the roe can be removed and incorporated into a sauce. The most direct method is to purée the roe in a food processor, strain it through a drum sieve, and combine it with butter, heavy cream, or egg yolks (as for the Sea Urchin Sauce, page 213) before using it to finish a fish sauce base. Sea scallop roe can also be poached for 2 to 3 minutes before it is puréed and then used to flavor a compound or whipped butter to be served with grilled or sautéed scallops or other seafood.

Red Wine Fish Sauces

Red wine sauces are excellent when served with full-flavored fish such as salmon, fresh mackerel, squid, and tuna. Most recipes for fish sauces discourage using salmon bones for making fish stock because of their strong, sometimes aggressive flavor. Red wine sauces are an exception; a sauce made with a full-bodied red wine and salmon bones makes an assertive yet complex and subtle sauce.

The following recipe can also be prepared with squid. Replace the salmon bones with 2 pounds (1 kilogram) of fresh squid that has been cleaned, well rinsed, and finely sliced.

Red wine fish sauces prepared in this way are similar to the classic sauce genevoise that was made with reduced fish stock bound with roux (sauce espagnole maigre) and finished with anchovy butter.

●━━● RED WINE SAUCE FOR SALMON

YIELD: 2 CUPS (500 MILLILITERS)

bones from an 8- to 10-pound (3.5 to 4.5 kilogram) salmon (including head)		
butter	4½ ounces	140 grams
carrot, coarsely chopped	1 medium	1 medium
onion, coarsely chopped	1 medium	1 medium
garlic cloves, coarsely chopped	3	3
red wine	5 cups	1.2 liters
medium bouquet garni (page 51)	1	1
chopped herbs (parsley, chervil, chives)	2 tablespoons	30 milliliters
red wine or sherry vinegar	1 tablespoon	15 milliliters
salt and pepper	to taste	to taste

1. Remove the gills from the base of the salmon head and chop the head and the spine into 2-inch (5 cm) sections.
2. Melt 1½ ounces (50 grams) of butter in a saucepan and add the carrots, onions, garlic, and salmon bones. Stir over low to medium heat until the vegetables soften and a brown layer of caramelized juices begins to form on the bottom of the pan.
3. Deglaze the pan with 1 cup (250 milliliters) of the red wine. Slowly simmer the mixture, stirring occasionally, until all the wine evaporates and caramelizes a second time on the bottom of the saucepan.
4. Add the rest of the wine and the bouquet garni. Slowly simmer the sauce for 45 minutes.
5. Strain the sauce and reduce it until 1½ cups (375 milliliters) remain.
6. Finish the sauce with the remaining 3 ounces (90 grams) of butter (a smaller amount of beurre manié may be used instead).
7. Add the chopped herbs. (If the sauce must be held before it is served, add the herbs 10 minutes before serving.) Add the vinegar and adjust the seasonings.

Raïto

The Provençals have their own methods of finishing red wine sauces; *raïto* is one of the best known. The sauce is garnished in various ways—sometimes with olives, sometimes capers, and sometimes a combination of the two—but tomato purée is always used to thicken a full-flavored red wine base like the one described above. Walnuts are also occasionally used as an additional liaison. Fish served *en raïto* is usually lightly sautéed before being finished in the sauce.

To make raïto, combine 1 cup (250 milliliters) of the reduction described for red wine sauce for salmon with ½ cup (125 milliliters) of tomato coulis. Finish the sauce by adding 2 to 4 tablespoons (30 to 60 milliliters) of capers, pitted black olives, or both. Although traditional recipes do not suggest it, raïto can also be finished with black olive purée.

CONTEMPORARY FISH SAUCES

Today the best restaurants prepare either integral fish sauces or lightened versions that contain only a small amount of cream and butter—or even none at all. Although many of the ingredients and techniques called for in classic French fish sauces are still used by chefs, roux, large amounts of cream and butter, and even fish stock are giving way to more contemporary methods. Contemporary fish sauces differ from older versions in several important ways:

1. Fish stock and fish glace have largely been replaced by court-bouillon or the cooking liquid from bivalves such as mussels, clams, or cockles. Many chefs feel that fish stock and especially fish glace is too aggressive and fishy tasting.

2. The consistency of fish sauces is often much thinner than in the past. Contemporary sauces often have a consistency similar to unreduced heavy cream.

3. Much less sauce is given per serving. Today, a small amount of fish sauce is often served *around* the fish. Two to 3 tablespoons (30 to 45 milliliters) of sauce per serving is typical.

4. Vegetable purées such as tomato concassée, sorrel purée, and mushroom purée often constitute both the base and liaison of the sauce.

5. Sauces are more direct and intensely flavored than in the past. Because much less sauce is used, an intensely flavored sauce will not overwhelm the fish.

6. Acidic ingredients, such as lime juice, lemon juice, assorted vinegars, and most recently, verjuice, are used in higher proportions.

7. Court-bouillon is no longer prepared using a single standard set of ingredients. Chefs are eager to emphasize the character of specific vegetables, such as fennel or leeks, and will often prepare a court-bouillon with only one or two ingredients. Some chefs are even experimenting with vegetable juices as sauce bases and flavorings.

8. Vinaigrette-like emulsions of oils and acidic ingredients are often used.

9. Combinations of already prepared sauces such as beurre blanc, hollandaise-type sauces, vinaigrettes, and vegetable purées are often used. When butter is added to these sauces, it is usually whisked into an emulsion with water or a small amount of court-bouillon (see Beurre Fondu, page 412) and then spooned or ladled into the sauce rather than being whisked into the sauce while cold.

10. Spices are more widely used. Chefs are looking toward the cooking of India and the Far East as well as the European cooking of the Middle Ages to devise new flavor combinations.

VINAIGRETTE- AND COURT-BOUILLON-BASED CHIVE SAUCE

This sauce is based on court-bouillon that is lightly thickened with butter. It is acidulated with vinaigrette and flavored at the end with chives. The flavor of the sauce can be varied by modifying the court-bouillon and the components in the vinaigrette. The chives may be replaced or augmented with other herbs or spices.

Because vinaigrette is unstable, the court-bouillon, emulsified butter, and the vinaigrette itself should be combined at the last minute. The flavor of the sauce will vary depending on the ingredients used in the vinaigrette.

YIELD: 1 CUP (250 MILLILITERS), ABOUT 10 SERVINGS

court-bouillon (page 102)	2 cups	500 milliliters
lemon juice	1 tablespoon	15 milliliters
water	2 tablespoons	30 milliliters
butter, in chunks	2 ounces	60 grams
basic vinaigrette (page 437)	¼ cup	60 milliliters
finely chopped chives	2 tablespoons	30 milliliters
salt and pepper	to taste	to taste

1. In a 2-quart (2 liter) saucepan, reduce the court-bouillon to 6 tablespoons (90 milliliters).
2. In a 1-quart (1 liter) saucepan, combine the lemon juice and water and bring the mixture to a simmer. Whisk in the butter. Keep this sauce warm.
3. Remove the reduced court-bouillon from the stove and whisk in the emulsified butter.
4. Whisk in the vinaigrette and the chives.
5. Adjust the seasonings. It may also be necessary to adjust the flavor by adding more vinaigrette.

CORIANDER-SCENTED CLAM SAUCE

This sauce is closer to a broth in consistency than a traditional sauce. The basic flavors—clam cooking liquid and mushrooms—give the sauce much of the same character as a classic sauce normande, but the fennel and the coriander give it an exciting, nervous complexity.

To crush the coriander seeds, a small coffee grinder works well. Or use a mortar and pestle or a saucepan on a cutting board.

YIELD: 1½ CUPS (375 MILLILITERS), ABOUT 10 SERVINGS

fennel trimmings (including 1 tablespoon/ 15 milliliters chopped leaves)	4 ounces	125 grams
white wine	½ cup	125 milliliters
water	as needed	as needed
clam cooking liquid	½ cup	125 milliliters
sliced mushrooms or mushroom trimmings	4 ounces	125 grams
heavy cream	6 tablespoons	90 milliliters
coriander seeds	2 teaspoons	10 milliliters
juice of ½ lemon		
or	or	or
verjuice	2 tablespoons	30 milliliters
salt and pepper	to taste	to taste

1. In a 1-quart (1 liter) saucepan, prepare a court-bouillon with the fennel trimmings (without the chopped leaves), white wine, and water. Strain the court-bouillon and reduce it to ½ cup (125 milliliters).
2. Combine the clam cooking liquid and mushrooms in a second 2-quart (2 liter) saucepan and simmer for 5 minutes. Strain the mixture.
3. Combine the clam-mushroom liquid with the reduced court-bouillon.
4. Whisk in the cream.
5. Crush the coriander seeds and add to the sauce. Add the lemon juice or verjuice, a bit at a time. Strain through a fine chinois.
6. Add the chopped fennel leaves. Adjust the seasonings.
7. The sauce can be reduced slightly if necessary, but it should remain light-textured and delicately flavored.

TOMATO-BASED VINAIGRETTE/HOLLANDAISE SAUCE FOR FISH

In classic French cooking, a tomato sauce for fish would be based on fish velouté, which would then be flavored with tomato purée (see Sauce Aurore for Fish, page 209). In the following sauce, the tomato purée becomes the base of the sauce by contributing not only flavor but body. It also functions as an emulsifier for the vinegar and oil. This sauce could also be described as an elaborate vinaigrette finished with sauce hollandaise.

This sauce can be modified by using different vegetable purées as the base, by altering the ingredients in the court-bouillon (or replacing the court-bouillon with shellfish cooking liquids), and by using emulsified or butter sauces other than hollandaise (sauces finished with crustacean and coral butters work well).

YIELD: 2 CUPS (500 MILLILITERS), ABOUT 10 SERVINGS

court-bouillon (page 102)	2 cups	500 milliliters
thick tomato coulis (page 461)	½ cup	125 milliliters
dijon mustard	1 teaspoon	5 milliliters
sherry vinegar	2 tablespoons	30 milliliters
extra-virgin olive oil	¼ cup	60 milliliters
sauce hollandaise (page 381)	½ cup	125 milliliters
salt and pepper	to taste	to taste

1. Reduce the court-bouillon to ½ cup (125 milliliters).
2. Whisk together the tomato coulis, mustard, and vinegar.
3. Whisk the olive oil into the tomato mixture as though you were preparing a vinaigrette.
4. Just before serving, whisk the hot, reduced court-bouillon into the coulis-based vinaigrette.
5. Whisk the vinaigrette into the sauce hollandaise and adjust the seasonings.

SMOKED SALMON AND SHRIMP SAUCE

Smoked salmon can be used to flavor fish sauce in the same way that ham is used along with mirepoix to prepare red wine sauces for meats. The rich, smoky flavor of the smoked salmon is best accented with hot peppers or hot pepper sauce (such as Tabasco), which give it a welcome spiciness. This sauce uses shrimp shells to give it an extra dimension of flavor, but the sauce can be prepared without them. The thickness of the sauce can be adjusted by reducing the cream in varying amounts.

The sauce is best served with full-flavored fish or grilled fish.

shrimp shells	12	12
butter	½ ounce	15 grams
court-bouillon or fish stock	½ cup	125 milliliters
tomatoes, peeled and seeded	3 medium	3 medium
or	*or*	*or*
tomato purée	3 tablespoons	45 milliliters
fresh tarragon sprig	1	1
excellent-quality smoked salmon	2 ounces	50 grams
heavy cream	½ cup	125 milliliters
hot pepper sauce	to taste	to taste

1. Cook the shrimp shells in the butter for about 10 minutes, until they turn pale orange.
2. Add the court-bouillon or fish stock, the tomatoes or purée, and the tarragon sprig to the shrimp shells. Simmer the mixture for 15 minutes and strain it into a second saucepan.
3. Cut the smoked salmon into thin strips about 1 inch (2.5 cm) long. Add the strips to the sauce and simmer for 10 minutes more.
4. Add the cream to the sauce and reduce to the desired consistency.
5. Add hot pepper sauce to taste.

IMPROVISING FISH SAUCES

When improvising any sauce, it is always helpful to have the actual foods that are available within view. Foods that are fresh and in season are almost always appropriate. Some of the best ideas for new dishes or fresh interpretations of old dishes happen while shopping in a large market. Many chefs miss this opportunity because hectic schedules compel them to order food by telephone and have it delivered unseen.

Sometimes a single ingredient will be impossible to pass by because of its beauty, freshness, or rarity and will become the focal point of the sauce. As a rule, the more perfect or inspiring the ingredient, the simpler the preparation need be. Some example approaches follow.

Tomatoes

Perfectly ripe late-summer tomatoes can be lightly stewed into a soup-like base, which is then used as a simple sauce for fish. On those few occasions when perfect tomatoes can be found, little needs to be done to amplify or alter their flavor, but variations might include stewing them with the trimmings from the fish; augmenting their flavor with garlic, fennel, or onions and serving the preparation directly as a sauce; or finishing it with mayonnaise (aïoli, saffron, or another full-flavored type), cream, butter (either directly or after the butter has first been worked into a beurre blanc–like emulsion), compound butters, or vinaigrettes. The tomato can also be cooked down to a naturally thick sauce (see "Tomatoes," page 459) and used as the base for a vinaigrette. Yellow tomatoes can also be used for these sauces and served alone or together with a red tomato sauce for contrast.

A tomato sauce for fish can also be approached from the other direction, by preparing a sauce base such as a cream- or butter-based sauce Aurore and then finishing it with tomato purée or a variation.

Mushrooms

The cooking liquid from mushrooms gives almost any sauce an ineffable finesse and is sometimes used in contemporary kitchens as a replacement for fish stock. When wild mushrooms are available, they can be used to give a deep, mysterious flavor to sauces. Their shapes also provide interesting contrasts for the presentation of the finished plate.

Depending on the types available, mushrooms can be gently stewed in a small amount of water or court-bouillon to provide a liquid sauce base; the stems can then be puréed and used as a liaison and to contribute flavor or serve as the base for a vinaigrette, while the caps can be used to garnish the plate.

Peppers

Grilled or stewed sweet peppers have become a popular addition to fish dishes. Some examples follow.

1. Peppers are stewed, puréed, and strained to convert them into a coulis and then worked into butter. The resulting compound butter is then served with grilled fish.
2. Finely diced (brunoise) peppers are used to coat the surface of grilled or sautéed fish fillets. The diced peppers are sometimes combined with other diced vegetables or lightly bound with other sauces, such as beurre blanc, vinaigrettes, or vegetable purées.
3. Peppers are stewed until soft, moistened with court-bouillon, and strained. The resulting coulis is then converted into a sabayon, which can be served as is or finished with butter (plain, compound, or crustacean) and olive oil and flavored with herbs.
4. Reduced pepper coulis can be used as the base for a hot vinaigrette.
5. Chopped and stewed peppers can be used to flavor a mayonnaise (either a classic andalouse or some variation). The mayonnaise can then be served as accompaniment to cold or deep-fried fish or whisked just before serving with hot fish stock or court-bouillon and used as a hot sauce.
6. The peppers can be grilled (preferably over wood), peeled, and then infused in a small amount of court-bouillon; the infusion is then enriched with butter for a beurre blanc–style butter sauce.

INTEGRAL MEAT SAUCES

Integral sauces are made from the natural juices released by meats, fish, and vegetables during cooking. The methods used to prepare these sauces depend on whether the food is sautéed, poached, braised, roasted, or grilled. A well-made integral sauce is an extract of a food's natural flavors and should capture and heighten the flavor of the food being prepared. Many contemporary chefs have at least partially abandoned many traditional stock-based sauce-making methods in favor of integral sauces, which often have a fuller, more direct, more spontaneous, home-cooked flavor.

INTEGRAL SAUCES FOR SAUTÉED MEATS

Meats are sautéed by rapid cooking in a small amount of hot fat. The technique should not be confused with frying, where meat is cooked by being partially or entirely submerged in hot fat, or with stewing, where meats are often sautéed first in hot fat but then finish cooking in liquid. When meats are sautéed, they should fit neatly into the sauté pan with no extra room. If the pan is too large, so that part of its surface is exposed during sautéing, the meat juices, which are essential to pan-deglazed sauces, will burn. An overcrowded pan, on the other hand, will prevent the meat from browning evenly and may even cause it to release its juices too quickly, so that it simmers in its own juices rather than browns. Meat should always be thoroughly dried with a towel before sautéing, as any moisture left on the meat will create steam and will prevent browning.

Meats should always be sautéed in a heavy-bottomed pan, which distributes heat evenly. If the pan is too thin, it will be too hot in the area directly over the flame and in any section not in contact with the meat. This uneven heating in turn results in uneven browning and may cause the meat juices to burn in areas where the pan is too hot. Heavy-gauge copper or aluminum sauté pans are best for sautéing. Iron skillets conduct heat well, but because of their black surface, it is difficult to see the juices that adhere to the bottom, to determine whether they are burning. Nonstick and enameled pans should be avoided because the juices released by the meat will not adhere to their surfaces.

When meats are sautéed, they release juices that caramelize and attach to the bottom of the sauté pan. These caramelized juices are intensely flavorful and are the basis for pan-deglazed integral sauces. Once the meat is removed from the pan, the first step in preparing a sauce is to remove the fat used for sautéing. If the meat has been sautéed properly, the juices will have formed a sticky, caramelized glaze adhering to the bottom of the pan; the fat remaining in the sauté pan is then simply poured off and discarded.

Once the fat has been removed from the sauté pan, the caramelized juices are dissolved in liquid by deglazing the pan with water or with a flavorful liquid such as wine or stock. The bottom of the pan is then scraped with a wooden spoon to dissolve the juices into the deglazing liquid. The wide range of possible deglazing liquids makes this technique extremely versatile.

Although an acceptable sauce can be made by simply deglazing a sauté pan with wine, water, or stock, most professionals add other ingredients to give the sauce greater depth of flavor and a richer consistency. Using meat stocks either alone or in conjunction with wine will give a more complex flavor to a pan-deglazed sauce. Most stocks, however, require considerable reduction to concentrate their flavors and give them the consistency needed for a sauce. For this reason, meat glace or demi-glace (in older recipes) is often used by professionals to give consistency, body, and flavor to a sauce without requiring time-consuming last-minute reduction. In lighter sauces the meat glace can be replaced by veal or chicken stock that has been well reduced in advance.

Once the sauté pan has been deglazed and the body of the sauce rounded out with stock or meat glace, the sauce can be served as is or be lightly bound. Most contemporary pan-deglazed sauces are finished with cream or butter, which gives them a rich texture and flavor. When used in moderation, cream and butter will also lengthen a sauce without diluting it and weakening its taste. Pan-deglazed sauces can also be lightly thickened with vegetable purées (see Chapter 17, "Purées and Purée-Thickened Sauces," page 457), yogurt, or fresh cheese (see "Yogurt and Fresh Cheese," page 132).

Some chefs prefer unbound versions of pan-deglazed sauces, which contain no butter or cream. Excellent sauces can be prepared by simply deglazing the pan and adding meat glace or reduced stock until the sauce has the desired consistency. The one danger with this method is that too much meat glace or stock will give the sauce a sticky, gluey consistency. Light-textured versions of pan-deglazed sauces prepared with very little or no cream or butter are often presented *under* the meat in a deep plate or wide bowl. When a pan-deglazed sauce has the desired consistency (through reduction or adding liaisons such as cream, butter, or vegetable purées), it can be finished with an almost infinite variety of additional flavorings. Vinegar, Cognac, freshly chopped herbs, tomato purée, mustard, and chopped truffles are just a few examples.

Sautéed meats are usually accompanied by vegetables or other garnitures. Depending on the style and presentation of the sautéed meats, vegetables and other accompaniments are either served separately or combined with the sauce used to cover or surround the meat. Most sautéed dishes are completed by heating a garniture, such as mushrooms, small strips of bacon (lardoons), turned vegetables, baby vegetables, or pearl onions, in the sauce before it is poured over or placed under the sautéed meats.

Even experienced cooks are sometimes confused by careless nomenclature that confuses stews and sautés. In strict culinary parlance, a *sauté* is composed of pieces of meat (including poultry) that have been browned in hot fat and finished cooking, without added liquid, either on top of the stove or in the oven. The sauce for a sauté is then prepared in the pan used to brown the meat and combined with the cooked meat just before serving—not sooner. When pieces of meat are browned but then cooked in liquid, the preparation is an authentic *stew*.

Model for a Pan-Deglazed Sauce

MEATS FOR SAUTÉING

Lamb (chops, medallions, noisettes)

Pork (chops, medallions, noisettes)

Veal (loin and rib chops, scallops, medallions)

Chicken parts (quarters or smaller)

Steaks (tenderloin, strip, club, other tender parts)

Calves' livers

Kidneys

Game (boneless breasts from wild ducks, partridges, pheasants, or other game birds; whole small birds such as quail; venison steaks)

FATS FOR BROWNING

Oil (pure olive, safflower, grapeseed)

Rendered poultry fat (goose, duck, chicken)

Clarified butter

Whole butter (at lower temperatures)

DEGLAZING LIQUIDS
ALONE OR IN COMBINATION

Water

Wine (red, white, fortified)

Vinegar (good-quality wine or cider)

Stocks (white or brown, depending on the desired sauce color and flavor intensity)

Cider

Beer

Brandies (Cognac, Calvados)

ADDITIONAL STOCK OR GLACE
ALONE OR IN COMBINATION

Reduced chicken, veal, or beef stock

Alternative Coulis (page 163)

Meat glace

Demi-glace (classic and natural)

Roasting juices

LIAISONS
ALONE OR IN COMBINATION

Butter

Cream

Starches

Vegetable purées

Mayonnaise-based sauces

Béarnaise-based sauces

Foie gras

Yogurt

Fresh cheese

FINAL FLAVORINGS

Spirits (Cognac, Calvados, eau-de-vie, marc, whiskey)

Freshly chopped herbs

Vinegar

Mustard

Truffles

Salt and pepper

Spices (saffron, curry, juniper berries, green peppercorns)

GARNITURES

Mushrooms

Assorted vegetables (baby or turned)

Lardoons

Pearl onions

Fruits

Shellfish

Quenelles

POULET SAUTÉ À LA MARENGO
Chicken with Tomatoes, Olives, and Mushrooms

Although chicken sautés can be varied almost infinitely by changing the garniture, the cooking method for the chicken sauté remains the same. Chicken Marengo was originally served with deep-fried eggs and crayfish, but most restaurants and home cooks usually serve the version that follows.

YIELD: 8 SERVINGS

chickens, 2	6 to 8 pounds	3 to 4 kilograms
salt and pepper	to taste	to taste
olive oil	¼ cup	60 milliliters
small mushrooms	8 ounces	250 grams
chicken stock	1 cup	250 milliliters
garlic cloves, crushed, peeled	2	2
tomatoes, peeled, seeded, and chopped	4 to 6 medium	4 to 6 medium
white wine	1 cup	250 milliliters
green olives	24	24
chopped parsley	1 tablespoon	15 milliliters

1. Cut the chickens into quarters. Pat the pieces dry with paper towels and season with salt and pepper.
2. Heat the olive oil in a 4-quart (4 liter) straight-sided sauté pan and brown the chicken, skin side first. If the pieces stick when turning them, they probably are not brown enough; wait a few minutes and try again. The pieces usually require about 8 minutes of cooking on each side. When the chicken is cooked, transfer it to a plate and keep it warm while preparing the sauce.
3. While the chicken is browning, cook the mushrooms in ½ cup (125 milliliters) of the chicken stock in a covered 2-quart (2 liter) saucepan for 5 minutes.
4. After removing the chicken, pour off the hot fat from the sauté pan and add the crushed garlic, chopped tomatoes, white wine, mushroom cooking liquid, and remaining stock. Reduce until about 2 cups (500 milliliters) remain. (Some recipes suggest thickening the sauce at this point with beurre manié, but this step is not necessary.) Remove the pieces of garlic.
5. Heat the olives and cooked mushrooms in the sauce for 1 or 2 minutes.
6. Serve the chicken napped with the sauce. Sprinkle with parsley.

STEAK WITH GREEN PEPPERCORN SAUCE

Any good cut of steak—such as beef tenderloin (filet), sirloin strip, or rib steak—can be lightly cooked in a straight-sided sauté pan, with the drippings used as the sauce base. The following recipe calls for meat glace and a reduction of cream as a liaison. It can also be made as a butter-enriched version by replacing the cream with 1½ ounces (45 grams) of butter or as a classic version by leaving out both cream and butter and finishing with demi-glace.

YIELD: 4 SERVINGS

steaks	4	4
clarified butter (see Note)	3 tablespoons	45 milliliters
shallot, finely chopped	1	1
port	2 tablespoons	30 milliliters
cognac	¼ cup	60 milliliters
meat glace (page 104)	3 tablespoons	45 grams
heavy cream	6 tablespoons	90 milliliters
green peppercorns in brine, drained	1 tablespoon	15 milliliters
butter	1 ounce	30 grams
salt and pepper	to taste	to taste
red wine vinegar	few drops	few drops

1. Dry the steaks thoroughly. In a straight-sided 2-quart (2 liter) sauté pan, sauté the steaks in the clarified butter. When they are cooked to the desired doneness, remove them from the pan and keep warm.
2. Pour the fat from the sauté pan. Whisk in the chopped shallot. Let the pan cool slightly, then add the port and Cognac to deglaze the pan. Tilt the pan and ignite the fumes. Reduce the liquids until the flames die out.
3. Add the meat glace, cream, and green peppercorns. Reduce the sauce to the desired consistency and swirl in the butter.
4. Adjust the seasonings and add a few drops of red wine vinegar.

Note: The clarified butter used to brown the steaks may be replaced by ½ ounce (15 grams) of whole butter and 2 tablespoons (30 milliliters) of oil.

PORK CHOPS WITH MODERN SOUBISE

This sauce demonstrates a method of finishing an integral pan sauce with vegetable purée—in this case onions, a modern version of the classic soubise.

YIELD: 2 TO 4 SERVINGS

rib or loin pork chops	4	4
clarified butter (see Note)	3 tablespoons	45 milliliters

brown pork or chicken stock	½ cup	125 milliliters
stewed onion purée (page 472)	6 tablespoons	90 milliliters
additional stock, or heavy cream	as needed	as needed
salt and pepper	to taste	to taste

1. Dry the pork chops. In a 2-quart (2 liter) straight-sided sauté pan, sauté the chops in the clarified butter until well browned and cooked through. Transfer them to a plate and keep warm.
2. Pour the fat from the pan and deglaze with the stock.
3. Reduce the stock by about one-fourth and whisk in the onion purée. Adjust the thickness by reducing the sauce slightly (to thicken) or adding stock or cream (to thin). Adjust the seasonings.

Note: The clarified butter may be replaced by ½ ounce (15 grams) of whole butter and 2 tablespoons (30 milliliters) of oil.

INTEGRAL SAUCES FOR ROASTS: THE JUS

Unlike pan-deglazed sauces for sautéed meats, which can be flavored and bound in many different ways, sauces for roasts are best kept simple and should capture the flavor of the roast. Additions that distort or weaken the natural flavor of the roast should be kept to a minimum.

The best method for roasting meats is on a spit in front of a wood fire. When this method is used, a dripping pan (*lèchefrite*) placed in front of the fire directly under the roasting meat is used to capture the drippings. Most of the fat is removed from the drippings, and the remaining jus is served as is. If the jus is pale, it can be rapidly cooked down on top of the stove until it caramelizes; the fat is then poured off and the caramelized juices are deglazed with an appropriately flavored or neutral stock.

When oven-roasting meats, be sure to select a heavy-bottomed roasting pan (a sauté pan will work in a pinch) that closely fits the size of the roast. If the roasting pan is too large, the juices will spread out over its surface and burn. If the pan is too thin, any surface that is not in direct contact with the meat will overheat, also causing the drippings to burn. Many recipes, especially in the United States, recommend setting roasts on top of special racks, presumably to expose them to the heat of the oven and help them brown evenly. Unfortunately, when the roast is suspended over the pan on a rack, the drippings fall into an overheated roasting pan and burn. A better method is to set the roast on a layer of meat trimmings and vegetables. These contribute flavor to the finished jus and keep the meat from sticking to the pan.

When the roast is done, the flavor and color of the drippings can be improved by heating the roasting pan on top of the stove so that the drippings caramelize. The fat is then easily poured off and the pan deglazed with water or stock. When dealing with large roasts that release large amounts of natural juices, it is usually impractical and unnecessary to caramelize the juices. The fat is simply skimmed off and the jus served as is.

The flavor of natural roasting juices, when skimmed of fat, cannot be surpassed. The problem that most often confronts professional chefs is that most roasts do not provide enough full-flavored jus to go around. This problem can be resolved in several ways. In classic French cooking, roasting pans are often deglazed with *jus de veau lié*—brown veal stock that has been reduced and lightly bound with arrowroot. Arrowroot, when used sparingly, gives a light sheen to the jus and looks more like a natural, unthickened jus than stock thickened with roux. Contemporary chefs, who are usually less compelled to use thickeners, are more likely to stretch a natural jus with unthickened, full-flavored stock. A stock with a natural jus-like flavor can also be prepared in advance with meat trimmings and used to deglaze the roasting pan.

The flavor of a jus can be reinforced with additional meat trimmings and aromatic vegetables. Some chefs surround roast meats with chopped onions, carrots, and meat trimmings that cook along with the roast and contribute to the flavor of the meat juices. This method requires a certain amount of skill and judgment to determine when to add the vegetables and trimmings and how finely they should be chopped. If they are chopped too finely or added too soon, they are liable to burn; if chopped too coarsely or added too late, they will remain undercooked and not contribute any flavor. Finely chopped vegetables can also be added to the roasting pan and caramelized on top of the stove along with the juices. In general, moisture should never be introduced into the oven during roasting (which by definition is cooking with dry heat), but if the meat juices or chopped vegetables start to overcook during the roasting, a small amount of water or stock can be added to the bottom of the roasting pan to prevent burning.

Cooks are often baffled as to whether or not roasts should be basted. The purpose of basting is to prevent the surface of the roast from drying out and to give the roast an even color and sheen. In some instances, especially for poultry and game birds, a dry, crispy skin may be desirable and basting should be avoided. In true roasting, meats are basted with fat. Basting meats with liquid such as wine or stock may prevent browning and cause the meat to braise rather than roast. The choice of basting liquids depends to a large extent on intuition and skill. A chicken or game bird may benefit from basting with reduced stock or meat glace near the end of roasting, which will give it sheen, moist skin, and a full-bodied jus.

Gravies and Thickened Jus

In classic French restaurants, a natural jus or one that has been only lightly thickened with arrowroot is traditionally served in a sauce boat either offered by the waiter or placed on the table where guests usually help themselves. This is both a simple and elegant method for serving roasts. In less formal cooking or in people's homes, a gravy is likely to be served instead of a jus. A gravy is simply a jus that has been thickened with flour in the roasting pan.

Most gravy recipes suggest removing most but not all of the grease from the roasting pan, stirring in flour with a wooden spoon, cooking the mixture for 4 or 5 minutes, and then adding water or stock. Although there are more refined and sophisticated methods for dealing with meat drippings, one of the most reassuring is a simple flour-thickened gravy.

Model for Preparing a Jus

MAIN INGREDIENT

The meat to be roasted, placed in a heavy-bottomed roasting pan

AROMATICS

ALONE OR IN COMBINATION, ADDED TO THE ROASTING PAN WITH THE MEAT

Carrots
Celery
Onions
Garlic

MEAT TRIMMINGS

Ham
Bones or carcasses

DEGLAZING LIQUIDS

ALONE OR IN COMBINATION

Water
Stock (either neutral or the same kind as the meat being roasted)
Wine (should be complemented with stock)

LIAISONS

ALONE OR IN COMBINATION

Jus de veau lié (reduced brown veal stock bound with arrowroot)
Flour (to convert jus into gravy)
Vegetable purée (made from the vegetables roasted with the meat or separately)
Butter
Cream
Puréed livers (from poultry or game)
Foie gras

FINAL FLAVORINGS

Chopped fines herbes (chervil, parsley, chives, tarragon)
Other herbs (marjoram, savory, thyme, alone or in combination)
Spices (curry, juniper berries, saffron)

A natural jus can also be thickened with puréed vegetables. The easiest and most flavorful method is to roast the meat with chopped aromatic vegetables such as carrots, turnips, onions, or garlic, degrease and deglaze the pan, and force the vegetables and cooking jus through a food mill or strainer. In restaurants or other professional settings where this is impractical, vegetable purées can be prepared on the side and used as thickeners for the jus (see Chapter 17, "Purées and Purée-Thickened Sauces," page 457), but the vegetables will not have benefited from being cooked with the fat and drippings from the roast.

Most Americans are familiar with giblet gravy, which is finished with the precooked and chopped heart, liver, and gizzard of turkeys or chickens. Although this is an excellent method—the chopped meats provide textural contrast and flavor—a different and somewhat more flavorful jus is obtained by puréeing the giblets (a food processor works well) while still raw with an equal amount of butter. The purée is then beaten into the jus at the last minute. Another refinement is to replace the giblet mixture with a purée of foie gras (see page 124).

The natural cooking liquid from game, rabbits, and poultry is sometimes thickened with blood, usually used in combination with the puréed liver and a few drops of Cognac or marc and vinegar (see page 130). Sauces for roast game also benefit from a few crushed juniper berries infused in the jus before the addition of the blood.

OVEN-ROASTED CHICKEN WITH NATURAL JUS

In kitchens with professional-quality stoves and hot ovens, it is rarely necessary to brown the chicken on top of the stove before roasting. The smaller the bird being roasted, the more likely will be the necessity for prebrowning—by the time a quail browns in the oven, it will have dried out and overcooked. The following recipe suggests browning the chickens in a mixture of butter and oil; clarified butter may be substituted for that mixture.

Older recipes suggest covering the breast of a roast chicken with a sheet of fatback (bard) for the first stage of roasting so the thighs and breasts will be done at the same time. This is still a good idea but a bit of a nuisance when sheets of fatback are not on hand. An easy alternative is to double up a small sheet of aluminum foil and place it over the breast while the chicken is roasting. The foil can then be removed 10 minutes before the end of roasting to allow the breast to brown.

YIELD: 8 SERVINGS

chickens, 2	3 to 4 pounds	1.5 to 2 kilograms
butter	1 ounce	30 grams
olive oil	2 tablespoons	30 milliliters

meat trimmings or chicken bones (optional)		
shallots, chopped	2 medium	2 medium
chicken stock	2 cups	500 milliliters
salt and pepper	to taste	to taste

1. Remove the giblets from the chickens. Truss the chickens with string.
2. Heat the butter and olive oil in a heavy-bottomed roasting pan or sauté pan on top of the stove. Brown the chickens on all sides.
3. Place the chickens in the oven, breast side up. Cover the breasts with folded sheets of aluminum foil. Surround the chickens with giblets, except the liver, which may give the jus a strong taste. If a few extra meat trimmings or bones from other chickens are available, add them as well. Roast for 30 minutes.
4. Remove the foil and roast for 15 to 20 minutes more, until the juices from a thigh run clear when it is poked with a trussing needle or sauté fork.
5. Transfer the chickens to a plate or platter. Lift them in such a way that any juices contained in the cavities run out into the roasting pan.
6. Heat the roasting pan on the stove until the juices caramelize on the bottom of the pan and the fat separates. Do not stir.
7. Remove the fat from the roasting pan with a ladle, or lift the roasting pan and pour it off. Stir the chopped shallots into the hot pan and stir them around for a minute until they release their aroma.
8. Add 1 cup (250 milliliters) of the chicken stock to the roasting pan and reduce until the stock caramelizes.
9. Add the remaining stock. Gently heat until all the caramelized juices dissolve in the stock.
10. Strain the jus through a fine chinois.
11. Adjust the seasonings. The jus may then be thickened and flavored in a variety of ways, as described earlier in this chapter.

ROAST SADDLE OF VEAL

This is a roast that almost no one serves, partly, no doubt, because of its expense. But for this very reason it is a very special roast suitable for a crowd or a large table in a restaurant. It should be carved at the table (see step 5 for how to carve it). The saddle is the whole loin section of the calf and comes untrimmed (#331 in *The Meat Buyer's Guide* put out by the North American Meat Processors Association) or trimmed (#332). If you buy it untrimmed, there will be plenty of veal meat to use for producing a jus.

saddle of veal (#331)	1	1
carrot, chopped	1 large	1 large
onion, chopped	1 large	1 large
salt and pepper	to taste	to taste

1. Preheat the oven to 450°F (230°C). Cut the flaps off both sides of the saddle, being careful not to cut into the loin muscle on each side. Cut out the two bones, one on each side of the saddle. Trim the fat off the flaps, cut the meat into small strips, and use it to prepare a jus.

2. Spread the veal strips in the roasting pan for the veal along with the carrot and onion and slide the pan into the oven. Roast until lightly browned, about 30 minutes.

3. Season the saddle and place it, loin muscles up, on top of the roasted meat trimmings. Slide into the oven and roast for 30 minutes or until well browned and then turn the oven down to 300°F (150°C) and continue roasting to an internal temperature of 130°F (55°C). If at any point the juices in the roasting pan threaten to burn, add 1 cup (250 milliliters) of water or broth to the pan.

4. Transfer the roast to a platter and cover it loosely with aluminum foil. Inspect the juices in the pan to see if they've all caramelized and have formed a crust on the bottom of the pan. If they have, pour off and discard the liquid fat. If not, put the roasting pan on the stove and boil down the juices until they caramelize, then ladle out and discard the liquid fat. Deglaze the pan with about 2 cups (500 milliliters) of water and scrape up the dissolved juices with a wooden spoon over medium to high heat. Strain and reserve as the jus.

5. Carve the saddle by cutting one of the loin muscles crosswise in the center and then carving, with the knife on its side, lengthwise, along the length of the loin such that you end up with long rectangular strips. Repeat on the second side. Turn the saddle over and carve the tenderloin into long strips and serve.

ROAST RACK OF LAMB WITH NATURAL JUS

A rack of lamb, being a red meat, is roasted to a lower internal temperature than chicken, veal, or pork, meaning that it releases little in the way of juices during the roasting process. To supplement the jus, spread the roasting pan with the trimmings from the rack (with the fat trimmed off) or a pound or so of lamb stew meat cut into small pieces and brown these in a hot oven before setting the rack on top. The flavor of the jus can also be accentuated by caramelizing the juices once or more after deglazing as described above for the saddle of lamb.

YIELD: 4 MAIN-COURSE SERVINGS

american rack of lamb	1	1
or	or	or
new zealand racks of lamb	2	2
salt and pepper	to taste	to taste
trimmings from the rack		
or	or	or
lamb stew meat cut into ½-inch (1 cm) pieces	1 pound	450 grams
broth or water	as needed	as needed

1. Season the lamb and allow it to come to room temperature. Preheat the oven to 450°F (230°C).
2. Spread the lamb trimmings or stew meat over the bottom of a roasting pan just large enough to hold the rack and roast until lightly browned, about 30 minutes.
3. Place the rack on top of the trimmings (this base of trimmings is called a *fonçage*) and slide into the oven. Roast until springy to the touch, about 25 minutes. Let rest, loosely covered with aluminum foil, for 15 minutes.
4. Put the roasting pan on top of the stove and pour over a cup (250 milliliters) of broth. Bring to a boil and boil until a brown crust of caramelized juices forms on the roasting pan. Pour out any liquid fat floating on top. Deglaze again with a cup (250 milliliters) of broth and scrape up the juices. Repeat the caramelization as many times as practical before deglazing a final time. Pass the jus in a sauce boat at the table. See the photograph in the color plates.

ROAST SADDLE OF LAMB WITH NATURAL JUS

While many of us are enamored with a rack of meat, be it lamb, veal, or pork, many of us forget the most dramatic cut, the saddle. The saddle is lower down on the animal, below the ribs. The cut looks in fact vaguely like a saddle because it has a flat long center section with flaps hanging down the sides. Many recipes call for partially boning the saddle, rolling up the loins in the flaps before roasting, and serving the roast in round medallions. This method is problematic because the fat and gristle contained in the flaps doesn't get cooked enough to render. A better approach is to use the meat contained in the flaps to augment the meat juices and then slice the loin into small rounds or, with great drama, lengthwise into strips. Since many butchers aren't used to having orders for whole saddles of lamb, it helps to have the number of the cut designated by the North American Meat Processors Association to give to your butcher.

saddle of lamb (NAMP #231), 1	6 pounds	2.75 kilograms
onion, quartered	1 small	1 small
garlic cloves, crushed	6	6
salt and pepper	to taste	to taste
dry white wine	1 cup	250 milliliters
lamb, veal, or chicken broth	1 quart	1 liter
dried or fresh thyme or marjoram leaves	½ teaspoon	2 milliliters
cold unsalted butter, sliced (optional)	3 ounces	90 grams

1. Cut the one or two ribs that remain attached to each side of the saddle away from the loin by following along the inside of the ribs with a boning knife and then cutting through where they join the loin. Cut the flaps away from the saddle.

2. Trim the meat away from the fat on the flaps by sliding a flexible knife along one side of the meat. Cut the meat into strips about ¼ inch (5 mm) thick.

3. About an hour before serving, preheat the oven to 425°F (220°C). Spread the lamb trimmings, onion, and garlic in a roasting pan just large enough to hold the saddle, and roast for about 25 minutes.

4. Season the saddle on both sides with salt and pepper. About 40 minutes before serving, place it upright on the trimmings. Roast until the meat feels firm to the touch or a meat thermometer stuck into one of the loins reads 125° to 130°F (50° to 55°C). Transfer the roast to a platter, cover it loosely with aluminum foil, and keep it in a warm place.

5. Examine the roasting pan to see if the juices have caramelized and formed a brown crust on the bottom of the pan. If they have, pour out the fat while holding the trimmings in place with an oven mitt. If not, boil down the juices on top of the stove until they caramelize and form a crust.

6. Add the wine to the pan and boil it down until it completely evaporates. Add 1 cup (250 milliliters) of broth to the pan and boil it down, repositioning the pan over the stove every couple of minutes, until it caramelizes. Pour out any fat released by the trimmings and deglaze with a second cup (250 milliliters) of broth. Boil down to caramelize a second time. Deglaze with the remaining broth. Scrape the bottom of the pan with a wooden spoon, add the thyme, and let the broth simmer for no more than 3 or 4 minutes or it will lose flavor. Whisk in the butter, if using, and season to taste with salt and pepper.

7. Strain the jus. Carve the roast in lengthwise strips or in rounds (don't forget the tenderloins on the underside) and pass the jus in a sauce boat at the table.

Variation

In hot weather, leave the butter out of the jus; chill the jus and the roast. Slice the roast lengthwise, arrange the slices on chilled plates, and spoon over the gelled jus.

INTEGRAL SAUCES DERIVED FROM POACHED MEATS

Poaching is one of the most fundamental and straightforward techniques for cooking meat. In English-speaking countries, we have the habit of speaking of boiled dishes, but when prepared correctly, so-called boiled dishes are actually poached—the poaching liquid is never allowed to reach a full boil. In France, dishes such as *pot au feu* ("boiled" beef with vegetables), *poule au pot* (poached hen with vegetables), and innumerable *potées* (poached meats, usually pork with beans or potatoes and vegetables, almost always including cabbage) have long been the mainstay of the rural diet. More refined poached dishes, such as *blanquette de veau* (poached veal stew with cream), *boeuf à la ficelle* (tender cuts barely poached in broth), and *petite marmite* (a rich consommé with vegetables and marrow) have made their way into middle-class homes and elegant restaurants. The age-old technique of serving poached meats surrounded with flavorful broth instead of a thickened sauce is popular with contemporary chefs because the dish is light and digestible.

The difference between poaching and stewing or braising is largely a question of the amount of liquid used for cooking the meat. Stewed and braised meats are cooked in and thus produce a small amount of concentrated liquid, whereas poaches, because the meat is completely submerged in liquid, provide a relatively dilute, soup-like broth. Consequently, most sauces derived from poached meats require reduction or the addition of reduced stock, demi-glace, or meat glace to intensify their flavor.

For some poached meats—the French pot au feu is a prime example—the poaching liquid is left alone and either served as a separate course or around the meat (here the distinction between soup and sauce is a bit cloudy). In a potée, the meat (often pork) is gently simmered with starchy foods such as beans or potatoes, which give substance to the dish, and if they do not completely absorb the surrounding liquid, at least they lightly thicken and contribute body to the broth.

There have been many so-called refinements (refinements, yes; improvements, not necessarily) of fundamental poached dishes such as potées and pot au feu. Boeuf à la ficelle consists of poaching beef tenderloin (or another tender cut) in the pot au feu broth and serving the still-rare beef with the pot au feu vegetables and broth. Contemporary chefs have taken this refinement several steps further, often serving game, pigeon, or even lobster and crayfish in a carefully reduced and clarified poaching liquid.

Poaching liquids can also be thickened and finished with a wide variety of flavorful ingredients. The traditional French blanquette de veau is composed of chunks of veal poached in water or stock flavored with aromatic vegetables and a bouquet garni. When the meat is cooked, the broth is then thickened with roux and finished with heavy cream combined with egg yolks.

Today, the term *blanquette* is often applied to any meat or fish that has been poached and surrounded by a sauce derived from the poaching liquid and finished with cream.

Poached chicken also provides a flavorful broth that can be reduced and finished with cream or, more traditionally, converted into a velouté and finished with cream or vegetable purées and a variety of flavorful ingredients.

Poached cooking liquids thickened with vegetable purées are analogous and sometimes almost identical to puréed soups. This is one area where the distinction between soup and sauce is sometimes difficult to discern. The usual difference, however, is that a sauce is more intensely flavored and can be richer, simply because there is less of it.

Model for Preparing Sauces for Poached Meats

BASIC INGREDIENTS
ALONE OR IN COMBINATION

Stewing hens or roosters (potées, poule au pot)
Pork shoulder, loin, sausage (potées)
Beef shank, rump, short ribs (pot au feu)
Beef tenderloin, sirloin strip (boeuf à la ficelle, petite marmite)
Veal stewing meat (blanquette de veau)
Game, duck, pigeon (potées, contemporary pot au feu derivatives)

AROMATICS

Onions
Celery
Carrots
Turnips
Garlic
Cabbage (for potées; blanched separately first)
Bouquet garni (classic—parsley, thyme, bay leaf—or with regional herbs such as marjoram or rosemary)

STARCHY INGREDIENTS
FOR LIAISON AND BODY

Potatoes
Beans (such as white beans, fava beans, lentils)

MOISTENING LIQUIDS

Water
Stock
Wine (in combination with stock or water)
Cider

LIAISONS

Cream
Egg yolks (in combination with cream)
Roux
Vegetable purées (derived from aromatic vegetables poached with the meat or cooked separately)

FINAL FLAVORINGS AND GARNITURES

Chopped herbs
Mushrooms
Vegetables (cut or turned into appropriate sizes or small to begin with, such as pearl onions and button mushrooms)
Truffles

POT AU FEU

A pot au feu is an example of poached meats par excellence. There was a day when every farmhouse had a pot of broth simmering on the stove or in the hearth to which various meats could be added and gently simmered. Traditionally a pot au feu is served in two courses—the broth followed by the meat. In this version the meat is served surrounded with the broth. Traditional accompaniments are mustard, cornichons (sour gherkins), and coarse salt, but the Mostarda di Cremona and Green Sauce on pages 239 and 240 are delicious with the various meats. When buying short ribs, be sure to buy them cut crosswise so the ribs themselves are only a couple of inches (5 cm) long.

YIELD: 12 MAIN-COURSE SERVINGS

cloves	2	2
onion	1 large	1 large
large bouquet garni (page 51)	1	1
beef or veal shanks	4 rounds	4 rounds
chuck roast, tied in two directions	4 pounds	2 kilograms
beef short ribs	4 pounds	2 kilograms
beef or veal broth or water, as needed to cover	8 quarts	8 liters
carrots, halved lengthwise, cut into 2-inch (5 cm) sections	4 medium	4 medium
leeks, greens removed, whites halved lengthwise and rinsed	6 medium	6 medium
turnips, peeled, each cut into 6 wedges	3 large	3 large
marrow bones, each about 2 inches (5 cm) long (optional)	12	12
mustard		
cornichons		
coarse salt		

1. Stick the cloves into the onion and put the onion in a large pot with the bouquet garni.
2. Arrange the meats on top and pour in enough broth to cover.
3. Put the pot over medium to high heat. When it reaches a simmer, turn the heat down to maintain it at the barest simmer—the top of the meat should barely vibrate.
4. Simmer for 2 hours, add the vegetables, and simmer about an hour more, until a knife slices easily in and out of the shanks, short ribs, and chuck roast. Add the marrow bones, if using. Simmer for 20 minutes more.
5. Slice the chuck roast and arrange the slices on a large platter with the rest of the meats, the marrow bones, and the vegetables and march triumphantly into the dining room. Ladle broth over each serving. Pass the condiments at the table. See the photograph in the color plates.

BEEF À LA FICELLE

A beef à la ficelle is made simply by poaching a piece of tenderloin in a pot au feu and then serving it in slices with the other pot au feu meats and the vegetables. To make a simplified version, simply poach the beef in good beef stock and then serve the slices in heated soup plates on mounds of spinach or on a piece of bread cooked in butter.

YIELD: 6 MAIN-COURSE SERVINGS

beef tenderloin in 1 piece	2½ pounds	1.2 kilograms
pot au feu (page 237) or broth to cover	3 quarts	3 liters

Submerge the tenderloin in the simmering pot au feu or broth about 20 minutes before serving. Arrange the pot au feu in heated soup plates and serve tenderloin slices on top. If you don't have a pot au feu, arrange the beef on vegetables such as lightly creamed spinach.

DUCK À LA FICELLE

This simple dish is a derivative of beef à la ficelle (above) made by poaching a duck breast, preferably a thick moulard duck breast, in a pot au feu or in broth. One trick, used here, is to render the skin in a sauté pan before poaching; this eliminates the fat more efficiently than the poaching.

YIELD: 4 MAIN-COURSE SERVINGS

pot au feu or broth to cover		
moulard duck breasts	2	2

1. When the pot au feu is just about ready, sauté the duck breasts, skin side down, for about 20 minutes to render their fat.
2. Poach the duck breasts for 3 minutes in the simmering pot au feu or broth.
3. Serve the duck breast sliced on top of the pot au feu ingredients or some other mounded-up vegetable such as spinach.

BOLLITO MISTO

You can make a bollito misto starting out with water, but making it with broth, especially veal broth, will take it to new heights. Making a bollito misto—an assortment of poached meats—in veal broth is an ultimate luxury because you end up with a double broth that's almost as clear as consommé. While you can make a bollito misto as sybaritic as you like by poaching fancy tender cuts of meat in the broth during the last 30 minutes or so of cooking, the soul of a bollito misto is based on slow-cooking tough cuts of meat that provide flavor and sapidity to the broth. Osso buco is de rigueur, and oxtail and tongue are good additions. A piece of pork shoulder—have the butcher cut off the four shoulder ribs attached to the pork loin—also adds flavor and plenty of juice meat. Ideally the meat is served with two sauces, a tangy tartar-like green sauce based on homemade mayonnaise, and mostarda di cremona, a sauce of candied fruits that sometimes is made with mustard oil or mustard seeds. (*Mostarda* refers to the wine must that was used in the sauce in centuries past.)

YIELD: 12 SERVINGS

veal tongues	2	2
2-inch-thick (5 cm) rounds of osso buco	6	6
oxtail pieces	12 large	12 large
pork shoulder section (last four ribs of the pork loin), tied in two directions with kitchen string	3 pounds	1.5 kilograms
leeks, greens removed, whites halved lengthwise, rinsed, and tied together	6	6
large carrots, cut in half lengthwise and cut into 2-inch (5 cm) sections	3	3
or	or	or
medium carrots, cut into 2-inch (5 cm) sections	2 bunches	2 bunches
large bouquet garni (page 51)	1	1
cold veal broth or water to cover	8 quarts	8 liters
mostarda di cremona (below)		
green sauce (page 240)		

1. Put the veal tongues in a pot with enough cold water to cover and bring to the boil over high heat. Drain and rinse with cold water. Remove any loose or unsightly veins hanging from the tongue. Don't worry about peeling off the membrane covering the tongue; it will be easier to remove when the tongue is finished cooking.
2. Put all the ingredients except the sauces in a pot with enough cold veal broth to cover. Bring to a gentle simmer and simmer until the meat pulls away from the oxtails with no resistance, about 3 hours. Take out the tongues and peel away the membrane, covering the tops and sides.
3. To serve, slice the tongue and the pork shoulder and serve them on heated soup plates with the vegetables—give everyone half a leek and a couple of carrot sections—and pieces of the oxtail and osso buco. Ladle some broth into each soup plate. Pass the sauces at the table.

Mostarda di Cremona

This ancient fruit sauce is the classic accompaniment to bollito misto. It is sold by online gourmet stores, but you can also make it yourself if it's the summer and you have access to the fruit. If you can't find all the fruit, just substitute more of the others.

underripe pears, peeled, cored, cut into wedges	2	2
quince or large apple, peeled, cored, cut into wedges	1	1
sugar	3 cups	600 grams
white wine vinegar or sherry vinegar	2 cups	500 milliliters
cherries, pitted	1 cup	250 milliliters
apricots, halved and pitted	½ pound	225 grams
peach, pitted, cut into wedges	1 large	1 large
fresh figs, halved	5 large	5 large

Simmer the pears and apples with the sugar and vinegar until soft. Add the remaining fruit and simmer gently for 10 minutes. Gently remove the fruit with a skimmer or spider and reserve in a bowl while you boil down the poaching liquid until it is syrupy. Put the fruit back in the syrup and simmer for 5 minutes. Put the fruit in sterile jars and pour over the syrup. The mostarda should keep in the refrigerator for weeks.

Green Sauce

A quick trick for making this sauce is to use bottled mayonnaise as a base. When you add additional olive oil and vinegar, no one will ever know you started with the bottled variety.

minced chives	3 tablespoons	45 milliliters
chopped capers	3 tablespoons	45 milliliters
chopped parsley	3 tablespoons	45 milliliters
chopped tarragon	2 tablespoons	30 milliliters
chopped chervil (optional)	2 tablespoons	30 milliliters
chopped sorrel (optional)	3 tablespoons	45 milliliters
mustard	1 tablespoon	15 milliliters
wine vinegar	1 tablespoon or more	15 milliliters
mayonnaise, homemade (page 393) or bottled	¼ cup	60 milliliters
extra-virgin olive oil	1 cup	250 milliliters
salt and pepper	to taste	to taste

Whisk the herbs, mustard, and vinegar (as needed for acidity and thinning the sauce) into the mayonnaise. Whisk in the oil in a steady stream. Season to taste with salt and pepper. For a greener, more subtly flavored sauce, purée the sauce with an immersion blender.

POACHED CHICKEN

If you're repeating this dish with any frequency, save the poaching liquid from the previous batch for poaching each new chicken. Its flavor will continue to improve. By serving the poaching liquid around the chicken, you have a dish that's perfectly lean, but you can also enrich it with a little cream and flavor it with herbs, especially chopped tarragon. You can also thicken the poaching liquid with egg yolks as described below.

YIELD: 4 MAIN-COURSE SERVINGS

chicken, 1	4 pounds	2 kilograms
carrots, sectioned, turned (turning optional)	2 large	2 large
turnip, cut into wedges, turned (turning optional)	1 large	1 large
cold chicken broth or water to cover	6 quarts	6 liters
bouquet garni (about 7 sprigs fresh tarragon, 1 bay leaf, 1 bunch parsley)	1	1
string beans, ends snapped off	½ pound	225 grams
peas, fresh or frozen (optional)	½ cup	125 milliliters
salt and pepper	to taste	to taste

1. Truss the chicken and put it in a pot surrounded with the carrots and turnips.
2. Add enough cold chicken broth to cover and nestle in the bouquet garni. Bring to a gentle simmer and simmer until the juices are clear when you poke the joint between the thigh and the drumstick. During the poaching, skim off any fat and scum that float to the surface.
3. Add the string beans to the poaching liquid and simmer until they lose their crunch, about 5 minutes. Add the peas, if using, and simmer 1 minute.
4. Season the broth to taste with salt and pepper and ladle it around the quartered chicken in soup plates. Distribute the vegetables among the servings. See the photographs in the color plates.

POACHED CHICKEN WITH CREAM AND EGG YOLKS

This classic method for poaching chicken and finishing the poaching liquid with roux and a liaison of cream and egg yolks is the same as preparing a white veal stew (blanquette). It is also similar to a fricassée, except that a fricassée is made with cut-up chicken that is usually cooked gently in butter before being moistened with stock.

Contemporary interpretations of this recipe use the same technique for poaching the chicken, but the roux, egg yolks, and often the cream will likely be missing. A simple and satisfying version can be presented by simply serving the sliced chicken in wide soup bowls with the reduced broth. The broth can be scented with whole leaves of basil, chopped herbs, truffles, cubes of ham, and the like.

onion, quartered	1 medium	1 medium
clove	1	1
carrot, sliced	1 medium	1 medium
celery, chopped	1 small stalk	1 small stalk
butter	5 ounces	150 grams
chickens, 2	6 to 8 pounds	3 to 4 kilograms
large bouquet garni (page 51)	1	1
white chicken or veal stock, warm but not hot	2 quarts	2 liters
flour	¼ cup	40 grams
heavy cream	¾ cup	185 milliliters
egg yolks	5	5
salt and pepper	to taste	to taste

1. Select a pot or casserole that will just hold the chickens. Stud one of the onion quarters with the clove. Gently sweat the carrot, onion, and celery in 1½ ounces (45 grams) of the butter in the pot or casserole. They must not color at all.
2. Place the chickens and bouquet garni on top of the vegetables. Add enough stock to cover the chickens by about ½ inch (1 cm).
3. Gently bring the stock to a simmer and skim off any froth or fat that floats to the surface. Partially cover the casserole with a lid. Check the broth every few minutes to make sure it is not boiling. After about 20 minutes, when the chickens are cooked (the juices run clear when the middle of a thigh is poked with a trussing needle), transfer them to a plate and cover with aluminum foil to keep warm.
4. Strain the broth into a 4-quart (4 liter) saucepan.
5. Reduce the broth until 1 quart (1 liter) remains. Skim carefully.
6. In a 2-quart (2 liter) saucepan, prepare a roux with the flour and 2 ounces (60 grams) of the butter. Add the broth.
7. Gently simmer the thickened broth for 15 minutes, skimming off any froth that rises to the surface.
8. Whisk together the cream and egg yolks.
9. Pour half of the thickened broth into the cream–egg yolk liaison and return this mixture to the remaining broth. Heat to just a simmer and whisk in the remaining 1½ ounces (45 grams) of butter. Adjust the seasonings.

Variation

Try turning the vegetables, cutting them into decorative shapes, and setting them over and around the chicken, with its broth as the sauce; see a photograph in the color plates.

INTEGRAL SAUCES MADE FROM BRAISED MEATS

Meat is braised by slow cooking in a small amount of liquid. The main difference between braising and poaching is that braising is accomplished in a minimum amount of liquid, whereas poaching requires a relatively large amount of liquid, enough to cover the meat completely. Usually herbs and aromatic vegetables are braised along with the meat for extra flavor and complexity. As meat cooks, it releases juices into the surrounding liquid, which becomes intensely concentrated and flavorful. If the braising has been done carefully, little if anything needs to be done to improve the flavor and consistency of the braising liquid.

Braising Terminology

There are many different techniques and approaches to braising, as well as an elaborate and contradictory terminology that often confuses even experienced cooks.

Stews are simply braises in which the meat has been cut up into small pieces, browned or not depending on recipe or whim, and covered with water, stock, or aromatic liquids such as wine, cider, beer, or vinegar. Stews are infinitely varied and are subcategorized into an endless variety of daubes, estouffades, coq au vin variations, and fricassées.

Until the middle of the nineteenth century, braising and stewing always implied that the meat was cooked for long periods—until the muscle tissue had completely broken down and the meat was tender. This technique is called "brown braising." Since then, many chefs also use a technique known as "white braising" for tender cuts of white meat, such as veal or pork. Meats that are white braised are not browned and are cooked in a small amount of liquid only long enough to reach a relatively low internal temperature, like a roast. An *étouffée* (sometimes *étuvé*) is a type of braise in which the meat is cooked covered with no or only a small amount of liquid. When meat is cooked covered with no liquid—only butter—the technique is called *poêlage*.

Brown braising is the more traditional technique and is best used for relatively tough cuts of meat, either white or red. There are several ways that large pieces of meat (3 to 7 pounds/1.5 to 3.25 kilograms) can be brown braised, but the oldest and most sophisticated uses a two-stage process that works well for both red and white meats. In brown braising, the meat is carefully larded to prevent it from drying out, browned in fat along with aromatic vegetables, placed in a close-fitting casserole, and covered halfway with water or stock. The casserole is then covered (with the lid inverted so that moisture accumulates, drips down over the meat, and bastes it from inside the pot), and the pot is placed in the oven for 2 to 3 hours, depending on the weight of the meat.

When the meat is easily pierced with a skewer, it is gently transferred to a clean casserole, and the braising liquid is strained into a saucepan, where it is reduced slightly and carefully degreased. The braising liquid is then placed in the new casserole with the meat, and the whole thing is returned to the oven. The braising continues, uncovered, and the meat is basted with the reduced liquid until a shiny glaze forms on its surface.

In traditional brown braising, relatively large pieces of meat are braised long enough for the fibers to break down and soften, a minimum of 2 hours. Some recipes call for slow cooking of meat for much longer periods, even to the point where the meat can be served with a spoon (*à la cuillère*).

A quicker and more straightforward technique for braising meats is simply to tie the meat, brown it in butter, and bake it slowly in a tightly covered pot with aromatic vegetables. From time to time the pot should be checked so that a few tablespoons of water can be added if needed to prevent the juices on the bottom of the pot from drying up and burning. This is the method most often used for American pot roasts or French étuvés. Meats braised in this way can be cooked to a relatively low internal temperature (as for roasts and white braises), or the process can be continued until the meat fibers soften in the same way as brown braises, in which case the meat should be larded to prevent it from drying out.

When meat is cooked with butter and no additional liquid, the technique is called poêlage, sometimes translated as "pot roasting." Because this technique provides little liquid from which to prepare a sauce, the bottom of the pot or casserole is deglazed with water, stock, or wine after removing the meat, and the liquid is then gently simmered to extract the flavor of the juices and aromatic ingredients left in the bottom of the pot. Poêlage is very similar to oven roasting, the only difference being that a covered pot is smaller than an oven.

In white braising, the meat is moistened with water, stock, wine, or a combination. The simplest approach is to place the meat in a casserole or close-fitting pot along with aromatic vegetables, a bouquet garni, and enough liquid to come halfway up the sides of the meat. The pot is then set on top of the stove until the liquid comes to a boil. The whole thing is then baked in the oven, with or without a lid, and basted regularly. The meat is cooked to the same degree of doneness as a roast.

Methods and Ingredients for Braises and Stews

Preliminary Browning

Classic French cookbooks claim that preliminary browning of braised meats is necessary to create a seal, to retain the meat's natural juices during the first stage of braising. The reasoning behind this theory is that, as the internal juices are released within the meat, pressure is generated that separates the meat fibers and aids in the cooking. All theory aside, perfectly acceptable braises and stews can be prepared without preliminary browning.

Preliminary browning does, however, improve the color of the braising liquid and, especially if the aromatic vegetables are browned as well, will give the braised meat or stew a somewhat more complex flavor. Initial browning also offers the chef the opportunity to flour the meat, which will help bind the finished liquid without giving it a floury taste. Browning cubes of meat for stews requires a certain amount of care and attention. If the meat is cold or added to the hot pan all at once or the pan or pot used for browning is not hot enough to begin with, the meat will not brown properly and may even release liquid and begin to boil in its own juices. This has a disastrous effect on the meat, so it is best to add the meat to the pan in increments, about a quarter at a time, to prevent sudden cooling of the pan. Care should also be taken when turning the meat. If it is turned haphazardly or all at once, it may cool the pan too quickly, causing the juices to release. When browning large amounts of meat, it may be necessary to change pans during browning so that the caramelized juices do not overheat and burn.

Moistening Liquids and Aromatic Vegetables

Moistening liquids for stews and braised meats have traditionally evolved out of necessity. Germans have long used vinegar; the French, wine (or cider in Normandy); the Irish have had to rely on water (with potatoes contributing body); and Caribbean cooks sometimes use rum. Some recipes augment these liquids with various types of tomatoes, purées of capers, pickles or olives, and, of course, stock. Standard aromatic vegetables—onions (often studded with a clove or two), celery, and carrots—are sometimes replaced or augmented with garlic, turnips, or chiles, depending on nation or region. The combinations of moistening liquids and aromatic vegetables used in stews and braised meats are almost limitless, which is probably why no braise or stew tastes exactly like another.

Bouquet Garni

The bouquet garni has become so standardized that chefs often add it to a stew with little thought as to how the herbs meld with the stew's other components. (See page 51 for a basic version in different sizes.) Rarely will parsley, thyme, and bay leaf—the standard components of a bouquet garni—clash with the other aromatic ingredients in a stew, but often a bouquet garni can be used to give a stew individuality and distinction, with the addition of other herbs. Early French recipes often called for basil and hyssop in a bouquet garni; Italian and southern French cooks will often add marjoram, wild thyme, or oregano. In Mexico, a piece of cinnamon stick will sometimes make its way into the bouquet garni. Medieval cooks, more attuned to spices than herbs, often simmered their meats in elaborate combinations of saffron, ginger, cinnamon, and other spices.

Marinades

Meat for stews and braises is often given added flavor by being first marinated in various mixtures, usually containing wine or vinegar, herbs, a small amount of oil, and sometimes spices such as cloves, juniper berries, and crushed pepper-corns. Although some contemporary chefs feel that marinades sometimes distort the natural flavor of meats, when used discreetly they give aromatic support and character to stews and larger pieces as well. Marinades are usually composed of the liquids, aromatic vegetables, herbs, and spices that will be braised along with the meat. If strong liquors, such as Cognac, grappa, or whiskey, are being used in the braise, they should not be added to the marinade—they will give the meat an odd, unnatural taste.

When the meat is finished braising or stewing, the chef should be left with an intensely aromatic, flavorful liquid. Often this liquid, after an initial degreas-ing, is complete—it is simply served with the stew or atop slices or spoonfuls of the braised meat.

Liaisons for Braising Liquids

At times, especially when no flour has been used to brown the meat and no pork trotters or rinds have been added during braising, the braising liquid may be too thin or not flavorful enough. The most straightforward approach is simply to re-duce it until it has the proper flavor and texture. If this is impractical, there are several methods that can be used to thicken the liquid. In classic French cook-ing, a beurre manié is the thickener most often used for red wine–moistened stews and braises. This solution has the advantage of being quick and, if carried out properly, of not giving the stew a starchy taste. For veal and pork that has not been cooked with red wine, the resulting clear, jus-like braising liquid can be thickened with cornstarch or arrowroot (first worked to a thin paste with a little water or stock), which will contribute a natural jus-like sheen and consistency if used carefully. In some recipes, such as a classic chicken fricassée, the thickener (in this case cream and egg yolks) is inherent in the definition of the dish. Well-reduced stocks or meat glace can also be added to braising liquids to give them body and lengthen them if not enough is available to moisten the meat.

The modern aversion to flour and other starch-based thickeners has led chefs to experiment with new and sometimes very old methods of thickening braising liquids. An obvious and wholesome approach is to purée the aromatic vegetables that have cooked with the stew and to whisk this purée into the strained braising liquid until it has the desired thickness. The Irish stew, in which potatoes give body to the liquid, exemplifies how a vegetable can give body to the surrounding liquid as an integral part of the braising process.

Some chefs reduce braising liquids or add meat glace to give them a thicker consistency, almost like demi-glace. The liquid is then finished with butter.

These sauces have great depth of flavor and considerable finesse, but many chefs find them too rich and think their refinement detracts from the satisfying earthiness of a hearty stew. Red wine stews can also be finished with a small amount of foie gras puréed with butter.

Braises and stews prepared from rabbit, game, and rooster (an authentic coq au vin) are sometimes thickened with the animal's blood, either alone or combined with the puréed liver of the animal. The French call such dishes *civets* (see "Blood" and Civet de Lapin, pages 128 and 129).

Adjusting the Flavor of Braising Liquid

Although a properly made stew or braise will always produce a full-flavored liquid, the chef may wish to enhance the flavor of the liquid by underlining one or more of its elements or by finishing it with distinct and assertively flavored ingredients to give it an individual or regional character. Many of the techniques suitable for brown sauces (see Chapter 7, "Brown Sauces," page 157) can be used to improve the flavor of braising and stewing liquids. Careful additions of vinegar, Cognac, or marc will often bring up the flavors inherent in the stew without distorting them. The most common and useful final flavorings for stews and braises are freshly chopped herbs. Chopped fines herbes—without tarragon—either alone or in combination, or tarragon alone, is best for flavoring delicate braises of chicken, pork, or veal cooked with water or stock. More assertive meats, such as beef, lamb, or venison, especially if they have been braised with red wine or vinegar, can do with more assertive treatment. Freshly chopped marjoram or oregano will give the dish a southern French or Italian character, and chopped cilantro will give final distinction to a Mexican-style stew.

A skilled saucier is likely to use a combination of methods to adjust the consistency and flavor of a finished braising liquid. He or she may reduce the liquid slightly, thicken it with aromatic vegetable purée, and finish it with a final touch of butter; or he or she may prefer to leave the braising liquid alone and serve the stew or braise in the style of a hearty red wine soup.

Garnitures

The term *garniture* is somewhat confusing because it is used in so many different ways. In America, a garniture often means a bit of decoration, usually not meant to be eaten, that is put on the side of the plate to give added color—most commonly, a sprig of parsley. In French terminology, a garniture is usually a vegetable or vegetables served as an accompaniment to meat or fish.

Garnitures for braised meats and stews are often served over the sliced meat or along with the pieces of meat in the stew, to give the impression that the garniture has been cooked with, and is an intrinsic component of, the braise or stew.

In some cases, especially in home cooking, stews and braised meats are served along with the aromatic vegetables used in the cooking. In most professional settings, however, the aromatic vegetables are separated from the meat at the end of cooking and either discarded or puréed as a sauce thickener. New garnishing vegetables are then either cooked along with the meat near the end of the braising, simmered in some of the braising liquid, or cooked entirely separately, to be added to the meat as it is served.

Garnitures for stews and braises are almost endless. For many home-cooked stews, the aromatic vegetables are cut into same-size shapes and added to the stew during the last 45 minutes of cooking. A somewhat more sophisticated approach, more often used in restaurants, is to cook the aromatic vegetables (sometimes turned or cut into decorative shapes) on top of the stove in some of the cooking liquid drawn off the stew or braise. Certain garnitures, such as wild mushrooms, are sautéed on top of the stove and added to the stew or over the braised meat just before serving. This method is useful for accenting and giving character to the finished stew without altering the flavor of the braising liquid. A beef daube, for example, covered at the last minute with wild mushrooms sautéed with lavender flowers and garlic purée, will benefit from the heady aroma of the mushrooms while the delicate suavity of the braising liquid is left intact.

Classic Garnitures for Stews and Pot Roasts

The classic French literature is filled with classic garnitures for stews and pot roasts. Remember that the basic stewing or braising method stays the same and the aromatic garniture (the onions, carrots, etc., cooked with the meat) is strained out before the final garniture is added. While many of these garnitures are dated, they provide plenty of ideas for more contemporary interpretations. Garnitures are always expressed in the feminine because the "à la" is short for *à la façon de*, which is feminine. Here are a few of the classics:

Algérienne. Potatoes croquette made with sweet potatoes and rolled into cork shapes and fried, and baked tomato halves

Alsacienne. Surrounded with tartlets filled with braised cabbage

Andalouse. Surrounded with grilled peppers, rice, and rounds of eggplant sautéed in olive oil, and topped with sautéed tomatoes

Berrichonne. Braised cabbage in little rounds the size of an egg, bacon, pearl onions, and glazed chestnuts

Bouquetière. Turned carrots and turnips, château potatoes, peas, diced string beans, cauliflower florets

Bourgeoise. Turned carrots, glazed onions, diced bacon

Bréban. Artichoke bottoms filled with fava bean purée, cauliflower, fingerling potatoes

Châtelaine. Artichoke bottoms filled with thick soubise (onion purée bound with béchamel), noisette potatoes (sautéed potatoes cut out with a melon baller)

Dubarry. Cauliflower coated with Mornay sauce and gratinéed

Financière. Quenelles made from chicken or veal, button mushrooms, cockscombs, and kidneys, truffles, olives

Jardinière. Carrots, turnips, string beans, flageolet beans, peas, cauliflower

Judic. Stuffed tomatoes, baby lettuces, château potatoes

Macédoine. Just like à la jardinière, but all the vegetables are arranged in artichoke bottoms

Printanière. Like jardinière except noisette potatoes also included

Renaissance. Baby artichokes filled with miniature turned carrots and turnips, string beans, peas, asparagus tips, and cauliflower, everything coated with hollandaise sauce

Sarladaise. Sautéed sliced potatoes and truffles

Braised Veal, Beef, and Pork Recipes

There are so many methods of braising, each with its own nuances that cause variations in the texture of the meat and the flavor of the sauce, that it is sometimes difficult to sort out the various techniques. The first few of the following recipes are all for a tied shoulder clod of veal to make comparison easy, but veal round will work well for white braising and pot roasting (poêlage) when the meat is not cooked long enough to dry it out.

American butchers usually use the meatiest section of the shoulder, called the *clod*, which is tied up for roasts and braises. The smaller pieces of the shoulder are cut into chunks and used as stew meat. The shoulder clod is tender enough to be used for roasting, but it can also be braised.

Model for Preparing Braises and Stews

MEAT

Beef
  Braising: bottom round, rump (well larded)
  Stewing: shank, short ribs, chuck, round
  (well larded)
Lamb
  Braising: whole shoulder
  Stewing: shoulder, leg (well larded), shanks
Veal
  Braising: shoulder clod, round (well larded),
  breast
  Stewing: shoulder, shank
Pork
  Braising: shoulder
  Stewing: shoulder, shank
Poultry
  Stewing: older hens or roosters, duck legs, goose
  (larding of breasts is suggested)
Game
  Braising and Stewing: older animals or tougher
  cuts from large animals such as deer or boar

MARINADE INGREDIENTS
OPTIONAL

Liquids
  Red or white wine
  Vinegar (good-quality wine or cider)
Oils
  Olive
  Grapeseed
  Inert-tasting peanut or safflower
Aromatic Vegetables
  Onions
  Garlic
  Carrots
  Celery
  Turnips
Herbs
  Parsley
  Bay leaf
  Thyme
  Tarragon
  Hyssop
  Basil

Spices
  Juniper berries
  Cloves (usually stuck into onions)
  Peppercorns

MOISTENING INGREDIENTS

Water
Wine (white, red, and fortified wines, alone or
  in combination)
Stock (neutral, such as veal or chicken, or the
  same type as the meat being braised)
Spirits (brandy, whiskey, marc), flamed
Beer
Cider

AROMATIC VEGETABLES

Same as those used in the marinade

HERBS

Same as those used in the marinade

SPICES

Same as those used in the marinade

LIAISONS
OPTIONAL

Flour (used to coat meat before browning or
  sprinkled over during browning; beurre manié
  used at the end to finish the braising liquid)
Arrowroot or cornstarch (combined with water,
  used to finish the braising liquid; produces a
  glossy appearance)
Vegetable purée (puréed aromatic vegetables taken
  from the braise or stew, or vegetable purées prepared on the side from garlic, beans, mushrooms,
  potatoes, turnips, celeriac root, and the like)
Liver (usually for poultry, game, or rabbits)
Blood (usually for game and rabbit civets, but
  also coq au vin)
Butter
Foie gras (puréed with butter)

FINAL FLAVORINGS

Fines herbs (without tarragon, or tarragon alone, usually for chicken, pork, or veal)

Assertive herbs (thyme, marjoram, oregano, basil, usually for red meats or game)

Spirits (Cognac, Armagnac, marc or grappa, eau-de-vie, whiskey)

GARNITURES

The following are heated in the braising liquid:

Carrots (cylinders with core removed, turned, julienne, or bâtonnets)

Turnips (turned, julienne)

Pearl onions

Garlic cloves (peeled)

Mushrooms

Truffles

These garnitures are sautéed or heated separately and added at the end of cooking:

Wild mushrooms (with herbs, garlic, shallots)

Artichoke hearts

Poultry or rabbit livers

Olives

Croutons

Bacon lardoons

ÉTOUFFÉE OF VEAL SHOULDER CLOD

Most recipes for white braising suggest moistening the braise with enough stock to come halfway up the meat and then cooking, uncovered, with frequent basting. In an étouffée, the stock is added a bit at a time so that it can gently caramelize during the braising. If too much stock is added at the beginning, the finished jus will have the flavor of a poaching liquid and may require reduction. If too little stock is added, the juices will caramelize and burn.

YIELD: 8 TO 10 SERVINGS

veal shoulder clod	4 to 5 pounds	1.8 to 2.3 kilograms
onion, chopped	1 medium	1 medium
carrot, chopped	1 medium	1 medium
celery, chopped	½ stalk	½ stalk
veal or pork trimmings, pancetta, or prosciutto, chopped	5 ounces	150 grams
clarified butter	¼ cup	60 milliliters
white or brown meat stock	2 quarts	2 liters
medium bouquet garni (page 51)	1	1

1. Tie the meat into an even shape.
2. Select an oval casserole that will just hold the tied shoulder clod. Sweat the onion, carrot, celery, and meat trimmings in the clarified butter in the casserole until the vegetables are shiny and translucent.

3. Place the tied shoulder clod on top of the vegetables and cook it on all sides on the stove over a low heat for 15 to 20 minutes, until it is a pale golden brown but not dark. Meanwhile, preheat the oven to 350°F (175°C).

4. Add ½ cup (125 milliliters) of the meat stock to the bottom of the casserole. Turn the heat onto high and reduce the stock to a glaze on the bottom of the casserole; do not allow it to caramelize.

5. Add ½ cup (125 milliliters) of the remaining stock to the casserole and bring it to a slow simmer on top of the stove. Add the bouquet garni. Place the casserole, covered, in the oven.

6. Baste the meat every 10 minutes. If the braising liquid evaporates and starts to caramelize on the bottom of the casserole, add another ½ cup (125 milliliters) of stock. Continue in this way until the veal is done (see Note). The veal is done when the juices run clear when the clod is poked in the center with a skewer, at an internal temperature of 135° to 140°F (57° to 60°C), the same as a roast. This takes about 45 minutes.

7. Transfer the meat to a platter and strain the braising liquid. Skim off any fat that floats to the surface of the strained liquid, and serve the remaining liquid over the meat or in a sauce boat alongside.

Note: The jus for an étouffée is best when the cooking liquid is kept constantly on the verge of caramelizing. The amount of stock that must be added during the last stage of cooking depends on the oven temperature and the amount of liquid released by the veal.

POT-ROASTED VEAL SHOULDER CLOD
Poêlage

In authentic poêlage, no moisture comes in contact with the meat during cooking; the meat is cooked in a covered casserole with mirepoix vegetables and butter alone. At the end of cooking, it is transferred to a platter while a jus is prepared by moistening the mirepoix with stock. The oven temperature must be carefully controlled: If it is too hot, the juices released by the veal will burn; if it is not hot enough, the juices will not caramelize and the veal will stew in its own juices.

YIELD: 8 TO 10 SERVINGS

veal shoulder clod	4 to 5 pounds	1.8 to 2.3 kilograms
onion, chopped	1 medium	1 medium
carrot, chopped	1 medium	1 medium
celery, chopped	½ stalk	½ stalk
veal or pork trimmings, pancetta, or ham, chopped	5 ounces	150 grams
clarified butter	½ cup	125 milliliters
large bouquet garni (page 51)	1	1
white or brown meat stock	2 cups	500 milliliters

1. Tie the meat into an even shape. Preheat the oven to 350°F (175°C).
2. Select an oval casserole that will just hold the tied shoulder clod.
3. Combine the onion, carrot, celery, and meat trimmings in the casserole. Add ¼ cup (60 milliliters) of the clarified butter and sweat the vegetables and meat trimmings for about 10 minutes, until the vegetables are translucent.
4. Put the tied shoulder clod on top of the vegetable-meat mixture (mirepoix). Pour over the remaining clarified butter.
5. Cover the casserole and place it in the oven. Baste the veal with the butter in the pan every 10 minutes, while checking the condition of the jus. If the vegetables and jus start to brown on the bottom of the casserole during the first 20 minutes of cooking, turn down the oven. If, on the other hand, the veal is sitting in a pale colorless liquid, turn up the oven. (It may be necessary to adjust the oven temperature several times during the cooking.) The veal is done when the juices run clear when the clod is poked in the center with a skewer, at an internal temperature of 135° to 140°F (57° to 60°C), the same as a roast. This takes about 1 hour.
6. Transfer the meat to a platter. Add ½ cup (125 milliliters) of stock to the casserole. Simmer it until it caramelizes. Do not pour off the butter.
7. Add the remaining 1½ cups (375 milliliters) of stock to the caramelized juices and bring it to a slow simmer for 5 minutes.
8. Strain the jus into a saucepan and skim off excess fat with a ladle. Serve the jus over the meat or in a sauce boat alongside.

BROWN-BRAISED VEAL SHOULDER CLOD

Brown-braised meats are cooked until the muscle fibers break down, leaving the meat tender. When this method is carried to its logical extreme, it is called *à la cuillère,* which implies the meat is so tender that it can be cut with a spoon.

YIELD: 8 TO 10 SERVINGS

fatback	1 pound	500 grams
garlic cloves, chopped	2	2
veal shoulder clod	4 to 5 pounds	1.8 to 2.3 kilograms
onion, chopped	1 medium	1 medium
carrot, chopped	1 medium	1 medium
celery, chopped	½ stalk	½ stalk
veal or pork trimmings, pancetta, or prosciutto, chopped	5 ounces	150 grams
clarified butter	¼ cup	60 milliliters
white or brown meat stock	2 quarts	2 liters
large bouquet garni (page 51)	1	1

1. Cut the fatback into 6 × ⅜-inch (15 cm × 5 mm) strips. Toss the strips in a stainless-steel bowl with the chopped garlic. Cover and refrigerate for 2 to 3 hours.

2. Open the shoulder clod and lay it out on a cutting board. Insert the strips of fatback into the various muscles with a larding needle (an *aiguille à piquer;* not a *lardoire;* see page 29). Turn the meat over and lard the outside. Tie the larded shoulder clod into an even shape. Preheat the oven to 350°F (175°C).

3. Select an oval casserole that will just hold the tied shoulder clod. Put the chopped onion, carrot, celery, meat trimmings, and clarified butter in the casserole. Set the tied shoulder clod on top.

4. Roast the shoulder, uncovered, in the oven for approximately 40 minutes, until it is golden brown and there are caramelized meat drippings on the bottom of the casserole. Turn down the oven to 300°F (150°C).

5. Add 1 cup (250 milliliters) of the meat stock to the bottom of the casserole. Place the casserole on top of the stove on high heat. Heat on high until the stock reduces to a glaze and caramelizes on the bottom of the casserole.

6. Add the bouquet garni and enough of the remaining stock to come halfway up the sides of the meat. Bring it to a slow simmer on top of the stove. Cover the casserole with a sheet of aluminum foil that is pressed down in the middle (which causes liquid to condense and drip down over the meat, so it is basted from the inside), and put on the lid. Place the casserole in the oven.

7. As the veal braises, check the casserole every 20 minutes to make sure the liquid is not boiling. Continue cooking the veal in this way for 2 to 3 hours, until a skewer inserted in the veal slides in and out with no resistance.

8. Carefully remove the meat (at this stage it is very fragile) from the braising liquid, and place it in a clean oval casserole. Turn the oven back up to 350°F (175°C).

9. Strain the braising liquid and place it in a saucepan on top of the stove. Bring it to a simmer and skim off any froth and fat that floats to the surface. Continue skimming and reducing for 20 minutes.

10. Pour the reduced and degreased braising liquid over the veal, and place the veal, uncovered, in the oven. Baste the veal every 5 minutes with the surrounding liquid. Continue in this way until the braising liquid has a lightly syrupy consistency and the veal is shiny and reddish brown.

11. Transfer the veal to a plate or platter and strain the braising liquid.

Note: Unlike roasts, white braises, and pot roasts, which cannot be reheated without causing them to overcook, slices of braised meats can be reheated to order in a small amount of braising liquid in a covered sauté pan.

ROUND OF VEAL ÉTOUVÉ

The term *etouver* refers to roasting in the oven or, sometimes, in a closed vessel. The only thing added to the meat being treated in this way is butter, preferably clarified butter that poses no risk of burning. The secret to success requires understanding what happens to a roast such as a veal round when it gets hot.

Essentially it releases juices that should caramelize as soon as they reach the hot outer surface of the meat. If the oven isn't hot enough, the juices accumulate in the bottom of the pan and cause the roast to steam. If the oven is too hot, the juices burn. The secret is to maintain a kind of homeostasis in which the juices are constantly caramelizing on the surface of the meat. If you see liquid in the pan, turn up the oven. If, on the other hand, you see any signs of excessive darkening, add a little broth to the roast to stop the caramelization.

Be aware when buying round of veal that it comes "cap on" or "cap off." It costs less per pound with the cap on, and you can then use the cap to prepare the jus for the roast.

YIELD: 8 MAIN-COURSE SERVINGS

round of veal, cap on	5 pounds	2.5 kilograms
carrot, chopped	1	1
onion, minced	1	1
broth or water	1 cup	250 milliliters
salt and pepper	to taste	to taste
clarified butter	½ cup	125 milliliters

1. Preheat the oven to a 450°F (230°C). Take the cap off the veal, cut the cap into small pieces, and put in a pan with the carrot and onion in the oven until it browns and any juices it releases caramelize on the bottom of the pan. Deglaze the pan with the broth or water. Reserve this liquid, the jus. Rinse out the pan. Leave the oven on at 450°F (230°C) for the roast.

2. Season the veal round with salt and pepper and brown it, over high heat, in 2 tablespoons (30 milliliters) of the butter until browned on all sides.

3. Put the veal in a pot just large enough to hold it and pour over the remaining clarified butter. Roast the veal to an internal temperature of 130°F (55°C); as the veal rests it will reach 135°F (57°C) and become firm to the touch. Follow the directions above for adjusting the oven temperature according to what the veal is doing. Cover the veal loosely with aluminum foil and let it rest for 20 minutes before carving.

5. Serve the veal by carving on a bias and serving "scaloppine." Serve the juices in the pot combined with the jus you made from the cap.

OSSO BUCO WITH JULIENNED VEGETABLES

Almost all braised dishes include aromatic vegetables, particularly onions, carrots, celery, and often garlic. In traditional French cooking, these vegetables are taken out of the dish before serving or left in depending on whether the style is *ménagère*, meaning "housewife," *bourgeoise*, as in *cuisine bourgeoise*, or *classique*. In cuisine ménagère the aromatic vegetables are left in and served with the braised or stewed meat. In cuisine bourgeoise the vegetables are strained out and discarded and new vegetables are added to the braising during the last hour or so of cooking. In cuisine classique, the vegetables are cooked separately, on the stove, and added to the dish at the very end.

This dish, in the tradition of la cuisine ménagère, leaves the vegetables in but in deference to more refined styles, the vegetables are julienned so they end up in a decorative tangle on top of the meat.

YIELD: 6 MAIN-COURSE SERVINGS

osso buco rounds, 12 to 14 ounces (335 to 400 grams) each	6	6
salt and pepper	to taste	to taste
olive oil	3 tablespoons	45 milliliters
dry white wine	1 cup	250 milliliters
veal or chicken broth or water	3 cups	750 milliliters
large bouquet garni (page 51)	1	1
leeks	3 medium	3 medium
turnips	2 medium	2 medium
carrots	3 large	3 large
celeriac (optional)	1 medium	1 medium
fennel (optional)	1 bulb	1 bulb

1. Season the osso buco on both sides with salt and pepper and brown the rounds in the olive oil on both sides over high heat in a pan with high straight sides just large enough to hold them in a single layer.
2. Take them out of the pan and pour out the fat. Put the osso buco back in the pan, pour over the wine, and bring it to a simmer. Simmer for 5 minutes and add the broth and the bouquet garni. Adjust the heat to maintain a very gentle simmer and cover loosely with aluminum foil pressed down slightly over the osso buco so condensation forms on the underside of the foil and bastes those parts of the osso buco that aren't submerged. Cover the pan and simmer for 1 hour.
3. While the veal is braising, julienne the vegetables. After the veal has simmered for 1 hour, pile the vegetables on top of the veal, replace the foil and the lid, and simmer another hour. Slide a paring knife into the meat and lift straight up. When the meat no longer clings to the knife as you lift, the meat is ready.
4. Take the vegetables out of the pan with tongs, discard the bouquet garni, put the osso buco in heated soup plates, ladle over the braising liquid, and cover with a tangle of vegetables. See the photograph in the color plates.

BRAISED SWEETBREADS

Regardless of how sweetbreads are cooked—they're usually braised or sautéed—they first undergo a blanching and weighting process to compact them. Sweetbreads come in two forms. One, long and a bit ragged, is called in French the *gorge*, meaning "throat," while the other, compact and spheroid, is called the *noix*, meaning "nut." Always choose the noix, which will look neater on the plate.

YIELD: 6 MAIN-COURSE SERVINGS

sweetbreads, preferably noix pieces	2½ pounds	1.25 kilograms
carrot, cut into small dice	1 large	1 large
onion, minced	1 medium	1 medium
garlic clove, minced	1	1
butter	1 ounce	30 grams
white wine	½ cup	125 milliliters
meat glace (page 104; optional)	2 tablespoons	30 milliliters
heavy cream	1 cup	250 milliliters
salt and pepper	to taste	to taste

1. Put the sweetbreads in a pot with enough cold water to cover and bring to a boil over high heat. As soon as the water comes to a boil, take out the sweetbreads and put them on a sheet pan. Put a cutting board on top with some cans or pots on top of that to weight the sweetbreads. Store in the refrigerator for 6 hours or overnight. Trim off loose pieces of fat and tissue.

2. In a pan just large enough to hold the sweetbreads in a single layer, cook the carrot, onion, and garlic in the butter over medium heat until the onion is translucent but not brown, about 10 minutes. Preheat the oven to 400°F (200°C).

3. Arrange the sweetbreads over the vegetables in the pan. Place a round of parchment paper or aluminum foil on top of the sweetbreads and slide the pan into the oven. Check every 10 minutes to make sure none of the juices are burning. If the juices are caramelizing and threatening to burn, add half the wine.

4. Bake for about 25 minutes or until firm to the touch. Take the sweetbreads out of the pan and keep them warm. Add the wine to the pan along with the meat glace and cream and bring to a simmer. Season to taste with salt and pepper. Slice the sweetbreads and top with the sauce. Here the vegetables are left in the sauce, but they may also be strained out.

Variations

This technique for braising sweetbreads and building a sauce is almost universal, but various ingredients can be added to the sauce to give it a different character. Chiffonade of sorrel, chopped fines herbs, sautéed or reconstituted dried porcini mushrooms, morels, and truffles are just a few possibilities. In the early twentieth century, sweetbreads were often served à la financière with truffles, chicken quenelles, and cockscombs. It's also possible to use a brunoise of carrots and turnips along with the minced onions to braise the sweetbreads and then use this as part of the garniture. Michel Guérard serves a dish of sweetbreads in which the sweetbreads are separated into pieces—virtually all the connective membrane is removed—and the braised pieces served in a sauce made with morels and truffles. Wedges of artichoke bottoms are served with the sweetbreads to provide a subtly contrasting texture. The whole thing is served in a rectangle of puff pastry to further add to the interplay of textures.

BRAISED SHORT RIBS

Short ribs are a perfect braising cut because they contain a lot of natural fat and gelatin. The fat slowly renders during braising and is later skimmed off, but during the process keeps the meat moist. Short ribs come in two forms: left long or cut crosswise into 2-inch (5 cm) lengths. Here we use long-cut short ribs, but the short form will also work.

YIELD: 8 SERVINGS

short ribs, 4 ribs each piece, ribs about 6 inches (15 cm) long	2 7 pounds	2 3.2 kilograms
salt and pepper	to taste	to taste
carrots, cut into sections	2 large	2 large
onion, sliced	1 large	1 large
garlic head, cut crosswise in half	1	1
red wine	3 cups	750 milliliters
chicken broth, as needed	2 cups or more	500 milliliters
large bouquet garni (page 51)	1	1

1. Preheat the oven to 400°F (200°C).
2. Roast the short ribs in the oven with the carrots, onion, and garlic until browned and any juices released caramelize on the bottom of the roasting pan, about 90 minutes. Turn off the oven.
3. Transfer the ribs and vegetables to a pot that holds them as compactly as possible. Deglaze the roasting pan with 1 cup (250 milliliters) of red wine and pour this into the pot. Pour over the rest of the red wine and broth and add the bouquet garni. Cover the pot with aluminum foil and the lid and simmer very gently for an hour. Rearrange the ribs so any that were protruding above the liquid are now submerged. Simmer in the same way for another hour or more, until a knife slides easily in and out of the ribs.
4. Turn the oven back on to 400°F (200°C). Put the short ribs in a clean pot. Strain the braising liquid and skim off any fat. Pour the braising liquid

over the ribs and glaze in the oven by basting, uncovered. When the glaze is syrupy and the ribs shiny, they're ready to serve.

5. Carve the ribs, one rib per serving, and serve surrounded with the braising liquid.

CHINESE-STYLE BRAISED SHORT RIBS

The idea of braising short ribs with cinnamon and star anise comes from Susanna Foo, one of our foremost writers about Chinese cuisine. For a more generic flavor, braise the ribs in red wine and broth and omit the spices and soy sauce. Keep in mind that short ribs come in two cuts: one consists of relatively long pieces of ribs—6 inches (15 cm) or so—and the other, used here, cut transversely into strips of 4 or so ribs about 1 inch (2.5 cm) long.

YIELD: 6 MAIN-COURSE SERVINGS

short ribs, cut crosswise so the ribs are 2 inches (5 cm) long	6 to 8 pounds	3 to 3.5 kilograms
onion, sliced	1 large	1 large
carrot, sliced	1 large	1 large
chicken or beef broth	1 quart	1 liter
garlic cloves, crushed, peeled	6	6
fresh ginger, peeled, sliced into thin rounds	2-inch piece	5 centimeters
star anise, crushed	5	5
honey	¼ cup	60 milliliters
soy sauce	¼ cup	60 milliliters
sherry vinegar	¼ cup	60 milliliters
cinnamon stick, 3 inches (8 cm) long	1	1

1. Preheat the oven to 400°F (200°C).
2. Place the ribs on top of the carrot and onion in a single or double layer in a round pan with a lid (rondeau). Bake in the oven until the meat is brown, the fat has rendered, and the juices have caramelized at the bottom of the pot. Pour out and discard the fat. Turn off the oven.
3. Pour and sprinkle over the remaining ingredients and cover with a sheet of aluminum foil and then the pot lid. Bring to a gentle simmer on the stove and let simmer until a knife slides easily through the ribs, about 2 hours.
4. Turn the oven back on to 400°F (200°C). Transfer the ribs to a clean pot and strain the braising liquid into a saucepan. Bring the liquid to a simmer and skim off any fat and froth that floats to the top. Reduce the braising liquid by about a third and pour it over the ribs.
5. Bake the ribs in the oven, basting with the braising liquid, until they are covered with a lightly syrupy glaze. Pass the braising liquid at the table in a sauce boat.

RED WINE POT ROAST

The most important step in making a pot roast is to choose the right cut of meat. A blade roast from the shoulder is best and can be cut into a large chunk suitable for braising.

In French cooking there are all sorts of ways to finish a pot roast including the classic Burgundian garniture of mushrooms, pearl onions, and bacon lardoons. Other variations including braising the beef with a substantial number of sliced carrots and then leaving them in as the garniture. The aromatic garniture (those vegetables stewed with the meat) can be left in or strained out. Here we strain it out.

YIELD: 6 SERVINGS

blade roast from the shoulder, 1	5 pounds	2.25 kilograms
onion, chopped fine	1 large	1 large
carrots, sliced	2 large	2 large
red wine	3 cups	750 milliliters
meat glace (page 104; optional)	¼ cup	60 milliliters
large bouquet garni (page 51)	1	1
salt and pepper	to taste	to taste
red wine vinegar to taste	2 tablespoons	30 milliliters

1. Preheat the oven to 450°F (230°C).
2. Tie up the roast and spread the vegetables in a pot just large enough to hold the roast. Place the roast on top.
3. Roast the meat until it browns and any juices it releases caramelize on the bottom of the pot, about an hour. Be careful at this last stage not to burn the juices. Turn the oven off or turn it down to 300°F (150°C).
4. Put the pot on the stove and pour over the wine. Add the meat glace, if using, and the bouquet garni; bring to a simmer. Cover the pot with aluminum foil and braise gently on the stove or in the oven until the meat is easily penetrated with a skewer, about 3 hours.
5. Take out the meat and strain the juices into a saucepan. Discard the vegetables or save them to serve with the roast. Discard the bouquet garni. Clean out the pan and put the roast back in. Turn the oven to 400°F (200°C).
6. Simmer the braising liquid on the stove and skim off the fat. Pour the liquid over the roast, slide the roast into the oven, and baste every 5 minutes for about an hour, or until it becomes shiny and the braising liquid syrupy. Season the braising liquid to taste with salt, pepper, and vinegar.
7. Serve with a spoon or knife and fork in soup plates and spoon over the braising liquid.

Mixed Shellfish Fricassée (PAGE 348)

Asparagus with Sauce Hollandaise
(PAGE 381)

Salmon en Papillotte with
Julienned Vegetable and
Chive Butter (PAGE 310)

Duck Breasts with Peaches or
Other Fruits (PAGE 281)

Osso Buco with Julienned
Vegetables (PAGE 255)

Pot au Feu (PAGE 237)

Duck Breast with Red Currants (PAGE 281)

Chicken with Morels (PAGE 278)

Coq au Vin (PAGE 268)

Chicken with Capers and Oysters (PAGE 14)

Sea Scallops with Butter-Enriched Nage (PAGE 292)

Shrimp Cocktail (PAGE 424)

Halibut Braised with Cockles (PAGE 303)

OPPOSITE: Oysters with Champagne Sauce (PAGE 319)

Sautéed Pigeon Breasts
with Giblet Sauce
(PAGE 123)

Steak with
Sauce Bordelaise,
Meat-Glace Method
(PAGE 179)

Braised Lamb Shanks with Shallots (PAGE 112)

Salmon with Basic Japanese Broth-Like
Sauce (PAGE 522)

Poached Chicken with Vegetables (PAGE 241)

Braised Duck Thighs (PAGE 280)

Boiled Lobster with Sauce Cardinal (PAGE 334)

Spaghetti with Clams (PAGE 504)

Tournedos Rossini (PAGE 192)

Fettuccine with Peas (PAGE 511)

Raspberries with
Sabayon (PAGE 564)

Roast Pears with
Pear-Butterscotch
Sauce and Ganache
(PAGES 569 AND 566)

Foie Gras "en Gelée" (PAGE 365)

Steak with Sauce Béarnaise (PAGE 378)

Poached Chicken (PAGE 241)

Roast Rack of Lamb with Natural Jus (PAGE 232)

Pork Shoulder Chops with White Wine and Prunes (PAGE 261)

Shrimp with Tropical Fruit Salsa (PAGE 448)

Lobster à la Nage II (PAGE 340)

Poached Eggs with Meurette Sauce (PAGE 181)

PORK SHOULDER CHOPS WITH WHITE WINE AND PRUNES

This French country dish demonstrates an excellent method for braising. Here we use shoulder chops, which require long braising; if you're using loin chops, short-braise them by cooking them only long enough for the heat to penetrate them. Here the garniture is simple, prunes steeped in water, then simmered in white wine, traditionally Vouvray, but this dish is a model for braising shoulder chops and can be garnished with virtually anything.

YIELD: 6 MAIN-COURSE SERVINGS

shoulder pork chops	6 large	6 large
salt and pepper	to taste	to taste
oil	3 tablespoons	45 milliliters
butter	1½ ounces	45 grams
carrot, chopped	1 medium	1 medium
onion, chopped	1 medium	1 medium
dry or semi-dry white wine such as Vouvray	1 cup	250 milliliters
chicken broth, preferably concentrated, or water	2 cups	500 milliliters
large bouquet garni (page 51)	1	1
prunes, pitted	1 cup	250 milliliters
heavy cream	1 cup	250 milliliters

1. Season the chops with salt and pepper. Brown them in the oil in a heavy-bottomed pan over high heat. Put the chops on a plate and pour the oil out of the pan. Add the butter, carrot, and onion to the pan and cook gently for about 10 minutes.
2. Add the chops back to the pan and pour in the wine and broth. Bring to a gentle simmer. Nestle in the bouquet garni. Cover the chops with a sheet of aluminum foil almost touching their surface. Cover with the lid. Simmer gently for about 2 hours, until a knife stuck into one of the chops goes in and out with no resistance.
3. Meanwhile, soak the prunes in just enough water to cover for 30 minutes.
4. Gently transfer the chops to a plate and keep them warm in a low oven while you make the sauce. Take out the bouquet garni and strain the braising liquid into a saucepan. Simmer gently, skimming off any fat and scum that floats to the surface, until the sauce cooks down by about three-quarters or takes on a lightly syrupy consistency. Add the cream and simmer again until the sauce thickens just slightly—it should be kept light. Drain the prunes and add them to the sauce.
5. Simmer the prunes in the sauce for a minute to soften them and then season the sauce to taste with salt and pepper. Arrange the chops on heated plates and spoon over the prunes and sauce. See the photograph in the color plates.

Stews are braises made with pieces of meat or poultry instead of whole birds or large cuts. The best meat stews are made from gelatinous and relatively fatty cuts. When leaner, more tender cuts are used, the stew is greatly improved by inserting a strip of fatback into each piece so that the meat is moistened from the inside while cooking.

The character of a finished stew is determined not only by the type and cut of meat or poultry used but by several other factors: whether or not it is browned before being moistened, the type of moistening liquid, the types of aromatic vegetables used, the herbs used in the bouquet garni, the final liaison if any, and the final garniture. Strips of pork rind, split and blanched pork, or veal trotters are also sometimes added to stews and braises to support the texture of the finished liquid.

In French classical and regional cooking a variety of terms describe stews. Some of the names indicate only that a dish has a regional character, whereas others give hints as to the techniques used in its preparation. The term *ragoût* can refer to almost any stew but has negative connotations, as does *galimafrée*, a completely acceptable term for a medieval stew. In modern French, however, it translates roughly as "mess."

Stews can be divided into two categories: brown stews, for which the meat or poultry is cooked in fat before moistening, and white stews, for which the meat or poultry is directly moistened without preliminary cooking. In brown stews, the meat or poultry is often dredged in or sprinkled with flour before being cooked in fat.

There is very little difference between a white stew and pieces of meat that have been poached—the only distinction is the amount of liquid used. The terms "white" braise or stew and "brown" braise or stew refer to whether the meat has been browned, not to the final color of the sauce. Thus, a beef stew made with red wine, without browning the meat, is still a white braise, even though the final color of the sauce is dark.

RED WINE BEEF STEW

YIELD: 8 TO 10 SERVINGS

fatback, rind removed	8 ounces	250 grams
garlic cloves, chopped	2	2
cognac	2 tablespoons	30 milliliters
beef shank (4 pounds/1.8 kilograms when cut from the bone)	6 pounds	3 kilograms
carrots, chopped	2 medium	2 medium

onions, chopped	2 medium	2 medium
garlic cloves, crushed	2	2
red wine	3 cups	750 milliliters
large bouquet garni (page 51)	1	1
olive oil	6 tablespoons	90 milliliters
butter	1½ ounces	45 grams
flour (optional)	¼ cup	40 grams
brown meat stock	3 cups	750 milliliters
liaison such as beurre manié, arrowroot, or vegetable purée (optional)		

1. Cut the fatback into 2 × ⅜-inch (5 cm × 5 mm) strips.
2. Marinate the fatback strips in the chopped garlic and Cognac for at least 3 hours.
3. Cut the beef into 3-ounce (75 gram) cubes. Insert a strip of fatback into each beef cube using a larding needle or paring knife.
4. Marinate the meat cubes for several hours with the carrots, onions, crushed garlic, red wine, and bouquet garni.
5. Preheat the oven to 300°F (150°C). Drain the meat in a colander set over a bowl and separately reserve the marinade liquid, vegetables, and bouquet garni. Thoroughly dry the meat. Heat the olive oil in a straight-sided sauté pan and brown the meat.
6. Transfer the meat to a bowl and discard the oil. Sweat the reserved chopped vegetables and crushed garlic in the butter in the sauté pan. Sprinkle the vegetables with flour, if using, and cook gently for 5 minutes more.
7. Add the reserved marinade liquid, the stock, and the reserved bouquet garni to the sweated vegetables and bring the mixture to a simmer while scraping the bottom of the pan with a wooden spoon.
8. Transfer the contents of the sauté pan to a 4-quart (4 liter) pot. Add the meat. Cover and cook in the oven for 2 to 3 hours, until the meat cubes are easily pierced with a fork.
9. Strain the stewing liquid into a 2-quart (2 liter) saucepan. Bring it to a slow simmer and skim off any froth or fat that floats to the surface. The stewing liquid can be reduced to the desired thickness or bound with beurre manié (the most traditional method), arrowroot, vegetable purées, or other liaison.
10. Spread the solid ingredients on a baking sheet. Separate the meat from the chopped vegetables, which should be discarded or can be puréed for use as the liaison. Reheat the meat cubes in the thickened stewing liquid. Serve with an appropriate garniture.

⊶● BOEUF BOURGUIGNON

Don't confuse boeuf bourguignon, a stew, with boeuf à la bourguignonne, which is a pot roast. The stewing is a standard method used for virtually all stews; the name comes from the garniture of pearl onions, bacon, and mushrooms added at the end.

YIELD: 8 TO 10 MAIN-COURSE SERVINGS

beef stew meat, cut into 1-inch (2.5 cm) cubes	6 pounds	2.5 kilograms
salt and pepper	to taste	to taste
carrots, cut into ½-inch (1 cm) slices	4 medium	4 medium
onions, halved	2 medium	2 medium
broth or water	as needed	as needed
full-bodied red wine	3 cups	750 milliliters
large bouquet garni (page 51)	1	1
concentrated chicken, veal, or beef broth	1 cup	250 milliliters
pearl onions, peeled	1 pint	500 milliliters
butter (for glazing the onions)	½ ounce	15 grams
mushrooms, preferably cremini, ends cut off, quartered vertically unless very small	1¼ pounds	600 grams
butter (for sautéing the mushrooms)	1 ounce	30 grams
or	or	or
olive oil (for sautéing the mushrooms)	2 tablespoons	30 milliliters
bacon, cut crosswise into 1 × ¼-inch (2.5 cm × 5 mm) lardoons	4 thick slices	4 thick slices
flour (to thicken the stew; optional)	2 tablespoons	30 milliliters
softened butter (to thicken the stew; optional)	1 ounce	30 grams
good wine vinegar, as needed	1 teaspoon up to a few tablespoons	5 milliliters or more

1. Preheat the oven to 500°F (260°C). Season the meat on all sides with salt and pepper and spread it, with the carrots and onions, in a heavy-bottomed roasting pan just large enough to hold everything in a single layer.
2. Roast until well browned, turning the meat and vegetables with tongs every 5 to 10 minutes to brown evenly. Continue until the meat and vegetables are well browned, about 40 minutes. If the meat has released liquid on the bottom of the pan, continue roasting until the juices caramelize into a crust. If a crust has formed before the meat is browned and it threatens to burn, add 1 cup (250 milliliters) of broth.
3. When the meat is browned and all the juices have caramelized on the bottom of the pan—don't confuse the clear fat floating on top with

juices—take out the meat and vegetables with tongs and put them in a tall narrow pot. Spoon or pour out the clear liquid fat—discard it—and deglaze the pan with 2 cups (500 milliliters) of the wine.

4. Put the pan on the stove and scrape the bottom with a wooden spoon to dissolve the juices in the wine, about 5 minutes. Pour the juices over the meat and vegetables. Nestle in the bouquet garni and add the rest of the wine and concentrated broth. The meat should be completely covered; if it isn't, add more broth.

5. If you're making the stew in the oven, turn the oven down to 325°F (160°C). Otherwise, turn it off. Bring the stew to a simmer on the stove and maintain at a gentle simmer for at least 10 minutes, even if you're putting the stew in the oven. Cover the pot and put it in the oven or over a low flame so that a bubble or two rises to the surface in about a second. Continue in this way for about 3 hours but for as many as 5 hours, until the meat, when poked through with a skewer, just falls off without clinging.

6. When the meat is approaching readiness, prepare the garniture. Glaze the pearl onions by cooking them partially covered with butter and enough broth or water to come halfway up their sides. Sauté the mushrooms in butter or oil. Cook the bacon gently until it's lightly crispy, and drain on paper towels.

7. Strain the stew into a wide pan and boil down the braising liquid, on one side of the flame, to quickly reduce it. Spoon off any froth or scum that forms on the side opposite the flame. When reduced to about 2½ cups (625 milliliters), pour this liquid back in with the meat.

8. If you want to thicken the stewing liquid, work the flour and softened butter together with the back of a fork to form beurre manié. Whisk this into the simmering stew (it won't work if the stew isn't simmering) a bit at a time until the stew has the right consistency.

9. Season the stewing liquid to taste with a little salt and pepper. Add the vinegar a tiny bit at a time to taste. Add the garniture ingredients to the stew or arrange them on each serving.

BEEF IRISH STEW

Not surprisingly, Irish stew is all about potatoes. The secret is to use two kinds: Yukon Golds, which dissolve and give a silky body to the stew, and waxy potatoes, which keep their shape and give texture to the stew. Most recipes say to slice the potatoes, but you can also shape them into miniature egg shapes. As for a daube, the meat for Irish stew isn't browned. Usually Irish stew is made with lamb, but it's delicious with beef.

beef stew meat, cut into 1-inch (2.5 cm) cubes	4 pounds	2 kilograms
onions, minced	2 medium	2 medium
beef broth, chicken broth, or water to cover	3 cups	750 milliliters
large bouquet garni (page 51)	1	1
Yukon Gold potato, peeled, sliced as thin as possible with a plastic vegetable slicer (keep the slices in water to keep them from darkening)	1 large	1 large
white or red waxy potatoes, peeled	3 large	3 large
pearl onions or walnut-size boiling onions, peeled (optional)	2 cups	500 milliliters
heavy cream (optional)	¼ to 1 cup	60 to 250 milliliters
salt and pepper	to taste	to taste

1. If you'll be cooking the stew in the oven, preheat the oven to 325°F (160°C).
2. Place the meat, minced onions, and enough broth or water to cover in a tall pot and nestle in the bouquet garni. Bring to a simmer on the stove and skim off any froth or scum that floats to the surface. Add the Yukon Gold potato, cover, and maintain at a gentle simmer on the stove or in the oven.
3. After an hour, stir with a wooden spoon to dissolve the sliced potato.
4. Slice the waxy potatoes into ¼-inch-thick (5 mm) rounds or shape the potatoes into elongated football shapes, 4 to 8 out of each one. When the stew has been simmering for 2 hours, add the waxy potatoes and the pearl onions, if using.
5. Simmer until the meat and potatoes are both easily penetrated with a skewer. Stir in the cream, if using, bring back to a simmer, and season to taste with salt and pepper. Serve in heated soup plates.

Poultry Braises and Stews

The techniques for stewing poultry and rabbit are essentially the same as for veal and red meats. The term *fricassée* traditionally refers to a chicken dish in which the chicken has been cut up, gently cooked in butter without being browned, and stewed with water or stock. The cooking liquid is then finished with heavy cream and egg yolks. The term is sometimes used more loosely to define any chicken or white meat that has been cooked in a small amount of liquid after a gentle preliminary cooking in fat.

Fricassées differ from sautés in that the chicken is finished cooking in liquid, whereas sautés are cooked entirely with a small amount of fat either on top of the stove or in the oven.

Older poultry can be braised, either cut into pieces as for a coq au vin or left whole.

One excellent method for cooking a whole chicken or other small- to medium-size poultry is to cook it covered in a close-fitting casserole with a small amount of liquid. When poultry is prepared in this way—the French call it *en cocotte*—it is cooked to the same doneness as roasts and white braises.

Brown braising of poultry is unusual, partly because the older birds, which lend themselves best to the technique, are not readily available. In addition, long-braised poultry white meat tends to dry out. The only way to prevent this problem is to lard the meat thoroughly with strips of fatback—a laborious (but worthwhile) task that few restaurants are willing to undertake. Most of what is served as coq au vin (rooster braised in red wine) in American restaurants is really a red wine chicken sauté.

POULET EN COCOTTE
Whole Chicken in a Casserole

Chicken cooked in this way is first browned either in the oven or on top of the stove before it is placed into an oval casserole along with vegetables, strips of bacon, and so on. Some recipes suggest then cooking the chicken with butter alone (poêlage), whereas others suggest adding a small amount of liquid, such as water or wine. The casserole is then covered, and the chicken baked for approximately 1 hour.

YIELD: 4 SERVINGS

bacon	3 ounces	75 grams
chicken, 1	3 to 3½ pounds	1.4 to 1.6 kilograms
pearl onions, peeled	20	20
potatoes, turned to the size of large olives	12	12
concentrated chicken or veal stock	3 tablespoons	45 milliliters

1. Preheat the oven to 350°F (175°C). Cut the bacon into 1 × ⅜-inch (2.5 cm × 5 mm) lardoons and blanch them in boiling water for 5 minutes. Gently brown the lardoons in a straight-sided sauté pan. Remove them with a slotted spoon.
2. Truss the chicken and brown it in the fat rendered by the bacon.
3. Remove the chicken from the sauté pan and brown the pearl onions and potatoes.
4. Place the chicken, lardoons, onions, potatoes, and stock in a close-fitting casserole and cover. Bake the casserole in the oven for approximately 1 hour.
5. Transfer the chicken and garniture to a plate or platter and strain the liquid in the casserole into a small bowl, pitcher, or fat separator. Skim off most of the fat and serve the sauce in a sauce boat.

COQ AU VIN
Rooster Braised in Red Wine

Traditional recipes for coq au vin finish the sauce with the rooster's blood, which is still a good idea if starting with a live bird (see "Blood," page 128). Coq au vin is usually thought of as Burgundian, and some cooks underline this fact by using a good marc de Bourgogne to deglaze the pan after browning and again to finish the braising liquid. Another approach is to give the dish the local character of where it is being prepared by using the appropriate wine and herbs for the bouquet garni, and finishing with the appropriate spirit (such as California Zinfandel or Napa Valley brandy).

In the recipe that follows, the pieces of rooster are coated with flour, browned, and moistened with red wine (traditionally, Burgundy). The consistency of the braising liquid is adjusted at the end by reduction and with beurre manié. For flourless versions, the flour and beurre manié can be omitted and the braising liquid lent natural body by including blanched pork rinds in the braise. The finished braising liquid can also be combined with concentrated chicken stock, or meat glace can be added to give it body. With either method, the braising liquid is then reduced to the desired consistency.

Coq au vin is traditionally finished with a garniture of separately cooked small mushrooms, pearl onions, and triangular croutons.

YIELD: 4 TO 6 SERVINGS

lean salt pork	5 ounces	150 grams
rooster, cut into serving pieces, 1	5 to 6 pounds	2.3 to 2.7 kilograms
salt and pepper	to taste	to taste
flour	1 cup	150 grams
carrot, chopped	1 medium	1 medium
onion, chopped	1 medium	1 medium
red wine	3 cups	750 milliliters
large bouquet garni (page 51)	1	1
brandy or marc	½ cup	125 milliliters
button mushrooms	8 ounces	250 grams
butter	2 ounces	60 grams
pearl onions, peeled	8 ounces	250 grams
triangular croutons	6	6
clarified butter	¼ cup	60 milliliters
beurre manié	¼ cup	60 grams
chopped parsley	2 tablespoons	30 milliliters

1. If you'll be cooking the coq au vin in the oven, preheat the oven to 300°F (150°C).
2. Cut the salt pork into thick lardoons and blanch them in boiling water for 5 minutes. Render the lardoons in a 4-quart (4 liter) heavy-bottomed pot. Remove them with a slotted spoon and reserve.

3. Season the rooster pieces with salt and pepper and dredge them in the flour.

4. Brown the chopped carrot and onion in the rendered pork fat. Remove them with a slotted spoon and brown the pieces of rooster. When the rooster pieces are well browned, remove them and discard the fat in the pot.

5. Place the sautéed vegetables, the browned rooster pieces, the red wine, the bouquet garni, and the brandy or marc in the pot. Cover and bring to a simmer on top of the stove. Cook either in the oven or on top of the stove for 1½ hours.

6. Sauté the mushrooms in 1 ounce (30 grams) of the butter for about 5 minutes, until lightly browned, and set aside. Gently cook the pearl onions in the remaining 1 ounce (30 grams) of butter for about 20 minutes, until they soften, and set aside. Lightly brown the croutons in the clarified butter and set aside.

7. Carefully remove the cooked pieces of rooster from the pot with a slotted spoon. Strain the braising liquid into a saucepan.

8. Slowly reduce the braising liquid, skimming off any fat or froth that floats to the surface. Continue reducing until the braising liquid has a deep, full flavor.

9. Whisk the beurre manié 1 tablespoon (15 milliliters) at a time into the liquid until the braising liquid has the desired consistency. Adjust the seasonings. (The flavor of the braising liquid can usually be improved by adding a tablespoon or two/15 to 30 milliliters of good vinegar and Cognac.) Gently heat the rooster with the mushroom and pearl onion garniture and the lardoons in the sauce. Dip the tips of the croutons in the sauce and then in the parsley. Arrange the croutons around the serving platter. See the photograph in the color plates.

CHICKEN WITH RED WINE SAUCE
Sometimes Called Coq au Vin

An authentic coq au vin is almost unheard of nowadays since roosters aren't easy to come by and are of questionable quality when they can be found. The traditional blood finish for the sauce is illegal for restaurants in most states. If you do find yourself with an old rooster and want to stew it as described opposite, be sure to lard the breast and stew it gently as you would the beef for the Boeuf Bourguignon on page 264.

What we usually eat instead of coq au vin is chicken with red wine sauce. But the inherent problem with cooking chicken in red wine is that a regular chicken cooks too fast for the wine's tannins to soften and for the flavors of the braising liquid to meld into something tasty and complex. The secret is to make a broth with chicken parts and red wine and then use this liquid to cook the chicken.

red wine chicken stock (page 93)	2 quarts	2 liters
chicken, quartered, 1	4 pounds	2 kilograms
butter	2 ounces	60 grams
mushrooms, trimmed of any grit or dirt, rinsed, quartered if large	10 ounces	300 grams
pearl onions, peeled	1 cup	250 milliliters
broth or water	as needed	as needed
thickly sliced bacon, cut crosswise into 1 × ¼-inch (2.5 cm × 5 mm) strips	6 ounces	170 grams
butter (for bound sauce; optional)	2 ounces	60 grams
parsley, finely chopped at the last minute	2 tablespoons	30 milliliters
salt and pepper	to taste	to taste

1. Simmer the stock, skimming any froth or scum that floats to the surface, until only 2 cups (500 milliliters) remain.
2. Brown the chicken on both sides in 1 ounce (30 grams) of the butter for about 5 minutes on each side in a large sauté pan over medium to high heat. Take out the chicken, discard the fat in the pan, and put the chicken back in along with the reduced stock. Cover the pot and bring to a gentle simmer for about 10 minutes.
3. Sauté the mushrooms in the remaining butter.
4. Glaze the onions with enough water or broth to come halfway up their sides.
5. Render the bacon until crispy. Drain.
6. Take the chicken out of the braising liquid as soon as it's firm to the touch and keep it warm while cooking down the liquid in the pan to about 1 cup (250 milliliters).
7. You can serve the chicken in heated soup plates (this allows for the sauce to remain unbound) and spoon over sauce, mushrooms, bacon, and onions, or you can reduce the braising liquid to ½ cup (125 milliliters) and whisk in the butter, if using. Sprinkle with parsley, salt, and pepper. You can also reduce the sauce until it's lightly syrupy, finish it with the butter, and serve the sauce over the chicken.

COLD RED WINE-CHICKEN DAUBE

You can skip the nineteenth-century touch of larding the chicken with prosciutto, but it does make the dish special and a little exotic. The secret to the gelée is to make a red wine stock as you would regular brown stock but replace the water with red wine.

prosciutto slice, about ⅛ inch (3 mm) thick, cut into strips	1	1
chicken, quartered, 1	4 pounds	2 kilograms
red wine chicken stock (page 93)	2 quarts	2 liters
butter	1½ ounces	45 grams
salt and pepper	to taste	to taste
parsley, finely chopped at the last minute	2 tablespoons	30 milliliters

1. Insert the strips of prosciutto under the surface of the chicken parts with a hinged larding needle.
2. Simmer the stock, while skimming off any froth or scum that floats to the surface, until 3 cups (750 milliliters) remain.
3. Cook the chicken in the butter in a nonstick sauté pan until well browned and firm to the touch. Remove from the pan and drain on paper towels.
4. Season the hot stock with salt and pepper and add the parsley. Let cool.
5. Arrange the chicken in a baking dish just large enough to hold it in a single layer and pour over the gelée. Chill until the gelée sets. Serve with the gelée.

CHICKEN FRICASSÉE

A fricassée differs from a sauté in that the chicken is gently cooked without browning and then finished in liquid. Although some contemporary recipes have stretched the traditional definition—thoroughly browning the chicken and using a variety of moistening liquids and garnitures—a classic fricassée should be almost perfectly white and the braising liquid always finished with heavy cream and egg yolks.

In the recipe that follows, flour is sweated with onions in the butter used for searing the chicken to form a roux. A more intensely flavored sauce can be prepared by eliminating the flour, moistening the chicken with a well-concentrated white stock, and reducing the braising liquid to an almost demi-glace consistency before finishing with the cream and egg yolks. It is also possible to eliminate the egg yolks, reduce the cream alone, and finish the sauce with 1 to 1½ ounces (30 to 45 grams) of butter.

chickens, 3 pounds (1.4 kilograms) each, cut in serving pieces	2	2
salt and pepper	to taste	to taste
butter	3 ounces	90 grams
onions, chopped	2 medium	2 medium
flour	2 tablespoons	30 milliliters
hot white chicken stock (page 93)	5 cups	1.25 liters

button mushrooms	8 ounces	250 grams
pearl onions, peeled	8 ounces	250 grams
heavy cream	¾ cup	185 milliliters
egg yolks	4	4
lemon juice (optional)	1 teaspoon	5 milliliters

1. If you'll be cooking the chicken in the oven, preheat the oven to 350°F (175°C). Season the chicken pieces with salt and pepper.
2. In a straight-sided sauté pan, gently cook the seasoned chicken pieces, skin side down, in 2 ounces (60 grams) of the butter. After about 10 minutes, turn them over and cook the flesh side. Cook gently to avoid browning the chicken or burning the butter. Remove the chicken from the pan.
3. Add the chopped onions to the butter in the pan and sweat them, without browning, until translucent. Add the flour and cook gently for 5 minutes.
4. Add 1 quart (1 liter) of hot chicken stock to the roux and bring to a simmer. Arrange the chicken pieces in the liquid. Cover. Cook the chicken in the oven or over low heat on the stove for 15 to 20 minutes.
5. Cook the mushrooms in ½ cup (125 milliliters) of the remaining chicken stock for 5 minutes.
6. Simmer the pearl onions in the remaining ½ cup (125 milliliters) of chicken stock for about 15 minutes, until they soften.
7. Strain the cooking liquid from both the mushrooms and onions and pour it into the cooking chicken. Keep the mushrooms and onions warm.
8. Strain the braising liquid from the chickens into a 2-quart (2 liter) saucepan. (Keep the chicken pieces warm.) Reduce the liquid, while skimming, until approximately 2 cups (500 milliliters) remain.
9. Whisk together the cream and egg yolks in a bowl. Whisk in half the reduced braising liquid. Return this mixture to the saucepan.
10. Gently heat the cream–braising liquid mixture, while stirring, until the egg yolks thicken it slightly and give it a silky texture. Don't let the mixture boil or the egg yolks will curdle (there's not enough flour to stabilize them).
11. Adjust the seasonings. (One teaspoon/5 milliliters of lemon juice, if using, will often enhance the finished sauce.) Serve the chicken coated with the sauce and topped with the mushrooms and onions.

CHICKEN WITH PRUNES AND SPICES

This dish from Padua shows influences of both the Middle Ages (the spices) and the Renaissance (the fruit). In medieval cooking, the cooking liquid would have been thickened with toast, but by the Renaissance a roux would have been used. Today we have the choice of leaving the braising liquid unthickened or we can reduce it and thicken it with cream or butter.

pancetta, cubed	¼ pound	110 grams
chicken, quartered, 1	4 pounds	2 kilograms
chicken broth, as needed to cover	2 cups	500 milliliters
orange juice	½ cup	125 milliliters
prunes, pitted	½ pound	225 grams
grated fresh ginger	1 tablespoon	15 milliliters
saffron threads, soaked in 1 tablespoon (15 milliliters) water for 30 minutes	1 pinch	1 pinch
nutmeg	1 tiny pinch	1 tiny pinch
orange zest, cut 3 inches (8 cm) long	1 strip	1 strip

1. Preheat the oven to 400°F (200°C).
2. In a pan large enough to hold the chicken and deep enough to hold the broth, render the pancetta cubes. Scoop them out with a slotted spoon, reserve them, and use the fat to brown the chicken on both sides. Take out the chicken, discard the fat, and put the chicken back in the pan.
3. Pour over the chicken broth and the orange juice. Add the prunes, the spices, the soaking liquid for the saffron, the cooked pancetta, and the orange zest and slide the pan into the oven.
4. Baste regularly for about 40 minutes until done. If at any point the braising liquid runs dry, let it caramelize on the bottom of the pan and add another ½ cup (125 milliliters) of broth or water. Serve the chicken surrounded or napped with the braising liquid and the prunes.

CHICKEN WITH VERJUICE, SAFFRON, MEDIEVAL SPICES, AND MINT

Verjuice (see page 43) was popular in medieval cooking as a source of acidity. It was usually made from underripe grapes. If you can't find verjuice, it's possible to make your own by puréeing sour grapes and straining the mixture. On the other hand, it can be hard to find sour grapes, in which case use regular grapes and combine their juices with an equal part wine vinegar. The saffron, of course, is typically medieval, while the mint and sugar are typical of the Renaissance. This dish is quite sour, also typically medieval, but you can attenuate it by adding cream.

chicken, quartered	1	1
salt and pepper	to taste	to taste
spice mixture (page 6)	1 teaspoon	5 milliliters
butter	1½ ounces	45 grams

verjuice	1 cup	250 milliliters
meat glace (page 104; optional)	3 tablespoons	45 milliliters
saffron, soaked in 1 tablespoon (15 milliliters) water	1 pinch	1 pinch
grated fresh ginger	1 tablespoon	15 milliliters
sugar	1 teaspoon	5 milliliters
fresh mint, chopped at the last minute	2 tablespoons	30 milliliters
heavy cream (optional)	½ cup	125 milliliters

1. Season the chicken with salt and pepper and then with the spice mixture. Brown the chicken on both sides in the butter, remove the chicken from the pan, and discard the cooked fat.
2. Put the chicken back in the pan with the verjuice, meat glace (if using), the saffron with its soaking liquid, ginger, and sugar and simmer gently, covered, for 10 minutes or until firm to the touch.
3. Whisk the mint into the sauce. Add the cream, if using, and adjust the seasonings. Spoon the braising liquid over the chicken in heated soup plates.

Variation

In medieval cooking, dishes were sometimes coated with gold or silver leaf much as Indian desserts are today. To gold-plate chicken, brush it with beaten egg yolk. Hold the gold leaf about an inch (2.5 cm) above the cooked chicken, with the paper backing toward you and the gold facing down, while blowing on the gold-leaf backing with a straw held in your mouth.

CHICKEN TAGINE

A tagine is typically a long-cooked stew-like dish, but the flavor called for in any tagine can be integrated into a chicken cooked like a fricassée so the chicken doesn't get overcooked. This tagine demonstrates the use of typically Moroccan ingredients.

YIELD: 4 MAIN-COURSE SERVINGS

chicken, quartered, 1	4 pounds	2 kilograms
salt and pepper	to taste	to taste
butter	1½ ounces	45 grams
onion, chopped	1 medium	1 medium
carrots, cut into rounds	2 medium	2 medium
grated fresh ginger	1 tablespoon	15 milliliters
ground cumin	1 teaspoon	5 milliliters
ground cinnamon	½ teaspoon	2 milliliters

ground turmeric	1 teaspoon	5 milliliters
ground cloves	¼ teaspoon	1 milliliter
saffron threads, soaked in 1 tablespoon (15 milliliters) water for 30 minutes	½ teaspoon	2 milliliters
tomatoes, peeled, seeded, chopped	4	4
chicken broth, preferably concentrated	1 cup	250 milliliters
cilantro, finely chopped	2 tablespoons	30 milliliters
white raisins	2 tablespoons	30 milliliters
slivered almonds, toasted in a 350ºF (175ºC) oven for 15 minutes	2 tablespoons	30 milliliters
preserved lemon, cut into ¼-inch (5 mm) dice	½	½
pomegranate seeds (optional)	½ cup	125 milliliters
harissa sauce (below)	1 cup	250 milliliters

1. Season the chicken with salt and pepper and cook it in the butter for about 5 minutes on each side. Take out the chicken and pour out the fat in the pan except for 2 tablespoons (30 milliliters). Add the onion and carrots and cook over medium heat for about 10 minutes to soften the carrots. Add the ginger and all the spices except the saffron and stir over medium heat for about 2 minutes to release their flavor.
2. Put the chicken back in the pan and add the saffron, tomatoes, and broth and simmer the chicken, covered, until it's firm to the touch, about 10 minutes.
3. Add the cilantro, raisins, almonds, and lemon, and stir. Put the chicken and sauce in hot soup plates. Sprinkle the pomegranate seeds, if using, on top and pass the harissa.

●—● Harissa Sauce

This chile paste, flavored with caraway, is the perfect accompaniment to a tagine. Experiment with different chiles to come up with different flavors.

YIELD: 1 CUP (250 MILLILITERS)

caraway seeds, ground to a powder in a coffee grinder	1 tablespoon	15 milliliters
ground coriander	1 tablespoon	15 milliliters
ground cumin	2 teaspoons	10 milliliters
dried ancho chiles, soaked in warm water for 1 hour, stemmed, seeded, chopped	15 / 3 ounces	15 / 90 grams
olive oil	½ cup	125 milliliters
salt	1 teaspoon	5 milliliters

Combine all the ingredients in a food processor and purée to a paste. This will require frequent scraping down of the sides of the processor with a rubber spatula.

CHICKEN MOLE

The same techniques are used to make a mole as are used to make a classic fricassée; just the flavors are different. Feel free to experiment with different chiles. The heart of a mole sauce is not, as some people assume, chocolate, but rather combinations of chiles with cinnamon and cloves. Raisins and almonds also enter into most moles. This mole makes enough for two chickens.

YIELD: 8 MAIN-COURSE SERVINGS

dried mulato chiles	5	5
dried ancho chiles	3	3
dried pasilla chiles	3	3
chipotle chile, either dried or canned in adobo sauce	1	1
sesame seeds	2 tablespoons	30 milliliters
coriander seeds	½ teaspoon	2 milliliters
chickens, quartered, 2	8 pounds	4 kilograms
salt and pepper	to taste	to taste
butter	1 ounce	30 grams
onion, chopped	1 medium	1 medium
garlic clove, chopped	1	1
ground cloves	¼ teaspoon	1 milliliter
ground cinnamon	½ teaspoon	2 milliliters
tomatoes, peeled, seeded, chopped	2 large	2 large
almonds with their skin, toasted in a 350°F (175°C) oven for 15 minutes	¼ cup	60 milliliters
sugar, to taste	1 tablespoon	15 milliliters
chicken broth	2 cups	500 milliliters
white raisins	3 tablespoons	45 milliliters
sherry vinegar, to taste	3 tablespoons	45 milliliters

1. Put the chiles, except the canned chipotle if that's what you're using, in a skillet over medium heat and toast them, about 5 minutes. Soak them in a bowl of warm water for 30 minutes until pliable. Discard the soaking water.
2. Toast the sesame seeds and coriander seeds in a skillet until fragrant. Grind in a coffee grinder. Reserve.
3. If you're using a canned chipotle chile, rinse the sauce off. Stem and seed all of the chiles.
4. Season the chicken with salt and pepper and cook in the butter in a large rondeau or in two sauté pans for about 5 minutes on each side over medium to high heat. Take out the chicken and pour out all but about 2 tablespoons (30 milliliters) of fat in the pan. Cook the onion and garlic in the fat for about 10 minutes. Stir in the cloves and cinnamon and cook for about 1 minute.

5. Combine the reserved spices, the chiles, the tomatoes, cooked onion mixture, almonds, sugar, and broth in a blender and purée for 1 minute.

6. Put the chicken back in the pan and pour over the sauce. Simmer, covered, for about 10 minutes or until firm to the touch. Take out the chicken and cook down the sauce, uncovered, until it starts to thicken to the consistency of a thick gravy. Sprinkle over the raisins. Season to taste with vinegar, salt, and pepper.

CHICKEN WITH TOMATILLO AND ASSORTED CHILE SAUCES

In this dish, the chicken is sautéed until completely done (there's no subsequent simmering in liquid) and the sauces poured over. This plate, which presents an opportunity to experiment with different chiles, actually comprises five sauces: the base tomatillo sauce and the four individual chile sauces.

YIELD: 4 MAIN-COURSE SERVINGS

4 different kinds of dried chiles	4 each	4 each
heavy cream	1 cup	250 milliliters
chicken broth, preferably concentrated	1 cup	250 milliliters
salt and pepper	to taste	to taste
chicken, quartered, 1	4 pounds	2 kilograms
butter	1 ounce	30 grams
onion, chopped	1 medium	1 medium
tomatillos, sheaths removed, halved	1 pound or 2 (15-ounce) cans, drained	450 grams
sour cream		

1. Prepare the individual chile sauces by toasting each type of chile in a dry iron skillet over high heat—don't use any oil. Turn the chiles with tongs. Soak each type of chile separately for 30 minutes in warm water. Remove the stems and rinse out the seeds. Chop the chiles to a paste, keeping each type separate.

2. Put each type of chile in a separate small saucepan with ¼ cup (60 milliliters) cream and ¼ cup (60 milliliters) broth and simmer gently, about 3 minutes. Strain each sauce, season with salt and pepper, and reserve.

3. Cook the chicken on both sides in the butter in a large sauté pan for about 7 minutes per side, until firm to the touch. Take the chicken out of the pan and keep warm.

4. Pour out all but 2 tablespoons (30 milliliters) of fat in the pan and add the onion. Cook the onion for about 5 minutes over medium heat and add the tomatillos. Cover the pan and cook gently for 20 minutes. Strain the sauce through a strainer or food mill and season to taste.

5. Serve the chicken with the tomatillo sauce poured over and either pass the chile sauces or spoon them over each serving. Pass the sour cream.

CHICKEN IN THE STYLE OF A VATAPÁ

This dish applies the classic principles of a fricassée with typical Brazilian flavors. Be sure to use all-natural peanut butter (there should be nothing hydrogenated in it or, for that matter, nothing but peanuts and salt) and unsweetened coconut milk.

YIELD: 4 MAIN-COURSE SERVINGS

chicken, quartered, 1	4 pounds	2 kilograms
salt and pepper	to taste	to taste
butter	1 ounce	30 grams
grated fresh ginger	1 tablespoon	15 milliliters
dried chipotle chile, soaked in cold water until soft, stemmed, seeded, finely chopped	1	1
onion, finely chopped	1 large	1 large
tomatoes, peeled, seeded, chopped	2	2
poblano chiles, charred, peeled, stemmed, seeded, chopped fine as to a paste	2	2
chicken broth, preferably concentrated	1 cup	250 milliliters
unsweetened coconut milk	1 (14-ounce) can	450 milliliters
peanut butter	2 tablespoons	30 milliliters
cilantro, finely chopped	2 tablespoons	30 milliliters

1. Season the chicken with salt and pepper. Brown it on both sides in the butter in a large sauté pan for about 5 minutes on each side. Take out the chicken and pour out all but 2 tablespoons (30 milliliters) of fat in the pan. Add the ginger, the chipotle, and the onion and cook gently for 5 minutes.
2. Add the tomatoes, poblanos, and chicken broth to the pan and put the chicken back in. Cover the pan and simmer until firm to the touch, about 10 minutes.
3. In a mixing bowl, work the coconut milk into the peanut butter a bit at a time until the mixture is smooth.
4. Take the chicken out of the pan. Add the coconut milk mixture and boil down until barely thickened. Add the cilantro and simmer for 1 minute. Season with salt and pepper. Serve over the chicken in soup plates.

CHICKEN WITH MORELS

This is prepared much like a classic fricassée except that morels replace the button mushrooms and the traditional egg yolk liaison is dispensed with. The chicken is floured, which gives a little consistency to the sauce, and the sauce is thickened with cream. Concentrated chicken stock is a real boon for the flavor of the dish and the consistency of the sauce.

fresh morels	1 pound	450 grams
or	*or*	*or*
dried morels, soaked in 1 cup (250 milliliters) water for 30 minutes	1 ounce	25 grams
chicken, quartered, 1	4 pounds	2 kilograms
salt and pepper	to taste	to taste
flour (for dredging)	as needed	as needed
butter	3 ounces	90 grams
chicken or veal broth, preferably concentrated white broth	2 cups	500 milliliters
heavy cream	1 cup	250 milliliters

1. Check the fresh morels for dirt or grit; rinse them off if necessary but don't soak them in water. Move the dried morels around in their soaking liquid so they soften evenly.
2. Season the chicken with salt and pepper and dredge it in flour. Brown it on both sides in 1½ ounces (45 grams) butter in a large sauté pan. Discard the cooked fat and pour the chicken broth (and the soaking liquid for dried morels, if using, leaving any grit behind) over the chicken. Cover and cook until firm to the touch, about 10 minutes.
3. Sauté the fresh morels in the remaining butter. (Reconstituted dried morels can simply be heated in the sauce.) Season with salt and pepper.
4. Take the chicken out of the cooking liquid with tongs and keep warm. Simmer down the cooking liquid to a syrup consistency. Pour in the cream and add the morels and simmer down to a sauce-like consistency. Season to taste with salt and pepper and serve over the chicken. See the photograph in the color plates.

Cooking Duck

Ducks available in the United States—the widely sold "Pekin" duck (not to be confused with Peking duck) and the moulard duck used to produce foie gras—are covered with a thick layer of fat that has to be rendered in some way before the duck is served. Such ducks cannot be roasted in the same way as a chicken because in order to get the fat to render the duck has to be overcooked, resulting in a "crispy" duck that's more like confit or braised duck than it is typical of a roast. Duck must be sectioned and the breasts cooked differently from the thighs. Usually, the breasts are sautéed, skin side down for the most part, to render the fat without overcooking the meat, which should be served rare to medium rare. The thighs are best braised or slow roasted. Slow roasting is really a kind of braising in which the only liquid is the liquid naturally released by the meat.

The best approach is to braise the thighs and use the braising liquid as the base for a sauce for both the breasts (called *magrets* when taken from a moulard duck) and the thighs.

BRAISED DUCK THIGHS

Restaurants are often stuck with leftover thighs. In fact, the thighs can make an even more impressive dish than the breasts; they just take a little more time. Ideally, the braising liquid from the thighs is used to sauce both the thighs and breasts (see opposite).

YIELD: 6 MAIN-COURSE SERVINGS

6 moulard duck thighs or 12 Pekin duck thighs		
salt and pepper	to taste	to taste
onion, sliced	1 large	1 large
carrot, sliced	1 large	1 large
garlic cloves, crushed	2	2
red wine	1 cup	250 milliliters
unsalted chicken broth, preferably homemade brown chicken stock (page 91)	1 quart	1 liter
large bouquet garni (page 51)	1	1

1. Preheat the oven to 400°F (200°C). Season the thighs with salt and pepper and arrange them, skin side up, in a heavy-bottomed sauté pan on top of the vegetables. Slide the pan into the oven and roast until the skin is golden brown, about 90 minutes for Pekin thighs and 2 hours for moulard thighs.

2. Turn off the oven or, if you want to braise in it, turn it down to 300°F (150°C). If the liquid in the pan is cloudy, place the pan over high heat and boil down the juices so they caramelize and form a shiny layer of liquid fat that floats on top. Pour or ladle off the fat.

3. Add the wine and broth, nestle in the bouquet garni, and bring to a gentle simmer on top of the stove. Cover the pan with a sheet of aluminum foil and press the foil down so it almost touches the tops of the thighs.

4. Cover the pan and simmer very gently, on top of the stove or in the oven, for 1 hour for Pekin thighs or 90 minutes for moulard thighs, or until the thighs offer no resistance when you poke at one with a knife. (If you pull up the thigh when you pull out the knife, the thighs aren't ready.)

5. Transfer the thighs, still skin up, into a clean pan that fits them in a single layer as closely as possible. Turn the oven to 400°F (200°C). Strain the braising liquid into a saucepan and bring to a gentle simmer with the pan to one side of the heat source. Skim off the fat with a ladle while you simmer the liquid for about 15 minutes.

6. Pour the degreased braising liquid over the thighs and slide them back in the oven. Baste every 10 minutes until the thighs are covered with a shiny glaze and the braising liquid is syrupy. Serve in heated soup plates surrounded with the braising liquid. The duck thighs can be garnished with vegetables. The duck breast can also be sliced before the sauce is poured over. See the photograph in the color plates.

DUCK BREASTS WITH PEACHES OR OTHER FRUITS

Because duck breasts are best sautéed rare to medium rare, they release little liquid with which to make a sauce. By braising duck thighs (see opposite), however, you'll have a rich and savory braising liquid that can be used to deglaze the pan used for sautéing the duck breasts. If you don't have braising liquid, it's also possible to make a duck stock with the duck carcass. (A good trick is to make duck stock with half the duck carcasses and then make a jus by roasting the remaining carcasses and deglazing the pan with the duck stock.)

The usual approach when making fruit sauces is to put the fruit in hot reduced demi-glace just long enough for the fruits to release liquid of their own. The fruits are then taken out of the sauce, the sauce reduced to compensate for the liquid released by the fruit and to concentrate its flavor, and the fruits returned to the sauce just before serving. Fruit sauces almost always benefit from a sweet-and-sour element provided by a gastrique or, when in a hurry, just a little sugar and vinegar.

YIELD: 6 MAIN-COURSE SERVINGS

6 Pekin duck breasts or 3 moulard duck breasts		
duck broth or duck braising liquid	1 cup	250 milliliters
peaches, peeled, pitted, cut into wedges	3	3
meat glace (page 104; optional)	2 tablespoons	30 milliliters
gastrique (see page 185), to taste	2 tablespoons	30 milliliters
butter	1½ ounces	45 grams
salt and pepper	to taste	to taste

1. Make a series of about 20 slashes into the duck skin, penetrating as deeply into the skin as possible without going all the way to the meat. Keep the knife leaning on an angle so you're cutting into the skin sideways, which allows for a deeper cut without cutting through. Make a second series of slashes at a 90-degree angle from the first.
2. Put the duck breasts, skin side down, in a sauté pan and cook over medium heat for about 12 minutes for Pekin duck breasts and about 20 minutes for moulard breasts. Turn the ducks over and cook them on the meat side for about 2 minutes over high heat. Take them out of the pan and keep warm while preparing the sauce.
3. Pour the fat out of the pan and deglaze the pan with the broth. Add the peaches and bring to a simmer. Simmer for 3 minutes, remove the peaches with a skimmer, and reserve. Boil down the sauce base, add the meat glace, if using, and when the sauce has a lightly syrupy consistency, add gastrique to taste. Whisk in the butter, reheat the peaches in the sauce, and season with salt and pepper. Slice the duck breast and spoon over the sauce. See the photographs in the color plates.

STEAMED MEATS

Although recipes for steamed meats are less common than those for roasting, poaching, or braising, the technique has several advantages over these other methods. Meat is best steamed in a *couscoussière*, which has a wide-mouthed pot for the steaming liquid and a second pot with a perforated base that fits on top of the pot of boiling liquid and holds the meat. Meats, however, should not be steamed in an industrial steamer, which uses pressure and temperatures above the boiling point. These steamers generate too much liquid of their own and make it impossible to capture any juices released by the steaming meats.

By adding aromatic ingredients, such as herbs, aromatic vegetables, wines, truffles, and spices, to the steaming liquid, steaming can be used to impart delicate flavors to meat. Restaurant chefs often prefer steaming to poaching (which produces similar results) because it is quick, neat, and easy to organize.

In most settings a relatively large amount of liquid is used to generate steam in the base of the steamer. As the meats cook in the basket above the boiling liquid, they release juices that in most cases are not used because they are diluted in the steaming liquid. If a small amount of liquid is used in the bottom of the steamer, it will simultaneously reduce and capture the juices being released by the steaming meats. This liquid can then be served as a broth around the steamed meats or converted into a sauce in the same way as a poaching or braising liquid. When a small amount of liquid is used for steaming meats, the steamer has to be watched carefully so the liquid does not run dry and burn.

Another useful method for steaming meats, especially chicken, is to seal the meats in a plastic roasting bag (or a pig's bladder) along with reduced stock or aromatic liquids. The wrapped meat is then baked, or poached in simmering water, and steam is generated within the bag. In this way none of the flavorful liquid is lost.

POULARDE À LA VAPEUR
Steamed Chicken

In Lucien Tendret's original recipe for this dish (1892), a stuffing is prepared with cubed truffles and the chicken's liver. In the following modification, truffle slices are slipped under the chicken's skin and added to the steaming liquid. French chefs are predisposed to using black truffles, but the method is at least equally as exciting with fresh white truffles. The method can be adapted and the truffles replaced with herbs such as tarragon (again, slipped under the skin) or with wild mushrooms chopped and placed under the skin or left whole or coarsely chopped and placed in the steaming liquid (morels are especially good).

The original recipe finishes the steaming liquid like a fricassée with roux, cream, and egg yolks, but in this modification, the chicken is served surrounded with the well-truffled steaming bouillon.

fresh black or white truffles	2 large	2 large
chickens, 2½ to 3 pounds (1.25 to 1.75 kilograms) each	4	4
excellent brown chicken stock	1 quart	1 liter

1. Peel the truffles; chop and save the peelings. Slice the truffles with a Japanese mandoline.
2. Slip three-quarters of the truffle slices under the skin of the thighs and breasts of the chickens.
3. Truss the chickens, cover well with plastic wrap, and store overnight in the refrigerator (to permeate the meat with the truffle flavor).
4. Pour the chicken stock, the remaining truffle slices, and the chopped peelings into the bottom of a steamer and bring to a simmer. Unwrap the chickens and arrange them in the basket of the steamer and cover with a sheet of crumpled aluminum foil (this makes a tighter seal) and the lid. It is imperative that the lid fit tightly. (The original recipe sealed the lid on with a luting paste of flour and water.)
5. Steam the chickens over low to medium heat for 1½ hours. If any steam starts to escape from under the lid, turn down the heat. Do not remove the lid during the cooking.
6. Carve the chickens and serve in deep plates or wide soup bowls surrounded with the steaming liquid.

POULET "EN VESSIE"
Steamed Chicken with Stuffed Morels

French regional cooks have long steamed chickens in sealed pigs' bladders. More recently, variations on the dish have taken center stage in France's choicest restaurants. Unfortunately, health regulations in the United States do not allow the sale of pigs' bladders (which in France are meticulously cleaned), and American cooks must make do with transparent oven bags, which are equally efficient but less picturesque.

This method is usually used with delicate ingredients such as fresh morels, truffles, and foie gras, whose aroma would suffer if cooked in a less roundabout way. Contemporary cooks have also used the method for capturing the perfume of herbs.

chicken, 1	3½ pounds	1.6 kilograms
fresh morels	4 ounces	125 grams
terrine of foie gras	2 ounces	50 grams
concentrated brown chicken stock	½ cup	125 milliliters
salt and pepper	to taste	to taste

1. Truss the chicken.
2. If the morels are sandy, quickly rinse them off in cold running water. Dry them immediately on towels.
3. Cut the foie gras into small strips and, with the end of a chopstick, push a strip of foie gras into the stem of each morel.
4. Select a pot that is large enough to hold the chicken and fill it half full with water. Bring the water to a simmer.
5. Gently warm the stock; it should not be too hot to touch.
6. Place the chicken and the morels inside a roasting bag and pour the warm stock into the bag. Seal the bag tightly with string. Seal the bag in a second bag, and then seal again in a third one. Do not entrap too much air in the bag.
7. Place the chicken in the simmering water and cover. Poach for 1¼ hours.
8. Remove the chicken from the water. Just before serving, open the bag and transfer the chicken to a cutting board to carve.
9. Pour the stock and morels into a 2-quart (2 liter) saucepan and bring to a simmer. Adjust the seasonings.
10. Present the chicken in deep plates surrounded by the morels and stock.

GRILLED MEATS

Grilled meats are traditionally served with stock-based sauces (such as Sauce Diable, page 170), simple sauces that function as condiments, or compound butters. These sauces are used because the juices released by grilled meats normally fall into the grill and are lost, making it impossible to prepare an integral sauce.

To prepare sauces that capture the flavor of the grill, partially grill the meat and then finish it in stock or other aromatic liquids. The method is somewhat analogous to braising (where meats are first browned on top of the stove and then moistened) or to a salmis, a technique in which meat, usually game or poultry, is partially roasted, a jus is prepared with the trimmings, and the cooking of the meat is completed by gentle reheating in the flavorful jus.

GRILLED GAME BIRDS IN SMOKE-SCENTED BROTH

YIELD: 4 SERVINGS

quails, about 6 ounces (150 grams) each	2	2
squabs, about 1 pound (450 grams) each	2	2
excellent brown stock	2 cups	500 milliliters
large bouquet garni (page 51), with several sprigs of fresh marjoram	1	1
duck breast (see Note)	1	1
pheasant or partridge breast, 1	6 ounces	150 grams
salt and pepper	to taste	to taste
mushrooms	4 ounces	125 grams
extra-virgin olive oil	2 tablespoons	30 milliliters

1. Remove the breasts from the quails and squabs and grill the carcasses over wood coals. When the carcasses are nicely browned, transfer them to a 4-quart (4 liter) saucepan. Add just enough brown stock to cover. Add the bouquet garni.

2. Gently simmer the carcasses for 20 minutes. Skim off any froth or fat that floats to the surface.

3. Strain the broth through a fine chinois and then through a cloth napkin.

4. Season the breasts from the quails, squabs, duck, and pheasant and grill them, skin side down first, over high heat. Leave the meat rare in the center. The quail breasts will take about 1 minute, the squab breasts about 2 minutes, and the larger breasts from 4 to 6 minutes.

5. Slide the mushrooms onto skewers, roll them in olive oil, and grill.

6. Pour the reserved broth into a 4-quart (4 liter) straight-sided sauté pan and poach the grilled breasts for 30 seconds to 2 minutes, depending on their size. Remove the breasts and adjust the seasoning of the broth.

7. Present the breasts (slice the duck and pheasant breasts) and mushrooms (removed from the skewers) in deep plates surrounded by the smoke-scented broth.

Note: Some duck breasts have a thick layer of fat, which makes them difficult to grill. To prevent this problem, first score the breast finely with a very sharp paring knife and sauté it, skin side down, for 5 to 7 minutes, to render most of the fat before grilling. The skin can also be removed entirely from the breast before grilling, but be careful not to overcook skinless breasts, as they dry out quickly.

TIPS FOR THE RESTAURANT CHEF

In fast-paced professional kitchens, many chefs find that integral sauces require too much last-minute preparation. Roasting a chicken and preparing a jus to order is impractical in all but the most well-staffed restaurants. Stock-based sauces were originally invented to free the cook from the last-minute difficulties inherent in preparing integral sauces. Unfortunately, stock-based sauces, especially the way they are prepared in today's economy-oriented kitchens, rarely have the satisfying direct flavor of a well-made integral sauce. It is, however, possible to organize a kitchen so that some of the elements necessary to an integral sauce can be accomplished in advance.

Roasts

Large roasts, such as turkeys or large cuts of beef, veal, or game, present little problem in a professional kitchen because they are roasted ahead of time, giving the chef ample time to prepare a jus. For smaller roasts, especially chicken and small game birds, which are often roasted to order, last-minute preparation of an individual jus is cumbersome and often impractical. For this reason, chefs often prepare a jus with appropriate trimmings just before the restaurant service (see "Jus," page 105).

Braises

Braised meats present little problem in a professional kitchen because they rarely suffer from, and are often improved by, advance preparation and reheating to order. The braising or stewing liquid can be stretched if necessary by adding well-flavored stock. Extra body can be given to the liquid with meat glace.

Certain liaisons, such as foie gras or butter, can be used only at the last minute, whereas others, such as arrowroot or flour, can be incorporated into the sauce ahead of time.

When reheating a stew or a piece of braised meat, place it in a tight-fitting covered pan with a little of the braising liquid. Heat it very gently so the surrounding liquid never comes to a boil. If a last-minute liaison is required, simply transfer the meat to a plate and finish the sauce in the pan. If the stewed or braised meat is particularly fragile, wrap each piece carefully in a sheet of caul fat after the initial braising and after it has thoroughly cooled.

Poached Meats

It is rarely practical to prepare sauces to order from poached meats, because the liquid is usually so diluted that too much last-minute reduction is required to make a flavorful sauce. Usually integral sauces for poached meats are prepared from the poaching liquid used the day before. In any case, meats are usually poached in advance—pot au feu, blanquettes, and potées are not last-minute affairs.

Poached meats should be reheated in the same way as stews and braises are: gently, in a covered pan, with a little stock.

Sautés

Preparing integral sauces for sautéed meats is a quick and straightforward process, provided that any necessary stocks and glaces are on hand. Any necessary stocks should be reduced to the proper degree ahead of time to avoid time-consuming last-minute reduction. If, on the other hand, the stocks are very reduced, the saucier will be constantly thinning the sauce with stock to adjust its consistency.

One problem with pan-deglazed sauces is that they are usually speckled with particles of coagulated meat that have adhered to the bottom of the pan. The obvious solution is to strain the sauce into a bowl or saucepan, but in a busy professional kitchen, this task is a nuisance. In some cases, especially if the sauce is garnished with chopped ingredients such as shallots, herbs, or mushrooms, straining is not necessary.

10
INTEGRAL FISH AND SHELLFISH SAUCES

Integral fish and shellfish sauces are made at the last minute from the natural juices released during cooking. Fish and shellfish are especially suited to last-minute integral sauces because they cook quickly and release flavorful liquid as soon as they are heated. Because the best method for preparing an integral sauce depends on the technique used for cooking the fish, this chapter is organized around the various cooking techniques. Although shellfish comprise crustaceans as well as mollusks and sea urchins, the term is used here for only the last two. Because the techniques for cooking crustaceans are so specific, they are treated separately, in Chapter 11.

BASIC PREPARATIONS AND INGREDIENTS

Fish Stock

To prepare Fish Stock, see page 100. Traditional recipes often call for fish stock as the cooking medium for fish and shellfish. If the fish stock is not overcooked and is prepared from impeccably fresh fish, it will help reinforce the sea-like flavor of an integral sauce.

Unfortunately, fish stock is often prepared from stale fish and allowed to sit for too long before use. Such a stock will give any sauce a strong, fishy taste.

Fish Glace

To prepare Fish Glace, see page 105. Fish glace is often used to reinforce the flavor of fish sauces that have been finished with butter or reduced cream. The advantage of fish glace is that it can be prepared ahead of time and refrigerated until needed. Unlike fish stock, it requires no last-minute reduction. Fish glace should be used very sparingly or it will give the sauce a strong, fishy taste.

Many contemporary chefs feel that fish glace, even when correctly prepared and used, detracts from the character of a sauce by giving it a nondescript fish flavor. The trend in the finest restaurants is to try to capture the individuality of a specific fish, which often means sacrificing convenience.

Shellfish Cooking Liquids

The liquid released by mussels, cockles, or clams during steaming has a delicious, forthright flavor and is excellent as a base for fish sauces. To prepare 1 cup (250 milliliters) of the cooking liquid, place 1 pound (500 grams) of mussels, cockles, or clams and ½ cup (125 milliliters) of white wine in a pot and cover with a tight-fitting lid. Heat the pot on the stove over a high flame and shake it from time to time to redistribute the shellfish. After about 5 minutes, open the lid. When the mussels or clams have all opened, they should be scooped out, and the cooking liquid should be strained through a fine chinois or, if the liquid seems gritty, through cheesecloth. When using shellfish cooking liquids, remember that they are very salty, so avoid too much reduction and be careful if adding additional salt.

Court-Bouillon

Court-bouillon is popular with contemporary chefs because of its lightness and the subtle fresh flavor it gives to sauces. A traditional recipe is given on page 102, but, as noted there, different herbs and vegetables can be used, depending on the type of fish being prepared, the region, and the whim of the chef. Court-bouillon can also be reduced and used as a flavor base when thicker sauces are needed.

Wines

Wine almost always works well in fish sauces, which are accented by its natural acidity.

Coral

The roe and coral from sea urchins, sea scallops, and lobsters are sometimes used as a flavorful finish for shellfish sauces.

Although sea urchin roe can be bought already removed from the shells, it is best to remove it just before cooking from perfectly fresh, living urchins. The best method is to take a pair of heavy scissors, cut halfway down the side of the sea urchin starting from the hole on the top, and then cut all around the spiny shell and remove the top half. The roe, which is pale orange or brown, can then be easily removed with a spoon. Some sea urchins have a strong iodine flavor, so be sure to taste the roe before incorporating it into a sauce.

Sea scallop coral can be simply cut off from the side of the meaty white part of the scallop.

Both sea urchin roe and scallop coral should be combined with an equal amount of butter and pushed through a drum sieve before they are used to finish a sauce. These coral butters can then be used as a final flavoring and light liaison for flavorful sauce bases. To prepare and use lobster coral, see page 328.

POACHING

Fish is poached by keeping it completely submerged in simmering liquid. As the fish cooks, it releases juices into the surrounding liquid. Integral sauces are then prepared from all or a portion of the poaching liquid. Some recipes suggest starting the poaching in cold liquid, whereas others suggest that the liquid should be at a simmer before adding the fish. Larger fish should be started in cold liquid so the heat will penetrate them slowly and they will cook evenly. Small fish, sections of fish, and shellfish should be started in hot liquid, both to seal in their juices and ensure rapid cooking.

The simplest, most direct method of serving poached fish is to place the fish in a bowl and pour over a ladleful of the poaching liquid, which can then be sipped with a spoon as though it were a soup or, in less formal settings, be mopped up with chunks of crusty bread.

Court-bouillon is the liquid most often used for poaching fish. When the vegetables used to make the court-bouillon are left in the broth and served along with the fish, the term *à la nage* (loosely translated "in the swim") is used. When fish is to be served à la nage, the vegetables should be chopped carefully so they create a decorative effect in the bowl. Some chefs like to cut grooves in the sides of the carrots with a channel knife so that the sliced carrots have a distinct cog-like look. A more contemporary look can be obtained by cutting the court-bouillon vegetables into julienne. The flavor and color of the poaching liquid can also be improved by adding finely chopped or whole leaves of herbs, such as chervil, parsley, or chives, just before serving.

Poaching does not lend itself well to making sauces with the traditional consistency—thick enough to coat the fish—because these sauces require long reduction to concentrate the flavor of the poaching liquid or an excessive amount of starch or other thickener. Either of these methods requires keeping the fish warm for too long a period while the sauce is being prepared. For this reason, it is best to serve poached fish with light broth-like sauces. If a thicker sauce is needed, a stock-based sauce should be used (see Chapter 8, "Stock-Based and Nonintegral Fish Sauces," page 201). Some chefs save the poaching liquid to use as a base for a sauce for the next service.

When converting the poaching liquid for fish into a sauce, it is best to combine the poaching liquid with a sauce that has been made in advance. Older recipes sometimes suggest combining some of the poaching liquid with a fish velouté made in advance and then reducing the mixture until it has the correct consistency. A similar method can be used for butter- or cream-based sauces. If the poaching liquid is to be finished with butter, it is best to prepare a butter-enriched sauce (such as a beurre blanc or one of its derivatives) and to combine the sauce with the poaching liquid after the fish is cooked, just before it is served. In this way, last-minute swirling of butter into the poaching liquid is avoided. This is especially practical in fast-paced professional settings.

Fish poaching liquid can also be combined at the last minute with emulsified egg-yolk-and-butter sauces, such as hollandaise and its derivatives. The resulting sauce is light and broth-like but still full flavored. Usually, equal parts of fish poaching liquid and emulsified sauce are used. The richness of the emulsified sauce can be adjusted by varying the ratio of butter to egg yolk, from a classic butter-rich hollandaise-style sauce to a sabayon containing no butter at all.

Another method for preparing sauces with fish poaching liquid is to combine the liquid with mayonnaise. This method has long been used in Provence to prepare the traditional *bourride*, which combines a full-flavored fish poaching liquid with a Sauce Rouille (page 135) or Saffron-Flavored Aïoli (page 396). Almost any flavor mayonnaise can be used, as long as it does not completely overpower the flavor of the fish or the poaching liquid (see Chapter 14, "Mayonnaise-Based Sauces," page 391). Because sauces made with mayonnaise tend to be unstable, the poaching liquid should be combined with the mayonnaise just before serving. When combining hot poaching liquid with mayonnaise, put the mayonnaise in a stainless-steel bowl and whisk in the hot poaching liquid. The ratio of poaching liquid to mayonnaise can be adjusted according to whether a thin broth-like sauce or a thicker version that will coat the fish is desired.

The hot poaching liquid from a fish or shellfish can also be combined with a small amount of vinaigrette just before serving. The vinaigrette will give the fish an agreeable tang and will limit the richness of the sauce.

Poaching liquid can also be combined with heavy cream, reduced cream, or reduced-cream-based white sauces. For example, a sauce consisting of reduced cream and flavorful ingredients such as sorrel or tomato purée can be prepared ahead of time and then combined as needed with the poaching liquid.

SEA SCALLOPS À LA NAGE

Almost any fish or shellfish can be prepared à la nage in a court-bouillon made from practically any kind of vegetable or herb. The vegetables used in the version that follows are those most commonly used, but many chefs add lemons (zest and pith removed), limes, cayenne pepper, or a variety of spices, such as coriander and fennel. Remember that à la nage always means that the vegetables used to prepare the court-bouillon are served with the fish, so they should be cut in a decorative way and cooked perfectly.

YIELD: 6 SERVINGS

sea scallops	2 pounds	1 kilogram
carrot, julienned	3 ounces	75 grams
leek, white part, julienned	2 ounces	50 grams
celery, julienned	2 ounces	50 grams
turnip, julienned	3 ounces	75 grams
large bouquet garni (page 51)	1	1
water	1½ cups	375 milliliters
white wine	1½ cups	375 milliliters
sea salt	1 tablespoon	15 milliliters
chopped parsley	1 tablespoon	15 milliliters
whole chervil leaves	1 tablespoon	15 milliliters

1. Prepare the scallops by shucking them (if they are still in the shell) and removing the small muscle running up the side of each one.
2. Place the julienned carrot, leek, celery, and turnip and the bouquet garni in the bottom of a 2-quart (2 liter) saucepan and moisten them with the water and white wine. Add the sea salt. Bring the liquids to a simmer and cook the vegetables for approximately 15 minutes.
3. Strain the vegetables, reserving the liquid until needed. Spread the julienned vegetables on a tray to cool them quickly and prevent them from overcooking.

4. Taste the court-bouillon and adjust the seasonings if necessary. If it seems to lack flavor, it can be reduced.

5. Poach the scallops in the court-bouillon to order. Heat portions of the julienned vegetables with a small amount of the court-bouillon, the parsley, and chervil. Spoon the scallops into bowls or deep plates and pour over the court-bouillon until it reaches halfway up the sides of the scallops. Place the julienned vegetables and herbs atop and around the scallops.

Sea Scallops with Butter-Enriched Nage

The cooking liquid for sea scallops à la nage can be converted into a rich broth-like sauce by reducing it and finishing it with butter.

After straining out the vegetables, reduce the court-bouillon by half, to about 1½ cups (375 milliliters). To finish the liquid with butter, two approaches can be used. If the dish is being prepared all at once and served right away, simply whisk 4 to 8 ounces (125 to 250 grams) of butter, cut into chunks, into the hot liquid. If the dish is being served over an extended period, as during a restaurant service, it is best to whisk the amount of butter anticipated for the service into a small amount of the nage liquid and keep it warm. The nage liquid is then combined with the necessary amount of emulsified butter when the order is placed. This method is preferable because the butter is more stable in a less liquid mixture. It also avoids last-minute whisking of butter into the nage. See the photograph in the color plates.

SEA SCALLOPS À LA NAGE WITH VINAIGRETTE

The forthright flavor and bright acidity of vinaigrettes have made them a recent favorite among contemporary chefs who are eliminating the butter and cream that replaced flour twenty years ago. The most difficult problem in working with hot vinaigrettes is their instability. Some chefs find this appealing—a brightly colored oil separating on the plate can be attractive—whereas others stabilize the emulsion with mustard, vegetable purées (often tomato), or even a tiny amount of cream. In the recipe that follows, the nage and vinaigrette are emulsified at the last minute in a blender, and basil oil is dribbled over just before serving to accent both color and flavor. The court-bouillon is flavored with fennel. Court-bouillons scented with only one vegetable have been made popular in recent years by chefs who find the flavor of a classic court-bouillon lacking in character because the individual flavor of each vegetable is obscured.

sea scallops	2 pounds	1 kilogram
fennel bulbs with branches	2	2
white wine	1 cup	250 milliliters
water	as needed	as needed
cooked or raw tomato coulis (page 461)	3 tablespoons	45 milliliters
champagne vinegar or excellent balsamic vinegar	3 tablespoons	45 milliliters
dijon mustard	1 tablespoon	15 milliliters
olive oil	5 tablespoons	75 milliliters
salt and pepper	to taste	to taste
basil oil (page 429)	2 tablespoons	30 milliliters

1. Prepare the scallops by shucking them (if they are still in the shell) and removing the small muscle running up the side of each one. Leave any coral attached.
2. Remove the top branches from the fennel. Save the leaves. Coarsely chop the branches. Cut the fennel into thin wedges. Be careful to leave a piece of the center core attached to each wedge; otherwise, they will fall apart.
3. Layer the fennel wedges and chopped branches in a 4-quart (4 liter) saucepan, pour over the white wine, and add enough water to cover. Cook the fennel court-bouillon, covered, for about 20 minutes, until the fennel softens but is not mushy.
4. Strain the court-bouillon into a straight-sided sauté pan and poach the scallops in it.
5. Remove the scallops and strain the court-bouillon into a 2-quart (2 liter) saucepan. Reduce the liquid to ½ cup (125 milliliters). Whisk in the tomato coulis, vinegar, and mustard.
6. Blend the sauce on high speed for 15 seconds while adding the olive oil.
7. Taste the sauce; it may be necessary to add more of any of the components—the coulis, vinegar, or mustard—to balance the flavors. Adjust the seasonings.
8. Coat the bottoms of deep plates or wide bowls with the sauce and place the scallops on top. Dribble the basil oil around and over the scallops and sauce. Garnish the plate with the fennel wedges and chopped fennel leaves.

Sea Scallops à la Nage with Vegetable Purée

The court-bouillon is reduced as for preparing a vinaigrette-finished sauce, then finished with a vegetable purée such as sorrel, tomato, garlic, or potato (see Chapter 17, "Purées and Purée-Thickened Sauces," page 457).

⊶ LOBSTER À LA NAGE I

Lobster is great cooked à la nage but has the disadvantage of requiring an inordinate amount of court-bouillon to submerge the lobsters. For this reason, here court-bouillon is made in advance and the liquid is used to steam the lobsters. The steaming liquid is then poured over the lobster and vegetables as a sauce.

YIELD: 4 MAIN-COURSE SERVINGS

carrots, julienned	2 large	2 large
leeks, white part, julienned	2 large	2 large
turnip, julienned	1 medium	1 medium
large bouquet garni (page 51)	1	1
white wine	½ cup	125 milliliters
water	2 cups	500 milliliters
lobsters, about 1½ pounds (675 grams) each	4	4

1. Simmer the vegetables and bouquet garni with the white wine and water until softened, about 25 minutes. Drain the liquid off into a pot large enough to hold the lobsters. Discard the bouquet garni. Set aside the vegetables and keep them hot.
2. Use the court-bouillon to steam the lobsters over medium heat until they turn bright orange, about 10 minutes.
3. Spread the hot vegetables in heated soup plates and place the lobsters—the bodies halved lengthwise, shelled claw meat placed on top—over the vegetables. Pour over the steaming liquid and serve.

⊶ BOURRIDE
Nage Bound with Mayonnaise

A *bourride* is a Provençal dish prepared by poaching fish in a fish stock prepared with aromatic vegetables and the trimmings from the fish. When the fish is cooked, the poaching liquid is then strained and whisked into an aïoli, which lightly binds it and contributes to its flavor. The bourride is a model for finishing the poaching liquid for fish with mayonnaise. Any of the classic mayonnaises given in Chapter 14 can be used, as well as improvised mayonnaises using different oils and flavorings for new variations.

One variation is *bourride sétoise*, which is made exclusively from monkfish (*baudroie*). Traditional recipes finish the sauce with the puréed monkfish liver. Considering that monkfish is a bottom dweller and scavenger and its habitat is often polluted, it is probably not a good idea to use the liver in sauce making.

firm white-fleshed whole fish	6 pounds	3 kilograms
olive oil	2 tablespoons	30 milliliters
onion, coarsely chopped	1 medium	1 medium
fennel bulb, coarsely chopped	1 small	1 small
or	*or*	*or*
fennel branches, 12 inches (30 cm), chopped	2 or 3	2 or 3
large bouquet garni (page 51), with a strip of dried orange rind	1	1
water	3 cups	750 milliliters
sauce aïoli (page 396)	½ cup	125 milliliters
egg yolks (optional)	3	3
french bread (large round or fat loaf)	6 slices	6 slices
salt and pepper	to taste	to taste

1. Scale and bone the fish; reserve the bones and heads. Cut the fillets into chunks; if only one variety of fish is being used, the chunks of fish need to be larger than if three types are being served at once. If you prefer to leave the skin on, score each fillet with a sharp knife in two directions to prevent it from curling up during the poaching.
2. Remove the gills and eyes from the fish heads, coarsely chop the heads and bones, and rinse under cold running water to eliminate traces of blood.
3. Gently heat the olive oil in a 2-quart (2 liter) saucepan and sweat together the chopped onions and fennel and the fish bones for about 10 minutes. Do not allow them to color.
4. Add the bouquet garni and water to the fish bones and vegetables and slowly simmer for 20 minutes. Strain through a fine chinois.
5. Prepare the aïoli. If a thicker, more stew-like sauce is wanted, stir the egg yolks into the aïoli.
6. Toast the slices of French bread.
7. When it is time to present the bourride, put the fish stock into a straight-sided sauté pan and bring it to a simmer on top of the stove. Place a slice of the toasted French bread in the bottom of each serving bowl. Poach the fish fillets in the stock, flesh side down. (If the skin side is poached first, the skin will contract and cause the fillets to curl.) When they are done, place the pieces of fish over the bread in the serving bowls.
8. Place the aïoli in a stainless-steel bowl and ladle the poaching liquid into the aïoli while whisking. Adjust the seasonings and pour the sauce over the hot poached fish.

BRAISING

Fish is braised by cooking it in a limited amount of liquid. In fish cookery the essential difference between poaching and braising is the amount of liquid used. When fish is poached, it is completely submerged in hot liquid. When it is braised, the liquid should come only halfway up the sides of the whole fish or fish fillets. Typically, fish to be braised is placed in a flat container that fits its shape as closely as possible; oval-shaped fish pans work especially well for this. Liquid such as fish stock, court-bouillon, white or red wine, or shellfish cooking liquid is added to the pan until it comes halfway up the sides of the fish. The pan is then placed on the stove and the liquid quickly brought to a simmer. As soon as the liquid is simmering, the fish is loosely covered with a sheet of aluminum foil or parchment paper and placed in a moderately hot oven. When the fish is cooked, it should be quickly transferred to a plate or platter while a sauce is prepared with the braising liquid.

The advantage of braising over poaching is that the flavorful juices released by the fish are released into a relatively small amount of liquid. Because braising liquid is more concentrated and flavorful than poaching liquid, it can quickly be reduced (or not) and used as the base for a wide variety of integral fish sauces.

The most common methods for converting the braising liquid for fish into a sauce are by adding heavy cream and reducing the mixture to the desired consistency or by reducing the braising liquid if necessary and whisking in butter. It is also possible to finish the braising liquid for fish with mayonnaise-based sauces, sabayons, and hollandaise-based sauces.

Most of the classic sauces for braised fish are based on the Sole Bercy recipe that follows. Variations usually consist of adding to or changing some of the ingredients in the braising liquid and using cream, whipped cream, butter, or egg yolks, either alone or in combination.

In traditional French recipes, fish is more often cooked and served whole. Nowadays many chefs prefer to use fillets, which are easy for the customer to eat. Many diners, especially in the United States, do not know how to bone fish, and it is often not economically practical to have a waiter bone the fish at tableside. In the traditional parlance of French classic cooking, the term *braising* is used only for whole fish, whereas the expression *en sauce* refers to the braising of fillets. To add to the confusion, American chefs often call the en sauce technique "shallow poaching."

FILLETS OF SOLE BERCY

This recipe uses sole fillets, but any lean white fish will work.

shallot, finely chopped	1 medium	1 medium
parsley, finely chopped	1 tablespoon	15 milliliters
sole fillets	4 medium	4 medium
salt and pepper	to taste	to taste
white wine	¼ cup	60 milliliters
fish stock	¼ cup	60 milliliters
cold butter	1 ounce	30 grams

1. Preheat the oven to 400°F (200°C). Sprinkle the chopped shallot and parsley over the bottom of a sauté pan. Add the fillets, with the white bone side up, to the pan. (The fillets should completely cover the surface of the sauté pan without overlapping.) Season the fillets with salt and pepper and pour over the white wine and fish stock.

2. Cover the fillets loosely with a piece of aluminum foil or parchment paper.

3. Heat over a high flame until the liquids come to a simmer.

4. Immediately place the pan containing the fillets in the oven. As soon as the fillets are cooked (this will take from 2 to 7 minutes, depending on the size and quality of the fish), carefully remove them from the sauté pan and keep them warm.

5. Put the sauté pan on the stove and reduce the braising liquid to a lightly syrupy consistency.

6. Whisk the cold butter into the reduced braising liquid and adjust the seasonings.

7. Place the fillets on a plate or platter and nap them with the sauce. Slide the plate or platter rapidly under the broiler to give the fillets an attractive glaze.

Sole Bercy Derivatives

The classic French repertoire includes long lists of Sole Bercy derivatives, most of which are rarely served today, at least under their original names. A few of the more important classic derivatives follow.

BRAISED WHOLE FLATFISH WITH COCKLES AND NORMAN BUTTER

The briny liquid released by cockles or clams as they cook is one of the divine substances of the kitchen. Use it as the base for fish sauces and no one will fail to be seduced by their intense sea-like flavor. To guild the lily, as it were, whisk French butter into the shellfish cooking liquid, grind in a little pepper, and serve.

You can use this same method to braise fish fillets, but it's more dramatic and you'll get more flavor if you leave the fish whole. As concerns skin, the normal European approach is to scale the white bottom skin and peel off the dark top skin. This is fine when you have Dover sole, but American fish is more fragile and likely to tear if you try to yank off the skin. With American fish, cut away the dark skin in strips with a flexible knife.

YIELD: 4 FISH-COURSE OR 2 MAIN-COURSE SERVINGS

whole flatfish, 16 to 20 ounces (450 to 625 grams), such as dover sole or fluke, top dark skin removed, bottom white skin scaled	1	1
salt and pepper	to taste	to taste
white wine	½ cup	125 milliliters
shallots, minced very fine	2	2
new zealand cockles	2 pounds	1 kilogram
or	or	or
littleneck or cherrystone clams	2 dozen	2 dozen
cold butter, preferably french butter such as beurre d'isigny or beurre de charantes	3 ounces	90 grams

1. Preheat the oven to 400°F (200°C). Season the fish with salt and pepper and keep chilled until you're ready to cook it.
2. Place the wine and shallots in a pot large enough to hold the shellfish. Rinse the cockles and add them to the pot. Cover the pot and cook over medium to high heat until steam shoots out the sides. Turn the heat down to low. Cook a total of 3 minutes for cockles and 7 to 9 minutes for clams.
3. When all the shellfish have opened—if there are cockles still closed, coax them open with a knife; they're probably fine—pour them into a strainer set over a bowl.
4. Take the meats out of the shells. Leave a few in the shells for decoration. Cover the meats with a little of the strained liquid and keep warm until needed.
5. Pour the shellfish cooking liquid into a pan that can go in the oven and that fits the size of the fish as closely as possible. An oval pan is perfect. Bring the liquid to a simmer on the stove and put in the fish, skin side down.
6. Put the pan on high heat until the liquid returns to a simmer. Cover the fish loosely with aluminum foil and slide the pan into the oven.
7. Bake for about 9 minutes per inch (2.5 cm) of thickness at the thickest point. Check the doneness by sliding a knife along the side of one of the top fillets and trying to lift it. It should barely cling to the bone.

8. Transfer the fish to a heated platter. Whisk the butter into the braising liquid over high heat. Serve over the fish, garnished with the cockles.

Variation

Fish can be steamed (the steaming liquid integrated into the sauce) or sautéed and then be finished in the same way. See the photograph of Halibut Braised with Cockles in the color plates.

SOLE MARGUERY

Made famous by the nineteenth-century Parisian Restaurant Marguery, this sauce is essentially a hollandaise made with the braising liquid from fillets of sole or other flatfish (or, for that matter, roundfish). If you have whole sole, make a fish broth with the bones and use that instead of the wine (use wine to make the fish broth).

YIELD: 4 MAIN-COURSE SERVINGS

fillets of sole, 2 to 3 ounces (60 to 90 grams) each	8	8
salt and pepper	to taste	to taste
shallots, minced	2	2
white wine or fish broth made from the sole bones	½ cup	125 milliliters
egg yolks	2	2
clarified butter	6 tablespoons	90 milliliters

1. Preheat the oven to 375°F (190°C). Season the sole with salt and pepper. Sprinkle an oval pan just the size of the fillets with the shallots and place the fish on top. Pour over the white wine. Cover loosely with aluminum foil and slide the pan into the oven.
2. Bake until the fish is white and firm to the touch, about 5 minutes. Transfer the fish to a heated platter or plates.
3. Whisk together the braising liquid and egg yolks in a saucepan with sloping sides over medium heat until the mixture turns fluffy and stiffens. Remove from the heat and whisk in the butter. Season to taste with salt and pepper and pass at the table.

Variation

By leaving out the butter or by using less, this sauce turns into a sabayon sauce that is fluffy, light, and less rich.

SKATE WITH CAPERS, MUSHROOMS, ARTICHOKES, AND POMEGRANATE SEEDS OR RED CURRANTS

This combination is typically seventeenth century and continues to show the medieval fondness for acidic ingredients such as vinegar, verjuice (see page 43), and the juice of underripe fruit such as red currants, gooseberries, or pomegranate seeds.

YIELD: 4 MAIN-COURSE SERVINGS

skate fillets	4	4
salt and pepper	to taste	to taste
flour (for dredging)	as needed	as needed
butter	3½ ounces	100 grams
verjuice, red currant juice (purée the fruit in a blender and strain), cider vinegar, or white wine vinegar	½ cup	125 milliliters
minced chives	1 tablespoon	15 milliliters
button mushrooms, sautéed in 1 ounce (30 grams) butter	10 ounces	290 grams
cooked artichoke hearts, cut into wedges	3	3
capers, drained	2 tablespoons	30 milliliters
pomegranate seeds or red currants	½ cup	125 milliliters

1. Season the skate with salt and pepper and dredge it in flour.
2. Sauté the skate in 1 ounce (30 grams) of the butter in a large sauté pan for a couple of minutes on each side, until firm to the touch. Take out the skate, reserve on a plate, and pour the cooked fat out of the pan.
3. Add the verjuice and the chives and boil the mixture down to half its volume. Add the mushrooms and artichoke hearts. Whisk in the remaining butter and add the capers and the pomegranate seeds. Spoon the sauce over the skate.

Fillets of Sole Bonne Femme

Spread a thin layer of shallots on the bottom of the sauté pan and add 3 sliced medium-sized mushrooms. (In a restaurant, these can be cooked in advance and the liquid added to the braising liquid to save time.) Some recipes finish the sauce with butter in the same way as a traditional Sole Bercy, whereas others add heavy cream and then reduce the sauce to the desired consistency. The fish is napped and glazed in the same way as Sole Bercy.

Fillets of Sole Bordelaise

Replace the white wine in the Sole Bercy recipe with a full-bodied red wine.

Fillets of Sole Crécy

In today's kitchens, this dish is rarely served, but it provides one of the few examples of a classic French recipe for braised fish in which the braising liquid is thickened with a vegetable purée.

Braise the fish in the same way as for Sole Bercy. Reduce the braising liquid slightly and finish it with carrot purée until it has the desired thickness. The sauce can then be finished with butter. Traditionally, Sole Crécy is served surrounded with braised artichoke hearts that have been filled with glazed carrots cut into little balls.

Fillets of Sole Dugléré

Sprinkle the bottom of the sauté pan with 1 minced shallot; 3 peeled, seeded, and chopped tomatoes; and 1 tablespoon (15 milliliters) of finely chopped onions. Finish the sauce with butter in the same way as for Sole Bercy.

Fillets of Sole Foyot

Prepare the sole in the same way as for Sole Bercy but add 1 tablespoon (15 milliliters) of meat glace to the braising liquid after removing the fish.

Fillets of Sole Thermidor

Prepare Sole Bercy but finish the sauce with 1 to 2 teaspoons (5 to 10 milliliters) of Dijon mustard.

Fillets of Sole Véronique

Prepare the sole in the same way as for Sole Bercy but replace the white wine with an equal amount of additional fish stock and 1 teaspoon (5 milliliters) of orange Curaçao. After the fillets have been removed from the pan, add 4 ounces (125 grams) of peeled and seeded grapes. Reduce the liquid and finish with the butter.

Modern Methods for Preparing Braised-Fish Sauces

The traditional system for braising whole fish and fish fillets is excellent because it provides a small amount of concentrated cooking liquid that can be rapidly converted into a variety of sauces. The juices released by freshly cooked fish will inevitably have a better flavor than a sauce made in advance from fish stock.

The cooking liquid from braised fish can be finished in the same way as the court-bouillon (nage) used for poached fish. Finishing the cooking liquid from braised fish is even easier because the liquid is more concentrated and does not require as much reduction. The methods and ingredients used for braising fish can be broken down into several stages, as follows.

1. **Ingredients added to the pan before the braising liquid is added.** In classic recipes these are most commonly shallots, mushrooms, and chopped parsley, but the inventive cook should feel free to add whatever ingredients seem appropriate that are at hand. A few examples are garlic, grilled and peeled peppers, almost any chopped herb, wild mushrooms (either chopped, sliced, or left whole), truffles (sliced or chopped), tomatillos, and mirepoix.

2. **The braising liquids.** In classic recipes, these often include fish stock, white wine, and mushroom cooking liquid, but almost any liquid can be used to give the sauce individuality and excitement. The cooking liquids from mussels or clams can replace fish stock (be careful of the salt). Other alcoholic beverages, such as hard cider, beer, red wine, flamed whiskey, or Cognac can replace the white wine. Flavorful liquids, such as verjuice or lemon juice, can also be added at this stage. Reduced meat stocks or meat glace can be used to give flavor and texture to the sauce.

3. **The liaisons.** Until recently, the liquid from braised fish was almost exclusively finished with either butter or heavy cream. Although these are both excellent methods, the resulting sauce is quite rich and sometimes heavy. In some instances it is possible to serve the braising liquid directly over the fish without thickening or enriching it with a liaison. Some chefs like to finish the braising liquid with yogurt, fresh cheese, or a vegetable purée.

4. **Final flavorings.** As is true with any sauce, certain ingredients whose flavor rapidly dissipates are best added near the end of a sauce's preparation. This is true of delicate herbs, such as chervil and chives, as well as delicately perfumed spirits such as fruit brandies, old Cognacs and Armagnacs, and delicately flavored wines. Some ingredients, such as lemon juice, vinegar, and salt and pepper, may also have to be added near the end, after the sauce has been tasted, to balance the sauce's flavors.

Braised Fish Fillets with Crustacean Sauces

The technique of cooking fish fillets in a small amount of liquid can be adapted to making crustacean-flavored fish sauces. The fish fillets are cooked with the aromatic liquid extracted from lobster as one of the steps in preparing Sauce Américaine (page 330) or one of its variations. The crustacean-flavored braising liquid is then finished using any of the methods appropriate for cooking en sauce—one excellent method is to finish the sauce with crustacean butter. Any type of crustacean cooking liquid can be used and the finished dish served with the appropriate crustacean garniture.

FILLETS OF SOLE WITH LOBSTER SAUCE

In this recipe, sole fillets are braised in lobster cooking liquid prepared as the base for Sauce Américaine (page 330). The braising liquid is then finished with cream, lobster butter, and chopped chives. Topping the fillets with lobster medallions is an elegant touch.

YIELD: 2 TO 4 SERVINGS

sole fillets	4 medium	4 medium
lobster cooking liquid	½ cup	125 milliliters
heavy cream	¼ cup	60 milliliters
lobster butter (page 329)	2 teaspoons	10 milliliters
chives, finely chopped	2 teaspoons	10 milliliters
salt and pepper	to taste	to taste
lobster medallions (optional)	1 to 3 per serving	1 to 3 per serving

1. Preheat the oven to 400°F (200°C). Heat the fillets with the lobster cooking liquid in a sauté pan. As soon as the cooking liquid comes to a simmer, cover the fillets with a sheet of aluminum foil or parchment paper and place them in the oven.
2. When the fillets have cooked (2 to 7 minutes), remove the pan from the oven and transfer the fillets to hot plates or a hot platter.
3. Add the cream to the cooking liquid.
4. Adjust the consistency of the sauce by reducing it (to thicken) or by adding lobster cooking liquid (to thin it). Whisk in the lobster butter and chives and adjust the seasonings.
5. Place the lobster medallions on the fillets, if using, and serve the sauce over or around the fillets on a hot platter or plates.

Other Braising Liquids

If you don't have lobster cooking liquid on hand, other braising liquids can be used, such as the cooking liquid from clams, mussels, or cockles, but also white wine, mushroom cooking liquid, or hard cider.

HALIBUT BRAISED WITH COCKLES

The liquid released by cockles or clams makes a perfect braising liquid for delicate fish such as sole, flounder, or halibut. When the fish has finished braising, the braising liquid can be finished with cream or butter as well as chopped fines herbes, alone or in combination.

cockles	1 pound	450 grams
or	or	or
clams	12	12
white wine	½ cup	125 milliliters
halibut fillets, 6 ounces (180 grams) each	4	4
heavy cream	½ cup	125 milliliters
parsley or chives, finely chopped (optional)	2 tablespoons	30 milliliters
butter (optional)	2 ounces	60 grams
salt and pepper	to taste	to taste

1. Preheat the oven to 350°F (175°C).
2. Steam the cockles open in the white wine by heating them in a covered pot over medium heat for about 5 minutes, until they all open.
3. Put the fillets in a pan just large enough to hold them in a single layer and carefully pour over the steaming liquid from the cockles, leaving behind any grit. Bring to a simmer over high heat. Cover loosely with aluminum foil and slide the pan into the oven. Bake until done, about 9 minutes per inch (2.5 cm) of thickness.
4. Transfer the halibut to heated soup plates. Add the cream to the braising liquid along with the herbs and butter, if using. Season to taste with salt and pepper and pour over the halibut. Arrange the cockles around. See the photograph in the color plates.

FILLETS OF SOLE WITH TOMATILLO AND PEPPER SAUCE

This recipe demonstrates how a classic French technique—in this case, braising en sauce—can be used to prepare a dish with completely different flavors and cultural associations from its own.

sole fillets, 2 to 3 ounces (60 to 90 grams) each	4 medium	4 medium
tomatillo sauce (page 464)	½ cup	125 milliliters
heavy cream	¼ cup	60 milliliters
salt and pepper	to taste	to taste

1. Preheat the oven to 400°F (200°C). Heat the fillets with the tomatillo sauce in a sauté pan. As soon as the sauce comes to a simmer, cover the fillets with a sheet of aluminum foil or parchment paper and place them in the oven.

2. When the fillets are cooked (2 to 7 minutes), remove the pan from the oven and transfer the fillets to hot plates.

3. Add the cream to the sauce.

4. Adjust the consistency of the sauce by reducing it (to thicken) or by adding liquid such as court-bouillon or cream (to thin). Add salt and pepper to taste.

5. Serve the sauce over the fillets.

ROASTING

Both whole fish and fish fillets can be roasted, and the juices that are released during the process can be converted to a sauce. Traditional roasting is done on a spit in front of a roaring fire, but more typically, fish is roasted in a hot oven.

The techniques for oven-roasting fish are similar to those for roasting meats. The roasting pan should be heavy and closely fit the size of the fish being roasted, so that no part of the pan's surface overheats and burns the juices released during cooking. The main difference between roasting fish and meats is that fish cooks more quickly. Consequently, any flavorful ingredients placed in the roasting pan with the fish to flavor the sauce must release their flavor almost immediately. For this reason, ingredients such as mirepoix or garlic must be chopped very finely or be slightly precooked ahead of time. Roasting works best with whole fish, probably because the skin helps seal the juices. Some chefs recommend using unscaled fish, but others like to serve the crispy skin. When roasting large fish, be sure to keep an eye on any aromatic vegetables on the bottom of the roasting pan to make sure they do not burn. If they start to burn, add a small amount of liquid to the bottom of the roasting pan. Once the fish is done, it can be removed from the pan and the roasting pan deglazed in the same way as for roasting meat. The pan can be deglazed with fish stock, court-bouillon, or white wine.

The deglazing liquid, or jus, from the roasted fish should be kept light and relatively simple, like a jus for roast meats, so the natural flavor of the fish stays intact. Some chefs simply finish the jus with freshly chopped herbs, such as parsley, chives, and chervil, and perhaps a small chunk of butter to give it a velvety consistency and a richer flavor. Others may convert it into a sauce by reducing it with cream or finishing it with vegetable purée, sea urchin roe, or scallop coral.

In some cases a roast fish releases so little liquid that it is impractical to try to prepare an integral sauce from the drippings. In this case the fish must be served with a sauce prepared independently, such as a butter or hot emulsified sauce. Some chefs "roast" fish in heat-resistant plastic bags. This is an excellent method but is more akin to braising or steaming than roasting (see "Steaming," page 308).

SAUTÉING

Whole fish, fish steaks, and fish fillets can all be sautéed in the same way as meats. The main difference between sautéing meat and fish is that fish cooks much more quickly, tends to stick to the sauté pan, and becomes extremely fragile once cooked. The best pans for sautéing fish are iron sauté pans that have been carefully seasoned with salt and oil so they have developed a nonstick surface. It is also convenient to have oval pans, which will easily hold whole fish and fillets. Nonstick pans also work well for sautéing fish and can be used with very little fat. The disadvantage to using a nonstick pan is that the juices released by the fish do not adhere to the bottom of the pan, from which they can later be deglazed to provide the beginnings of a sauce. (This is also somewhat true of well-seasoned iron pans. In any case, deglazing a seasoned iron pan may damage the nonstick surface.)

Whichever type of sauté pan you decide to use, make sure the butter or oil is hot before adding the fish, and move the pan back and forth for a few seconds after adding the fish so that its surface cooks slightly, making it less likely to stick. When the fish is cooked, transfer it to a plate and keep it warm while preparing the sauce. The stages in preparing a pan-deglazed sauce for fish are almost identical to those used for preparing meat sauces, but there is a logical succession that should be followed:

1. **Solid ingredients.** Any ingredients that need relatively high heat to release their flavor quickly should be added while the pan is still hot, before any liquid is added. The most common example is finely chopped shallots, but other ingredients, such as garlic and mirepoix, should also be added at this stage.

2. **Wines and spirits.** Because of the alcohol and natural acidity in wine (and tannin in red wine), it should be quickly and rapidly reduced before other liquids are added. If it is added at a later stage, it may give the sauce an aggressive flavor of raw wine.

   Some recipes suggest deglazing a pan with Cognac, whiskey, or some other spirit. If the flavor of a particular spirit forms the predominant flavor of the sauce, then a relatively large amount of that spirit should be used to deglaze the pan. Be careful when deglazing a hot pan with brandy or whiskey. Pull the pan away from the flame, move the bottle away, and stand back when returning the pan to the stove. If the spirit does not ignite immediately, tilt the pan slightly to ignite the alcohol. Flaming the alcohol does not affect the flavor of the sauce, but it prevents unexpected flare-ups in the kitchen.

3. **Stocks and glaces.** If stocks or glaces are being used, they should be added after the wine has been heated for a few seconds to cook off its alcohol. The stocks should be reduced along with the wine and any solid ingredients until the liquids in the bottom of the pan have the desired consistency for the finished sauce.

4. **Liaisons.** Liaisons should be added to the sauce at the end, only after the aromatic liquids in the pan have been reduced as much as necessary. This is especially true of butter, lobster coral, sea urchin roe, and egg yolks, which would break if the sauce were heated after they were added.

5. **Final flavorings.** The flavor of some ingredients is so fleeting that they are best added at the very end. This is true of very delicate herbs such as finely chopped chervil and parsley and also of certain delicate and expensive spirits such as brandies (eaux-de-vie), Calvados, old Cognac, Armagnac, and the like. Once these ingredients are added, the sauce should be heated for only a few seconds to evaporate the alcohol or give the flavor of the herbs a chance to infuse.

The methods for sautéing described above are for sautéing in its strictest sense. Many chefs will use the word in a less rigid way to mean a kind of made-to-order stew. This is especially common with small shellfish, such as shrimp, sea scallops, and bay scallops, where the deglazing of the pan, the addition of flavorful ingredients, and the final liaison all take place while the seafood is still in the pan. This can be an excellent method provided that excess fat is discarded before the pan is deglazed and cooking times are closely watched.

SAUTÉED SALMON FILLET WITH SORREL CREAM SAUCE

This dish was first presented at the Troisgros brothers' restaurant in Roanne in the early 1970s, and at the time was considered extremely innovative. The following recipe differs somewhat from the original in that it is prepared in the pan used to sauté the fish and the sorrel is added without a preliminary blanching. Obviously, each of the components—moistening liquid, butter and cream liaison, and sorrel garniture—can be varied.

YIELD: 6 SERVINGS

salmon fillet	2½ pounds	1.1 kilograms
salt and white pepper	to taste	to taste
butter	3 ounces	90 grams
dry white vermouth	¼ cup	60 milliliters
dry white wine	¼ cup	60 milliliters
heavy cream	½ cup	125 milliliters
sorrel leaves, cut into chiffonade	18	18

1. Slice the salmon fillet on a bias into 6 even portions. Sprinkle with salt and white pepper.
2. Gently sauté the salmon in 1½ ounces (45 grams) of the butter in a large sauté pan. Transfer the salmon to a plate covered with a towel (to absorb excess butter). Traditionally, fish is cooked for a total of 9 minutes per inch

(2.5 cm) of thickness (4½ minutes per side), but nowadays chefs often cook it less so that it remains shiny and moist inside.

3. Pour the fat out of the sauté pan. Gently mop out any remaining fat with a paper towel.

4. Deglaze the pan with the vermouth and white wine and reduce by two-thirds.

5. Add the cream and reduce to the desired consistency. If the sauce contains unsightly specks from the bottom of the pan, it can be strained through a fine chinois into a small saucepan.

6. Add the sorrel chiffonade to the sauce and cook for 30 seconds, until the sorrel melts. Finish the sauce by whisking in the remaining 1½ ounces (45 grams) of butter. Adjust the seasonings and serve over or around the salmon.

STEAMING

In most situations, steamed fish cannot be served with an integral sauce because a steamer is usually filled with a relatively large amount of water or an aromatic liquid such as court-bouillon. The natural juices from the fish drip into this liquid and can never be retrieved.

There are, however, methods that can be used to steam fish and at the same time capture the liquid released by the fish during cooking for an integral sauce. The first and most obvious method is simply to put a very small amount of liquid in the steamer and then convert the liquid at the end of cooking into a sauce. This is the method used for steaming mussels *marinière*. The disadvantage to this method is that it requires constant pouring of the liquid from the bottom of the steamer and replenishing of the liquid for each batch of fish. This method is rarely practical in professional settings. The other disadvantage is that it is easy to let the steamer run dry, ruining both steaming liquid and the fish.

A more practical method for steaming fish is to cook the fish in a tightly covered sauté pan (with straight sides) and a tight-fitting lid. (In classic French cooking parlance, this is referred to as *étuver*.) A small amount of liquid is poured into the sauté pan and brought to a rapid boil over high heat. The fish is then placed in the pan and the lid sealed tightly. The pan can then be left on the stove or transferred to a hot oven. When the fish is cooked, a small amount of flavorful liquid should remain in the bottom of the pan, which can be quickly converted to a sauce with little or no reduction.

Almost any liquid can be used to steam fish, but it is practical to use something that will contribute a desirable flavor to the finished sauce. Some common steaming liquids are fish stock, court-bouillon, red or white wine, spirits (flamed ahead of time), cider, and beer. Once the fish has been steamed, the liquid can be converted into a sauce.

One method used to steam fish is called *en papillote*. A fish fillet is sealed in a parchment-paper or aluminum-foil sack with lightly precooked aromatic vegetables and a small amount of liquid. The sack is then quickly baked in the oven and usually opened in front of the diner. The fish is served surrounded with its own cooking liquid. A similar method, used for whole fish, is to wrap the fish in a heat-resistant plastic roasting bag before it is roasted in the oven. The bag is then opened in the kitchen, and the juices are served unadorned or are converted into a sauce.

STEAMED BASS FILLETS WITH YOGURT CURRY SAUCE

This recipe illustrates how a steaming liquid can be converted into a sauce with yogurt and flavored with curry. The steaming liquid can also be converted into a sauce using any of the methods for finishing poaching and braising liquids. This technique can be used for practically any fish.

YIELD: 6 SERVINGS

court-bouillon	1 cup	250 milliliters
melted butter	1 tablespoon	15 milliliters
bass fillets, 6 ounces (175 grams) each	6	6
curry powder	1 to 2 teaspoons	5 to 10 milliliters
whole butter	½ ounce	15 grams
leben yogurt	3 tablespoons	45 milliliters
finely chopped cilantro	2 tablespoons	30 milliliters
salt and pepper	to taste	to taste
lime juice and hot pepper sauce (optional)	to taste	to taste

1. Pour the court-bouillon into the bottom of a steamer and bring it to a simmer.
2. Brush the inside of the steamer basket with melted butter. Set the fish fillets in it; make sure none of them overlap. Place the basket on the steamer.
3. Cover, and cook the fish for about 10 minutes per inch (2.5 cm) of thickness, but check them before this much time has elapsed in case they are done sooner. (In fact, it is a good idea to leave them slightly underdone, because they will continue cooking while the sauce is being prepared.) Transfer the fish to a plate to keep warm while preparing the sauce.
4. Strain the court-bouillon from the bottom of the steamer into a 2-quart (2 liter) saucepan with sloping sides. There should be about 5 fluid ounces (150 milliliters) remaining. (If there is more, reduce it; if less, thin with additional court-bouillon.)

5. Cook the curry powder in the whole butter for about 30 seconds, and then combine it with the yogurt in a stainless-steel bowl. Whisk the hot court-bouillon into the curry-yogurt mixture until the sauce has the desired flavor and consistency.

6. Add the chopped cilantro and adjust the seasonings. This sauce is good when it is quite hot and sour—lime juice and hot pepper (Tabasco) sauce are often welcome additions. It may be necessary to heat the sauce slightly before it is served, but be careful not to let it boil. Serve the sauce over or around the fish fillets.

SALMON EN PAPILLOTE WITH JULIENNED VEGETABLES

YIELD: 6 SERVINGS

salmon fillet	2 pounds	1 kilogram
leek, white part, cut into fine julienne	1	1
carrot, cut into fine julienne	1 medium	1 medium
turnip, cut into fine julienne	1	1
butter or herb butter	2½ ounces	75 grams
tarragon leaves	18	18
dry vermouth	6 tablespoons	90 milliliters
egg white	1	1

1. Preheat the oven to 350°F (175°C). Cut the salmon on a bias into 6 equal portions.

2. Gently sweat the julienned leek, carrot, and turnip in 1 ounce (30 grams) of the butter until they soften, but do not brown.

3. Cut 6 sheets of parchment paper, 18 × 18 inches (45 × 45 cm). Arrange each salmon piece slightly to the right of center on a square of parchment paper.

4. Spoon the julienned vegetables over each piece of salmon. Place ½ table-spoon (7 milliliters) of butter or herb butter atop each. Place 3 tarragon leaves on top of the butter on each serving. Sprinkle each serving with about 1 tablespoon of vermouth.

5. Lightly beat the egg white so that it breaks up, but do not cause it to foam. Brush the outer edges of the parchment paper squares with the egg white, fold over, and seal them by making a series of straight folds all along the edge of the paper. Brush the folds with egg white and make another set of folds. It is imperative that the packet be perfectly sealed. The finished pa-pillotes should form half-circles.

6. Bake the papillotes on a sheet pan in the oven until they puff. (It is difficult to determine exactly when the fish is done, so it is a good idea to test one or two in advance to determine exact baking times.)

7. The papillotes are best cut open in the dining room with scissors and transferred to hot plates in front of the diner. The natural juices in the bottom of the parchment paper sack are spooned over. See the photograph in the color plates.

COMBINING METHODS: FISH STEWS

The difference between a fish stew and a soup is often difficult to define; the most important difference is that soups usually have a higher proportion of liquid to solid than do stews. Because stews contain less liquid, they may also be more boldly flavored than soups.

The table on page 312 provides a sense of the diversity of fish stew recipes. There exist almost as many varieties of fish stews as there are combinations of fish, most of which are the natural outcome of combining ingredients available in a particular region, although many of the stages of preparation are the same. The simplest fish stews are made by first preparing an aromatic liquid with vegetables such as onion, garlic, and fennel, the trimmings from the fish, and wine. When the flavors of the vegetables and trimmings have infused in the wine, the liquid is then strained into a straight-sided saucepan, and the pieces of fish are then poached in the liquid. When the fish is finished poaching, it is removed with a skimmer and kept warm while the poaching liquid is converted into a sauce. In traditional French recipes where red wine is used, beurre manié is most often used, but more modern versions will often simply reduce the cooking liquid and finish it with butter. White wine–based fish stews are most often finished with cream or a mixture of cream and egg yolks.

Although traditional recipes for fish stews usually suggest poaching the fish in a premade aromatic liquid, this method is often impractical in a professional setting because reducing the poaching liquid takes too long. It is more practical to prepare fish stews to order by cooking them in a tightly covered pan with a small amount of aromatic liquid that has been reduced in advance. In this way the pieces of fish release flavorful liquids into the surrounding aromatic base, and little if any reduction is necessary before converting the liquid into a sauce. To prepare a fish stew to order, it is best to cook the precut pieces of fish in a covered pan with a small amount of appropriate liquid (see the discussion of *étuver* under "Steaming," page 308). In some cases, as for Red Wine Matelotes (page 314), preparing an aromatic red wine reduction in advance and using it to cook the fish is an excellent method. When the pieces of fish are cooked, they should be quickly transferred to hot plates or bowls; the liquid remaining in the pan is then converted into a sauce.

Traditional Fish Stews and Soups

	ORIGIN	AROMATIC BASE/FLAVORINGS	MOISTENING LIQUID(S)	FISH AND SHELLFISH	LIAISON	GARNITURE
Anguille au Vert	Belgium	Butter, onions	White wine	Eel	Eggs	Herbs
Bouillabaisse	Provence (France)	Onions, leeks, fennel, garlic, tomatoes, saffron, bouquet garni with oregano, thyme, etc., dried orange rind	Fish stock made with trimmings, pastis	Mediterranean	Aïoli	Croutons, aïoli
Bourride	Provence (France)	Onions, fennel, thyme, bay leaf, orange zest	Fish stock made with trimmings	Mediterranean	Aïoli	Aïoli
Bourride Sétoise	Languedoc (France)	Leeks, onions, Swiss chard, bouquet garni	Fish stock, white wine	Monkfish, monkfish liver	Aïoli	Aïoli
Calderada	Portugal	Onions, sweet green peppers, garlic, tomatoes, thyme	Fish stock made with trimmings and white wine	Saltwater fish: sea bass, cod, monkfish, etc., squid, bay scallops	None	Basil cut in strips (chiffonade)
Caldereta Asturiana	Spain	Olive oil, onions, sweet red peppers, nutmeg	Sherry, water	Cod, sea bass, monkfish, etc.	None	None
Caudière	Flanders (Belgium)	Onions, cloves, bouquet garni, garlic	Fish stock made with trimmings and water, white wine, mussel cooking liquid	Small Atlantic fish, baby sole, flounder, conger eel, mussels	Cream	Mussels
Chaudrée	Charente (France)	Bouquet garni, pepper	White wine, water	Squid or cuttlefish, baby skate, eel, mullet	Butter	Buttered croutons
Clam Chowder	New England (United States)	Pork, onions	Milk	Clams	Potatoes	None
Cotriade	Brittany (France), Cornwall (England)	Onions, sorrel, potatoes	Water, vinegar	Conger, eel, cod, mackerel	Butter	Stale bread
Matelote Alsacienne	Alsace (France)	Leeks, carrots, onions, bouquet garni	Fish stock made with vegetables and fish trimmings, Riesling	Freshwater fish: carp, eel, perch, etc.	Cream, egg yolks, beurre manié	Buttered croutons
Matelote à la Canotiere	Alsace (France)	Leeks, carrots, onions, bouquet garni	Fish stock made with vegetables and fish trimmings, Riesling or Sylvaner	Carp and eel only	Butter	Mushrooms, crayfish
Matelote Normande	Normandy (France)	Onions, garlic, bouquet garni	Cider, Calvados	Saltwater fish: sole, flounder, conger eel	Beurre manié, cream	Croutons, mussels

Meurette	Burgundy (France)	Onions, garlic, bouquet garni	Red wine, marc de Bourgogne	Freshwater fish: trout, eel, perch, etc.	Beurre manié, butter	Garlic-rubbed croutons
Pauchouse	Burgundy (France)	Onions, garlic, cloves, bouquet garni	White wine (Bourgogne Aligoté)	Freshwater fish: trout, perch, eel, pike, etc.	Beurre manié, cream	Pearl onions, bacon, mushrooms, croutons
Shchi	Russia	Butter, onions, carrots	Water	White fish	Flour	Sour cream, green onions, cabbage
Ttorro	Basque country (Spain)	Olive oil, onions, garlic, sweet red pepper, hot peppers, saffron, bouquet garni	Stock made with fish trimmings and vegetables	Saltwater fish and shellfish: mussels, langoustines, monkfish, conger eel, shrimps, lobster, etc.	None	Croutons cooked with olive oil, chopped parsley
Vatapá	Brazil	Onions, hot peppers, tomatoes, ginger	Coconut milk, water	Small ocean fish, shrimps	Coconut purée, peanut purée, rice	Chopped cilantro
Waterzooï	Flanders (Belgium)	Butter, onions, bouquet garni, sage	Stock made with fish trimmings and vegetables	Freshwater fish: trout, eel, perch, pike, etc.	Butter or heavy cream	Chopped parsley, croutons
Zarzuela	Catalane (Spain)	Onions, sweet red peppers, sweet green peppers, garlic, ham, tomatoes, saffron, bouquet garni	White wine	Lobster, large shrimps, mussels, bay scallops, sea scallops	None	Almonds, chopped parsley
Zuppa di Pesce	Italy	Olive oil, garlic	Water, wine vinegar	Firm fish, mussels, shrimps		

Some recipes for fish stews suggest browning the fish first in a small amount of butter or oil and then deglazing the pan with liquid and returning the pieces of fish to the pan. The method, roughly analogous to a chicken fricassée, is best reserved for relatively large pieces of fish; cooking thin fish fillets and other small pieces in two stages will usually cause overcooking. When prebrowning fish on the stove, it is a good idea to coat the pieces lightly with flour (any excess carefully shaken off) so that they brown quickly.

RED WINE MATELOTES

Traditional red wine matelotes have always been made from freshwater fish. The same methods, however, can be adapted to saltwater fish or even a combination of the two. Traditional matelote recipes almost invariably call for poaching the fish in a large amount of red wine, usually flavored with onions, a bouquet garni, and maybe some garlic. The fish is then removed, kept warm, and the poaching liquid thickened with beurre manié. In the version that follows, the red wine is cooked with the trimmings and bones from the fish, aromatic vegetables, and herbs and reduced ahead of time. The sections of fish are then cooked to order in a covered pan with a small amount of the flavored and reduced red wine broth. When the pieces of fish are cooked, the base mixture is quickly finished with butter and used to sauce the fish. Some chefs like to give further body to the aromatic red wine broth by browning squid, chunks of fish, pork, or ham along with the vegetables and fish trimmings.

The traditional garniture for red wine matelotes usually consists of pearl onions, mushrooms, small strips of bacon (lardoons), and heart-shaped croutons.

YIELD: 6 MAIN-COURSE OR 8 FIRST-COURSE SERVINGS

whole fish (such as trout, salmon, perch, pike, or eel)	6 pounds	3 kilograms
butter	5 ounces	150 grams
onion, coarsely chopped	1 large	1 large
garlic cloves, coarsely chopped	4	4
cleaned squid or extra fish (optional)		
red wine	6 cups	1.5 liters
large bouquet garni (page 51)	1	1
pearl onions, peeled	18 to 30	18 to 30
small mushrooms	6 ounces	175 grams
heart-shaped croutons browned in clarified butter	6	6
chopped parsley	2 tablespoons	30 milliliters
cognac, armagnac, or marc	few drops	few drops
salt and pepper	to taste	to taste

1. Scale (unless fillets are to be skinned), fillet, and gut the fish. Reserve the heads and bones.

2. Score the skin side of the fillets in two directions with a sharp knife to prevent them from curling. Cut the fillets into appropriate-size pieces (size depends on the number of fish being used and the importance of the matelote in the meal—whether it is being served as a main course or first course). Keep the fillets covered and refrigerated until needed.

3. Remove the gills from the fish heads and split the heads in half. Rinse the fish bones and split heads under cold running water for 15 minutes. Make sure that any remaining organs or bits of coagulated blood are removed.

4. Melt 1 ounce (30 grams) of the butter in a 2-quart (2 liter) saucepan, and add the chopped onion, garlic, and fish bones. If squid or extra pieces of fish are being used, add them. Gently cook the bones and vegetables for about 15 minutes, until they brown slightly.

5. Add 1 cup (250 milliliters) of the red wine to the browned bones and vegetables.

6. Cook the bones and vegetables with the wine, stirring with a wooden spoon until all the wine has evaporated. Add the rest of the wine and the bouquet garni. Simmer the mixture for 30 minutes.

7. Strain the cooked red wine through a fine chinois into a 1-quart (1 liter) saucepan. Reduce the wine until 1½ cups (375 milliliters) remain. Skim off any froth that floats to the surface.

8. Glaze the pearl onions in ½ ounce (15 grams) of the butter and enough water to come halfway up their sides until they soften slightly, usually about 15 minutes. Keep warm.

9. Sauté the mushrooms in ½ ounce (15 grams) of the butter until they are well browned, usually after 5 to 10 minutes. Keep warm.

10. If you will be cooking the fish in the oven, preheat the oven to 400°F (200°C).

11. Ladle the reduced wine mixture into a straight-sided sauté pan. Bring the mixture to a simmer.

12. Place the fish in the simmering wine. If the pieces of fish are of different thicknesses, add the thickest pieces first. Cover the pan. Place the pan over a low to medium flame or in the oven. Quickly add thinner pieces of fish as necessary. Cook the fish for about 9 minutes per inch (2.5 cm) of thickness. When the fish is done, quickly transfer it to plates or bowls.

13. Check the consistency of the red wine sauce in the sauté pan. If it is overly reduced, it can be thinned with court-bouillon, fish stock, or water.

14. Whisk ½ ounce (15 grams) of the butter per serving (3 ounces/90 grams for all the fish) into the red wine mixture.

15. Dip the pointed ends of the croutons into the chopped parsley. Finish the sauce with the remaining parsley and a few drops of Cognac. Season it with salt and pepper to taste, and pour it over the fish. Arrange the onions, mushrooms, and croutons over and around the fish.

SQUID WITH RED WINE SAUCE

Squid is best cooked either very quickly, such as when it is fried, or slowly, by braising. It is delicious braised in red wine and served in soup plates with plenty of French bread and a tub of aïoli.

YIELD: 4 MAIN-COURSE OR 6 FIRST-COURSE SERVINGS

olive oil	2 tablespoons	30 milliliters
carrot, chopped	1 medium	1 medium
onion, chopped	1 medium	1 medium
garlic cloves, minced	4	4
squid, cleaned, hoods cut into ½-inch (1 cm) rings	3 pounds	1.5 kilograms
red wine	2 cups	500 milliliters
large bouquet garni (page 51)	1	1
flour	1 tablespoon	15 milliliters
butter, at room temperature	½ ounce	15 grams
salt and pepper	to taste	to taste
aïoli (page 396)		

1. Heat the olive oil in a saucepan large enough to hold the squid and add the carrot, onion, and garlic. Over medium heat, gently cook the vegetables until they soften and lightly brown, about 10 minutes.
2. Add the squid and turn the heat to high. Stir the squid around as they release liquid and keep over high heat until all the liquid evaporates and caramelizes on the bottom and sides of the pan. Don't let it burn.
3. Add the red wine and nestle in the bouquet garni. Simmer for about 45 minutes, uncovered, so the wine reduces a little.
4. Work the flour and butter together into a smooth paste (beurre manié) and whisk into the simmering sauce a bit at a time until the sauce has the consistency you like. Season to taste with salt and pepper. Pass the aïoli.

OCTOPUS DAUBE

Octopus takes to slow, long cooking in the same way as tough cuts of meat. It releases so much natural gelatin that it always gives the sauce a lovely consistency. After about 90 minutes of cooking, it becomes melt-in-your-mouth tender.

YIELD: 4 MAIN-COURSE SERVINGS

octopus, cleaned	1	1
onion, peeled, chopped	1 medium	1 medium
carrot, chopped	1 medium	1 medium
garlic cloves, chopped	3	3

olive oil	2 tablespoons	30 milliliters
full-bodied red wine	3 cups	750 milliliters
medium bouquet garni (page 51)	1	1
finely chopped parsley	2 tablespoons	10 milliliters
baguette toasts		
aïoli (page 396)		

1. Cut the octopus into 1-inch (2.5 cm) sections.
2. In a pot large enough to hold the octopus, cook the onion, carrot, and garlic in the oil over medium heat for about 12 minutes, or until the onion is softened but not browned.
3. Add the octopus pieces, pour in the red wine, and nestle the bouquet garni in the center of the pot. Bring to a gentle simmer and simmer, covered, for about 1½ hours, or until a skewer slides easily in and out of a large piece of the octopus. If some of the octopus is above the liquid, turn the octopus around after 45 minutes of cooking to submerge what was protruding above.
4. Strain the octopus stew and discard the vegetables, sorting out the octopus. Simmer the braising liquid down to about 1 cup (250 milliliters), add the parsley, and serve with the octopus in heated soup plates. Pass the toasts and aïoli.

White Wine Fish Stews

White wine fish stews are prepared in almost the same way as red wine matelotes. In French regional cooking, the poaching liquid for white wine–based fish stews is usually thickened with roux rather than with beurre manié, and the stews are often finished with heavy cream and sometimes a mixture of heavy cream and egg yolks. Garnitures vary almost endlessly. Recently chefs have taken to naming these stews blanquettes, after the traditional veal stew finished with cream and egg yolks.

White wine fish stews can also be flavored and thickened using a variety of contemporary techniques.

Moistening Options

Court-bouillon (flavored with different wines, herbs, spices, or vegetables)

Fish stock (made from the fish carcasses)

Shellfish cooking liquids

Liaison Options

Egg yolks and cream

Vegetable purées such as potato, garlic, tomato

Coconut milk

Beurre manié

Mayonnaises such as aïoli or rouille

Butter, whole or worked into a butter sauce
such as beurre blanc or hollandaise

Vinaigrette

Yogurt

Mustard

Garniture Options

Pearl onions (glazed)

Mushrooms (cooking liquid added to fish poaching liquid)

Fennel (cut into wedges, braised)

Tomatoes (diced)

Garlic (whole cloves, blanched)

Fresh fava beans (peeled twice, blanched)

Artichokes (turned, precooked, cut into wedges)

Final Flavoring Options

Chopped herbs

Vegetable purées such as tomato, sorrel, or sweet pepper

Spirits such as Calvados, marc or grappa, eau-de-vie

COOKING MOLLUSKS

Once a particular fish or shellfish has released flavorful liquid during cooking, the methods used for manipulating the liquid are the same. Some shellfish, however, lend themselves better to certain techniques.

Oysters

The flavor of oysters varies considerably, depending on the variety and the region where they were harvested. Often the smallest oysters, such as Belons from Maine and Pigeon Points from California, will contribute a more intensely flavored cooking liquid than fatter, more impressive looking types.

Recipes and chefs often disagree as to whether the liquid contained in the oyster when it is first shucked should be used for sauce making. The best guide is to taste the liquid first, but since it often has only a salty taste with little of the sea-like character of the oyster, it is usually discarded.

The most flavorful component of the oyster is released when it is very gently stewed in almost no liquid. Oysters should never be allowed to boil, only to warm.

OYSTERS WITH CHAMPAGNE SAUCE

These oysters can be served individually as hors d'oeuvres or in larger groupings as a fish course. A still Champagne is excellent for this sauce (see page 77), but if this is unavailable, a dry white wine with high acidity, such as a French Chablis, Sancerre, or Muscadet, can be substituted and the dish renamed accordingly.

YIELD: 3 TO 4 FIRST-COURSE SERVINGS

oysters	12	12
heavy cream	1 cup	250 milliliters
spinach, blanched, excess water squeezed out	1 bunch	1 bunch
sorrel leaves	1 handful	1 handful
salt and pepper	to taste	to taste
still champagne or dry white wine	½ cup	125 milliliters
finely chopped parsley or chives	1 tablespoon	15 milliliters

1. Shuck the oysters into a bowl. Refrigerate until needed. Discard the top shells and scrub the bottom shells under running water with a brush. Turn them upside down on a sheet pan to drain and dry.
2. Reduce ⅓ cup (80 milliliters) of the cream in a saucepan until it is on the verge of breaking. Heat the blanched spinach and the sorrel leaves in the cream. Season with pepper and a little salt (the sauce will be salty from later additions).
3. Heat the oyster shells in a 250°F (120°C) oven.
4. Poach the oysters in their own liquid in a small saucepan for about 1 minute. Do not let them boil, even for a second.
5. Remove the oysters from their cooking liquid with a slotted spoon. Put them on a clean cloth napkin on a plate to remove specks of shell. Fold the napkin over them to keep them warm.
6. Strain the poaching liquid through a fine chinois into a saucepan and add the still Champagne. Reduce by two-thirds.
7. Add the remaining ⅔ cup (165 milliliters) of cream to the oyster liquid–Champagne reduction and reduce the sauce until it has the consistency of a beurre blanc. Add the chopped parsley and adjust the seasonings.
8. Spoon the spinach-sorrel mixture into the bottom of each oyster shell. Place a hot oyster on top and nap with the sauce. See the photograph in the color plates.

Sea Scallops

It is a sad fact that truly fresh sea scallops are rarely if ever sold in the United States. The only way to be assured of their freshness is to buy them in their shells and shuck them almost to order. The amount of cooking they require is inversely proportionate to their freshness.

A popular method for preparing scallops is to sauté them in hot fat, usually butter. Unfortunately, when scallops are sautéed, their flavor is often altered — they take on a vaguely cloying sweet taste — and much of their delicate sea-like flavor is lost. When truly fresh scallops are available, they are best when lightly poached or braised and served immediately. Avoid methods that require holding the scallops for long periods while the poaching liquid is being reduced.

Because sea scallops are often thick, many chefs make the mistake of trying to submerge them completely in poaching liquid. This technique will work only if the scallops are nestled into a perfectly fitting sauté pan with straight sides. A better method is to cook them in a covered pan with a small amount of aromatic liquid. Another excellent method is to slice the scallops into ⅜-inch (9 mm) disks and poach them for no more than 30 seconds. They can then be served on a wide, shallow plate with a few tablespoons of their poaching liquid, which may be finished with the usual sauce-finishing options such as fresh herbs, tomato concassée, vinaigrette, cream, or butter.

SCALLOPS ÉTOUFFÉES WITH CHIVES

YIELD: 6 FIRST-COURSE SERVINGS

scallops, preferably with roe	18 ounces	500 grams
mussel or clam cooking liquid	6 tablespoons	90 milliliters
freshly chopped chives	2 tablespoons	30 milliliters
salt and pepper	to taste	to taste

1. Cut the scallops crosswise into ⅜-inch (9 mm) disks.
2. Put the mussel or clam cooking liquid in a 2-quart (2 liter) straight-sided sauté pan, and distribute the scallops in a single even layer.
3. Cover the sauté pan and place it over high heat for approximately 45 seconds, until the liquid comes to a simmer.
4. Remove the lid and transfer the scallops to hot plates.
5. Whisk the chopped chives into the hot cooking liquid. Adjust the seasonings. Pour over the scallops.

Bay Scallops

Like sea scallops, bay scallops should be bought in their shells and shucked just before cooking. Once shucked, they quickly lose their delicacy and ocean-breeze flavor. When available, they are beautiful when served individually in their shells. Making a sauce to order can be impractical, so a good method is to poach them in a limited amount of liquid and, from time to time, remove enough of the poaching liquid to make enough sauce for several orders.

Mussels

Mussels should be checked carefully to eliminate dead ones before they are cooked; one bad one can spoil an entire dish. The best way to check them is to scrub them thoroughly with a brush under cold running water and press firmly on the two shells in opposing directions—any dead ones will immediately break apart. Many recipes insist that mussels that have opened slightly cannot be used. This is rarely true, as most mussels will close again if the two shells are squeezed together. If in doubt, give the mussel a sniff—it should smell like a clean beach. If it smells like anything else, throw it out.

Occasionally a recipe will insist that mussels be shucked while still raw. Considering the difficulty of the task, it is rarely worth it, especially since mussels are so easily steamed open and their delicious essence so easily captured. It is, of course, best to steam them open to order, but if a somewhat complicated gratin (like the following one) is being prepared, this is not practical. They can be steamed open an hour or two before serving, the top shell removed, and the bottom shells containing the mussels covered with plastic wrap and refrigerated until needed. Remove any pieces of beard once they have been steamed open.

In some areas, sand-free cultivated mussels, which are small, flavorful, and of uniform size, are available.

GRATINÉED MUSSELS WITH SAFFRON HOLLANDAISE

In this recipe the mussels are steamed open and their cooking liquid captured, reduced, and used as the base for a sauce hollandaise. The sauce is then napped over the mussels, which are then gratinéed for 5 to 10 seconds under the broiler.

YIELD: 10 FIRST-COURSE SERVINGS

mussels	60	60
white wine	½ cup	125 milliliters
saffron threads	1 pinch	1 pinch
egg yolks	4	4
clarified butter	1½ cups	375 milliliters
heavy cream	¼ cup	60 milliliters
pepper	to taste	to taste
fresh spinach, leaves only, blanched, refreshed, and wrung out	1 large bunch	1 large bunch
coarse salt	as needed	as needed

1. Scrub and sort through the mussels to eliminate any dead ones. Put the mussels and white wine in a covered pot. Bring the wine to a simmer on the stove and simmer until the mussels open, for about 5 minutes.
2. Strain the mussel cooking liquid through a fine chinois or cheesecloth into a saucepan. Remove the mussels from the shells. Save half of the shells and wash them thoroughly. Dry them on a sheet pan in a 250°F (120°C) oven.
3. Reduce the mussel cooking liquid by three-quarters.
4. Combine ¼ cup (60 milliliters) of the reduced mussel cooking liquid with the saffron. Let the saffron soak for 15 minutes.
5. Whisk the cooled saffron-scented mussel cooking liquid with the egg yolks in a 2-quart (2 liter) saucepan with sloping sides until the mixture froths, usually about 20 seconds. Place the saucepan over a medium flame and continue whisking over the heat until the mixture becomes even more frothy and stiffens.
6. Whisk the clarified butter into the egg yolk base. Adjust the consistency by adding more clarified butter to thicken or by adding more mussel cooking liquid, cream, or other liquids to thin.
7. Reduce the cream in a saucepan until it is almost ready to break. Season it with pepper (but no salt); stir the spinach into the cream to heat it.
8. Place a small amount of the hot creamed spinach in the bottom of each mussel shell, add a mussel, and coat with the saffron hollandaise.
9. Cover a sheet pan with a thick layer of coarse salt and arrange the mussels in rows on the sheet pan. Gratiné the mussels under the broiler for about 5 seconds.

Clams

Depending on their size, clams are adaptable to the methods used to cook oysters (shucking, poaching lightly out of their shells) or mussels (steaming open, capturing their cooking liquid *à la marinière*).

Snails

Although there are hundreds of varieties of land snails, most require careful cleaning and a long preliminary cooking in court-bouillon before they can be used. Rarely is their cooking liquid converted into a sauce; instead, they are almost always served with a nonintegral sauce, such as the ubiquitous garlic and parsley butter (snail butter) or a lightly creamed mushroom duxelles. Wild mushrooms go especially well with the earthy flavor of land snails.

The miniature sea snails (periwinkles), so popular in Europe, are rarely eaten in the United States, although they are beginning to catch on. Unlike land snails, periwinkles will cook in about 10 minutes. A popular method for preparing an integral sauce is to simmer the snails *à la nage* and serve them with the cooking liquid with lots of crusty bread. Any of the methods used to finish court-bouillon—with butter, vinaigrette, mustard, herbs—can also be used.

Sea Urchins

Used for their roe, sea urchins should be cut open with scissors and the pale orange or brown roe removed shortly before it is to be used. Usually the roe is puréed and used as a flavorful liaison to finish and enrich fish sauces. Occasionally, whole pieces of the roe will appear in fish stews or as garniture for sauced fish fillets.

11

CRUSTACEAN SAUCES

Crustaceans are members of the class *Crustacea,* a Latin word that means "shell." Crustaceans have jointed bodies, appendages (which may be legs), and antennae. Mollusks, including clams, mussels, scallops, oysters, snails, squid, and octopus, have unsegmented bodies and thus are classified differently from crustaceans, though both groups are considered shellfish. Crustaceans are treated separately from fish and other shellfish because they have certain characteristics that require special treatment by the sauce maker. A wide variety of techniques is used to extract the natural flavors from crustaceans and to convert them into sauces;

traditional techniques for cooking crustaceans as well as contemporary innovations are presented in this chapter.

Flavor can be extracted from three major parts of the crustacean: the flesh itself; the organs, including the tomalley and coral; and the shell. The techniques used for extracting flavor from each of these parts are different and will be analyzed separately.

Flavor is extracted from the fleshy parts of crustaceans in the same way that natural flavors are derived from cooking fish and meat: Juices are released during cooking into the surrounding cooking liquid. This liquid is then reduced to concentrate its flavor and usually thickened with some type of liaison. The thickened sauce can then be flavored with additional ingredients such as herbs, Cognac, and tomatoes. Most traditional recipes call for browning or gently sautéing the cut-up crustaceans with flavor components such as mirepoix or chopped onions and shallots before any liquid is added.

The shells of crustaceans contain components that can be used to provide color and flavor to a finished sauce. The techniques for extracting these components differ from most sauce-making methods because the components are soluble in oil and fat rather than water. The traditional technique for extracting flavor and color from crustacean shells is by preparing a crustacean butter. Crustacean butters can be prepared in advance and used to finish sauces in the same way as regular butter.

The most flavorful parts of crustaceans are the tomalley (liver) and coral (the ovary, with eggs, or roe). In many types of crustaceans, it is impractical to try to remove the coral for use in the sauce. Lobster, however, has coral that is accessible and easy to remove. Lobster coral and tomalley must be handled carefully, as they are extremely perishable and sensitive to heat. Coral and tomalley have a pronounced sea-like flavor that is lost when cooked. Consequently, these components should be used at the very end of the sauce-making process.

Fortunately, crustacean recipes are largely interchangeable. Recipes for lobster can be prepared using crabs, for instance. Some of the techniques (such as the use of the tomalley and cleaning) vary, depending on the type of crustacean.

TYPES OF CRUSTACEANS

Crabs

All of the many varieties of crabs can be used for sauce making except soft-shell crabs, which would be exorbitantly expensive. Although there are few sauce recipes designed specifically for crabs, crabs are useful for making crustacean sauces because they are easy to clean and are usually inexpensive. To clean them, turn them over and make an incision directly behind the eyes with a sharp knife or ice pick. Turn the crab over and unfold the apron—the small flap clinging to the underside of the body—and make another incision into the body of the crab; this cuts the major ventral nerves and kills them instantly. Twist off the apron while pulling. The crab's intestine should come with it. Grip the crab firmly and pull off the top shell. This will expose the gills clinging to the bottom section and allow the inedible intestines to fall out. Pull the gills off with your fingers. After cleaning, the crab can be used in the same way as other crustaceans.

Crayfish

Crayfish live in freshwater and vaguely resemble miniature lobsters. Their flavor, however, is distinctly different. They have long been popular in France and Italy, where they have been almost completely fished out. Nowadays, European crayfish comes mostly from eastern Europe. The United States still has an abundance of crayfish in its streams and lakes, probably because Americans (Louisianans are an exception) have ignored them for so long. They are becoming increasingly popular as interest in European and regional American cuisine increases. Although some suppliers market crayfish tails, these are useless for sauce preparation.

Because removing the meat from crayfish is labor intensive, many restaurant chefs buy a quantity of live crayfish with which to prepare sauce along with some of the prepared tails for use in the final dish. When buying whole crayfish, make sure they are alive. Many cookbook authors insist that a gritty vein—actually the intestine—running through the tail be removed from the live crayfish before it is used in sauce making. Not only is this inhumane, it is unnecessary, as the intestine is easily removed after cooking.

Langoustines

Also known as Dublin prawns, Norway lobsters, or scampi (singular, scampo), langoustines are similar in appearance to crayfish except that they swim in salt water. Although langoustines can be found all over the world, only three American species are large enough to be marketable, and even these are hard to find. Most of the langoustines found in American markets have been flown in from Europe, where they are more widely available, though never inexpensive. The tails can be used in the same way as shrimp or crayfish tails. The shells are pale and so contribute little color to a crustacean sauce.

Lobsters

There are two primary species of lobster, *Homarus americanus*, which is found in American waters, and *Homarus gammarus*, found in European waters. These two types are similar and can be cleaned and cooked in the same way. Many recipes call for cooking lobster in a pot of boiling water for 10 to 15 minutes, depending on its size. Although the result may be suitable, the lobster's juices are lost in the pot, the coral is cooked to a red, hard, practically tasteless mass, and none of the flavor is extracted from the shell. The recipes in this chapter are designed so that the flavors from the lobster can be converted into sauces. To accomplish this, the lobster is usually cut apart while alive (not as brutal as it sounds—the lobster is killed instantly).

Practically all of the lobster can be used. Only the small stomach sac in the middle of the head should be discarded (see Classic Sauce Américaine, page 330).

Selecting lobsters depends on eventual use. It is not necessary to buy perfect 2-pound (1 kilogram) lobsters to use in a lobster salad. For salads, sauces, and lobster ragoûts, it is a good idea to buy culls—lobsters that are missing a claw or have one claw that has atrophied. They are considerably less expensive and, provided they are still alive, work just as well as larger, more expensive lobsters for making sauces.

Always use female lobsters for sauce making, because they usually contain coral, which contributes to the sauce. To tell the difference between a male and female lobster, turn the lobster over and examine the small legs lining each side of the bottom of the tail. The pair of legs closest to the head (where the tail and head join) are hard and firm on the male and soft and flexible on the female. European recipes sometimes call for lobsters that are spawning. The underside of a spawning lobster's shell is thickly encrusted with eggs. Marketing of spawning lobsters is, however, illegal in the United States.

Rock Lobsters

Also known as spiny lobsters, rock lobsters are similar to regular lobsters but have no claws. They are available fresh in Europe and on the Pacific coast of the United States. Frozen rock lobster tails from South America, South Africa, and New Zealand are often served in the United States, but they have little value in sauce making.

Shrimps

Unfortunately, shrimps are usually marketed with their heads removed, which leaves little that can be used for sauce making. In a pinch, however, a suitable stock can be made with the shells, providing the shrimps are impeccably fresh. Certain wholesalers sell frozen shrimp heads to use for soups and sauces.

⬤— CRUSTACEAN BUTTER

Crustacean butter is used for finishing and adding complexity not only to crustacean sauces but to fish and certain meat sauces as well. It is also useful for last-minute sauces, to which the flavor of crustaceans can be added without starting an américaine-style sauce from scratch.

Crustacean butter is prepared from cooked crustacean shells. Shells with a bright orange color, such as lobster and crayfish, are best. Because crustacean butter takes considerable time to prepare, it is best to save the shells when preparing lobster salads and other dishes in which the shells are removed, freezing them until needed.

Crustacean butter is valuable in sauce making not only for its flavor but for the bright color it gives to sauces. By cooking crustacean shells with butter, flavor and color are extracted that would be left behind if the shells were cooked only in stock or other water-based liquids.

Because crustacean butter is intensely flavored, a little goes a long way. It can be prepared in batches and refrigerated or frozen until needed. It keeps in the refrigerator for up to a month and can be frozen almost indefinitely.

YIELD: 1 POUND (450 GRAMS)

butter	1½ pounds	675 grams
crustacean shells, preferably lobster or crayfish	3 pounds	1.3 kilograms
hot water	2 quarts	2 liters

1. Cut the butter into large chunks and combine it with the lobster or crayfish shells in the bowl of an electric mixer. (The shells should not come more than halfway up the sides of the bowl or they might fly out while the mixture is being worked.)
2. Attach the paddle blade to the mixer and start on slow speed. Work the shells with the butter at slow speed until the mixture starts to hold together in a single mass, usually after about 5 minutes.
3. Turn the mixer up slightly and work the shells with the butter for 20 to 30 minutes. The butter should take on a salmon color.
4. Preheat the oven to 250°F (120°C). Transfer the butter to a heavy-bottomed pot. Place the pot on the stove and gently heat it while stirring until the butter has melted.
5. Put the pot containing the butter in the oven for 1 hour. Check it every 15 minutes to make sure that the butter is not getting too hot, which would

cause it to lose its color and flavor. If there is any sign of boiling or if the butter starts to brown around the edges, immediately turn down the oven.

6. Remove the pot from the oven and add enough hot water to cover the shells by about 2 inches (5 cm). (The hot water is added so that the shells will sink to the bottom while the butter floats to the top, where it can be easily removed.)

7. Chill the pot containing the butter in the refrigerator or in a bowl of ice until the butter floating on the surface congeals into a solid mass.

8. Carefully remove the butter (which should be bright orange) from the surface of the liquid in the same way as removing fat from a chilled stock. Discard the crustacean shells and the liquid.

9. Put the congealed butter into a small saucepan and gently bring it to a simmer. Be careful not to overheat it or it may brown and lose its flavor and color.

10. When the butter has completely melted, strain it through a fine-mesh sieve (fine chinois) to remove fragments of shell and other particles.

11. The crustacean butter is best stored in small, tightly sealed mason jars. If more has been prepared than will be needed over a month, the excess can be frozen.

Crustacean Oil

Crustacean butter cannot be used in cold sauces such as mayonnaise and vinaigrette because it congeals. For these sauces it is better to prepare a crustacean oil. Crustacean oil is prepared by replacing the butter in the crustacean butter recipe with the same amount of inert-tasting oil. When preparing crustacean oil, break up the shells by wrapping them in a kitchen towel and beating them with a rolling pin before combining them in the mixer with the oil. The mixer will not break them up as it would when butter is used.

Butters with Whole Crustaceans

Occasionally a classic recipe will call for a compound butter made with the flesh of cooked crustaceans. To prepare these butters, purée equal parts butter and cooked and shelled crustacean meat in a food processor. Work the butter through a drum sieve with a plastic pastry scraper.

Sauce Américaine

Although there are many variations of this classic sauce, the recipe that follows serves as a model because it demonstrates many of the techniques used for preparing crustacean sauces. This recipe uses lobster, which is the traditional crustacean used for sauce américaine. Other crustaceans such as crabs, shrimps (if they have their heads), and crayfish can be substituted. Originally, américaine-type sauces were integral sauces, served with the lobster or other crustaceans.

Sauce américaine can be thickened and flavored in many ways (although some will argue it is then no longer sauce américaine). Many recipes include either veal or fish stock. Older recipes usually call for thickening the sauce with beurre manié or roux. Some contemporary chefs use other starches, such as arrowroot or cornstarch. This recipe uses no starch but relies on reduction to concentrate the sauce's flavors and on whole butter and crustacean butter to give a smooth texture and a final thickening. Cream is added to the lobster coral (more traditional recipes combine it with butter) to prevent it from curdling on contact with the hot sauce. Although classic recipes for sauce américaine do not usually use crustacean butter, the butter adds an extra note of complexity and contributes to the color.

Recipes for sauce américaine always call for Cognac, which has an amazing affinity for crustaceans. Other sauces use other flavorful liquids (Madeira is common), but again, if the Cognac is replaced, the sauce is usually given another name. Tarragon and fennel, which both have similar anise-like notes, go extremely well with crustaceans (and, in fact, with most seafood). Herbs such as chervil and parsley, whose flavor is fleeting, especially when they come in contact with heat, should be worked with butter first. Other more intensely flavored herbs, such as marjoram, oregano, or wild thyme, should be added earlier and can be bundled into a bouquet garni.

Although traditional sauce américaine is normally quite thick, so that it can coat pieces of lobster, modern chefs and their clientele are often pleased to have lobster in a sauce with a more broth-like consistency. If a lighter sauce is wanted, reduction of the lobster cooking liquid should be stopped earlier.

CLASSIC SAUCE AMÉRICAINE

YIELD: 3 CUPS (750 MILLILITERS)

female lobsters	6 pounds	2.5 kilograms
wine vinegar	1 tablespoon	15 milliliters
cognac	9 tablespoons	140 milliliters
olive or vegetable oil	¼ cup	60 milliliters
shallots, finely chopped	5	5
garlic cloves, crushed	2	2
white wine	1 cup	250 milliliters
large bouquet garni (page 51)	1	1
tomato purée	1 cup	250 milliliters
chicken or good-quality fish stock (optional)	½ cup	125 milliliters
heavy cream	½ cup	125 milliliters

butter, cut into chunks	3 ounces	90 grams
lobster or other crustacean butter	1 ounce	30 grams
parsley, chopped	½ bunch	½ bunch
tarragon sprig, chopped	1	1
chervil, chopped	¼ bunch	¼ bunch
reduced tomato paste, tomato purée, or paprika (for color; optional)	as needed	as needed

1. Rinse the lobsters under cold running water (lobsters are often kept in tanks for long periods and should be thoroughly rinsed). To save the coral and tomalley from the lobsters, the lobsters must be cut up alive. The best way to do this is to cut into the underside of the head with a paring knife to kill the lobster quickly, and then twist the tail off while holding the lobster over a strainer over a bowl. Hold the lobster firmly by the back of the head with one hand and the back of the tail with the other. Twist quickly while holding both the tail and the head over the strainer. Squeeze the head firmly so that any juices run into the strainer. (If the lobster is cut with a knife on a cutting board, some of the juices run out and are lost.) The clear juices that run out of a freshly killed lobster tend to clot. To avoid this, put 1 tablespoon (15 milliliters) of wine vinegar and 1 tablespoon (15 milliliters) of the Cognac into the bottom of the bowl used to retrieve the lobster juices.

   Reach into both the head and the tail of the lobster with a forefinger, pull out the coral and tomalley, and place them in the strainer over a bowl. (The tomalley is pale grayish green, and the coral is very dark green, almost black, when raw, turning bright orange when cooked.)

2. Press the coral and tomalley from all the lobsters through the strainer. Use a small ladle at first; since the mixture tends to be slippery, it can be worked through the strainer with the fingers.

3. When all the tomalley and coral have been strained, put the bowl immediately over ice. Do not try to keep them for more than a few hours. (The mixture will probably have an ugly blue-green color, but it will turn bright orange once heated.)

4. Cut the lobster tails into sections about 1 inch (2.5 cm) long. (They can be cut smaller to extract more flavor, but if cut too small, they cannot be saved for another use.) Cut the heads in half lengthwise and remove the stomach sacs. Crack the claws with a chef's knife.

5. Heat the olive oil in a flat sauté pan that will hold all the pieces of lobster in one layer. Sauté the lobster sections, including the cracked claws, the pieces of tail, and the halved heads, until they turn red (usually in about 5 minutes).

6. Sprinkle the lobster with the shallots and the garlic and stir over the heat for 2 to 3 minutes.

7. Place the remaining ½ cup (125 milliliters) of Cognac in a small saucepan and bring it to a simmer. Tilt the pan slightly over the flame to ignite it. (Cognac should always be flamed before adding to hot mixtures; otherwise, it can cause the tiny hairs on the lobster shells to burn and give a bitter taste to the sauce. It can also flare up dangerously.)

8. Add the flamed Cognac, white wine, bouquet garni, and tomato purée to the lobster. Cover the pan and cook the lobster for 10 minutes more.

9. Remove the lobster from the pot and extract the meat for another use. Return the shells to the pot and break them up (the end of a cleaver or a plain European-style rolling pin works well for this). Continue to cook the shells, covered with the liquid ingredients, for about 20 minutes.

10. Strain the liquid through a coarse chinois and then through a fine chinois, into a small saucepan; there should be about 2 cups (500 milliliters) of liquid. If there is less, stock should be added. Reduce the sauce by half, until 1 cup (250 milliliters) remains. Check to see whether further reduction is necessary: The sauce should be full flavored and have a lightly syrupy consistency. (It is better to overreduce the sauce slightly at this point rather than to underreduce it, because once the butters and lobster coral are added, further reduction will be impossible.)

11. Whisk in the cream and reduce slightly if the sauce seems too thin.

12. Whisk in the chunks of whole butter and then the crustacean butter. Add the parsley, tarragon, and chervil.

13. Put the lobster coral and tomalley in a stainless-steel bowl. Carefully ladle the hot sauce in while whisking. (Notice that the blue-green organs will first discolor the sauce, but once they are heated by the hot sauce they will turn orange. If this color change does not occur, it means that there was not enough coral, as only the coral, not the tomalley, changes color. Although the color of the sauce will be a pale green instead of orange, its flavor will still be excellent.)

14. It is unlikely that the sauce will require additional salt. The color, however, may be reinforced by adding a small amount of reduced tomato purée or tomato paste. Paprika can also be used. Be careful with these ingredients, however; too much can interfere with the sauce's flavor.

Sauce Cardinal and Sauce Nantua

Sauce Cardinal and sauce Nantua are crustacean-flavored white sauces. They are similar in that they are both based on sauce béchamel, which is finished with lobster or crayfish butter, for Cardinal and Nantua, respectively. Sauce Cardinal also contains fish fumet and truffle essence, whereas sauce Nantua contains a large proportion of heavy cream. Contemporary versions never contain flour but are usually based on reduced cream flavored with reduced court-bouillon, reduced fish stock, or the cooking liquid from the steamed or stewed crustaceans.

CLASSIC SAUCE CARDINAL

YIELD: 2 CUPS (500 MILLILITERS)

sauce béchamel (page 139)	1½ cups	375 milliliters
fish fumet	¼ cup	60 milliliters
truffle juice or cooking liquid (page 108)	¼ cup	60 milliliters
heavy cream	6 tablespoons	90 milliliters
lobster butter (page 329)	1½ ounces	45 grams
salt and white pepper	to taste	to taste

1. Combine the sauce béchamel, fish fumet, truffle juice, and cream in a 2-quart (2 liter) saucepan.
2. Reduce the sauce if necessary to bring it to the desired consistency.
3. Whisk in the lobster butter and adjust the seasonings. See the photograph in the color plates.

CLASSIC SAUCE NANTUA

YIELD: 2 CUPS (500 MILLILITERS)

heavy cream	1 cup	250 milliliters
sauce béchamel (page 139)	2 cups	500 milliliters
crayfish butter (page 329)	2 ounces	60 grams
salt and white pepper	to taste	to taste

1. Combine half the cream with the béchamel in a 2-quart (2 liter) saucepan and reduce the mixture until 2 cups (500 milliliters) remain.
2. Thin the sauce with the remaining cream and whisk in the crayfish butter.
3. Adjust the seasonings and strain through a fine-mesh sieve.

CONTEMPORARY SAUCE CARDINAL AND SAUCE NANTUA

This recipe is based on the classic sauces but is finished with chopped fines herbes. It is presented as a model and can be varied following the needs and whims of the cook.

full-flavored court-bouillon, full-flavored fish stock, or crustacean or shellfish cooking liquid	1 cup	250 milliliters
heavy cream	1 cup	250 milliliters
crustacean butter (page 329)	2 ounces	60 grams
parsley, finely chopped	½ bunch	½ bunch
tarragon sprig, finely chopped	1	1
chervil, finely chopped	½ bunch	½ bunch
salt and pepper	to taste	to taste

1. Combine the flavor base liquid with the cream in a 2-quart (2 liter) saucepan. Reduce the mixture until it takes on a sauce-like consistency.
2. Whisk in the crustacean butter and strain the sauce through a fine chinois.
3. Add the chopped herbs. Adjust the seasonings.

CRAYFISH SAUCE

Although crayfish are prepared like lobsters and other crustaceans, certain techniques differ. Because crayfish are available whole, the tails can be lightly cooked, and the remaining parts of the crayfish—the head and claws—can be cooked and used to create a crayfish sauce base. The basic technique resembles the method used for the preparation of sauce américaine. In this recipe the crayfish heads and claws are puréed after cooking and used to prepare a rich, full-flavored crayfish sauce.

If the tails contain an unsightly intestine, it can be easily removed after they are cooked by pinching the tip of the tail and pulling it out.

live crayfish	3 pounds	1.4 kilograms
olive or vegetable oil	¼ cup	60 milliliters
shallots, finely chopped	5	5
carrot, finely chopped, 1 small	3 ounces	75 grams
celery, finely chopped	2 ounces	60 grams
garlic cloves, crushed	2	2
large bouquet garni (page 51)	1	1
cognac	½ cup	125 milliliters
white wine	1½ cups	375 milliliters
tomato purée	1 cup	250 milliliters
heavy cream	2 cups	500 milliliters
parsley, finely chopped	½ bunch	½ bunch
tarragon sprig, finely chopped	1	1
chervil, finely chopped	¼ bunch	¼ bunch
butter, cut into chunks	2 ounces	60 grams
crayfish or other crustacean butter (page 329)	2 ounces	60 grams

1. Eliminate any dead crayfish. The best way to do this is to spill them out on a large table and quickly sort through them. Throw out any that are limp or obviously dead. Rinse the crayfish in cold running water.

2. Heat the olive oil in a 5-quart (5 liter) pot and sweat the shallots, carrot, celery, and garlic in it. When the vegetables begin to soften, add the bouquet garni and continue sweating the mixture for 5 minutes more.

3. Place the Cognac in a small saucepan and flame off the alcohol.

4. When the vegetables have softened but not browned, add the white wine and flamed Cognac and bring the mixture to a rapid boil.

5. Add the crayfish to the pot, cover the pot firmly, and steam the crayfish. While the crayfish are steaming, toss them several times so they are redistributed and cook evenly. Check the crayfish after 5 to 10 minutes. When they have all turned red, remove the pot from the heat.

6. Place a large colander over a bowl and drain the crayfish, reserving the cooking liquid.

7. Let the crayfish cool for several minutes and then twist off their tails. Remove the meat from the tails by gently squeezing them to crack the shells and then pulling the shells away from the meat. Reserve both the meat and the shells.

8. Traditionally, crayfish heads and claws are crushed with a heavy mortar and pestle, but today a food processor is often used. (If using a food processor, however, be sure to remove the claws from the crayfish—they are extremely hard and can damage the blade.) Put the crayfish heads and tail shells into the food processor and purée them to a coarse paste. Crack open the claws with a heavy mortar and pestle or by wrapping them in a cloth and hitting them with the side of a cleaver.

9. Combine the paste and cracked claws with the cooking liquid from the crayfish, the vegetables and bouquet garni left from cooking the crayfish, and the tomato purée. Bring the mixture to a slow simmer and simmer for 15 minutes.

10. While the puréed crayfish mixture is simmering, reduce the cream in a saucepan on the stove. Stir it every minute or so to keep it from breaking. Reduce it by one-third to one-half, depending on the desired consistency of the final sauce.

11. Strain the crayfish mixture through a coarse chinois and then through a fine chinois. Finally, the cooking liquid should be strained through a carefully rinsed wet cloth napkin. The best way to do this is to line a chinois with the napkin, add the liquid, and then carefully twist the napkin at the top. Continue twisting to squeeze out the liquid. There should be about 2 cups (500 milliliters) of strained liquid.

12. Add the reduced cream to the strained crayfish liquid. Reduce the sauce more if necessary.

13. Add the chopped parsley, tarragon, and chervil.

14. Swirl in the butter and crustacean butter.

Classic Crustacean Sauce Variations

Sauce américaine, sauce Nantua, and sauce Cardinal are the classic crustacean mother sauces from which other sauces are derived. Other variations are based on classic fish sauces, such as sauce normande, which can be finished with crustacean butter and truffles to produce Sauce Diplomate and Sauce Joinville (pages 212 and 213).

Sauce Homard (Lobster Sauce)

Lobster sauce (sauce homard) differs from a classic sauce Cardinal in that the sauce béchamel base is replaced with a fish velouté. If the sauce Cardinal is based on reduced cream, as is the contemporary version of the recipe, a small spoonful of fish glace would be added to give the sauce the character of a classic lobster sauce.

Sauce Newburg

The technique for preparing a sauce Newburg is essentially the same as that for a sauce américaine except that the tomatoes are replaced with Madeira and cream. The sauce is then finished with the lobster coral and tomalley in the same way as the américaine.

Sauce Orientale

A sauce orientale is a sauce américaine to which a small amount of curry powder, first heated in butter, is added at the end.

Sauce Bavarian

A sauce bavarian is based on an infusion of horseradish, thyme, bay leaf, and parsley in wine vinegar. The mixture is then beaten with egg yolks into a sabayon and finished with Crustacean Butter (page 329).

TIPS FOR THE RESTAURANT CHEF

Crustacean sauces can be expensive to prepare. Much of the cost can be defrayed by using the crustacean meat for other dishes, especially cold dishes such as salads, in which it will not require reheating. Crustacean shells can also be saved and converted into crustacean butter. If lobster is being presented in lobster stews or in other dishes for which it is cut into pieces, buying lobster culls instead of perfectly intact whole lobsters is far more economical. If you are using lobster for sauce making but saving the meat for another dish, or as a garniture, a helpful method is to leave the lobster tails whole and tie them together with two pieces of string with the bottoms facing each other. This will prevent them from curling in the pot and makes it easier to slice presentable medallions.

Depending on the style of restaurant service, the sauce can be finished to order. It is very difficult to keep coral-thickened sauces warm during a restaurant service. Even when they can be kept from curdling (with very careful attention to temperature), they lose a great deal of finesse. To prevent these problems, the base tomato mixture can be thickened with the whole butter and the crustacean butter, kept warm, and combined with a small amount of the coral mixture only after an order is placed. Remember, the coral mixture should be kept on ice at all times.

As mentioned earlier, a crustacean sauce base can be prepared with different crustaceans. Blue-claw crabs are inexpensive and produce a delicious sauce.

Sauce Cardinal and sauce Nantua, although lacking the complexity of sauce américaine and crayfish sauce, are convenient to prepare and keep well during a restaurant service. They also lend themselves well to last-minute variations for special crustacean and fish dishes. Provided a reserve of crustacean butter is on hand, sauce Cardinal variations can be made with only a few minutes' notice.

Some crustacean sauces, if left over after a restaurant service, can be used the next day. Sauce Cardinal and sauce Nantua can be reheated and brightened with a few freshly chopped herbs and a few drops of lemon juice. Américaine-style sauces, especially when they contain lobster coral, cannot be reused but they should be saved and added to the moistening liquids in the next batch of sauce américaine.

TIPS ON COOKING LOBSTERS

Novice cooks usually cook lobsters by throwing them into a pot of boiling water—usually longer than necessary—and then serving them with melted butter. This method is straightforward and gives satisfactory results, but unfortunately many of the lobster's flavorful juices are released in the boiling water during cooking and never recovered. Melted butter contributes flavor and richness but does little to underline or accent the natural flavors of the lobster.

An equally efficient but more versatile method is to steam lobsters in a small amount of white wine, court-bouillon, stock, or even water. The briny lobster juices are thus released into the steaming liquid during cooking. Because relatively little liquid remains in the pot after the lobster has been steamed, the liquid can quickly and easily be converted into a sauce. Once a natural cooking liquid is available as a base for a sauce, a wide variety of sauce-making techniques can be used to vary the sauce's consistency and shape its final flavor. In the recipe that follows, the steaming liquid is lightly reduced and finished with heavy cream and freshly chopped parsley.

STEAMED LOBSTER WITH PARSLEY SAUCE

live lobsters, preferably female	4	4
white wine	1 cup	250 milliliters
shallots, finely chopped	3	3
heavy cream	½ cup	125 milliliters
parsley, finely chopped	1 bunch	1 bunch
white pepper	to taste	to taste

1. Lobsters require little preparation before steaming, but they should be rinsed in cold running water and then quickly and painlessly killed by inserting a sharp knife in the underside where the tail and head join. Do not kill the lobsters until the last minute; otherwise they will lose juices and flavor while waiting to go into the pot.

2. Into a pot with a tight-fitting lid that holds the lobsters without too much leftover space, pour in the wine and chopped shallots, put on the lid, and simmer for 2 to 3 minutes, to infuse the shallot flavor into the wine.

3. Add the lobsters and replace the lid. (Even though the lobsters have been killed, they may still kick around a bit, so be careful to secure the lid. It might even be necessary to hold it down during the first few minutes of cooking.)

4. After 5 minutes of steaming, remove the lid and toss the pot to rotate the lobsters, so that the ones on the bottom are shifted to the top of the pot (those directly in the steaming liquid cook faster). Continue cooking the lobsters until they are all bright red—no longer. The whole process usually takes 10 to 12 minutes. Do not remove the lid any more often than necessary or too much steam will be released and the cooking will be slowed.

5. Remove the lobsters from the pot using a kitchen towel wrapped around your hand (wait 30 seconds or so after removing the lid for the steam to dissipate—steam can burn you very quickly). Cover the lobsters with a towel to keep them warm and prevent them from drying out while finishing the sauce.

6. Add the cream to the cooking liquid from the lobster. Bring to a simmer.

7. Strain the liquid mixture through a fine-mesh strainer into a 2-quart (2 liter) saucepan. Taste the mixture to see if it needs reduction. (It is usually quite salty, so reduction should usually be avoided.) Add the chopped parsley, simmer the sauce for about 1 minute to infuse the parsley flavor, and grind in the white pepper.

8. Cut the lobsters lengthwise down the middle. Remove the stomach sac from each side of the head.

9. Because the parsley sauce is very thin, it is best to serve the lobster in large, flat soup bowls with the sauce either underneath it in the bowl or passed at the table in a sauce boat.

Variations

Other possibilities for converting the lobster steaming liquid into a sauce include:

- Beating it with an egg yolk to convert it into a sabayon, which can be left as is or finished with whole butter, clarified butter, crustacean butter, herb butter, or yogurt.
- Finishing the steaming liquid with less cream and using butter to produce a sauce with more luster and a richer consistency.
- Finishing the steaming liquid with flavored mayonnaise.

LOBSTER À LA NAGE II

One popular way of serving lobster is in a lobster-scented court-bouillon or, more extravagantly, with an intensely flavored lobster consommé. The lobster is garnished with finely julienned vegetables. No liaison is used. This method can be used for shrimp, crayfish, and other crustaceans as well.

YIELD: 6 SERVINGS

full-flavored court-bouillon	3 cups	750 milliliters
lobsters	6	6
carrot, finely julienned	1 large	1 large
leek, finely julienned	1 large	1 large
turnip, finely julienned	1	1
chives, finely chopped	1 bunch	1 bunch
flat parsley, leaves removed and washed	½ bunch	½ bunch

1. Bring 2 cups (500 milliliters) of the court-bouillon to a rapid boil in a 6-quart (6 liter) pot.
2. Rinse the lobsters, place them in the pot with the court-bouillon, and cover with a tight-fitting lid. Cook for about 5 minutes, or until the lobsters have turned completely red. Remove the pot from the heat but do not remove the lid for 10 minutes.
3. While the lobsters are steaming, cook the julienned carrot, leek, and turnips in the remaining court-bouillon until they are soft but not mushy.
4. Remove the lobsters from the pot, cut them in two lengthwise, and remove the stomach sacs (on the head). Place the two halves, meat side up, in wide soup bowls.
5. Strain the lobster cooking liquid into the court-bouillon and julienned vegetables. Add the chopped chives and the parsley leaves and bring the mixture to a simmer for 3 minutes.
6. Distribute the julienned vegetables over the lobster halves and pour over the hot court-bouillon. See the photograph in the color plates.

USING CRUSTACEAN FLAVORS
WITH MEAT AND FISH

In traditional classic and regional French cooking, the flavorful liquid extracted from lobster, crayfish, or other crustaceans is usually converted into an integral sauce, such as sauce américaine, served with the crustaceans themselves. Crustacean butter, on the other hand, is used as a staple ingredient in professional kitchens as a last-minute flavoring for both classic sauces (Joinville, diplomate) and contemporary or improvised variations.

In certain older or regional recipes, crustacean cooking liquid is also used to moisten fish and poultry. This excellent technique will give a finished dish a deeper, more complex flavor than simply swirling in crustacean butter at the end.

CHICKEN WITH CRAYFISH

The flavors of crayfish and chicken can be combined by browning or lightly searing the pieces of chicken in crayfish butter, moistening the chicken pieces with crayfish cooking liquid in the manner of a fricassée, or cooking the pieces of chicken completely in the crayfish butter and making the sauce in the pan with crayfish cooking liquid in the manner of a sauté. The chicken can also be roasted in the oven and basted with crayfish butter; the drippings are caramelized at the end of cooking, the roasting pan is deglazed with crayfish cooking liquid, and cream is whisked in along with more crayfish butter. Crayfish tails are the obvious garniture for either version. The following version is a fricassée.

YIELD: 8 SERVINGS

chickens, 2	7 pounds	3½ kilograms
crustacean butter (page 329)	3 ounces	90 grams
strained crayfish cooking liquid	2 cups	500 milliliters
butter	2 ounces	60 grams
finely chopped fines herbes	2 tablespoons	30 milliliters
salt and pepper	to taste	to taste
crayfish tails	40	40

1. Quarter the chickens and lightly brown them on both sides in 2 ounces (60 grams) of the crustacean butter in a straight-sided sauté pan.
2. Add the crayfish cooking liquid to the pan, cover, and gently simmer the chicken for 15 to 20 minutes, until it is done. Transfer the chicken to a platter and cover it with aluminum foil to keep it warm.
3. Reduce the cooking liquid until 1 cup (250 milliliters) remains. Carefully skim off any fat or froth that floats to the surface.

4. Whisk the butter and remaining 1 ounce (30 grams) of crustacean butter into the reduction. (The sauce can be served as a light-textured broth or reduced so that it can be served over the chicken.)
5. Strain the sauce through a fine chinois into a 1-quart (1 liter) saucepan.
6. Whisk in the fines herbes. Adjust the seasonings.
7. Heat the crayfish tails in the sauce. Serve over or around the chicken.

Japanese-Style Crustacean Sauces for Seafood

Japanese cooks flavor dashi with mirin and soy sauce and then thicken it with a small amount of potato starch to come up with a sauce base that is then varied by adding shredded crustacean, often crab. These sauces are light and elegant alternatives to French-style butter sauces.

JAPANESE-STYLE CRAB SAUCE

This very fluid sauce is best served around and under seafood rather than on top.

YIELD: 6 SERVINGS

dashi (page 520)	2 cups	500 milliliters
mirin	1 tablespoon	15 milliliters
soy sauce	1 tablespoon	15 milliliters
potato starch	2 tablespoons	30 milliliters
water	2 tablespoons	30 milliliters
shredded crab meat, preferably snow or king crab	1 cup	250 milliliters

1. Bring the dashi to a simmer and add the mirin and soy sauce. Work the starch to a smooth paste with water and whisk the mixture into the barely simmering dashi.
2. Whisk in the crab meat and serve immediately over fish or shellfish such as scallops.

IMPROVISING CRUSTACEAN SAUCES

After analyzing and preparing the classic crustacean sauces—Cardinal, américaine, and Nantua—the basic techniques used for crustacean sauces should be familiar. Once the techniques have been mastered, it is relatively simple to change one or more of the ingredients to give a sauce a new twist or a personal touch.

One of the components most frequently replaced when preparing an américaine- or Nantua-style sauce is the preliminary moistening liquid. In a sauce américaine, tomato pulp, flamed Cognac, and white wine are used. It is possible to replace these moistening liquids with various table wines (Sauternes adds a subtle sweetness and complexity to the sauce), fortified wines such as Madeira or sherry, or hard cider. The flamed Cognac can be replaced with other liquors, such as whiskey or Armagnac. Remember, however, that complex, expensive liquors and wines should not be added during the early stages of preparing a sauce, because their nuances will be lost.

Recipes for crayfish sauce and sauce américaine usually call for stock, typically fish or veal stock. Be especially careful when using fish stock: It must be made from only the freshest fish or bones. Because the sauce will undergo reduction, if only fish stock is used, the resulting sauce may have a strong fishy taste that will overwhelm the more subtle flavors of the crustaceans. If you are uncertain about the quality of available fish stock, it is better to use a more subtle stock, such as veal or chicken. Some chefs like to use some mussel cooking liquid in crustacean sauces. Mussel liquor gives a lively, sea-like flavor to a sauce, but be careful, especially if the sauce is going to be reduced at a later stage—mussel cooking liquid is very salty.

When preparing sauce américaine and crayfish sauce, shallots and garlic are used for the américaine and a mirepoix—in this case, a mixture of chopped carrots, shallots, garlic, and celery—is used for the crayfish sauce. These elements provide complexity and help round out the flavors of the sauces. It is possible to add other flavorings to these initial ingredients, such as extra garlic, chopped fennel (which accents beautifully the flavors of crustaceans), and a variety of herbs. Once the sauce américaine and crayfish sauce are moistened, a classic bouquet garni of parsley, fresh thyme, and bay leaf is added during the cooking. This bouquet garni can be altered to give the sauce a different character. Sprigs of fresh marjoram, wild thyme, or oregano can be used to give it an Italian or southern French accent. Fennel greens or tarragon can also be used to liven up the sauce. Remember, again, when flavoring a sauce at this early stage, only the more aggressively flavored herbs (see "Herbs," page 50) will contribute flavor that will last through all the stages of making the sauce. When using delicate herbs, such as chervil and chives, or herbs whose flavor is extremely volatile, such as basil, add them near the end of the sauce's preparation.

Once the crustaceans have been cooked in a moistening liquid, the chef must decide on the consistency he or she wants for the final sauce. If the final dish is to be presented in the style of a soup, light stew, or pot au feu, then obviously little liaison is necessary—a few tablespoons of cream or a swirl of butter will be sufficient to smooth out the sauce's texture and give it an appealing sheen. If, however, it is important that the sauce coat the final preparation, then a greater amount of liaison must be used. In the classic recipe for sauce américaine, beurre manié is used. Beurre manié provides a quick, inexpensive liaison without making the sauce overly rich. Be sure to reduce the sauce to concentrate its flavors before adding the beurre manié. Roux can also be used.

When beurre manié or roux is used to thicken a crustacean sauce, the resulting sauce often has a slightly matte appearance. In some cases, where a certain rusticity is wanted—in regional French, Italian, or Spanish cooking—this effect is desirable. If, however, you want a sauce with more sheen without resorting to butter, another starch, such as cornstarch or arrowroot, can be used. Be sparing in the use of either of these, as too much will give the sauce a slippery texture and an artificial appearance. Remember, when using starch, to bring the sauce to a full boil.

Crustacean sauces can also be thickened with cream, butter, or both. Remember the techniques for using butter: It should be added only after the sauce has been reduced. If you add the butter and then discover that the sauce is too thin or its flavor is not concentrated enough, you will not be able to reduce it further to thicken it. If cream is used, it is advisable to reduce it separately before adding it to the crustacean sauce reduction—long reduction with the sauce can cause the cream to turn granular or break. Remember, never cover a sauce containing cream while it is cooking.

Classic sauces are often thickened with egg yolks. Although the classic method (beating the egg yolks with a small amount of the sauce liquid and returning the mixture to the hot sauce) works for crustacean sauces, the resulting sauce is often undesirably rich. Alternative methods using egg yolks can also be used to thicken crustacean sauces (see "Contemporary Variations," page 384). The reduced crustacean cooking liquid (finished or not with the shell purée) can be beaten with egg yolks to form a sabayon, an extremely light, almost dietetic sauce. This sabayon can also be finished with butter, crustacean butter, and herb butters to produce a crustacean-flavored hollandaise-type sauce.

A second method for binding a crustacean sauce with egg yolks is to finish the sauce with a mayonnaise (see "Mayonnaise-Based Shellfish Sauces," page 404). This method will not only lightly bind the sauce but can be used to incorporate final flavorings and nuances into the finished sauce. A saffron-flavored mayonnaise works particularly well.

Once the liaison has been added to the sauce (or the decision has been made to dispense with it), it is time for the final shaping of the sauce's flavor. In some cases the liaison and final flavoring of the sauce will occur simultaneously, such as when herb butter, crustacean butter, or a flavored mayonnaise is being used. The final flavorings of a crustacean sauce should never mask the intrinsic crustacean flavors that the chef has worked so hard to extract, but should bring them into focus. Fines herbes are especially useful for this. Fines herbes without tarragon can always be used to finish a crustacean sauce, regardless of the ingredients used to flavor the sauce. Their flavor is so delicate that they add subtlety, freshness, and complexity to the sauce while never taking over. If tarragon is used, more thought should be given to whether it complements the other flavor components (usually it does—tarragon and crustaceans work extremely

Crustacean Sauce Variations

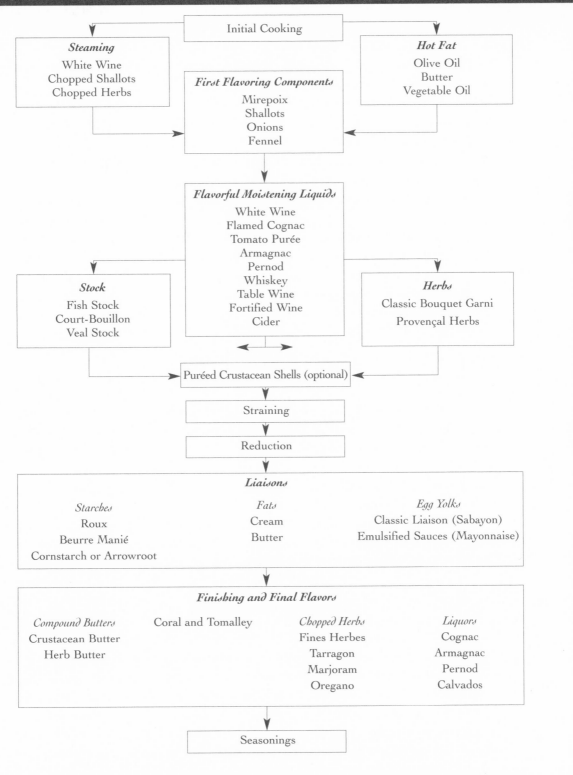

Initial Cooking

Steaming
White Wine
Chopped Shallots
Chopped Herbs

First Flavoring Components
Mirepoix
Shallots
Onions
Fennel

Hot Fat
Olive Oil
Butter
Vegetable Oil

Flavorful Moistening Liquids
White Wine
Flamed Cognac
Tomato Purée
Armagnac
Pernod
Whiskey
Table Wine
Fortified Wine
Cider

Stock
Fish Stock
Court-Bouillon
Veal Stock

Herbs
Classic Bouquet Garni
Provençal Herbs

Puréed Crustacean Shells (optional)

Straining

Reduction

Liaisons

Starches	*Fats*	*Egg Yolks*
Roux	Cream	Classic Liaison (Sabayon)
Beurre Manié	Butter	Emulsified Sauces (Mayonnaise)
Cornstarch or Arrowroot		

Finishing and Final Flavors

Compound Butters	Coral and Tomalley	*Chopped Herbs*	*Liquors*
Crustacean Butter		Fines Herbes	Cognac
Herb Butter		Tarragon	Armagnac
		Marjoram	Pernod
		Oregano	Calvados

Seasonings

well together). If you want a more assertive, direct sauce, other herbs and herb butters can be used to contribute a final accent. Chopped fresh marjoram or oregano (used sparingly) gives the sauce a distinct, unmistakable character.

One of the classic flavorings used for crustaceans is Cognac. It is a magic marriage, as the flavors merge in amazing, subtle ways. However, if Cognac is used in the preliminary moistening of the crustaceans, many of its nuances will have been lost by the time the sauce is ready for final flavoring. Toward the end of cooking, depending on the budget, a finer Cognac can be used. In any case, avoid an extremely old Cognac. It is preferable to use a young, full-bodied Cognac with considerable fruit.

The classic Cognac used in flavoring crustacean sauces can be replaced with other liquors, such as Armagnac, whiskey, Calvados, aquavit, or Pernod, to give the sauce individuality. Remember, when choosing these flavorings, to use good judgment—do not use whiskey to finish a sauce moistened with cider, use Calvados. Do not use Calvados to finish a sauce that has been moistened largely with tomato pulp. Be careful when using Pernod or other anise flavors: Unlike with Cognac or whiskey, if you add too much, their flavor is difficult to cook off.

Regardless of what other flavors are used to finish a sauce, lobster coral should be added at the very end, because it is so sensitive to temperature.

GARNITURES FOR CRUSTACEANS

Many chefs and home cooks like to vary the classic crustacean preparations by adding various vegetables or even fruits and presenting these with the finished crustaceans. When preparing dishes such as these, you should decide whether to incorporate the flavor of these components into the crustacean sauce or simply serve these garnitures to the side. If, for example, you want to serve a lobster with fresh morels (or other wild mushrooms), there are two routes to follow. The mushrooms can be sautéed in an appropriate oil or fat, sprinkled with herbs, and simply presented on the side of the plate along with the lobster. This is a perfectly acceptable method. On the other hand, morels have a delicate complexity that works well in sauces. If you want to exploit that flavor, the morels should be cooked so that their flavor can be incorporated into the sauce. To do this, take a few tablespoons of the crustacean cooking liquid (or other liquid, such as cream, fish stock, or court-bouillon if another base is being used), and cook the morels in a covered saucepan with the liquid. When they are finished cooking, this liquid should be returned to the crustacean sauce base.

A current trend is to serve crustaceans with fruits—mango is especially popular and surprisingly good. When using fruit, the cooking liquid from the fruit can be returned to the sauce to give it a subtle, underlying sweetness. Fruit-based eau-de-vie can also be used to finish the sauce when the flavor is appropriate (for example, do not finish your crayfish with pineapples with Poire William).

Stew-like preparations that contain two or more types of crustaceans have become extremely popular in French restaurants, because the customer can taste a variety of different crustaceans on the same plate. When well prepared, they are extremely labor intensive, both in preparation and when the order is placed. When preparing several crustaceans at once, do not try to combine too many flavor components (such as lobster cooking liquid with crayfish cooking liquid), or the nuances of each will be lost. The resulting generic crustacean sauce will be much less interesting than either of the two would have been alone.

ADDITIONAL SAUCES FOR CRUSTACEANS

The sauces described above are based on flavors extracted from crustaceans such as lobster, crayfish, crab, and shrimp. They follow the French tradition of using a sauce to accentuate, nuance, and extend the flavors of the basic ingredients. Because these sauces are time consuming and expensive to prepare, the home cook or restaurant chef may want to resort to a simple sauce that can be prepared at the last minute and served with the crustacean as an alternative to the ubiquitous drawn butter. Some ideas follow. (Other chapters in this book describe the methods for making these sauces.)

Emulsified Sauces

Hollandaise: plain, flavored with garlic, finished with crustacean butter, finished with tomato purée, flavored with curry or saffron

Béarnaise-style: practically any of the classic versions

Beurre Blanc and Derivatives

Beurre blanc: finished with crustacean butter, Pernod, Cognac, tomato coulis; flavored with garlic, Provençal herbs

Mayonnaise-Finished Sauces

Hot fish or chicken stock finished with appropriately flavored mayonnaise; saffron- and herb-flavored mayonnaises work especially well

Reduced-Cream Sauces

Reduced cream infused with herbs, green peppercorns, white wine and shallot reductions

Brown Sauces

Brown sauces containing wild mushrooms, truffles, or herbs, lightly finished with crustacean butter

COMBINING CRUSTACEANS WITH OTHER SHELLFISH

All the techniques used for extracting the flavor from crustaceans are used to create braising liquids that are in turn used to cook other shellfish. The complexity of flavor, when combining shellfish in this way, is overwhelming and well worth the (considerable) effort.

MIXED SHELLFISH FRICASSÉE

This dish is called a fricassée because it sounds prettier than "stew," not because it follows the stricter definition given on page 266. The idea is to cook each shellfish in a way that suits it best and then combine the liquids released by all the shellfish to form the sauce.

YIELD: 4 MAIN-COURSE SERVINGS

cockles	1 pound	450 grams
or	or	or
littleneck clams	12	12
mussels, preferably green-lipped new zealand	4 large	4 large
white wine	½ cup	125 milliliters
water	1 cup	250 milliliters
lobster, 1	1½ pounds	600 grams
tomatoes, chopped	2 large	2 large
heavy cream	½ cup	125 milliliters
sea scallops	4 large	4 large
shrimp, peeled, deveined	4 jumbo	4 jumbo

1. Steam open the cockles and mussels in the white wine and water. Remove the cockles and mussels and set aside. Put the lobster in the pot with the steaming liquid. Steam it, covered, over medium heat until it turns bright red, about 10 minutes.
2. Take the meat out of the lobster.
3. Combine the tomatoes with the steaming liquid and simmer gently for 10 minutes. Work through a strainer and combine with the cream. Simmer slightly to concentrate its flavor but not so much as to thicken it or make it too salty. Poach the scallops and shrimp in the sauce for about 3 minutes.
4. Arrange the shellfish in heated soup plates and pour the sauce over and around them. See the photograph in the color plates.

12

JELLIES AND CHAUDS-FROIDS

Natural meat and fish jellies (sometimes called aspics) are among the most subtle and delicious of foods, and can be the most beautiful: A breast of chicken or fillet of fish surrounded by a golden herb-specked jelly is a delightful sight. Because aspics lend themselves to manipulation—their intrinsic quality compromised by the addition of excess gelatin—they are thought of more as building materials for the far-flung fantasies of late-nineteenth-century French cooking than as delicate accompaniments to cold meats or fish. An authentic jelly is the natural cooking liquid from meat or fish, which sets when cold. In France, the term *aspic* usually refers to a meat or fish preparation that has been molded and held together with the appropriate *gelée*, or jelly. In the United States, where the word "jelly" brings to mind fruit preserves, the term "aspic" is most often used to refer to any dish that includes meat or fish jelly.

The most common way to prepare a meat jelly is to take clear meat stock and add enough gelatin to set it. The resulting jelly may look passable but will have less flavor than the stock would if served hot. If the stock is weak flavored initially, the peculiar flavor of commercial gelatin will come through, and the too-stiff texture given the jelly by the commercial gelatin creates a nauseating glue-like mass.

Unfortunately, the dining public has grown to dislike jellies because few people have ever tasted an authentic meat or fish jelly. A properly prepared jelly should be deeply flavored and only slightly gelatinous; it should barely hold together when served.

NATURAL MEAT JELLY

In most professional settings, meat and fish jellies are prepared, or at least begun, independently of what they will accompany, in the same way that stocks are prepared in advance and eventually used in stock-based (nonintegral) sauces or in integral sauces. Several methods can be used to make a natural meat jelly. Most jellies are best prepared by starting with brown stock, which lends the jelly a deeper color and more assertive flavor. Like the best stocks, good jellies are prepared exclusively with meat. A meat broth is first prepared and then used as the moistening liquid for more meat. The process is repeated until the liquid contains the right amount of natural gelatin.

Natural jellies can also be prepared by reducing stocks or braising liquids to concentrate both the flavor and the natural gelatin, but this method tends to cook out much of the aromatic flavor of the stock and give it a flat taste.

The jelly also can be prepared with meat (veal or beef shanks, pork shoulder, turkey wings, duck thighs, for example) and a split and blanched veal foot or pork rinds. The veal foot provides natural gelatin and gives a somewhat more fragile texture to the stock than commercial gelatin, but does little to enhance its flavor.

In a restaurant setting, if cold meats are poached for other dishes, the jelled poaching liquid can be used when it contains enough natural gelatin. This method not only provides the best jelly but costs nothing more to prepare. It can be used only in settings where poached meats and poultry are served *without* jelly or an integral sauce of their own (such as cold poached beef, chicken for chicken salad, poached turkey breast, or veal shank with tomato sauce).

Begin by preparing a full-bodied white or brown stock using meat and appropriate trimmings. The meat and trimmings can be browned or not, along with aromatic vegetables, depending on the use and style of the jelly (see Chapter 4,

"Stocks, Glaces, and Essences," page 87). Remember to moisten the stock with *cold* water and to prevent it from boiling at any point. If the stock is kept at a slow simmer and not allowed to boil during its initial preparation and during the subsequent poaching of the meats, and if it is carefully skimmed, it will not require clarification.

Use the stock over the course of several days for poaching meats. To keep it clear, it is best to start poaching the meats in cold or lukewarm stock. If the stock is already simmering when the meat is added, it may cloud. Again, be careful not to let the stock boil while poaching the meat. When the stock has been used several times for poaching, it should be tested to determine whether it is ready to be used as a jelly. Taste it to see if it is full flavored. It may be necessary to revitalize it from time to time by adding additional aromatic vegetables or a bouquet garni.

The consistency of the jelly also needs to be checked constantly by placing a few tablespoons of the liquid in a small bowl and putting it in the refrigerator or over a bowl of ice. When the jelly has set, remove it from the refrigerator or ice for about 5 minutes and check the consistency. It should be as delicate as possible without being liquid. If the jelly is too thick (this is unlikely if it has not been reduced), it can be lightened with some clear stock. If it is too thin, continue to poach more meat in the poaching liquid or gently reduce it until it has the necessary consistency when set.

When the jelly has the correct consistency, salt and other flavorings can be added. Remember that salt is much less assertive in cold preparations than hot, so be certain to adjust the salt *after* the jelly has cooled but not set.

CLASSIC MEAT JELLY

Classic recipes for meat jellies are almost identical to basic brown and white stocks except that a gelatinous element is added. It is then clarified with additional meat and egg whites, although properly made stock—carefully skimmed and never allowed to boil—should not require the addition of egg whites.

The following recipe calls for moistening 3 pounds (1.5 kilograms) of meat, such as veal or beef shanks, stewing hens, or chicken carcasses, with water or stock. If water is used, extra gelatin is provided by combining a split and blanched veal foot with the meat. One veal foot, split in 2 halves, when cooked for 6 hours, will set 4 quarts (4 liters) of liquid, so it is necessary to gauge the amount of gelatin that will be in the finished jelly; if gelatinous cuts of meat are used or an already gelatinous stock is used to moisten the meat, then adding a veal foot will make the finished jelly too gelatinous.

As the jelly cooks it loses a certain natural vitality that is best restored by adding a small amount of chopped mirepoix or coarsely chopped fines herbes.

veal foot (for water-based jelly only)	1 split	1 split
meat	3 pounds	1.5 kilograms
onion, halved	1 medium	1 medium
clove	1	1
carrot, coarsely chopped, 1 medium	4 ounces	125 grams
cold clear veal, beef, or chicken stock, or water	4 quarts	4 liters
large bouquet garni (page 51)	1	1

1. If using water to moisten the meat, split and blanch the veal foot, starting in cold water.
2. (If a very pale jelly is wanted, omit this step.) Preheat the oven to 400°F (200°C). Place the meat, onion halves—one studded with the clove—and carrot in a roasting pan, and lightly brown them in the oven.
3. Transfer the meat and vegetables (and blanched veal foot, if used) to a 15-quart (14 liter) stockpot and add the cold stock. Slowly bring the mixture to a simmer (this should take at least 20 minutes; it should *never* boil). Skim off any scum or fat that floats to the surface.
4. Add the bouquet garni and continue simmering the stock for 5 hours.
5. If the jelly stock is perfectly clear, carefully ladle it through a coarse chinois, then a fine chinois, and finally a fine chinois lined with cheesecloth. If, for some reason, the stock is cloudy, it will need to be clarified (see "Clarifying Jellies," opposite).

Finishing the Jelly

Once the jelly stock has been strained, chill some of it in the refrigerator or over a bowl of ice so that it sets and its consistency can be checked. If a fairly gelatinous stock was used to moisten the meats or a veal foot was used, the jelly will probably set firmly and in fact may need to be lightened. If water alone was used, however, the jelly may not be stiff enough, in which case its consistency can be adjusted by:

1. Putting it back on the stove, reducing it by one-fourth, and rechecking its consistency, repeating the process again if necessary.
2. Using the jelly stock to moisten additional meat or lean meat trimmings and cooking it again for 2 to 4 hours (preparing a double or triple stock).
3. Adding powdered or sheet gelatin (soaked first in cold water and drained) to the still-hot jelly stock. Use the gelatin sparingly, adding only a small amount at a time. Remember that even if the jelly stock does not set, it still contains natural gelatin of its own.

When jellies are prepared using carefully defatted meat, clarification takes place naturally: The proteins contained in the meat combine with any loose fat in the surrounding stock, float to the surface, and are skimmed off. When jellies are prepared with carcasses or with stock whose clarity has been compromised by inadequate skimming or by boiling, the final jelly must be clarified.

Often a stock that is only slightly cloudy can be clarified by straining through a chinois lined with a cloth napkin, a sheet of muslin, or a triple layer of cheesecloth. When using any of these, be sure to rinse the cloth thoroughly to eliminate any traces of soap or bleach. After several minutes of straining, the cloth will become clogged with minute particles. When this happens, gently pull on one side of the cloth so the liquid moves to a clean section. It may be necessary to do this several times during the straining.

The traditional method for clarifying stocks (also used for consommé) is to combine the lukewarm jelly with perfectly lean chopped meat and egg whites. The meat and egg whites are whisked with the stock while it is being gently heated, and the whole mixture is cooked long enough to coagulate any soluble protein. The finished jelly is then strained through cheesecloth.

Many authors suggest combining the chopped meat with mirepoix and fresh herbs to compensate for the flavor lost during long cooking and clarification, but these ingredients should be added judiciously, taking into consideration the flavor of the stock and its eventual use.

CLARIFICATION FOR MEAT JELLY

YIELD: TO CLARIFY 5 QUARTS (5 LITERS) OF STOCK

lean beef (such as rump)	1 pound	500 grams
egg whites	3	3
fresh tarragon sprigs (optional)	3	3
onion, finely chopped (optional)	1 small	1 small
celery, finely chopped (optional)	½ stalk	½ stalk
carrot, finely chopped (optional)	½	½
warm jelly stock	5 quarts	5 liters

1. Carefully remove any fat from the beef, and chop the meat finely. (A meat grinder or food processor can be used to chop.)
2. Stir together the meat, the egg whites, and the tarragon and chopped vegetables, if using.
3. Place the mixture in the bottom of a 10-quart (10 liter) stockpot and add the warm stock to be clarified. Whisk the chopped meat mixture into the stock to ensure that the egg white is evenly distributed throughout.

4. Bring the mixture slowly to a simmer, and let it simmer slowly for 20 minutes, without disturbing it.

5. Cut a hole in the crust (known as a "raft") that will have formed on the surface of the jelly to see whether the mixture is clear. Once the stock is perfectly clear (don't worry about larger particles floating around in it), strain it through a coarse chinois lined with three layers of well-rinsed cheesecloth.

FISH JELLIES

Fish jellies are prepared with essentially the same methods used for meat jellies, except that veal feet are never cooked with the fish bones (fish bones cook in 30 minutes and veal feet take 6 hours). Because the gelatin contained in fish bones rapidly dissolves into the surrounding liquid, it is rarely necessary to add extra gelatin.

Fish jelly has traditionally been prepared by making a double fish stock (moistening inexpensive fresh fish with a previously made fumet) and then clarifying with puréed whiting flesh (Escoffier called for fresh caviar!) and egg whites in the same way as for meat stock. Excellent fish jelly can still be prepared using this method, but the danger lies in the unavailability of fresh ingredients. Because the fish flavors will be intensified by three moistenings, it is essential that the fish be impeccably fresh (caught the same morning), or the resulting jelly will have a strong fishy taste.

Because fish stock contains finely divided particles of protein that are hard to strain out, it is usually clarified with lean chopped fish flesh and egg whites. If the fish stock is carefully prepared, clarification can be dispensed with, as the jelly is simply strained through cheesecloth or a napkin. If only a small amount of fish jelly is needed, a double fish stock can be allowed to settle and the clear liquid on the top carefully drawn off with a ladle.

●━━━● CLASSIC FISH JELLY

YIELD: 4 QUARTS (4 LITERS)

very fresh lean fish or fish trimmings (no skin)	3 pounds	1.5 kilograms
onion, chopped	1 medium	1 medium
cold fresh fish stock (page 100)	5 quarts	5 liters
medium bouquet garni (page 51)	1	1
lean white fish, finely chopped (optional)	8 ounces	250 grams
egg whites (optional)	2	2

1. Make sure the gills, skin, and all traces of blood have been removed from the fish. Combine the fish with the chopped onion in a 10-quart (10 liter) stockpot. Cover with the cold fish stock. Add the bouquet garni.

2. Slowly bring the mixture to a very slow simmer. Skim off any froth that floats to the surface.
3. Strain the stock through a fine chinois after 30 minutes.
4. The stock can now either be strained through a napkin or cheesecloth, allowed to settle, and the top half carefully drawn off with a ladle; or it can be clarified with the fish and egg whites.
5. To clarify the stock, allow the strained stock to cool slightly (it can be tepid but should not be boiling hot).
6. Combine the chopped fish and egg whites, if using.
7. Cover the mixture with the strained fish stock. Bring the mixture slowly to a simmer. When it has reached a simmer, gently scrape against the bottom of the pot with a long spoon to make sure the fish–egg white mixture has not formed a clump and stuck to the bottom, where it might burn. Allow the mixture to simmer for 30 minutes.
8. When the stock is clear, carefully ladle it through a strainer lined with cheesecloth. (Be sure to rinse the cheesecloth in cold water first to eliminate any chemical taste.)

Alternatives to Traditional Fish Jelly

Because the fresh fish for fish jelly is difficult to obtain, many chefs have worked out alternative jellies to accompany cold fish dishes in the same way as traditional fish jelly. One excellent method is to prepare a light jelly by simply cooking a veal foot with water and then using the resulting jelly to moisten an abundance of herbs and vegetables combined with a small amount of egg white and acidulated with lime juice, lemon juice, or verjuice.

This jelly can also be prepared by adding commercial gelatin to court-bouillon, but a certain suaveness of texture and flavor is lost.

COURT-BOUILLON JELLY

YIELD: 3 QUARTS (3 LITERS)

veal foot, split and blanched	1	1
water	4 quarts	4 liters
onion, cubed	1 large	1 large
leeks, including several inches of green, cubed	2	2
carrots, cubed, 2 medium	8 ounces	250 grams
garlic cloves, chopped	2	2
fennel bulb, cubed	1 small	1 small
tarragon sprigs, chopped	3	3
parsley, chopped	½ bunch	½ bunch
thyme sprigs, chopped	2	2
egg whites	4	4
juice of 2 to 3 limes or lemons, or verjuice	to taste	to taste
salt and pepper	to taste	to taste

1. Combine the veal foot with the water and simmer it for 6 hours. Skim carefully, adding cold water from time to time to compensate for evaporation.

2. Combine the onion, leeks, carrots, garlic, fennel, tarragon, parsley, and thyme. Add the egg whites and the lime or lemon juice or verjuice. Thoroughly work the egg whites into the mixture with a wooden spoon or with clean hands.

3. Stir in the lukewarm veal jelly. (The jelly should be heated just enough to melt it, to facilitate pouring.)

4. Place the mixture in a 6- to 8-quart (6 to 8 liter) stockpot and slowly bring it to a low simmer. Allow it to simmer for 20 minutes.

5. Cut into the raft of coagulated egg white that forms on the surface with a spoon to make sure the liquid beneath is clear.

6. Strain the stock through a coarse strainer and then again through a wet napkin or a cheesecloth-lined chinois.

7. Chill some of the mixture to verify its consistency. If it is too stiff, it can be thinned with court-bouillon. If the jelly is too light, add additional reduced light-flavored veal jelly or commercial gelatin. (The mixture can also be reduced but much of its vitality will be lost.)

8. Season to taste with salt and pepper, and adjust the acidity of the jelly if necessary.

FLAVORING JELLIES

Because they are served cold, jellies can be flavored using a wide variety of techniques and ingredients, some that would be destroyed in a sauce served hot. Many ingredients, such as wines, herbs, truffles, and wild mushrooms, can be added to the jellies either near the end of cooking or when the jelly has completely cooled.

The same principles apply to determining a jelly's final flavor as to preparing hot sauces. In most cases the jelly should enhance and extend the flavor of the food it accompanies. For example, a jelly made to accompany a dish of cold rabbit should capture the flavor of the rabbit and not be dominated by wine, herbs, or other ingredients. In some cases, however, the jelly's flavor can be manipulated to contrast with the flavor of the central ingredient rather than extend it, such as an acidic jelly based on court-bouillon and verjuice served with a cold fish fillet.

Wines

When wine is used to prepare jellies, it is often added at the end so that volatile compounds such as alcohol and certain flavor components remain in the jelly;

these would be lost if the wine were added to a hot sauce. For this reason, jellies are an exception to the informal rule that expensive, rare, and old wines have no place in cooking.

Choose a wine with little or no tannin. Be careful also with very acidic white wines, which will sometimes cloud the jelly (the acidity denatures the soluble proteins contained in the jelly). If this happens, bring the jelly to a simmer and reduce it slightly while skimming; if it still remains cloudy, strain it through a napkin. As a general rule, the ratio of wine to jelly should be one part wine to nine parts jelly, but the real criterion is taste. Avoid adding so much wine that the flavor of alcohol remains in the jelly.

Because the flavor of the wine used for making jellies is well diluted, it is best to use wine with an assertive character. Fortified wines, such as port, sherry, and Madeira, work especially well. Wines with a distinct varietal character, such as Gewürztraminer, late-harvest Rieslings, and Sauternes, can also be used.

Red wine–flavored jellies are somewhat more complicated. Jellies are best flavored with a mature red wine whose tannin has almost completely disappeared. Avoid red wines that contain a high percentage of alcohol. Big-bodied California wines or Rhône wines that work beautifully in red wine sauces, because their alcohol is cooked off, are often too alcoholic for jellies. To obtain a deeply colored jelly, a full-bodied, deeply colored red wine should be used, but such a wine will usually be too tannic to be added to a jelly at the end. It should first be simmered with meat trimmings or stock. The cooked wine, which will give body and color to the jelly, can be used in conjunction with raw wine that will contribute individuality and finesse.

After adding wine, check the consistency of the jelly. The gelatinous components will be diluted, and the alcohol may also interfere slightly with setting. If the jelly refuses to set, use a small amount of commercial gelatin, or remove one-fourth of the jelly, reduce it by half, and return it to the original batch.

RED WINE MEAT JELLY

The best red wine meat jelly is a natural by-product of braising a large quantity of beef in red wine (as in Boeuf Mode, page 367), but this method is expensive and not often practical. A simpler version can be made with red wine and jelly stock. When red wine is combined with meat jelly, the resulting mixture often tastes acrid and acidic. The best way to deal with this problem is to combine the red wine with a light jelly stock (the stock should not contain too much gelatin or it will end up being overreduced), and reduce the two together. As the acid contained in the red wine combines with the stock, soluble proteins will coagulate and make the stock cloudy, so the jelly will have to be strained through cloth.

deep-colored, full-bodied red wine	2 cups	500 milliliters
medium bouquet garni (page 51; optional)	1	1
onion, chopped (optional)	1 small	1 small
carrot, chopped (optional)	1 small	1 small
garlic clove, crushed (optional)	1	1
light-bodied clear jelly stock	1 quart	1 liter

1. In a 4-quart (4 liter) saucepan, combine the red wine with the bouquet garni and the aromatic vegetables, if using.
2. Reduce the wine by half.
3. Add 2 cups (500 milliliters) of jelly stock to the wine and reduce the mixture for about 20 minutes, until only 1 cup (250 milliliters) remains.
4. Add the remaining stock to the reduction and reduce again for 20 minutes, until 2 cups (500 milliliters) remain.
5. Strain the jelly through a wet napkin or a triple layer of cheesecloth.
6. If desired, additional raw wine can be added to the strained jelly to give the final jelly complexity and finesse. When using raw wine, which is often unpredictable, work with a small amount of the jelly at first, adding wine and tasting as you go, before flavoring the whole batch.

PORT AND CRACKED-PEPPER JELLY FOR FOIE GRAS

Some recipes for preparing fresh foie gras suggest wrapping it tightly in a clean towel and poaching it. If you are using this method, be sure to poach the foie gras in the natural jelly to enhance the jelly's flavor. If the foie gras is baked in terrines, be sure to add the natural jelly that floats to the top of the terrine to the jelly in this recipe.

To crack the black pepper, crush it under a heavy-bottomed pot on a cutting board or hard surface.

natural veal, chicken, or game jelly	2 cups	500 milliliters
cracked black pepper	1 teaspoon	5 milliliters
tawny or mature vintage port	½ cup	125 milliliters
salt and pepper	to taste	to taste

1. Bring the jelly to a simmer. Add the cracked pepper and turn off the heat. Cover the hot jelly with a lid so that it cools slowly, giving the pepper time to infuse.
2. When the jelly has cooled to room temperature, add the port to taste. The exact amount will depend on the flavor and style of the port.

3. Strain the jelly. Adjust the seasonings as it cools. Serve the chopped jelly on the plate next to slices of the foie gras.

LOBSTER WITH SAUTERNES JELLY

YIELD: 2 CUPS (500 MILLILITERS), FOR 4 LOBSTERS

lobsters	4	4
natural veal or chicken jelly	enough to cover	enough to cover
finely chopped parsley (optional)	2 tablespoons	30 milliliters
sauternes, to taste (see Note)	½ cup	125 milliliters
salt and pepper	to taste	to taste

1. Separate the heads, tails, and claws of the lobsters while they are still alive. Remove the stomach sacs and save any juices that run out, but leave the tomalley and coral in the lobster.
2. Tie the lobster tails together with string in sets of two. (This keeps them straight while they are cooking, making it easier to slice even medallions.)
3. Combine the lobster parts, lobster juices, and the jelly in a large saucepan; the parts should be completely covered with the jelly. Bring the jelly to a slow simmer and poach the lobster parts until they turn red (about 4 minutes after they reach a simmer).
4. Turn off the heat, remove the lobster parts, and let them cool slightly. Remove the meat from the claws and tails, reserving it to serve with the jelly. Coarsely chop the lobster shells and return them to the hot jelly.
5. Gently cook the chopped shells in the jelly for 20 minutes. (The chopped shells should flavor and clarify the jelly.)
6. Strain the jelly through cheesecloth, stir in the chopped parsley, if using, and let it cool to room temperature.
7. Add the Sauternes to taste (the exact amount will depend on the particular Sauternes being used).
8. Chill the jelly and check its flavor and consistency. Adjust the seasonings. If the jelly is too thin or refuses to set, add some reduced jelly or commercial gelatin.
9. Slice the reserved lobster meat into medallions and spoon over the jelly.

Note: Other sweet wines, such as a Beerenauslese, late-harvest California Riesling, or Muscat de Beaumes de Venise, may be used instead of Sauternes, with the recipe title changed accordingly.

SHERRY DUCK JELLY

This full-flavored, golden jelly, although never inexpensive to prepare, is an excellent way for a restaurant to use extra duck thighs. Use a good-quality dry sherry—a fino, Manzanilla, or amontillado would work well.

YIELD: 2 CUPS (500 MILLILITERS)

duck thighs	6	6
dry sherry	2 cups	500 milliliters
brown chicken, beef, or veal jelly	2 cups	500 milliliters
salt and pepper	to taste	to taste

1. Trim all the skin and fat off the duck legs, and separate the drumsticks from the thighs.
2. Place the thighs and drumsticks in a 2-quart (2 liter) pot with a tight-fitting lid. Add the sherry, making sure it completely covers the duck, and put on the lid.
3. Place the pot in a larger pot that contains enough water to reach halfway up the sides of the small pot.
4. Place the lid on the large pot and bring the water to a simmer. Simmer in this way for 5 hours. Replace water in the outer pot as needed. Do not open the inner pot.
5. While the duck legs are cooking, place the brown jelly in a 1-quart (1 liter) saucepan and carefully reduce it by three-quarters, until it is almost a glace. Strain it through a chinois if necessary.
6. Remove the inner pot and cool, covered, in the refrigerator or in an ice bath.
7. When the contents of the inner pot have cooled, carefully separate the liquid and solid ingredients. The solid ingredients can be saved for another use. The liquid should be either completely liquid or barely set.
8. Melt the reduced brown jelly and stir it into the cold sherry-duck liquid. Strain through a chinois lined with a wet napkin or a triple layer of cheesecloth. Chill the mixture to adjust its consistency. Adjust the seasonings if necessary.

Herbs

Herbs can be used in jellies in much the same way as when preparing hot sauces. Some herbs, such as thyme and savory, should be included in the bouquet garni while the jelly is cooking so they can meld into the flavor structure. Fines herbes, whose volatile flavors dissipate quickly when exposed to heat, are best freshly chopped and added as the jelly is cooling to freshen and enliven it. If they are added when the jelly is cool, however, they will be raw, and their flavor will not infuse in the jelly. Others, such as marjoram, become an assertive accent when a generous amount is infused in the jelly near the end, then strained out.

FINES HERBES JELLY

To capture the flavor of delicate herbs, many chefs like to infuse the hot jelly with the herbs in tightly sealed containers, as this recipe demonstrates.

YIELD: 1 QUART (1 LITER)

jelly	1 quart	1 liter
fresh chervil	1 bunch	1 bunch
flat parsley	1 bunch	1 bunch
chives	1 bunch	1 bunch

1. Bring the jelly to a slow simmer in a 2-quart (2 liter) saucepan.
2. While the jelly is heating, finely chop the herbs. (This must be done at the last minute.)
3. Put the chopped herbs in a large mason jar and pour the simmering jelly over them. Seal the lid.
4. Let the jelly cool at room temperature in the mason jar. Gently turn the jar over from time to time during cooling to redistribute the herbs.
5. When the jelly is completely cool but not set, the herbs can be strained out with a chinois. If you decide to retain the herbs, continue to turn the jar while the jelly is setting so they are distributed evenly throughout.

Spirits

When preparing jellies and hot sauces, spirits are used at two stages. Full-bodied spirits, such as young Cognac or whiskey, can be added near the beginning so that they blend into the background; more delicate spirits, such as older Cognacs, Calvados, and marc or grappa (especially good with game), can be added almost near the end so their nuances are not lost from prolonged exposure to heat. Many of the nuances of old or delicate spirits that would be lost if used to finish a hot sauce can be better appreciated in a jelly. When using spirits, experiment with a small amount of the jelly before adding spirits to the whole batch. Choose the most flavorful spirits available so that you do not have to add too much; otherwise, the jelly will have an unpleasant taste of alcohol.

Other Flavorings for Jellies

Because of their delicacy, jellies can be flavored with almost any ingredient that will not cause them to cloud or interfere with their appearance. Cracked pepper is popular with chefs. If you are tempted to substitute green peppercorns, make sure they are well rinsed, and do not crush them or they will cloud the jelly.

Wild mushrooms, and even cultivated mushrooms, lend depth and complexity when added near the end of cooking. Dried morels are particularly excellent, but dried cèpes (porcini) also work well. The stems from cultivated mushrooms can be used, but be sure they are fresh or they will color the jelly an unpleasant gray.

Jellies used for fish can be enhanced by adding saffron (preferably in threads) while the jelly is still warm. When used by itself in jellies or cold sauces, saffron has an aggressive quality that is not as apparent when used in hot sauces. It is therefore best used in conjunction with typically Provençal flavors, such as basil, tomatoes, fennel, and marjoram.

MOREL JELLY

YIELD: 2 CUPS (500 MILLILITERS)

fresh morels	8 ounces	225 grams
or	or	or
dried morels, 20 medium	½ ounce	14 grams
port or madeira (for dried morels)	sprinkling	sprinkling
hot brown meat jelly	2 cups	500 milliliters

1. If fresh morels are being used, inspect them for sand and dirt. Check the insides for bugs. If they need to be cleaned, put them in a colander and quickly rinse them with cold running water.

   If dried morels are being used, rinse them quickly in cold running water and place them in a bowl. Sprinkle them with the port or Madeira and let them soften for 20 minutes. When they are soft, gently squeeze them to eliminate grit.
2. Infuse the morels in the hot jelly in a covered 1-quart (1 liter) saucepan for 10 minutes. Strain the jelly through a fine chinois. The morels can then be served as a garniture or chopped and stirred into the finished jelly.

SAFFRON AND TOMATO FISH JELLY

This jelly is analogous to a Mediterranean fish soup and is excellent when served with an assortment of cold poached fish. Although the recipe calls for concentrated fish stock (which should be made from very fresh fish), the jelly is even better if the poaching liquid from several batches of fish is used as a base. This jelly can also be used in the layers of a cold terrine, or *hure* (see page 369).

YIELD: 2 CUPS (500 MILLILITERS)

warm concentrated fish stock	2 cups	500 milliliters
or	or	or
warm fish poaching liquid	2 cups	500 milliliters
finely chopped fresh marjoram leaves	1 tablespoon	15 milliliters
saffron threads	1 pinch	1 pinch
peeled, seeded, and diced tomatoes	½ cup	125 milliliters
salt and pepper	to taste	to taste

1. Let the fish stock settle in a glass jar. Carefully ladle off the top, clear portion and strain it first through a fine chinois and then through a chinois lined with a wet napkin or a triple layer of cheesecloth.
2. Tie the marjoram leaves in a small square of cheesecloth.
3. Heat the jelly in a 1-quart (1 liter) saucepan and stir in the saffron, tomatoes, and the packet of marjoram leaves. Remove the pan from the heat and cover it with a lid. Let the flavors infuse for 10 minutes.
4. When the jelly has cooled, remove the packet of marjoram and check the jelly's consistency. Adjust the seasonings.

WORKING WITH JELLIES

Meat and fish jellies can be used to accompany cold foods in several ways. The simplest method is to serve the chopped jelly next to the food being served, such as a terrine or slice of foie gras. When chopping jelly, some chefs like to sprinkle a few drops of Cognac over it before chopping to help prevent the little chunks of jelly from melting back together. Chopped jelly will also contribute suavity when tossed with cold cooked vegetables to form a kind of salad.

When chopped jelly is served with vegetables, the distinction between jelly-accompanied vegetables and cold consommé is simply a matter of proportion. A cold consommé consists traditionally of mostly consommé with an almost insignificant amount of garniture incorporated into the consommé at the last minute. When jellies are used in vegetable, meat, or fish salads, the solid elements are in the forefront and the jelly in the background.

SALADE GRECQUE IN COURT-BOUILLON JELLY

Because court-bouillon contains no gelatin of its own, it must be combined with commercial gelatin or jelly stock made with veal feet (see page 351). A delicate court-bouillon jelly, lightly acidulated with lime juice or verjuice, not only makes an excellent accompaniment to cold raw or poached fish (it can even be served atop raw oysters), but it can be a semiliquid medium for a salad grecque. A traditional salade grecque is prepared by gently braising vegetables with herbs, white wine, olive oil, and coriander seeds. In this *en gelée* version, a pre-made court-bouillon jelly stock is used to moisten the vegetables, and the salad is served in its own glistening jelly.

YIELD: 8 SERVINGS

fennel bulb	1	1
juice of 1 lemon		
artichokes	2 large	2 large
pearl onions	24	24
zucchini	2 medium	2 medium
carrots	2 medium	2 medium
coriander seeds	1 tablespoon	15 milliliters
court-bouillon jelly	3 cups	750 milliliters
cayenne pepper	to taste	to taste
flat parsley leaves	2 tablespoons	30 milliliters
chervil leaves	2 tablespoons	30 milliliters

1. Preheat the oven to 300°F (150°C). Cut the fennel bulb into 8 wedges. Make sure to leave some of the central core attached to each wedge to hold it together. Put the wedges in a 4-quart (4 liter) bowl; sprinkle and toss them with a few drops of lemon juice.
2. Turn the artichokes and rub them with lemon juice. Add them to the bowl with the fennel.
3. Peel the pearl onions.
4. Cut each zucchini lengthwise into 4 sections. Bevel the edges for a decorative effect.
5. Peel and slice the carrots.
6. Spread the vegetables in a single layer over the bottom of a 6-quart (6 liter) rondeau or straight-sided sauté pan. Add the coriander seeds, the court-bouillon jelly, and the cayenne. Cover with a sheet of parchment paper cut into a round, and put the lid on the pan.
7. Bring the vegetables to a slow simmer; as soon as they simmer, place them in the oven. Braise in the oven for about 20 minutes. Check the vegetables after 20 minutes; be careful not to cook out all of their texture.
8. When the vegetables are done (slightly crunchy), take the pot out of the oven and remove the artichokes with a slotted spoon; reserve them.
9. While the mixture is cooling at room temperature, add the parsley and chervil leaves.
10. Remove the choke from each artichoke bottom with a spoon. Cut each bottom into 4 or 8 wedges and return them to the other vegetables.

11. When the vegetables have cooled, transfer them with the braising liquid to a mixing bowl or a decorative terrine (if the salad is being served at the table), and let set in a cool place or in the refrigerator.

Coating Foods with Jellies

In more formal French cooking, jellies have long been used to coat fish and meats, such as trout, chicken breasts, and game. The piece of meat is first chilled and then placed on a rack over a sheet pan. The cold but still-liquid jelly is spooned over and allowed to set; the process is repeated until the meat or fish is coated with a smooth layer. Most diners today are more excited by a piece of meat or fish taken from a terrine or gratin dish embedded in its own natural jelly than by the presentations of the past, but a slice of cold meat coated with a sparkling herb jelly is still a striking sight.

Jellies that are used to coat chilled meats, fish, or vegetables or that are chopped and presented as an accompaniment to pâtés and terrines, or that are integrated into salads, can often be enhanced with the addition of chopped or cubed ingredients, such as truffles, carrots, mushrooms (diced or left whole if small), grilled peppers of various colors, tomatoes (peeled, seeded, chopped, and degorged with salt), chopped herbs, prosciutto, or cubes of foie gras. Some of these garnitures (peppers, tomatoes, foie gras) are best stirred into the jelly just before it sets, whereas others, such as morels, truffles, or prosciutto, should be stirred into the jelly while it is still hot, so their flavors can infuse into the jelly. These garnished jellies can then be used in the same ways as plain jellies.

Jellies are also used to coat the insides of molds that can then be filled with mousses, vegetables such as artichokes or mushrooms, pieces of lobster, crayfish tails, and the like. The molds should first be chilled, and the cold-but-not-set jelly spooned over the insides of the molds in several stages.

FOIE GRAS "EN GELÉE"

The ideal gelée for foie gras would be derived from the poaching liquid for the foie gras itself, but since this is rarely practical, here we use a classic brown meat jelly. If you like, add chopped morels or truffles to the jelly.

YIELD: 4 FIRST-COURSE SERVINGS

terrine of foie gras, 3-ounce (100 gram) slices	4	4
brown meat jelly, as needed	1 cup	250 milliliters

1. Assemble four ramekins that are just large enough to hold the slices of foie gras. Pour about a third of the jelly into the ramekins and let it set in the refrigerator.

2. When the jelly is well set, arrange the foie gras slices on top in the ramekins and pour over the rest of the jelly. Allow to set in the refrigerator.

3. Unmold the foie gras en gelée onto cold plates and serve immediately. See the photograph in the color plates.

JAMBON PERSILLÉ
Parsleyed Ham Terrine

Jambon persillé is a terrine of cooked ham, chopped parsley, and jelly. The ham is cut into cubes and placed in alternating layers with the meat jelly and a large amount of chopped parsley. In the traditional version from Burgundy, the terrine is sliced, necessitating a rather stiff jelly to hold it together. Although the traditional version is wonderful, the variation that follows is prepared in individual portions, so the jelly can be kept fragile and trembling.

YIELD: 10 SERVINGS

raw cured ham such as prosciutto, Westphalian, or Smithfield, thinly sliced	8 ounces	250 grams
brown meat jelly	3 cups	750 milliliters
flat parsley, finely chopped	1 large bunch	1 large bunch

1. Cut the ham slices into strips about ¼ inch (5 mm) wide.
2. If the ham is salty, soak the strips in cold water for 10 minutes to eliminate the salt; pat them dry with paper towels.
3. Melt the jelly in a 2-quart (2 liter) saucepan, holding it at a temperature that keeps it on the verge of setting.
4. Chill 10 dariole molds and line them with jelly. Coat them as often as necessary to produce a ⅛-inch-thick (3 mm) layer of jelly.
5. Fill the jelly-lined dariole molds with alternating layers of ham strips and chopped parsley (about 1 tablespoon/15 milliliters of parsley per mold). Fill them with the chilled-but-not-set jelly. Tap the molds firmly against a table to eliminate air pockets.
6. Refrigerate the molds for 2 to 3 hours to set.
7. Unmold the jambon persillé onto cold plates and serve.

Integral Jellies

A jelly that is the natural outcome of a preparation that has been allowed to set is an excellent method of presentation. Cold leftover stews can be spooned out as they are, provided all fat is taken off the top. A slightly more sophisticated method is to melt the natural jelly surrounding the meat and add decorative garnitures, such as freshly chopped herbs, freshly cooked baby carrots (stewed in some of the melted jelly), turnips, fennel, or julienned vegetables. The whole thing can then be reconstructed in an attractive dish (a copper *braisière,* perhaps) and presented at the table. The boeuf mode en gelée that follows exemplifies this method.

·──● BOEUF MODE
Cold Braised Beef

This home-style French dish is a model of simple, natural cooking, in which the braising liquid is served along with the cold beef. The dish can also be prepared in the same way using white wine instead of red (it is then called *boeuf à la bourgeoise*).

In rustic preparations of this dish, the carrots and onions used in the braising are returned to the jelly and constitute part of the garniture for the finished dish. In a restaurant, a new set of carrots (center core removed, or turned) and sometimes onions (pearl onions are most attractive) are simmered in the degreased braising liquid and used as the garniture.

YIELD: 8 SERVINGS

fatback	7 ounces	200 grams
cognac	¼ cup	60 milliliters
parsley, chopped	1 small bunch	1 small bunch
garlic cloves, chopped	3	3
red wine	7 fluid ounces	200 milliliters
onions, chopped coarsely	6 ounces	175 grams
carrots, chopped coarsely	8 ounces	250 grams
large bouquet garni (page 51)	1	1
boneless rump roast	4 pounds	1.8 kilograms
split veal foot, halved crosswise (4 pieces)	1	1
vegetable oil	3 tablespoons	45 milliliters
brown stock	1 quart	1 liter
salt and pepper	to taste	to taste
carrots, sliced crosswise	4 medium	4 medium

1. Cut the fatback into strips for larding. Combine the Cognac, parsley, and garlic, and marinate the fatback overnight in the mixture.
2. (This marinating step is optional.) Combine the red wine, the coarsely chopped onions and carrots, and the bouquet garni, and marinate the beef in the mixture for 6 hours.
3. Lard the rump roast in the direction of the grain with the strips of fatback.
4. Blanch the veal foot pieces and rinse them in cold water. Preheat the oven to 275°F (135°C).

5. In a 4-quart (4 liter) heavy-bottomed pot, brown the rump roast in the vegetable oil. Discard the oil and add the red wine, chopped carrots, onions, veal foot, stock, and bouquet garni. The liquid should reach just to the top of the meat.

6. Bring the liquid to a slow simmer, skimming any froth that floats to the surface. Cover the pot with a sheet of aluminum foil and then with a lid. Continue cooking in the oven for 4 hours, or until the meat is easily penetrated with a skewer. Remove the lid and foil every 15 minutes and check to make sure the liquid is not boiling. If it starts to simmer, turn down the oven.

7. Remove the meat from the pot and cover it with plastic wrap to prevent it from drying out.

8. Strain the cooking liquid and carefully skim any grease from it. (The easiest way to do this is to let it set in the refrigerator overnight, removing the solidified grease when it is cold.) Reserve the veal foot pieces.

9. If the jelly is too light or does not jell when it is cool, it can be reduced by one-fourth to one-third to concentrate its natural gelatin. When it sets to the correct consistency, it should be seasoned with salt and pepper.

10. Strain the jelly through a fine chinois lined with a wet cloth napkin or a triple layer of cheesecloth.

11. Simmer the sliced carrot rounds in the jelly until they are soft.

12. Bone the cooked veal foot. Cut the gelatinous flesh into strips or cubes and stir into the jelly.

13. When the braised beef has cooled, it can be sliced and layered in a terrine with the carrots and barely melted jelly and served sliced or spooned (like an hure—a jelly-based terrine; opposite) or molded in oval gratin dishes.

Variations

A larded and braised piece of beef assembled in a terrine with its natural jelly and aromatic garniture can be used as a model for an almost infinite variety of cold meat terrines and hures. The jelly can be flavored with wines, which can be added at the beginning of the braising or at the very end during the final flavoring of the jelly.

In a traditional boeuf mode, carrots and onions constitute the principal garnitures, but obviously these can be modified according to season, location, and occasion. A southern French or California version might be garnished with tomatoes (peeled, seeded, degorged with salt), fennel (cut into wedges, precooked in braising liquid or stock), garlic cloves (peeled and poached), or wild mushrooms, for example.

The jelly almost always benefits from a generous quantity of freshly chopped herbs added while it is cooling. Parsley works beautifully, but chervil, tarragon, or a combination of classic fines herbes also works well.

Hures (Terrines in Jelly)

Meat, vegetable, and fish terrines held together with jelly (in French, *hures*) have become increasingly popular; they are beautiful, require no cream or butter, and can be adapted to a wide range of ingredients. Their one drawback is that to produce firm, even slices of these terrines, the jelly must be stiff enough to bind the various components. If a jelly is too stiff, its cool, melting suavity is lost, and it instead feels rubbery in the mouth.

An alternative to jelly-based terrines is to make individual portions in small ramekins or molds. They can then be unmolded at the last minute. Because no slicing is involved, the jelly can be left fragile and shimmering.

⬤━ SALMON AND TRUFFLE HURE

This hure is made by layering very thin, lightly cooked slices of salmon with sliced truffles and truffle-flavored meat jelly. The hure is then allowed to set in a truffle-lined bowl so that, once unmolded, it is completely black and shining with jelly. It is best served with a spoon.

YIELD: 4 FIRST-COURSE SERVINGS

salmon fillet	8 ounces	250 grams
extra-virgin olive oil	2 tablespoons	30 milliliters
salt and pepper	to taste	to taste
fresh black truffle	1 large	1 large
brown veal or beef jelly	1 cup	250 milliliters

1. Preheat the oven to 300°F (150°C). Slice the salmon into squares about 5 inches (12.5 cm) on each side and ⅛ inch (3 mm) thick. Place each slice on a small individual sheet of aluminum foil that has been very lightly brushed with the olive oil.
2. Sprinkle the slices with salt and pepper. Place the sheets of aluminum foil with the salmon slices on a sheet pan and place in the oven for approximately 20 seconds, until the surface of the salmon begins to cook slightly. Do not cook the slices all the way through. Remove from the oven and let cool.
3. Peel the truffle, chop and reserve the peelings, and slice the truffle with a Japanese mandoline. (A large truffle should yield approximately 60 paper-thin slices.)
4. Cover each of the salmon slices with the sliced truffles, reserving 20 to 30 truffle slices to line the mold. Gently stack the truffle-covered slices of salmon, leaving them on the foil. Place the stack on a plate and cover with plastic wrap. Refrigerate for 2 to 3 hours, so the truffles permeate the salmon with their perfume.

5. Bring the jelly to a simmer in a 1-quart (1 liter) saucepan. Remove it from the heat and add the chopped truffle peelings and the reserved truffle slices. Cover the saucepan and let it cool.

6. Strain the infused jelly into a mixing bowl, reserving the truffle slices. Place the bowl with the jelly over a bowl of ice. Stir the jelly until it is just on the verge of setting.

7. Place a 2-cup (500 milliliter) round-bottomed bowl in another bowl containing ice. Line the inside surface of the bowl with jelly. Coat the bowl as often as necessary to produce a ¼-inch-thick (5 mm) layer of jelly around the inside of the bowl.

8. Line the inside of the bowl with the reserved truffle slices until none of the interior of the bowl is visible.

9. Layer the inside of the bowl with the truffled salmon slices and the almost-set truffle jelly. Continue until the bowl is full and all the ingredients have been used.

10. Cover the bowl with plastic wrap and refrigerate for 2 hours.

11. Place the bowl of truffled salmon in another bowl of hot water for 10 to 15 seconds. Turn the salmon hure onto a round silver tray. (Silver contrasts well with the black truffles.) Serve the hure at the table with a spoon.

Note: This salmon and truffle hure can also be made in ramekins and served in individual portions.

Smoked Jellies

A natural jelly flavored with the smokiness of grilled foods is analogous to the smoke-scented broth that accompanies grilled game birds (see page 284). To prepare a smoke-flavored jelly, a natural jelly is prepared in advance; smoked or grilled meats or fish are then gently stewed in the melted jelly until they impart the flavor of the smoker or grill. The jelly can be used to coat or accompany the grilled or smoked meats or fish or as an accent to other cold foods.

CHICKEN BREASTS WITH SMOKED JELLY

In this recipe, chicken wings and backs are grilled and used to prepare a smoke-flavored jelly. The jelly can then be used to coat the poached chicken breasts. The breasts can also be grilled, but the smoke-flavored jelly will provide a less striking contrast.

YIELD: 8 SERVINGS

split boned breasts, wings, and backs from 4 chickens		
clear brown chicken stock (see Note)	6 cups	1.5 liters
salt and pepper	to taste	to taste

1. Poach the chicken breasts for about 5 minutes in 2 cups (500 milliliters) of the stock. They are done when they bounce back to the touch. Remove them from the stock and chill on a plate in the refrigerator.
2. Grill the chicken wings and backs over wood coals (aromatic woods—fruitwoods, hickory, vine cuttings, and mesquite—are best).
3. Place the grilled chicken wings and backs in a 2-quart (2 liter) saucepan and cover them with the remaining clear stock. (Do not use the poaching stock for the jelly, as it will be cloudy.) Bring the stock to a slow simmer for 15 minutes. Skim off any fat or froth that floats to the surface.
4. Strain the stock first through a fine chinois and then through a chinois lined with a wet napkin or a triple layer of cheesecloth. Chill the stock in a bowl over ice or in the refrigerator until it barely starts to set. It will set on the sides of the bowl first.
5. Place the cold chicken breasts on a cake rack placed on a sheet pan. Spoon a layer of jelly over the breasts and return them to the refrigerator for 10 minutes to give the jelly time to set. Repeat this process until there is a ¼-inch-thick (5 mm) layer of jelly on the top of each breast. It may be necessary to melt the jelly gently in the bowl from time to time by placing it over the stove or a bowl of hot water. Do not let it get too hot or it will melt the jelly on the breasts and you will have to start over.
6. Serve the jelly-coated breasts on chilled plates. Surround each of the breasts with additional chopped jelly.

Note: The chicken stock should be gelatinous enough to set firmly in the refrigerator; if it is not, reduce it.

Variation

Smoked jelly can be used to coat the chilled chicken breasts or can be served chopped on the side or used to construct an hure. Garnishing elements, such as diced grilled peppers, ham, tomatoes, mushrooms, or even fruits such as peaches can be incorporated into the jelly or served on the side. Avoid using tropical fruits, however, because the protease they contain will break down the natural gelatin contained in the jelly, causing it to melt.

IMPROVISING JELLIES

Because of their subtlety, natural jellies can be used as a medium for virtually any flavor. As with hot sauces, the aesthetic spectrum for making jellies runs between two poles. At one end of the spectrum are jellies prepared so that they are actually or seemingly derived from the meats or fish they accompany. Remember that a jelly was originally created directly from the cooking process—stews left to set in their own juices or chicken sautés allowed to congeal and then spooned out the next day.

On the opposite end of the spectrum are jellies designed to contrast with the foods they accompany. Popular in eighteenth-century France, dishes with contrasting jellies, such as pigeon with crayfish jelly, are still served in contemporary French restaurants. Between these two poles are jellies whose flavor is gently shaped so that the flavor of the ingredient they accompany is accented while remaining intact, such as the braising liquid from a rabbit accented with a grassy-flavored Sauvignon Blanc or Sancerre.

It is always valuable for the chef to keep in mind a historical, regional, or well-known dish as a reference point during improvisation. As an example, imagine preparing a dish of cold chicken to be accompanied by a jelly. It may be useful to think first of hot chicken dishes appropriate to the setting or style of the restaurant. A chicken sautéed with mushrooms and tarragon (*chasseur*) could be reinterpreted as a cold dish by deglazing the pan with a natural jelly stock and infusing the mushrooms and tarragon. In the hot version, the sauce would often be finished by swirling in a chunk of butter; for the cold version, the surrounding jelly would simply set. The traditional mushrooms could be set in the jelly as components in an *hure* or cut into cubes as garniture.

CHAUDS-FROIDS

The fundamental difference between jellies and chauds-froids is that chauds-froids are opaque, usually because they contain cream, although some older versions contain egg yolks or even mayonnaise. Originally, chauds-froids were leftover cream-finished stews, such as chicken fricassée, served cold, surrounded by their congealed cooking liquid. The spontaneity of serving cold chicken with its congealed sauce has been replaced over the years with the elaborate and tasteless presentation pieces so popular at food shows. It is little wonder that chaud-froid is rarely served in restaurants when its origin as a natural cold sauce has been forgotten. Like jellies, if it is prepared at all, it is done with characterless stock and too much gelatin.

In classic French cooking, chauds-froids are divided into white and brown. White chauds-froids are analogous to white sauces and are prepared with white stock, without browning any of the components. Brown chauds-froids have been almost entirely abandoned because they form a less impressive backdrop for decoration than the white versions; their flavor, however, is at least as good.

The intrinsic quality of the chaud-froid has been forgotten in favor of appearance, but the contrived presentations of the past are rarely appealing. Food is far more pleasing when decorative elements appear as natural components of good cooking—because they are essential to the flavor of the dish.

It is possible to elaborate on a natural chaud-froid by incorporating garnishing elements in the same way as for natural jellies. Finely chopped herbs are among the easiest and most appealing of garnitures, but cubes of mushrooms, grilled peppers, truffles, and other ingredients can be folded into the chaud-froid just before it sets.

For a chaud-froid to be good (and when they are good, they are wonderful), the same precautions must be followed as when preparing hot sauces and jellies.

Preparing Chauds-Froids

Chaud-froid is made by adding heavy cream to either white or brown meat or fish jelly. Usually one-eighth to one-tenth cream by volume is the appropriate amount. Because cream softens the flavors of the jelly, be sure to adjust the seasonings and flavorings after the cream is added. Also, both the seasonings and flavorings are more subtle when the chauds-froids and jellies have set, so chauds-froids should be slightly overseasoned. In some ways, chauds-froids are easier to prepare than aspics because the jelly used as the base need not be perfectly clear.

Adding Purées to Chauds-Froids

The color and flavor of chauds-froids can be enhanced by stirring in a full-flavored vegetable purée just before adding the cream. Tomato purée gives the chaud-froid a lovely pink color and a touch of sweetness and acidity that goes well with chicken and fish. Sorrel purée gives the chaud-froid an irresistible acidity that offsets its richness (the color is somewhat drab, but the flavor compensates for it). A chaud-froid to which a quantity of puréed grilled red or yellow peppers has been added is an excellent accent to strongly flavored meats or grilled foods (using a smoke-flavored jelly as the base would make a worthwhile experiment).

Puréed black truffles infused in a small amount of still-hot jelly before the cream is added provides a sublime coating for game.

SORREL CHAUD-FROID

This chaud-froid is an excellent coating for cold barbecued chicken.

YIELD: 2 CUPS (500 MILLILITERS)

full-flavored jelly	1½ cups	375 milliliters
heavy cream	½ cup	125 milliliters
sorrel leaves, 2 large handfuls	3 ounces	75 grams
salt and pepper	to taste	to taste

1. Combine the jelly, cream, and sorrel leaves in a 2-quart (2 liter) saucepan.
2. Bring the mixture to a simmer for 5 minutes.
3. Purée for 30 seconds in a blender. (Be careful when blending hot liquids. Never fill the blender more than half full, and wrap a towel around the top so the hot liquid does not force its way out. On the other hand, do not try to blend the mixture when it is cold or the cream may curdle.)
4. Strain through a fine chinois and season well with salt and pepper.

13
HOT EMULSIFIED EGG YOLK SAUCES

Hot emulsified egg sauces are made by quickly beating egg yolks and liquid over heat to form an airy emulsion. Fat, usually melted or clarified butter, is then added. The sauce can then be flavored with a wide range of ingredients and preparations. Hot emulsified egg yolk sauces are among the richest and most luxurious sauces, and they can be the most difficult to make well. The technique of emulsifying egg yolks with fats and liquids can also be adapted and used for contemporary sauce innovations. Sauce béarnaise and sauce hollandaise are the best known of the hot emulsified egg sauces, but there are many classic and contemporary variations.

The technique of combining flavor components into a hot emulsion of egg yolks, liquid, and air remains the same regardless of the particular sauce being prepared.

Hot emulsified egg sauces usually consist of three elements: a sabayon, a fluffy mixture prepared by whisking the egg yolks with water or another liquid over heat to incorporate air; a flavoring element, usually added to the sauce at the end (this can be a flavorful reduction, as is used for béarnaise, or a single flavor component, such as saffron); and fat, usually melted or clarified butter.

PRECAUTIONS FOR MAKING HOT EMULSIFIED EGG YOLK SAUCES

1. Remember that one egg yolk can absorb about ½ cup (125 milliliters) of clarified butter (the equivalent of 5 ounces/150 grams of whole butter). If too much butter is added, the sauce will likely break.
2. Egg yolks curdle above 185°F (85°C), so make sure the butter is not too hot before stirring it into the sabayon.
3. Do not add the butter to the sabayon all at once, or the sauce will break. Conversely, it should not be added too slowly or the sauce will be heavy.
4. Make sure that the sabayon is completely cooked. If it is not cooked enough, it will separate, and the sauce will be too thin or will break completely.
5. Keep the sauce at the correct temperature, about 145°F (63°C), during restaurant service. If it gets too hot, it will break. The best way to keep it at the correct temperature is to place it in a pan of water on a low flame or somewhere near the back of the stove. Check it from time to time to make sure that it is not too hot.
6. Keep emulsified sauces covered while they are being held before use. Otherwise, a skin may form on the surface. Stir them gently before serving.
7. Hot emulsified sauces tend to cook and thicken while being held warm before service. They should be thinned about every hour with a little water or heavy cream. If allowed to sit for too long without being thinned, they will break.

REPAIRING BROKEN SAUCES

If an emulsified egg yolk sauce is prepared incorrectly—if the clarified butter is too hot or too much is added at once—the tenuous emulsion will destabilize and the sauce will "break." A broken sauce is easy to recognize because it suddenly thins and takes on a grainy appearance. Broken emulsified sauces can usually be repaired by beating the warm sauce into an egg yolk that has first been beaten with a little cold water or 1 tablespoon (15 milliliters) of heavy cream. The resulting sauce will not be as light as a sauce made correctly initially, but it will be acceptable for most uses.

When confronted with a broken emulsified sauce, it is important to diagnose the problem first. Check the temperature of the sauce by feeling the outside of the saucepan. If it seems too hot, let the sauce cool before trying to repair it.

If the problem seems to be that the butter was added too quickly, gradually beat the broken sauce into 1 tablespoon (15 milliliters) of heavy cream, adding a bit at a time. Once the repaired sauce starts to thicken, the broken sauce can be added more quickly. Provided that the broken sauce contains a minimum amount of egg yolk (1 yolk per ½ cup/125 milliliters of clarified butter), any amount of sauce can be repaired starting with 1 tablespoon (15 milliliters) of heavy cream. If doubtful whether the broken sauce contains enough egg yolk, work the broken sauce into an egg yolk instead of the heavy cream.

If a sauce seems to be only on the verge of breaking, it can often be brought back together by slowly whisking in 1 tablespoon (15 milliliters) of cold water or heavy cream.

STORAGE

When preparing hot emulsified egg yolk sauces, make only what is needed. Although these sauces can be stored overnight in the refrigerator and melted and beaten into a fresh egg yolk the next day, the longer a sauce is kept, the greater the danger of bacterial contamination. Because these sauces are kept warm rather than hot while being held before service, they become perfect media for bacteria. If sauce has been kept warm for more than 2 or 3 hours, it is best to discard any that is left over. If only a small amount of sauce was prepared and it was not held for more than 2 hours, it can be stored overnight and reconstituted the next day. Remember, when storing emulsified egg yolk sauces overnight, to date the container with the date the sauce was *first* made. An emulsified egg yolk sauce should never be reconstituted more than once.

To reconstitute a hot emulsified egg yolk sauce, gently heat it in a pan set over another pan containing warm water. While the sauce is melting, put 1 egg yolk into a sloping-sided saucepan. Beat the yolk with 1 tablespoon (15 milliliters) of cold water. Put the saucepan over high heat. Continue whisking until the yolk begins to stiffen. When the sauce has melted—it will be severely broken with bits of egg yolk floating around in the melted butter—whisk it gradually into the beaten egg yolk. A reconstituted sauce will never be as light as the original sauce was.

SERVING

These sauces are traditionally served with grilled meats, poached or grilled fish, and hot vegetables. The tangier sauces, such as béarnaise and Choron, go well with meats, whereas more delicate variations accompany vegetables or fish. Sauce maltaise is almost always used to accompany hot asparagus. In traditional restaurant service, foods should never be served already coated with a hot emulsified egg yolk sauce. These sauces should be either served in a sauce boat or to the side of the meat or fish on the plate. In this way the diner can regulate the amount of sauce he or she wants to eat.

CLASSIC HOT EGG YOLK SAUCES

Sauce Béarnaise

Sauce béarnaise is made by preparing an intensely flavored infusion of tarragon, chopped shallots, white wine, wine vinegar, and cracked pepper. These ingredients are simmered and slowly reduced to extract the flavor from the herbs and shallots and to concentrate the acidity of the vinegar and white wine.

Many chefs and cooks know how to prepare an acceptable béarnaise or hollandaise but rarely understand what is required to prepare a perfect airy sauce. Many recipes for hot emulsified sauces simply say to beat melted butter into gently warmed egg yolks. Sauces prepared in this way contain no air and thus tend to be heavy and thick. To prepare a light, delicate, emulsified sauce, it is essential to first prepare a frothy emulsion of egg yolks, liquid, *and* air. This emulsion is called a *sabayon*. Once the sabayon is correctly prepared, the addition of flavorings and fat is a straightforward process.

Chefs sometimes differ as to whether to use cold butter, melted butter, or clarified butter. There are advantages and disadvantages to each. Clarified butter gives the smoothest-textured sauce, but many flavor components and nutrients, which are contained in the milk solids, will be lost. If a thick sauce is required, however, it is essential to use clarified butter. Clarified butter is almost always necessary if a sabayon, which contains water or another liquid, is being used as the sauce base. Whole butter, either cold or melted, contains only 75 percent pure fat; the remaining 25 percent is mostly water, which results in a thinner sauce. Melted butter will give a more delicate-tasting sauce but can often make the sauce runny. Emulsified sauces made with cold butter will often have the best flavor, but much of the airiness of the sauce will be lost because the butter will require more whisking as it is added to the sabayon.

When using clarified butter for hot emulsified egg yolk sauces, allow approximately ½ cup (125 milliliters) of clarified butter per egg yolk. When using whole or melted butter, use 6 egg yolks for approximately 1 pound (500 grams) of butter. For either method, use 1 to 1½ tablespoons (15 to 25 milliliters) of liquid (usually water) per egg yolk when preparing the sabayon. If clarified butter is used, the sauce will be extremely thick—the consistency of a traditional mayonnaise—but since the base is usually thinned by adding other liquids to flavor it, it is better to start out with a thick mixture than one that is too thin. It is also possible to add less than the full amount of butter, which will result in a lighter, airier sauce. One tablespoon (15 milliliters) of liquid added to ½ cup (125 milliliters) of an emulsified sauce base made with clarified butter will result in a perfect texture for most dishes.

Either of two methods can be used to flavor emulsified egg yolk sauces. Some recipes suggest whisking the basic flavors, such as a lemon juice, tarragon, and vinegar infusion or orange zests, with the egg yolks when preparing the sabayon and then straining the sauce after adding the butter. The disadvantage to this method is that the sauce loses some airiness when it is strained. In the recipes that follow—the béarnaise recipe is a model for the others—a sauce base is prepared with clarified butter and the flavoring is added at the end. This eliminates the need for straining the sauce and also makes it possible to prepare a quantity of flavoring to be added to the sauces as they are prepared over the course of several days. See the photograph in the color plates.

SAUCE BÉARNAISE

The emulsified sauce base that is prepared here is used for all of the sauces that follow; the flavor reduction of herbs, vinegar, white wine, and shallots makes this sauce specifically a sauce béarnaise. Traditional recipes for sauce béarnaise call for chervil in the flavor reduction, but in this recipe it is optional. The flavor of tarragon is so much more assertive that the flavor of the chervil is usually overpowered and lost.

YIELD: 1 QUART (1 LITER)

whole butter	21 ounces	600 grams
shallots	3 medium	3 medium
fresh tarragon	1 bunch	1 bunch
fresh chervil (optional)	½ bunch	½ bunch
whole black peppercorns	1 teaspoon	5 milliliters
white wine	¾ cup	185 milliliters
tarragon or white wine vinegar	¾ cup	185 milliliters
egg yolks	6	6
cold water	6 tablespoons	90 milliliters
salt and white pepper	to taste	to taste

1. To clarify the butter, melt it in a straight-sided saucepan over medium heat. Check it from time to time to make sure that it does not become too hot and burn. Remove it from the heat and skim off any froth that has floated to the top with a ladle; then carefully remove the clarified butter (the water contained in the butter will be on the bottom) with a ladle. There should be about 2 cups (500 milliliters). Keep the clarified butter warm until needed.

2. To prepare the flavor reduction, peel and chop the shallots. This should be done as close to the last minute as possible. (If the shallots are chopped more than a few hours in advance, they should be kept in a plastic or stainless-steel container and covered with wine vinegar to help keep their flavor intact.)

3. Remove the leaves from the tarragon and the chervil, if using, and reserve. They will later be chopped and added to the sauce at the end. Reserve the stems.

4. Crush the peppercorns by placing them on a cutting board and crushing them with the bottom of a small pot or saucepan.

5. Combine the white wine, vinegar, herb stems, shallots, and the peppercorns in a 1-quart (1 liter) straight-sided saucepan. Heat the mixture over a medium flame until it comes to a simmer. Continue reducing the mixture for 15 to 20 minutes until it is reduced by about two-thirds—about ½ cup (125 milliliters) will remain. Be careful to prevent the flame from wrapping around the outside of the saucepan, which can cause any of the mixture that has stuck to the sides of the saucepan to brown, giving an off flavor and color to the finished sauce.

6. Strain the reduction through a fine chinois and reserve until needed. (Some recipes suggest combining the unstrained reduction with the sauce and then straining the entire sauce. This method has the disadvantage of forcing air out of the sauce.)

7. Combine the egg yolks with the cold water in a 2-quart (2 liter) saucepan with sloping sides. Whisk the mixture until it becomes light and frothy. This usually takes about 30 seconds.

8. Heat over a medium to high flame, whisking rapidly (see Note). The mixture will triple in volume. As the sabayon approaches the correct temperature, it will suddenly thicken—you will start to see the bottom of the saucepan while whisking. When the sabayon starts to stiffen, continue whisking as rapidly as possible over the heat for about 5 seconds, to ensure it is completely cooked. (If the sabayon is undercooked, the process tends to reverse itself and the sauce will be runny and may even break.)

9. Remove the sabayon from the heat and whisk for about 20 seconds to cool it. (Otherwise it may curdle, being overcooked by the residual heat in the saucepan.)

10. Ladle the clarified butter into the sabayon while gently stirring with the whisk. (At this stage it is not necessary to work the butter into the sabayon drop by drop, because the sabayon is already an emulsion that will readily combine with fat. In fact, the butter should be added fairly rapidly to avoid overworking the sauce, which would force out air.)

11. When all the butter has been added, the sauce will have a very stiff texture. Add the tarragon-vinegar reduction until the sauce has the right flavor and desired consistency. If it is too stiff, it can be thinned with water or with the water released by the butter when it was clarified. Do not thin the sauce until the flavor has been adjusted. (Some recipes suggest combining the reduction with the egg yolks before cooking them into a sabayon. Because the reduction is extremely acidic, it tends to cook the yolks prematurely, so the resulting sabayon contains less air and is heavier.)

12. Chop the reserved tarragon leaves and chervil leaves, if using, and add them to the sauce.

13. Adjust the sauce's flavors. It may need salt, white pepper, or additional vinegar. If the sauce is too acidic, it will need to be lengthened with extra fat or liquid. This can be accomplished by adding more butter or by simply thinning the sauce with water or cream. If you do not want to thin the sauce and are afraid of causing it to break by adding more butter, quickly stir in another egg yolk before adding more butter.

Note: Some restaurants prepare enough flavor reduction (steps 2 through 6) to last several weeks (it keeps well) instead of preparing a batch for each sauce.

Many recipes suggest cooking the egg yolks over low heat or even over a pan of simmering water. This is a nuisance in a professional kitchen, where these sauces often must be prepared at the last minute. Slow heating of the sabayon is also detrimental to the sauce. A sabayon should be completely cooked in about 2 minutes. If whisked and cooked any longer, the egg yolks lose their ability to emulsify with air, and the resulting sauce is heavy. If you are not confident working with high heat, practice making sabayons with 2 or 3 egg yolks at a time.

Sauce Hollandaise

This sauce is one of the simplest and most delicious of the emulsified sauces. Because the flavor of hollandaise is subtle—only a bit of lemon juice is used—it is especially important to use the best butter available. It is best to use clarified butter; melted whole butter will produce a sauce that is too thin once the lemon juice has been added.

Prepare a sabayon using only water and egg yolks, as in steps 7 through 9 for Sauce Béarnaise (page 379). (Older recipes use a vinegar reduction, but most modern chefs dispense with it.) Stir in clarified butter to prepare a sauce base, as in step 10 for sauce béarnaise. Finish the sauce with approximately 2 tablespoons (30 milliliters) of lemon juice per 2 cups (500 milliliters) of sauce. (If using the quantities in the sauce béarnaise recipe, add ¼ cup/60 milliliters of lemon juice to the sauce, of which there will be 1 quart/1 liter.) Taste the sauce while adding the lemon juice, so as not to add too much. If the sauce is too lemony, much of the subtlety and buttery nuances will be lost. Adjust the seasoning with salt and freshly ground white pepper. See the photograph in the color plates.

Derivatives of Béarnaise and Hollandaise

Most classic emulsified egg yolk sauces are prepared in the same way as béarnaise or hollandaise—only the flavoring is different. Each of the following classic recipes makes approximately 2 cups (500 milliliters) of sauce.

Sauce Choron (Sauce Béarnaise with Tomato)

The natural sweetness of ripe tomatoes goes well with the vinegar and tarragon flavor of sauce béarnaise. Prepare a tomato purée by slicing the tomatoes crosswise and squeezing the seeds out over a bowl. (It is not necessary to peel the tomatoes, because the purée will be strained.) Coarsely chop the seeded tomatoes and gently stew them in a small amount of olive oil. They will first release water. Continue cooking until the water has evaporated and the purée begins to thicken. Strain the purée and stir it into the sauce béarnaise. Use approximately one part strained tomato purée to three parts sauce béarnaise (for 2 cups/500 milliliters of sauce Choron, use 1½ cups/375 milliliters of sauce béarnaise and ½ cup/125 milliliters of tomato purée—two medium tomatoes will produce this much purée). Taste while adding the purée because the amount of purée to use will depend on the ripeness and flavor of the tomatoes and on personal taste.

Sauce Maltaise (Orange-Flavored Sauce Hollandaise)

Sauce maltaise is prepared in the same way as hollandaise except that orange juice cooked with orange zests is added to the sauce instead of lemon juice. Traditionally blood oranges, which give this sauce a distinctive reddish tint, are used, but if they are unavailable, a delicious sauce can still be made with regular oranges. In classic French cooking, this sauce is served with asparagus.

Prepare an infusion from the juice of 2 large oranges (about 5 fluid ounces/150 milliliters) and the julienned zest from half of 1 orange. Gently reduce this infusion until ¼ cup (60 milliliters) remains. Stir this reduction into 2 cups (500 milliliters) of unflavored sauce base.

Sauce Mousseline (Hollandaise with Whipped Cream)

Sauce hollandaise can be lightened with whipped cream just before serving. To lighten 2 cups (500 milliliters) of hollandaise, whip approximately ½ cup (125 milliliters) of heavy cream. The whipped cream should be folded into the hollandaise just before serving. (If added earlier, it will release water into the sauce, and the air contained in the whipped cream will be lost.) Be sure to adjust the seasoning after adding the whipped cream. This sauce is traditionally served with hot vegetables, but it also makes an excellent accompaniment for fish.

Sauce Noisette (Noisette Butter Sauce)

Although this sauce is traditionally based on hollandaise, any hot emulsified egg sauce can be given added complexity by finishing it with a small amount of noisette butter. Reserve one-fourth of the whole butter being used to prepare the base, and cook it gently to the noisette stage. Do not add lemon. Strain the beurre noisette through a fine chinois and use it to finish the sauce. To prepare 2 cups (500 milliliters) of sauce, use 2 egg yolks, 2 tablespoons (30 milliliters) of water, 2 ounces (60 grams) of butter cooked to the noisette stage, ¾ cup (185 milliliters) of clarified butter, and salt and pepper to taste. (For a description of how to prepare Beurre Noisette, see page 412.)

Because noisette butter gives sauces an intensely buttery flavor, it can be used to flavor emulsified sauces that have less than the full amount of butter. These sauces, although they will taste very buttery, will actually be lighter.

Sauce Foyot or Valois (Sauce Béarnaise with Meat Glace)

Sauce béarnaise can be given a fuller, meaty flavor by adding meat glace (*glace de viande*). The amount to add depends on the consistency and flavor of the glace, but 3 tablespoons (45 milliliters) added to 2 cups (500 milliliters) of sauce béarnaise is usually correct. This sauce is excellent with grilled or sautéed meats.

Sauce Tyrolienne (Oil-Based Sauce Béarnaise)

Although this sauce is technically a mayonnaise (because oil is used instead of butter), it is included here because it is served hot and because it is traditionally classified in the béarnaise family. Prepare the reduction and sabayon used for sauce béarnaise (steps 2 through 9), but instead of finishing the sabayon with butter (step 10), use the same amount of oil instead. The sauce should then be completed with 3 tablespoons (45 milliliters) of reduced tomato purée for every 2 cups (500 milliliters) of sauce base. A pinch of cayenne pepper added at the end helps enliven the sauce and bring out the flavor of the other ingredients. Traditionally, this sauce is used for grilled fish and meats. The sauce is very thick and may be thinned with stock, cooking liquids, or other liquids.

Sauce Rubens (Anchovy and Crustacean Sauce for Fish)

This unusual sauce is an excellent accompaniment to fish. It is based on an infusion of chopped onions, carrots, and celery (a mirepoix) and white wine, which is then combined with egg yolks and finished with crustacean butter and anchovy paste.

Gently stew ½ cup (125 milliliters) of mirepoix in ½ ounce (15 grams) of butter. Do not let the mirepoix brown. When the mirepoix is cooked, after about 10 minutes, add 1 cup (250 milliliters) of white wine and 1 cup (250 milliliters) of fresh fish stock. Gently reduce this mixture until only 3 tablespoons (45 milliliters) of syrupy glaze remain in the saucepan. Add 1 tablespoon (15 milliliters) of Madeira to this mixture. Cook the mixture for 1 minute more, to remove the alcohol from the Madeira. Strain this mixture through a fine strainer, let it cool, and combine it with 2 egg yolks. Whip this mixture into a sabayon and finish it with ½ cup (125 milliliters) clarified butter and 1 ounce (30 grams) of Crustacean Butter (page 329). Traditionally, 1 teaspoon (5 milliliters) of anchovy paste is called for, but for some, it detracts from the sauce.

CONTEMPORARY VARIATIONS

The techniques used to prepare classic hot egg yolk sauces can be modified to make lighter contemporary variations. There are no rules about serving contemporary hot emulsified egg yolk sauces, but often they are served on the plate rather than on the side, because they are lighter than their classic cousins. The first step in preparing a classic emulsified sauce is the preparation of the sabayon. In classic recipes, the egg yolks are combined with a small amount of cold water and the mixture is beaten over heat to form a preliminary, extremely airy emulsion, the sabayon. Water works well because it contains no acid, which tends to stiffen the yolks prematurely, or gelatin, which can make the sabayon too heavy. It is possible, however, to prepare a sabayon with a more flavorful liquid. If the sauce is to be served with poached fish, it makes good culinary sense to use some of the poaching liquid instead of water to give the sauce more character. If the sauce is to be used for meat, then a small amount of appropriate stock or the liquid from a deglazed roasting or sauté pan can be used to give the sauce extra flavor and complexity.

Fats

Classic emulsified sauces call for a large amount of fat, usually butter, added to a given number of egg yolks. In the nineteenth century, when these sauces were standardized, people were less concerned with eating fat and in fact associated rich sauces with luxury and wealth. One of the most obvious modifications of classic egg yolk sauces is simply to add less fat. The result is a sauce that contains a higher proportion of air and hence fewer calories.

Because much of the flavor of these sauces depends on the type and quality of the fat used, serious thought should be given to which type of fat to use, even if the proportion of fat is less than in a traditional sauce. When using butter, use the best quality available. Never use salted butter in sauce making; the salt interferes with the seasoning of the sauce, and salted butter has a less delicate flavor and is often less fresh than sweet butter.

It is also possible to replace butter with oils or other fats to lighten the sauce and give it a different flavor. A delicious emulsified egg yolk sauce can be made with olive oil instead of butter. The resulting sauce is identical to a mayonnaise except that it is served hot. Olive oil has a full, distinctive flavor, however, so it should replace butter only when its flavor is appropriate. In Gascony, a region in southwestern France, the butter for these sauces is sometimes replaced with a small amount of goose fat. A small amount of the fat that is rendered when preparing terrines of foie gras will give a wonderful flavor to a sauce. Because the flavor of foie gras is extremely full and intense, very little is needed to make a deeply flavored sauce. A small amount of Beurre Noisette (page 412) also can be whisked into butter sauces to give them a full, buttery taste, without using too much butter.

The idea of reducing the amount of fat added to the initial sabayon can be taken to its logical extreme. It is possible to make a sabayon and add no fat at all. Such a sauce will be extremely light and airy, containing only a small amount of fat from the egg yolks.

This technique can be used to thicken cooking liquids. A classic preparation, sole bonne femme, can be used to exemplify the technique. To prepare sole bonne femme, either a whole sole (with the dark skin removed) or sole fillets are quickly baked with some chopped shallots, sliced mushrooms, chopped parsley, white wine, and fish stock. As soon as the sole is done, it is transferred to a plate or platter and the cooking liquid is quickly reduced on top of the stove. Heavy cream is then added, the sauce is again reduced until it thickens, and butter is swirled in to finish the sauce. The sole is then coated with the sauce and quickly glazed under the broiler before serving (see page 300 for the full recipe.)

To lighten this recipe, the cooking liquid needs to be reduced only slightly, allowed to cool, and then combined with an egg yolk and beaten into a sabayon. Butter can then be added to the sabayon before glazing, but this is optional. The recipe for Braised Fillets of Sea Bass with Sabayon Sauce (page 387) also exemplifies this technique.

Alternative Flavors

Many chefs have neglected the wide range of flavoring possibilities that can be used for hot emulsified sauces. These sauces can be strongly flavored (such as a sauce Choron) or very delicately flavored (sauce mousseline). One flavor that has become justifiably popular with contemporary chefs is saffron. Curry also works extremely well, as do truffles.

Adding Vegetable Purées

Much of the butter or oil used to prepare these sauces can be replaced with various purées, which contribute flavor without making the sauce excessively rich. Mushroom purée, carrot purée, onion purée (*soubise*), garlic purée, freshly prepared parsley purée, asparagus purée, artichoke purée, watercress purée, puréed tomatoes, puréed tomatillos, and truffle purée can all be used to finish emulsified sauces (see Chapter 17, "Purées and Purée-Thickened Sauces," page 457).

Adding Whipped Cream, Sour Cream, Yogurt, or Fresh Cheese

For a lighter effect, hot emulsified egg yolk sauces can be finished with sour cream, yogurt, or fresh cheese in the same way that a classic sauce mousseline is finished with whipped cream. Use these ingredients sparingly, however. Yogurt and sour cream will give an unpleasant acidity to the sauce if too much is used. Fresh cheese will give delicacy and lightness to a sauce, but again, be careful not to use too much, or the sauce will have a fine graininess or a chalky texture.

Combining Emulsified Sauce with Stock or Other Sauces

One of the most fundamental changes in the aesthetics of sauce making has been an acceptance of thinner sauces. Not too many years ago, it would have been unacceptable to serve a sauce that would not cling to the surface of whatever food was being served. Nowadays, it is acceptable for a sauce to be served under or around a piece of meat, fish, or vegetable. Modern sauces often resemble an intensely flavored broth that captures or accents the flavor of the dish being served without masking either its appearance or flavor.

Hot emulsified sauces can be readily combined with other liquids—sauces, broths, and stocks. These thinned sauces will be lighter textured but have the intensity of flavor of the original thicker versions. It is often convenient, especially in a restaurant setting, to prepare a standard sauce and whisk it with another liquid—broth, stock, or another, lighter sauce—to order. Emulsified sauces, hot sauces, and mayonnaise have a tendency to break if too thin—the emulsion can exist only in a particular range of densities. For this reason, thinner emulsified sauces should be prepared to order.

Emulsified sauces can be combined with other sauces, providing an excellent method of making use of broken butter sauces, which would be difficult to reconstitute. Leftover beurre blanc can be melted and used instead of melted butter to finish a hot emulsified egg yolk sauce.

Special Flavors and Finishes for Fish Sauces

Hot emulsified sauces work well with fish and shellfish. Fish sauces are traditionally based on fish stock (usually reduced or thickened with roux) or the natural cooking liquid derived from cooking the fish itself (integral sauces). Fish stock, because it is usually made with fish bones, often has a fishy taste instead of the delicate sea-like flavor that gives fish sauces their finesse and vitality.

To impart a natural sea-like flavor to a hot emulsified sauce, several ingredients and techniques can be used. One technique, discussed opposite, is to prepare a sabayon with the cooking liquid from the fish. The sauce is then seasoned and served as a light, almost fat-free sabayon, or butter is added in the style of a more traditional sauce.

If it is impractical to prepare an integral hot emulsified sauce with the cooking liquid from the fish, the cooking liquid from clams, mussels, or oysters works extremely well—far better than ordinary fish stock does. If full-flavored, briny oysters are available (Belons from Maine are excellent), shuck one directly into the saucepan of the finished sauce. The oyster will give the sauce the delicate flavor of the sea. A small quantity (1 tablespoon/15 milliliters per 1 cup/250 milliliters of sauce) of sea urchin roe, first strained through a fine-mesh sieve, can be used to finish hot emulsified sauces for fish. Sea urchin roe must be impeccably fresh and should have a delicate, slightly sweet taste, vaguely reminiscent of milk chocolate. Always taste it before using it in a sauce. If scallops with roe are available, the roe can be puréed, strained through a fine-mesh sieve, and used to finish the sauce.

Hot emulsified sauces can also be finished with Crustacean Butter, page 329 (about 1 ounce/30 grams per cup/250 milliliters of sauce) or with lobster coral and tomalley that have first been strained through a fine-mesh sieve.

Sabayon Sauces

When a cooking liquid is allowed to cool, it can be combined with egg yolks and quickly whisked over heat to form a sabayon. In classic sauce making, the sauce would then be completed by adding fat, usually melted butter. It is possible to eliminate most or all of the fat. The resulting sauce is extremely light and airy. Although egg yolks are extremely rich, two or three egg yolks form enough sabayon sauce to serve six to eight diners.

BRAISED FILLETS OF SEA BASS WITH SABAYON SAUCE

YIELD: 6 SERVINGS

shallot, chopped	1	1
sea bass fillets, 6 to 8 ounces (150 to 225 grams) each	4	4
fish stock or court-bouillon	½ cup	125 milliliters
white wine	¼ cup	60 milliliters
egg yolks	2	2
whole butter (optional)	1 ounce	30 milliliters
or	or	or
extra-virgin olive oil (optional)	2 tablespoons	30 milliliters
or	or	or
crème fraîche (optional)	1 tablespoon	15 milliliters
salt and pepper	to taste	to taste

1. Preheat the oven to 500°F (260°C). Place the shallots in the bottom of a straight-sided sauté pan or oval baking dish. Use a container that fits the dimensions of the fish fillets as closely as possible or too much liquid will

be needed to moisten the fish. (The natural flavors of the fish will then be lost, and an inordinate amount of time will be needed to reduce the cooking liquid before it is combined with the egg yolks.) Place the fillets atop the shallots.

2. Add fish stock and the wine until the liquid comes halfway up the sides of the fish fillets. (If you do not use all the liquids called for in the ingredients, do not worry. It is best to use as little liquid as possible, to concentrate the flavors of the fish and the resulting sauce.)

3. Heat the fish on top of the stove until the liquid comes to a slow simmer. Cover the pan loosely with aluminum foil and place it in the oven.

4. While the fillets are still slightly underdone, after about 8 minutes of cooking per inch (2.5 cm) of thickness (they will continue cooking while the sauce is being prepared), remove them from the oven and transfer them to a plate. Cover them with aluminum foil to keep warm while preparing the sauce.

5. Strain the fish cooking liquid into a measuring cup. If more than ½ cup (125 milliliters) remains, reduce it on top of the stove to concentrate its flavors.

6. Transfer the fish cooking liquid to a mixing bowl, to cool it more rapidly. (If a large number of these sabayon sauces is being prepared during a restaurant service, it might even be convenient to keep a bowl of ice handy to speed up the cooling.) When the liquid is cool, combine it with the egg yolks in a sloping-sided saucepan.

7. Heat the mixture over high heat while quickly beating with a sauce whisk.

8. When the sabayon begins to stiffen and the bottom of the saucepan starts to be visible while whisking, remove the pan from the heat. Continue whisking for about 20 seconds more, to cool the sabayon slightly.

9. The sabayon can be served as is, or it can be finished with the butter, olive oil, or crème fraîche (see Note). Season with salt and pepper.

Note: Sabayon sauces contain such a high proportion of air that they do not pour easily—they are too light. It is often best to serve them on the plate with the fillets rather than at the table, as is traditional with classic emulsified sauces. One method that works well is to coat the tops of the fish fillets with the sabayon and then quickly slide the fillets under the broiler to brown them lightly.

IMPROVISING EMULSIFIED SAUCES

Improvisation requires an ability to imagine in gustatory rather than visual images—a kind of thinking with the mouth and stomach. The technique of recalling tastes, textures, and colors takes practice, but once mastered it allows the chef to review mentally a variety of flavor combinations, checking and discarding until some exciting juxtaposition begins to form. Because the art of cookery relies on an aesthetic invariably linked with appetite, this technique works best on an empty stomach. The stomach and salivary glands are quick to respond to mental taste images and, when it comes to cooking, are far more reliable than the intellect.

The modern urban chef is often overwhelmed by the variety of available ingredients and finds it difficult to cook in a cohesive way with a kind of natural culinary logic underlying his or her cuisine. Many a chef has made the mistake of inventing for invention's sake in this era when something seemingly new and outlandish is revered more than a well-prepared classic. The best way to keep this wayward tendency in check is to work within limits. Regional cooks have always had the natural advantage of working with a limited variety of ingredients, restricted by what nature provides.

One useful method for improvising a sauce is to consider whether the ingredients grow (or could grow) in the same region. Nature usually shows good taste, so that ingredients that grow in the same region are likely to work well together in the kitchen.

An example of this method of checking the regionality of a dish can be used when devising modifications to a classic sauce béarnaise. Perhaps the béarnaise is to be served with a grilled steak, and the more assertive fresh marjoram is used to replace the tarragon. Marjoram is a Mediterranean herb. In traditional Mediterranean cooking, butter is rarely used; rather, extra-virgin olive oil is the cooking fat most often used. So perhaps the butter in the "béarnaise" can be replaced with olive oil. Technically it would no longer be sauce béarnaise but rather a hot mayonnaise or a kind of sauce tyrolienne, but in the realm of improvisation, these designations become cloudy.

An improvised sauce will often start as a modification of a classic or traditional recipe. Sometimes the improvisation stems from a happy accident—a missing ingredient, an apprentice using the wrong herb, or just the sudden whim of adding something because it seems good.

A classic sauce can often be personalized by changing one or more of the ingredients. For example, try replacing the tomato purée in a sauce Choron with a purée of tomatillos.

When altering a classic sauce, be sure that the newly improvised sauce is appropriate. Do not try to make a sauce delicate and subtle if it is going to be served with a full-flavored piece of meat such as a steak grilled over vine cuttings or mesquite. On the other hand, a piece of poached fish should not be served with a sauce that has been too strongly flavored with herbs.

If a sauce is being invented from scratch, the chef should consider several key points:

With what is the sauce to be served? A sauce intended to accompany a leg of lamb grilled over vine cuttings and fresh herbs should obviously be more assertive than a sauce served with shoots of freshly picked wild asparagus. Here is where the chef needs to envision the flavors of a sauce, trying to determine whether they work with the food being served.

What is the setting? Taste and flavor are not independent of other experiences. Certain sauces are better served in a formal restaurant setting, where foods are carefully presented to the diners, than at outdoor barbecues. The reverse is also true: A delicate and subtle sabayon may be wasted on a socializing barbecue crowd, whose food needs to be more assertive for its flavor to be noticed. Conversely, a full-flavored, straightforward sauce may seem ordinary in a fancy restaurant where diners may be looking to be surprised.

Who are the diners? Some people are so intimidated by fats that a classic béarnaise will frighten them off. If this is so, a lightened version of an emulsified sauce may be appropriate.

Should an integral sauce be used? If the cooking method used provides flavor components, such as the cooking liquid from braised or poached fish or a pan to deglaze from sautéed steaks, then it might be valid to base the sauce on these components. Preparations that provide none of these components, such as boiled green vegetables and grilled meats or fish, obviously cannot be accompanied by integral sauces.

14

MAYONNAISE-BASED SAUCES

Mayonnaise is an emulsion of oil and water-based liquid. Because liquids such as lemon juice, vinegar, and wine do not mix readily with oil, a third component, egg yolks, is required to bind the two. The egg yolks are first seasoned with salt and pepper, and a small quantity of lemon juice or vinegar is added. Oil is then slowly stirred or beaten into the yolks until the mixture starts to thicken. At this point, the emulsion is established and the oil can be added more quickly. Many home cooks and beginning chefs associate mayonnaise with the commercial bottled variety. Bottled mayonnaise is made with whole eggs and a high proportion of oil, giving it little of the flavor of authentic freshly made mayonnaise. Fresh mayonnaise made with fresh egg yolks and good-quality oil is often a revelation.

Mayonnaise is a versatile sauce. Its flavor, texture, and color can all be adjusted according to traditional recipes (of which there are many) or the whim of the chef. Traditionally, mayonnaise has been used to accompany cold meats, fish, and vegetables and to bind composed salads, in which each of the components is cut into a predefined shape.

Many chefs now prepare mayonnaise with a lightly cooked egg yolk base called a sabayon, which not only produces a lighter sauce but kills bacteria such as salmonella that sometimes exist in eggs. When preparing mayonnaise, make sure the egg yolks are fresh. Always use a good-quality oil. Many commercially available vegetable oils have an unnatural taste or may even taste rancid (see "Oils," page 41). Safflower or canola oil is recommended in the recipes that follow. Carefully taste and smell any oil before using it in the mayonnaise.

PRECAUTIONS FOR PREPARING MAYONNAISE

1. All the ingredients for making mayonnaise should be at room temperature.
2. Never use aluminum bowls or saucepans to prepare mayonnaise, as they will turn it gray.
3. Add the oil very slowly, especially at the beginning.
4. Use a maximum of 1 quart (1 liter) safflower oil to 6 egg yolks. If too much oil is added, the mayonnaise will break.

REPAIRING BROKEN MAYONNAISE

If mayonnaise breaks at any point, it can be brought back together by beating the broken mixture bit by bit into a fresh egg yolk. As soon as this new mixture begins to thicken, the broken mayonnaise can be added more quickly. Mayonnaise frequently breaks when stored overnight in the refrigerator and should be reconstituted before being used.

STORING MAYONNAISE

Many cases of food poisoning have resulted from improperly handled and stored mayonnaise. When correctly stored, mayonnaise is less perishable than people usually assume. It most often becomes contaminated when used in salads or other prepared dishes that are left for long periods at room temperature. An additional danger is that contaminated mayonnaise may smell and taste perfectly normal. To keep mayonnaise fresh and safe, it should be kept cool and well covered in a plastic container with a tight-fitting lid. Never use aluminum containers to store mayonnaise—they will turn it gray. Mayonnaise should be stored for no more than 4 days in the refrigerator and never for more than 24 hours at room temperature. Make small batches so there is no temptation to store it for too long a period.

TRADITIONAL MAYONNAISE

This mayonnaise uses a high proportion of oil to egg yolks, making it quite thick.

YIELD: 1 QUART (1 LITER)

egg yolks	6	6
mustard (optional)	2 tablespoons	30 milliliters
fine salt	1 to 2 teaspoons	5 to 10 milliliters
finely ground white pepper	1 pinch	1 pinch
wine vinegar or lemon juice	1 to 2 tablespoons	15 to 30 milliliters
safflower oil	3 cups	750 milliliters

1. Combine the egg yolks, mustard, if using, salt, pepper, and half of the wine vinegar. Lightly stir or whisk until the mixture is smooth. If using an electric mixer, use the whisk attachment on medium speed.
2. Slowly beat the oil into the egg yolk mixture. Pour in about a tablespoon (15 milliliters) at a time while beating, and wait for the oil to combine with the yolks before adding more. (This is much easier to accomplish when using an electric mixer.) If preparing the mayonnaise by hand, it is best to pour several tablespoons of oil down one side of the bowl and whisk the yolks in such a way as to avoid stirring more than a tablespoon of oil into the mixture at once.
3. When the mixture begins to thicken, the emulsion has been established, meaning the mixture is now relatively stable. The oil can now be added in a steady stream.
4. As more oil is added, the mayonnaise will become so thick that it will be difficult to work. Add the remaining wine vinegar. If the mayonnaise is still too thick, other liquids can be added. (The choice of liquid depends on the eventual use of the mayonnaise. If the mayonnaise is being used as a base for a variety of uses, then a neutral-tasting liquid, such as heavy cream, court-bouillon, stock, or even water can be added.) Continue beating and adding oil until all the oil has been incorporated. Adjust the seasonings.

SABAYON-STYLE MAYONNAISE

A light basic mayonnaise can be prepared by first beating the egg yolks with a small amount of liquid over a carefully controlled heat source. The technique is the same as that used for preparing hot emulsified sauces such as béarnaise and hollandaise. This method causes the egg yolks, water, and air to emulsify (in classic sauce making, this preliminary emulsion is called a sabayon), so that when oil is added to the mixture the resulting sauce has a light, airy consistency. Conveniently, heating the egg yolks also kills any salmonella bacteria that may be in them.

A sabayon-based mayonnaise should contain far less oil than traditional mayonnaise. If too much oil is added, the sauce will be heavy and the air that has been beaten into the sabayon will be lost. Although a sabayon-based mayonnaise is usually prepared by first combining water with the egg yolks, it is also possible to use other flavorful liquids appropriate to the sauce's final flavor. Cooking liquids from fish or meat or various stocks can all be used. Acidic ingredients, such as vinegar or lemon juice, however, should not be added at the beginning. They cause the egg yolks to thicken prematurely and result in a heavier sauce; they should be added at the end. Judging the amount of liquid to use (anywhere from 1 to 1½ tablespoons/15 to 25 milliliters per egg yolk) requires experience. Egg yolks vary in size, regardless of the designated size of the egg, and different yolk sizes require different amounts of water to produce the correct frothiness of a sabayon. Once the sabayon-based mayonnaise is prepared, it can be flavored in the same way as a traditional mayonnaise. (Recipes and techniques for hot sabayon sauces are given in Chapter 13, "Hot Emulsified Egg Yolk Sauces," page 375.)

Because sabayon-based mayonnaise is relatively unstable, it should not be kept for more than a few hours or it will lose its airiness and light texture. Consequently, it is best to prepare only a small amount at a time.

YIELD: 2 CUPS (500 MILLILITERS)

egg yolks	6	6
cold liquid	6 to 9 tablespoons	90 to 135 milliliters
safflower oil	1 cup	250 milliliters
lemon juice or wine vinegar	to taste	to taste
salt and pepper	to taste	to taste

1. Combine the egg yolks with the cold liquid in a 2-quart (2 liter) sloping-sided saucepan or a stainless-steel mixing bowl. (Do not use a regular straight-sided saucepan or the egg yolks will coagulate where they cannot be reached with a whisk.) If using a mixing bowl, have a towel handy to protect your hand, as the bowl gets hot when held over the heat.

2. Whisk the yolks and liquid together *off* the heat for 30 seconds to 1 minute, until the mixture becomes frothy.

3. Heat the mixture over medium heat, beating constantly with a whisk. (Some chefs use a pot of simmering water as a bain-marie, but it is a good habit to become accustomed to using direct heat. As long as the yolks are beaten continuously and are not allowed to overheat, there is little risk of them curdling.) Beat the mixture until it froths and stiffens slightly. The bottom of the saucepan or mixing bowl will start to show through while you are whisking.

4. Immediately remove the sabayon from the heat. Continue whisking off the heat for about 20 seconds more, to cool the mixture slightly and keep it from curdling.

5. Add the oil in a steady stream, beating constantly. (It is not necessary to add the oil bit by bit as when preparing traditional mayonnaise, because the egg yolks have already formed an emulsion during the preparation of the sabayon. In fact, it is best to whisk the sauce as little as possible once the sabayon has been prepared. Overworking will drive out the air and result in a heavier sauce.)

6. Transfer the mixture to a clean container and allow it to cool. Flavorful ingredients (such as lemon juice or wine vinegar) and seasonings can now be added as desired.

CLASSIC MAYONNAISE-BASED SAUCES

Basic unflavored mayonnaise is useful because of its versatility, but other ingredients are usually added to flavor it and make it useful for a particular preparation. Many different flavorings can be incorporated into the mayonnaise base as need and inspiration suggest. Some flavored mayonnaises, however, have become standards, and their recipes follow. Most have French names but can also be named for the principal flavoring.

Sauce Verte (Green Mayonnaise)

This mayonnaise tastes the same as basic unflavored mayonnaise—only the color is different. Stir ½ teaspoon (3 milliliters) of chlorophyll into 1 cup (250 milliliters) of mayonnaise (to extract chlorophyll from spinach leaves, see page 416). It may be necessary to add more chlorophyll, but it is best to start with a small amount; surprisingly little is needed.

Mayonnaise can also be colored directly with the juice from spinach, watercress, or parsley. Blanch the greens in a large pot of rapidly boiling salted water. Quickly rinse the greens in cold water, pat dry, and finely grind in a blender or food processor. Place the puréed greens in the middle of a kitchen towel and tightly wring the juice out into a bowl. This juice can then be used for coloring the mayonnaise. The purée can also be combined directly with the mayonnaise and the sauce strained.

Sauce Aïoli (Garlic Mayonnaise)

This mayonnaise is a specialty of Provence, where it accompanies platters of hot vegetables, poached salt cod, and octopus daube. To prepare 1 cup (250 milliliters) of aïoli, peel 3 medium-size cloves of garlic and work them into a smooth paste with a pinch of coarse salt with a mortar and pestle. If a mortar and pestle are not available, finely chop the garlic and then crush it on a cutting board with the side of a chef's knife. Combine the garlic paste with 2 egg yolks and gradually work 1 cup (250 milliliters) of extra-virgin olive oil into the mixture. If using a mortar and pestle, do this directly in the mortar. Add 1 tablespoon (15 milliliters) or more of lemon juice or water to the mayonnaise after adding half the oil, to prevent the mayonnaise from becoming too thick.

Although garlic mayonnaise is traditionally prepared directly in a mortar while the oil is gently worked in with the pestle, modern recipes frequently suggest using a blender, electric mixer, or hand whisk. Olive oil is a surprisingly fragile substance and will often turn bitter if beaten or overworked. When using extra-virgin olive oil, work it into the yolks with a wooden spoon if a mortar and pestle are not available.

Saffron-Flavored Aïoli

Aïoli can be flavored with saffron by adding a pinch of saffron threads or powder to the garlic–egg yolk mixture before adding the oil. When using saffron threads, soak them for 30 minutes in a tablespoon (15 milliliters) of warm water and then add both water and threads to the egg yolks. Do not add the saffron to the mayonnaise after the oil has been added, as it will take too long for the color and flavor of the saffron to dissolve into the mayonnaise.

Sauce Andalouse
(Tomato and Sweet Red Pepper Mayonnaise)

This lively flavored mayonnaise is prepared by adding reduced tomato purée and peeled and diced sweet red peppers to basic mayonnaise. It is, of course, possible to prepare the sauce with canned pimentos and tomato paste, but much of the spirit and vitality of the sauce is then lost. Use 1½ sweet red peppers (4 ounces/125 grams, peeled and chopped) and ¼ cup (60 milliliters) of reduced tomato purée for each cup (250 milliliters) of mayonnaise base. This sauce also benefits from the addition of an extra tablespoon or two (15 to 30 milliliters) of good wine vinegar and a good pinch of cayenne pepper or hot pepper sauce.

To peel peppers, the skin must first be burned off. To do this, grill the peppers over a wood fire. If this is impractical, the peppers can be placed directly over the flame of a gas stove or under the broiler. The skin must be completely charred before it can be removed. After the peppers have cooled, simply pull off the charred skin. Sections of peel that still adhere can be removed by scraping the pepper with the blade of a paring knife. Carefully cut the pepper in half from top to bottom and remove and discard the inner pulp and seeds. Lay each half on a cutting board, and dice.

Sauce Chantilly (Mayonnaise with Whipped Cream)

Mayonnaise can be lightened by folding it at the last minute with whipped cream. Although traditional recipes suggest folding the mayonnaise with only one-fourth its volume of whipped cream, it is possible to use more—up to one part cream (before whipping) to two parts mayonnaise. Mayonnaise lightened with whipped cream has a delicate, melting texture, making it an excellent accompaniment to cold or warm vegetables and fish. When folding mayonnaise with whipped cream, it is best to lighten the mayonnaise by thoroughly stirring a third of the whipped cream into the mayonnaise before folding it with the last two-thirds. The whipped cream, medium stiff, should be seasoned with salt and white pepper before being combined with the mayonnaise.

Whipped cream should never be combined with mayonnaise until the last minute, as it tends to break down and lose its airiness after the two are combined.

Mustard-Flavored Mayonnaise

Mustard is an excellent and surprisingly subtle flavoring for mayonnaise. When used in small amounts, it brightens the flavor of the mayonnaise while remaining in the background. Any variety of mustard can be used. Maille brand Dijon mustard, homemade, and Meaux-style whole-grain mustard all provide different nuances. Green mustard can also be used for color and flavor. Flavored mustards can also be used in mayonnaise, but a better flavor is often obtained by adding the fresh flavor component directly to the mayonnaise instead of relying on the mustard to provide it. For example, tarragon-flavored mustard will not provide as clear and bright a flavor as mayonnaise flavored with plain mustard and fresh tarragon. The total amount of mustard to use—including any that was added when preparing the mayonnaise base—depends on the strength of the mustard and the whim of the chef, but 4 teaspoons (20 milliliters) per cup (250 milliliters) of mayonnaise is a good place to start.

Sauce Rémoulade (Caper and Herb Mayonnaise)

This sauce can accompany cold meats, fish, and vegetables. Although sauce rémoulade can be combined with julienned celeriac with delicious results, a
traditional celeriac rémoulade is prepared with mayonnaise well flavored with
mustard rather than with sauce rémoulade. To prepare sauce rémoulade, flavor
1 cup (250 milliliters) of basic mayonnaise with 2 tablespoons (30 milliliters) of
mustard and ¼ cup (60 milliliters) of chopped capers. Add 1 teaspoon (5 milliliters) of anchovy paste and 2 tablespoons (30 milliliters) of a mixture of finely
chopped parsley, chervil, and tarragon. If fresh chervil and tarragon are not
available, it is better to leave them out rather than use dried. Tarragon preserved in vinegar, however, makes an acceptable substitute for fresh.

Sauce Suédoise (Apple-Horseradish Mayonnaise)

Although this may sound like a bizarre juxtaposition, the combination of apple
purée and mayonnaise makes an excellent sauce for cold meats, especially pork
and game. It is best to use sour baking apples (Reinettes de Canada are among
the best), but if they cannot be found, Granny Smiths will produce a very satisfactory sauce. Prepare the apple purée by first peeling, coring, and slicing the
apples. Coat the sliced apples with a few drops of lemon juice to prevent them
from turning brown, as well as to add a note of acidity to the finished sauce.
(Never soak sliced apples in water, or their natural sugars and flavor will leach
out.) Cook the apples in a covered saucepan with 1 tablespoon (15 milliliters)
of white wine. This may seem like a small amount of liquid, but remember that
the apples themselves will release liquid as soon as they are heated by the steaming wine. As soon as the apples are soft, usually after about 10 minutes, purée
them in a food processor, food mill, or drum sieve. Return the purée to the
saucepan and reduce it until it is stiff and no liquid remains. Be careful to stir
the mixture constantly with a wooden spoon and not allow it to burn.

The proportion of apple purée to mayonnaise will vary depending on the
apples' flavor; anywhere from one part apple purée and three parts basic mayonnaise to equal parts of each will work. One pound (450 grams)—about 2
large apples—provides approximately 1 cup (250 milliliters) of purée. Flavor
the apple mayonnaise with grated horseradish, about 1 tablespoon (15 milliliters) per cup (250 milliliters).

Mayonnaise Made with Hard-Boiled Egg Yolks

Traditionally, mayonnaise made with hard-boiled yolks is prepared by working oil
into the hard-boiled egg yolks. Creating an emulsion with cooked yolks is difficult
and unreliable; it is better to cheat a little and begin with a combination of raw and
cooked yolks—or for that matter, with raw egg yolks alone. Sauces prepared

using all raw egg yolks will differ only slightly from the cooked-yolk variety. In any case, cooked yolks will absorb not even half as much oil as raw yolks, so adjust proportions accordingly. Be sure to sieve the cooked egg yolks to eliminate lumps.

Sauce Gribiche

Although this sauce is traditionally served with cold fish, its tangy acidity works well with deep-fried foods (even french fries). Both the whites and yolks of hard-boiled eggs are used. Prepare a mayonnaise base with 3 sieved hard-boiled egg yolks, 1 raw egg yolk, 1 tablespoon (15 milliliters) of mustard, 1 tablespoon (15 milliliters) of wine vinegar, 1 teaspoon (5 milliliters) of fine salt, pepper to taste, and 1 cup (250 milliliters) of safflower oil. Make sure the hard-boiled yolks are worked with the raw yolk and mustard to a smooth paste before adding the oil. Add 2 tablespoons (30 milliliters) of chopped capers, 2 tablespoons (30 milliliters) of chopped sour gherkins (cornichons), and 2 tablespoons (30 milliliters) of a mixture of chopped fresh parsley, chervil, and tarragon. (If all three are not available fresh, do not substitute dried herbs; just add a little more of the other two.) Finish the sauce with a julienne of 3 cooked egg whites.

Sauce Tartare (Tartar Sauce)

Traditional recipes for sauce tartare vary: Some call for a mayonnaise made with hard-boiled egg yolks, whereas others use all raw yolks. Flavorings for tartar sauce also differ: Older recipes call for puréed scallions or chives (a food processor cannot be used for this purée—you need a mortar and pestle), whereas others prepare tartar sauce with the same ingredients as Sauce Rémoulade (opposite) but replace the anchovy paste with a teaspoon or two (5 to 10 milliliters) of mustard. Although not classic, probably the easiest and most satisfying method is to flavor 1 cup (250 milliliters) of mayonnaise base with 2 finely chopped shallots and then finish the sauce with a heaping tablespoon (20 milliliters) of finely chopped chives and 2 teaspoons (10 milliliters) of mustard.

CONTEMPORARY MAYONNAISE VARIATIONS

Contemporary chefs have explored new ingredients and methods to devise new, often lighter variations of traditional mayonnaise. Several techniques that are not used in traditional mayonnaise recipes have worked themselves into the professional kitchen.

Using Various Oils

Basic mayonnaise can be prepared or flavored with a wide variety of oils, including extra-virgin olive oil, nut oils such as walnut or hazelnut, sesame oil, and relatively flavorless oils such as grapeseed oil, as well as certain brands of vegetable oil and peanut oil.

Because nut oils and sesame oil are strongly flavored and expensive, it is usually best to prepare a base mayonnaise with three parts inert oil (grapeseed, safflower, or canola) and then finish the mayonnaise with one part of the more strongly flavored oil.

A Note on Using Extra-Virgin Olive Oil

Extra-virgin olive oil imparts an unmistakable full flavor to mayonnaise, which lovers of olive oil find hard to resist. Some chefs find the flavor overbearing and prefer to use half olive oil and half safflower oil. Mayonnaise containing extra-virgin olive oil should be gently worked by hand, using a wooden spoon or a mortar and pestle, once the olive oil has been added. Strange as it may seem, when olive oil is beaten with a whisk or in a machine, it loses its fruitiness and turns bitter. Some chefs hesitate to use Italian olive oils for making mayonnaise because of their deep green color, which looks odd when combined with the yolks.

Hazelnut Mayonnaise

This sauce works extremely well when lightly brushed on grilled or quick-broiled fish (full-flavored fish, such as salmon, are the best). Prepare a mayonnaise using three parts safflower oil and one part hazelnut oil. Stir mustard into the sauce (Dijon or Meaux-style work equally well)—about 2 tablespoons (30 milliliters) per cup (250 milliliters) of mayonnaise. Thin the sauce with a little fish stock or court-bouillon and a good-quality wine vinegar; the sauce should be quite acidic, to give it lightness and to bring out the flavor of the fish. Make sure the sauce is well seasoned with salt and white pepper. This sauce can be colored green by adding chlorophyll or by using a commercially available green mustard (the Maille brand of fines herbes also works well).

SALMON WITH HAZELNUT MAYONNAISE

The trick to this dish is to broil the salmon, for just seconds, at the last minute and brush with hazelnut mayonnaise. To prepare this dish, use heatproof plates that you can slide under the broiler and preheat in the oven. While this dish calls for only 1½ pounds (675 grams) of salmon, it's easier to work if you have a whole salmon fillet. Keep in mind that the mayonnaise is the only seasoning so it should be well seasoned and quite acidic to bring out the flavor of the fish and counteract its richness.

YIELD: 6 FIRST-COURSE OR 4 MAIN-COURSE SERVINGS

scaled, skin-on salmon fillet	1½ pounds	675 grams
hazelnut mayonnaise (above)	¾ cup	185 milliliters

1. Cut the salmon in the same way as smoked salmon. Preheat one oven to 200°F (95°C). Preheat the broiler in another oven. If you have only one oven, heat the plates in the oven with the broiler.

2. Place a sheet of waxed paper on one of the plates you'll be using and cover over the plate with thin sheets of salmon, skin side up. Repeat with the remaining plates so you have four or six sheets of waxed paper with circular patches of salmon on them.

3. Preheat the plates in a 200°F (95°C) oven.

4. Immediately before serving, take out two of the plates, turn the salmon out onto the plates, and peel away the waxed paper. Slide under the broiler and continually rotate the plate. Broil for about 30 seconds, just until the salmon loses its sheen. Repeat with the other plates.

5. Brush with the hazelnut mayonnaise and serve.

Alternative Flavors

Because the flavor and consistency of mayonnaise are so malleable, mayonnaise makes the perfect medium for a variety of both subtle and assertive flavorings and garnitures. With the increased popularity of ethnic cuisines, American diners have grown accustomed to direct and forthright flavors that would have seemed overwhelming even as recently as twenty years ago. Many of these flavors can be used for boldly flavored and appealing mayonnaise-based sauces.

Cilantro and Hot Pepper Mayonnaise

This mayonnaise is excellent with grilled or deep-fried fish or vegetables. Combine 1 cup (250 milliliters) of mayonnaise with 1 bunch of finely chopped cilantro, ¼ cup (60 milliliters) of cooked Tomato Coulis (page 461), 1 clove of garlic that has been crushed in a mortar or with the side of a knife on a cutting board, and 2 seeded and finely chopped jalapeños. Finish with 1 to 2 tablespoons (15 to 30 milliliters) of wine vinegar, to taste. Season with salt. Yield: 1½ cups (375 milliliters).

Morel Mayonnaise

This mayonnaise works better with dried morels (which have an intense smoky flavor) than with fresh. It is excellent with grilled vegetables and fish. Prepare ½ ounce (15 grams) of dried morels by rinsing them quickly in cold running water and then soaking them in a bowl with ½ cup (125 milliliters) of Madeira. When the morels are soft, put them in a covered saucepan with the Madeira (be careful to leave any grit in the bottom of the bowl) and cook them for 5 minutes to soften them more and eliminate the alcohol. Remove the morels and cook down the Madeira until only 1 tablespoon (15 milliliters) remains. Chop the cooked morels and add them and the reduced Madeira to 1 cup (250 milliliters) of mayonnaise. Add 1 to 2 tablespoons (15 to 30 milliliters) of wine vinegar, to taste. Season with salt and pepper. Yield: 1 cup (250 milliliters).

Thinning Mayonnaise with Liquids

The thick texture of traditional mayonnaise limits its use as a sauce and is sometimes unappealing. Fortunately, traditional mayonnaise can be thinned to virtually any consistency. Thinning mayonnaise with either hot or cold liquids is a useful sauce-making technique. When mayonnaise is thinned and correctly flavored, it becomes a light, digestible sauce that can be varied almost endlessly.

Hot Liquids

An example of combining hot liquids with mayonnaise is using mayonnaise-based sauces for fish. Cooking liquids from fish soups and stews can be lightly thickened with mayonnaise. When poaching or braising fish, place ¼ cup (60 milliliters) of flavored mayonnaise in the bottom of a saucepan or a stainless-steel mixing bowl. Slowly pour 1 cup (250 milliliters) of the hot poaching or braising liquid over the mayonnaise, whisking rapidly. Whisk the mixture continuously while pouring in the hot liquid; otherwise, the mayonnaise may break. When all the hot liquid has been added, place the bowl or saucepan over low heat or a bain-marie and continue whisking until the mixture begins to thicken. Do not overheat the mixture (by no means should it boil). The sauce, which has the consistency of heavy cream, can then be served over or under the fish. This technique works especially well with full-flavored mayonnaises such as saffron, garlic (aïoli), or curry (see also Bourride, page 294).

The ratio of mayonnaise to cooking liquid can, of course, be varied, depending on the desired final consistency of the sauce. The foregoing method uses mayonnaise to lightly thicken the cooking liquid from fish. It is also possible to prepare a light-style mayonnaise by replacing the water in a sabayon mayonnaise with a flavorful liquid, such as the cooking liquid from fish, crustaceans, or meat.

Cold Liquids

Mayonnaise can be thinned with a wide variety of flavorful cold liquids, such as mushroom cooking liquid, cold stocks (provided they are not too gelatinous), court-bouillon, truffle juice, and vinegar (sherry and balsamic are especially good). Wine can be used to thin and flavor mayonnaise, provided the alcohol is cooked off first. Fortified wines, such as Madeira and sherry, work the best. Cognac and anise-flavored spirits such as Pernod or Ricard can provide flavor, but they should be used sparingly.

Lightening Mayonnaise with Beaten Egg Whites

If mayonnaise is being served on the side as an accompaniment to cold meats, fish, or vegetables, it can be lightened by folding it with beaten egg whites. The beating of the egg whites and the final folding with the mayonnaise should be done as near to the last minute as possible. One egg white can be used to lighten approximately ½ cup (125 milliliters) of mayonnaise. The resulting sauce is extremely light and works well with delicate flavorings. One excellent flavoring is ½ teaspoon (3 milliliters) of grated orange zest and 1 tablespoon (15 milliliters) of orange juice per cup (250 milliliters) of lightened mayonnaise. The lightened, orange-flavored mayonnaise is excellent with cold asparagus.

Mayonnaise that has been lightened with beaten egg whites should not be used to prepare hot mayonnaise-finished sauces, because the egg whites will coagulate when they come in contact with hot liquid.

Combining Mayonnaise with Vegetable Purées

The fat content and richness of mayonnaise can be reduced by combining it with one or more vegetable purées (see Chapter 17, "Purées and Purée-Thickened Sauces," page 457). The ratio of purée to mayonnaise depends on the purée, the final use of the sauce, and the desired consistency, but using equal parts of each is a good place to start. Make sure that the purée is perfectly smooth and not too liquid. It is better to produce a sauce that is too thick than one that is too thin, as a thick sauce can easily be thinned. If using a green-vegetable purée, do not add vinegar to the sauce until the last minute or it will turn the sauce gray. One of the oldest combinations of mayonnaise and a vegetable purée is aïoli made with a cooked potato, a method popular in Provence.

Extending Mayonnaise with Yogurt and Fresh Cheese

Freshly made cheese or yogurt can be added to mayonnaise to give it a lighter texture and make it less caloric. The ratio of yogurt or cheese to mayonnaise should be adjusted according to taste, but one part yogurt to four parts mayonnaise is usually about right. Yogurt gives the mayonnaise a pleasant tang, which makes it an excellent medium for spicy flavorings and curries. Plain regular or Middle Eastern leben yogurt can be used.

Curry Yogurt Mayonnaise

Gently cook 2 tablespoons (30 milliliters) of good-quality curry powder with 2 tablespoons (30 milliliters) of safflower oil for 30 seconds to 1 minute. Combine the curry mixture with 1 cup (250 milliliters) of mayonnaise. Stir in ¼ cup (60 milliliters) of yogurt.

Eggless "Mayonnaise"

Mayonnaise-like sauces can be made without eggs, using breadcrumbs, vegetable purées, and fresh cheese as a medium for olive oil and flavorings (see the recipes for Sauce Rouille, page 135, and Skorthaliá, page 470). Aïoli is sometimes made using a boiled potato as the base instead of egg yolks. Several contemporary food writers have used fresh cheese (*fromage blanc*) or cream cheese for so-called eggless mayonnaises.

MAYONNAISE-BASED SHELLFISH SAUCES

Mayonnaise, long used as an accompaniment to shellfish, can be enhanced with braising liquids, stocks, tomalley, and coral. Cooking liquids from shellfish can be used to flavor mayonnaise by one of two methods. The first is to simply whisk the cooking liquid into a mayonnaise made in advance. The second is to prepare a sabayon-style mayonnaise by whisking the shellfish cooking liquid in with the egg yolks over heat before adding any oil.

Both traditional and sabayon mayonnaise bases can be flavored with cooking liquid from bivalves. The cooking liquid that results from steaming mussels or clams in a small amount of wine or other liquid, or from poaching or steaming scallops, can be reduced and used to flavor a plain or flavored mayonnaise base. Be sure to strain the cooking liquid from clams and mussels through a cloth or fine-mesh sieve to eliminate sand. Also, remember that cooking liquid from clams and mussels is extremely salty, so do not add salt to the mayonnaise at the beginning, and keep tasting while adding the cooking liquid, to regulate the saltiness.

Mayonnaise made with shellfish cooking liquid can be served either hot or cold. When preparing hot mayonnaise, remember to whisk the cooking liquid into the mayonnaise, rather than the other way around. This sauce can be used as a base for light fish and shellfish stews or simply as a sauce for fish. Various mayonnaises have long been used in elaborately presented cold lobster dishes. Unfortunately, the mayonnaise used is often thick and carelessly flavored, so it does little more than mask both the appearance and taste of the lobster and add unwanted richness and calories.

It is possible to prepare delicately textured, full-flavored mayonnaise from crustaceans. One method of making these sauces is to prepare a sabayon-based mayonnaise using the cooking liquid from the crustaceans. This sauce can then be further flavored with herbs, Cognac, Pernod, crustacean oil, and sea urchin roe, as in the recipe for Sabayon-Based Lobster Mayonnaise (opposite).

Crustacean-flavored mayonnaise can be finished with Crustacean Oil (page 330), which is prepared in the same way as crustacean butter, with olive oil replacing the butter. Crustacean oil can be used in cold sauces where crustacean butter would congeal.

Sea urchin roe that has first been forced through a fine-mesh sieve gives a delicate, sea-like sweetness to seafood sauces. Be sure that the sea urchins are impeccably fresh. Some sea urchin roe has an aggressive taste of iodine, so be sure to taste it before adding it to a sauce.

SABAYON-BASED LOBSTER MAYONNAISE

YIELD: 2 CUPS (500 MILLILITERS)

lobster cooking liquid	1 cup	250 milliliters
egg yolks	6	6
safflower oil	½ cup	125 milliliters
extra-virgin olive oil	6 tablespoons	90 milliliters
cooked tomato coulis (page 461)	½ cup	125 milliliters
crustacean oil (page 330; optional)	2 tablespoons	30 milliliters
wine vinegar	to taste	to taste
salt and pepper	to taste	to taste

1. Reduce the lobster cooking liquid to ½ cup (125 milliliters). Let it cool.
2. Combine the concentrated lobster cooking liquid with the egg yolks in a 2-quart (2 liter) saucepan with sloping sides. Whisk off the heat until frothy.
3. Beat the mixture over medium heat until it froths and stiffens slightly. Immediately remove from the heat and continue whisking for about 20 seconds, to cool it slightly.
4. Whisk in the safflower and olive oils, the tomato coulis, and the crustacean oil, if using.
5. Add vinegar to taste. Season to taste with salt and pepper.

Lobster Coral Mayonnaise

A sublimely flavored mayonnaise can be prepared by simply whisking strained raw lobster coral and tomalley into a traditional or sabayon-based mayonnaise. The color will be a somewhat odd gray green, but the sauce will be complex, with an intense lobster taste. If you cannot bear the color, the coral can be whisked with an egg yolk over a low heat until it turns orange and then folded into the mayonnaise base. The color will now be appetizing, but the sauce will not have the complexity or finesse of a sauce made from the raw coral. Raw lobster coral should never be kept for more than a few hours either before or after it has been combined with mayonnaise, as it is extremely perishable.

MAYONNAISE-BASED MEAT SAUCES

Highly flavored mayonnaise is wonderful with grilled and sautéed meats. An assortment of flavored mayonnaises can even be served in lieu of the more typical American condiments, mustard and ketchup. A more elaborate approach is to prepare one or more hot mayonnaises, which can be made by deglazing the sauté pan with wine, stock, or even water and whisking the hot deglazing liquid into an appropriate flavored mayonnaise. The mayonnaise should then be whisked over medium heat until it begins to thicken (see "Thinning Mayonnaise with Liquids," page 402).

IMPROVISING MAYONNAISE-BASED SAUCES

A walk-in refrigerator containing fruits and vegetables, leftover sauces, varieties of fish and shellfish, and perhaps an array of well-made stocks can be a powerful inspiration to a chef looking to devise a new and interesting mayonnaise-based sauce. Often a particular ingredient will stand out and suggest itself as the focal point of the sauce. Perhaps there are some wild mushrooms, some smoked fish, or too many sweet peppers—any of which can be used to make an original sauce. Once the central flavor of the sauce has been decided, peripheral ingredients and components can be added to the sauce to shape its final flavor, texture, and color.

Traditional recipes are also a valuable source of ideas. One method for inventing sauces is to imagine a traditional dish (one you do not like will often work the best) and think about what can be done to improve it. A Waldorf salad is an American innovation that traditionally consists of diced apples, celery, and walnuts bound together with mayonnaise. The principle of binding cubes of fruit and vegetables with mayonnaise has been used for centuries but is less popular than it used to be because people find that the mayonnaise is a needless addition of fat and calories. The mayonnaise contributes little to the final flavor of the dish and in fact does more to obscure the clean flavor and crisp texture of the salad's components than to lend them finesse or excitement. The chef must decide whether mayonnaise is a worthwhile addition to the dish as a whole—a vinaigrette may be a better choice. Sometimes the added richness and calories of mayonnaise are justified if the mayonnaise contributes more flavor—for example, if it is flavored with herbs, curry, truffles, or wild mushrooms. Perhaps the mayonnaise can be flavored with walnut or hazelnut oil to accentuate the walnuts, or maybe a teaspoon (5 milliliters) of Calvados or reduced cider can be added to underline the character of the apples. The chef may even decide to change the salad's ingredients entirely and retain only the principle of combining diced fruits and vegetables with mayonnaise. Another possibility is to convert the Waldorf salad into a sauce by chopping the nuts, apples, and celery very finely and combining them with a mayonnaise that has been thinned with a little cider or cream. The sauce can then be used for cold fish or meats.

Once the basic flavor of the sauce has been determined, the chef should decide its use and its final texture and color. Are lightness and delicacy important? Will the diners be calorie conscious, or are they more interested in robust, traditional fare? In some cases a traditional mayonnaise with classic flavoring may be more appropriate than a modern improvised version, no matter how delicious. The chef should decide early on whether the sauce will be constructed from a traditional mayonnaise base or a sabayon-based mayonnaise. The type of oil must be determined before either of these bases can be prepared. If the flavor of the oil is not needed to contribute to the final flavor of the mayonnaise, an inert-tasting oil, such as safflower oil, French peanut oil (*huile d'arachide*), or grapeseed oil should be used for the base. If the oil will give character to the sauce, then the chef must determine how assertive the final flavor should be and what proportion of flavorful oil to use.

Once the base mayonnaise has been prepared, the chef must decide whether the sauce should be lightened, perhaps with vegetable purées, whipped cream, beaten egg whites, fresh cheese, or yogurt. Should the finished sauce be light and frothy? Thin, with a soup-like consistency? Stiff, in the traditional style? A colored mayonnaise is often more appealing than the pale yellow of traditional plain mayonnaise. Chlorophyll, green mustard, chopped tomatoes, reduced tomato purée, tomato paste, saffron, curry, and finely chopped truffles can all be used to provide color (provided, of course, that the flavor is appropriate). Avoid preparing sauces with too deep or intense a color, as they may look artificial and unappetizing.

When all the major components have been integrated into the sauce, its flavor and texture should be fine-tuned. It may need only something obvious, such as salt or pepper (always use freshly ground white pepper). If you are uncertain about adding a particular ingredient, work with only a small amount of the mayonnaise until you have a sense of how the ingredient will behave and work in the finished sauce. Good-quality vinegar and mustard will almost invariably enliven the flavor of mayonnaise. If the mayonnaise tastes flat, try adding these ingredients first. They will often bring out the flavor of other ingredients in the sauce. Finely chopped fresh herbs add subtlety and an ineffable complexity to a finished sauce. They will often make the difference between a very good sauce and a great sauce. Mushroom cooking liquid, truffle cooking liquid, or good-quality truffle juice will usually give a seemingly complete sauce a whole new dimension. As extravagant as it may sound, good truffle juice will go a long way in sauce making, especially in cold sauces, in which none of the flavor is lost in cooking.

While the final flavor of the sauce is taking shape, pay close attention to its color and texture. Do not become so carried away by adding liquid flavorings that you find the sauce has suddenly become too thin—this can be a difficult problem to fix. If adding stock or mushroom cooking liquid, keep an eye on the sauce's color. As delicious as mushroom cooking liquid is, it can give an unsightly gray cast to the finished sauce.

If you have decided to lighten the sauce, remember that some lightening agents, such as beaten egg whites or whipped cream, should be added to the sauce only just before serving.

TIPS FOR THE RESTAURANT CHEF

Because mayonnaise is a cold sauce, it is easy to work with in a restaurant setting. It need not be kept on the stove or in a steam table during a restaurant service, and it can usually be prepared well in advance. It will sometimes break when held overnight in the refrigerator, but it can be easily reconstructed by gently working it into an egg yolk or a tablespoon or two (15 to 30 milliliters) of heavy cream.

In restaurants where a large number of mayonnaise-based sauces are being prepared, it is often convenient to prepare a relatively large quantity of mayonnaise base and then flavor it as needed to construct derivative sauces.

Because mayonnaise can be reconstituted almost indefinitely, kitchen personnel are often tempted to keep it on hand for too long. Mayonnaise, especially when left unrefrigerated, can become contaminated with staphylococci and other bacteria—particularly treacherous because they do not produce an off-odor or taste in the mayonnaise. Mayonnaise should never be kept on hand for more than three days.

Light-style mayonnaises based on sabayon or that contain beaten egg whites or whipped cream must be finished just before serving. When these mayonnaises are being used, the lightening component should be prepared and folded with the base almost to order. Sabayon-based mayonnaise should be prepared just before the restaurant service.

15 BUTTER SAUCES

Butter sauces can be classified into four categories. In *beurre blanc–type sauces*, cold butter is whisked into a flavorful liquid base. *Broken butter sauces* are made by cooking whole butter in a sauté pan so that the butter breaks. These sauces are then usually finished with lemon juice or wine vinegar. *Compound butters* are prepared by working cold whole butter with flavorful ingredients, such as herbs or reduced vegetable purées. *Whipped butters* are prepared in almost the same way as compound butters, except that a hot flavorful liquid is also incorporated into the butter.

BEURRE BLANC SAUCES

Until the late 1960s, beurre blanc (also called *beurre nantais*) was little known outside Brittany, the Loire valley, and a few specialized Parisian restaurants. Because it contains no emulsifier other than butter itself, it was considered extremely difficult to make. In fact, there was a certain amount of mystique surrounding its preparation, usually concerning magic wrists or the need for a half-century's experience. Gradually, a few of the more adventurous Parisian chefs discovered that the sauce was not so difficult to make after all, and beurre blanc, along with an array of obvious derivatives, took Paris by storm. Whether this sudden mass discovery of beurre blanc started flour's banishment from the kitchens of starred restaurants or coincided with it is hard to say, but once beurre blanc emerged from obscurity, it played a leading role in French kitchens in much the same way as béchamel and velouté had years before.

As beurre blanc became firmly established in contemporary kitchens, chefs realized that the technique used to whip the sauce into an emulsion (*monter au beurre*) was applicable to an almost infinite variety of sauce bases, including traditional and newly innovated brown and white sauces.

TRADITIONAL BEURRE BLANC
Beurre Nantais

The original version, from Brittany, is almost always prepared with Muscadet wine, which is made from grapes grown in the area surrounding the city of Nantes on France's Atlantic coast. Muscadet has the crisp, clean flavor and the acidic edge essential to a successful beurre blanc. If Muscadet is unavailable, other wines can be used, but if only wines containing relatively little acidity are available, it may be necessary to add a few drops of additional vinegar to wake up the sauce at the end.

The recipe that follows contains a small amount of heavy cream, which, although not essential, will help start the emulsion. A great deal of myth still surrounds the addition of the butter to the flavor base. Many authors insist that the butter be added in tiny increments, often as little as a tablespoon (15 milliliters) at a time, over low heat, and imply that the sauce will break if the butter is added any faster. In fact, the butter can be cut into relatively large cubes (about 1 inch/2.5 cm on each side) and added all at once over high heat. The keys are not to stop whisking and not to let the sauce boil. Seasonings can be added at the end. Traditionally, 1 teaspoon (5 milliliters) of fine salt is added per 2 cups (500 milliliters) of sauce, but diners today often find this to be slightly too much.

shallots, finely chopped, 4 medium	3 ounces	75 grams
white wine	½ cup	125 milliliters
white wine vinegar	½ cup	125 milliliters
heavy cream (optional)	¼ cup	60 milliliters
butter, cut into 1-inch (2.5 cm) cubes	1 pound	500 grams
salt and pepper	to taste	to taste

1. Combine the shallots with the white wine and vinegar in a heavy-bottomed saucepan. Gently simmer the mixture until practically all the liquid has evaporated (reduce by about 90 percent).
2. Add the cream. (If the cream is not being used, the same amount of another liquid, such as water, must be added, or the sauce will be too thick.)
3. Check the inside of the saucepan to make sure it has not browned, which would discolor the sauce. Wipe off any browning with a wet towel.
4. Add the butter to the shallot infusion. Whisk the sauce over high heat until all the butter has been incorporated.
5. Adjust the seasonings. If the sauce seems flat, add wine vinegar, a few drops at a time. If the sauce tastes harsh or overly acidic, whisk in more butter.
6. Most chefs prefer to strain the beurre blanc, but for some dishes the minced shallots provide an appealing contrast to the pale sauce.

Holding and Saving Beurre Blanc

If held properly, beurre blanc prepared just before a restaurant service or lengthy meal will stay intact for several hours. Leave it in the saucepan, covered, in a warm area such as a warm oven, plate warmer, or on the back of the stove. If necessary, the saucepan can be placed in a pan of hot water.

When beurre blanc is held for any length of time, it will begin to thicken and must be thinned periodically with heavy cream, water, court-bouillon, or another appropriate liquid. If it is not thinned and stirred approximately every 30 minutes, it is likely to break. Broken beurre blanc can be repaired by whisking it into several tablespoons of reduced heavy cream, but this can be done only once.

Leftover beurre blanc can be used in hollandaise- or béarnaise-type sauces. It can also be cooked on the stove until it breaks completely and separates; it can then be used for clarified butter.

Beurre Blanc Variations

Beurre blanc lends itself to several obvious variations, such as beurre rouge (red wine replaces the white), beurre citron (lemon juice replaces wine and vinegar), beurre à l'ail (garlic replaces the shallots). Any of the flavor bases for emulsified egg sauces can be used as the base for beurre blanc–style sauces.

Beurre Rouge (Red Wine–Butter Sauce)

The most obvious variation of beurre blanc involves replacing the white wine with red wine and the white wine vinegar with red wine vinegar. The resulting sauce has a pale purple cast that reminds some people of Pepto-Bismol. To deepen the color of the sauce, use a full-bodied red wine with no tannin and low acidity and replace both the white wine and the vinegar called for in beurre blanc with twice as much red wine. Unfortunately, beurre rouge often has a one-dimensional flavor and may even have an unpleasant metallic taste, because the wine is reduced without any protein, which would remove the astringent tannins and deepen the flavor.

Beurre Citron (Lemon Beurre Blanc)

This sauce is prepared in the same way as a beurre blanc except that the white wine and vinegar are replaced with lemon juice. Use the juice of 1 lemon for 1 pound (500 grams) of butter. Many beginning chefs incorrectly assume that lemon juice will impart a distinct lemon flavor to the sauce. In fact, lemon juice contributes only acidity—a more direct, less subtle acidity than that provided by vinegar. For lemon flavor, grated or julienned lemon zests can be infused in the lemon juice before whisking in the butter.

Beurre Fondu (Emulsified Butter)

In many sauce-making settings, it is convenient to have on hand already emulsified butter, which does not necessarily have the distinct character of a classic beurre blanc. Butter can be emulsified by whisking it into almost any liquid, such as court-bouillon, various stocks or cooking liquids, and of course, lemon juice or vinegar. Whatever liquid base is used, some acidity derived from wine, vinegar, verjuice, or citrus juice will help stabilize the emulsion. Emulsified butter is handy for finishing last-minute sauces or cooking liquids, rather than enriching with cold butter each time.

BROKEN BUTTER SAUCES

These sauces are prepared by cooking butter until it breaks and then flavoring it with an acidic ingredient, such as lemon juice or wine vinegar. Broken butter sauces are less popular than they used to be, probably because the undisguised broken butter makes calorie-conscious diners feel guilty. Yet there are preparations for which no other kind of sauce will do quite as well.

Beurre Noisette

The French name for this butter sauce translates literally as "hazelnut butter," not because it contains nuts but because of the characteristic nutty smell, like butterscotch, of the butter when it is cooked to just the right stage. Do not confuse beurre noisette with *beurre de noisette*, which is actually made with puréed hazelnuts.

Usually beurre noisette is prepared directly in the pan used for cooking fish or white meats *à la meunière* (as in the recipe that follows), but it can also be prepared separately, especially for banquets or when large numbers of guests are being served at one time.

To prepare beurre noisette separately, on the stove, slowly melt whole butter in a heavy-bottomed saucepan. Continue cooking the butter over medium heat until the water has cooked off (usually 20 to 25 percent of whole butter is water). When the water has evaporated—the milk solids will begin to coagulate into small white specks—turn down the flame. Watch the specks carefully while the butter is cooking. When the specks turn pale brown, remove the saucepan from the heat. If a large amount of the butter is being prepared at once or if the saucepan is particularly heavy, plunge the bottom of the saucepan into a bowl of cold water to stop the cooking. When the butter has cooled slightly, add lemon juice. Usually the juice of one lemon is sufficient for every 4 ounces (125 grams) of whole butter. Be sure to add the lemon juice *after* the butter has cooled somewhat, or the butter will burn as soon as the juice is added.

FILLETS OF SOLE À LA MEUNIÈRE

This recipe illustrates how beurre noisette is most often prepared and used.

Beurre noisette can be garnished with different ingredients to provide variations. The most well-known variations on the *meunière* theme are *à la grenobloise*, which is beurre noisette to which capers, miniature croutons, and lemon cubes have been added, and *amandine*, which contains slivered almonds that have been cooked in the hot butter. *A la polonaise* is beurre noisette with breadcrumbs.

YIELD: 2 SERVINGS

fillets of sole, 3 to 4 ounces (100 to 125 grams) each	4	4
salt and pepper	to taste	to taste
flour (for dredging)	as needed	as needed
clarified butter	¼ cup	60 milliliters
whole butter	2 ounces	60 grams
juice of ½ lemon		
chopped parsley	1 tablespoon	15 milliliters

1. Season the fillets with salt and pepper and dredge them in flour. Pat them to remove any excess.
2. Sauté the fillets in the clarified butter (oval sauté pans are best for this), and transfer them to serving plates or a platter. Discard the cooked butter and wipe out any particles of burned flour with a paper towel.

3. Let the sauté pan cool slightly, then add the whole butter. Cook the whole butter until it froths and the froth begins to subside. While the butter is cooking, sprinkle the cooked fillets with the lemon juice (see Note) and chopped parsley.
4. Pour the hot beurre noisette over the fillets.

Note: The lemon juice can also be added directly to the butter in the sauté pan, but be sure to let the cooked butter cool slightly before adding the lemon juice, which can cause the butter to burn if it is too hot.

Beurre Noir

Many chefs confuse *beurre noir*, which literally means "black butter," with burned butter. Correctly prepared beurre noir is made in the same way as beurre noisette except that the lemon juice is replaced with vinegar. It is best to reduce the vinegar by half before adding it to the cooked butter, which should be allowed to cool slightly in the same way as beurre noisette cools before the lemon juice is added. Full-flavored vinegars, such as sherry and balsamic vinegar, work especially well. In classic French cooking, beurre noir is most often served with fish (especially skate) and also as a sauce for poached brains.

Alternative Flavorings

Beurre noisette and beurre noir can be garnished with herbs other than the traditional chopped parsley. Tarragon, chervil, marjoram, and oregano all provide different nuances. Other components, such as chopped garlic, diced gherkins (cornichons), diced mushrooms (wild or otherwise), diced truffles, and chopped shallots can be added to the butter while it is being heated. Acidic liquids, such as verjuice or reduced red or white wine, can replace the traditional lemon juice and vinegar.

COMPOUND BUTTERS

Compound butters are prepared by working whole butter with flavorful ingredients such as herbs, vegetable purées, reduced wines or stocks, anchovies, spices, or coral. They can be used by themselves as "sauces" for grilled meats, fish, and vegetables, or swirled in at the end to complete more complex sauces.

It is often convenient to add compound butters, rather than flavoring ingredients alone, to sauces. This is especially true for herbs such as basil or tarragon, which will turn black if chopped in advance. If the herbs are chopped into butter, they will be protected from the air, and their color and flavor will stay intact. It is also useful to prepare a compound butter when using fragile ingredients that may coagulate in contact with a hot liquid. Sea urchin roe, sea scallop coral, and foie gras should be combined with at least one-third of their weight in butter before being whisked into a sauce.

Compound butters served over grilled or sautéed meats or fish can be presented in one of two ways. The first is to roll the softened compound butter in a sheet of aluminum foil to form a compact cylinder. The cylinder of butter is then chilled and sliced into miniature disks and placed over the hot meat or fish just before serving. The second method is to warm the butter slightly and then work it with a wooden spoon or even whip it with a whisk. Avoid overworking the butter, or it will develop an unpleasant clinging feel in the mouth. The flavor of the butter itself will also lose some of its finesse. Worked or whipped compound butters are traditionally served on the side in a sauce boat, but today's chefs will often put them directly on the meat or fish.

Compound butters are also useful as a decorative and flavorful finish for hot soups.

The flavor base for compound butters was traditionally prepared with a mortar and pestle and then usually strained through a fine-mesh drum sieve after being combined with the butter. Today a food processor is usually used instead of the mortar and pestle, but to obtain a perfectly smooth texture, a fine-mesh drum sieve is still necessary for straining the butter at the end.

Compound butters are almost always seasoned with salt and pepper. Recipes vary and suggest anywhere from ½ teaspoon to 1 tablespoon (3 to 15 milliliters) of fine salt to 1 pound (500 grams) of butter. If a whole tablespoon is used, the butter will be extremely salty; this is appropriate only if the butter is being used as the only seasoning on grilled or deep-fried foods. Cayenne pepper, wine vinegar, and lemon juice will often wake up the flavor of a compound butter.

Crustacean butters, which are compound butters, are found in Chapter 11, "Crustacean Sauces," page 325.

Classic French Compound Butters

The classic French repertoire contains approximately forty compound butters. Some of these, such as maître d' butter (*beurre maître d'hôtel*) and Montpellier butter, continue to be widely used, whereas others, though more obscure, remain useful.

Almond Butter

Finely grind 5 ounces (150 grams) of peeled and lightly toasted almonds in a food processor for 5 minutes (this sounds like a long time but is necessary to achieve the right texture). Scrape the inside walls of the food processor from time to time, grinding until a smooth paste is obtained. Add 8 ounces (250 grams) of cold butter cut into cubes to the almond paste, and process the mixture until it is perfectly homogeneous. Season with salt. The butter can be used as is or made perfectly smooth by working it through a fine-mesh drum sieve with a plastic pastry scraper or rubber spatula. This butter is excellent on grilled fish and vegetables.

Anchovy Butter

Select the best anchovies available (see page 81). Soak 24 anchovy fillets (2½ ounces/60 grams) in cold water for 5 minutes to eliminate excess salt and oil. Dry the anchovies on paper towels and purée them in a food processor with 8 ounces (250 grams) of butter. Work the butter through a fine-mesh drum sieve with a plastic pastry scraper or rubber spatula. When used sparingly, anchovy butter is excellent for finishing fish sauces.

Bercy Butter

Reduce 1 cup (250 milliliters) of white wine with 2 finely chopped shallots until only 2 tablespoons (30 milliliters) remain. Let the reduction cool (do not strain it), and then work it into 7 ounces (200 grams) of creamed butter. Add 1 tablespoon (15 milliliters) of chopped parsley and 2 teaspoons (10 milliliters) of lemon juice. Season the butter with salt and pepper. Older recipes incorporate diced and poached marrow into the butter along with the other ingredients. The only difference between a Bercy butter without marrow and a shallot butter is that the Bercy butter is flavored with reduced white wine. Season with ½ teaspoon (2 milliliters) of salt.

Chivry Butter

This butter is also sometimes called *ravigote butter.* Blanch 1 heaping tablespoon (20 milliliters) each of fresh tarragon, chervil, parsley, chives, and salad burnet in boiling salted water for 15 seconds. Mince 1 shallot and blanch for 1 minute. Quickly refresh the herbs and minced shallot in a strainer with cold running water, and dry them on towels. The herbs and shallot are best ground with a mortar and pestle before being worked with 4 ounces (125 grams) of butter, but if a mortar and pestle are unavailable, the herbs can be puréed along with the butter in a food processor. After the herbs have been puréed with the butter, force the butter through a fine-mesh drum sieve.

Chlorophyll Butter

This butter is good to have on hand for coloring hot sauces green. (Plain chlorophyll can be used for cold sauces.) First prepare 1 ounce (25 grams) of chlorophyll. To do this, grind 1 pound (500 grams) of raw spinach leaves with ½ to 1 cup (125 to 250 milliliters) of water in a blender or food processor. Put the green paste in the center of a clean kitchen towel and twist the towel to extract green liquid from the spinach. Gently heat the green liquid in a saucepan until it coagulates. Strain the liquid through a strainer lined with a wet towel.

Gently scrape the chlorophyll away from the inside of the towel with a spoon or metal spatula. Chlorophyll can be stored in the refrigerator, covered with a thin coating of oil.

To prepare chlorophyll butter, work the chlorophyll with four times its volume of butter.

Colbert Butter

Work 2 tablespoons (30 milliliters) of melted meat glace and 1 tablespoon (15 milliliters) of chopped and blanched tarragon leaves into 8 ounces (250 grams) of maître d' butter (below).

Garlic Butter

Traditional recipes call for blanching peeled garlic cloves and combining them with an almost equal weight of butter (7 ounces/200 grams of garlic to 8 ounces/ 250 grams of butter) before straining the butter through a drum sieve. For some applications, such as snail butter or for garlic bread, garlic butter can be prepared by grinding and working unblanched cloves with butter, 2 cloves per 4 ounces (125 grams) of butter.

Maître d' Butter (Beurre Maître d'Hôtel)

This is probably the best known of the compound butters, as it is the usual accompaniment to *steak frites* (grilled steak with french fries), long popular in France and more recently *the* thing to eat in the United States. Work 8 ounces (250 grams) of butter with ¼ cup (60 milliliters) of finely chopped parsley and 1 teaspoon (5 milliliters) of lemon juice. Season the butter with salt and pepper. Some recipes suggest adding mustard to the butter.

Marchand de Vin Butter

This butter is excellent when served on top of grilled steaks. Reduce 1 cup (250 milliliters) of full-bodied red wine with 1 minced large shallot and 5 cracked peppercorns. When the wine is three-quarters reduced, add 1 tablespoon (15 milliliters) of meat glace and a good pinch of salt. Continue reducing until a few tablespoons of syrupy mixture remain. Work the mixture with 5 ounces (150 grams) of butter, 2 teaspoons (10 milliliters) of lemon juice, and 1 tablespoon (15 milliliters) of finely chopped parsley.

Montpellier Butter

This, the most elaborate of the classic compound butters, is excellent served on both hot and cold fish and meats. It has a softer texture than most compound butters because of the olive oil it contains.

Blanch the leaves from ½ bunch each of parsley, watercress, chervil, chives (chopped before blanching); 1 sprig of tarragon, 1 small handful of spinach leaves; and 2 chopped shallots in boiling salted water. Rinse the blanched greens and shallots in cold water, dry them in a towel, and grind them with a mortar and pestle or in a food processor. Add 2 cornichons (gherkins), 1 heaping tablespoon of capers (20 milliliters), 1 peeled garlic clove, and 4 anchovy fillets (soaked in cold water for 5 minutes to remove salt and oil). Grind the mixture until it is smooth. Add 2 raw egg yolks and 3 cooked egg yolks to the mixture and work again until smooth. Add from 4 to 8 ounces (125 to 250 grams) of butter (depending on how assertive you want the butter to be), and work through a drum sieve. Gently work ½ cup (125 milliliters) of extra-virgin olive oil into the butter with a wooden spoon (remember, whisking turns olive oil bitter). Season the butter with salt, pepper, cayenne, and a little lemon juice or good wine vinegar.

Mustard Butter

This simple butter is excellent served atop grilled foods for which straight mustard would be too strong. Mustard butter can be prepared with smooth Dijon mustard or with whole-grain Meaux-style mustard. Traditional recipes call for 2 to 3 tablespoons (30 to 45 milliliters) mustard per 8 ounces (250 grams) of butter, but more can be added according to taste.

Paprika Butter

Most commercially available paprikas have so little flavor that the spice is used in the kitchen primarily for its color. Some chefs prepare paprika butter, using 1 teaspoon (5 milliliters) of paprika to 8 ounces (250 grams) of butter, for coloring sauces at the last minute or for decorating soups.

Smoked Salmon Butter

This butter can be used to add an extra dimension to fish sauces or can be served as is atop grilled or sautéed fish. Purée 4 ounces (125 grams) of smoked salmon in a food processor. Work the paste with 8 ounces (250 grams) of butter and strain the mixture through a drum sieve.

Snail Butter

Combine 2 finely chopped shallots, 1 garlic clove worked to a paste (in a mortar or crushed with the side of a knife on a cutting board), and 2 tablespoons (30 milliliters) of finely chopped parsley with 12 ounces (350 grams) of butter. Season the butter with salt and pepper.

Sweet Red Pepper Butter

This butter is excellent on grilled fish and vegetables or for finishing more complex fish sauces. Combine 4 ounces (125 grams) of grilled and peeled sweet red peppers with 8 ounces (250 grams) of butter. Force the butter through a drum sieve.

Tarragon Butter

This is, justifiably, one of the most popular of the herb butters. Blanch 4 ounces (125 grams) of fresh tarragon leaves for 1 minute in boiling salted water. Rinse the leaves and dry them on a towel. Grind the blanched leaves with a mortar and pestle or in a food processor. Combine the tarragon paste with 8 ounces (250 grams) of butter.

Tomato Butter

Combine ¼ cup (60 milliliters) of thick Tomato Coulis (page 461) with 8 ounces (250 grams) butter. This butter is excellent on all grilled foods and as a decorative finish for hot soups. Adding 1 teaspoon (5 milliliters) of good wine vinegar will enhance its flavor.

Truffle Butter

Traditional recipes combine 4 ounces (125 grams) of fresh black truffles with 8 ounces (250 grams) of butter strained through a drum sieve. This is an extravagance that few restaurants (even those that serve truffles) can afford. A more economical method, which is exciting in its subtlety, is to unwrap sticks of butter and store them overnight in a tightly sealed jar with the fresh truffles. The next day the butter will reek of the truffles and can be used on top of grilled or sautéed foods or to give an ineffable, fleeting complexity to other sauces.

Coral Butters

Coral butters can be approached in several ways, depending on how they are going to be used. When destined to finish a sauce, the raw coral is simply worked with an equal amount of butter and forced through a fine-mesh drum sieve. When coral butters are served as an accompaniment to foods such as grilled fish, some chefs prefer to cook the coral for a minute or two before working it with the butter. Raw coral will, however, always have more subtlety and a brighter flavor than cooked. When using raw coral to prepare compound butters, it must be impeccably fresh. Some raw coral, especially lobster coral, is extremely perishable and should be used within hours of killing the lobsters.

When a hot sauce is finished with coral butter, do not allow the sauce to come to the boil or the coral will coagulate.

Sea Scallop Coral Butter

In the United States, sea scallops are usually sold already shucked without their bright orange coral. Not only is the coral wasted but the scallops are never fresh, because, once removed from the shell, they die and are extremely perishable.

When fresh scallops are available, they can be served with their coral, or the coral can be converted into a compound butter and used to finish a sauce or the scallops' poaching liquid. Purée equal parts of scallop coral and butter. Cream the two together and force the butter through a fine-mesh drum sieve.

Sea Urchin Roe Butter

Sea urchin roe has a delicate, almost sweet sea-like flavor, making it perfect for fish sauces. If incorporated directly into a hot sauce, it will curdle, so it should first be strained through a drum sieve with an equal amount of butter. Taste the sea urchin roe before using it in a sauce. If it has a strong, iodine flavor, it should not be used.

Caviar Butter

Caviar butters have recently become popular, unjustifiably. To make an authentic caviar butter with sturgeon caviar is an extravagance whose sum is worth less than its parts. The delicacy and complex flavor of sturgeon caviar is lost when it is heated, and its texture is completely eradicated when preparing the butter. Some chefs have prepared "caviar" butters with lumpfish roe, trout roe, salmon roe, and others, but the resulting butters can be only as good (and are rarely as good) as the raw ingredients.

Using Lobster Coral

Many recipes suggest creaming lobster coral with butter before incorporating it into a sauce. This is often difficult because coral that has been forced through a sieve along with the lobster tomalley is too liquid to be added in any quantity to butter. The coral is best combined with a small amount of cream rather than butter before being used in sauce making.

Spice Butters

Practically any spice can be ground and creamed with butter so that it can be easily incorporated into a sauce at the last minute without the risk of forming lumps. Spices can be freshly ground in a small home coffee grinder. Some spices, such as those contained in curry—cardamom, fenugreek, coriander, cumin, turmeric, nutmeg—should be cooked for about a minute in a small amount of butter on the stove before being incorporated into the rest of the butter. This wakes up their flavor, especially if they are a bit stale.

Herb Butters

Almost any herb can be chopped and worked with butter to form a compound butter. The method works especially well with such herbs as basil, thyme, and tarragon, which quickly turn black once chopped. Certain classic green butters, such as Chivry Butter and Montpellier Butter (pages 416 and 417), make use of several herbs that are first blanched in boiling salted water before being chopped or crushed in a mortar and worked with the butter. Traditionally, herb butters were prepared by first crushing the herbs with a mortar and pestle before being combined with the butter and strained through a drum sieve. Nowadays most chefs chop the herbs, combine them with the butter in a food processor, and omit the last step of straining through a drum sieve. Whichever method is used, it is best to let herb butters sit for an hour or two before they are used to allow the herb flavors to permeate the butter.

Liver Butters

Many sauces, especially deeply flavored sauces for game, benefit by being finished at the end with a compound butter prepared from the animal's liver. Sometimes the heart and gizzard can also be used, as well as a small amount of ground juniper berries, which help reinforce the sauce's gamy flavor. Sauces finished with liver butter have an opaque, almost muddy texture that is sometimes startling to people used to translucent brown sauces finished with butter.

Pigeon Sauce

The most obvious method for cooking a tender young pigeon is to roast it and prepare a jus. The jus can then be finished with a compound butter prepared with equal weights of butter and the pigeon's liver, heart, gizzard, and lungs. In a restaurant setting, it is often more practical to remove the pigeon suprêmes and to prepare the giblet-juniper butter and a jus with the pigeon carcass in advance. The suprêmes are then sautéed to order, the pan deglazed with the jus, and the sauce finished with the giblet-juniper butter.

Foie Gras Butter

Foie gras is excellent for finishing sauces. Because of its high fat content, it will thicken a sauce and remain smooth provided it is not allowed to boil. When using partially cooked foie gras (*mi-cuit*) or terrine of American foie gras, mash together equal parts foie gras and butter, and then force the mixture through a fine-mesh drum sieve. When using raw foie gras, a higher percentage of foie gras (about two parts foie gras to one part butter) should be used, because of its higher water content. In restaurants where terrines of foie gras are prepared on a regular basis, the trimmings obtained when removing the veins from inside the raw livers can be worked through a drum sieve and reserved for finishing sauces.

WHIPPED BUTTERS

These butters are essentially compound butters that have been lightened and flavored with a relatively large amount of flavorful liquid and to which whipped cream is added. They are usually served in a sauce boat, so diners can serve themselves. Whipped butters offer a greater range of possibilities than the better-known compound butters because of the flavorful liquids they contain.

WHIPPED BUTTER FOR GRILLED OR SAUTÉED FISH

YIELD: 8 TO 10 SERVINGS

whole butter	8 ounces	250 grams
warm flavorful liquid (see Note)	½ cup	125 milliliters
good-quality wine vinegar, to taste	3 tablespoons	45 milliliters
heavy cream	½ cup	125 milliliters
salt and pepper	to taste	to taste

1. Soften the butter with an electric mixer equipped with a paddle blade.
2. When the butter is soft, put the whisk attachment on the mixer and whip the butter while slowly adding the warm but not hot flavoring liquid. Slowly add the vinegar to taste. Whip the butter until it is light and airy, usually for about 8 minutes. Adjust the seasonings.
3. Season the cream with salt and pepper. Whip the cream and fold it with the butter.

Note: Any appropriate flavorful liquid, such as mussel or clam cooking liquid, reduced court-bouillon, good fish stock, or fish cooking liquid, can be used.

Whipped Butter Variations

Whipped butters can be based on stocks, cooking liquids, vegetable purées, or infusions and then finished with appropriate compound butters. A whipped butter for grilled chicken might consist of brown chicken stock reduced with shallots or garlic and finished with tarragon, tomato, sweet red pepper, or mustard butter. Whipped butters for fish can be based on court-bouillon, fish stock, or the fresh cooking liquid from the poached or braised fish. Red wine whipped butter for fish can be prepared using red wine fish sauce (see page 214) as a base and then finishing with herb butters, crustacean butters, or coral butters.

16

SALAD SAUCES, VINAIGRETTES, SALSAS, AND RELISHES

These sauces are also called simple or independent sauces because they are prepared independently of the foods they accompany. They are the opposite of integral sauces because they derive none of their character from the preparation itself. They do not require stock, because they are designed to contrast and complement rather than underline and reinforce a food's basic flavors. Other sauces, such as mayonnaise, béchamel, and hollandaise, also function in this way. Independent sauces can be simple or complex. Sometimes the most simple natural products make the best sauces.

Cold-pressed extra-virgin olive oil dribbled over a piece of grilled fish can be more appropriate and satisfying than a complicated, artfully prepared lobster sauce.

Independent sauces can be prepared from an infinite variety of flavorful ingredients that are usually infused in an appropriate medium such as cream, vinegar, oil, or vegetable purée. They can also be simple mixtures of finely chopped fruits and vegetables (as in salsas), combinations of pickled ingredients (relishes), or more elaborate sweet-and-sour concoctions (chutneys).

SHRIMP COCKTAIL

The classic sauce for shrimp cocktail will have another notch of flavor if you grate your own horseradish.

YIELD: 6 FIRST-COURSE SERVINGS

shrimp	24 jumbo or large	24 jumbo or large
olive oil	2 tablespoons	30 milliliters
ketchup	⅔ cup	165 milliliters
chile sauce	⅔ cup	165 milliliters
grated horseradish, preferably fresh, to taste	¼ cup	60 milliliters
hot pepper sauce, to taste	1 tablespoon	15 milliliters
lemon juice, to taste	1 tablespoon	15 milliliters
lemon wedges		

1. Sauté the shrimp in olive oil until they turn color, about 3 minutes, and allow to cool. Peel and, if necessary, devein.
2. Combine the remaining ingredients, except the lemon wedges, and serve in cocktail glasses with the shrimp and lemon wedges arranged around the edges. See the photograph in the color plates.

CREAM-BASED COLD SAUCES

Heavy cream has replaced béchamel and velouté as the base for most contemporary white sauces (see "White Sauces Based on Reduced Cream," page 144). It is also an excellent medium for cold sauces. Because of its delicate, almost neutral flavor, it is a useful backdrop for flavorful ingredients that would be too aggressive if used alone.

American heavy cream is usually too thin to be used directly for a cold sauce base. Several methods can be used to thicken it to the desired consistency. One of the simplest is to combine it with a small amount of acidic liquid, such as lemon juice, lime juice, verjuice, or vinegar. Cream thickened in this way can then be used as a medium for a wide variety of flavorful ingredients and can then be served with cold meats, fish, and vegetables and as a salad dressing. Heavy cream can also be thickened in the same way as crème fraîche, by inoculating it with an active culture found in buttermilk, sour cream, or yogurt. The bacteria secrete lactic acid that causes the cream to thicken. The quickest method for thickening cream is, of course, to whip it lightly. When whipping cream, make sure that the cream, the bowl, and the whisk have been well chilled. In hot weather, it is a good idea to whisk the cream over ice.

HERB-SCENTED THICKENED CREAM FOR SALADS

Several kinds of herbs can be infused and used to flavor heavy cream or crème fraîche. The herbs are first crushed with a mortar and pestle or finely chopped with lemon juice, lime juice, or vinegar. The cream is then whisked into the infusion. If regular heavy cream is used, it will thicken after a few minutes.

Herb-scented cream can be lightly spooned over cold fish and meats, but it is most often used as a sauce for salads. When flavored with mint or dill, it can be served with sliced cucumbers that have been seeded and degorged with salt. When flavored with freshly chopped cilantro and Tabasco, it makes an excellent dressing for a salad of tomatoes, cucumbers, grilled peppers, onions, garlic, and fennel. Or it can be used as a dressing for a simple green salad.

YIELD: 1 CUP (250 MILLILITERS)

fresh herb leaves (see Note)	1 to 2 tablespoons	15 to 30 milliliters
coarse salt	½ to 1 teaspoon	3 to 5 milliliters
lemon or lime juice, wine vinegar, or verjuice	2 tablespoons	30 milliliters
heavy cream	1 cup	250 milliliters

1. Combine the herb leaves and coarse salt in a mortar or wooden bowl. Grind the herbs with the salt (the salt helps work the mixture into a purée) using a pestle or the back of a wooden spoon.
2. Stir in the lemon juice. Continue stirring until the salt dissolves. Stir in the cream.
3. Let the mixture rest for 5 to 10 minutes, until the cream thickens.

Note: Marjoram, oregano, mint, thyme, and dill are some of the possibilities. The amount to use depends on the strength of the herb's flavor; for example, marjoram is stronger than mint, so less marjoram would be used.

Cultured Cream

When Americans see crème fraîche, the French equivalent of American heavy cream, they usually assume that, because it is thick, it is richer and more flavorful than the American equivalent. The thick texture results not from the richness of crème fraîche but from the bacterial culture it contains, which contributes acidity. The acidity in turn causes the cream to thicken and gives it a delicate tang.

Although the flavor of authentic crème fraîche cannot be duplicated with American ingredients, heavy cream can be cultured so that it thickens. Combine 2 tablespoons (30 milliliters) of buttermilk or sour cream with 2 cups (500 milliliters) of heavy cream, and gently heat the mixture to body temperature in a saucepan. Transfer the cream to a stainless-steel, glass, or porcelain container. Keep it covered in a warm place until it thickens, usually about 24 hours. As soon as the cream thickens, refrigerate it. It will keep for at least a week.

YOGURT-BASED COLD SAUCES

In addition to its usefulness as a thickener for hot sauces, yogurt is an excellent medium for cold sauces and can be used in much the same way as thickened cream. It is less rich than cream and has a refreshing tang that is especially pleasant in the summer. It is often used in Indian and Middle Eastern cooking.

There are several types of yogurt available, ranging from very light yogurt made from skimmed milk to thick Middle Eastern–style yogurt that almost has the consistency of fresh cheese. When using yogurt in salads, a thicker yogurt works best because the vegetables in the salad will continue to release liquid into the sauce, thinning it and diluting its flavor.

One of the simplest yogurt sauces is for the Indian *raita,* a cucumber salad flavored with mint or cilantro and sometimes minced garlic and hot peppers. The Greeks have another version, a sort of light-style *skorthaliá* that contains garlic, almonds, and parsley, which they serve over cold vegetables. Yogurt can also be flavored with herbs, with colorful purées made from sweet peppers or tomatoes, with onions, or with shallots to create a variety of light spreads for cold or grilled foods. These simple sauce variations can also be used to finish hot sauces for fish and vegetables (see "Finishing Sauces with Yogurt," page 132).

MINT AND CILANTRO YOGURT SAUCE

This bright green sauce is excellent served with barbecued foods such as chicken or full-flavored fish.

YIELD: 1½ CUPS (375 MILLILITERS)

yogurt	5 fluid ounces	150 milliliters
finely chopped onion	2 tablespoons	30 milliliters
finely chopped fresh ginger	¼ teaspoon	2 milliliters
jalapeños, finely chopped	2	2

mint, leaves only	1 bunch	1 bunch
cilantro, leaves only	1 bunch	1 bunch
salt and pepper	to taste	to taste

Combine all the ingredients in the food processor. Process for 15 to 30 seconds, until the ingredients are finely chopped and the mixture is smooth.

OILS, VINEGARS, AND VINAIGRETTES

Oil and vinegar have long been used as condiments for grilled foods and salads. First-pressed extra-virgin olive oil has a finesse and depth of flavor that surpass those of many a more complicated sauce. Because it is a completely natural product subject to variations in climate and soil, its flavor, like that of wine, is never completely predictable. Perhaps it is these subtle variations in flavor that make it possible to use olive oil throughout the year in all sorts of preparations without the flavor ever becoming monotonous.

Other flavorful oils, such as nut oils, can of course be used alone as condiments or combined with vinegar in vinaigrettes. Inert-tasting oils, such as grapeseed or safflower oil, are sometimes used to attenuate their more assertive cousins.

Flavored Oils

For centuries Mediterranean cooks have been putting sprigs of herbs in jars of olive oil and using the infused oils for salads, to baste roasting meats, and as condiments for grilled fish. Recently chefs have taken a more aggressive approach to infused oils and have been experimenting with blanching and puréeing a wide variety of herbs and vegetables to create full-flavored and brightly colored oils that can be emulsified with other ingredients in vinaigrettes or simply dribbled over foods as sauces themselves. Flavored oils can also be prepared from a variety of spices and from concentrated vegetable juices. Although no less rich than butter, these oils contain no cholesterol and have a brightness of color and flavor that are a welcome relief to the butter-weary diner.

Several approaches can be used when preparing flavored oils. The first and more traditional method is a simple infusion: Flavorful ingredients are left to steep in the oil for up to several weeks, and the oil is then strained or poured off as it is needed. Another method involves combining various purées with the oil (for example, basil, truffle, stewed red pepper). The purées are then either strained out or left dispersed in the oil, resulting in a full-flavored and often brightly colored oil that can be used alone or in combination with other ingredients as a decorative sauce. Spice-scented oils can also be prepared by first moistening the ground spice and then combining it with oil and allowing it to infuse for several days. Crustacean-flavored oils can be prepared in the same way as crustacean butter, by simply replacing the butter with an inert oil or a good olive oil. Some infused oils are best if the oil is kept cool while it is infusing— the delicacy of herbs such as basil or chervil is damaged by heat—whereas other ingredients require that the oil be warm so that it extracts the flavor of the ingredients more efficiently.

Oils for Infusing

Select an oil whose flavor goes well with the ingredient being infused. Extra-virgin olive oil makes sense when the infusion is made with full-flavored herbs such as marjoram, thyme, lavender, rosemary, sage, basil, and oregano— typically Mediterranean flavors—but might take over the flavor of more delicate herbs such as chervil or parsley. For these, a less flavorful "pure" olive oil, perhaps with a small amount of extra-virgin olive oil added, allows the flavors of the herbs to come through more clearly. For other ingredients, such as spices, it makes more sense to use a completely neutral oil such as canola, safflower, or grapeseed oil. For Asian ingredients such as ginger, Szechuan peppercorns, lemongrass, or star anise, a neutral oil or peanut oil, perhaps with some dark sesame oil added for flavor, is far better than olive oil.

Cold-Infused Method

This is the most straightforward method for making infused oils and usually consists of simply shoving sprigs of herbs or coarsely chopped ingredients (such as orange rinds) through the neck of a bottle of oil. Some cold infused oils (for example, basil oil) take only a day to make because the ingredients release their aroma and flavor very quickly into the surrounding oil. Other ingredients may require a week or two of infusing to reach optimum flavor. If the herbs are finely chopped or the leaves are detached from the branches, the oil will need to be strained through a fine-mesh strainer before it is used. Never use powdered herbs. Because herb oils, especially cold-infused versions, may strengthen or weaken over time, it is best to taste them each time before they are used.

COLD-INFUSED HERB OIL

This oil is one of the simplest to make. Simply slide sprigs of full-flavored herbs through the neck of the bottle into the oil.

YIELD: 1 QUART (1 LITER)

4 bunches of fresh or dried marjoram, thyme, sage, lavender, rosemary, or oregano (enough so that the herbs loosely fill the bottle)		
or	*or*	*or*
loose (off the branch) dried herbs	¼ cup	60 milliliters
extra-virgin olive oil	1 quart	1 liter

1. Wash the herbs under cold running water (use a strainer if the herbs are off the stem). Dry the herbs on a towel.
2. Combine the herbs with the olive oil (simply slide sprigs of herbs through the neck of the bottle).
3. Cork the bottle and store in a cool place (but not in the refrigerator) for at least a week or two and up to several months.

BASIL OR CHERVIL OIL

Basil and chervil have delicate flavors that infuse quickly into the surrounding oil. The herbs can be chopped in a blender or food processor, but they should not be processed for too long or the moisture contained in the herbs will emulsify with the oil and the finished oil will be cloudy.

YIELD: 1 QUART (1 LITER)

leaves from 6 large bunches fresh basil	6 tightly packed cups	1.4 liters
or	or	or
15 large bunches fresh chervil	6 tightly packed cups	1.4 liters
extra-virgin olive oil	4½ cups	1.1 liters

1. Wash and dry the herbs.
2. Sprinkle the herbs with a tablespoon (15 milliliters) of the olive oil to prevent them from turning dark, and chop them finely by hand or chop them—not too finely—in a blender or food processor. If using a blender or food processor, add enough of the olive oil to help the herbs to circulate but don't use more oil than necessary.
3. Combine the chopped herbs with the rest of the olive oil and allow to sit at room temperature for 24 hours.
4. Strain through a fine-mesh strainer (chinois) or through a triple layer of cheesecloth. Don't push on the herbs in the strainer because too much moisture will be extracted. Instead, let the oil drain through naturally, for about an hour. Basil and chervil oil keep for up to two weeks in a cool place.

Hot-Infused Method

Some ingredients release their flavor into the surrounding oil so slowly that it's impractical to use them to make infused oils using the cold method. For these ingredients, the oil is gently heated—but not so much that the delicacy of the oil or ingredients is lost—and the ingredients are allowed to lightly sizzle for between 10 seconds (for finely chopped herbs and ground spices) and up to 1 hour (for vegetables such as tomatoes).

Chile and Fresh Pepper Oils

Because chiles come fresh, dried, and smoked in so many varieties and colors, they can be used to make an array of subtly flavored oils that in turn can be used as seasonings in vinaigrettes, as additions to purée sauces (such as tomato sauce) or to emulsified sauces (such as hollandaise-based sauces, reduced-cream sauces, beurre blanc and its derivatives), as components in pasta sauces, or in Chinese cooking.

Chinese chile oils generally contain additional ingredients such as ginger, and usually include dark sesame oil. Sweet red peppers can be infused in olive oil for a sweet and delicate oil that makes a perfect component in vinaigrettes, or that can simply be sprinkled on sliced tomatoes or fresh Italian-style cheeses such as mozzarella. Dried and smoked chiles are used to make hot and spicy yet subtly flavored oils that can be used as sauces for grilled meats and seafood.

Fresh pepper oil keeps for 2 weeks in a cool place and dried pepper oils for several months.

ANCHO CHILE OIL

Because ancho chiles (dried ripe poblano chiles) are easy to find, flavorful, and give a deep ruby glow to infused oils, they make a perfect starting point for experimentation. But almost any dried or fresh chile can be used to make a distinctive oil. Chipotle chiles or pasillas di Oaxaca (both of which are smoked) make especially delicious hot and smoky oils. Adjust the chile amounts depending on the size of the chiles. Dried pasillas, for example, are at least twice the size of dried chipotles. Adjust the proportions of "pure" olive oil and extra-virgin olive oil to taste.

YIELD: 1 QUART (1 LITER)

dried chiles such as ancho, guajillo, mulato, pasilla, chipotle, or pasillas di Oaxaca	20 to 40	20 to 40
pure olive oil	3 cups	750 milliliters
extra-virgin olive oil	1 cup	250 milliliters

1. Rinse and dry the chiles or wipe them with a moist towel. Cut off their stems.
2. Chop the chiles for about 30 seconds in a food processor (until they flake but aren't powdered) or chop them finely by hand. There should be 1½ cups (375 milliliters) of flakes, so if necessary, grind or chop a few more.
3. Combine the chile flakes with the pure olive oil in a saucepan and place over medium heat. When the chiles are sizzling and begin to float, turn the heat down very low and let the chiles sizzle gently for 3 to 10 minutes. Keep sniffing the oil and as soon as the chiles begin to smell toasty, take the pan off the heat. Let cool for 30 minutes.

4. Stir the extra-virgin olive oil into the chile mixture and strain the mixture through a fine-mesh strainer (chinois) or through a triple layer of cheesecloth. If there are still specks floating around in the oil, strain the oil again through a sheet of fine cloth spread over a strainer.

CHINESE-STYLE CHILE OIL

Because most commercial Chinese chile oil is harsh (and often rancid), conscientious Chinese cooks make their own. Recipes for the oil range from simple (hot chiles heated in peanut oil) to relatively complex (garlic, ginger, sesame oil, and black beans added to the mix). This recipe falls between the two extremes.

The chiles suggested below can be combined for different flavor nuances and degrees of heat. Chipotles and pasillas di Oaxaca will lend a characteristic smoky note to the oil. If using all small or relatively mild chiles, add a few extra.

YIELD: 1 QUART (1 LITER)

dried chiles such as ancho, guajillo, mulato, pasilla, chipotle, pasillas di Oaxaca	20 to 40	20 to 40
coarsely chopped fresh ginger	3 tablespoons	45 milliliters
garlic cloves, peeled	5	5
peanut oil	1 quart	1 liter
dark Asian sesame oil	½ cup	125 milliliters

1. Rinse and dry the chiles or wipe them with a moist towel. Cut off their stems.
2. Chop the chiles, ginger, and garlic for about 30 seconds in a food processor or chop everything finely by hand. If there is less than 1¾ cups (450 milliliters) of mixture, add more chiles.
3. Combine the chile-garlic-ginger mixture with the peanut oil in a saucepan. Place the pan over medium heat. When the solids are sizzling and begin to float, turn the heat down to low and allow the ingredients to sizzle gently for about 5 minutes or until they smell toasty. Take the pan off the heat and let cool for 30 minutes.
4. Strain the mixture through a fine-mesh strainer or triple layer of cheesecloth and combine with the sesame oil.

SWEET RED PEPPER OIL

This brightly colored oil captures the flavor of sweet red peppers. Unlike chile oil, which is hot and spicy, red pepper oil is mild and sweet. It is best when served with grilled fish or used as the oil in preparing a vinaigrette.

sweet red peppers	1 pound	500 grams
olive oil	2 cups	500 milliliters

1. Halve the peppers, remove the stems and seeds, and chop coarsely.
2. Combine the chopped peppers with the olive oil in a 2-quart (2 liter) saucepan. Cook the peppers over a low flame for about 1 hour, until they are soft.
3. Let the peppers and oil cool. Pour into a blender and blend for 30 seconds.
4. Return the mixture to the saucepan and cook gently for 15 to 20 minutes, until the grains of pepper separate from the oil. Do not overcook the oil or its flavor will be compromised.
5. Strain the oil through a fine chinois. The oil will keep for months in the refrigerator.

Vegetable-Infused Oils

Aromatic vegetables, especially garlic, tomatoes, and mushrooms, make marvelous oils that in turn can be used in vinaigrettes, as flavorings in vegetable purées, or as simple sauces for vegetables, seafood, or even meats.

TOMATO OIL

Tomato oil makes a lovely accent in vinaigrettes that in turn can be used as sauces for grilled seafood, chicken, or vegetables. Tomato oil can also be used alone.

YIELD: 2 CUPS (500 MILLILITERS)

ripe red tomatoes	7 pounds	3 kilograms
extra-virgin olive oil	2 cups	500 milliliters

1. Preheat the oven to 400°F (200°C). Wash the tomatoes, cut them in half crosswise, and squeeze out the seeds. Oil a heavy-bottomed roasting pan with 1 tablespoon (15 milliliters) of the olive oil and spread over the tomato halves, flat side down, in a single layer.
2. Bake the tomatoes in the oven for 1½ to 2 hours, until the juices released by the tomatoes have evaporated into a small amount of syrupy liquid. Do not allow the liquid on the bottom of the pan to brown.
3. Scrape the tomatoes into a heavy-bottomed saucepan and add the remaining olive oil. Cook over low heat (the tomatoes should slowly release small bubbles) for 1 to 1½ hours until the bubbles dissipate and the tomatoes begin to darken very slightly. Be careful at this point not to burn the tomatoes or oil.
4. Gently pour the ingredients in the pan into a fine-mesh strainer set over a bowl and let drain, without pushing on the tomatoes, for about 1 hour.

(The cooked tomatoes can be worked through a food mill or strainer to eliminate peels; they make a delicious sauce.)

5. Reserve the oil in a cool place for up to 2 weeks. If liquid settles to the bottom of the bottle, the oil can be carefully transferred to another bottle, leaving the liquid behind.

MOREL OR PORCINI OIL

Most dried mushrooms infuse oil with a surprisingly full-flavored yet delicate aroma, but dried morels and porcini (cèpes) work the best. Dried mushroom oil can be used in salad dressings, pasta sauces, or in emulsified egg, butter, or cream sauces. Mushroom oils can be kept in a cool place for up to 2 weeks.

YIELD: 1 QUART (1 LITER)

dried morels or porcini, rinsed, patted dry	3 to 6 ounces	90 to 175 grams
pure olive oil	1½ cups	375 milliliters
extra-virgin olive oil	3½ cups	875 milliliters

1. Combine the mushrooms with the pure olive oil in a blender and purée to a coarse paste, about 1 minute.
2. Transfer the mushroom paste to a 2-quart (2 liter) saucepan and place over low heat while stirring gently. One minute after the mushroom mixture has started bubbling, take the pan off the heat and let cool.
3. Stir the extra-virgin olive oil into the mushroom mixture and strain the mixture through a fine strainer (chinois) and again through a triple layer of cheesecloth or carefully cleaned and rinsed kitchen towel.

SPICE-INFUSED OILS

Pungent and finely ground spices can be quickly infused in oil by heating the spices in the oil until the spices sizzle and then straining the mixture. Any of the spices used in Indian curry mixtures (pages 549 to 553), as well as the mixtures themselves, can be infused into an inert-tasting oil, such as French *huile d'arachide*, grapeseed oil, or good-quality safflower oil. If experimenting with an unknown spice or spice mixture, heat the spices in a small amount of oil so that if you accidentally overheat the spices you won't waste a large amount of oil.

YIELD: 1 QUART (1 LITER)

ground spices such as cardamom, cumin, star anise, cinnamon, cloves, or spice mixtures such as garam masala (page 550)	1 cup	250 milliliters
tasteless oil such as grapeseed, safflower, or canola	4½ cups	1.1 liters

1. Combine the spices with 2 cups (500 milliliters) of the oil in a small, heavy-bottomed saucepan. Heat, while stirring over medium heat, until the spices begin to sizzle. Continue cooking for about 2 minutes until the spices smell aromatic. Remove from the heat and let cool.

2. Taste the oil to make sure it hasn't burned (in which case it has to be thrown out) and that it tastes strongly of the spices. If it isn't very spicy, repeat the heating and cooling until the oil is intensely flavored (remember, this oil-spice mixture will be diluted with the rest of the oil).

3. Combine with the remaining oil and strain first through a fine-mesh strainer (chinois) and again through a triple layer of cheesecloth or through a carefully washed and rinsed kitchen towel.

Infused Vinegars

Like cold-pressed natural oils, vinegar can be used as a condiment in itself. It can be especially lovely when sprinkled over grilled or sautéed fish instead of the ubiquitous squeezed lemon. Many people like to sprinkle both vinegar and olive oil over grilled foods. Depending on the setting, the effect can be far more satisfying than that of a premade vinaigrette.

Vinegars infused with herbs, garlic, and flowers have long been kitchen staples. Fruit vinegars, popular in the seventeenth and eighteenth centuries, have re-entered the culinary mainstream, with sometimes dubious results. Whether the flavor of a particular herb or ingredient is best introduced into a sauce by first infusing it in vinegar or by using the herb directly depends on the herb or ingredient. Infused vinegars may have first been used as a method of preserving seasonal herbs, rather than ends in themselves. Tarragon and Provençal herbs such as thyme, rosemary, oregano, marjoram, savory, and lavender seem to take best to preservation in vinegar. The flavor of certain other herbs, such as basil, is distorted by vinegar and would be more likely to stay intact if the herb were puréed and held in oil.

PROVENÇAL HERB VINEGAR

Vinegars can be made from single herbs or from combinations, as in this recipe. This method is also excellent for preserving herbs.

YIELD: 1 QUART (1 LITER)

thyme	1 bunch	1 bunch
savory	1 bunch	1 bunch
marjoram	1 bunch	1 bunch
bay leaf	1	1
garlic clove, peeled	1	1
shallot, peeled and halved	1	1
good-quality wine vinegar	1 quart	1 liter

1. Force the thyme, savory, marjoram, bay leaf (all of which should be left on the stems), garlic, and shallot through the mouth of a vinegar or wine bottle.
2. Fill the bottle with the vinegar, and cork. Let the vinegar steep for at least 1 week before use.

ORANGE VINEGAR

Vinegar can be flavored with orange or other citrus fruits by allowing strips of zest to infuse in the vinegar for several days. Citrus vinegars are especially lovely when used with endive.

YIELD: 1 QUART (1 LITER)

oranges	4	4
good-quality wine vinegar	1 quart	1 liter

1. Peel the zests from the oranges with a sharp paring knife or vegetable peeler.
2. Push the zests through the mouth of a wine or vinegar bottle. Pour over the vinegar, and cork.
3. Let the zests infuse in the vinegar for 1 week before use.

RASPBERRY VINEGAR

Practically any fruit, chopped or left whole, can be infused in a bottle of vinegar. Commercially available raspberry vinegar is often made with raspberries that have been cooked to concentrate their sweetness and flavor. Unfortunately, the result is often too sweet and strongly flavored. A more subtle version can be made by simply steeping fresh raspberries in good-quality wine vinegar. The vinegar should have a good concentration of acetic acid (7 percent) because the water contained in the raspberries tends to dilute it.

YIELD: 1 QUART (1 LITER)

fresh raspberries	1 cup	250 milliliters
white wine vinegar	3 cups	750 milliliters

1. Crush the raspberries in a stainless-steel bowl with the back of a wooden spoon.
2. Add the vinegar, stir the mixture, and funnel it into a bottle. Cork it.
3. Let the raspberries steep in the vinegar for a week, and then strain the vinegar through a fine chinois or, if it needs to be perfectly clear, through cheesecloth.

Vinaigrettes

Strictly speaking, vinaigrettes are emulsions of vinegar and oil, but in contemporary kitchens the definition is often stretched to include an emulsion of an acid, such as lemon juice or verjuice, containing not only oil but sometimes cream. Long relegated for use as dressings for green salads and cold foods, vinaigrettes have come into their own as both hot and cold sauces that can be served with meats, fish, and vegetables. Vinaigrettes are relatively unstable emulsions that break down if left to sit. The most common emulsifier is mustard, but many contemporary vinaigrettes are constructed around vegetable purées, such as tomato, sweet pepper, or garlic. So-called vinaigrettes that have been stabilized with egg yolks are, strictly speaking, light-style mayonnaises.

In addition to using vegetable purées as starting points for contemporary vinaigrettes, chefs often use vinaigrettes in conjunction with other sauces, such as beurre blanc and its derivatives. Because vinaigrettes, especially when served hot, are unstable, combining them with emulsified butter sauces helps stabilize the emulsion.

Integral sauces made from roasting juices and cooking liquids can also be quickly finished as vinaigrettes by combining the cooking liquid in a blender with cooked vegetables or herbs, which act as emulsifiers, and slowly adding vinegar and oil.

Vinaigrettes for Green Salads

Beginning cooks often prepare vinaigrette by nervously whisking oil into a mixture of vinegar and mustard, ever fearful that the tenuous emulsion will break. It often does. Since the components in a vinaigrette will be evenly spread over the surface of a salad anyway, it is not necessary to work them into an emulsion. In fact, extra-virgin olive oil loses much of its delicacy and may even turn bitter if overbeaten. The easiest and most obvious sauce for a tossed green salad is to dribble over a few tablespoons of good extra-virgin olive oil, sprinkle over about one-third as much good wine vinegar (infused herb vinegar is great), sprinkle on some salt and freshly ground pepper, and toss.

The most important flavors of a vinaigrette are usually those provided by the vinegar and oil. The best-quality extra-virgin olive oil and good aged vinegar are the most natural sauces, although some chefs find extra-virgin olive oil too characteristic (or too expensive) and insist that it be used exclusively for Provençal cooking. Nut oils can also be used but can become monotonous if used regularly. They are best served with distinctly bitter or particularly aggressive greens. Some people think that a vinaigrette should be almost tasteless and insist on using inert, chemically extracted vegetable oils, either alone or in conjunction with natural full-flavored oils.

To vary the flavor of a salad vinaigrette beyond the natural characteristics of the oils and vinegars, flavored vinegars and oils can be used, or additional ingredients can be infused in the vinegar before the salad is tossed. Two of the most common ingredients are mustard and garlic. Garlic should be worked to a paste along with or before it is combined with the vinegar, or it should be finely chopped. It is then allowed to infuse and is strained out before the vinegar is added to the salad. Herbs should be finely chopped and allowed to infuse in the vinegar for varying lengths of time: Provençal herbs, such as marjoram, thyme, and savory, for several hours; fines herbes (tarragon, chives, parsley, and chervil), for 5 to 10 minutes. It is best to avoid using mustard in delicately flavored salad sauces containing extra-virgin olive oil, as the delicacy of the oil will be lost.

BASIC VINAIGRETTE FOR GREEN SALADS

Plain vinaigrette can be varied by balancing the flavors of various vinegars and oils. Some chefs use only extra-virgin olive oil for their salads, whereas others like to attenuate the full flavor of olive oil with relatively tasteless oils such as safflower or French *huile d'arachide*. Some chefs are fond of nut oils, such as walnut or hazelnut. Most people use mustard when making a vinaigrette (not only for flavor but because it acts as an emulsifier), but mustard can obscure the flavor of good-quality oils and is best left out when using the sauce for green salads. When preparing vinaigrette to be served with cold meats, mustard is a welcome addition. Either finely ground Dijon or whole-grain Meaux-style mustard can be used.

Depending on taste and the strength of the vinegar, most vinaigrettes contain one part vinegar to three or four parts oil.

YIELD: 2 CUPS (500 MILLILITERS)

vinegar	½ cup	125 milliliters
mustard (optional)	2 tablespoons	30 milliliters
salt and pepper	to taste	to taste
oil	1½ to 2 cups	375 to 500 milliliters

1. Combine the vinegar, mustard, and salt and pepper in a stainless-steel bowl.
2. Slowly stir in the oil with a whisk. Do *not* beat. When most, but not all, of the oil has been added, start tasting the vinaigrette. It may not be necessary to add all the oil. Do not worry if the vinaigrette separates. When it is tossed with the salad greens, all of its components will coat the greens even if the vinaigrette has not been thoroughly emulsified.

CREAMY VINAIGRETTE FOR SALADS

Heavy cream, alone or in conjunction with oil, can be added to vinegar and mustard, producing a vinaigrette that is excellent with delicately flavored salads. Because of its subtlety, creamy vinaigrette can be flavored easily with delicate herbs, such as mint, chives, or chervil. It is also an excellent sauce for showcasing the quality of a special vinegar.

YIELD: 1½ CUPS (375 MILLILITERS)

mustard	2 teaspoons	10 milliliters
salt and pepper	to taste	to taste
vinegar	¼ cup	60 milliliters
heavy cream	1 cup	250 milliliters
extra-virgin olive oil	¼ cup	60 milliliters
chopped chervil (or other delicate herb)	2 tablespoons	30 milliliters

Combine the mustard, salt and pepper, and vinegar. Whisk in the cream and gently stir in the olive oil. Stir in the chopped chervil.

HONEY-MUSTARD VINAIGRETTE

This savory vinaigrette is delicious in salads and when tossed with cold cooked vegetables.

YIELD: ¾ CUP (185 MILLILITERS)

garlic clove, minced	1	1
minced fresh ginger	½ teaspoon	2 milliliters
balsamic, homemade, or Banyuls vinegar	3 tablespoons	45 milliliters
honey	1 tablespoon	15 milliliters
dijon or meaux (whole-grain) mustard	1 tablespoon	15 milliliters
soy sauce	2 tablespoons	30 milliliters
Japanese sesame oil	1 tablespoon	15 milliliters
extra-virgin olive oil	¼ cup	60 milliliters
bonito flakes (optional)	½ cup	125 milliliters

Combine all the ingredients. If you're including the bonito flakes, let the mixture sit for an hour or overnight and then strain them out.

More Elaborate Vinaigrettes

Vinaigrettes often provide the necessary accent for leftovers and have long been popular with cold foods such as brains, leftover poached meats, and cold roast chicken. Because no cooking is involved, the preparation of an impromptu sauce based on oil and vinegar lends itself to improvisation. Vinaigrettes for cold meats and fish are usually best when more aggressively flavored than a vinaigrette for a green salad. Mustard is one of the best and most obvious flavorings, but other briny ingredients, such as cornichons (sour gherkins), capers, anchovies, and grilled peppers, are excellent when finely chopped and incorporated into the sauce. Herbs, finely chopped or crushed at the last minute into a paste with a mortar and pestle, provide exciting flavor and color.

Cold vinaigrettes can also be constructed around vegetable purées (which act as emulsifiers), bits of leftover roasting juices or braising liquids, reduced court-bouillon, or leftover cream sauces.

WILD MUSHROOM–WALNUT OIL SALAD

Be sure to use walnut oil made from roasted nuts (see "Nut Oils," page 41) when flavoring this salad. The greater your collection of wild mushrooms the tastier the salad. The confit is optional.

YIELD: 4 FIRST-COURSE SERVINGS

wild mushrooms	1½ pounds	675 grams
duck fat, olive oil, or bacon fat	3 tablespoons	45 milliliters
red wine vinegar or sherry vinegar	¼ cup	60 milliliters
walnut oil	3 tablespoons	45 milliliters
extra-virgin olive oil	3 tablespoons	45 milliliters
confit duck legs, meat shredded (optional)	2	2
salt and pepper	to taste	to taste
salad greens	as needed	as needed

1. Clean the mushrooms and cut them into thick slices; if they are small, leave them whole. When cutting them in pieces, follow the contours of the mushroom to respect its shape.
2. Heat the duck fat in a large sauté pan until it ripples and toss in the mushrooms. Sauté over high heat until browned and fragrant, about 10 minutes.
3. Pour the vinegar and walnut and olive oils into the pan, add the confit, if using, and season with salt and pepper. Dump over the salad greens and toss gently.

Green Sauces

Some of the oldest European sauces are vinaigrettes (older recipes also used verjuice) containing finely chopped herbs. These were usually called green sauces. Any of the many herb-anchovy-caper-cornichon–hard-boiled egg combinations found as the basis for mayonnaises and compound butters such as Montpellier Butter (page 417) can be used for vinaigrettes.

SALSA VERDE

Recipes for this Italian green sauce vary widely, depending on the source, but the sauce is basically a vinaigrette that is well flavored with herbs and pickled vegetables such as capers and cornichons (sour gherkins). It often contains mustard and anchovies, but these are not essential. Breadcrumbs are sometimes worked into the sauce to give it a thicker texture, so it can be dolloped onto foods at the table. It is excellent with cold boiled meats and grilled foods, especially full-flavored fish such as tuna and mackerel.

YIELD: 3 CUPS (750 MILLILITERS)

garlic cloves, peeled	2	2
flat parsley leaves	3½ ounces	100 grams
basil leaves	3½ ounces	100 grams
extra-virgin olive oil	9 fluid ounces	280 milliliters
capers, drained	3 tablespoons	45 milliliters
cornichons	2 ounces	50 grams
mustard	1 tablespoon	15 milliliters
wine vinegar	½ cup	125 milliliters
salt and pepper	to taste	to taste
breadcrumbs (optional)	4 to 8 tablespoons	60 to 120 milliliters

1. Chop the garlic and crush it into a paste in a mortar or on a cutting board with the side of a knife.
2. Wash and dry the parsley and basil. Sprinkle the leaves with 2 tablespoons (30 milliliters) of the olive oil (to prevent the basil from turning black during chopping). Chop the herbs, capers, and cornichons together until they are the size of large grains of sand.
3. Put the mixture in a bowl and combine it with the mustard and vinegar.
4. Gently stir in the remaining cup (250 milliliters) of olive oil. Add salt and pepper to taste. If a thicker vinaigrette is desired, work in the breadcrumbs until the appropriate consistency is achieved.

SAUCE RAVIGOTE

There are two classic versions of sauce ravigote, one a velouté flavored with herbs and served hot (page 151) and this, probably earlier version, which is a type of vinaigrette, served cold. This French version of green sauce is similar to the Italian *salsa verde*, except that it contains onions and is never bound with breadcrumbs.

wine vinegar	½ cup	125 milliliters
drained capers, chopped	2 heaping tablespoons	40 milliliters
flat parsley	1 bunch	1 bunch
chopped chervil	2 heaping tablespoons	40 milliliters
chopped chives	2 heaping tablespoons	40 milliliters
onion, finely chopped	1 medium	1 medium
extra-virgin olive oil	1 cup	250 milliliters
salt and pepper	to taste	to taste

Combine all the ingredients except the olive oil, salt, and pepper. Whisk the olive oil into the mixture. Adjust the seasonings.

MINT SAUCE FOR LAMB

Older recipes for English green sauce vaguely recommend finely chopping or grinding together herbs, vinegar or verjuice, and usually a bit of sugar or sometimes orange juice. Sorrel was most frequently called for, but parsley, spinach, and sometimes mint were also used. Green sauces were usually served with veal or roast lamb. The mint in this green sauce can be replaced with dill, sorrel, parsley, or spinach.

YIELD: ½ CUP (125 MILLILITERS)

mint	1 large bunch	1 large bunch
coarse salt	½ teaspoon	2 milliliters
sugar	1 teaspoon	5 milliliters
vinegar, lemon juice, or verjuice	¼ cup	60 milliliters

1. Remove the leaves from the mint. Wash them if necessary, and make sure they are perfectly dry.
2. Grind the mint leaves with the salt and sugar with a mortar and pestle.
3. When the mint has been ground to a fine paste, add the vinegar. If the sauce seems too acidic, dilute it with water.

Hot Vinaigrettes

Because vinaigrettes are relatively unstable emulsions, they have been little used as hot sauces for fear they will separate on a hot plate — even though vinegar and oil have long appeared separately as condiments on Mediterranean tables. For vinegar and oil to remain combined, it is necessary to have an ingredient that will stabilize an emulsion of the two. Mustard is the emulsifier most often used, but it is too aggressive to use with delicate sauces and oils. Vegetable purées and herbs combined in a blender just before serving with the other ingredients are being used more and more by chefs. Because the flavor of extra-virgin olive oil is distorted when the oil is worked in a blender, it is often necessary to use another type of oil for the first stage of the blending and then to stir in extra-virgin olive oil by hand.

Several factors in the changing aesthetic of how a sauce should look and taste have contributed to the acceptance of hot vinaigrettes in contemporary kitchens. At one time, a trace of fat on the surface of a sauce meant that the sauce had broken, because it had been carelessly prepared. Nowadays, certain foods are sometimes presented surrounded with a small amount of fat. This is especially true for naturally fatty foods such as foie gras or vegetables cooked *à la grecque* with olive oil. Hence it is acceptable to serve the components of a vinaigrette—oil and vinegar—so that they appear separately on the plate. Moreover, diners no longer expect foods to be served swimming in sauce or napped with a sauce that covers the food. A small amount of sharply flavored, tangy sauce on the bottom of the plate has become acceptable. Finally, chefs have taken to combining vinaigrettes with other sauces to stabilize them. For example, the hot tomato vinaigrette recipe that follows is stabilized with hot emulsified butter.

HOT TOMATO VINAIGRETTE

This vinaigrette uses hot tomato coulis as the emulsifier and is given extra flavor and complexity with reduced court-bouillon. The vinaigrette is then combined with emulsified butter (Beurre Fondu, page 412), and the flavor is adjusted with seasonings or by adding more of certain ingredients. This vinaigrette is best served with fish or shellfish.

YIELD: 2 CUPS (500 MILLILITERS)

court-bouillon	2 cups	500 milliliters
shallot, minced	1 medium	1 medium
garlic clove, crushed, peeled	1	1
extra-virgin olive oil	5 tablespoons	75 milliliters
ripe tomatoes	4	4
fresh thyme sprig	1	1
lemon juice	2 tablespoons	30 milliliters
water	1 tablespoon	15 milliliters
butter	2 ounces	60 grams
sherry or balsamic vinegar	2 tablespoons	30 milliliters
salt and pepper	to taste	to taste

1. Reduce the court-bouillon to ½ cup (125 milliliters).
2. Sweat the minced shallot and the garlic with 1 tablespoon (15 milliliters) of the olive oil in a 2-quart (2 liter) saucepan.
3. Cut the tomatoes in half crosswise and squeeze out their seeds. Chop them coarsely and add them to the shallots and garlic. Add the thyme.
4. Cook the tomatoes until any excess liquid evaporates. Strain the mixture through a fine chinois.
5. While the tomatoes are cooking down, prepare the emulsified butter (beurre fondu) by heating the lemon juice and water and whisking in the butter.
6. Pour the strained tomato mixture (coulis) into a 2-quart (2 liter) saucepan with the reduced court-bouillon, and add the vinegar. Whisk in the emulsified butter and then the remaining ¼ cup (60 milliliters) of extra-virgin olive oil.
7. Adjust the sauce's flavors by adding additional vinegar, olive oil, or whole butter. Season with salt and pepper.

WARM SWEET RED PEPPER AND GARLIC VINAIGRETTE

This sauce illustrates the use of infused oils and garlic purée in a hot vinaigrette. The vinaigrette can be served hot on grilled foods, or it can be used as a thickener for roasting juices or for poaching liquids for fish.

YIELD: 1 CUP (250 MILLILITERS)

garlic cloves, peeled	10	10
champagne vinegar	3 tablespoons	45 milliliters
finely chopped marjoram	1 tablespoon	15 milliliters
sweet red pepper oil (page 431)	5 fluid ounces	150 milliliters
roasting juices (optional)	to taste	to taste
salt and pepper	to taste	to taste

1. Simmer the garlic cloves in enough water to cover by 2 inches (5 cm) for about 20 minutes, until they are soft. Force the garlic through a drum sieve with a plastic pastry scraper.
2. Combine the garlic pulp with the vinegar and marjoram in a stainless-steel bowl.
3. Whisk in the oil and stir in the roasting juices, if using. Adjust the seasonings to taste.

Finishing Integral Sauces as Vinaigrettes

The cooking liquids from braised fish, vegetables, and meats and the roasting juices from meats can be converted into savory vinaigrettes by last-minute puréeing in a blender with vinegars, oils, cooked vegetables (such as the mirepoix vegetables used in cooking the meat or fish), and herbs. These delicate yet full-flavored sauces are excellent alternatives to flour-thickened gravies or butter-enriched roasting juices.

BASIL VINAIGRETTE FOR ROAST LAMB

In this recipe a jus prepared from a roast leg, rack, saddle, or shoulder of lamb is finished as a basil-flavored vinaigrette. The resulting sauce may be served hot or cold. The recipe can be adapted by using roasting juices from other meats, different herbs, and various oils.

Because the only emulsifier is basil, a blender is used to quickly homogenize the mixture. Because the flavor of extra-virgin olive oil is compromised by the action of the blender, pure olive oil is used first and then extra-virgin olive oil is whisked in by hand. It is also possible to omit the oils completely.

YIELD: ¾ CUP (185 MILLILITERS)

hot full-flavored lamb roasting juices	¼ cup	60 milliliters
wine vinegar	3 tablespoons	45 milliliters
salt and pepper	to taste	to taste
basil leaves	20 large	20 large
pure olive oil	2 tablespoons	30 milliliters
extra-virgin olive oil	2 tablespoons	30 milliliters

1. Combine the hot roasting juices, wine vinegar, salt and pepper, and basil leaves in a blender. Blend the mixture for 15 to 20 seconds, until the basil is finely chopped.
2. Pour the pure olive oil into the mixture in a steady stream while blending.
3. Transfer the sauce to a mixing bowl and stir in the extra-virgin olive oil by hand.
4. Taste the sauce to see whether it needs additional vinegar or oil. Adjust the seasonings.

HOT HAZELNUT AND PARSLEY VINAIGRETTE

This is an excellent method for finishing the cooking liquids from roast meats or braised fish and fish fillets cooked *en sauce* (see Chapter 10, "Integral Fish and Shellfish Sauces," page 287). The sauce, which is bound and flavored with parsley, can be flavored with different oils, vinegars, lemon or lime juice, verjuice, and herbs. Because the sauce is unstable and its flavor fragile, serve it immediately after blending. Fish and meats can be lightly brushed with this sauce, or they can be surrounded with a thin layer of sauce spread on the plate.

YIELD: ¾ CUP (185 MILLILITERS)

flat parsley, leaves only	1 bunch	1 bunch
hot meat roasting juices or fish braising liquid	¼ cup	60 milliliters
vinegar	2 tablespoons	30 milliliters
hazelnut oil	¼ cup	60 milliliters
salt and pepper	to taste	to taste

1. Combine the parsley leaves with the hot meat juices in a blender. Add the vinegar and blend on high speed for 15 to 20 seconds.
2. Pour the hazelnut oil into the liquid through the top of the blender, while blending. Strain the sauce through a regular mesh strainer to eliminate any large pieces of parsley or through a chinois to eliminate the parsley completely.
3. Taste the sauce and adjust with the salt and pepper. More oil or vinegar can be added if necessary.

SALSAS

Mexican salsas are combinations of more or less finely chopped vegetables and sometimes fruits. They are seasoned and flavored in many different ways, but usually contain hot peppers, cilantro, lime juice, and tomatoes. The ingredients, instead of being puréed or infused into a liquid, are allowed to retain their texture and individuality within the mixture. Salsas are usually brightly colored and have a direct and refreshing flavor. Because of this, the more traditional salsas are excellent with grilled and highly flavored foods.

MEXICAN SALSA

There are many recipes and variations for Mexican salsa, some cooked, some raw. The following recipe is a mixture of raw ingredients that are allowed to infuse.

YIELD: 1 QUART (1 LITER)

plum tomatoes, peeled, seeded, and coarsely chopped	6 large	6 large
garlic clove, crushed to a paste	1	1
sweet red pepper, seeded and finely chopped	1	1
jalapeño, seeded and finely chopped	1	1
cuban long pepper, seeded and finely chopped	1	1
red onion, chopped	1 medium	1 medium
avocado, chopped	1	1
cilantro, chopped	1 small bunch	1 small bunch
juice of 2 limes		
extra-virgin olive oil	3 tablespoons	45 milliliters

Combine all the ingredients and let the mixture steep for an hour or two before serving.

Variations

There are many possible variations of Mexican salsa. One of the best is to replace the tomatoes in the recipe with cooked small tomatillos, which give the salsa a delightful sour taste and characteristic green color. Yellow tomatoes and different-colored chiles and peppers can be used for exciting color combinations. Cilantro is the most commonly used Mexican flavoring for salsa. Other herbs, such as parsley, freshly chopped thyme, or oregano, can be substituted, giving the salsa a Mediterranean rather than a Mexican character.

Improvising Salsas

The concept of chopping ingredients and then serving the mixture as a sauce opens up a whole range of possibilities for sauce making. The ingredients retain their color, texture, and individual flavor but are cut small enough for the mixture to take on an identity of its own. It can then be spread over foods and eaten like a sauce.

Almost any vegetable or fruit can be chopped and served in the juices it releases during maceration; vegetables and fruits such as cucumbers, tomatoes, papayas, and mangoes release liquid when tossed with salt. Vegetables and fruits can also be lightly bound with another sauce. Although no one would ever call it a salsa, a mushroom duxelles lightly bound with cream could be thought of as an extension of this concept.

When improvising salsas, the difference between soup, salad, and salsa becomes hazy. Gazpacho, a spicy Spanish soup of raw chopped garlic, onions, cucumbers, and tomatoes, can be served as a summer sauce for grilled foods. Fruit salads can be converted to sauces by chopping or cutting the fruits into smaller pieces and seasoning them with herbs. The ingredients in guacamole, instead of being mashed, can be coarsely chopped so they retain their color and texture. The mixture can then be served as a sauce for other foods instead of always being relegated to before-dinner chips and dip.

Chefs in France have started using a mixture of vegetables cut into brunoise (cubes measuring 2 millimeters, or between ⅛ and 1/16 inch, on each side) as a light and decorative treatment for grilled or sautéed meats and fish. Likely vegetables for this treatment are tomatoes, sweet peppers, cucumbers, mushrooms, truffles, and cornichons (sour gherkins). Capers are also sometimes added to these mixtures for their direct flavor and contrasting shape. These mixtures of vegetable brunoise are usually scented with a variety of herbs and moistened with an acidic ingredient, such as lemon or lime juice, various vinegars, or, most recently, verjuice. Olive oil and nut oils as well as stocks and roasting juices are also used.

VEGETABLE BRUNOISE FOR GRILLED FOWL OR FISH

The thyme called for in this recipe can be replaced with another flavorful herb such as savory, marjoram, mint, or cilantro. This sauce can be served either hot or cold. If served hot, heat it just before serving and carefully spread it over the surface of the grilled fowl or fish with a tablespoon.

YIELD: 1 CUP (250 MILLILITERS), SERVING 8

leek, white part only	1	1
fennel bulb	¼ small	¼ small
lemon juice, wine vinegar, or verjuice	2 tablespoons	30 milliliters
zucchini	1	1
extra-virgin olive oil	2 tablespoons	30 milliliters
sweet red pepper	½	½
cucumber	¼	¼
tomato	1 small	1 small
small capers, drained	2 tablespoons	30 milliliters
freshly chopped thyme leaves	1 teaspoon	5 milliliters
salt and pepper	to taste	to taste

1. Wash the leek, separate the leaves, and cut them carefully into julienne and then into brunoise.
2. Cut the core out of the fennel section. Carefully pull apart the peel-like sections of the bulb, julienne them, and cut them into brunoise. Put the fennel brunoise in a bowl with 1 tablespoon (15 milliliters) of the lemon juice.
3. Only the outside of the zucchini, with the peel, is used. Slice the outside of the zucchini into strips between ⅛ and 1⁄16 inch (2 mm) thick. Cut these into brunoise.
4. Gently sweat the brunoise of leeks, fennel, and zucchini in the olive oil until the vegetables soften and release their liquid. Drain the vegetables in a strainer and return any liquid to the saucepan.
5. Burn the skin off the red pepper, and cut it into brunoise.
6. Peel and seed the cucumber. Cut it into brunoise.
7. Peel the tomato and cut it into wedges. Remove the pulp from the wedges with a small paring knife. Cut the flesh into brunoise.
8. Combine all the vegetables, the capers, the thyme, the remaining lemon juice, and the vegetable cooking liquid (with olive oil). Add salt and pepper.

TRUFFLE SALSA

When truffles are chopped and used to finish a classic brown sauce, the sauce is called *Périgueux;* the same sauce, finished with sliced truffles, becomes a *périgourdine* (see page 192). When the truffles are puréed with a natural jus, contemporary (and seventeenth-century) chefs call it a truffle coulis. To call the following recipe a truffle salsa may be carrying poetic license too far, but the term is used here to imply that the truffles are cut into tiny cubes. The salsa may be served hot or cold, spread over hot or cold meats or fish.

YIELD: 1 CUP (250 MILLILITERS)

fresh or preserved black truffles	7 ounces	200 grams
full-flavored stock	2 tablespoons	30 milliliters
heavy cream	2 tablespoons	30 milliliters
extra-virgin olive oil	1 tablespoon	15 milliliters
excellent vinegar (sherry or authentic balsamic)	several drops	several drops
salt and pepper	to taste	to taste

1. Peel the truffles and slice them into ⅟₃₂-inch (1 mm) slices with a Japanese mandoline. Julienne the slices and then cut them into a tiny dice.
2. Combine the stock and cream and bring the mixture to a simmer. Add the diced truffles and stir the mixture over low heat for 5 minutes.
3. Cover the saucepan and remove the salsa from the heat. Let it sit for 15 minutes.
4. Stir in the olive oil and the vinegar. Add salt and pepper.

TROPICAL FRUIT SALSA

The idea for making salsas with fruit stemmed from a delicious summer salad of tropical fruit highly seasoned with grilled peppers and cilantro and tossed with lime juice and olive oil. Barbecued chicken or shrimp is tossed into the salad just before serving.

To convert a salad into a salsa, simply cut the pieces of fruit or vegetable small enough so that the mixture, although comprising small pieces of solid food, gives the impression of being semiliquid, so it can be poured or spooned over foods.

If preparing the salsa in advance, it is best to keep the fruits separate. The cilantro should be chopped just before serving, and the fruits seasoned only at the end. In this recipe the fruit is cut into ¼-inch (5 mm) cubes—the French call this size cube *macédoine*—but for less formal presentations, the ingredients can simply be chopped until the salsa has the right consistency.

This tropical fruit salsa comprises several different fruits. The fruits can also be kept separate, each seasoned differently, and a variety of fruit salsas served with grilled meats or fish. In restaurant settings or in situations where this is impractical, the individual fruit salsas flavored with different herbs or tossed with different-colored peppers and tomatoes can be arranged directly on the plate.

This recipe is only a model; almost any type of fruit can be used.

pineapple	¼ small	¼ small
Hawaiian papaya	1	1
kiwis	2	2
mango	1	1
sweet red pepper, grilled, skinned, and seeded	1	1
hot chiles, seeded	2 or 3 small	2 or 3 small
cilantro	1 small bunch	1 small bunch
red onion, finely chopped	1 medium	1 medium
juice of 2 limes		
salt	to taste	to taste

1. Cut the fruits into small cubes or chop until they come together to produce a semiliquid consistency.
2. Chop or cube the red pepper and the chiles. Chop the cilantro.
3. Combine all the ingredients. Add salt to taste. See the photograph in the color plates.

CHUTNEYS AND RELISHES

The distinction among chutneys, relishes, salsas, pestos, and purées is often hard to establish because the terms are all used somewhat interchangeably.

Although in some languages the term *salsa* describes any sauce, it is used here to refer to a Mexican-style sauce of chopped herbs, vegetables, and sometimes fruits. Mexican salsas are usually served raw or only lightly cooked. Salsas can be made exclusively with Mexican-style ingredients or the concept and style can be stretched and used with other ingredients for a distinctly non-Mexican result (such as Truffle Salsa, page 447).

A *relish* is similar to a salsa except that some of the ingredients have usually been pickled in brine or vinegar—pickles (often French cornichons), capers, pickled onions, peppers, and pickled beets are likely candidates.

Chutneys are usually divided into three types. The most familiar kind (Major Grey's is the best-known example) is sweet and sour and usually contains fruit cooked with a sweetener (such as sugar or molasses), spices, and an acidic ingredient, such as vinegar. A second variety, made by tossing vegetables such as onions with herbs (usually mint or cilantro), spices, chiles, and acidic ingredients such as lemon juice, vinegar, or tamarind, is more akin to a relish or simple salad designed to accompany richer foods. A third kind consists mostly of finely chopped herbs (again, usually cilantro or mint) simply tossed with lemon juice or given body with coconut or mango.

Pesto is the Italian word for "pestle," which makes the term applicable to sauces other than the familiar Genoese version made of basil, cheese, and pine nuts. Any mixture that has been ground to a paste with a mortar and pestle or food processor can be called a pesto (see "Pestos," page 485).

Sweet-and-Sour Chutneys

Almost any fruit or vegetable can be cooked and seasoned with sugar, vinegar, and spices to provide an acceptable chutney. Sweet-and-sour chutneys make a perfect vehicle for underripe fruits such as pears, peaches, or mangoes. Because of the sugar and vinegar they contain, sweet-and-sour chutneys will keep for several months, tightly covered, in the refrigerator.

SWEET-AND-SOUR FRUIT CHUTNEY

Although many Indian classics have been carefully standardized, it's possible to improvise a sweet-and-sour chutney by adjusting some of the standard ingredients to taste and by using virtually any underripe fruit.

YIELD: ABOUT 2 CUPS (500 MILLILITERS)

sugar	2 tablespoons	30 milliliters
good-quality white wine vinegar, cider vinegar, or sherry vinegar	½ cup	125 milliliters
underripe fruit cut into ¼ × ½-inch (5 mm × 1 cm) dice	2 cups	500 milliliters
such as		
pears, 8 ounces (225 grams) each	2	2
or	*or*	*or*
mangoes, 14 ounces (400 grams) each	2	2
or	*or*	*or*
peaches, 6 ounces (175 grams) each	3	3
serrano chile, stemmed, seeded, finely chopped	1	1
or	*or*	*or*
thai chiles, stemmed, seeded, finely chopped	2	2
grated fresh ginger	2 teaspoons	10 milliliters
garam masala (page 550) or basic curry powder (page 552)	1 tablespoon	15 milliliters
white or dark raisins (optional)	½ cup	125 milliliters

1. Combine the sugar and vinegar in a stainless-steel saucepan large enough to hold the diced fruit, and simmer gently to dissolve the sugar.
2. Stir the fruit cubes into the sugar-vinegar mixture and simmer gently until the cubes soften but retain some texture, 5 to 15 minutes. Drain the cubes in a strainer set over another saucepan. Combine the chiles, ginger, and spice mixture with the liquid released by the fruit and, if necessary, reduce the liquid by two-thirds to three-quarters, until it is syrupy.
3. Stir the raisins, if using, into the hot reduced liquid and let the mixture cool. Stir the fruit into the cooled mixture.

GREEN TOMATO CHUTNEY

This chutney—using underripe tomatoes, not tomatillos—is flavored with garam masala (pages 550 and 551), a mild curry powder, but other spices and flavors can be used. It is served cold with meats and curries.

YIELD: 3 CUPS (750 MILLILITERS)

onion, finely chopped	1 large	1 large
olive oil	¼ cup	60 milliliters
green (underripe) tomatoes	2 pounds	1 kilogram
garam masala or good-quality mild curry	1 ounce	25 grams
sugar	6 tablespoons	90 milliliters
vinegar	¼ cup	60 milliliters
salt and pepper	to taste	to taste

1. Gently sweat the onion in the olive oil for 20 minutes. Do not allow it to brown.
2. Peel the tomatoes by plunging them into boiling water, then into cold water, and sliding off the skins. Cut them in half crosswise and squeeze out the seeds. Chop them coarsely.
3. Add the garam masala to the onions and cook for 1 minute.
4. Add the chopped tomatoes, the sugar, and the vinegar to the mixture, and cook the mixture for about 30 minutes, until it thickens.
5. Taste the mixture and adjust the seasonings, the sugar, and the vinegar. Allow to cool.

KUMQUAT RELISH

Kumquats are not to everyone's taste but their tartness coupled with a subtle bitterness makes them perfect for relishes that can be served with grilled foods or leftover roast meats. This relish is a little like a marmalade but not as sweet and with more texture.

YIELD: 2 CUPS (500 MILLILITERS)

kumquats	1 pound	450 grams
sugar	⅓ cup	80 milliliters
star anise, crushed and tied up in cheesecloth (optional)	3	3
orange juice	3 cups	750 milliliters

1. Rinse the kumquats and slice them the thickness of quarters.
2. Combine the kumquats with the sugar, star anise, if using, and juice and bring to a gentle simmer. Skim off any froth that floats to the surface.

3. When the kumquats soften, after about 15 minutes, drain them in a colander set over a clean saucepan. Boil down the liquid until it's thick and syrupy, to about ½ cup (125 milliliters), and combine it with the kumquats. Serve cold.

Vegetable Chutneys

Some chutneys function as relishes or even salads and provide a bright, refreshing flavor and crunchy texture that contrasts with the main course. Although many of these chutneys are traditional and don't allow for much variation, the concept of thinly slicing, cubing, or grating raw vegetables such as cucumbers, tomatoes, onions, and carrots and then flavoring them with spices lends itself to improvisation. In addition to spices, most Indian vegetable chutneys contain chiles to provide heat and an acidic ingredient such as lemon juice or vinegar.

CAPER AND CORNICHON RELISH

This relish is excellent with barbecued chicken and pork.

YIELD: 2 CUPS (500 MILLILITERS)

red onion	1	1
capers, drained	4 ounces	125 grams
cornichons (sour gherkins)	4 ounces	125 grams
vinegar	¼ cup	60 milliliters
extra-virgin olive oil	¼ cup	60 milliliters
chopped dill	2 tablespoons	30 milliliters

Finely chop the onion, capers, and cornichons. Combine them with the vinegar, olive oil, and dill. Cover the mixture and let it steep overnight in the refrigerator.

TOMATO AND ONION CHUTNEY

The combination of onions and tomatoes is an Indian favorite. Each region, or even cook, stamps a unique identity on the mixture by using different spices, and sometimes yogurt, grated coconut, or nuts. This version is one of the simplest and most popular.

YIELD: ABOUT 1 QUART (1 LITER), ENOUGH FOR 6 TO 8 SIDE-DISH SERVINGS

red onions, thinly sliced	2 medium	2 medium
tomatoes, peeled, seeded, chopped	4 medium	4 medium
coarsely chopped cilantro leaves	¼ cup	60 milliliters

lemon juice	1 tablespoon	15 milliliters
serrano chiles, stemmed, seeded, very finely chopped	2	2
or	or	or
thai chiles, stemmed, seeded, very finely chopped	4	4
or	or	or
jalapeños, stemmed, seeded, very finely chopped	4	4
fine salt	1 teaspoon	5 milliliters

1. Soak the onion slices for 1 hour in ice water to give them crunch and attenuate their flavor.
2. Heat the tomatoes in a small heavy-bottomed saucepan over medium heat, and stir until they thicken into a sauce. Remove from the heat and stir in the cilantro, lemon juice, chiles, and salt.
3. Within an hour of serving, drain the onions, spin them dry in a lettuce spinner (or pat them with towels), and stir them into the cooled tomato sauce.

Herb Chutneys

Anyone who's eaten in an Indian restaurant has encountered the runny but flavorful green sauces served as relishes at the beginning of the meal. Mint and cilantro are the herbs most often used in these sauces, but the idea of puréeing fresh green herbs, sweetening them slightly, and thinning the mixture with water, yogurt, or coconut milk can be used to improvise very light sauces with other herbs.

CILANTRO OR MINT CHUTNEY

YIELD: 1 CUP (250 MILLILITERS), ENOUGH FOR 4 TO 6 SERVINGS

cilantro or mint leaves, tightly packed	1 cup	250 milliliters
sugar (optional)	1 teaspoon	5 milliliters
cold water, plain yogurt, or coconut milk	¾ cup	185 milliliters
onion, peeled, finely chopped	1 small	1 small
serrano chile, stemmed, seeded, finely chopped	1	1
or	or	or
thai chiles, stemmed, seeded, finely chopped	2	2
or	or	or
jalapeños, stemmed, seeded, finely chopped	2	2
lemon juice	2 tablespoons	30 milliliters

Within an hour of serving the sauce, purée the herbs in a blender with the sugar, if using, and water for 1 minute on high speed. Stir in the rest of the ingredients.

FRUIT SAUCES

Savory fruit sauces have long been popular in England and the United States as accompaniments to roasts and pâtés. Everyone is familiar with mint jelly served with roast lamb, and cranberry sauce served with roast turkey. The more elaborate Cumberland sauce, although less well known, has long been served with pâtés and cold roast meats.

Most cold fruit sauces contain pectin, a naturally occurring sugar-like substance that causes acidic fruit mixtures to jell. Because most fruits contain insufficient pectin, most fruit sauces contain jelly to help them set.

CUMBERLAND SAUCE

This sauce is traditionally served with cold venison.

YIELD: 1 CUP (250 MILLILITERS)

shallot, minced	1	1
zest of 1 orange, finely julienned		
zest of 1 lemon, finely julienned		
red currant jelly	¼ cup	60 milliliters
port	6 tablespoons	90 milliliters
juice of 1 orange		
wine vinegar	2 tablespoons	30 milliliters
dijon mustard	1 teaspoon	5 milliliters
powdered ginger	1 pinch	1 pinch

Blanch the shallots and orange and lemon zests for 2 minutes in boiling water and drain in a strainer. Combine with the remaining ingredients in a small saucepan. Bring the sauce to a slow simmer and simmer long enough to cook the alcohol off the port and to dissolve the red currant jelly. Serve cold.

CRANBERRY SAUCE

This straightforward sauce is the one served in England and the United States with roast turkey. It should not be confused with more elaborate French cranberry sauces, which are actually brown sauces garnished with whole cranberries.

YIELD: 1 QUART (1 LITER)

cranberries	1 pound	500 grams
sugar	1 cup	200 grams
water	to cover	to cover

1. In a heavy-bottomed saucepan, combine the cranberries, sugar, and enough water to cover the mixture by 1 inch (2.5 cm).
2. Bring the mixture to a slow simmer and cook for about 20 minutes. Stir every couple of minutes to keep the sauce from sticking.
3. Taste the sauce; more sugar may be needed.
4. The sauce can be allowed to cool and served as is. For a smooth sauce, strain through a food mill or drum sieve. Serve cold.

TAMARIND SAUCE

This sauce is excellent as a dipping sauce condiment for grilled fish and poultry.

YIELD: 1 CUP (250 MILLILITERS)

tamarind pulp	2 walnut-size pieces	2 walnut-size pieces
water	1 cup	250 milliliters
garlic clove, minced	1	1
sugar	3 tablespoons	45 milliliters
fish sauce	3 tablespoons	45 milliliters
thai chiles, stemmed, seeded, minced	3	3
grated fresh ginger	3 tablespoons	45 milliliters

1. Combine the pulp and water in a small saucepan and bring to a simmer. Poke at the pulp with a wooden spoon to get it to dissolve. Strain into a clean saucepan.
2. Add the rest of the ingredients and bring to a simmer. Simmer gently for 3 minutes and let cool. Serve at room temperature.

17
PURÉES AND PURÉE-THICKENED SAUCES

Purées of vegetables, nuts, legumes, and sometimes fruits are used as either sauces in themselves or to thicken and flavor more complex sauces or cooking liquids. Tomato and sorrel sauces are examples of purées providing the base and essential character of the sauce; the purée functions both as a thickener and as the primary flavor. Purées can also be used to finish sauces, or to lightly thicken braising liquids or roasting juices without distracting from the cooking liquid's intrinsic flavor. Because most purées, depending on the amount and type of starch they contain, are less efficient emulsifiers than purified starches such as flour, cornstarch, or arrowroot, they give body to a sauce by dispersing large amounts of insoluble components—often proteins or cellulose-related compounds—into the liquid medium. For this reason sauces based on or thickened with vegetable purées usually have a matte appearance rather than the smooth, transparent look associated with starch- and butter-thickened sauces.

The advantage of using vegetable purées rather than starch as thickeners is that they provide flavor of their own and a natural, wholesome texture to the sauce. Diners have become wary of starch-thickened sauces that have the texture of a carefully reduced jus, stock, or cooking liquid but that when tasted show themselves for what they are—thin, carelessly prepared stocks thickened at the last minute with cornstarch or arrowroot. A purée-thickened sauce will have a more rustic appearance but a more natural flavor than a starch-thickened one will. Purées are also almost completely free of fat; a purée-thickened sauce will be much less rich than one thickened with butter or cream. Purées can also be used in conjunction with starches or cream and butter. In this way the finished sauce will not be as rich as one thickened with cream and butter alone nor completely lean as a sauce thickened with purée alone would be.

One of the simplest and most obvious ways that a purée can be used to give body to a sauce is to purée the aromatic vegetables used in a stew or the mirepoix cooked along with a roast to enhance the flavor of the finished jus. The purée is then stirred bit by bit into the roasting juices or braising liquid to achieve the desired thickness. As a result, the aromatic vegetables are not wasted, and the sauce is lightly thickened without resorting to flour or other flavorless starches. The one drawback to this method, however, is that the aromatic vegetables used in roasting or braising often contain fat released by the meat during cooking. They should, therefore, be heated with the jus or braising liquid and the fat carefully skimmed off before the vegetables are puréed.

In large restaurants and catering operations, last-minute thickening of roasting and braising juices is rarely practical. Consequently, purées are often prepared in advance and used to thicken sauces or cooking liquids as they are needed.

Some sauces derive not only their texture but their flavor and color from a purée. The best-known examples of this are tomato sauces, but almost any vegetable, legume, nut, or fruit can be cooked, puréed, and converted into a sauce. Some purée-based sauces combine the purée with other thickeners, such as reduced cream, sauce béchamel, or sauce velouté. The best-known example of this is sauce soubise, which is sauce béchamel combined with onion purée.

EQUIPMENT FOR PREPARING PURÉES

A mortar and pestle can always be relied on for grinding nuts, puréeing vegetables, and converting various ingredients into pastes and purées. They are a most reliable tool because they allow easy control of the consistency of ingredients and avoid the sometimes brutal action of machines, which can damage the flavor of certain ingredients, such as extra-virgin olive oil and basil. Their main disadvantage is that using them can be time consuming when preparing large quantities; moreover, a large, good-quality mortar and pestle can be hard to find.

Blenders work extremely well for moist purées, when there is no danger of making the purée too thin or smooth. Some mixtures, if too dry or stiff, are difficult to work in a blender. When puréeing a thin purée (such as watercress sauce), put the solid ingredients in first, turn on the blender, and slowly add the liquid through the top. If too much liquid is added at the beginning, the solid ingredients may churn around and escape the blades. When adding cream to a purée, remember to make sure it is hot; otherwise it will turn into butter. Do not use a blender for potatoes or other starchy vegetables because it tends to overwork the mixture and make it gluey. Do not make sauces containing extra-virgin olive oil in a blender.

Food processors often are the most efficient tools for chopping and puréeing. When using a food processor, it is very easy to overwork certain mixtures and eliminate texture completely. When preparing coarse mixtures (such as pesto), use the pulse mechanism on the food processor and continually scrape the sides with a rubber spatula so that none of the mixture escapes the blade. Do not use a food processor for starchy vegetables or mixtures containing extra-virgin olive oil.

Food mills, the hand-driven precursors to the food processor, are excellent for puréeing and simultaneously straining a variety of mixtures. Their action is more delicate than that of a blender or food processor, making them useful for starchy purées, tomato sauces, sorrel mixtures, and other purées for which the ingredients are already soft and do not require much force to crush them into a paste.

Drum sieves provide the only reliable means of obtaining perfectly smooth purées. They are also excellent for making perfect mashed potatoes: The vertical pressure used to force the potatoes through the sieve does not cause the purée to become sticky and elastic, as will the rotary action of a food mill or food processor.

A fine chinois can be used to strain very liquid purées and sauces. The main disadvantage to using a chinois is that it tends to eliminate practically all the texture from a purée-thickened sauce.

TOMATOES

There are many types of basic tomato sauces: Some are uncooked lumpy mixtures of raw tomatoes, whereas others are delicate, smooth purées or long-cooked variations flavored with meats, aromatic vegetables, and herbs. The best way to approach a tomato sauce depends on the time of year and the type and quality of tomatoes that are available. One axiom of cooking might be: The better the ingredients, the less treatment they require. This is especially true when preparing tomato sauce.

The best tomatoes for sauces are usually the small pear-shaped plum tomatoes, but more important than the type are ripeness and gardening methods. Most tomatoes on the market are picked and used before they are ripe. Tomatoes are best used when they are so ripe that they seem ready to burst out of their skin and are so soft that they must be handled very carefully (a condition that is not optimum for mass shipping to the nation's supermarkets). Most tomatoes are also overwatered before they are picked. The water dilutes their flavor and must be eliminated later.

Most tomato sauces are spoiled by overcooking and by using too many ingredients, so that the natural delicacy of the tomato is lost, although admittedly a tomato sauce made with canned tomatoes or pale winter fresh tomatoes will need some reinforcement.

Raw Tomato Concassée

The simplest tomato sauce is a raw or barely cooked concassée. *Concasser* means "to crush, break, or grind" and, when applied to cooking, implies that the original texture of the food is still somewhat intact.

When ripe end-of-summer tomatoes are in season, the best way to prepare them and keep all their bright, natural flavor intact is to prepare a raw concassée. Raw tomato concassée can be served as a cold sauce for meats and fish or gently warmed and served with hot foods. Because raw tomato concassée is not strained, the tomatoes must be peeled and seeded before they are chopped. The best way to peel tomatoes is to plunge them in boiling water for 10 or 15 seconds (the exact amount of time depends on how ripe they are—the riper they are, the shorter the time) or, if only one or two tomatoes are involved, rotate them over a gas flame with a fork. Plunge the tomatoes immediately into cold water to prevent the pulp from cooking, and then pull off the peel with your fingers.

To seed tomatoes, cut them in half crosswise and squeeze the seeds from each half. Chop the tomatoes coarsely with a chef's knife. When raw tomato concassée is made with ripe summer tomatoes, any additional flavoring other than salt and pepper may seem superfluous, but a sprinkling of freshly chopped parsley or basil and a dribble of extra-virgin olive oil will not do any harm.

When preparing tomato concassée with less-than-perfect tomatoes, several methods can be used to reduce the water content and concentrate the tomatoes' flavor. Coarse salt can be used to eliminate excess liquid. After peeling the tomatoes, cut them into wedges as for a salad. Pull the seeds from each of the wedges with the tip of a finger and place the wedges in a colander set over a bowl. Sprinkle them with coarse salt and toss them thoroughly. Let the tomatoes sit for 30 minutes; toss them every 10 minutes. After they have drained, chop them to the desired texture.

Cooked Tomato Concassée

Excess liquid can also be eliminated from a tomato concassée by gentle cooking. Most cooks make the mistake of cooking down the whole concassée to eliminate the water and thicken the mixture, thus destroying its texture and delicacy. A better method is to bring the concassée to a slow simmer for 5 to 10 minutes (depending on ripeness) and then to transfer it immediately to a strainer and capture the liquid that drains off in a saucepan. The liquid alone is then reduced until it is syrupy. It then is returned to the chopped, drained tomatoes.

Tomato Coulis

The term *coulis* describes any sort of purée that has been strained to eliminate seeds and bits of peel and to smooth the texture. A tomato coulis is perfectly smooth and can be used alone, either hot or cold, or to flavor other sauces, such as Aurore and Choron, mayonnaises, and beurre blanc. Depending on the quality of the tomatoes, tomato coulis can be raw or cooked. When preparing tomato coulis, you need only seed the tomatoes to eliminate excess liquid; peeling is not necessary because the skins will be strained out anyway.

Raw Methods. To prepare raw tomato coulis, cut the tomatoes in half crosswise, squeeze out the seeds, and chop the halves with a chef's knife. It is best to chop the tomatoes by hand; if dealing with a large quantity, a food processor can be used, but work the mixture as little as possible or the blade will break up any remaining seeds, making the mixture bitter. Strain the mixture through a fine strainer or a food mill with the finest attachment.

Raw tomato coulis contains a large proportion of water, which will tend to separate out as the coulis sits or, worse, while the coulis sits on the plate. Excess water can be eliminated in several ways:

- Coarsely chop and salt the tomatoes, as for tomato concassée, and allow them to drain before they are strained.

- Place the tomato coulis in a chinois suspended in a pot for 2 to 3 hours. Stir the mixture inside the chinois gently every 20 minutes.

- Let the coulis settle in a tall container and skim off the water from time to time with a ladle.

Even when excess water has been eliminated from a raw tomato coulis, the microscopic particles of pigment tend to separate from the surrounding liquid. In some situations this will probably not even be noticed, but in more formal settings, in which a coulis is spread over the bottom of a large plate, it can be unsightly. For this reason some chefs combine raw tomato coulis with an emulsifier such as reduced heavy cream or a very small amount of egg yolk.

Cooked Method. Rinse the tomatoes, cut them in half crosswise, and squeeze out the seeds. Chop them coarsely, skins and all, and stew them with olive oil or another fat until they are completely soft and release all their liquid. Strain the mixture and reduce the liquid that runs through the strainer until it is syrupy. Purée the solids by working them through a food mill or a drum sieve. Combine the purée with the reduced liquid.

Traditional Tomato Sauces

Most of the better-known Italian sauces, such as *sugo finto*, *salsa di pomodoro*, and *ragù*, are constructed around a flavor base of one or more mirepoix vegetables (celery, carrots, onions), in some cases pork or veal, sometimes garlic, various herbs, and a bouquet garni.

In French cooking, tomatoes are more often used as a flavoring or secondary component added to a more complex sauce, rather than as a sauce base. Despite this seemingly secondary role, tomatoes enter into a classic sauce espagnole and hence into practically every classic French brown sauce. Tomato concassée and coulis are also used to moisten meat and chicken stews, such as Marengo and chasseur, but in each of these examples the sauce is balanced with other ingredients and flavors. Mexican and Spanish tomato sauces, such as salsa (see page 445), are often raw concassées seasoned with appropriate herbs and spices.

Improving the Flavor of Tomato Sauces

Regardless of the type of tomato sauce being prepared, its flavor can usually be improved in several ways:

1. Use the best, ripest, fresh tomatoes. When this is not possible, canned tomatoes can be used. There is much argument as to the best brands of canned tomato or tomato purée, but Redpack, Hunt's, Pomi, and Delverde are well rated and seem like good ones to start using and comparing. Fresh tomato coulis or concassée can also be prepared in the summer and frozen for winter use if there is enough freezer space available for this to be practical.
2. Avoid overcooking the tomatoes. Most recipes suggest preparing some kind of flavor base, adding the tomatoes, and cooking the mixture down until it thickens. It is best to precook and strain the liquid released by the tomatoes (as described for Tomato Concassée, page 461) and cook the liquid down with the flavor base before adding the tomato pulp.
3. The better the tomatoes, the less they benefit from additional flavoring and manipulation. But less-than-excellent tomatoes can still be used in an almost endless

variety of ways. They can be cooked with meats and vegetables (either as a flavor base or in a stew); different herbs can enter into the bouquet garni (sage, oregano, marjoram, hyssop, basil) or be chopped and added to the sauce near the end (tarragon, chives, parsley, chervil); the sauce can be finished with cream, butter (plain or compound), or olive oil (flavored or not, or emulsified into a mayonnaise such as aïoli or rouille). The sauce can be lent body and suavity by adding reduced stock or by combining it with stock and carefully reducing and skimming the two together (as in a classic espagnole). White or red wine can be added at the beginning and simmered with the flavor base. Tomato coulis can be used as the starting point and emulsifier for a hot or cold vinaigrette or stirred into whipped cream or crème fraîche and served as a cold sauce; mustard whisked in at the end lends a discreet tang.

4. Some tomato sauces, especially pasta sauces, are made by slowly roasting tomatoes in the oven, where they release a surprising amount of liquid. This liquid is ladled off, simmered down to a syrup on top of the stove, and combined with the more or less finely chopped roasted tomatoes. This "open air" cooking of the peeled tomato halves lightly caramelizes the tomatoes and magnifies their flavor in a way that simple stove-top stewing will not.

Caramelization also enhances the flavor of sauces made with tomato paste (whole tomatoes contain so much water that they can be caramelized only by very long cooking). An excellent method for starting a traditional French or Italian tomato sauce is to sweat onions, carrots, celery, and garlic in olive oil until lightly caramelized, stir in tomato paste, and continue cooking (on top of the stove for small amounts, in the oven for large amounts) until the tomato paste browns and smells toasty. A small amount of wine can be stirred in and quickly reduced to dryness before relatively neutral liquids such as stock or water are added and the sauce simmered just long enough to extract the flavor of the caramelized ingredients.

5. The flavor of a tomato sauce can usually be improved by increasing both its sweetness and acidity and making sure the two are in balance. Chefs and home cooks have long added sugar to tomato sauces, especially when the tomatoes are underripe. What is less obvious is that even the flavor of acidic tomatoes is improved by adding a small amount of wine vinegar. Start by adding sugar, a small amount at a time, while tasting. As soon as you can taste the sugar, add vinegar a bit at a time, until you can taste it. Then balance the taste of the vinegar with an additional small amount of sugar. By increasing both the acidity and sweetness of the sauce, the flavor of the tomatoes will come into focus.

TOMATILLOS

Despite their name, tomatillos, or green tomatoes, are more closely related to gooseberries than to regular tomatoes. They are not underripe tomatoes but are a separate fruit entirely. They have long been popular in Mexican cooking, where they are usually lightly stewed and flavored with various combinations of garlic, peppers, onions, and cilantro.

Tomatillos can be prepared in much the same way as tomatoes, except that their paper-like sheath should be removed, and they should be lightly cooked, as they are usually too tough to eat raw. They can be gently stewed and puréed into a colorful tangy sauce that can be flavored with traditional Mexican flavors or adapted in other ways.

●━━● TOMATILLO SAUCE

YIELD: 2 CUPS (500 MILLILITERS)

fresh or canned tomatillos	1 pound	500 grams
onion, chopped	1 small	1 small
garlic cloves, chopped	2	2
hot peppers, seeded and chopped	2 small	2 small
olive oil	3 tablespoons	45 milliliters
chopped cilantro	¼ cup	60 grams
heavy cream (optional)	½ cup	225 milliliters

1. If using fresh tomatillos, remove the papery sheath from the outside. If using canned, drain them. Chop the tomatillos coarsely.
2. Sweat the onion, garlic, and hot peppers in the olive oil for 10 minutes.
3. Add the chopped tomatillos and stew the mixture until completely soft.
4. Add the chopped cilantro and cook for 2 to 3 minutes.
5. For a smoother, more refined sauce, strain the mixture and finish it with a bit of cream before adding the cilantro.

SORREL

Sorrel is undeservedly ignored by American cooks, who in all fairness have little access to it, even in summer when it is in season and easy to grow. It has a sharp, tangy flavor that makes it an excellent accompaniment to fish and white meats. It softens as soon as it comes in contact with heat, so it is easy to purée and use as both a flavoring and a thickener.

When sorrel is available, usually in summer, it is best to buy it in large quantities (it is not expensive), stew it for 10 minutes in its own juices, and freeze it in tightly sealed plastic bags. Sorrel is used in sauce making in two ways. In one method the raw leaves are rolled and cut into thin strips (chiffonade) and added to white sauces at the end; in the other method, the sorrel is stewed by itself or with a touch of cream or butter, finely chopped or puréed with a food processor, and forced through a fine-mesh sieve.

SORREL PURÉE

This is a simple purée used for finishing sauces. It must be thinned and enriched with butter or cream if it is to be used alone to accompany meats or fish.

YIELD: 2 CUPS (500 MILLILITERS)

fresh sorrel leaves	1 pound	500 grams
butter	1 ounce	30 grams

1. Wash the sorrel leaves and drain them thoroughly.
2. Melt the butter in a straight-sided sauté pan and add the sorrel leaves. If they do not all fit, wait a minute until the first batch starts to wilt.
3. When all the sorrel leaves have softened and turned a dull green-gray, take them out of the pan with a slotted spoon, pressing them against the side of the pan to extract any liquid. Put the leaves in a bowl.
4. Reduce the liquid remaining in the sauté pan until it becomes syrupy, and add it to the sorrel leaves.
5. The leaves can be puréed in a food processor or blender, or they can be chopped by hand. Force the mixture through a fine-mesh drum sieve.

Note: If the purée is to be used within a day or two, keep a sheet of plastic wrap directly on its surface; otherwise a black crust will form. To store the purée longer, keep it in a jar, refrigerated, covered with a thin film of oil, or freeze it in resealable plastic freezer bags.

Sorrel Sauces

Sorrel purée is used in sauce making as both a flavoring and thickener. Depending on the style of a restaurant, sorrel purée can be kept on hand and stirred into last-minute reductions or used to thicken and flavor sauces made in advance. It is almost always used in conjunction with butter or cream.

The amount of sorrel purée to use will vary, depending on the desired thickness of the finished sauce. For a thick purée that should be served on the side, add 1 cup (250 milliliters) of liquid to 2 cups (500 milliliters) of purée. For a thin, almost soup-like consistency, 1 cup (250 milliliters) of purée can be used to thicken 3 cups (750 milliliters) of liquid.

SORREL SAUCE FOR FISH

YIELD: 2 CUPS (500 MILLILITERS)

flavorful liquid (see Note)	1 cup	250 milliliters
sorrel purée	¾ cup	185 milliliters

heavy cream	¼ cup	60 milliliters
butter	1 ounce	30 grams
juice of 1 lemon		
salt and pepper	to taste	to taste

1. Heat the flavorful liquid base.
2. Whisk in the sorrel purée until it is evenly distributed.
3. Add the cream and check the consistency. If the sauce is too thin, add more purée. If it is too thick, thin it with more of the liquid base or cream.
4. Whisk in the butter. Whisk in the lemon juice and adjust the seasonings.

Note: The liquid base can be any appropriate flavorful liquid, such as fish stock, shellfish cooking liquid, court-bouillon, or mushroom cooking liquid, alone or in combination. The lemon juice may seem redundant in an already acidic sauce, but it sharpens and brings into focus the flavor of the sorrel without making it aggressively acidic.

GARLIC

When raw garlic cloves are crushed or chopped, a series of chemical reactions produces their familiar assertive aroma and flavor. By cooking garlic cloves whole, either peeled or unpeeled, these reactions are bypassed, and the resulting flavor is surprisingly mild.

The easiest and most flavorful method for preparing cooked garlic purée is to wrap four or five heads together in aluminum foil and roast them for about 1 hour, until they are soft. The pulp is then extracted with a food mill or drum sieve. If a paler purée is needed for finishing cream sauces, the unpeeled garlic cloves can be cooked in simmering water until they are soft. Some recipes suggest peeling the cloves and simmering them in several changes of water to attenuate their flavor. This usually is not necessary because, again, whole cooked cloves are quite mild.

Buy garlic with large cloves surrounded with white skin and preferably a little violet near the base. The best garlic is the freshly harvested spring garlic, which has large fresh-smelling cloves and is sticky to the touch. Do not confuse this with elephant garlic, which also has large cloves but a peculiar taste; it should be avoided.

Garlic purée is delicious when served alone as a condiment to smear on grilled foods or on croutons. It should be well seasoned and is best when finished with extra-virgin olive oil or a little heavy cream. It also goes well with Provençal herbs such as thyme, marjoram, or oregano.

Garlic purée can also be used to finish soups and sauces or to thicken roasting juices or braising liquids. It works especially well with full-flavored fish and chicken dishes. One very direct method of using garlic purée for thickening roasting juices is to surround the uncooked roast with unpeeled garlic cloves and strain the roasted cloves along with the roasting juices through a sieve or food mill.

When garlic is puréed raw, it is so strong that it is used primarily as a flavoring for mayonnaise (aïoli) or in conjunction with more mild purées such as potatoes. Raw garlic can also be worked to a paste with a mortar and pestle or with the side of a knife and combined with finely chopped herbs, to sprinkle over sautéed vegetables. A *persillade* is a classic mixture of raw garlic purée, chopped parsley, and sometimes breadcrumbs, but this mixture can be made with almost any full-flavored herb, such as thyme, marjoram, oregano, or lavender.

Garlic purée can be kept in jars, covered with a layer of olive oil, in the refrigerator.

BAKED GARLIC PURÉE

YIELD: 1 CUP (250 MILLILITERS)

garlic heads	15	15
olive oil	1 tablespoon	15 milliliters

1. Preheat the oven to 325°F (160°C). Peel the outside papery skin off the garlic heads. Create 3 or 4 packets of garlic by wrapping 4 or 5 heads together in aluminum foil.
2. Bake the garlic in the oven until the cloves are soft, usually about 1 hour.
3. Extract the purée from the cloves with a food mill or drum sieve or by pushing the cloves through a strainer with the back of a ladle.
4. To store the purée in the refrigerator, smooth the top with the back of a spoon and dribble over the olive oil. Cover with plastic wrap or seal in mason jars. The purée darkens when exposed to air.

SWEET PEPPERS

In recent years, many different-colored sweet bell peppers have become available in American markets. Chefs have taken to them not only for their flavor but for the sunny, summery look they give to a finished plate. Sweet pepper purée can be used to finish cooking liquids, to give them color, flavor, and texture. It works especially well in sauces for grilled or sautéed foods. It can be incorporated into an already prepared sauce, such as a mayonnaise, or it can be used as a sauce base in itself, with ingredients added to it (such as for vinaigrette). The simplest way to use sweet pepper purée is to whisk it into a flavor base such as a stock, wine used to deglaze a sauté pan, or a little heavy cream. Exciting presentations can be made using different-colored sweet pepper purées together on the plate.

Thick sweet pepper purée can be chilled and stirred into whipped cream to form a delicate cold sauce for meats or fish.

Sweet pepper purée can also be served alone as a condiment for barbecued or other full-flavored foods.

SWEET PEPPER PURÉE

When served alone, this sauce can be made hotter and more exciting by including some hot peppers, fresh Provençal herbs (fresh thyme, marjoram, or oregano), chopped garlic, or onions or hot pepper (Tabasco) sauce.

YIELD: 3 CUPS (750 MILLILITERS)

sweet peppers of a single color	6 to 8	6 to 8
extra-virgin olive oil	¼ cup	60 milliliters

1. Cut around and remove the stems from the peppers. Cut the peppers in half lengthwise and pull out the seeds and pulp.
2. Chop the cleaned peppers coarsely and add them to a heavy-bottomed pot with the olive oil.
3. Gently stew the peppers in the oil until they soften, usually about 20 minutes.
4. The cooked peppers can be puréed with a food processor, food mill, or drum sieve. If an extremely stiff purée is needed, it can be cooked further in a saucepan to thicken it. The color of sweet peppers (except for green, which turns gray) is quite stable and will not be destroyed by long cooking.

SWEET RED PEPPER VINAIGRETTE

This vinaigrette is prepared in the same way as more traditional versions except that the red pepper purée replaces the mustard as an emulsifier.

YIELD: 1 CUP (250 MILLILITERS)

sweet red pepper purée	3 tablespoons	45 milliliters
fine salt	1 teaspoon	5 milliliters
good-quality wine vinegar	3 to 4 tablespoons	45 to 60 milliliters
extra-virgin olive oil	½ cup	125 milliliters

1. Combine the sweet pepper purée with the salt and vinegar in a bowl.
2. Gently stir in the extra-virgin olive oil.
3. Adjust the proportions of oil and vinegar to taste.

POTATOES

Potato purée is used as a thickener for sauces and cooking liquids and as the base for strongly flavored sauces, especially those containing garlic. In hot sauces it is often used in conjunction with cream and butter, but it can also be used alone. Sauces thickened with potato purée lack the perfectly smooth texture of starch-thickened sauces or of sauces thickened with cream and butter. Potato purée does, however, give a sauce a satisfying subtlety and depth of flavor without being too rich.

Potato purée can be used in varying amounts to thicken sauces. Sauces that have been lightly thickened with potato purée can also be strained through a chinois to eliminate some of its mealy texture.

Although the recipes that follow all use cooked potato purée, a raw purée can also be prepared and stirred into sauces at the last minute as a thickener. The best potatoes for making purées for sauces are Yukon Golds or Yellow Finns.

POTATO PURÉE

YIELD: 2 CUPS (500 MILLILITERS)

potatoes	1 pound	500 grams
salt and pepper	to taste	to taste

1. Peel the potatoes. Keep them in a bowl of cold water until needed. If they are large, cut them into quarters.
2. Put the potatoes in a pot, and add just enough cold water to cover. Cook the potatoes at a slow simmer for 30 to 40 minutes, until they are easily penetrated with a knife.
3. Drain the potatoes, being sure to save the cooking liquid. (If a thinner purée is desired, the cooking liquid can be used instead of cream or butter to thin the finished purée.)
4. Purée the cooked potatoes by forcing them through a drum sieve or by using a food mill. Using a drum sieve produces the finest texture and is also the least likely to work up the gluten and give the purée a gluey consistency. Never use a blender or food processor, as these would overwork the purée.

Lightening Mayonnaise with Potato Purée

Potato purée is often used in Provence to lighten strong mayonnaises such as aïoli so they can be dolloped more generously on the hot vegetables, fish, and eggs served at a traditional aïoli dinner. The method can also be used for other types of full-flavored mayonnaises to make them less rich.

To lighten a Sauce Aïoli (page 396), combine two parts of the sauce with one part potato purée. If the mayonnaise becomes too stiff, it can be thinned with an appropriate liquid, such as fish broth, stock, potato cooking liquid, cream, or lemon juice. Peeled and still-warm red potatoes can also be added directly along with the oil when preparing aïoli with a mortar and pestle.

SKORTHALIÁ
Potato-Garlic Purée

Stiff purées redolent of raw garlic can be found all along the Mediterranean, where they are used to accompany grilled and sautéed vegetables (eggplant, zucchini), cold vegetables (beets and artichokes), meat, and fish (especially poached salt cod). A variety of ingredients are used to give the sauces body. An aïoli may contain only egg yolks and oil as thickeners, whereas the Greek version, *skorthaliá*, may contain ground almonds. The recipe that follows uses potatoes for body, but some versions use breadcrumbs—probably older versions, because potatoes were not widely used around the Mediterranean until the nineteenth century. The consistency of the skorthaliá can be adjusted by adding stock or cooking liquid. The flavor and color can also be enhanced by adding Sweet Red Pepper Purée (page 468) to taste. Basil Oil (page 429) can also be added for flavor and color.

YIELD: 1 QUART (1 LITER)

small, firm-fleshed unpeeled potatoes	2 pounds	1 kilogram
garlic cloves, peeled	8	8
fine salt	1 tablespoon	15 milliliters
extra-virgin olive oil	1 cup	250 milliliters
wine vinegar or lemon juice	½ cup	125 milliliters
white pepper	to taste	to taste

1. Cover the potatoes with cold water and bring to a simmer. Cook for 20 to 30 minutes, until easily penetrated with a knife but before the skins begin to split.
2. Work the garlic to a paste with a mortar and pestle or by crushing the cloves with the side of a knife on a cutting board.
3. When the potatoes are done, peel them while they are still warm and add them a few at a time to the garlic paste in a mortar or bowl. Crush them with a pestle or the back of a wooden spoon, adding the salt while crushing them.
4. When the potato mixture is smooth, gradually work in the olive oil and the wine vinegar. Add pepper to taste.

POACHED CHICKEN WITH TARRAGON

Potato purée can be used to thicken the poaching liquid for chicken or fish.

YIELD: 4 SERVINGS

whole chicken, 1	4 pounds	2 kilograms
tarragon	1 bunch	1 bunch
warm white chicken stock, as needed	1 quart	1 liter
heavy cream	¼ cup	60 milliliters
potato purée	½ cup	125 milliliters

1. Separate the chicken skin from the meat of the chicken with the forefinger. Do not try to pull the skin away from the breast bone or from the back, or it may tear.

2. Remove the tarragon leaves from the branches and place them between the skin and meat of the chicken.

3. Truss the chicken and place it in a tight-fitting tall but narrow pot. Pour over just enough of the chicken stock to cover the chicken. The stock should be warm but not hot.

4. Slowly bring the stock to a simmer, skimming off any froth that floats to the surface. Poach the chicken for approximately 40 minutes. Transfer it to a plate and cover it lightly with foil to keep it warm.

5. Reduce the poaching liquid while skimming carefully, until 1½ cups (375 milliliters) remain.

6. Add the cream to the reduced poaching liquid and whisk in the potato purée a bit at a time, until the sauce has the desired consistency. The sauce can be left very light—almost the consistency of a soup—or made thick enough to coat the pieces of chicken. For a very thin, light-textured sauce, strain through a chinois.

7. Remove and discard the skin from the chicken, carve the meat, and serve it with the sauce in hot bowls or wide deep plates.

POTATO-THICKENED SAUCE FOR PORK

Potato purée can be used as a light thickener for pork sauces, added to the cooking juices from a roast loin of pork, or used to thicken pan-deglazed sauces.

YIELD: 2 TO 4 SERVINGS

pork chops	4	4
clarified butter or oil	2 tablespoons	30 milliliters
full-bodied brown pork or chicken stock	¾ cup	185 milliliters
heavy cream	¼ cup	60 milliliters
waxy-potato purée	3 tablespoons	45 milliliters
salt and pepper	to taste	to taste

1. Sauté the pork chops in the clarified butter. Transfer them to a plate and keep them warm while preparing the sauce.

2. Discard the fat in the sauté pan. Deglaze the pan with the stock and reduce by about one-third.

3. Whisk in the cream and the potato purée. Reduce the sauce if it is too thin or add more stock if it is too thick. Adjust the seasonings and serve the sauce over the pork chops.

ONIONS

Onions that have been gently stewed develop a delicate sweetness and depth of flavor that makes them a perfect foil for roast meats. The best-known onion sauce is Sauce Soubise I (page 141), which is made especially delicate and discreet by preliminary blanching of the onions that are then puréed and combined with a large proportion of sauce béchamel. A more rustic and assertive sauce can be prepared by simply stewing onion slices in butter until they are soft, cooking them for a few minutes longer with some heavy cream, and puréeing the mixture in a food processor. Both sauce soubise and a simple stewed onion purée can be flavored with roasting juices or stock and enriched with varying amounts of cream and butter. Onion purée served with grilled foods can be made more assertive by adding tomato purée, wine vinegar, or Provençal herbs.

Variations of sauce soubise and onion purée can be prepared with leeks, shallots, rocambole, and other similarly flavored vegetables.

Sauce Soubise II

Peel and slice 2 medium onions (1 pound/500 grams), and blanch them for 10 minutes in boiling salted water. Drain the onion slices and gently cook them in butter until they are completely soft, usually in about 20 minutes. Do not allow them to brown. Add 2 cups (500 milliliters) of sauce béchamel to the onions, and season the mixture with salt, white pepper, and a pinch of sugar. Cover the pot or saucepan and put it in a 300°F (150°C) oven for 1 hour. Strain the sauce and finish it with ½ cup (125 milliliters) of heavy cream and 1 ounce (30 grams) of butter. Yield: 1 quart (1 liter).

Stewed Onion Purée

Traditional sauce soubise is quite thick by today's standards because it was often used to coat roasts (veal Orloff) or chops. A more contemporary version can be made by puréeing the stewed onions with heavy cream and omitting the béchamel. This sauce can then be served as is or reduced to the desired consistency.

Peel and slice 5 pounds (2.25 kilograms) of onions, and sweat them in 4 ounces (125 grams) butter. Be sure to use a heavy-bottomed pot and stir the onions almost constantly to prevent them from browning. The onion slices will shrink to about one-sixth of their original volume. When the onions are completely soft and there is no liquid left on the bottom of the pot, add ½ cup (125 milliliters) heavy cream. The sauce can be seasoned and served as is or puréed in a blender or food processor and strained. Be sure to purée it while it is still hot, or the cream will turn to butter. For a tangy sauce that is more appropriate for grilled foods, wine vinegar, red pepper purée, or tomato purée can be added to the onion sauce. The sauce can also be made more complex by adding reduced stock or roasting juices. Yield: 1 quart (1 liter).

PARSLEY

Parsley that is puréed in a blender just before serving is an excellent flavoring for fish sauces or delicate meat sauces, especially for sweetbreads. Its flavor is robust yet subtle and complex. Parsley, once puréed, quickly loses its pungent aroma and flavor and so should be used immediately. Parsley purée can be presented in two ways: as a stiff purée to be served alongside fish and meats, or as a thickener, blended directly into a sauce at the last minute.

STIFF PARSLEY PURÉE

This purée can be dolloped directly on the plate alongside hot foods, passed at the table in a sauce boat, or used as a thickener for thinner sauces and cooking liquids.

YIELD: 2 CUPS (500 MILLILITERS)

flat parsley	2 large bunches	2 large bunches
heavy cream	½ cup	125 milliliters
stiff potato purée	1 cup	250 milliliters
salt and pepper	to taste	to taste

1. Remove the parsley leaves and discard the stems (or save for stock). Wash and dry the leaves thoroughly.
2. Bring the cream to a simmer.
3. Put the parsley leaves in a blender. Turn the blender to slow speed and slowly pour in the hot cream through the hole in the center of the lid.
4. When all the cream has been added, turn the blender to high speed and purée for 1 minute.
5. Strain the purée through a fine chinois.
6. Transfer the parsley purée to a saucepan and whisk in the potato purée until the mixture has the desired consistency. Adjust the seasonings.

Finishing Sauces and Cooking Liquids with Parsley Purée

In addition to accompanying hot meats and fish, parsley purée can be used as a thickener and flavoring for light-textured sauces. Sauces finished with parsley purée can be approached using one of two methods.

The first method consists of blanching and puréeing parsley and then working it through a fine-mesh drum sieve. The purée is then whisked into made-to-order sauces as needed. Although this method is convenient to use at the last minute, the process of working the purée through the sieve is laborious and time consuming.

The second method involves pouring hot cooking liquids, stocks, or court-bouillon over raw parsley leaves in a blender and puréeing at high speed for 2 minutes. The hot sauce is then quickly strained through a strainer or chinois. This method sidesteps the drum sieve and captures the flavor of the parsley at its freshest, but it has the disadvantage of requiring considerable last-minute manipulation.

PLAIN PARSLEY PURÉE FOR FINISHING SAUCES

Method 1: Using a Drum Sieve

YIELD: 2 CUPS (500 MILLILITERS)

flat parsley	1 large bunch	1 large bunch
court-bouillon or stock	¼ cup	60 milliliters
flavorful liquid sauce base	1½ cups	375 milliliters

1. Remove the parsley leaves and discard the stems (or save for stock). Blanch the leaves for 1 minute in boiling salted water. Drain the parsley in a colander and rinse it with cold running water. Gently squeeze dry.
2. Put the blanched parsley in the blender with the court-bouillon and blend at high speed, stopping every 10 to 15 seconds to scrape the inside of the blender. Blend until the liquid is green and contains only tiny specks of parsley; this usually takes about 2 minutes.
3. Work the purée through a fine-mesh drum sieve with a plastic pastry scraper.
4. Heat the flavorful base in a saucepan and whisk in purée to taste.

Method 2: Using a Blender Alone

YIELD: 1 CUP (250 MILLILITERS)

flat parsley	1 large bunch	1 large bunch
flavorful liquid sauce base	¾ cup	185 milliliters

1. Wash the parsley and remove the leaves, discarding the stems (or save for stock). Dry the leaves in a towel.

2. Bring the flavorful base to a simmer in a saucepan. Add the leaves and bring the liquid back to a simmer.

3. Strain the leaves from the liquid and return the liquid to the saucepan on the stove.

4. Put the leaves in a blender. Turn the blender on high and slowly pour in the simmering liquid through the small hole on top. Blend for 15 to 30 seconds. Strain through a medium-mesh strainer. Serve immediately.

Note: Liquids finished with parsley purée tend to be quite thin. If a thicker sauce is desired, it can be finished with reduced cream, butter, egg yolks, or other purées (such as Mushroom Purée, page 476). The perfume of parsley purée is lost after about 15 minutes, so if another liaison is being used, work quickly and do not overcook the purée. In a restaurant, these purées must be made to order or at regular intervals.

WATERCRESS

Like parsley, watercress can be puréed, thickened with potatoes, and served as an accompaniment, or it can be used directly to finish cooking liquids and sauces.

Sauces finished with watercress purée have become popular because of their bright color and delicate flavor. Like parsley, watercress purée to finish sauces can be prepared in two ways: The first and easiest is to add the hot sauce base to blanched watercress in a blender (see method 2 for parsley purée). The second is to prepare a separate watercress purée and whisk it into the sauce base at the last minute. Watercress sauces and purées should not be kept hot for more than 1 hour or they lose their vibrant color and flavor.

Watercress Purée

When watercress purée is served on the side, as an accompaniment to meat or fish, its texture is reinforced by combining it with a starchy purée, usually potato, like the Stiff Parsley Purée (page 473). If the purée is being used to finish a sauce, it can be used alone. Usually, however, watercress sauces contain cream, butter, or other purées that attenuate watercress's sometimes bitter flavor. Watercress purée is prepared in the same way as parsley purée: Simply blanch the watercress leaves (the stems tend to be bitter) for 2 minutes in boiling salted water, drain, and refresh them in cold running water. Purée them in a blender with a small amount of court-bouillon or stock, and force the mixture through a drum sieve. This purée will keep for several days in the refrigerator and can be used for finishing sauces (such as mayonnaise, hot emulsified egg sauces, beurre blanc–type sauces) or cooking liquids from fish, chicken, and delicately flavored meats. Keep the purée well covered until it is needed.

MUSHROOMS

Fresh or dried mushrooms can be puréed and used as flavorful thickeners for a variety of sauces and cooking liquids. The mushrooms can first be cooked in a small amount of stock or water and drained; the cooking liquid is then reduced and puréed with the mushrooms in a blender or food processor. Or the mushrooms can be puréed raw and cooked in butter with lemon juice over high heat to eliminate their moisture.

For a fine-textured purée, the mushrooms should be worked through a drum sieve. Almost any type of mushroom can be used to make purée, but always try to use them when they are fresh, especially when using the ordinary cultivated kind, which give an off-gray cast to the purée if they are old. Cooking mushrooms with lemon juice helps prevent them from turning dark, but too much juice may affect the final flavor. Dried wild mushrooms should be well rinsed and soaked; they can then be used in the same way as fresh.

Purées made from more assertive mushrooms such as morels, cèpes (porcini), and chanterelles make an excellent flavoring and thickener for brown sauces, red wine sauces, meat stews, or even as a finish for roasting juices. Cultivated mushrooms and delicately flavored wild varieties are excellent for finishing fish sauces.

Although many chefs often use vegetable purées as a way to avoid adding too many rich ingredients to their sauces, mushroom purées are best used in conjunction with a small amount of cream or butter.

MUSHROOM PURÉE

YIELD: 2 CUPS (500 MILLILITERS)

mushrooms	20 ounces	550 grams
stock, water, or madeira (for wild mushrooms)	½ cup	125 milliliters
juice of 1 lemon		
butter (method 2 only)	1 ounce	30 grams

Method 1: Using Cooked Mushrooms

1. Thoroughly rinse the mushrooms. If they are large, they can be halved or quartered.
2. Put the mushrooms in a saucepan with the stock and the lemon juice. Cover the saucepan and simmer for 10 minutes.
3. Drain the mushrooms and reduce the cooking liquid to about 2 tablespoons (30 milliliters).
4. Purée the mushrooms and the cooking liquid in a food processor for about 3 minutes. Scrape the sides of the food processor every 15 seconds. Force the purée through a drum sieve with a plastic pastry scraper. Keep the purée well covered with plastic wrap until needed.

Method 2: Using Raw Mushrooms

1. Rinse the mushrooms and cut them into quarters.
2. Purée the mushrooms with the stock in a blender.
3. Combine the puréed mushrooms, lemon juice, and butter in a straight-sided sauté pan. Cook the purée until all the moisture evaporates.
4. Use the purée as is or work it through a drum sieve if a very fine purée is needed.

Red Wine–Mushroom Sauces

Deeply flavored brown sauces and red wine sauces take especially well to thickening with mushroom purée. The braising liquid from a red wine stew or the concentrated red wine base for Sauce Bordelaise or Meurette Sauce (pages 180 and 181) can be thickened using this method.

Use approximately one part mushroom purée to thicken three parts braising liquid or sauce base. Heat the liquid or sauce base to a simmer and whisk in the mushroom purée until the sauce has the desired consistency.

CAULIFLOWER

Cooked cauliflower can be puréed with a blender and then strained to give body and a subtle flavor to sauces. In the sauce below, we combine it with coconut milk and flavor it with galangal.

CAULIFLOWER AND GALANGAL SAUCE

This exotic sauce captures the flavor of galangal, a rhizome that looks a lot like ginger but has a different flavor (see page 71). The cauliflower and coconut milk give consistency to this sauce, which is best on seafood.

YIELD: 1½ CUPS (375 MILLILITERS) OF BROTH-LIKE SAUCE

cauliflower	½ small	½ small
white onion, chopped	1 small	1 small
coconut milk	1 cup	250 milliliters
chicken broth	1 cup	250 milliliters
fresh or frozen galangal rhizome	1	1

1. Cut the small cauliflower florets away from the large stem at their base. Toss the florets into a pot of boiling water and simmer for 1 minute. Drain.
2. Combine the cauliflower, onion, coconut milk, and chicken broth and simmer gently until the cauliflower softens, about 15 minutes.
3. Cut the peel off the galangal and slice the galangal into rounds the size of quarters. Add these to the cauliflower mixture and simmer for 5 minutes more. Purée with an immersion blender and strain.

ROOT VEGETABLES

Flavorful root vegetables such as turnips, celeriac, and carrots can be puréed either alone or in combination and used to thicken sauces. One of the most useful techniques for thickening a braising or stewing liquid is to purée the aromatic vegetables included in the mirepoix and use these as the thickener. In this way the vegetables are not wasted; they will always provide more flavor than a thickener based on starch.

Root vegetables can also be glazed with stock and a small amount of butter before being puréed and used to finish sauces for roasted meats.

Thickening Meat Stews

Most meat stews contain aromatic vegetables—usually carrots, onions, and garlic—which are used to flavor the marinade and are eventually cooked along with the meat. In homemade versions, the aromatic vegetables are left in the stew when it is served. In more formal settings, the stewed meat, poultry, or fish is sorted out, and the aromatic vegetables are discarded and replaced with more "presentable" vegetables that have often been turned and cooked separately. The braising liquid is then usually reduced and thickened with beurre manié, or cream and egg yolks (for a blanquette).

To thicken the stew with its own vegetable purée, sort the cooked meat from the vegetables. Put the vegetables in a pot with the braising liquid. Bring the liquid to a slow simmer and skim off the fat over a period of about 20 minutes. This step is designed to eliminate most of the fat contained in the vegetables. Strain out the vegetables and continue reducing the braising liquid (unless too little is left or it is already thick enough). Purée the vegetables in a blender or food processor or by forcing them through a drum sieve. When the braising liquid has been reduced enough and has a full flavor, whisk in the vegetable purée bit by bit, until the liquid has the desired consistency. To obtain a perfectly smooth texture, the liquid can be strained through a chinois. Because straining will make the sauce much thinner, it may be necessary to add more purée and strain again until the consistency is right.

NUTS

Nuts have been used in sauce making since Roman times and are still used in rough-textured purées—the best known is pesto—and to thicken Indian curries. In medieval European cooking, they were often used in conjunction with bread and sometimes cooked egg yolks to thicken sauces and cooking liquids. In seventeenth-century recipes for roux, almond flour was often included along with the wheat flour. Gradually, classical French cooking abandoned nuts as thickeners in favor of starches and eventually cream and butter, but the use of nuts in sauce making is still common in European regional cooking and in Indian cooking. Sauces made with almonds, pine nuts, pistachios, chestnuts, hazelnuts, and walnuts are the most common.

Always buy shelled nuts in cans or tightly sealed bags. Taste them as soon as possible—a surprisingly large percentage of commercially available nuts are rancid. Nuts should be stored in a cool place.

Some nuts, such as hazelnuts, almonds, and walnuts, are covered with a thin brown skin that usually must be removed before the nuts are used. To peel the skin from almonds, plunge them into boiling water for 1 minute, drain them, and rub them in a wet towel. Hazelnuts are best toasted for 5 minutes and then worked together with the hands while still hot. Walnuts are more tricky and require longer blanching and meticulous scraping—most cooks do not bother peeling them. The flavor of nuts is often improved by lightly toasting them in a 350°F (175°C) oven for 5 to 10 minutes.

Nut Butters

In rough-hewn sauces, such as pestos, the nuts are ground or pounded with the other ingredients. When nuts are used as a thickener, they are puréed into nut butters. To prepare a nut butter, purée peeled and lightly toasted nuts in a food processor for 3 to 5 minutes, stopping every 30 seconds to scrape the sides with a rubber spatula. To produce 1 cup (250 milliliters) of nut butter, use 8 ounces (250 grams) of nuts. Nut butters can be used to give a velvety texture to sauces that might otherwise be thickened with cream, butter, or starch. The subtle flavor of the nuts goes especially well with spices and curries.

CARDAMOM-NUT BUTTER SAUCE

YIELD: 1 CUP (250 MILLILITERS)

full-flavored stock or cooking liquid	1 cup	250 milliliters
husked cardamom seeds	1 teaspoon	5 milliliters
almond, hazelnut, or cashew butter	1 tablespoon	15 milliliters
heavy cream (optional)	2 tablespoons	30 milliliters

1. Heat the stock in a 1-quart (1 liter) saucepan and add the cardamom seeds. Gently simmer the stock with the cardamom seeds for 15 minutes to infuse their flavor.
2. Whisk in the nut butter and the cream, if using. Thin the sauce as needed with additional stock, or thicken it with slightly more nut butter.
3. Strain through a fine chinois.

NUT CURRY SAUCE

YIELD: 1 CUP (250 MILLILITERS)

onion, chopped	1 small	1 small
butter	½ ounce	15 grams
curry powder	2 teaspoons	10 milliliters
freshly grated coconut	¼ cup	60 milliliters
stock or cooking liquid	1½ cups	375 milliliters
nut butter	1 to 2 tablespoons	15 to 30 milliliters
salt and pepper	to taste	to taste

1. Sweat the onion in the butter until it is translucent. Do not allow it to brown.
2. Add the curry powder and cook for 3 minutes more.
3. Add the grated coconut and the stock and cook at a slow simmer for 15 minutes.
4. Whisk in the nut butter until the sauce has the desired consistency.
5. Adjust the seasonings and strain through a fine chinois.

CASHEW SAUCE

In Southern India, cashews are ground to a paste and used to thicken sauces. Here is a typical Keralan sauce used for chicken.

YIELD: ENOUGH SAUCE FOR 4 SERVINGS

cardamom pods, crushed	6	6
minced fresh ginger	1 teaspoon	5 milliliters
minced garlic	1 teaspoon	5 milliliters
ground cumin	1 teaspoon	5 milliliters
minced onion	3 tablespoons	45 milliliters
clarified butter	3 tablespoons	45 milliliters
salt and pepper	to taste	to taste
sugar	¼ teaspoon	2 milliliters
dried fenugreek leaves (optional)	1 big pinch	1 big pinch
milk	½ cup	125 milliliters
cashew paste (opposite)	2 tablespoons	30 milliliters

1. Gently sauté the cardamom, ginger, garlic, cumin, and onion in the butter for about 5 minutes.
2. Season with salt and pepper, sugar, and dried fenugreek leaves, if using, and stir in the milk and cashew paste. Whisk until smooth.

Cashew Paste

YIELD: 1 CUP (250 MILLILITERS)

Combine 1 cup (250 milliliters) of roasted cashews with ½ cup (125 milliliters) water in a food processor and purée for about 2 minutes until smooth. Store in a jar in the refrigerator.

Almonds

Almonds have long played a role in European, Middle Eastern, and Indian cookery. In European cooking, ground almonds, along with egg yolks and breadcrumbs, were used to give body to sauces before the development of roux.

A large number of sauces containing almonds can be found in Europe's regional cuisines. Spanish romesco is a well-seasoned purée of almonds, hazelnuts, peppers, garlic, and breadcrumbs, often flavored with tomatoes. It is usually served with grilled or poached fish and shellfish. Picada (below) is a similar mixture, used to thicken soups and stews.

Bitter almonds are unavailable in the United States because of their high cyanide content, so here only sweet almonds are used. For a more pungent almond flavor, a drop or two of almond extract can be added, but be careful, or it may mask the flavor even of garlic.

Almonds are excellent in curry sauces, where they soften the flavor of the spices and add an ineffable subtlety to the sauce. They are surprisingly efficient as thickeners, so they can be used to thicken without making the sauce too rich.

PICADA
Garlic-Almond Purée

This mixture is used as a thickener. All of the ingredients except the olive oil can be puréed in a food processor until smooth. The olive oil is stirred in at the end by hand.

Picada can be used as a thickener for meat and fish stews and soups in much the same way as an aïoli is used to thicken a bourride. To thicken fish soups and stews, it is best to whisk the hot cooking liquid into the picada in a bowl. To thicken meat stews, be sure to strain and thoroughly remove the grease from the liquid before adding the picada. Again, the liquid should be whisked into the picada, not the other way around. For a perfectly smooth sauce, strain through a fine chinois. About 1 to 2 tablespoons (15 to 30 milliliters) of picada can be used to thicken ½ cup (125 milliliters) of broth or liquid.

garlic cloves, peeled	4	4
peeled and toasted almonds	4 ounces	125 grams
flat parsley	1 bunch	1 bunch
white bread, lightly toasted, crusts removed	3 slices	3 slices
water	½ cup	125 milliliters
extra-virgin olive oil	½ cup	125 milliliters

1. Put the garlic, almonds, parsley, and bread into a food processor. Purée the mixture for 4 to 5 minutes, until smooth.
2. Add the water, 2 tablespoons (30 milliliters) at a time, and continue mixing until the picada is stiff but no longer oily. Scrape down the sides of the food processor from time to time for an evenly textured mixture. Transfer the picada to a mixing bowl and slowly stir in the olive oil with a wooden spoon.
3. Keep the picada covered until needed. It is best used the same day.

Chestnuts

Chestnut purée has long been the traditional accompaniment to roast game. It usually has the texture of mashed potatoes and is eaten along with the meat as a vegetable. The chestnuts are often glazed with a flavorful stock and sometimes port wine to underline their natural sweetness before they are puréed. Bacon or smoked ham is sometimes cooked along with the chestnuts to accent the purée with an agreeable smoky flavor.

Chestnut purée is commercially available—do not confuse it with the sweetened version, *crème de marrons*—or can be prepared from scratch. Chestnuts are best peeled by making a slit on the rounded outer side with a sharp paring knife (essential to keep them from exploding) and then roasting them for about 10 minutes in a 400°F (200°C) oven in a roasting pan containing just enough water to cover the surface. It is easiest to peel the chestnuts while they are still hot, so work quickly or take only a few out of the oven at a time. The inner skin can be removed at the same time by rubbing the hot chestnuts in a towel. If the inner skin sticks, plunge the peeled chestnuts into boiling water for 1 or 2 minutes, or simply leave it.

CHESTNUT PURÉE

peeled chestnuts	1 pound	500 grams
celery, 1 stalk	3 ounces	100 grams
full-flavored brown stock	2 cups	500 milliliters
port	½ cup	125 milliliters
butter	2 ounces	60 grams

1. Combine all the ingredients in a straight-sided sauté pan and bring to a simmer. Cover the chestnuts with a round of parchment paper or half-cover the pan with a lid. Simmer until the chestnuts are soft (easily crushed with a fork) and the liquids have reduced and formed a syrupy glaze on the bottom of the pan.
2. Purée the chestnut mixture in a food processor until smooth, for about 3 minutes. (The resulting purée is very fine, so it is not necessary to force it through a drum sieve.) When storing chestnut purée, be sure to cover it with a sheet of plastic wrap directly on its surface, to prevent a skin from forming.

Coconuts

Coconut water taken from the inside of the coconut and coconut milk extracted from grated coconut pulp have long been used as a moistening liquid and flavoring for Curry Sauce (page 148). The coconut pulp, finely puréed in a food processor and forced through a drum sieve, can also be used as a thickener. The shrimp sauce that follows is a variation of the traditional Brazilian fish stew *vatapá*.

SHRIMP WITH COCONUT AND PEANUT SAUCE

YIELD: 8 FIRST-COURSE SERVINGS

shrimp, preferably with heads	32	32
onion, chopped	1 small	1 small
garlic cloves, crushed, peeled	2	2
fresh ginger slice	¼ inch	5 millimeters
peanut oil	2 tablespoons	30 milliliters
fish stock, chicken stock, or court-bouillon	1 cup	250 milliliters
tomatoes, peeled, seeded, and coarsely chopped	3 medium	3 medium
jalapeños, seeded and finely chopped	1 or 2	1 or 2
peanuts	4 ounces	125 grams
puréed pulp from 1 coconut		
cilantro, finely chopped	1 small bunch	1 small bunch
salt and pepper	to taste	to taste

1. Peel and devein the shrimp, saving the shells and heads (if available).
2. Gently sweat the shrimp shells and heads and the onion, garlic, and ginger in the peanut oil for 15 minutes.
3. Moisten the mixture with the fish stock and simmer for 15 minutes. Strain the mixture through a chinois into a second saucepan. Discard the solids.
4. Add the tomatoes and jalapeños to the sauce base. Simmer for 15 minutes.
5. Purée the peanuts in a food processor for 3 minutes and combine the purée with the coconut pulp (or purée the two together).

6. Force the purée through a drum sieve with a plastic pastry scraper.

7. Put the shrimp in a straight-sided sauté pan and cover with the hot sauce base. Poach for 3 minutes. Transfer the shrimp to hot plates.

8. Whisk the coconut-peanut purée and the chopped cilantro into the hot poaching liquid. Adjust the seasonings.

Pine Nuts

Pine nuts, sometimes called *pignolia* or *pignoli,* are the actual seeds of pine trees. They are used in Mediterranean sauces, for which they are crushed with a mortar and pestle with a variety of herbs and sometimes olives. They are best known as one of the ingredients in Genoese pesto sauce (opposite). Pine nuts are expensive. In some recipes, walnuts can be substituted.

Pistachios

Pistachios are sometimes used in the same way as almonds or walnuts, as the basis for pestos. Like pine nuts and almonds, they were often called for in medieval cooking. Even though they were more expensive than almonds, they were appreciated for their distinctive green color. Pistachios turn green only after they are cooked. They should be blanched and peeled in the same way as almonds.

Walnuts

Like pine nuts and pistachios, walnuts are excellent when coarsely pounded or chopped, contributing both texture and flavor to a finished sauce. They are often used in Italian cooking, in sauces for pasta.

WALNUT AND PARMESAN CHEESE SAUCE FOR PASTA

A dry, well-aged goat or sheep's milk cheese may be substituted for the Parmesan cheese in this sauce.

YIELD: 2 CUPS (500 MILLILITERS)

shelled walnuts	8 ounces	250 grams
extra-virgin olive oil	½ cup	125 milliliters
heavy cream	¼ cup	60 milliliters
freshly grated parmigiano-reggiano	2 ounces	50 grams
finely chopped parsley	3 tablespoons	45 milliliters
salt and pepper	to taste	to taste

1. Chop the walnuts in a food processor; use the pulse mechanism to avoid turning the walnuts into a purée. The pieces should be about the size of peppercorns.
2. Gently heat the chopped walnuts in the olive oil and cream. Do not let the sauce boil.
3. Stir in the grated cheese and the parsley. Adjust the seasonings.

PESTOS

Although most people think of the traditional Genoese version of crushed pine nuts, garlic, basil, cheese, and olive oil, *pesto* simply means "pestle," so the term can be stretched and applied to a whole family of sauces made of solid ingredients crushed to a paste in a mortar or food processor.

Pistou is the southern French version of pesto and differs from Genoese pesto only in that it sometimes contains tomatoes but never pine nuts. It is used almost exclusively to finish the French version of minestrone, called *soupe au pistou*. Perhaps it is the rough-and-tumble last-minute character of these sauces or the brightly flavored ingredients they contain that make them among the most satisfying of foods.

Although tapenades and anchoïades are usually not referred to as pestos, the principles and techniques used to prepare them are the same: A variety of solid ingredients are worked to a paste with a mortar and pestle. A food processor should be used for preparing tapenade only when the chunks of olive are left relatively coarse; if the olives are overworked, the sauce will lose much of its finesse and may even turn bitter.

GENOESE PESTO

Genoese pesto is not only wonderful over pasta but makes an excellent sauce for grilled meats, fish, and vegetables. It can also be stirred into soups at the last minute.

YIELD: 1 QUART (1 LITER)

basil leaves	1 pound	500 grams
garlic cloves, peeled	5	5
toasted pine nuts	3 tablespoons	45 milliliters
coarse salt	1 tablespoon	15 milliliters
freshly grated parmigiano-reggiano	8 ounces	250 grams
extra-virgin olive oil	1 cup	250 milliliters

1. Wash the basil leaves and make sure they are well dried. (If they are wet, some of their pungent flavor will be lost.)

2. Put all the ingredients except the olive oil in a mortar or blender. If not all of the basil fits, it may be necessary to start grinding and add it a bit at a time. Work or blend the mixture to a paste. If using a blender, scrape the paste into a mixing bowl.
3. Gently work in the olive oil with a pestle or wooden spoon.

Pistou/Pesto Variations

Thick, intensely flavored pastes can be made with other ingredients using pesto and pistou as models. In French cooking, many of these mixtures have an *-ade* ending and are used in various ways, sometimes for finishing more complex sauces and sometimes served atop strongly flavored grilled or sautéed foods.

INDIAN MINT PESTO

YIELD: 1 CUP (250 MILLILITERS)

mint leaves, tightly packed	1 cup	250 milliliters
finely chopped jalapeños	2 tablespoons	30 milliliters
finely chopped onion	2 tablespoons	30 milliliters
finely chopped fresh ginger	½ teaspoon	3 milliliters
lemon juice	4 teaspoons	20 milliliters
almond butter (page 415)	3 tablespoons	45 milliliters
salt	to taste	to taste

Combine all the ingredients in a food processor and purée until the mixture is smooth, about 20 seconds.

ANCHOÏADE

An anchoïade can be prepared by chopping or crushing salted or canned anchovies into a paste with garlic and sometimes other ingredients such as herbs and olives. Olive oil is then stirred into the mixture, and the finished anchoïade is served with grilled vegetables or on croutons. Salted or canned anchovies should be soaked in cold water and then drained on towels to eliminate the salt or oil before using.

TAPENADE

This mixture of finely chopped olives makes a marvelous spread for toasted croutons, hot pasta, and grilled vegetables, fish, and meats. This recipe uses a mortar and pestle, but a food processor can be used, although the texture will be more homogeneous and much of the rustic, rough-hewn quality of the sauce will be lost. Tapenade recipes always contain capers—*tapéno* means "caper" in the Provençal dialect—but the dried currants, which add a note of sweetness that relieves the saltiness of the mixture, are not traditional.

YIELD: 1 QUART (1 LITER)

dried currants	6 ounces	175 grams
oil-cured Moroccan olives	2 pounds	1 kilogram
salt-cured or canned anchovy fillets	4 ounces	125 grams
garlic cloves, peeled	2	2
capers, drained	3 ounces	75 grams
extra-virgin olive oil	½ cup	125 milliliters
salt and pepper	to taste	to taste

1. Soak the currants in just enough warm water to cover for 1 hour, to plump and soften them.
2. Pit the olives by first tapping them with a mallet or a full tin can to push the pits through the flesh.
3. Soak the anchovies in cold water to eliminate salt and oil (see Note).
4. Work the garlic and anchovies to a paste with a mortar and pestle.
5. Drain the currants and add them, the pitted olives, and the capers to the anchovy-garlic paste. Work the mixture to the desired consistency with the mortar and pestle; the sauce is always better when left coarse, containing irregular bits and pieces of olive.
6. Work in the olive oil and adjust the seasonings.

Note: Salted anchovies should be soaked for 30 minutes, canned anchovies for 10 minutes.

GREEN OLIVE AND CAPER TAPENADE

The green olives in this recipe are unusual, as is the hard-boiled egg, which softens the flavor and helps bind the mixture. Green olive and caper tapenade can be used on grilled foods and as a quick finish for full-flavored fish broths and poaching liquids.

YIELD: 2 CUPS (500 MILLILITERS)

green olives (see Note)	1 pound	500 grams
capers, drained	4 ounces	125 grams
garlic clove, peeled	½	½
parsley, chopped	1 small bunch	1 small bunch
hard-boiled eggs	3	3
whole-grain mustard	2 tablespoons	30 milliliters
extra-virgin olive oil	¼ cup	60 milliliters
salt and pepper	to taste	to taste

1. Pit the olives by first hitting them with a mallet or a full tin can and cutting around them with a paring knife if necessary.
2. Put all the ingredients except the olive oil in a mortar or food processor. Work the mixture to a stiff paste, making sure that little pieces of each component are left intact; the mixture should not be a purée.
3. Stir in the olive oil by hand and adjust the seasonings, adding salt and pepper as needed.

Note: Use Picholine or other natural olives; do not use canned California varieties of green olives.

BEANS AND OTHER LEGUMES

Almost any variety of bean or legume can be cooked, puréed, and whisked into a sauce to give it body, flavor, or color. In most areas of the United States, dried beans are the only ones available, but occasionally fresh lima beans, cranberry beans, or fava beans will appear. Fresh and frozen peas can also be used as sauce thickeners.

Dried beans must be soaked for 2 or 3 hours in warm water to soften them before cooking. They have soaked long enough when the skin starts to wrinkle. Longer soaking can cause the beans to start germinating, so it is best not to soak beans overnight. Lentils do not require softening. Dried beans will not soften if cooked with acidic ingredients, so do not add wine or tomato purée until the beans have already completely softened. Some chefs add a pinch of baking soda to the water, which makes it alkaline and helps soften the beans.

Dried beans usually require about three times their weight of water for cooking: For example, 1 pound (500 grams) of beans should be cooked in 6 cups (1.5 liters) of water. Always start dried beans in cold water and bring the water to a simmer over a 45-minute period. Do not rush the cooking or the beans will harden.

Depending on how the bean purée is to be used, other ingredients, such as onions, celery, carrots, garlic, and fennel, can be added. A bouquet garni is almost always a welcome addition. Many recipes for bean purées suggest adding smoked meats, such as ham, ham hocks, or bacon, but these are inappropriate if the purée will be used to finish a delicate sauce.

Bean purées should be kept covered with plastic wrap pressed down against the surface.

Fava Beans

Fava, or broad, beans are one of the few varieties of bean that are not native to the Americas but have been used in European cooking for centuries. They are often available fresh in the United States in Spanish or Italian markets. When properly prepared, they have a bright green color and a subtle, complex flavor. The main disadvantage to fava beans is that they must be peeled twice, so preparing a substantial amount of purée can be time consuming. Much of the weight of the unshelled bean will also be lost: 2 pounds (1 kilogram) of unshelled beans will yield 1 pound (500 grams) of beans, which in turn yields 20 percent less (13 ounces/400 grams) when the inner skin is removed. Unlike dried beans, which are slowly simmered, fresh fava beans should be cooked like most green vegetables, uncovered in a large pot of boiling salted water (a sprig of fresh winter savory in the water will add an interesting note). The recipe that follows can be used for thickening sauces; if the purée is to be served alone as an accompaniment, it should be enriched with butter or cream.

FAVA BEAN PURÉE

This recipe can also be used to prepare a purée of fresh or frozen peas. The peas need to be peeled only once. If using frozen peas—which can be excellent—skip the preliminary blanching and simply purée the thawed peas.

YIELD: 1 CUP (250 MILLILITERS)

fresh fava beans in the shell	1 pound	500 grams
appropriate liquid (see Note)	½ cup	125 milliliters

1. Remove the beans from the pods.
2. Remove the skin from each of the beans. This is best done with a small paring knife or a thumbnail.
3. Cook the beans for about 5 minutes in a pot of rapidly boiling salted water. Drain the beans in a colander and rinse them with cold running water to cool them.
4. Purée the beans in a food processor with the appropriate liquid. (If using cream, make sure it is hot or it will turn to butter.)
5. Force the purée thorough a drum sieve and keep it in a bowl covered with plastic wrap until needed.

Note: Cream, butter, stock, roasting juices, or braising liquids are some of the possible liquids to use to thin the purée.

Lentils

Lentils are easy to cook (they require no presoaking) and come in several colorful varieties. The type most familiar to Americans is the common brown lentil, but the French have a tiny green variety called *le puy* that is particularly tasty. In India a striking orange variety is sometimes used. Lentils cook faster than most types of dried beans, usually within 1 hour.

Lentil purée can be served as an accompaniment to red meats (it is best with game) or used to finish sauces. When served as a purée, it should be well enriched with butter or cream and preferably some roasting or braising juices. It can also be improved by gently sweating mirepoix with ham or bacon before adding the lentils. A note of sweetness from Madeira, port, or sugar will often enhance the flavor of the purée.

LENTIL PURÉE

YIELD: 2 CUPS (500 MILLILITERS)

lentils	1 cup	250 milliliters
carrot (optional)	½	½
onion (optional)	1 medium	1 medium
medium bouquet garni (page 51)	1	1
butter	2 ounces	60 grams
water	3 cups	750 milliliters

1. Rinse the lentils and peel and coarsely chop the carrot and onion, if using.
2. Combine all the ingredients in a heavy-bottomed saucepan. Bring to a slow simmer and cook until the lentils crush easily between thumb and forefinger.
3. Remove the bouquet garni and purée the mixture in a food processor or food mill.
4. Force the purée through a drum sieve. Keep it well covered with plastic wrap until needed.

Red Wine Sauce Finished with Lentil Purée

The earthy flavor of lentils makes them an excellent liaison for full-bodied brown and red wine sauces. Thicken 1 cup (250 milliliters) of either the Sauce Bordelaise or Meurette Sauce base (pages 180 and 181) with ½ cup (125 milliliters) of lentil purée. Strain the finished sauce through a chinois.

White Beans and Flageolet Beans

After soaking for 2 hours, white beans and flageolet beans can be softened and made easier to digest by precooking them for 15 minutes with a pinch of baking soda, draining them, and then moistening them again with fresh boiling water. If the purée is being used to finish other sauces, no other ingredients need be added, but if the purée is being served as a flavorful accompaniment in itself, then it can be enhanced by gently stewing the cooked beans with mirepoix vegetables, ham, bacon, or herbs before puréeing them. The purée can also be enriched with cream, butter, roasting juices, reduced stock, or other flavorful liquids if it is to be served as an accompaniment.

WHITE OR FLAGEOLET BEAN PURÉE

YIELD: 2 CUPS (500 MILLILITERS)

white or flageolet beans	1 cup	250 milliliters
baking soda	1 teaspoon	5 milliliters
onion, chopped (optional)	1 small	1 small
carrot, chopped (optional)	1 small	1 small
celery, chopped (optional)	½ stalk	½ stalk
ham, chopped (optional)	2 ounces	50 grams
butter (optional)	1 ounce	30 grams
large bouquet garni (page 51; optional)	1	1

1. Soak the beans for 2 hours in lukewarm water.
2. Drain the beans and put them in a pot with the baking soda and enough water to cover. Bring the water to a simmer, cook the beans for 15 minutes, and drain.
3. If using the vegetables and ham, sweat them in the butter until they have softened.
4. Add the precooked beans and the bouquet garni, if using. Cover with 3 cups (750 milliliters) of water. Cook the beans at a slow simmer for an hour more, or until they are easily crushed between thumb and forefinger.
5. Drain the beans, remove the bouquet garni, and purée the beans in a food processor. Force the purée though a drum sieve.
6. Put the purée in a bowl and cover it with plastic wrap until needed.

USING PURÉES WITH OTHER METHODS

Most purées have a distinct character of their own that can sometimes interfere with the flavor of a delicate sauce. For this reason chefs often combine different purées or use them with different types of liaisons. They are excellent when used in conjunction with butter, cream, or egg yolks because they lend support to the final texture of the sauce, so less of the rich ingredients needs to be used to achieve the same effect.

WATERCRESS AND MUSHROOM SAUCE FOR FISH

This sauce can be treated as a stock-based sauce, or the same method can be used to finish the cooking liquid for integral fish sauces.

YIELD: 2 CUPS (500 MILLILITERS)

fish cooking liquid, court-bouillon, or fish stock	¾ cup	185 milliliters
leben yogurt	4 teaspoons	20 milliliters

mushroom purée (page 476)	¼ cup	60 milliliters
watercress purée (page 475)	4 teaspoons	20 milliliters
salt and pepper	to taste	to taste

Heat the fish cooking liquid in a 1-quart (1 liter) sloping-sided saucepan. Whisk in the yogurt, mushroom purée, and watercress purée. Adjust the seasonings.

PARSLEY SABAYON SAUCE

This sauce can be used for either fish or white meat, such as veal. It goes especially well with sweetbreads. The method presented below uses purées prepared in advance, but the sauce can also be prepared by combining cooked mushrooms, blanched parsley, and egg yolks in a blender and then pouring in the simmering stock or cooking liquid and straining the sauce at the last minute.

YIELD: 1 CUP (250 MILLILITERS)

cool flavorful liquid (see Note)	½ cup	125 milliliters
mushroom purée (page 476)	¼ cup	60 milliliters
egg yolks	2	2
parsley purée (page 474)	2 teaspoons	10 milliliters
salt and pepper	to taste	to taste

1. Combine all the ingredients except the salt and pepper in a 2-quart (2 liter) sloping-sided saucepan.
2. Whisk the mixture over a medium flame until it expands in volume and begins to stiffen. (The bottom of the saucepan will become visible while whisking.)
3. Add salt and pepper. It may be necessary to add more of one or both the purées, to taste. Thin the sauce if necessary by adding more liquid.

Note: Meat or fish cooking liquid, court-bouillon, or meat or fish stock may be used as the liquid. The liquid should be cool.

18 PASTA SAUCES

Every region of Italy has its traditional pasta favorites. Although pasta sauces are easy to invent and improvise, it is helpful to keep in mind certain principles and time-proven traditions. All pasta dishes contain a liquid component that functions as a carrier for flavor and prevents the pasta from sticking to itself. Cooked and drained pasta tossed only with solid ingredients will soon become a gummy mess. In Italy, a popular method of serving pasta, especially stuffed pasta, is in a minestra. A *minestra* is simply a broth to which a simple garniture such as vegetable cubes, a spoonful of Parmesan cheese, or several pieces of stuffed pasta is added.

For stuffed pasta, the broth and a little grated Parmesan cheese are the only "sauce." We Americans, however, are more familiar with pasta served with a limited amount of savory sauce or sauce-like liquid. The most familiar sauces are based on tomatoes or olive oil, but other ingredients such as cream, butter, the cooking liquid from shellfish, meat juices, rendered fats (especially pancetta and prosciutto fats) are all used to create a flavorful medium for a pasta sauce. Once the basic liquid medium is established, the sauce can be augmented with herbs, vegetables, shellfish, salty condiments such as capers or olives, and chopped meats.

PASTA STYLES

Although cooks in America tend to combine sauces with any variety of pasta that comes to mind, most Italians associate particular kinds of pasta with a region's own specialties and sauces. In northern Italy, fresh pasta made with eggs is more popular than the dried pasta, often made only with water, usually served in the south. To delineate which sauces are traditionally served with what pasta would be the subject of an entire book, but there are a few principles and traditions that help make a judicious pairing of pasta and sauce.

Fresh pasta is usually cut in strands and served with the richer sauces—often containing cream, butter, and meats—associated with northern Italian cooking, whereas dried pasta, which comes in a myriad of shapes (often contorted) and sizes, is usually associated with the tomato-based and vegetable sauces of the south. One reliable approach when deciding what pasta to use is to consider how much of the sauce will cling to the pasta and how rich the sauce is. A pasta with a lot of nooks and crannies such as *radiotore* ("little radiators") will absorb too much of a very rich sauce based on butter or cream. A light tomato sauce, on the other hand, will slide off a smooth, slippery fettuccine or spaghetti. If pasta with a meat sauce is being served as a first course, a smooth-strand pasta and relatively little sauce will be appropriate, while the same dish served as a main course might be better with an irregularly shaped pasta and relatively more sauce.

A NOTE ABOUT SERVING SIZES

In Italy, pasta is always served in relatively modest amounts before the main course—never *with* the main course or *as* the main course as it is sometimes served in the United States. The amount of pasta served in Italy as a first course (or second course if it follows antipasti) is about two-thirds the amount served in the United States as a main course. One pound (450 grams) of dried pasta or 1½ pounds (675 grams) of fresh is usually about right for four main-course or six first-course (pasta course) servings.

Pasta Shapes

Acini de pepe	peppercorns	Orzo	barley
Anelli	little rings	Pappardelle	wide strips
Bucatini	little hollows	Penne	quill pens
Cannelloni	large reeds	Perciatelli	small pierced
Capellini	fine hairs	Radiatore	radiators
Conchiglie	shells	Rigatoni	large grooves
Ditali	thimbles	Rotelle	spiral shapes
Ditalini	little thimbles	Rotini	little spiral shapes
Elbow macaroni	dumplings	Ruote	wagon wheels
Farfalle	butterflies or bowties	Spaghetti	length of rope
Fettuccine	small ribbons	Stelline	little stars
Fusilli	twisted spaghetti	Tagliatelle	cut noodles
Gemelli	twins	Tripolini	little bows
Linguine	small tongues	Tubetti	little tubes
Mafalda	flat, ripple-edged	Tubettini	very little tubes
Manicotti	small muffs	Vermicelli	little worms
Mostaccioli	small mustaches	Ziti	bridegrooms
Orecchiette	little ears		

OLIVE OIL AND BUTTER: THE BASE FOR THE SIMPLEST SAUCES

One of the simplest and most satisfying ways to eat pasta is to toss it with the best extra-virgin olive oil or sweet butter and sprinkle it with freshly grated Parmesan cheese. Butter is the basis for the famous (or nowadays perhaps infamous) *fettuccine alfredo*, which is simply cooked fettuccine tossed with triple the amount of butter normally served with buttered pasta, plus reduced heavy cream, cheese, and other seasonings.

PASTA WITH BUTTER OR OLIVE OIL

YIELD: 6 PASTA-COURSE OR 4 MAIN-COURSE SERVINGS

fresh pasta	1½ pounds	675 grams
or	or	or
dried pasta	1 pound	450 grams
sweet butter, cut into small chunks, to taste	6 ounces	175 grams
or	or	or
extra-virgin olive oil, to taste	¾ cup	185 milliliters
salt and pepper	to taste	to taste
freshly grated parmigiano-reggiano		

Boil the pasta until al dente, drain, and toss with the butter or oil and salt and pepper. Pass the Parmesan cheese at the table.

Simple Additions to Basic Pasta with Butter or Olive Oil

Many of the best pasta sauces are made by adding one or more simple ingredients to cooked pasta that has simply been tossed with olive oil or butter. Much of the time, these ingredients can be tossed raw with the cooked pasta. Other ingredients (such as garlic or sage) may also be gently cooked first in the olive oil or butter before being tossed with the pasta. Remember, however, that extra-virgin olive oil should be cooked very gently so that its perfume isn't destroyed by the heat. The creamy texture of sweet butter is also lost when the butter is overheated rather than simply allowed to melt on the pasta. However, butter can be cooked to the noisette stage (until lightly browned) before being tossed with the pasta (see Pasta with Butter and Sage, page 498).

Anchovies. Italians, especially those from the south, are fans of both fresh and salted anchovies. In the United States, fresh anchovies are almost impossible to find, so we must rely on anchovies packed in oil. In Italy, anchovies are usually sold packed whole in salt and have a deeper, more complex flavor than anchovies packed in oil (see page 81).

Sweet Peppers. Grilled and peeled sweet red peppers—in Italian called *peperoni*—are cut into strips or cubes, quickly simmered with tomatoes and garlic, and used as a pasta sauce.

Capers. These miniature salted or brine- or vinegar-soaked berries give a savory accent to pasta sauces based on simple combinations of fresh tomatoes, herbs, olives, and anchovies. Italian cooks prefer the small nonpareil capers, which in Italy are available packed in salt but in the United States are usually found packed in brine and vinegar in jars.

Garlic. So often used in Italian cooking that it's almost universal, finely chopped or sliced garlic gently cooked in olive oil or butter makes a simple and satisfying sauce. Italian cooks often cut the garlic into paper-thin slices and then cook them very slowly until they turn pale brown and develop a nutty flavor.

Herbs. The simplest way to give distinction to simple butter- or olive oil–coated pasta is to add fresh herbs. Basil is the best known—just add a small handful of whole leaves with the basic pasta tossed with olive oil—but finely chopped marjoram (especially with garlic) works magic with pasta tossed with butter or olive oil. Throughout Italy, sage and butter are cooked together in one of the best and simplest of pasta sauces. Mint and oregano are also popular herbs for flavoring pasta.

Olives. A variety of green and black olives are found throughout Italy, and each variety can be used to give its own particular nuance to a pasta sauce. The olives are pitted—easy to accomplish by just squeezing the pointier ends together between thumb and forefinger—and left otherwise whole, coarsely chopped, or on occasion ground to a paste. Olives give a salty and bitter note to pasta sauces, which makes them excellent in combination with basil, tomatoes, garlic, and anchovies.

Peperoncini. These little dried red peppers, found in any Italian grocery, are a favorite condiment for simple Italian pasta sauces. The peppers are coarsely chopped and need very little if any cooking before being tossed with the pasta. Red pepper flakes make a good substitute.

Pine nuts. In addition to their use in pesto sauce, pine nuts are a popular ingredient in pasta sauces (especially those made with vegetables and garlic) to provide texture. The flavor of pine nuts is enhanced when they are lightly browned in a dry sauté pan or in the oven.

Tomatoes. In many Italian sauces, chopped tomatoes are gently stewed with aromatic vegetables, often combined with meats and wine, into deep-flavored and complex sauces such as ragù or bolognese sauce. But in simpler sauces, tomatoes can simply be peeled and seeded, cut into cubes, and tossed with pasta—often in conjunction with other condiments such as olives and anchovies, producing pasta sauces that are fresh and light.

Truffles. The most famous truffles used in pasta dishes are the pungent white truffles from the Piedmont region of northern Italy. Umbria, in central Italy, is also renowned for its winter black truffles, the same species (*Tuber melanosporum*) as French truffles from the Perigord and other regions. Tuscany is also gifted with summer truffles (*Tuber aestivum*), which, although less aromatic than white truffles or winter black truffles, are much less expensive. White truffles are shaved raw over simple dishes of fresh pasta tossed with butter or olive oil, whereas black truffles are more likely to be cooked in preparations such as Spaghetti alla Norcina (page 499).

PASTA WITH BUTTER AND SAGE
Fettuccine con Burro e Salvia

This simple but delicious pasta sauce shows off the combination of sage and garlic. The secret to success is that both the butter and garlic should be lightly browned before they're tossed with the pasta.

YIELD: 6 PASTA-COURSE OR 4 MAIN-COURSE SERVINGS

unsalted butter	6 ounces	175 grams
fresh sage leaves	12	12
garlic cloves, very thinly sliced	4	4
fresh pasta	1½ pounds	675 grams
or	*or*	*or*
dried pasta	1 pound	450 grams
salt and pepper	to taste	to taste
freshly grated parmigiano-reggiano		

1. Bring a large pot of water to a rapid boil for cooking the pasta.
2. Heat the butter in a small saucepan or sauté pan over medium heat with the sage leaves. When the butter starts to froth, stir in the garlic.
3. Cook the pasta in the boiling water while the butter is cooking.
4. When the butter stops frothing, the garlic is pale brown, and light brown specks of coagulated milk solids appear along the bottom and sides of the pan, toss the butter, garlic, and sage with the pasta. Season to taste with salt and pepper. Pass the Parmesan cheese at the table.

SPAGHETTI WITH STREETWALKER'S SAUCE
Spaghetti alla Puttanesca

This sauce, said to be from the island of Ischia (off the coast of Naples), has become popular not only in Naples but in all of Italy and even abroad. The name *puttanesca*, usually translated somewhat less delicately than "streetwalker," comes from the fact that the ladies of the night, after whom this sauce is named, had little time to shop and had to rely on ingredients such as olives and anchovies that would keep without spoiling. Or so the story goes.

YIELD: 6 PASTA-COURSE OR 4 MAIN-COURSE SERVINGS

extra-virgin olive oil	¼ cup	60 milliliters
garlic cloves, crushed to a paste	2	2
dried peperoncini, chopped	2 teaspoons	10 milliliters
or	*or*	*or*
red pepper flakes	2 teaspoons	10 milliliters
anchovy fillets, drained, patted dry, coarsely chopped	24	24

plum tomatoes, peeled, seeded, coarsely chopped	1½ pounds	675 grams
brine-cured black olives such as gaeta (not oil-cured), pitted, coarsely chopped, about 60	6 ounces	175 grams
capers, drained	¼ cup	60 milliliters
dried spaghetti or other strand pasta	1 pound	450 grams
or	or	or
fresh strand pasta such as fettuccine or linguine	1½ pounds	675 grams
salt	to taste	to taste

1. Bring a large pot of water to a rapid boil for cooking the pasta.
2. Heat the oil over medium heat in a sauté pan large enough to hold the cooked pasta, and stir in the garlic, peperoncini, and anchovies. Let the garlic sizzle for about 1 minute and stir in the tomatoes, olives, and capers.
3. Put the spaghetti on to cook while continuing to stir the sauce over medium heat. Season the sauce with salt—it many not need any because of the olives and anchovies—and toss with the boiled and drained spaghetti.

SPAGHETTI WITH BLACK TRUFFLES, GARLIC, AND ANCHOVIES
Spaghetti alla Norcina

This dish is named after Norcia, a town in Umbria famous not only for its black truffles but for its excellent pork and pork products. The slightly dissonant flavor of the anchovies is lovely with the truffles and garlic.

YIELD: 6 PASTA-COURSE OR 4 MAIN-COURSE SERVINGS

black truffle	1	1
extra-virgin olive oil	1 cup	250 milliliters
garlic cloves, crushed to a paste	2	2
anchovy fillets, soaked for 5 minutes in cold water (soaking optional), patted dry, finely chopped	12	12
dried spaghetti	1 pound	450 grams
or	or	or
fresh strand pasta such as fettuccine or linguine	1½ pounds	675 grams
salt and pepper	to taste	to taste

1. Bring a large pot of water to a rapid boil for cooking the pasta.
2. If the truffle has dirt in its crevices, scrub it with a small brush, quickly rinse it, and pat it dry. Grate it with the small teeth of a hand grater.
3. Gently heat ¼ cup (60 milliliters) of the olive oil over low heat in a pan large enough to hold the cooked pasta and stir in the garlic and anchovies. Stir the sauce for about 4 minutes, until the garlic sizzles and releases its

aroma. Stir the grated truffle in the hot sauce for 1 minute and pour in the rest of the olive oil.

4. Cook and drain the pasta and toss it in the pan with the sauce. Season to taste, while tossing, with salt and pepper.

CREAM-BASED PASTA SAUCES

Heavy cream, because it is so receptive and forms so perfect a medium for other flavors, is often simmered with one or more aromatic ingredients to make a rich and flavorful pasta sauce. Unlike butter, which turns oily if overheated, cream thickens just enough so that it coats the pasta with a suave and velvety sauce. Pasta cream sauces require little effort—ingredients are simply infused in the simmering cream until the sauce thickens slightly. Almost any flavorful ingredient can be infused in cream, but here are a few suggestions. The following ingredients can be used alone or in combination.

Dried Mushrooms. Dried mushrooms, especially porcini, rinsed and soaked in barely enough water to cover, make a full-flavored pasta sauce that is especially delicious when the chopped mushrooms and their soaking liquid are simmered in heavy cream. Dried mushrooms can also be tossed in butter- or olive oil–based sauces.

Prosciutto. Tiny slivers or cubes of prosciutto, simmered in cream, give pasta sauces an inimitable depth of flavor.

Walnuts. Ground walnuts are used in Genoa and the surrounding region of Liguria to make pasta sauces. Traditionally, raw walnuts are ground to a paste, but it's also possible to leave them slightly chunky so the sauce has some texture. The walnuts can also be roasted to bring out their flavor.

PAPPARDELLE WITH DRIED PORCINI MUSHROOMS
Pappardelle ai Porcini Secchi

Pappardelle are flat long noodles, originally from Tuscany, measuring about ¾ inch (2 cm) wide. Any flat strand pasta, such as linguine or tagliatelle, can be substituted. Dried porcini mushroom sauces often contain tomatoes, but the simplest and perhaps most delicious versions are made with only cream and seasonings.

YIELD: 6 PASTA-COURSE OR 4 MAIN-COURSE SERVINGS

dried porcini mushrooms (about 1½ ounces/45 grams)	1 cup	250 milliliters
heavy cream	2 cups	500 milliliters
salt and pepper	to taste	to taste

fresh pappardelle or strand pasta such as fettuccine or linguine	1½ pounds	675 grams
or	or	or
dried pappardelle or strand pasta	1 pound	450 grams
freshly grated parmigiano-reggiano		

1. Rinse the mushrooms under cold running water and place them in a small bowl with ¼ cup (60 milliliters) warm water. Turn the mushrooms around in the water every 5 minutes and soak for a total of 20 minutes until soft and pliable.
2. Bring a large pot of water to a rapid boil for cooking the pasta.
3. Heat the cream over medium heat in a pot large enough to hold the drained pasta.
4. Squeeze the soaking liquid out of the mushrooms and reserve both mushrooms and liquid.
5. Coarsely chop the mushrooms and pour the liquid slowly into the cream, leaving any grit or sand behind. Add the chopped mushrooms to the cream and simmer until the cream thickens slightly, about 5 minutes, and season to taste with salt and pepper.
6. Cook and drain the pasta, toss with the sauce, and serve. Pass the Parmesan cheese at the table.

RAVIOLI OR TAGLIATELLE WITH WALNUT SAUCE
Ravioli o Tagliatelle con Salsa di Noci

Traditional with ravioli or tagliatelle, walnut sauce is delicious on any flat strand, preferably fresh, pasta. The consistency of the chopped walnuts is largely a matter of taste; some Italian recipes recommend puréeing them to a paste, whereas some chefs leave them in lentil- to pea-size crunchy pieces.

YIELD: 6 PASTA-COURSE OR 4 MAIN-COURSE SERVINGS

shelled walnuts	1⅔ cups	400 milliliters
heavy cream	2 cups	500 milliliters
garlic cloves, finely chopped	2	2
finely chopped fresh marjoram or sage (optional)	2 teaspoons	10 milliliters
salt and pepper	to taste	to taste
small to medium ravioli	48	48
or	or	or
fresh fettuccine	1½ pounds	675 grams
or	or	or
dried fettuccine	1 pound	450 grams
freshly grated parmigiano-reggiano		

1. Preheat the oven to 350°F (175°C). Spread the walnuts on a sheet pan and bake in the oven for 15 minutes, until they smell fragrant and darken very slightly. Chop the walnuts by hand or in a food processor—the walnuts should be about the size of peas—and reserve.
2. Bring a large pot of water to a rapid boil for cooking the pasta.
3. Heat the cream over medium heat in a pot large enough to toss the drained pasta, and stir in the garlic, marjoram, if using, and walnuts. Simmer until the cream thickens slightly, about 5 minutes, and season to taste with salt and pepper. Cook and drain the pasta and toss with the sauce. (Ravioli can be tossed with a little butter and the sauce spooned over on the plates.) Pass the Parmesan cheese at the table.

SAUCES BASED ON PRESERVED PORK PRODUCTS

Although the best-known pasta sauces are based on olive oil, butter, or cream, Italy has delicious ham (prosciutto)—both cured (*crudo*) and cooked (*cotto*)—savory unsmoked bacon (pancetta), and a version of lard (*strutto*) far superior to the soapy-tasting American version. Good-quality American bacon can also be used in pasta sauces, but it will give the sauce a pronounced smoky flavor that, although not authentic, is quite tasty.

Pork products such as pancetta or prosciutto are gently cooked so they render their delicious fat, which is then incorporated into the sauce. Pancetta is quite fatty and can be cut into cubes or strips and rendered in the same way as bacon. Prosciutto, on the other hand, is very lean, except for a layer of fat surrounding the meat just under the rind. This fat can be finely chopped or puréed to a paste in a food processor and then gently rendered and used as a cooking fat for sauces. It's important that the fat from pancetta or prosciutto be exposed to only very gentle heat—as with extra-virgin olive oil—or it will lose flavor and finesse.

SPAGHETTI WITH PANCETTA, EGGS, AND PARMESAN CHEESE
Spaghetti alla Carbonara

This famous Roman dish is traditionally made with *guanciale,* a kind of unsmoked bacon made from pork cheeks. Guanciale is obtainable online, but if you cannot get it, pancetta or prosciutto make more than adequate substitutes.

YIELD: 8 PASTA-COURSE OR 4 MAIN-COURSE SERVINGS

guanciale, pancetta, or prosciutto such as prosciutto di parma with fat left attached, cut into ⅛-inch-thick (3 mm) slices	⅓ pound	150 grams
garlic clove, finely chopped	1 small	1 small

large eggs, beaten	3	3
salt and pepper	to taste	to taste
freshly grated parmigiano-reggiano	¾ cup	185 milliliters
dried spaghetti	½ pound	225 grams
or	*or*	*or*
fresh strand pasta such as fettuccine or linguine	1 pound	450 grams

1. Cut the guanciale or pancetta into 1-inch-wide (2.5 cm) strips. If using prosciutto, cut off and discard the rind (or save it for braises), remove and finely chop the fat, and cut the meat into 1-inch (2.5 cm) strips. Bring a large pot of water to a rapid boil for cooking the pasta.

2. Over low to medium heat, render the guanciale or pancetta strips or chopped prosciutto fat in a heavy-bottomed pan large enough to hold the cooked pasta, until the fat becomes slightly crispy, 10 to 15 minutes. If using a very fatty guanciale or pancetta, drain off all but ⅓ cup (80 milliliters) of the fat. Stir the garlic into the pan with the remaining fat and cook for 1 minute more.

3. Season the eggs with salt and pepper and stir in half of the grated Parmesan cheese. Cook and drain the pasta and quickly toss with the rendered fat and garlic; the beaten eggs; the guanciale, pancetta, or prosciutto; and the remaining cheese. Season to taste with salt and pepper and serve on hot plates.

SEAFOOD SAUCES

Fresh shellfish sauces and, to a lesser extent, sauces made from fresh fish—especially fresh anchovies and sardines—are popular in regions of Italy that border the sea. Preserved seafood, especially salted anchovies and tuna preserved in oil or brine, are more typical in those inland areas with limited access to fresh seafood.

Fresh shellfish sauces are approached in several ways. One typical method, usually used for clams and mussels, consists of steaming open the shellfish with a little water or white wine, combining the cooking liquid with olive oil, butter, or occasionally cream, and tossing the liquids (sometimes reduced but often not) with the cooked pasta. Crustacean sauces are often nothing more than the whole crustacean—shrimp, scampi (langoustines), or mantis shrimp (Mediterranean shrimp-like crustaceans)—sautéed in olive oil, sprinkled with chopped herbs, and perhaps some chunks of tomato. The whole combination is then tossed with the pasta. Occasionally, crustacean shells are infused in cream or used to make a crustacean butter, either of which is then used in the sauce (see Fettuccine with Shrimp and Crustacean Cream Sauce, page 506).

Italians are fond of tentacled creatures. Squid and octopus are familiar to Americans, but cuttlefish, which look like squid but are fatter and more squat, aren't found in American waters and must be imported—they're hard to find in the United States except in East Coast ethnic markets. Cuttlefish ink is much darker, thicker, and more abundant than squid ink, so it works better in black Italian sauces and as a coloring for fresh pasta. Squid and baby octopus are usually lightly sautéed with olive oil, herbs, and white wine (they can also be grilled) and simply tossed with the cooked pasta. Cuttlefish, which is meatier and tougher, is braised in stews with tomatoes and occasionally red wine, and finished with its ink in a method analogous to making a *civet*. Squid can also be trimmed, the hoods cut into rings, the cluster of tentacles sectioned (if it is large), and tentacles and rings braised in red wine, with the sauce reduced and tossed with pasta. Large octopus, a favorite Italian antipasto and salad ingredient, is also best when braised—much like a red wine beef stew—and the full-flavored and gelatinous braising liquid reduced and used as a sauce. The braised octopus sections can also be quickly grilled and combined with their reduced braising liquid just before tossing with the pasta.

Contemporary French-influenced sauces also crop up in Italian restaurants. Two examples are smoked salmon sauce, made by infusing slivers of smoked salmon in cream, and sauces based on caviar butter.

SPAGHETTI WITH CLAMS OR MUSSELS
Spaghetti alle Cozze o Vongole

Americans are probably most familiar with the classic linguini with clam sauce, but in Rome and Naples clams and mussels are usually served with spaghetti. Virtually any cooked pasta can be tossed with steamed mussels or clams and their delicious briny liquid. This version is based on olive oil, but it is also possible to combine the cooking liquid with butter or with heavy cream (reduced until slightly thickened), flavor it with chopped herbs—especially parsley—and toss with the pasta.

YIELD: 6 PASTA-COURSE OR 4 MAIN-COURSE SERVINGS

garlic cloves, finely chopped	2	2
small clams or mussels, scrubbed and sorted	4 pounds	1.8 kilograms
tomatoes, peeled, seeded, coarsely chopped	2 medium	2 medium
extra-virgin olive oil or heavy cream	⅔ cup	165 milliliters
finely chopped parsley or basil, chopped at the last minute	2 tablespoons	30 milliliters
salt and pepper	to taste	to taste
dried spaghetti or other strand pasta	1 pound	450 grams
or	*or*	*or*
fresh strand pasta such as fettuccine or linguine	1½ pounds	675 grams

butter	½ ounce	15 grams
or	or	or
olive oil	1 tablespoon	15 milliliters

1. Bring a large pot of water to a rapid boil for cooking the pasta.
2. Combine the garlic with ⅓ cup (80 milliliters) water in a pot large enough so that the shellfish come only halfway up its sides (to leave room for them to open). Add the shellfish, cover the pot, and cook over medium to high heat until all the shellfish have opened, about 10 minutes for clams and 6 minutes for mussels.
3. Remove the shellfish from the pot with a big spoon or skimmer, put them in a bowl or pot, cover them, and keep them warm. (The cooked clams or mussels can be taken out of the shell—or just remove the top shell—but the dish looks more festive when they're left in their shells.) Slowly pour the shellfish cooking liquid into a small saucepan, leaving any grit behind in the large pot (if the liquid is very gritty, strain it).
4. Combine the tomatoes, extra-virgin olive oil, and parsley with the cooking liquid and bring to a simmer. Season to taste with salt and pepper (salt may not be necessary).
5. Cook and drain the pasta, toss with the butter, and distribute it in hot bowls. Ladle the sauce over the pasta and arrange the shellfish over and around. See the photograph in the color plates.

SPAGHETTI WITH SQUID OR BABY OCTOPUS
Spaghetti al Ragù di Totano

This dish, from the southern Italian region of Calabria, can be made with squid (called *totani* in the regional dialect), baby octopus, or cuttlefish. Unlike many Italian pasta dishes that use quickly sautéed squid, this version calls for gentle braising in tomato sauce. One difference between this dish and classic French stews is that French stew recipes call for cooking the ingredients in a minimum of fat and skimming off the fat during or after cooking so that little if any ends up in the final sauce. In this stew, a large amount of olive oil is used, and the stew is gently cooked, uncovered, until the olive oil separates back out. This separated mixture, heresy to a French cook, becomes the sauce. The original version calls for braising the basil with the other ingredients, but the basil's flavor and freshness will remain more intact if it is chopped and added at the last minute.

YIELD: 6 PASTA-COURSE OR 4 MAIN-COURSE SERVINGS

squid or baby octopus	2 pounds	900 grams
onion, finely chopped	1 medium	1 medium
garlic cloves, finely chopped	2	2
extra-virgin olive oil	½ cup	125 milliliters

tomatoes, peeled, seeded, chopped	4 medium	4 medium
or	or	or
drained and chopped canned tomatoes	2 cups	500 milliliters
dried spaghetti or other strand pasta	1 pound	450 grams
chopped basil leaves (chopped at the last minute)	3 tablespoons	45 milliliters
salt and pepper	to taste	to taste

1. Clean the squid by pulling out the innards and cutting off the tentacles just above where they join into a cluster. Cut the hoods into ¼-inch-wide (5 mm) rings. (The purple skin may be scraped off before cutting the hoods into rings, but this is only for appearance—some cooks insist that the flavor is improved by leaving this skin attached.) Clean baby octopus in the same way as squid but leave the hoods and tentacle clusters whole.

2. Heat the onion and garlic over medium heat in 2 tablespoons (30 milliliters) of the olive oil in a heavy-bottomed pot until translucent, about 10 minutes. Stir in the tomatoes and the rest of the oil and bring to a gentle simmer. Stir in the squid or octopus, partially cover the pan, and simmer very gently, stirring the squid every few minutes, until the oil and tomatoes separate and the squid is tender, about 45 minutes. (If the squid is cooked before the sauce separates, continue cooking uncovered.)

3. While the squid is cooking, bring a large pot of water to a rapid boil for cooking the pasta. Cook and drain the pasta.

4. Stir the chopped basil into the squid, season to taste with salt and pepper, and toss with the pasta.

FETTUCCINE AND SHRIMP WITH CRUSTACEAN CREAM SAUCE
Fettuccine alla Crema di Scampi

Scampi are saltwater crayfish-like crustaceans, not the shrimp that are usually served as a substitute in the United States. The correct English name for scampi is "lobsterettes," but most of the time the French name, *langoustines,* is used instead. Although some langoustines are imported into the United States (mostly from New Zealand), they are difficult to find. Shrimp, crayfish, and lobster can all be substituted. This sauce is made with crustacean butter made from crustacean shells (the shells needn't be from the same crustacean; see page 329). This sauce is very similar to the Sauce Crevettes on page 212.

YIELD: 6 PASTA-COURSE OR 4 MAIN-COURSE SERVINGS

shelled raw shrimp tails, cooked shelled crayfish tails, or cooked lobster meat	1½ pounds	675 grams
heavy cream	1½ cups	375 milliliters

ripe tomatoes, seeded, finely chopped	2	2
or	or	or
drained and chopped canned tomatoes	1 cup	250 milliliters
chopped fresh thyme	½ teaspoon	3 milliliters
or	or	or
chopped fresh marjoram	1 teaspoon	5 milliliters
crustacean butter (page 329)	4 ounces	125 grams
salt and pepper	to taste	to taste
fresh fettuccine (tagliatelle) or linguine	1½ pounds	675 grams
or	or	or
dried fettuccine or linguine	1 pound	450 grams

1. Bring a large pot of water to a rapid boil for cooking the pasta. If the shrimp are very large, cut them into ½-inch (1 cm) sections. If using crayfish tails, leave them whole. Slice lobster tails into ¼-inch-thick (5 mm) medallions. Leave lobster claws whole.

2. Combine the cream, tomatoes, and chopped herbs in a medium saucepan over medium heat until the mixture thickens to a sauce-like consistency, about 10 minutes. Whisk in the crustacean butter and strain the sauce through a fine-mesh strainer. Season with salt and pepper, and reserve.

3. Just before serving, boil the pasta and very gently heat the shellfish in the sauce, never letting it boil for even a second—which would cause the shellfish to curl up, harden, and dry out. Toss the pasta with the sauce and shellfish and serve.

SPAGHETTI WITH TUNA
Spaghetti col Tonno

This Roman dish is traditionally made with tuna packed in oil, but nowadays in the United States fresh tuna is so widely available that it's worth making this dish with fresh tuna or, for that matter, any full-flavored, firm-fleshed fresh fish. Avoid overcooking fresh tuna or it will turn very dry.

YIELD: 6 PASTA-COURSE OR 4 MAIN-COURSE SERVINGS

garlic cloves, finely chopped	2	2
extra-virgin olive oil	½ cup	125 milliliters
tomatoes, peeled, seeded, coarsely chopped	3 medium	3 medium
or	or	or
drained, seeded, and chopped canned tomatoes	1½ cups	375 milliliters
dried spaghetti or other strand pasta	1 pound	450 grams
or	or	or
fresh spaghetti or other strand pasta	1½ pounds	675 grams

fresh tuna, cut into ½-inch (1 cm) cubes	1 pound	450 grams
finely chopped parsley (chopped at the last minute)	1 tablespoon	15 milliliters
finely chopped fresh basil (chopped at the last minute)	2 tablespoons	30 milliliters
salt and pepper	to taste	to taste

1. Bring a large pot of water to a rapid boil for cooking the pasta.
2. Sweat the garlic in 2 tablespoons (30 milliliters) of the olive oil over medium heat in a heavy-bottomed pot large enough to hold the drained pasta. When the garlic turns translucent and smells aromatic (don't let it brown), after about 5 minutes, add the tomatoes and the rest of the olive oil. Stew over medium heat, uncovered, until the tomatoes and oil separate, about 15 minutes.
3. Cook the pasta. Immediately before draining the pasta, add the tuna and chopped herbs to the sauce and stir over medium heat for 30 seconds. Season with salt and pepper and toss with the drained pasta.

VEGETABLE SAUCES

Many of the best pasta sauces are simple vegetable dishes made by chopping the vegetables somewhat more finely than if they were being served as a vegetable side dish and then tossing the vegetables with the cooked pasta. Tomatoes, chopped and gently stewed into a sauce, are the best-known examples, but greens such as spinach, chard, broccoli raab, kale, artichokes, asparagus, peas, green beans, and fennel can all be cooked and used alone or in combination as simple sauces. Mushrooms and truffles are also used to make simple but extraordinarily delicious sauces.

Most vegetable sauces are made by gently stewing the vegetable in olive oil or butter or sometimes cream; sometimes adding chopped garlic or other condiments such as anchovies, pine nuts, or raisins; and sometimes herbs such as sage or marjoram, and then tossing the whole mixture with the cooked pasta.

SPAGHETTI WITH ARTICHOKES, GARLIC, AND PARSLEY
Spaghetti e Carciofi

The suave delicacy of artichokes makes a luxurious pasta sauce that can be served with spaghetti—the pasta used for this dish in the far southern region of Calabria, where it is popular—but the sauce's richness makes it even better served with fresh flat strand pasta such as fettuccine. In typical southern Italian style, this sauce is based on olive oil—pancetta is optional—but the cubes of cooked artichokes can also be simmered in cream to make a delicate cream-based pasta sauce.

YIELD: 6 PASTA-COURSE OR 4 MAIN-COURSE SERVINGS

artichoke bottoms (leaves trimmed off the sides, top two-thirds of the artichoke cut off)	4 large	4 large
juice of 1 lemon		
olive oil (for cooking the artichokes)	2 tablespoons	30 milliliters
extra-virgin olive oil	⅔ cup	165 milliliters
or	or	or
heavy cream	1 cup	250 milliliters
garlic clove, finely chopped	1	1
dried spaghetti or other strand pasta	1 pound	450 grams
or	or	or
fresh spaghetti or other strand pasta	1½ pounds	675 grams
finely chopped parsley, chopped at the last minute	2 tablespoons	30 milliliters
salt and pepper	to taste	to taste
freshly grated parmigiano-reggiano		

1. Toss the artichoke bottoms with lemon juice immediately and put the artichoke bottoms, lemon juice, 1 tablespoon (15 milliliters) of the olive oil, and enough cold water to cover the artichokes by several inches in a large nonaluminum pot. Put a plate directly over the artichokes in the pot to keep them submerged. Simmer the artichokes for about 20 minutes from the time the water comes to a boil, until they can be easily penetrated on the bottom with a sharp knife. Drain and let cool.

2. While the artichokes are cooling, bring a large pot of water to a rapid boil for cooking the pasta.

3. Scoop the chokes out of the artichoke bottoms with a spoon and cut the bottoms into ⅓-inch (1 cm) dice. Toss the dice with the remaining 1 tablespoon (15 milliliters) of olive oil and reserve.

4. Heat the extra-virgin olive oil or the cream over medium heat in a pot large enough to hold the drained pasta. Add the garlic and cook until it smells aromatic, or the cream thickens to a sauce-like consistency, about 5 minutes. Meanwhile, cook and drain the pasta.

5. Stir the parsley and the reserved artichoke cubes into the sauce and bring it back to a simmer. Season to taste with salt and pepper and toss with the drained pasta. Pass the Parmesan cheese at the table.

ORECCHIETTE WITH COOKED GREEN AND LEAFY VEGETABLES

Orecchiette con Cime di Rapa

Orecchiette (the word means "little ears") are popular in Puglia, the region of Italy that Greece-bound travelers vaguely remember passing through on their way to the ferry in Bari. Many of Puglia's pasta dishes are based on vegetables and olive oil, and Puglia is famous for both. Although the Pugliese have their favorite greens—broccoli raab among them—this simple method of combining greens and pasta can be used for Swiss chard, arugula, kale, turnip or beet greens, or even spinach.

YIELD: 6 PASTA-COURSE OR 4 MAIN-COURSE SERVINGS

greens such as Swiss chard, kale, turnip or beet greens, or spinach	2 pounds	900 grams
or	or	or
arugula	4 bunches	4 bunches
or	or	or
broccoli raab	2 pounds	900 grams
garlic cloves, very thinly sliced	4	4
peperoncini, stemmed and chopped	2	2
or	or	or
red pepper flakes	2 teaspoons	10 milliliters
extra-virgin olive oil	½ cup	125 milliliters
dried orecchiette or short tubular pasta such as macaroni, ziti, or penne	1 pound	450 grams
salt and pepper	to taste	to taste
freshly grated parmigiano-reggiano		

1. Bring a large pot of water to a rapid boil for cooking the pasta. Remove the stems from the greens or broccoli raab, wash and drain, and chop the leaves or flowers coarsely.
2. Heat the garlic and peperoncini over medium heat in 2 tablespoons (30 milliliters) of the olive oil in a heavy-bottomed pot large enough to hold the drained pasta. When the garlic smells aromatic and begins to turn very slightly brown, about 3 minutes, stir in the chopped vegetables. Continue stirring over medium heat until the vegetables release their moisture and become tender, about 5 minutes.
3. Cook and drain the pasta. Season the vegetables with salt and pepper and stir in the remaining olive oil. Toss with the pasta. Pass the Parmesan cheese at the table.

FETTUCCINE WITH PEAS

Fettuccine con i Piselli

This simple dish, best known in the Veneto, the region surrounding Venice, is based on a mixture of pancetta and butter, but lightly reduced cream can replace the butter and even the pancetta. This approach need not be limited to peas; other delicately flavored green vegetables such as asparagus tips, baby string beans, or baby green onions or leeks can be quickly blanched or boiled and tossed with the pasta. Parsley is called for in the traditional recipe, but other herbs such as chervil or chives can be used to give this dish a vaguely French touch.

YIELD: 6 PASTA-COURSE OR 4 MAIN-COURSE SERVINGS

pancetta, 1 slice, finely chopped	2 ounces	60 grams
onion, finely chopped	1 small	1 small
fresh peas, 2 to 3 pounds (1 to 1.5 kilograms), shucked	2 to 3 cups	500 to 750 milliliters
or	or	or
frozen baby peas, thawed	2 (10-ounce) packages	600 grams
chicken broth	½ cup	125 milliliters
fresh fettuccine, linguine, pappardelle, or other strand pasta	1½ pounds	675 grams
unsalted butter	1 ounce	30 grams
finely chopped parsley, chopped at the last minute	1 tablespoon	15 milliliters
salt and pepper	to taste	to taste
freshly grated parmigiano-reggiano		

1. Bring a large pot of water to a rapid boil for cooking the pasta. Cook the pancetta over medium heat for about 5 minutes in a heavy-bottomed pot large enough to hold the drained pasta. Stir in the onion and continue cooking, stirring occasionally, until the onion turns translucent, about 7 minutes more.

2. If using fresh peas, boil them in a large pot of salted water for 1 to 2 minutes and drain.

3. Add the chicken broth and the peas to the onion mixture, turn the heat to high, and boil the peas for 3 to 5 minutes, while gently folding them over each other so they cook evenly.

4. Cook and drain the pasta. Toss the pasta with the butter and arrange in wide soup bowls (they must have rims because the sauce is very liquidy).

5. Stir the parsley into the peas and season to taste with salt and pepper. Ladle the peas and their cooking liquid over the pasta. Pass the Parmesan cheese at the table. See the photograph in the color plates.

MEAT SAUCES

Italian meat sauces, called *ragù*, are usually made by gently cooking chopped meat with aromatic vegetables (the Italian equivalent of a mirepoix is a *soffritto*) and then adding liquids such as red or white wine and chopped tomatoes. What distinguishes ragù from French sauces is that the meat is left *in* the sauce, whereas French brown sauces are based on the extract—the braising or poaching liquid (stock)—that has been separated from the cooking meats. This Italian method of including the meat right in the sauce makes ragù a substantial sauce, perfect for pasta. (A French brown sauce wouldn't cling to pasta and would lack substance.) Italian cooks do sometimes, however, serve pasta in the broth made from gentle simmering of meats (such combinations of pasta in broth are called *minestre*) and then serve the meat after the pasta with condiment-like sauces such as the Salsa Verde on page 440.

It's useful to think of a ragù as analogous to a *ragoût* (a "stew"), in which the meat is cut up so finely that it becomes an integral part of the sauce. In fact, many ragù recipes are far better if the meat is cut into small cubes, by hand, rather than being chopped. Better yet—and taking the ragù/ragoût analogy a step further—large pieces of meat or meat cubes can be braised and then chopped and combined with the reduced braising liquid *after cooking*. Using this system, any French stew or braise can be converted into a delicious pasta sauce. Italian meat sauces are not only based on the familiar beef or veal (Bolognese sauce) or pork (popular in Naples) but also on rabbit, duck, hare, and variety meats such as sweetbreads, brains, kidneys, and chicken and duck livers.

●━━● RAGÙ

Although recipes for this famous Bolognese sauce vary, they all begin with the preparation of a flavor base with ground beef (or sometimes leftover cubes of cooked beef) and mirepoix vegetables. This recipe is slightly different from the classic one in that the flavor base is first cooked with the liquid released by the tomatoes; the pulp is added later. This recipe calls for ground beef, but the sauce will have more texture and an appealing hand-hewn quality if the meat is cut by hand into ¼-inch (5 mm) cubes.

YIELD: 1 QUART (1 LITER)

onion, finely chopped	1 medium	1 medium
carrot, chopped	1 small	1 small
prosciutto, chopped	2 ounces	50 grams
extra-virgin olive oil	3 tablespoons	45 milliliters
lean chopped or ground beef	12 ounces	350 grams
large bouquet garni (page 51), with a few sprigs marjoram	1	1

raw tomato concassée (page 460), including liquid	3 cups	750 milliliters
heavy cream	¼ cup	60 milliliters
salt and pepper	to taste	to taste

1. Gently sweat the onion, carrot, and prosciutto in the olive oil until the vegetables soften. Add the beef and stir the mixture until the juices released by the meat evaporate and only oil is left. Do not cook beyond this stage.
2. Add the bouquet garni and the liquid released in preparing the tomato concassée to the meat and vegetables, and stew the mixture for about 30 minutes, until the liquid evaporates and again only fat is visible.
3. Add the tomato pulp and continue stewing the sauce until it has the right thickness. This should not take longer than 15 minutes.
4. Add the cream and cook for 2 minutes more.
5. Adjust the seasonings. If the sauce seems to lack flavor, follow the recommendations for using sugar and vinegar (see "Improving the Flavor of Tomato Sauces," page 462).

PAPPARDELLE WITH TUSCAN DUCK SAUCE
Pappardelle Aretine

Duck is cooked into pasta sauces in many regions of Italy. Each region has its preferred pasta shape and its own style of cooking and serving the duck. In some regions, the duck is left in large chunks—even on the bone—whereas in other places the duck flesh is finely chopped. This recipe falls somewhere in between.

Most Italian recipes call for removing the duck skin and cooking the whole duck, but this sauce is especially good when made with leftover duck thighs, which can be saved in the freezer if the breasts are being used for other dishes. In general, duck thighs are better for braising because the thighs tend to stay more moist, although if the duck meat is being finely chopped, any dryness will be imperceptible. Making a broth from the duck carcass, reducing it, and adding it to the sauce is an ultimate, but not essential, refinement.

YIELD: 1 QUART (1 LITER) SAUCE, ENOUGH FOR 6 PASTA-COURSE
OR 4 MAIN-COURSE SERVINGS

whole duck or thighs (including the drumstick) from 2 ducks	5 pounds	2.3 kilograms
olive oil	2 tablespoons	30 milliliters
onion, finely chopped	1 medium	1 medium
carrot, finely chopped	1 small	1 small
celery, finely chopped	½ stalk	½ stalk
garlic cloves, finely chopped	3	3
prosciutto, 1 slice ⅛ inch (3 mm) thick, finely chopped (optional)	2 ounces	50 grams

ripe tomatoes, peeled, seeded, chopped	3 pounds	1.35 kilograms
or	or	or
drained and seeded canned tomatoes, chopped	2 (28-ounce) cans	1 liter
red wine	1 cup	250 milliliters
sage leaves	3	3
fresh pappardelle, fettuccine (tagliatelle), or linguine	1½ pounds	675 grams
or	or	or
dried tubular pasta such as penne or rigatoni	1 pound	450 grams
salt and pepper	to taste	to taste
freshly grated parmigiano-reggiano		

1. If using a whole duck, remove the breasts, thighs, and the first (thicker) wing joints. Reserve the giblets. The carcass can be used for making broth or discarded.
2. Brown the giblets and the duck pieces, skin side down first, in the olive oil in a heavy-bottomed pot and reserve. Brown the duck as long as possible on the skin side without letting it burn, about 20 minutes. Turn the pieces over and brown them for 5 minutes more on the meat side. Take the duck pieces out of the pan and reserve. Pour off all but 2 tablespoons (30 milliliters) of the rendered fat and add the chopped vegetables and prosciutto. Sweat over medium heat until the onion turns translucent, about 10 minutes.
3. Put the browned duck pieces, except for the liver, back into the pot with the vegetables. Add the tomatoes, wine, and sage. Cover the pot and simmer very gently for 2 hours.
4. Remove the duck pieces. Reduce the sauce gently, skimming every 15 minutes, until only 1 quart (1 liter) of sauce remains.
5. While the braising liquid is reducing, bring a large pot of water to a rapid boil for cooking the pasta. Pull off and discard any fat and skin clinging to the duck pieces, take the meat off the bones, and chop the duck meat, giblets, and liver into roughly ¼-inch (5 mm) pieces.
6. Cook and drain the pasta.
7. Stir the chopped duck into the sauce. Just before serving, season to taste with salt and pepper. Toss the sauce with the boiled and drained pasta and serve immediately. Pass the Parmesan cheese at the table.

TOMATO SAUCES

Italian cooks use tomatoes in several ways: as a moistening liquid in braises, stews, and meat (*ragù*) and seafood sauces; raw, coarsely chopped and simply tossed with pasta, usually olive oil, and often with herbs or other ingredients such as olives, anchovies, or capers; added to a soffritto and gently simmered until thick; and baked or dried and more or less finely chopped to a sauce-like consistency (see also "Tomatoes" in Chapter 17, pages 459 to 463).

MACARONI WITH BAKED TOMATO SAUCE

Maccheroni con Pomidori al Forno

Tomatoes become intensely sweet and savory when gently baked—the oven baking seems to concentrate their flavor more than simply stewing or simmering them on the stove, as with most tomato sauces. This dish comes from Puglia.

YIELD: 6 PASTA-COURSE OR 4 MAIN-COURSE SERVINGS

ripe tomatoes, peeled	4 pounds	1.8 kilograms
extra-virgin olive oil	¼ cup	60 milliliters
dried macaroni or short tubular pasta such as ziti, rigatoni, or penne	1 pound	450 grams
or	or	or
fresh macaroni or pasta	1½ pounds	675 grams
garlic cloves, finely chopped	3	3
finely chopped parsley	2 tablespoons	30 milliliters
freshly grated parmigiano-reggiano		

1. Preheat the oven to 400°F (200°C). Cut the tomatoes in half crosswise, squeeze out and discard the seeds, and chop the tomatoes coarsely into chunks.
2. With 1 tablespoon (15 milliliters) of the olive oil, brush a baking dish or roasting pan that is just large enough to hold the chunks of tomato in a single layer.
3. Bake the tomatoes in the oven for 1½ to 2 hours, until the liquid released by the tomatoes has almost completely evaporated and only a couple tablespoons of syrupy liquid remain.
4. Bring a large pot of water to a rapid boil. Cook and drain the pasta.
5. Heat the remaining olive oil in a wide skillet and stir in the garlic. Stir the garlic for about 2 minutes, until it releases its aroma, and stir in the parsley and cooked tomatoes.
6. Stir the tomatoes with a wooden spoon—this will cause them to break down into a sauce—and toss with the pasta. Pass the Parmesan cheese at the table.

ASIAN SAUCES

Many classically trained cooks are perplexed when confronted with an Asian sauce recipe. Not only are the ingredients sometimes completely unrecognizable, but the approach and logic are profoundly different from those used in making "Western" sauces. Unlike European sauces, especially French classic sauces, which are designed to concentrate the flavors of the main ingredients (in integral sauces) or at least emulate the flavors of the main ingredients through the preparation and careful reduction of stocks (in nonintegral sauces), Asian sauces are designed to accent or contrast with the main ingredient. Japanese cooks use dashi, a smoky fish broth, for both meats and fish; Southeast Asian cooks flavor most of their curries, soups, and stews with fish sauce;

Indian cooks use elaborate combinations of spices; and Chinese cooks are likely to use an array of bottled sauces, often in subtle and delicious combinations, but again as an accent to, rather than intensification of, the main ingredient's inherent flavor. With this in mind, it's essential for the cook who sets out to make an Asian sauce to avoid masking the flavors of the main ingredient with too many strong or disparate flavors. Although Asian sauces don't emphasize the careful sculpting of the main ingredient's inherent flavors in the way of classic French sauces, the best Asian sauces use their own palate of ingredients with great subtlety and finesse to accent the main ingredient without masking its flavor or appearance.

Although many of the ingredients used are radically different, Western and Asian sauces share many of the same techniques. Asian sauces are often begun by "sweating" mixtures of aromatic ingredients in a small amount of fat before liquids are added—in much the same way as in making the sauce base for any number of classic European sauces. Whereas in France this basic mixture will likely contain onions, carrots, and celery (a classic mirepoix) or in Italy, a fair amount of garlic (a soffritto), Asian base mixtures may contain an array of exotic-sounding ingredients, including shrimp paste, galangal, ginger, chiles, curry leaves, and so on. Asian cooks sometimes add liquids directly to stir-fried meats, vegetables, and seafood in the same way a French chef adds broth and other liquids to a fricassée. In other instances, the stir-fried foods are completely removed from the wok (or sauté pan) before liquids are added, in the manner of a sauté. Thickeners are also used, but instead of flour, butter, or cream, Asian sauces may be thickened with coconut milk, cooked lentils, kuzu root (a starch much like arrowroot), or nut butters.

Fortunately, a trained cook who sets out to make an Asian sauce for the first time won't have to master an array of new techniques but will need only familiarize himself or herself with a new palate of ingredients. Other than painstakingly following basic recipes, it is useful for beginning cooks to travel, so in addition to tasting foods in situ, they can experience the context of how the food is served—to see and taste those foods that precede, follow, or accompany a particular dish—and to experience how the people eat and what foods give them pleasure. Short of traveling thousands of miles, eating in Asian restaurants in the United States will also introduce the beginning cook to the flavors and rituals of a particular cuisine. Once a palate of flavors and ingredients becomes familiar, the cook can work within it, improvising here and there, to come up with authentic dishes stamped with his or her own particular style.

Many cooks, having newly discovered an exotic-seeming Asian ingredient, set out to integrate it into the tried-and-true sauces of their own repertory with results that are bizarre at best. These attempts often fail because the context of the sauce is from one place and the flavors from another. But although this skewing of flavors and context has led to many of the most ill-conceived mishmashes of "fusion" cooking, it is possible to cautiously add an Asian ingredient to a Western sauce to provide a note of unfamiliar intrigue. (A few bonito flakes infused in a fish sauce do wonders.) The influence of Japanese cooking on French classic cuisine, one of the most successful interactions of two seemingly disparate approaches to food, led to the light touch and elegant simplicity of the most successful plates of the nouvelle cuisine. This Japanese influence, more an aesthetic seen in the almost stark simplification of presentations, has irreversibly influenced the refined cooking found in classic French restaurants. For those attempting the "fusion" of disparate cuisines, it's essential to keep the context of one cuisine intact. If the context becomes clouded such that no one particular cooking tradition predominates, the diner may be left weary and confused. A fine meal should follow a single tradition and aesthetic—and evoke a history, a place, and a people—not serve as an experimental testing ground for bizarre juxtapositions of flavors and styles.

JAPANESE SAUCES

Whereas most "Western" sauces are made by thickening a liquid, such as broth or milk, and infusing the mixture with flavorful ingredients, Japanese sauces are often served as light broths (Japanese foods are often served in small bowls) with little or no thickener. When Japanese sauces are thickened or reduced, they are used as savory glazes, often brushed on foods while they are cooking rather than as liquid sauces. Teriyaki sauce is the most familiar of these glazes. Japanese sauces are also often served as dipping sauces or as salad dressings containing no oil. And whereas European sauces are constructed using an almost infinite variety of ingredients, most Japanese sauces are made using relatively few.

Traditional European sauces rely on broths, either made in advance to serve as stocks or as the result of the cooking process, but Japanese cooks rely almost exclusively on a universal broth called *dashi*. Dashi is the most fundamental component in Japanese sauce making and, in fact, for most Japanese cooking. Although dashi's universality may surprise Western-trained cooks, who take great care and time to distill the flavor of a particular food into a broth or "jus," dashi takes only about 15 minutes to make and lends itself to great subtlety.

Only two ingredients are needed to make dashi: dried bonito (a fish closely related to tuna) and *konbu*, a variety of kelp sold dried in long strips. Bonito destined for making dashi is slowly and carefully dried and smoked until it shrinks and hardens into something looking vaguely like an overripe banana but with the texture of wood. In the most traditional kitchens, the hardened chunk of bonito, *katsuo-bushi*, is shaved as it is needed on a plane-like gadget with a drawer attached to its base. But nowadays, even serious Japanese cooks who insist that the flavor of hand-shaved bonito flakes is better often rely on preshaved flakes. Bonito flakes, *hana-katsuo* or *kezuri-katsuo*, are sold in cellophane bags and look like pink wood shavings. Large pink flakes are usually more subtle and inviting, whereas brownish or very small flakes sometimes have a fishy smell and flavor. Instant dashi (*dashi-no-moto*) is sold in little bags, and although it has none of the inviting subtlety of dashi made from bonito flakes, it's a usable substitute and infinitely better than the Western equivalent, the bouillon cube.

The second dashi ingredient, *konbu,* is a kind of dried kelp sold in dark brown, almost black, strips a couple of inches (2 cm) wide and about 18 inches (45 cm) long. The best strips come from Hokkaido, Japan's northernmost island, and are lightly coated with a thin white mineral layer that should be left on. These strips are gently wiped with a moist towel—never rinsed—before they are cooked.

Dashi is prepared in two stages. In the first stage, konbu is steeped in hot water for about 15 minutes as though making tea. This first infusion, *konbu dashi,* is sometimes used alone (it's a favorite of vegetarians), but bonito flakes are generally added to the hot mixture, steeped for about 1 minute, and strained out. The result is primary dashi. Secondary dashi, made by using the bonito flakes and kelp a second time, is sometimes used in long-simmering soups and stews, where the subtlety of primary dashi would be lost. Dashi will keep in the refrigerator for 2 weeks or it can be frozen indefinitely.

PRIMARY DASHI

YIELD: 1 QUART (1 LITER)

1 strip konbu (kelp)	18 inches	45 centimeters
cold water	5 cups	1.2 liters
hana-katsuo (shaved bonito flakes), about 4 loosely packed cups/1 liter	1 ounce	25 grams

1. Wipe the konbu with a barely moistened towel. Fold the konbu in half, place it in a 2-quart (2 liter) saucepan, and pour over the water. Place the pan over low to medium heat (or higher heat if you're making more than what's called for here) so that the water comes to a slow simmer after 15 minutes.
2. As soon as the water reaches a simmer, take out the konbu (reserve for secondary dashi or discard) and take the pan off the heat. Stir in the bonito flakes and let them infuse for 1 minute. Strain. The bonito flakes can be discarded or saved for secondary dashi.

Constructing a Japanese Sauce

Once the basic dashi is on hand, most Japanese sauces are easily constructed by adding two or three additional ingredients. Only rarely is additional cooking required, and never the long cooking needed to make Western stocks and reductions.

The four most popular additions to dashi are sake (rice wine), soy sauce, miso, and mirin. Sake is used in much the same way as wine is used in Western cooking. It's simmered long enough for the alcohol to cook off and, like grape wine, is appreciated for its ability to give a bright freshness to sauces and broths, especially those containing fish—no rarity in Japan.

Soy sauce is used in Japan much like salt is used in the West. It gives an intriguing savor to sauces and broths. Dark soy sauce can also be used to deepen the color of a sauce (Japanese soy sauce comes both light and dark).

Miso is made by fermenting soy beans with grains and then grinding the mixture to a peanut butter–like paste. It comes in a variety of colors, each with a different salt content and depth of flavor. Lighter misos, called "white" or "yellow" miso, are less salty than darker varieties and are often used for cold dressings; darker miso has a deeper flavor and is used for more strongly flavored, usually cold-weather, dishes. Japanese chefs usually combine more than one miso (as Western cooks might carefully balance mixtures of herbs) to come up with their own nuances of flavor. Because miso is salty and full flavored, it is used sparingly, with rarely more than a couple of tablespoons (30 grams) added to 1 cup (250 milliliters) of liquid.

Mirin, an extremely sweet type of sake, is sold in Japanese grocery stores (often in American groceries as well) as a cooking wine. Used in small amounts to give sweetness to Japanese sauces, it is a perfect counterpoint to the saltiness of ever-present soy sauce and dashi. Sugar can be used instead of, or in addition to, mirin (see Chapter 3, "Ingredients," for more about soy sauce, miso, and mirin).

Presenting and Serving Japanese Broth-Like Sauces

Much of the appeal of Japanese seafood and meat dishes is the lightness of an accompanying broth-like sauce that surrounds the food rather than covering it. It may be for this reason that so many Japanese dishes are served in small and elegant, often handmade, pottery or lacquer bowls.

Because broth-like sauces are served in a small bowl with hot foods, there is always the risk of the sauce causing the food (especially delicate seafood) to overcook while it makes its way from kitchen to dining room, and even while it sits in front of the diner. To avoid this, foods are often placed on mounds of cooked vegetables (such as julienned carrots or daikon, or over greens such as spinach or watercress) or atop Japanese noodles so the meat or seafood is held suspended above the hot broth.

BASIC JAPANESE BROTH-LIKE SAUCE WITH MIRIN, SOY SAUCE, AND SAKE

This sauce, actually a cross between sauce and soup, is fundamental to Japanese cooking. It can be subtly varied to taste or to go with particular ingredients by adding more or less of the three primary ingredients: soy sauce, mirin, and sake. In addition to these ingredients, the sauce is infused with extra bonito flakes to give it a more pronounced smokiness. Finely chopped scallions are added at the end for color and additional flavor.

YIELD: 2 CUPS (500 MILLILITERS), ENOUGH FOR 4 MAIN-COURSE
OR 8 FIRST-COURSE SERVINGS

dashi (page 520)	1¼ cups	300 milliliters
mirin	¼ cup	60 milliliters
sake	¼ cup	60 milliliters
dark Japanese soy sauce	¼ cup	60 milliliters
dried bonito flakes	¾ cup	185 milliliters
scallions, including green parts, finely sliced	2	2

Combine the dashi with the mirin, sake, and soy sauce in a small saucepan and bring to a simmer. Remove from the heat, stir in the bonito flakes, and let sit for 1 minute. Strain and stir in the scallions. Use immediately. See the photograph in the color plates.

SALMON WITH BASIC JAPANESE BROTH-LIKE SAUCE

This dish is inspired by a classic recipe in Shizuo Tsuji's excellent book, *Japanese Cooking: A Simple Art.* Mr. Tsuji uses steamed sea bream, but any firm-fleshed fish works well. Scallops are also excellent. Alternative cooking methods can also be employed—the seafood can be sautéed (the crispy skin provides textural contrast), poached, baked, or even grilled. Soba (buckwheat) noodles prop up the fish and provide starch; julienned vegetables or cooked leafy greens can also be used. Double the amounts to produce main-course servings.

YIELD: 8 FIRST-COURSE SERVINGS

squares of salmon fillet with skin (scaled) or other firm-fleshed fish, all the same thickness, 3 ounces (75 grams) each	8	8
dried soba noodles	8 ounces	225 grams
japanese broth-like sauce (above)	2 cups	500 milliliters

1. Steam, sauté, poach, bake, or grill the fish. If you sauté the fillets, pat off any excess oil with paper towels. (The fish can also be teriyaki-glazed; see page 524.)

2. Cook the noodles as you would pasta, and drain. Arrange the noodles in mounds in small hot bowls.

3. Place a piece of salmon, skin side up, on each mound and ladle the sauce around it. Serve immediately.

GRILLED SWORDFISH WITH CLAMS AND BROTH-LIKE MISO SAUCE

Miso provides a simple and savory addition to the cooking liquid from fish and shellfish. Keep in mind, however, that miso is very salty, so it must be used sparingly, especially with the salty cooking liquid from clams or mussels. This technique—of surrounding grilled seafood with miso- and shellfish-scented broth—can be used with any firm-fleshed fish. *Shiso* or *kinome* leaves (see pages 57 and 54) are typical Japanese garnitures, but tiny watercress or mint sprigs will also work. The swordfish steaks may also be glazed with Teriyaki Sauce (page 524). If the ingredient amounts in this recipe are halved (cut the clams down to 12), the dish works well as a first course.

YIELD: 4 MAIN-COURSE SERVINGS

littleneck clams, scrubbed	20	20
dashi (page 520)	3 cups	750 milliliters
swordfish steaks, 6 to 8 ounces (175 to 250 grams) each	4	4
peanut oil or vegetable oil	2 teaspoons	10 milliliters
sansho powder or freshly ground black pepper	1 teaspoon	5 milliliters
red miso	2 tablespoons	30 grams
kinome leaves, shiso leaves, or watercress sprigs	4	4

1. Simmer the clams in a covered pot with the dashi for about 12 minutes. When the clams have all opened, remove the top shell from each clam and reserve the clams, nestled in their bottom shells. Slowly pour the cooking liquid into a small saucepan, leaving any grit or sand behind.

2. Brush the swordfish steaks with oil and sprinkle with the sansho powder. Grill or sauté the swordfish.

3. While the swordfish steaks are grilling, work 2 tablespoons (30 milliliters) of the clam cooking liquid into the miso and return this mixture to the rest of the cooking liquid. Gently reheat the clams in the miso broth.

4. Place the grilled swordfish steaks in wide soup plates and ladle the miso broth around them. Place 5 clams around each serving. Garnish with the kinome leaves, shiso leaves, or watercress sprigs.

Using Japanese Sauces as Glazes

Because of the sugar or mirin they contain, Japanese sauces are easily cooked down into thick and syrupy, sweet and savory glazes.

TERIYAKI SAUCE

Teriyaki sauce, a mixture of mirin, sake, soy sauce, and sometimes sugar, may be brushed on meat, fish, or vegetables while they are grilling so that it concentrates on their surface into a thick syrupy glaze. It can also be prepared in the still-hot pan used for sautéing—in the same way a French sauce is made by deglazing—but instead of the sauce being then poured over the meat or fish, the meat or fish is put back in the pan and the sauce reduced to a glaze. The meat or fish comes out of the pan coated with a shiny sweet-and-savory glaze. This glazing method is especially effective on the crispy skin of chicken or salmon.

YIELD: ½ CUP (125 MILLILITERS)

sake	3 tablespoons	45 milliliters
mirin	3 tablespoons	45 milliliters
dark Japanese soy sauce	3 tablespoons	45 milliliters

Combine all the ingredients and refrigerate until needed—they'll keep indefinitely—or simply use all these ingredients at one time to deglaze the hot sauté pan, as in the following recipe.

TERIYAKI-GLAZED FISH, STEAK, OR CHICKEN

Teriyaki glazing works best for relatively thick cuts of fish, steak, or chicken. It's easy to overcook thinner cuts because they must be sautéed in two stages— the first in hot oil, the second with the teriyaki ingredients.

YIELD: 4 SERVINGS

thick fish or meat steaks	4	4
or	or	or
chicken, quartered	1	1
vegetable oil	2 tablespoons	30 milliliters
ingredients for teriyaki sauce (above) either combined or separate		

1. Sauté the fish, meat, or chicken in the oil in a large heavy-bottomed sauté pan over medium to high heat so they're well browned on both sides. Leave underdone by about 3 minutes. Remove from the pan.

2. Pour out the cooked oil and pour the teriyaki sauce or ingredients into the still-hot pan. Put the fish, meat, or chicken back in the pan and boil the teriyaki mixture over high heat for about 1½ minutes, until it looks thick and syrupy.

3. Turn over the meat or fish and boil for another 1½ minutes, until there's practically no sauce left in the pan. Be careful at this point (keep sniffing) to permit the glaze to caramelize only slightly, not to burn.

YAKITORI SAUCE

Yakitori are small skewers of meat, usually chicken but sometimes beef—or even horse—or vegetables, quickly grilled and glazed with a sweet and savory sauce. Yakitori sauce contains ingredients common to many Japanese sauces: sake, soy sauce, mirin, and sugar, but it is thicker than most Japanese sauces.

The skewers of yakitori are brushed with or dipped into the yakitori sauce at least twice during grilling: once when the food is three-quarters done and once again 1 minute before serving. If using wooden skewers, be sure to push the pieces of meat or vegetables right next to one another so the wood between the pieces doesn't burn. The ends of wooden skewers should also be wrapped in aluminum foil so they don't burn.

YIELD: 1 CUP (250 MILLILITERS)

sake	½ cup	125 milliliters
dark Japanese soy sauce	1 cup	250 milliliters
mirin	¼ cup	60 milliliters
sugar	3 tablespoons	45 milliliters

Combine all the ingredients in a small saucepan and simmer for about 10 minutes, until reduced by half. Let cool. Yakitori sauce keeps indefinitely in the refrigerator.

CHICKEN, MEAT, OR VEGETABLE YAKITORI

Yakitori make savory pre-dinner hors d'oeuvres and can be made with small cubes of meat or chicken or pieces of vegetables such as peppers, onions, or mushrooms.

boneless chicken breasts (both sides of the breast from 1 chicken), cubed	12 ounces	350 grams
or	or	or
beef steak such as sirloin, cut into ¾-inch (2 cm) cubes	12 ounces	350 grams
or	or	or
vegetables, cut into cubes or strips	12 ounces	350 grams
yakitori sauce (page 525)	1 cup	250 milliliters

1. Marinate the cubes of meat, chicken, or vegetables in the yakitori sauce for 30 minutes.
2. Thread the cubes on 8 presoaked wooden or metal skewers and grill over high heat until lightly browned but not cooked through, about 3 minutes, turning after 1½ minutes.
3. Brush the skewers with the yakitori sauce or roll the skewers in the sauce on a plate. Grill until almost done, about 2 minutes more, and again coat with sauce. Grill for 30 seconds more and serve.

Japanese Dipping Sauces

Although many of the best Japanese sauces are broth-like affairs, served hot, surrounding the food in small bowls, the Japanese also use an array of dipping sauces for raw fish and simmered meats and seafood. Some of these sauces are as simple as a tiny mound of wasabi combined with soy sauce by the diner at a sushi bar; others are more complex and thicker, containing miso, ground sesame seeds or peanuts, egg yolks (these sauces are thickened much like a crème anglaise), and kuzu starch (a root-derived starch that behaves much like arrowroot).

Many of the dipping sauces traditionally served with sashimi (raw fish) are also served with cold or hot grilled or fried seafood and meats or with cold vegetables—even as salad dressings. *Tosa* sauce is a smoke-flavored sauce made by infusing dark soy sauce with sake, mirin, konbu, and bonito flakes. The basic ingredients are almost the same as those used for making dashi, but instead of the bonito and konbu being simmered, they are left to infuse in the cold soy sauce for anywhere from a day to a year. Tosa sauce is more deeply flavored and complex than the simple soy sauce and wasabi usually served as an accompaniment to raw fish.

TOSA SAUCE

Tosa sauce is best after it has aged for 6 months, but it can be used right away or for up to 1 year.

konbu (kelp), 1 strip	3 inches	8 centimeters
mirin	¼ cup	60 milliliters
sake	¼ cup	60 milliliters
dark Japanese soy sauce	1 cup	250 milliliters
loosely packed bonito flakes (¼ ounce/7 grams)	1 cup	250 milliliters

1. Wipe the konbu with a barely moist towel and snap it into several pieces.
2. Combine all the ingredients in a stainless-steel mixing bowl, cover with plastic wrap, and let sit for 24 hours at room temperature. Strain through a fine-mesh strainer or cheesecloth. Refrigerate in a bottle with a tight-fitting lid.

PONZU SAUCE

In addition to many of the basic dipping sauce ingredients—soy sauce, mirin, bonito flakes, and konbu—ponzu sauce contains a large amount of lemon juice. In Japan, *yuzu*, a very sour lemon, is used, so recipes adapted for American readers usually call for a combination of lemon and lime juice.

In Japan, ponzu sauce is served as a dipping sauce for raw, very firm-fleshed fish that are sliced very thinly and traditionally served in a rosette pattern. (Fugu, the blowfish known to be fatal if improperly cleaned, is the most notorious and expensive example.) Very thinly sliced fish has too delicate a flavor to match the combination of soy sauce and wasabi or tosa sauce served with the more familiar thicker-sliced raw fish such as tuna. Ponzu sauce also lends a bright yet subtle complexity when dribbled over hot grilled or sautéed seafood in the same way as lemon juice. A drop or two also makes a delicious accent to a raw oyster.

Like tosa sauce, ponzu sauce is best when allowed to mature for several months, but it can be used right away or as long as 1 year after it is made.

lime juice	½ cup	125 milliliters
lemon juice	½ cup	125 milliliters
rice wine or sherry vinegar	2 tablespoons	30 milliliters
dark Japanese soy sauce	½ cup	125 milliliters
mirin	¼ cup	60 milliliters
loosely packed bonito flakes (¼ ounce/7 grams)	1 cup	250 milliliters

1. Combine all the ingredients in a stainless-steel mixing bowl, cover with plastic wrap, and let sit at room temperature for 24 hours.
2. Strain through a fine-mesh strainer and store in a bottle with a tight-fitting lid in the refrigerator.

MISO SAUCE

Miso, fermented soy bean sauce, is often used in both cold and hot Japanese sauces. Miso is often combined with mirin or sugar to provide a sweet relief to miso's strong saltiness. Sweetened miso combined with toasted and ground sesame seeds is a popular sauce for cold vegetables such as asparagus, string beans, or okra. Miso sauce can also be used as a dipping sauce for hot steamed or boiled vegetables. Don't use salt anywhere else—miso sauce is very salty.

YIELD: ²/₃ CUP (165 MILLILITERS), ENOUGH FOR 4 FIRST-COURSE OR SIDE-DISH SERVINGS

white sesame seeds	6 tablespoons	90 milliliters
red miso or a mixture of brown and white miso	2 tablespoons	30 grams
mirin	¼ cup	60 milliliters
water (optional)	1 to 2 tablespoons	15 to 30 milliliters

1. Toss the sesame seeds in a sauté pan over high heat until they smell toasty and turn pale brown, for about 5 minutes. Grind them to a paste in a coffee grinder or in a traditional suribachi (Japanese mortar and pestle; see page 30).
2. Stir the sesame paste with the miso and the mirin until smooth. Add water, if using, to thin to desired consistency.

Japanese Salad Dressings

Japanese salad dressings are acidic in the same way as Western dressings, but unlike "vinaigrette" and its variations, Japanese salad sauces rarely contain oil. In addition to the familiar Japanese standbys—soy sauce, dashi, and mirin—Japanese salad dressings almost always contain rice vinegar or lemon or lime juice to provide the necessary acidity. And although the most basic dressings contain no thickeners, more elaborate versions are thickened or given body with egg yolks, starch (kuzu starch or cornstarch), ground sesame seeds, puréed tofu, mustard (the closest equivalent to vinaigrette), and wasabi horseradish.

BASIC JAPANESE SALAD DRESSING

In the same way that a Western vinaigrette might be balanced, the amounts of each of the ingredients in a Japanese salad dressing can be varied to taste; more soy sauce can be added for a pronounced saltiness, more dashi to soften the effect of the vinegar and to lend a subtle smokiness, and more vinegar if the dressing needs an emphasized acidic zing. Rice vinegar is traditionally used, but sherry vinegar makes a delicious accent to the smokiness of the dashi.

Unlike Western vinaigrettes that take on a stale quality when stored overnight, Japanese salad dressings keep in the refrigerator almost indefinitely, unless they contain egg yolks.

YIELD: 1 CUP (250 MILLILITERS)

rice vinegar or sherry vinegar	6 tablespoons	90 milliliters
japanese soy sauce	1 tablespoon plus 1 teaspoon	20 milliliters
cold Japanaese broth-like sauce (page 522)	½ cup	125 milliliters

Combine all the ingredients.

Variations

Some salads or vegetables benefit from extra sweetness in the dressing (cold beets and cucumbers come to mind). Anywhere from 1 teaspoon (5 milliliters) to several tablespoons of mirin (or half as much sugar) dissolved into the basic salad dressing will give the sauce additional sweetness. The delightful smokiness of most Japanese salad dressings can be increased by infusing a handful of dried bonito flakes in the hot dressing and straining after 1 minute. (If infusing in a cold sauce, strain after 24 hours.) This is an alternative to adding dashi, which would dilute the sauce's acidity.

Japanese salad dressings can also be thickened and used to coat cooked vegetables or for dipping sauces. To thicken the basic dressing, bring it to a simmer, beat 3 egg yolks until pale, and whisk them into the sauce off the heat. Return the mixture to the heat and stir gently with a wooden spoon (as though making crème anglaise) until the sauce thickens. Let cool.

A basic Japanese salad dressing can also be thickened and flavored with sesame paste, a popular ingredient in Japanese sauces. To make a sesame-flavored and thickened salad sauce, toast two-thirds the amount of white sesame seeds as there are liquid ingredients (for example, ⅔ cup/165 milliliters seeds to 1 cup/250 milliliters liquid ingredients) by tossing the seeds in a hot skillet until lightly browned and fragrant, about 5 minutes. Grind the seeds to a flaky paste in a coffee grinder (or blender for larger amounts) or in a traditional Japanese suribachi (see page 30). (Peanut butter can also be substituted for the sesame paste with delicious, if not strictly authentic, results.)

Miso is also used as a thickener and flavoring for Japanese salad dressings. To make a miso-flavored dressing, work 2 tablespoons (30 milliliters) of the basic dressing into ¼ cup (60 milliliters) of brown, red, or white miso and stir this mixture into 1 cup (250 milliliters) of the basic dressing. (This sauce tends to be quite salty.)

KOREAN SAUCES

Korean cooking is more appreciated for its variety of side dishes, pickles, and condiments than for an elaborate system of sauce making. Most Korean sauces are simple dipping sauces or salad dressings (very similar to their Japanese equivalents) or seasoning mixtures for pickles, especially *kimchi*, which is pickled cabbage—a condiment present at virtually every meal.

In many ways, Korean cooking is similar to that of Japan, but there are two important and particularly Korean ingredients that give many Korean dishes a character that sets them apart. Red chile paste known as *kochujang* (see page 36), an everyday condiment in Korea, is used to flavor soups, one-pot dishes, and as a dipping sauce. Soy bean paste, or *twoenjang* (see page 40) is the Korean equivalent of Japanese miso, but Korean paste is stronger and more distinctive—no dish made with twoenjang would be mistaken for a Japanese relative made with miso.

KOREAN VINEGAR DIPPING SAUCE

Korean dipping sauces are similar to many Japanese dipping sauces in that they share the common ingredients of soy sauce, rice vinegar, sugar, ginger, and sesame (either sesame oil or ground sesame seeds). One difference, however, is that Korean sauces often contain hot chiles that are finely chopped, powdered, or in kochujang paste form. Another difference is that neither dashi nor bonito flakes ever appears in Korean sauces, whereas they are staple ingredients in Japanese sauces.

Recipes for Korean dipping sauces vary from household to household, and any of the ingredients in the following recipe can acceptably be adjusted to taste. This sauce is used for dipping grilled or fried meats, fish, or vegetables. It also makes a delicious condiment for leftover cold grilled or roasted meats or fish. It will keep at least a week in the refrigerator.

YIELD: ⅔ CUP (165 MILLILITERS)

sesame seeds	1 tablespoon plus 1 teaspoon	20 milliliters
Japanese dark soy sauce	6 tablespoons	90 milliliters
rice vinegar	¼ cup	60 milliliters
sugar	2 teaspoons	10 milliliters
grated fresh ginger	2 teaspoons	10 milliliters
or	or	or
grated garlic	2 teaspoons	10 milliliters
sesame oil	2 teaspoons	10 milliliters
serrano chiles, finely chopped	1 or 2	1 or 2
or	or	or
Thai chiles, finely chopped	2 to 4	2 to 4

or	*or*	*or*
kochujang (korean chile paste), to taste	1 teaspoon to 2 tablespoons	5 to 30 milliliters
chopped cilantro (optional)	2 tablespoons	30 milliliters
or	*or*	*or*
scallions, chopped (optional)	2	2

1. Toast the sesame seeds by tossing them in a skillet over high heat for about 5 minutes until they turn pale brown and smell toasty.
2. Combine all the ingredients and let sit for at least 30 minutes before serving.

THAI, VIETNAMESE, AND INDONESIAN SAUCES

To group these countries together is somewhat like trying to characterize in a few short pages the cooking of all of Europe. But there are certain ingredients and techniques that, if not identical, are similar enough to give these cuisines characteristics in common.

The ingredient most central to Thai and Vietnamese sauces is fish sauce, known respectively as *nampla* or *nuoc mam,* which is made from the liquid released by fermenting fish (see page 35 for buying tips). None of this sounds very appetizing, but surprisingly, when combined with other ingredients, fish sauce settles into the background in much the same way as salted anchovies lend a subtle note to Mediterranean sauces with garlic and perhaps tomatoes. But fish sauce has such a full flavor and is so much the heart and soul of Southeast Asian cooking that it allows for the creation of sauces and soups completely without broth or stock, much less the long-simmered reductions of "Western" sauce making.

Other ingredients used in Southeast Asian sauces, such as garlic and shallots, are familiar Western staples, but Southeast Asian cooks also rely on a variety of flavorings that until recently were never seen in the United States. Two aromatic ingredients—lemongrass and kafeer lime leaves—are used throughout Southeast Asia to give sauces a delicate citrus flavor. A stalk of lemongrass looks like an elongated, very immature ear of corn. Usually only the tender section (which is several inches long near the base) is thinly sliced and simmered in liquids or ground into a curry paste to lend a subtle lemony flavor and aroma. Kafeer lime leaves look like bay leaves but have a distinct lime aroma. They can be simmered whole in soups or sauces, they can be thinly sliced, or they can be ground up with other ingredients in curry pastes. Like Chinese cooks, Southeast Asian cooks use fresh ginger, but they are also fond of galangal (sometimes spelled "galanga"). This rhizome looks very much like ginger but has a subtle and distinctive pine-resin flavor.

Whereas European cooks use heavy cream to give body, richness, and unctuosity to their sauces, Southeast Asian cooks use coconut milk. Coconut milk has a gentle sweetness and richness that softens the often incendiary heat of the native sauces and soups. Shrimp paste is also popular in Southeast Asian cooking, although in many restaurants in America it seems to be left out or is used only in very small amounts. Made from fermented shrimp, shrimp paste gives a distinctive aroma to Southeast Asian foods, but most Westerners find the aroma too strong (the kitchen will smell like something went terribly wrong). Southeast Asian cooks also like to finish their sauces with herbs. Cilantro is probably the most popular—the leaves are typically added at the end—but the roots and stems are also used, ground into curry pastes. Mint and two Asian varieties of basil are also well liked (see Chapter 3, "Ingredients," for more about each of these ingredients).

Southeast Asian Dipping Sauces

Many of the most popular Southeast Asian sauces are simple dipping sauces, based on fish sauce of course, and made as everyday accompaniments to a bowl of rice, which is the main staple. In the West, these sauces are more likely to be served with richer fare such as fried or grilled fish or shellfish or chicken.

Every Southeast Asian country has its own classic dipping sauces, but the most-often-used dipping sauces in each country do have certain characteristics and ingredients in common. Most dipping sauces are simple mixtures of chopped herbs (cilantro is a favorite, but mint and basil are also popular), aromatic vegetables such as shallots and garlic (at times in prodigious amounts), and ginger. Burmese and Vietnamese sauces sometimes reveal their country's proximity to China by including soy sauce and even hoisin sauce.

Almost all Southeast Asian dipping sauces include an acidic ingredient, which makes them lovely accents to seafood. Vinegar (namely harsh, distilled white vinegar) is often used and is the one ingredient that might be better replaced with good cider or white wine vinegar. Lime juice is popular (in Southeast Asia the small kafeer lime is likely to be used, but the juice of Western limes works perfectly well). But the most distinctive acidic ingredient is tamarind. Tamarinds are beans that look vaguely like wizened fava beans surrounded in the husk with a brown sticky paste. It's the paste rather than the bean that is used as a souring agent, and since fresh tamarinds are sometimes difficult to find outside of ethnic markets, it is fortunate that the paste itself is sold inexpensively in small packages. The packaged paste, which also contains chunks of seeds and peel, must be soaked in boiling water and strained before it can be used.

Chiles are also an almost universal ingredient in Southeast Asian dipping sauces. The most popular chiles—the small bird chiles, sometimes called Thai chiles—make up in heat for what they lack in size. Larger serrano chiles are also used in Southeast Asian cooking and are easier to find than the Thai variety in some parts of the United States. Peanuts—either coarsely chopped and chunky, or roasted and ground into peanut butter—are also added to dipping sauces in small amounts to give the sauces a bit of texture and sweetness. Sugar is another popular ingredient used in Southeast Asian dipping sauces, often serving to strike the perfect balance between sour ingredients (vinegar, lime, or tamarind), savory ingredients (primarily fish sauce), hot ingredients (chiles), and aromatic ingredients (herbs, garlic, and ginger).

VIETNAMESE SPICY FISH SAUCE
Nuoc Cham

This basic sauce has the same essential flavors that are included in most Southeast Asian dipping sauces. Americans who are unfamiliar with Thai food may prefer a sauce with less fish sauce or a sauce made with Thai fish sauce, which is milder. In fact this sauce is very similar to one of the most popular Thai dipping sauces, *nam prik*. In Vietnam, *nuoc cham* might be served with a bowl of rice to constitute a simple meal, but it is also an almost universal sauce for salads—it's perfect with cucumbers—and grilled and fried seafood or meats. It will keep for up to 2 weeks, well covered, in the refrigerator.

YIELD: ¾ CUP (185 MILLILITERS)

garlic cloves, crushed to a paste	2	2
fresh red or green thai chiles, finely chopped	4	4
or	or	or
serrano chiles, finely chopped	2	2
sugar	3 tablespoons	45 milliliters
lime juice	6 tablespoons	90 milliliters
vietnamese or thai fish sauce	¼ cup	60 milliliters

Combine all the ingredients in a small bowl. Stir until the sugar is dissolved.

Variations

The amounts of each of the ingredients can be increased or decreased to produce spicier, hotter, more sour, or sweeter versions. The lime juice can be replaced with vinegar (distilled white vinegar is typically used, but white wine vinegar or cider vinegar will give the sauce more finesse), or with tamarind extract (see Note). Water can also be added to the sauce for a lighter version, and chopped cilantro will give the sauce a refreshing bite. A finely chopped 1-inch (2.5 cm) slice of peeled fresh ginger can be stirred into the sauce to make the classic Vietnamese *nuoc mam gung*—a sauce sometimes served with plain rice and also with seafood.

Note: To prepare ½ cup (125 milliliters) of tamarind extract, pour ½ cup (125 milliliters) of boiling water over 2 tablespoons (30 milliliters) of tamarind paste in a small mixing bowl. Let sit for 15 minutes, stir thoroughly, and strain.

Thai Curry Pastes

Unlike Indian curries, which are almost always made from a combination of dried and powdered spices, Thai curries are pastes with a consistency much like stiff peanut butter. Instead of relying entirely on dried spices, Thai cooks also include fresh ingredients such as chiles, garlic, and shallots in their pastes. Thai curry pastes are usually freshly made using a traditional mortar and pestle, so their pungent aroma and flavor stay intact.

Curry pastes are very strong and are never served alone. Rather, they are combined at the last minute with liquids such as water, seafood or meat stock, fish sauce, lime juice, and coconut milk. And although the ingredients that go into a Thai curry paste can be used separately as flavorings, a premade paste makes the complicated assortment of flavorings easier to use. And because the pastes have a relatively smooth consistency achieved from long pounding and grinding, they can be incorporated into sauces without interfering with the consistency.

Red curry paste—red because it contains a large number of red chiles—is the best-known and most popular Thai curry paste. Traditionally it is made by slow grinding with a mortar and pestle, but in modern kitchens the grinding is sometimes started in a food processor. Don't try to use the food processor for the whole process, because it won't grind the ingredients to a smooth enough consistency. Other curry pastes, made using the same techniques, contain additional ingredients and different proportions of many of the same ingredients found in red curry paste. Green curry paste contains green chiles (often serranos) instead of red chiles, and it is even hotter than red curry paste. Yellow curry contains many of the same ingredients contained in green and red curry pastes, but it also includes an array of Indian curry spices.

✎ THAI RED CURRY PASTE

Red curry paste (as all curry paste) is somewhat labor intensive because there is no adequate substitute for slow grinding with a mortar and pestle. Curry pastes do freeze well, however, so the slow grinding process isn't necessary every time a dish calls for a curry paste. It's worth making a large batch, freezing it in smaller batches, and using it as needed.

Dried guajillo chiles are suggested here, but it's worthwhile experimenting with different dried red chiles to come up with varying nuances and heat.

Shrimp paste, listed here as optional, is traditionally cooked in a skillet before it is combined with the other ingredients. To avoid an aroma that many Western cooks find unpleasant, do this in a well-ventilated kitchen, or simply add the shrimp paste to the curry without cooking it. (Some cooks wrap the shrimp paste in aluminum foil and toast it in a skillet so the aroma doesn't escape.)

YIELD: 1 CUP (250 MILLILITERS)

guajillo or ancho chiles, 10	2½ ounces	70 grams
coriander seeds	1 tablespoon	15 milliliters
lemongrass	2 stalks	2 stalks
thai chiles, stemmed and seeded	6	6
or	or	or
serrano chiles, stemmed and seeded	3	3
¼-inch-thick (5 mm) slices peeled galangal	8	8
shallots, peeled	4	4
garlic cloves, peeled	4	4
2 cilantro roots or stems from 1 bunch cilantro, chopped		
zest of 1 lime, cut in strips		
or		
kafeer lime leaf	1	1
shrimp paste (optional)	1 tablespoon	15 milliliters

1. Wipe the guajillo chiles with a dry towel. Cut off the stems and slice the chiles in half lengthwise. Shake out the seeds.
2. Put the dried chiles and coriander in the bowl of a food processor and grind to a powder, about 3 minutes.
3. Peel the outermost sheath off the lemongrass stalks and discard. Cut off 5 inches (12.5 cm) of the tender end and thinly slice. Add these slices to the chile mixture. Discard the rest of the stalks.
4. Add the rest of the ingredients to the chile mixture and purée for about 10 minutes, scraping the inside of the food processor bowl with a rubber spatula every minute.
5. Transfer a third of the paste to a mortar and grind with a pestle to a smooth paste, about 10 minutes. Repeat with the remaining two-thirds (a third at a time). (If a very large mortar and pestle are available, the paste can be ground all at once.)

THAI GREEN CURRY PASTE

Green curry paste is made in the same way as red curry paste—preliminary grinding in a food processor, final grinding with a mortar and pestle—but some of the ingredients and their proportions are different. Most important, green curry is made with fresh green chiles (usually serranos) rather than dried red ones. The proportion of chiles is also higher, so green curry is even hotter than red.

coriander seeds	1 tablespoon	15 milliliters
white peppercorns	1 teaspoon	5 milliliters
lemongrass, outer sheath removed and discarded	3 stalks	3 stalks
green serrano chiles, seeded, coarsely chopped	12	12
zest of 1 lime, coarsely chopped		
or		
kafeer lime leaf, coarsely chopped	1	1
shallots, coarsely chopped	6 medium	6 medium
garlic cloves, coarsely chopped	6	6
5 cilantro roots or stems from 1 bunch cilantro, coarsely chopped	about 2 heaping tablespoons	40 milliliters
¼-inch-thick (5 mm) slices peeled galangal	4	4
gently packed cilantro leaves	1 cup	250 milliliters
shrimp paste (optional)	1 tablespoon	15 milliliters

1. Put the coriander seeds and peppercorns in the bowl of a food processor and grind to a powder, for about 1 minute.
2. Thinly slice 3 inches (8 cm) of the tender ends of the lemongrass and add to the processor bowl. Discard the rest of the lemongrass stalks.
3. Put the remaining ingredients in the food processor bowl and purée for about 10 minutes, scraping the inside of the bowl with a rubber spatula every minute.
4. Transfer the paste to a mortar, about a third at a time, and grind with a pestle to a smooth paste, for a total of about 20 minutes.

Using Curry Pastes: Thai Meat and Seafood Sauces and Stews

Once Thai curry pastes are on hand, a Thai-style sauce can be assembled in minutes. Most Thai sauces are used as part of stew-like "curries" rather than sauces prepared separately for ladling, Western style, over cooked meats and seafood. Thai sauces are only lightly thickened with either curry paste or coconut milk, having the consistency of creamy soup. This characteristic makes Thai curries perfect for serving with rice.

There are numerous traditional and standard recipes for Thai curries, but these curries can be improvised once the function of the basic ingredients is grasped. Other than the curry paste itself, Thai curries almost always contain fish sauce and an acidic ingredient such as tamarind, vinegar, or lime juice. They also usually contain coconut milk (which gives them a delicate sweet richness), a little sugar, additional kafeer lime leaves (which add flavor and look pretty), chopped or whole basil, mint, or cilantro leaves, and perhaps most important, a vegetable or nut garniture to provide contrasting flavor and texture. Garnitures for Southeast Asian stews function in the same way as they do for European stews but instead of carrots, pearl onions, or mushrooms, a Southeast Asian stew might contain cashews, bamboo shoots, miniature eggplants, pineapple, long beans, or cucumbers.

IMPROVISING THAI CURRIES WITHOUT CURRY PASTES

Curry pastes offer an easy method for quickly incorporating a complex mixture of ingredients into stew-like curries. But these same ingredients can be finely chopped or even left whole and then be simmered directly in broth or even water to make a sauce.

Here is a broth-like sauce that's quick to make and can be served around pieces of cooked meat and fish. Adjust, add, or omit ingredients to taste.

YIELD: 3 TO 4 CUPS (750 MILLILITERS TO 1 LITER); 1 QUART (1 LITER) IF THE TOMATOES ARE USED; ENOUGH FOR 6 TO 8 MAIN-COURSE SERVINGS

chicken, fish, or meat broth, cooking liquid from meat stew, or water	1 cup	250 milliliters
coconut milk	1 (14-ounce) can	425 milliliters
peeled, seeded, chopped tomatoes (optional)	1 cup	250 milliliters
garlic cloves, crushed to a paste	4	4
shallots, finely chopped	2	2
thai chiles, seeded, finely chopped	2 to 8	2 to 8
or	or	or
serrano chiles, seeded, finely chopped	1 to 4	1 to 4
lemongrass, outer sheath removed and discarded, root end thinly sliced to 3 inches (8 cm) each	2 stalks	2 stalks
kafeer lime leaves	6	6
¼-inch-thick (5 mm) slices peeled galangal	6	6
lime juice or tamarind extract (see Note, page 534)	2 to 4 tablespoons	30 to 60 milliliters
thai fish sauce	2 to 4 tablespoons	30 to 60 milliliters
sugar	½ to 2 tablespoons	7.5 to 30 milliliters
cilantro, mint, or thai basil leaves	3 tablespoons	45 milliliters

1. Bring the broth, coconut milk, and tomatoes, if using, to a slow simmer in a medium pot.
2. Stir in the rest of the ingredients except the cilantro. Adjust the acidity with lime juice or tamarind, the saltiness with fish sauce, and the sweetness with sugar.
3. Stir in the cilantro, simmer for 30 seconds, and serve.

THAI CURRY MODEL

This basic model can be used for seafood, poultry, red meat, or vegetables. Meats, poultry, and seafood can be browned first or simply simmered directly with the stew's liquid ingredients. Poultry, seafood, and tender cuts of meat can be quickly stir-fried or sautéed before they are simmered in the curry, but tough cuts of meat should be gently braised in broth or water in the same style of a European-style stew. The stewing liquid is then used as the liquid component in the curry.

YIELD: 6 SERVINGS

Main Ingredient

2¼ pounds/1 kilogram (6 ounces/175 grams per serving) of one of the following, cut into 2 × ½-inch (5 × 1 cm) strips:

boneless chicken breasts

firm-fleshed fish such as swordfish or shark

tender cut of beef (such as sirloin, flank, or sirloin strip)

or

shellfish such as scallops, left whole or cut into disks

squid, cut into rings

shrimp (left whole)

peanut or vegetable oil (if meat or seafood is being browned first)	2 tablespoons	30 milliliters

Cooking Oil, Basic Flavoring, and Cooking Liquid

peanut or vegetable oil	1 tablespoon	15 milliliters
red or green thai curry paste	¼ to ½ cup	60 to 125 milliliters
appropriate broth or water	1 cup	250 milliliters
fish sauce	2 to 6 tablespoons	30 to 90 milliliters

Enrichener and Thickener

coconut milk	1 (14-ounce) can	425 milliliters
or	*or*	*or*
homemade coconut milk (see page 34)	2 cups	500 milliliters

Sweet-and-Sour Ingredients

juice of 2 limes		
or	*or*	*or*
tamarind extract (see Note, page 534)	½ cup	125 milliliters
or	*or*	*or*
wine vinegar or cider vinegar	2 tablespoons	30 milliliters
sugar (optional)	1 to 2 tablespoons	15 to 30 milliliters

Slow-Cooking Aromatic Ingredients

optional

kafeer lime leaves	6	6
¼-inch-thick (5 mm) slices peeled galangal	3	3

Garnitures

to be used alone or in combination

bamboo shoots

sweet bell peppers

broccoli (cut into florets)

cashews

eggplant, peeled, cut into 1-inch (2.5 cm) cubes

long beans or string beans

mushrooms

pineapple (cut into wedges or cubes)

spinach

tofu, cut into 1-inch (2.5 cm) cubes

Fast-Cooking Aromatic Ingredients

optional

cilantro or thai basil leaves, whole or coarsely chopped, or mint leaves	3 tablespoons	45 milliliters

1. Brown the main ingredient in peanut or vegetable oil in a skillet or wok and set it aside on a plate. Pour off the cooked oil.
2. Heat the cooking oil (in the same skillet used for browning the main ingredient) and stir in the curry paste over medium heat for about 4 minutes, until it smells fragrant. Stir in the broth or water and fish sauce and bring to a gentle simmer.
3. Stir in the coconut milk, the sweet-and-sour ingredients, and the slow-cooking aromatic ingredients, if using, and bring back to a simmer.
4. Add one or more of the garnitures and simmer until almost done.
5. Add the main ingredient and simmer until done or heated through.
6. Stir in the cilantro, or basil leaves, or mint, if using. Simmer for 30 seconds. Serve immediately.

Indonesian Sauces

Any cook familiar with Thai curry pastes and sauces will find the ingredients and techniques for making Indonesian sauces very similar to those used in Thailand. Indonesian cooks are forever grinding aromatic ingredients with a mortar and pestle—to create an Indonesian spice paste, generically called *bumbu*—and then heating the mixture in oil before adding liquids, usually coconut milk. But whereas Thai curries are somewhat standardized, Indonesians make a different spice mixture for every dish.

There are, however, several ingredients that give Indonesian dishes their own identity and make Indonesian cuisine distinct from other Southeast Asian cuisines. Bottled fish sauce, an indispensable flavoring in Thai and Vietnamese cooking, is rarely used in Indonesia. Indonesian cooks rely instead on shrimp paste, called *terasi*, to give dishes much of their depth of flavor. While it's possible to get by without shrimp paste in Thai and Vietnamese cooking (fish sauce fills the gap somewhat), it's an essential ingredient in Indonesian cooking. Traditional Indonesian recipes often include shrimp paste in the bumbu, which is fried before liquids are added. The aroma released by the shrimp paste is so pungent and unfamiliar to Western noses that a safer approach is to wrap the shrimp paste tightly in a square of aluminum foil, heat it in a dry sauté pan, and unwrap it and combine it with the other ingredients when it has cooled and the liquids have been added. Another trick—frowned upon by purists—is to simply stir the uncooked shrimp paste into the simmering sauce.

Kemiri nuts, sometimes called candlenuts, are another particularly Indonesian ingredient. These waxy nuts have very hard shells, but fortunately they're always sold out of the shell. They are ground to a paste using a mortar and pestle (although nowadays the grinding is sometimes initiated in a food processor) and used to thicken sauces. Macadamia nuts can be used as a substitute, but they don't thicken as well and won't impart the particular authentic flavor of kemiri nuts. Kemiri nuts are mildly toxic when raw and should always be cooked.

Salam leaves contain a subtly flavored oil that imparts a distinct character to Indonesian stews and sauces. They are used in the same way as bay leaves in Western cooking and curry leaves in Indian cooking. Imported bay leaves can be used as a substitute.

Like the Chinese, Indonesians are also fond of soy sauce and have two versions of their own: *kecap asin*, relatively light and salty, and a heavier, sweeter version, *kecap manis*. Both versions are used in marinades and in sauces. Kecap, pronounced "ketchup," is the origin of the word "ketchup," but Indonesian soy sauces are very different from tomato ketchup.

Indonesian cooks share the Thai passion for galangal, but they are more likely to buy it in powdered form (called *laos*) than they are in fresh or frozen chunks.

The satay (or *saté*) is the Indonesian preparation best known in the West. A satay is made by marinating cubes of meat or seafood with spices, kecap, and aromatic vegetables, and then skewering the cubes and grilling them. The distinct flavor of the marinade contributes to the satay's character, but much of its special character comes from the sauce. Most satay sauces are based on ground peanuts flavored with spices, made hot with chiles, and sweetened with sugar.

Indonesians also have their own set of relishes, most of them hot and spicy, called *sambals*. Most sambals are used as condiments for other foods.

CHINESE SAUCES

It's obviously difficult to describe even the most basic sauces of a country as huge and diverse as China in a few short pages. It can be helpful, however, to see how profoundly the Chinese approach to sauce making differs from the traditions of Europe.

Whereas many of the best European sauces are made by careful and systematic concentration of a product's natural flavors, many Chinese sauces are designed to accent and provide contrast to the ingredients rather than to distill their essence. And although few condiments are used in classic French cooking (mustard is the only one used with any regularity), Chinese kitchen cabinets are filled with bottled seasonings, sauces, oils, and relishes. Some are homemade, but others, having been made commercially for centuries, are trusted standby condiments much like mustard and ketchup are in the West.

Another well-known factor that has influenced the evolution of Chinese cooking is the scarcity of cooking fuel. Many Chinese sauces are the result of a quick stir-fry and a few simple seasonings or condiments sprinkled toward the end of cooking.

Making Sauces for Stir-Fries

Even though Chinese cooks rely on a variety of techniques, stir-frying is probably the one most associated with Chinese cooking. It's essential to understand stir-frying to get a sense of how Chinese sauces are made.

Stir-frying is almost identical to sautéing—sautéing in the most literal sense, wherein the foods are tossed in the hot pan over high heat—except that a wok is used instead of a frying pan and the foods are stirred (often with chopsticks) instead of being tossed. Chinese cooks introduce flavor into stir-fries by lightly frying aromatic ingredients (especially ginger and garlic) in the oil before the main ingredients are added. This technique is essentially what an Italian cook does when gently sautéing sliced garlic in olive oil before stirring in vegetables. These aromatic ingredients can also be finely minced and stir-fried along with the rest of the ingredients. To make a sauce for a stir-fry, the cooking oil is drained out and liquids are added—essentially the same method used in Western fricassée. A fricassée differs from an authentic sauté in that the ingredients are cooked in liquid at the end rather than entirely with dry heat (see "Integral Sauces for Sautéed Meats," page 222).

Liquids, which almost always include soy sauce, are then quickly stirred with the foods and served immediately. The liquids added to a stir-fry are sometimes left unbound—they remain completely liquid and surround the foods on the serving dish—but often a thickener is used, usually cornstarch, to get them to cling around the foods. Cornstarch can be added to a stir-fry in two ways. It can be dissolved in a small amount of liquid (typically 1 tablespoon/15 milliliters of cornstarch is dissolved in 2 tablespoons/30 milliliters of liquid) and then stirred into the stir-fry a minute before the cooking is completed. Alternatively, it can be incorporated into a marinade. In addition to cornstarch, marinades for stir-fries typically contain soy sauce.

BASIC STIR-FRY

There are dozens of variations on this basic theme, and a couple of different approaches for incorporating the cornerstone ingredients of ginger, garlic, and cornstarch. Both the ginger and garlic can be left in thick slices, gently fried for a minute or two in hot oil, and fished out before other ingredients are added, or they can be peeled, finely chopped, and added to the stir-fry with the other ingredients. The cornstarch is combined with soy sauce (or another cool liquid) and used as a marinade, or the mixture may be simply added to the stir-fry near the end so the cornstarch thickens the sauce. Stir-fries require very high heat so that the ingredients brown quickly without overcooking.

YIELD: 4 SERVINGS

Main Ingredients

boneless chicken breasts, beef (a medium-tender cut such as flank steak or sirloin steak), boneless and skinless duck breast, shrimp, or scallops	1½ pounds	675 grams
green vegetables such as bok choy, broccoli (domestic or Chinese), watercress, chard, or others	1 pound (after trimming)	500 grams (after trimming)

Marinade

dark soy sauce	2 tablespoons	30 milliliters
cornstarch	2 teaspoons	10 milliliters
dry sherry or chinese rice wine	2 tablespoons	30 milliliters

Ingredients for Stir-Frying

peanut or vegetable oil	2 tablespoons	30 milliliters
finely chopped fresh ginger	1 teaspoon	5 milliliters
finely chopped garlic	2 teaspoons	10 milliliters
chicken broth, seafood or fish broth, or water	¼ cup	60 milliliters
soy sauce (optional)	to taste	to taste

1. Cut the poultry or meat into strips about 2 × ⅜ inches (5 cm × 5 mm). Shellfish such as shrimp or scallops may be left whole or, if very large, cut into 1-inch (2.5 cm) sections or ½-inch-thick (1 cm) disks. Cut the vegetables into manageable pieces, but not so small that they lose their identity.

2. Work the marinade ingredients together into a smooth paste and work the mixture into the meat or seafood. Marinate for 10 to 30 minutes.

3. Heat the peanut oil in a large wok or skillet over very high heat. When the oil begins to ripple, stir in the meat or seafood, leaving any excess marinade behind in the bowl—don't throw it out yet. When the meat or seafood begins to brown, add the ginger, garlic, and vegetables.

4. Quickly stir the meat or seafood with the vegetables until both are done, for 3 to 6 minutes. (Chicken strips should lose their flexibility and become stiff to the touch; duck and beef should remain rare or medium rare; shrimp should turn orange). If there is oil left in the bottom of the wok or skillet after stir-frying, spoon it out and discard it.

5. Stir in the chicken broth and simmer for 30 seconds more. If the stir-fry needs salt, add a teaspoon (5 milliliters) or more of soy sauce. If the sauce is too runny, stir in a teaspoon or two (5 to 10 milliliters) of the marinade left in the bottom of the bowl. Stir while cooking for another 30 seconds and serve.

Basic Stir-Fry Sauce Variations and Flavorings

The foregoing basic stir-fry recipe is to Chinese cooking what a simple sauté recipe is to French cooking—a base upon which unlimited variations can be built. Here are some of the more common ingredients added to stir-fries (see Chapter 3, "Ingredients," for more information about best brands, and so on).

Chiles, Chile Pastes, and Chile Oil. Many stir-fries are enhanced by a little spicy heat. Depending on the regional cooking style, Chinese cooks may use black pepper (for example, in hot and sour soup), Szechuan pepper, chopped hot chiles, or chile oil. Hot chiles are most popular in the regions of Szechuan and Hunan. Chinese cooks also use bottled chile pastes. Chiles and chile-based condiments are added to stir-fries at different stages. Chile oil can replace the vegetable oil used for stir frying, or chopped dried or fresh chiles can be added at the same time as chopped garlic and ginger. Chile pastes can be stirred into the stir-fry, to taste, a minute or two before serving.

Fermented Black Beans. Rinsed and lightly chopped, fermented black beans are best when soaked in a little sherry before they are added to stir-fries near the end of cooking. Because fermented black beans are very salty, the soy sauce called for in the basic stir-fry recipe should be left out and then added to taste at the end of cooking. Two tablespoons (30 milliliters) rinsed and crushed or lightly chopped black beans, soaked in the same amount of sherry, is usually just about the right quantity for the Basic Stir-Fry (page 542). The black beans should be added at the same time as the meat. Their soaking liquid, which will be very salty, can be added near the end, to taste.

Ham. Slivers of salty ham can make the perfect accent to stir-fried foods, especially vegetables. China has an array of excellent hams, but none of them is imported into the United States, so Smithfield ham is the best available substitute. Black Forest ham runs a close second. These hams should be thinly sliced, cut into slivers, and added to stir-fries a minute or two before the end of cooking.

Hoisin Sauce. Like so many Chinese sauces, this sweet anise-scented sauce is made with soy beans. A tablespoon or two of hoisin sauce (15 to 30 milliliters) added to a stir-fry during the last minute of cooking will give the sauce a subtle sweetness. Hoisin sauce is best used in conjunction with sesame oil.

Orange Peel. Dried orange and tangerine peels are sold at Asian groceries as a seasoning for stir-fries. Slivers of dried orange peel (or in a pinch, slivered fresh zests) are especially good in stir-fries containing hot chiles (or chile paste) and sesame oil. Orange zests can be cut off in strips with a paring knife or vegetable peeler and allowed to dry for 2 or 3 days on a rack. Tightly sealed, they can then be stored for several months.

Oyster Sauce. One to 2 tablespoons (15 to 30 milliliters) of oyster sauce added to a stir-fry during the last minute of cooking will give the sauce a distinctive seafood character. Oyster sauce is especially good when used in conjunction with dark sesame oil.

Peanuts and Other Nuts. Szechuan cooks are fond of peanuts and like to combine them with garlic, sesame oil (or paste), and chile paste in fiery sauces for cold meats or noodles. Peanuts and other nuts are also added to stir-fries for their flavor, and to provide a contrasting texture. Peanuts (start out with raw peanuts) are best and are most easily incorporated into a stir-fry by frying them, with their papery red skins left on, in a few tablespoons of hot oil. Most of this oil should be drained off before adding and stir-frying the peanuts with the rest of the ingredients.

Sesame Oil. Dark Asian sesame oil has an intense flavor that gives stir-fries a savory accent and a characteristic northern Chinese character. Sesame oil is very powerful — ½ to 2 teaspoons (3 to 10 milliliters) added to a stir-fry the last few seconds of cooking is usually appropriate.

Sugar and Honey. Sauces for stir-fried meats or vegetables are often enhanced with a little sugar or honey. Start out adding ½ teaspoon (3 milliliters) of either to a stir-fry a minute before the cooking is completed.

Vinegars. Chinese cooks use a variety of vinegars and often combine them with sugar to come up with sweet-and-sour sauces. Rice vinegar, Chinese black vinegar, and balsamic vinegar can all be used to season stir-fries.

Chinese Cold Sauces

Whereas Western (especially French) cooks have for centuries emphasized the importance of warm and hot sauces and have come up with elaborate systems and hierarchies for their use, Chinese cooks have put much of their energy into developing cold sauces. The Chinese also lack the aversion to bottled sauces that Western chefs feel, and will often combine these bottled sauces and condiments to make variations. Many of these cold sauces can be tossed with cold meats, poultry, or noodles, and others can be used as simple dipping sauces for items such as wontons or deep-fried dishes, or as salad dressings (see also "Flavored Oils," page 427).

CHINESE GINGER- AND GARLIC-FLAVORED "VINAIGRETTE"

One of the easiest and most versatile dipping sauces is a simple mixture of soy sauce, vinegar, and fresh ginger. This sauce is excellent with Chinese black vinegar (see page 44), but balsamic vinegar makes an acceptable substitute.

YIELD: 1 CUP (250 MILLILITERS)

Japanese dark soy sauce (see Note)	⅔ cup	165 milliliters
chinese black vinegar or balsamic vinegar	⅓ cup	80 milliliters
grated fresh ginger	2 teaspoons	10 milliliters
finely chopped garlic	2 teaspoons	10 milliliters
sesame oil (see page 42)	1 teaspoon	5 milliliters

Combine all the ingredients. Let sit for an hour and serve. This sauce will keep for at least a week in the refrigerator.

Note: Japanese soy sauce is popular even in Chinese sauces because it is less salty. When substituting Chinese soy sauce, use half as much as called for and add more, if desired, to taste (see page 39).

SWEET AND SPICY SESAME SAUCE

Inspired from a recipe in Barbara Tropp's excellent *The Modern Art of Chinese Cooking*, this sauce has a complex sweetness but enough heat to prevent the sweetness from being cloying. This sauce can be tossed with or brushed on cold chicken, used as a dipping sauce for grilled foods, or used as a salad dressing.

sesame seeds	2 tablespoons	30 milliliters
or	*or*	*or*
asian sesame paste (see page 38)	¼ cup	60 milliliters
sesame oil (see page 42)	2 tablespoons	30 milliliters
hoisin sauce (see page 36)	1 tablespoon	15 milliliters
japanese dark soy sauce	¼ cup	60 milliliters
chile oil (page 34)	1 tablespoon	15 milliliters
or	*or*	*or*
thai chiles, very finely chopped	2 to 4	2 to 4
or	*or*	*or*
serrano chiles, very finely chopped	1 or 2	1 or 2
sugar, dissolved in 2 tablespoons (30 milliliters) hot water	1 tablespoon	15 milliliters

1. If using whole sesame seeds, toss them in a skillet over high heat until they are lightly brown and smell fragrant, about 5 minutes, and grind them to a paste in a coffee grinder.
2. Whisk all the ingredients into a smooth paste or purée them in a food processor. Scrape down the sides of the food processor with a rubber spatula a few times during the processing.

CHINESE MUSTARD SAUCE

Most Chinese mustard sauces are made with dried mustard and flavored with sesame oil and chile oil. Barbara Tropp (*The Modern Art of Chinese Cooking*) recommends replacing the dried mustard with Dijon (specifically Maille brand) for a truer mustard flavor. Ms. Tropp uses a sauce similar to this one for a number of cold salads (some with chicken, others with duck) and as a dipping sauce for fried pork balls. Dipping sauce keeps indefinitely in the refrigerator, but it is better if the fresh cilantro is added shortly before serving. For homemade Chinese-Style Chile Oil, see page 431.

YIELD: 1 CUP (250 MILLILITERS)

dijon mustard	¾ cup	185 milliliters
chile oil	3 tablespoons	45 milliliters
chinese black vinegar or balsamic vinegar	1 tablespoon	15 milliliters
finely chopped cilantro	3 tablespoons	45 milliliters

Combine all the ingredients 1 or 2 hours before serving.

INDIAN SAUCES

Because India is a huge and diverse country with well over a dozen languages and several major religions (each with its own culinary taboos and traditions), it would seem impossible to make generalizations about Indian cooking as a whole. And although any serious discussion of Indian cooking requires a close look at the cooking of individual regions, many of the same techniques and ingredients are used throughout the country, making it possible to take a broad overview and at least get a sense of how an Indian sauce is put together.

Curries

The most famous Indian sauces are the natural products of making curries. In essence, curries are stews made by simmering meat, seafood, or vegetables (or a combination) in flavorful liquid in much the same way as a French cook might simmer meat or seafood in wine and then add a variety of garnitures for flavor and contrasting texture and color. But whereas much of the subtlety and variety of the best French cooking lies in the careful combining of herbs, the genius of Indian cooking is based on the subtle use of spices, many of which are rarely if ever used in European cooking.

A European or American cook's experience with Indian cooking is likely to be throwing a dash of curry powder into an essentially Western dish (curry powder is in fact marvelous in cream and butter sauces), but in India, bottled curry powder—essentially an Anglo-Saxon adaptation—is never used. Instead, each region (and even each cook) relies upon a unique combination of spices that gives Indian sauces distinct regional character.

Except for the use of spices, an Indian curry is made in much the same way as any stew. Whereas European cooks start most stews by gently "sweating" aromatic vegetables such as onions, carrots, celery, and garlic as a gently flavored mirepoix or soffritto, Indian cooks rely most heavily on onions. And instead of the gentle sweating that prevents the onions from turning brown, Indian cooks use higher heat so the onions do brown. A French or Italian cook would probably sweat the vegetables in butter or olive oil, but an Indian cook might use ghee, mustard oil, coconut oil, or sesame oil, depending on the region where he or she lives. Nowadays, neutral-tasting vegetable oils are replacing many of these regional preferences.

Whereas a Western cook might add a little fresh or dried thyme or marjoram to an aromatic vegetable base, an Indian cook will most likely add chopped hot chiles, garlic, and ginger to the browning onions. At this point, the Indian cook may begin to add spices. Spices are typically added at different stages of cooking. Again, the incorporation of spices into an Indian curry is analogous to the use of herbs in European cooking. Herbs or spices that release their flavor slowly (such as thyme in France, cinnamon in India) are added first so they can meld with the flavors of other ingredients. Those spices whose flavor the cook wishes to magnify are stirred in the hot fat to accentuate their flavor. Other spices whose flavor the cook wishes to mollify may be worked to a paste with water and stirred into the stew later during cooking. Other spices may be worked to a paste with water or cooked in ghee and then stirred in at the very end so their delicacy or forthrightness isn't lost.

Meat, seafood, or vegetables are usually added to the curry after cooking the vegetables, aromatics (such as ginger, garlic, chiles) and usually the first round of spices. The meat or seafood may be lightly browned in the oily spice mixture, but much of the time this preliminary browning is minimal (much like a fricassée) or it is skipped entirely (much like a blanquette). At this point, a European cook is likely to add broth, wine, or water, or perhaps a mixture of wine and herbs used for marinating the meat, but the Indian cook may use one or more of an array of liquids. Tomatoes are well liked in India and often constitute the only liquid. In Southern India, coconut milk is often used, either in purely liquid form or as a pasty purée of whole coconut pulp (see Coconut Milk, page 34). In Northern India, yogurt and dairy products, including whole milk and cream, are also popular.

Once the meat, seafood, or vegetables are simmering in spice-flavored liquid, the Indian cook may add one or more ingredients to thicken the curry. A traditional European cook would have likely floured the meat before browning it (*singer*), or might whisk the finished braising liquid into a roux, as when making a blanquette. Indian cooks have a far more imaginative array of thickeners and techniques, many of which are only recently being incorporated into Western cooking. In some Indian curries the cooked onions are puréed into a thickening paste before being combined with the simmering meat. Nuts, especially cashews, peanuts, and almonds, and seeds such as sesame, poppy, mustard, or fenugreek, are ground into pastes and used as thickeners. Lentils, especially pink or yellow Indian lentils, are simmered, puréed, and added to curries. Coconut milk and coconut paste are often used as thickeners in Southern Indian cooking. Dairy products such as cream, milk, or yogurt, especially when drained in cheesecloth, are also effective thickeners.

It's appropriate to mention at this point that the criteria for an Indian curry differ somewhat from those for a Western stew. The fat contained in Western stews—for example, those containing cream—must never separate, but in Indian cooking the oil or fat used for the initial cooking of aromatic vegetables and the principal ingredient(s) may very likely separate out, especially during long cooking. When yogurt or other dairy products are used, this leaves a stew with the coagulated milk solids clinging to the solid ingredients (such as meat or seafood) and a rather oily sauce. This effect is often unappealing to Westerners but is quite acceptable in India. (In Western cooking, this problem could be remedied by spooning out and discarding the separated fat and adding liquid and an emulsifier such as heavy cream to at least partially re-emulsify the coagulated milk solids.)

Like a discerning European cook who understands how to wake up the flavor of a stew or brown sauce with a splash of good wine vinegar, or a white sauce with a squeeze of lemon, the use of acidic ingredients has long been recognized as an important element in Indian cooking. Some of the acidic ingredients used in Western cooking are also used in India: Underripe tomatoes, vinegar (introduced by Portuguese settlers in Goa), lime or lemon juice, and yogurt (used also as a moistening liquid and thickener) often provide curries with the essential acidic bite. Other ingredients, unfamiliar to Western cooks, are also used in India. Tamarind pulp, sold as a paste (see page 39) is especially popular in Southern India and also used throughout Southeast Asia. In some regions of India, the pulp is combined with spices. The pulp from fresh mangoes (abundant in India during the summer months) is sometimes simmered in curries for its freshness and tang. Dried mango and dried mango powders are also used when fresh mango is unavailable or when tradition dictates.

Indian cooks are keenly aware of color, and because many of the ingredients used in Indian curries sometimes give the stew an unpleasant off-gray or brown hue, some ingredients are used primarily for the bright colors they impart. Powdered turmeric, often included in commercial curry powders, will give a drab-looking curry an appealing yellow brightness; saffron is not only delicious but creates an exotic orange-colored sauce, even when used in very small quantities; a wide assortment of fresh herbs may be puréed with liquid ingredients, or just very finely chopped to add a green hue or green specks (cilantro is the most popular; and tomatoes contribute an appealing pink).

Finely chopped herbs are the most popular last-minute finishes for Western stews and sauces, but Indian cooks are more likely to use spices. The spices can be worked with water into pastes and added in the same way that spices are added earlier during the cooking, or they can be cooked into a flavorful *tadka* (also spelled *tarka*). A tadka is made by heating ghee in a skillet and stirring in spices—especially cumin seeds, mustard seeds, cloves, and asafetida—and aromatic vegetables such as chiles, garlic, and onions, and then quickly blending this mixture into vegetarian stews and lentil dishes.

Spice Mixtures

The subtlety and variety of Indian food reveals itself only when spices are carefully balanced to achieve a particular effect or to enhance a particular flavor. Spice mixtures, if used to the exclusion of other spices, or if used for every dish (the ubiquitous bottle of curry powder is the best example), will leave Indian dishes with a tiring sameness. On the other hand, it can be tedious to combine an array of spices for every dish. What is typical in India is to use a spice mixture—the particular blend will depend largely on the traditions of the cook's region—and then add one or more other spices or aromatic ingredients to give the dish distinction.

Indian cooks are fond of roasting spices. This is easy to do by stirring the raw whole spices in a hot skillet until they brown ever so slightly and smell fragrant, but it is also possible to cook the ground spices or finished spice mixtures, Western style, in a little butter or oil until they release their flavor. One disadvantage to this quick-and-easy method, however, is that some spices release their aroma and flavor more quickly than others. So-called sweet spices such as cinnamon and cloves release their aroma quickly and need no roasting, whereas "spicier" spices such as cumin or coriander are greatly enhanced by roasting. Consequently, sweeter and delicate spices can be left raw and spicier spices can be roasted and combined in the same spice mixture.

Although purists insist on roasting and combining their spices every day, roasted and ground spices and the derivative spice mixtures will keep with very little alteration in their flavor for several months, tightly wrapped, in the freezer.

TRADITIONAL GARAM MASALA
Moghul Garam Masala

Garam masala means "hot spice mixture," a somewhat misleading translation because Indian cooks talk about spices that either heat or cool the body—distinctions that have little to do with how hot they are in the mouth. Garam masala is the spice mixture most often used in Northern Indian cooking. None of the spices for the following garam masala need be roasted, because they are all intensely aromatic anyway.

YIELD: 1/3 CUP (80 MILLILITERS)

cinnamon sticks, 2 inches (5 cm) long, coarsely chopped	4	4
black peppercorns	1 rounded tablespoon	20 milliliters
whole cloves	1 tablespoon	15 milliliters
black cardamom seeds, husks removed	3	3
fennel seeds (optional)	1 rounded tablespoon	20 milliliters

Blend the spices in a blender at high speed for about 3 minutes. Work the mixture through a fine-mesh strainer. Zap what doesn't go through the strainer a second time in the blender and work it through the strainer. Reserve garam masala, tightly sealed, in the freezer.

MODERN GARAM MASALA
Punjabi Garam Masala

In addition to the "sweet" and aromatic spices combined to make traditional garam masala, many contemporary versions of garam masala contain green cardamom instead of the traditional black cardamom and also contain a large proportion of cumin and coriander—spices that give traditional garam masala a sharper and more "curry-like" flavor and aroma. It's possible to get by without roasting the spices (especially if the spice mixture is being cooked in fat before being combined with moist ingredients), but Punjabi garam masala will have more distinction if the coriander and cumin seeds are stirred in a hot skillet for a few minutes first, until they release their aroma.

YIELD: ¼ CUP (60 MILLILITERS)

black or white cumin seeds	2 tablespoons	30 milliliters
coriander seeds	2 tablespoons	30 milliliters
cinnamon sticks, 2 inches (5 cm) long, coarsely chopped	4	4
black peppercorns	1 tablespoon	15 milliliters
whole cloves	1 tablespoon	15 milliliters
green cardamom seeds, husks removed	1 tablespoon	15 milliliters

Stir the cumin seeds in a hot skillet until they smell aromatic and brown very slightly. Transfer the cumin seeds to a bowl and repeat with the coriander seeds. Grind all the spices together in a coffee grinder or blender on high speed for about 3 minutes. Strain through a fine-mesh strainer, grind again, and strain what doesn't go through. Punjabi garam masala may be frozen, tightly sealed, for several months.

BENGALI SPICE MIXTURE
Panch Phoran

This spice mixture is used in many Bengali vegetable dishes. The spices are left whole and added to hot oil at the beginning of cooking.

YIELD: ½ CUP (120 MILLILITERS)

fennel seeds	2 tablespoons	30 milliliters
brown mustard seeds	2 tablespoons	30 milliliters
fenugreek seeds	2 tablespoons	30 milliliters
cumin seeds	2 tablespoons	30 milliliters

Stir together all the ingredients and store in a tightly sealed container. Shake before using.

SAMBAAR POWDER

This is a spicy mixture based largely on the flavor of certain dried peas. Sambaar powder is especially popular in Southern India, where it is used to flavor an array of vegetarian dishes. It is often used in conjunction with cooked hulled mung beans (*moong dal*) and lentils, which are then puréed and used to thicken vegetarian stews. Three tablespoons (45 milliliters) of sambaar powder is usually enough to flavor about 1 quart (1 liter) of liquid.

YIELD: ½ CUP (125 MILLILITERS)

coriander seeds	¼ cup	60 milliliters
brown mustard seeds	1 teaspoon	5 milliliters
moong dal (split and hulled yellow variety)	1 teaspoon	5 milliliters
channa dal	1 teaspoon	5 milliliters
urad dal	1 teaspoon	5 milliliters
fenugreek seeds	1 teaspoon	5 milliliters
cumin seeds	2 teaspoons	10 milliliters
powdered asafetida	¼ teaspoon	1 milliliter
curry leaves	20	20
dried guajillo chiles, stems and seeds removed	6	6
black peppercorns	1 teaspoon	5 milliliters

Stir the coriander, mustard seeds, moong dal, channa dal, urad dal, fenugreek, and cumin in a hot skillet for about 3 minutes until the spices smell aromatic. Stir in the asafetida, curry leaves, and chiles and stir for another 2 minutes. Remove from the heat, let cool, and combine with the peppercorns. Grind in a coffee grinder or blender at high speed for about 3 minutes and work through a fine-mesh strainer. Store, tightly sealed, in the freezer.

BASIC CURRY POWDER

This homemade curry powder is far better than any commercial bottled version. Because the spices are roasted, this curry powder can be stirred into liquids, to taste, without first being cooked. Two teaspoons to 1 tablespoon (10 to 15 milliliters) is usually appropriate for 1 cup (250 milliliters) of liquid.

YIELD: ⅓ CUP (80 MILLILITERS)

coriander seeds	¼ cup	60 milliliters
cumin seeds	2 teaspoons	10 milliliters
brown mustard seeds	2 teaspoons	10 milliliters
fenugreek seeds	2 teaspoons	10 milliliters
green cardamom seeds (husks removed)	10	10

cloves	12	12
cinnamon sticks, 2 inches (5 cm) long, coarsely chopped	2	2
black peppercorns	2 teaspoons	10 milliliters
powdered turmeric	1 tablespoon	15 milliliters

Stir the coriander, cumin, mustard seeds, fenugreek, and cardamom in a hot iron skillet until the spices smell aromatic, for about 5 minutes. Combine with the rest of the spices in a coffee grinder or blender and blend at high speed for about 3 minutes. Strain through a fine-mesh strainer. Blend again and strain what doesn't go through the strainer the first time. Store, tightly sealed, in the freezer.

CURRY MODEL

Although it's impossible in a short space to include a collection of authentic Indian dishes and to explain the traditions that give each one its character and that dictate the spices, spice mixtures, and other ingredients that go into their preparation, it is possible to outline a basic system that is common to most Indian curries. The resulting dish may not be identical to any particular authentic and regional Indian dish, but the ingredients and techniques will be authentically Indian, and the cook who experiments with the basic ingredients will develop a sensitivity to the balance of spices in the same way a European-trained cook will have developed an almost instinctual sensitivity to herbs. The amounts of each of the following ingredients will vary enormously depending on which of the other ingredients are being included. Cooking times will also vary. Shellfish such as shrimp or scallops may only need a minute or two, strips of tender meats about 5 minutes, a quartered chicken about 40 minutes, and stewing meats about 2 hours. Slow-cooking meats should be gently stewed in broth or water following the techniques for any stew (that is, carefully degreasing, never allowing to boil; see "Braising Terminology," page 243) and the braising liquid then converted into a curry.

YIELD: 6 TO 8 MAIN-COURSE SERVINGS

Main Ingredient

2¼ to 4 pounds/1 to 2 kilograms (6 to 8 ounces/175 to 225 grams per serving) of one of the following:

chicken, quartered or sectioned into small pieces

lamb (leg or shoulder), cut into cubes or strips

stewing beef (chuck, shank, or other stewing cut), cut into cubes or thick strips tender beef (sirloin, strip, rib), cut into cubes or strips

shrimp and other shellfish (left whole)

firm-fleshed fish fillets, cut into cubes or strips

vegetables, cut into chunks, florets, strips, and so on

Cooking Fat

About 2 tablespoons/30 milliliters:

ghee

mustard oil (heat to smoking and let cool)

sesame oil

coconut oil

vegetable oil

Fresh Aromatic Ingredients

onions, thinly sliced, chopped, or puréed	2 large	2 large
finely chopped garlic	1 teaspoon to 3 tablespoons	5 to 45 milliliters
finely chopped fresh green chiles such as serrano	1 teaspoon to 3 tablespoons	5 to 45 milliliters
grated peeled fresh ginger	1 teaspoon to 1 tablespoon	5 to 15 milliliters

Spice Mixtures

1 teaspoon to 2 tablespoons/5 to 30 milliliters or more to taste:

traditional garam masala (page 550)

modern garam masala (page 551)

bengali spice mixture (page 551)

sambaar powder (page 552)

basic curry mixture (page 552)

Individual Spices and Herbs

any of the spices contained in spice mixtures above	¼ teaspoon to 2 tablespoons	2 to 30 milliliters
curry leaves	10 to 30	10 to 30
fenugreek leaves, soaked in water with a pinch of salt for 30 minutes to remove the slightly bitter taste	½ cup	125 milliliters
saffron	1 pinch	1 pinch
turmeric (for color)	1 teaspoon to 1 tablespoon	5 to 15 milliliters

cinnamon leaves, gently fried for 10 minutes	1 or 2	1 or 2
bay leaf	1 or 2	1 or 2
mace	⅛ to ½ teaspoon	1 to 3 milliliters
nutmeg	⅛ to ½ teaspoon	1 to 3 milliliters
star anise, crushed	1 or 2	1 or 2

Liquids and Moist Ingredients

1 to 3 cups/250 to 750 milliliters:

broth

tomatoes (peeled, seeded, chopped)

coconut milk

yogurt

milk

Nuts

optional

slivered almonds

cashews

pistachios

Thickeners

1 to 3 tablespoons/15 to 45 milliliters:

nut butter (peanut, almond, cashew)

ground seed paste such as sesame, poppy, mustard, or fenugreek

cooked and puréed onions

dried legumes, cooked separately and puréed; especially pink or yellow Indian lentils, hulled mung beans (*moong dal*), yellow split peas (*channa dal*), or split gram beans (*urad dal*)

coconut paste (ground coconut pulp)

Acidic Ingredients

2 teaspoons to 2 tablespoons/10 to 30 milliliters:

vinegar

lime juice

underripe tomatoes

tamarind extract (see Note, page 534)

green mangoes (fresh, dried, or powdered)

Aromatic Finishes (Taдka)

optional

cumin seeds	1 to 2 teaspoons	5 to 10 milliliters
brown mustard seeds	½ to 2 teaspoons	3 to 10 milliliters
cloves	¼ to ½ teaspoon	2 to 3 milliliters
asafetida	⅛ to ¼ teaspoon	1 to 2 milliliters
aromatic vegetables such as chiles, garlic, and onions		

Final Herbs

optional

1 to 3 tablespoons/15 to 45 milliliters whole or chopped leaves:
cilantro

mint

basil

Final Addition of Spices

any of the foregoing spices or spice mixtures worked to a smooth paste with water
(if the spices in the mixtures have not been roasted, the spice mixtures should be
gently cooked in oil or butter until they release their perfume)
salt

1. (Optional) Brown the meat or seafood in one of the cooking fats and reserve.
2. Cook one or more of the fresh aromatic ingredients in fresh cooking oil or in the fat left in the pan. The ingredients can be gently sweated or quickly sautéed.
3. Stir the spice mixture and the additional spices and herbs into the hot vegetables and cook gently until the spices release their aroma. If the base is being used for a long-cooking stew, the spices are better added at the end.
4. Return the meat to the pan (seafood should be added later because it cooks so quickly) and add one or more of the liquids. Simmer gently until the meat has finished cooking. Thickeners can be added at the same time as the meat or added when the meat is done.
5. Add nuts, if using, one of the thickeners, and an acidic ingredient.
6. (Optional) Cook one or more of the tadka ingredients in hot ghee until they release their aroma. Stir the hot tadka into the finished curry.
7. (Optional) Add chopped herb or whole leaves.
8. Season to taste with salt and, if necessary, final additional spices.

LAMB CURRY WITH GARAM MASALA AND MIXED VEGETABLES

This stew is an example of one of the many possibilities that can be derived from the foregoing curry model. One of the advantages to this dish is that it's self-contained, so there's no need to prepare an accompanying starch (new potatoes are simmered in the curry) or green vegetables, which are also cooked directly in the curry. The effect of including vegetables right in the curry is also an impressive sight.

YIELD: 6 MAIN-COURSE SERVINGS

lamb shoulder meat (from 3 pounds/1½ kilograms thick shoulder lamb chops)	2 pounds	1 kilogram
salt	to taste	to taste
ghee or vegetable oil	2 tablespoons	30 milliliters
onion, thinly sliced	1 medium	1 medium
garlic cloves, chopped	2	2
serrano chiles, stemmed, seeded, finely chopped	1 to 3	1 to 3
or	or	or
jalapeños, stemmed, seeded, finely chopped	2 to 6	2 to 6
finely chopped fresh ginger	1 tablespoon	15 milliliters
water	1 cup	250 milliliters
fingerling potatoes, about 1 ounce/25 grams each	1 pound	450 grams
coconut milk	1 (14-ounce) can	425 milliliters
or	or	or
fresh coconut milk (see page 34)	2 cups	500 milliliters
cremini or domestic mushrooms, quartered	½ pound	225 grams
garam masala (page 550)	1½ tablespoons	25 milliliters
cashew or other nut butter	3 tablespoons	45 milliliters
snap peas or snow peas, ends broken off	½ pound	225 grams
spinach leaves, blanched, drained, refreshed	1 bunch	1 bunch
coarsely chopped cilantro leaves	3 tablespoons	45 milliliters

1. Cut the lamb into 1-inch (2.5 cm) cubes. Sprinkle with salt and brown on all sides in a heavy-bottomed sauté pan, uncovered and over high heat, in ghee. Remove the meat from the pan and reserve.
2. Pour all but 2 tablespoons (30 milliliters) of fat out of the pan and stir in the onion, garlic, chiles, and ginger. Cook over medium heat while stirring for about 15 minutes, until the onions lightly caramelize.

3. Add the water and the potatoes to the onion mixture. Cover the pan and simmer gently over low to medium heat until the potatoes are barely done, about 20 minutes. Add the coconut milk and the mushrooms and simmer for 5 minutes more.

4. Work together the garam masala, the cashew butter, and 3 tablespoons (45 milliliters) of liquid from the pan into a smooth paste in a small bowl. Whisk this mixture into the rest of the liquid in the pan.

5. Stir in the snap peas and simmer for 2 minutes. Stir in the spinach and cilantro and simmer for 1 minute more. Season to taste with salt.

20 DESSERT SAUCES

Many desserts can be enhanced with an appropriate sauce, to provide contrast, extra sweetness or acidity, moistness, and extra color. Fruit tarts, especially if they do not contain too much sugar, are best served with a sweet sauce such as a crème anglaise or a sabayon that will round out the acidic flavor of the fruit. Very sweet desserts, such as cakes or pastries containing chocolate or elaborate creams, are best served with a relatively acidic sauce, such as an unsweetened fruit coulis. Dessert sauces can be served at the table in a sauce boat or directly on the plate.

CRÈME ANGLAISE

Crème anglaise is one of the most delicious and versatile of the dessert sauces. Although traditionally flavored with vanilla, it can also become an adaptable medium for a variety of flavor combinations. It is excellent when served with fruit tarts and pastries that are not too sweet. It is also the base for French-style ice cream.

Traditional crème anglaise is made with a vanilla bean, sugar, milk, and egg yolks. The amounts of each can be changed to taste. The recipe that follows contains less sugar and more vanilla than older recipes, which tend to be sweeter and less extravagant with the vanilla. Acceptable crème anglaise can be made with vanilla extract, but it will never have the depth of flavor that the cream has when infused with vanilla beans. The recipe that follows uses twelve egg yolks per quart (liter) of milk, which produces a fairly rich cream. Acceptable crème anglaise can be made with as few as eight yolks per quart (liter). Richer versions also exist, using as many as sixteen yolks per quart (liter) and replacing half of the milk with heavy cream.

CRÈME ANGLAISE

YIELD: 6 CUPS (1.5 LITERS)

vanilla beans	2	2
milk	1 quart	1 liter
sugar	¾ cup plus 2 tablespoons	175 grams
egg yolks	12	12

1. Cut the vanilla beans in half lengthwise and add them to the milk in a 2-quart (2 liter) saucepan. Bring the milk to a simmer.
2. While the milk is heating, whisk together the sugar and egg yolks until the sugar dissolves and the yolks are pale yellow.
3. As the milk approaches a simmer, remove the vanilla beans and scrape the inside of each half with a paring knife to release the tiny seeds. Return the seeds to the milk.
4. When the milk simmers, pour half of it over the egg yolk–sugar mixture, gently whisking.
5. Add the egg yolk–sugar-milk mixture to the saucepan and stir it over medium heat with a wooden spatula or spoon. Stir constantly, being careful to reach around and into the corners, where the cream is most liable to curdle.
6. *Do not let the cream boil.* Check the consistency of the cream by holding the spatula up sideways and making a streak along the back of the spatula with

your finger. When the streak remains without the cream running down and obscuring it, the cream is ready.

7. Immediately remove the cream from the heat. Continue stirring it for 1 or 2 minutes, so the heat retained in the bottom of the saucepan won't cause the crème anglaise to curdle.

8. Strain the cream through a strainer. Do not use a chinois or the specks of vanilla will be strained out.

9. Stir the cream over a bowl of ice to cool it quickly and prevent a skin from forming.

Crème Anglaise Variations

Crème anglaise is the most versatile of all the dessert sauces because it is a perfect medium for other flavors. Flavors should be added to taste, but a few parameters are listed below. The vanilla contained in the crème anglaise will usually enhance whatever additional flavor is used, but if pure flavor is wanted, the vanilla can, of course, be omitted.

Spirits

Make sure the crème anglaise is cool before adding spirits; otherwise their flavor, most of which is volatile, will evaporate.

- Whiskeys (such as bourbon or Scotch): Add ½ cup (125 milliliters) per quart (liter) of crème anglaise.
- Grape brandies (such as Cognac or Armagnac): Add ½ cup (125 milliliters) per quart (liter) of crème anglaise.
- Fruit brandies (such as framboise, mirabelle, Poire William, Calvados—not fruit-flavored brandies): Add 6 tablespoons (90 milliliters) per quart (liter) of crème anglaise.
- Liqueurs (such as Cointreau, Grand Marnier, Chartreuse, Amaretto, anisette): Add ½ cup (125 milliliters) per quart (liter) of crème anglaise; decrease the sugar contained in the crème anglaise by ⅓ cup (60 grams) per quart (liter).
- Rum (either white or dark pot-distilled rums—Martinique rum is the best): Add ½ cup (125 milliliters) per quart (liter) of crème anglaise.

Fruits

Crème anglaise can be flavored with fruit in several ways. The first and most obvious is to add fruit purée, but good-quality fruit brandy can also be used (see preceding list). The flavor of citrus fruits is best imparted by replacing the vanilla bean with the grated zest of the appropriate fruit.

- Berries (such as raspberries, strawberries, blueberries): Add ¾ cup (185 milliliters) of strained purée (coulis) per quart (liter) of crème anglaise.
- Citrus fruits (such as oranges, lemons, limes, tangerines): Replace the vanilla bean in the basic recipe with the grated zests of 2 oranges, 3 tangerines, or 4 lemons or limes. Strain the cream through a chinois.

Chocolate

Chocolate can be added to a crème anglaise in two ways. The first method is to stir cocoa powder into the egg yolks along with the sugar. The second method is to add chunks of chocolate to the finished cream while it is still hot and stir the mixture until they dissolve. Remember to use the best-quality chocolate (see page 83).

- Using cocoa powder: Combine ½ cup (125 milliliters) of the milk called for in the recipe with the egg yolks and sugar. Add 4 ounces (125 grams) of cocoa powder to the mixture and stir with a whisk until smooth. Continue as for a regular crème anglaise.
- Using bar chocolate: Break up 8 ounces (250 grams) of bittersweet chocolate into small chunks. Add these to the crème anglaise as soon as it thickens. Stir off the heat with a whisk until the chocolate is completely and evenly dissolved in the cream. Strain through a chinois. If bittersweet chocolate is not available, sweet or baking chocolate can be used, but remember to adjust the amount of sugar contained in the crème anglaise accordingly.

Coffee

Crème anglaise can be flavored with coffee in several ways: Strong espresso can be added to the crème anglaise at the end; ground coffee beans can be infused in the milk along with or instead of the vanilla (this method provides the best flavor); or coffee extract or dissolved instant coffee can be added to the cream at the end.

- Using espresso: Add ½ cup (125 milliliters) of strong espresso per quart (liter) of crème anglaise.
- Using coffee beans: Finely grind 3 ounces (75 grams) of dark-roasted coffee beans. Stir the cold milk into the ground coffee before heating.
- Using coffee extract or instant espresso coffee: Dissolve 2 heaping tablespoons (40 milliliters) of instant coffee granules in 3 tablespoons (45 milliliters) of water. Stir slowly into the finished crème anglaise, to taste. Coffee extract should be added in the same way.

Herbs

Herb-flavored crème anglaise is wonderful served with fruits and delicately flavored pastries. Mint, spearmint, lavender, verbena, thyme, and lemon thyme can all be used to replace the vanilla in a traditional crème anglaise. Simply tie up the herbs (like a bouquet garni or in cheesecloth if they are loose) and simmer them with the milk.

Caramel

Crème anglaise can be prepared with caramel syrup instead of sugar. Prepare a caramel, using 25 percent more sugar than normally called for in the crème anglaise (see the discussion of caramel sauces, page 567). Prepare a caramel syrup by dissolving the still-hot caramel in a small amount of water and then combining the resulting syrup with the hot milk for the crème anglaise.

Nuts

The two most common nut flavorings for crème anglaise are hazelnut and almond. Bitter almonds are unavailable in the United States because of the cyanide they contain. For this reason most chefs use almond extract, paste, or praline to impart the full flavor of bitter almonds.

The flavor of hazelnuts is best imparted using hazelnut praline, which is available from suppliers of imported foods. If imported hazelnut praline is unavailable, it can be prepared by cooking coarsely chopped hazelnuts in plain caramel for a minute or two, pouring the hot mixture onto an oiled marble, letting it cool and solidify, and pounding it with a rolling pin to prepare nougatine. The nougatine is then coarsely chopped with a knife and ground for 5 to 10 minutes in a food processor.

Spices

Cinnamon and cloves are often found in sweet desserts, but it is surprising how rarely other spices are used. Ginger (infuse fresh ginger in hot milk; combine powdered ginger with the egg yolks) is magnificent, as is a mixture of saffron and cardamom, a flavor combination used in India for ice cream.

The best way to experiment with flavoring with spices is to make small amounts of individual infusions, using ½ cup (125 milliliters) of milk and 1 teaspoon (5 milliliters) of spice for each and then combining the infusions to devise interesting flavor combinations.

Truffles

The flavor of black truffles has an amazing affinity for sweet, creamy desserts, including crème anglaise. Infuse ¾ ounce (20 grams) of grated or finely julienned fresh truffles (first sliced on a Japanese-style mandoline, then julienned with a knife) in a hot mixture of 1 cup (250 milliliters) milk and 1 cup (250 milliliters) heavy cream. Convert the infusion into a crème anglaise by cooking with 6 egg yolks in the usual way. Do not strain. Serve with poached or caramelized fruits. This crème anglaise can also be turned into ice cream; use only half as much heavy cream (and half again as much milk), or the ice cream may contain tiny lumps of congealed fat.

Alternative Sweeteners

Crème anglaise can be made with honey or maple syrup (great when flavored with bourbon) instead of sugar. When substituting either of these, use 1¼ cups (300 milliliters) to replace 1 cup (200 grams) of white sugar.

SABAYONS

Sabayons are among the few sauces in which the character of the wine used in preparation is not lost. They are delicious even when prepared with ordinary white wine, but when distinctively flavored wines are used, they are magnificent. Because of the acidity contained in wine (even sweet wines), a well-made sabayon will always have a nervous, vinous edge that makes it the perfect accompaniment to fruits and fruit pastries. If not made too sweet, it is also a good foil for a glass of dessert wine.

Even though the recipe that follows contains less sugar than classic versions, the amount of sugar should be decreased even more when sweet wines are used in its preparation. When Marsala is used, the sabayon becomes a traditional Italian zabaglione. Although traditional sabayons are prepared with wine as the only flavoring, some chefs like to flavor the sabayon with fruit brandies or liqueurs after it has cooled. Although the techniques are the same, sabayons, which always contain sugar, should not be confused with savory sabayons, or the preliminary stage in the preparation of emulsified egg sauces.

SABAYON

YIELD: 6 CUPS (1.5 LITERS)

egg yolks	12	12
sugar	1½ cups	300 grams
white wine	2½ cups	625 milliliters

1. Whisk together the egg yolks and sugar in a saucepan with sloping sides.
2. Pour in the wine and whisk the mixture continuously over medium heat. The sabayon will expand and become fluffy. As soon as it begins to lose volume, or if the bottom of the pan becomes visible while whisking, remove it from the heat. Whisk it for 15 seconds more to prevent it from curdling.
3. Transfer the sabayon to a bowl and cover it with plastic wrap to prevent a skin from forming. See the photograph in the color plates.

Variations

Although almost any wine can be used to make a suitable sabayon, white wines with good acidity and a distinctive character will give subtlety and nuance to the sauce. Many recipes suggest making sabayon sauce with Champagne, which is delicious. It is best to use a mature (even slightly madeirized) French Champagne, but since this is rarely practical, a good-quality Coteaux Champenois (see page 77) will produce excellent results. Do not substitute a sparkling wine other than Champagne. If Champagne is unavailable or too expensive, it is better to substitute a good-quality still wine.

Chablis, Vouvray (demi-sec), Riesling (German or Alsatian), Gewürztraminer, and Muscadet will all make interesting sabayon sauces. Sweet wines can also be used: Sauternes, late-harvest Rieslings (including German Beerenauslese and Trockenbeerenauslese), Muscat de Beaumes de Venise, and madeirized wines (Madeira, Marsala, and sherry) will all impart their own character and distinction to the sauce.

Sabayon can also be flavored with fruit brandies, such as Calvados, Poire William, or kirsch, after it has cooled; fruit purées and coulis (equal parts coulis and sabayon); and spices, first infused in a small amount of water or cream and strained into the sabayon. It can also be lightened by folding it with an equal volume of whipped cream.

CHOCOLATE SAUCES

Most chocolate sauces are made by combining melted chocolate with varying proportions of heavy cream, butter, egg yolks, or other liquids. The amount of each of these ingredients depends on the desired consistency of the sauce and whether the sauce is being served hot or cold.

Bittersweet (sometimes called semisweet) chocolate is the type of chocolate most often called for in chocolate sauce recipes, but other chocolates can be substituted and the recipe modified if bittersweet is unavailable. Always use the best-quality European chocolate.

When melting chocolate, make sure that all the utensils are perfectly dry. Even a drop or two of liquid will cause several ounces (60 grams) of chocolate to pull together into a lumpy mass. Once this occurs, extra liquid has to be added to the chocolate (at least 1 tablespoon/15 milliliters of liquid per ounce/30 grams of chocolate) to thin it out. In most sauce recipes this is not a problem because some type of liquid is usually added anyway. Chocolate is also sensitive to heat and will scald at relatively low temperatures. For this reason, it is best to heat chocolate in a double boiler when it is being melted alone. Chocolate can also be easily melted in a microwave oven. Place the chocolate in a microwave-safe dish and heat on the high setting. Allow 1 minute for the first ounce (30 grams) of chocolate, an additional 10 seconds for each additional ounce (30 grams). Heat until almost melted, stirring once, and then stir until smooth.

In addition to the following recipes, chocolate-flavored crème anglaise (page 562) can also be used as a chocolate sauce, especially when a less rich sauce is needed for fruits or fruit pastries or if the sauce is to be served cold.

GANACHE

This is the simplest and one of the best chocolate sauces. It can be made with different proportions of chocolate and liquid; equal parts heavy cream and bittersweet chocolate are most common for frosting cakes or for a chocolate filling for candies, where the ganache needs to be stiff. For chocolate sauce, a higher proportion of liquid can be used, or some milk can be substituted for the cream. In this recipe the ganache is finished with a small amount of butter to give it an appealing sheen. If the sauce is being used for ice cream (which causes it to get very thick), thin it to the appropriate consistency with an extra ½ cup (125 milliliters) of milk or cream.

YIELD: 1 QUART (1 LITER)

bittersweet chocolate (see Note)	1 pound	500 grams
heavy cream or crème fraîche	1 cup	250 milliliters
milk	1 cup	250 milliliters
butter	2 ounces	60 grams

1. Chop the chocolate into medium-size chunks.
2. Combine the cream and milk in a 2-quart (2 liter) saucepan and bring to a simmer.
3. As soon as the cream and milk come to a simmer, remove from the heat and add the chunks of chocolate.
4. Let the chocolate sit in the liquid for 5 minutes, and then stir the mixture with a rubber spatula until it is perfectly smooth.
5. Stir in the butter. See the photograph in the color plates.

Note: When using bitter (baking) chocolate, substitute 10 ounces (300 grams) of bitter chocolate and ¾ cup plus 2 tablespoons (175 grams) of granulated sugar for the bittersweet chocolate. Dissolve the sugar in the cream while the cream is heating. Make sure it is completely dissolved before adding the chocolate.

Flavoring Ganache

Ganache can be flavored at the end with liquid, such as spirits or extracts, added to taste. Ganache can also be flavored by infusing flavorings such as vanilla beans, orange zests, mint leaves, or ground coffee into the cream-milk mixture and then straining them out before the chocolate is added.

CHOCOLATE BUTTER SAUCE

Chocolate butter sauce has a richer texture and a more luxurious sheen than ganache. The liquid in this recipe can be anything with which the sauce might be flavored, such as strong coffee, brandy, whiskey, or liqueur; water can also be used for a plain chocolate flavor.

YIELD: 1 QUART (1 LITER)

bittersweet chocolate (see Note)	1 pound	500 grams
liquid	1½ cups	375 milliliters
butter	6 ounces	175 grams

1. Gently melt the chocolate with the liquid in a double boiler or in a heavy-bottomed saucepan over very low direct heat.
2. When the liquid and chocolate are combined and the mixture is perfectly smooth, add the butter, one-fourth at a time. Continue adding the butter until it is all worked into the sauce and the sauce is smooth and shiny.

Note: If using bitter (baking) chocolate, use 10 ounces (300 grams) of chocolate and dissolve ¾ cup plus 2 tablespoons (175 grams) of granulated sugar in 6 tablespoons (90 milliliters) of water before combining it with the chocolate.

White Chocolate

White chocolate can be substituted in either of the preceding recipes. It is even more sensitive to heat than dark chocolate because of the milk solids it contains. White chocolate that has been overheated will coagulate irreversibly. When preparing ganache with white chocolate, grate the white chocolate or chop it very finely. Let the heavy cream cool to 120°F (50°C) before stirring in the chocolate.

If preparing white chocolate butter sauce, carefully monitor the temperature of the liquids and melting chocolate. Do not let the temperature exceed 120°F (50°C).

White chocolate is extremely sweet, lacking the bitter flavors that balance the sweetness of dark chocolates. White chocolate sauces are best flavored with fruit brandies (eaux-de-vie) such as kirsch, framboise, or mirabelle.

CARAMEL SAUCES

The easiest way to prepare caramel is to simply stir granulated sugar in a heavy-bottomed saucepan over medium heat. When the sugar melts and turns deep brown, add water, cream, or fruit juice to dissolve the caramel into a sauce.

Many recipes for caramel suggest that the sugar first be dissolved in water and that any crystals that form on the inside of the saucepan be continuously brushed off with a pastry brush to prevent the sugar from recrystallizing. Both of these steps can be eliminated by simply melting the sugar without liquid. The most important precautions to follow when preparing caramel in this way are to stir the mixture continuously, and do not use too high a heat; otherwise the sugar will burn rather than caramelize evenly.

Because liquid caramel is burning hot (320°F/160°C), it must be combined with other liquids when it is used to flavor a sauce. Some recipes add heavy cream to the hot caramel, which dissolves the caramel and simultaneously reduces the cream. Other recipes first add water, fruit juice, or fruit purées to the caramel to dissolve it and then serve it as is or finish it with cream, butter, or both. Caramel sauces are often flavored with vanilla, but bourbon or malt whiskey can be used with excellent results.

CARAMEL CREAM SAUCE

YIELD: 2 CUPS (500 MILLILITERS)

granulated sugar	1 pound	500 grams
heavy cream	1 quart	1 liter
vanilla extract or other flavoring (optional)	2 teaspoons	10 milliliters

1. Melt the sugar in a 4-quart (4 liter) heavy-bottomed saucepan or copper poêlon. (A large saucepan or poêlon is necessary because the cream boils up when added to the caramel.) Stir the sugar constantly over medium heat with a wooden spoon until any lumps have melted. Continue stirring until the caramel is a deep reddish brown.
2. Standing back from the saucepan, add half the cream. The cream will boil vigorously and dissolve the hot caramel. When the boiling slows down, add the rest of the cream.
3. Whisk the sauce until the caramel is thoroughly dissolved in the cream. Check the consistency of the sauce and reduce it slightly if necessary. Add the vanilla extract or other flavoring if desired.

Caramel Butter Sauce

Caramel butter sauce is prepared in the same way as caramel cream sauce except that the heavy cream is replaced with 2 cups (500 milliliters) of water, fruit juice, coffee, or other flavored liquid, and the mixture is reduced to a syrup. It is then finished with 4 ounces (125 grams) of butter plus the vanilla extract. Interesting flavor combinations can be invented by infusing the water that is added to the sugar with spices, such as cloves and star anise. The butter can also be omitted and the sauce served simply as a caramel syrup.

BUTTERSCOTCH SAUCE

Butterscotch is similar to caramel sauce except that butter is cooked along with the sugar, so that the milk solids caramelize and impart the characteristic flavor of noisette butter (Beurre Noisette, page 412) to the sauce. Some recipes use brown sugar to give the sauce a deeper color and flavor, but brown sugar also tends to obscure the flavor of the butter, which is what makes butterscotch sauce so delicious.

This recipe uses a caramel base that is cooked a second time with butter. Cream is added near the end to emulsify the butter.

YIELD: 1 QUART (1 LITER)

granulated sugar	1 pound	500 grams
water	2 cups	500 milliliters
butter	4 ounces	125 grams
heavy cream	½ cup	125 milliliters
vanilla extract	2 teaspoons	10 milliliters

1. Prepare a caramel by melting the granulated sugar in a 4-quart (4 liter) heavy-bottomed saucepan (large enough to prevent boiling over). When it is a deep reddish brown, stand back and pour in half the water.
2. When the water has stopped boiling, add the rest of the water and the butter. Cook the mixture to the soft-ball stage (see Note).
3. Add the cream and the vanilla extract. Continue to simmer the sauce until it attains the desired thickness.

Note: To judge when sugar syrup has reached the soft-ball stage (234° to 240°F/112° to 116°C), dip the back of a spoon into the syrup and then quickly into a glass of cold (but not iced) water. Pinch the end of the spoon between two fingers. The syrup should form a gum-like mass on the end of the spoon.

PEAR-BUTTERSCOTCH SAUCE

This sauce is the natural outcome of caramelizing pears with sugar and butter. Pear-butterscotch sauce could be described as an integral dessert sauce. Pears prepared in this way are an exciting alternative to poached pears.

YIELD: 12 SERVINGS

pears	6	6
lemon	½	½
granulated sugar	1 cup plus 2 tablespoons	225 grams
butter	5 ounces	150 grams
heavy cream	1 cup	250 milliliters

poire william (optional)	to taste	to taste
raspberry coulis (optional; opposite)		
whipped cream (optional)		

1. Peel the pears, cut them in half lengthwise, and remove the cores with a paring knife. Rub them with the half lemon.
2. Spread the pear halves in a single layer in a heavy-bottomed pot. Do not leave any section of the pot bottom uncovered or the sauce will burn.
3. Sprinkle the pears with the sugar and the butter, cut into large chunks.
4. Bake the pears in a 375°F (190°C) oven until they soften and begin to brown slightly. This can take anywhere from 15 minutes to 1 hour, depending on the ripeness of the pears. Remove them from the pot with a slotted spoon.
5. When the pears are cooked, the butter should be clear and the sugar should be lightly caramelized on the bottom of the pot. If not, cook the mixture on top of the stove until the liquids on the bottom are well browned.
6. Pour in the cream while the pot is still hot. Whisk the mixture while scraping the bottom of the pot to dissolve the caramelized sugar.
7. Strain the sauce and let it cool slightly. It can be flavored with Poire William to taste if desired.
8. Serve the sauce over the hot pears. Raspberry coulis and whipped cream may be served alongside if desired. See the photograph in the color plates.

FRUIT SAUCES

Fruits can be used to prepare the simplest and most satisfying of dessert sauces. Although they can be sweetened to taste, their natural acidity makes them an excellent accompaniment to sweet desserts. The most straightforward fruit sauces are simple fruit purées. For a slightly more sophisticated version called a *coulis*, the purée is strained to eliminate seeds or fragments of peel.

Purées and coulis are prepared in different ways, depending on the type of fruit. Some fruits, such as raspberries or strawberries, can be simply forced through a strainer with a ladle or wooden spoon. Other fruits, such as ripe pears and melons, will be easier to strain if they are first puréed in a food processor or blender. Some firm fruits, such as underripe pears or apples, must be stewed with water and sugar before they are puréed or strained.

The flavor of fruit purées and coulis can be adjusted depending on the foods they are accompanying. When served with sweet desserts such as ice creams, an unsweetened fruit purée provides a welcome contrast. For less sweet desserts, such as brioche or certain fruit tarts, a sweetened fruit coulis may provide the appropriate sauce. Some chefs may decide to go even further and finish a fruit coulis with cream or butter, to produce a richer and fuller-textured sauce. When sweetening fruit coulis and purées, always prepare a sugar syrup with granulated sugar rather than adding the sugar directly to the purée, where it will take longer to dissolve. The sugar syrup should then be added to the coulis to taste; the amount will vary depending on the ripeness and natural acidity of the fruit. Most fruit coulis are improved by adding a small amount of lemon juice (oddly, this is true even for coulis that are initially acidic).

When good-quality ripe fruit is used to prepare purées and coulis, little needs to be done to improve their flavor. On the other hand, a purée or coulis made from underripe or out-of-season fruit can sometimes be improved by adding a small amount of appropriate-flavored fruit brandy, such as kirsch, framboise, or mirabelle. These flavorings should be added only when the fruit purées and coulis are cool, because heat quickly causes the volatile fruit flavors of these brandies to evaporate.

When fresh berries are out of season, coulis and purées can be prepared with frozen berries. There are also some excellent commercially available frozen purées, which are especially practical for out-of-season or tropical fruits. Quality varies; some of these purées have been cooked (which destroys much of their finesse) or contain too much sugar, so a bit of comparative testing is advisable before settling on a particular brand.

Raspberry Coulis

Force 2 cups (500 milliliters) of raspberries through a strainer with a ladle or large wooden spoon. When using frozen raspberries, make sure they are completely thawed before straining. To eliminate the tiny seeds, the coulis can be strained a second time through a chinois. Do not try to strain the raspberries through a chinois initially, as too much force may damage the fragile mesh screen. Adjust the flavor and consistency of the coulis with sugar syrup or plain water (when it needs to be thinned without being made any sweeter) and lemon juice. This technique can be used for strawberries, blueberries, black currants, and other soft berries. If any of the berries are hard or underripe, they can be puréed first in a food processor.

Cranberry Coulis

The preparation of cranberry coulis is similar to that for other berries, except that the cranberries must be cooked to soften them before they are strained. Put the cranberries in a heavy-bottomed saucepan with enough water or sugar syrup to cover, and simmer them for 20 to 30 minutes, until they are soft. Strain them and adjust the flavor with sugar syrup or water. Cranberry coulis is extremely acidic and almost always needs to be sweetened. When left on the sour side, it is excellent served with hot sweet desserts such as vanilla soufflé or bread pudding. This same technique can be used with fruits that need to be softened before they can be strained, such as underripe apricots and red currants.

Pear Coulis

Peel and core the pears and rub the cut sides with half a lemon. Poach them in a sugar syrup (equal parts sugar and water by weight) until they are soft. Purée them in a food processor and strain. Sweeten the pears with the syrup used for poaching.

Kiwi Coulis

Kiwis should not be puréed in a food processor before being strained. A food processor or blender causes the small black seeds to break open, giving the purée a peculiar bitter flavor. Crush the peeled kiwis in a bowl with a large wooden spoon and then force them through a strainer. To eliminate the seeds (which can be attractive), strain the mixture a second time through a chinois.

APPENDIX

THE RELATIVE THICKENING POWER OF LIAISONS

The chart that follows shows how much liaison is needed to thicken various cooking liquids, and how much of a thickener is necessary for the finished sauce to have a given thickness.

The leftmost column lists example liquids and sauces. To the right of the example liquids column are four columns that show the thickening power of different starches: flour, cornstarch, arrowroot, and potato starch. The numbers in these columns show how many ounces of the starch need to be added per quart of liquid (such as stock, milk, or water) to arrive at the thicknesses illustrated in the leftmost column.

Next to the four starch columns are four columns that illustrate the thickening power of egg yolks when used in different ways. The first two, cold crème anglaise and hot stock thickened with egg yolks alone, illustrate how many egg yolks are needed per quart of liquid to arrive at a given thickness. The second two columns, labeled Mayonnaise and Hollandaise, show what thickness these sauces will have when diluted with a given amount of cooking liquid. For example, in the Mayonnaise column, a classic mayonnaise containing 30 percent liquid will have approximately the same consistency as heavy cream.

The next column (Cream) shows the consistency of heavy cream when it is reduced by a given percentage. Notice that cream reduced by 40 percent is only slightly thicker than unreduced heavy cream but that as reduction approaches 50 percent, the cream thickens considerably.

The Butter column shows how butter added to a cooking liquid acts as a thickener. The figures in this column may vary considerably depending on the water content of the butter. Notice that as a mixture approaches 100 percent butter, the sauce breaks.

The thickening power of nut butters varies depending on the type of nut, but cashews are among the most effective and consistent as liaisons. This column shows the number of ounces of finely puréed nuts (nut butter) required to thicken a quart of liquid.

The last column illustrates the thickening power of highly reduced tomato purée. Notice that tomato purée in the example column is almost as thick as a thick béchamel.

A FEW THOUGHTS ABOUT WINE

People often ask me what to drink with this or that dish, and my answer leaves them looking as though they wish they'd kept their mouths shut. The flavor of wines and foods is so subjective—no one's reaction to a specific combination is the same—that a simple recommendation is fraught with uncertainty.

573

Relative Thickening Power of Liaisons

Examples	Flour (oz/qt)	Corn-starch (oz/qt)	Arrowroot (oz/qt)	Potato Starch (oz/qt)	Crème Anglaise (cold) yolks/qt	Egg Yolks/Stock (hot) yolks/qt	Mayonnaise % liquid	Hollandaise % liquid	Cream % reduct	Butter %	Cashews oz/qt	Tomato Purée % liquid
Water												
Stock												
Heavy Cream					6	6	30	30	0	70	2	
Beurre Blanc		0.5	0.5		8	8		15		80		
Light Béchamel	1			0.5	12	12	20	10	40	90	3	70
Thick Crème Anglaise		1	1		16	16				95	4	60
Medium Béchamel				1	20		10	0	50	breaks		40
Hollandaise	2	1.5	1.5								5	
Tomato Purée	3	2	2	1.5							6	0
Thick Béchamel									55			
Soufflé Base	3.5			2					65 breaks			
Mayonnaise							0					

Although it is true that on occasion a specific wine will enhance the subtleties of a particular dish in an almost magical reverberation of perfumes and flavors (an old Champagne with the Salmon and Truffle Hure on page 369 comes to mind), most of the time the choice of wine has more to do with the mood, the wines (if any) that come before or after, the succession of dishes, the formality of the setting, and of course, budget.

I remember a period when I was drinking a lot of very special wine at dinners hosted by wine professionals. Some of the wines were so rare and lovely that to this day I feel privileged to have tasted them. But I remember what a relief it was to sit at a meal where only a simple inexpensive wine was being served—what a pleasure to drink without having to swirl and sniff and think. Perhaps because many of us grew up in an environment where wine drinking was reserved for special occasions or formal dinners, we often forget that wine's first role is as a simple beverage. Instead of just drinking, eating, and enjoying, we reverently sniff and sip and all too often try to show off what we know. And although some of this may enhance our enjoyment of the finest wines, it can detract from the pleasures of a simple convivial meal by distracting us from the real business at hand: conversation with friends or family, and hearty and happy eating. So my first question when recommending a wine or wines is to ask what the setting will be and who will be there. An informal picnic or an outdoor barbecue requires wine that doesn't need a lot of thought, that goes down easily and refreshes, and that doesn't contain too much alcohol, so people can drink a lot without drinking too much. On these occasions I recommend inexpensive simple-tasting wines because people aren't going to be paying much attention to the wine while they're passing around plates of barbecued chicken and potato salad. If too expensive or complex a wine is served, there is always the danger that it will go unappreciated. As a host this may cause resentment, not a feeling conducive to happy conviviality. I often serve a simple Beaujolais, slightly chilled, or occasionally a commune Beaujolais such as a Juliénas or a St. Amour for the extra fruit they may offer, not because of a subtle complexity that demands attention. If I'm having more than a couple of people, I may also serve a white, often an inexpensive Italian Pinot Grigio with plenty of crisp acidity to keep everyone refreshed. I often may serve just red wine, but I almost never serve only white.

As meals become more formal, the question of wine and food pairing becomes more complex. The real purpose of formality and ritual should be to minimize needless distraction and to focus the diners' attention on the food and drink in an environment that's conducive to conversation. Wines that are perfect at a picnic may not fit in a more formal setting because too much attention will be focused on them and they may suddenly seem frivolous and uninteresting. I remember such an instance at a three-star restaurant in Paris. A friend and I had just spent a week in Paris, and having both realized that we were drastically over budget, decided that we would have one last extravagant meal but would compromise by ordering the least expensive wines. So instead of Chablis and red Burgundy or Bordeaux we had Sancerre and Beaujolais. Well, Sancerre and good Beaujolais are wines I'd drink happily every day, and, partly because they're no longer bargains, they're wines I never take for granted. But they didn't work. It wasn't that their flavors didn't go with the food, but the wines somehow seemed clumsy, overly straightforward, and out of place in the Baccarat glasses and next to the subtle succession of dishes and refined sauces.

But let's examine a meal somewhere in between a picnic and a French three-star restaurant. At all but the most casual dinners I serve at least two wines for the simple reason that it's more fun drinking two wines than one and, other than having a few more glasses to wash, no more work or expense. Even in a restaurant when I'm having dinner with only one other person I search the list for two half bottles (difficult in most places) instead of one whole. (Most restaurants serve an assortment of wines by the glass, but with a half bottle there's less worry about the condition of the wine and there's the lovely ritual of opening and pouring. American waiters also have the bad habit of pouring wines by the glass behind the scenes instead of pouring at the table.) At more elaborate dinners, I may serve as many as four wines, but rarely more.

The first decision when orchestrating a meal is whether first to choose the foods or the wines. Most of us decide what to cook (or order) and then set out to find an appropriate bottle or two. It's also possible to work in reverse: Decide what to drink first and then set out to prepare foods that put the wine(s) in the best light. This latter approach makes good sense when we're confronted with a rare or special bottle. In this instance, not only must the foods that accompany the star bottle be carefully selected but those wines that precede and follow must be well chosen too. It's useful to think of the meal as establishing the context for the most important wine; everything possible must be done to show the star bottle at its best. Let's imagine, for example, a meal designed to accompany a mature bottle of Bordeaux, say, a 1970 Château Lynch-Bages or an equivalent wine from a similar vintage. Instead of immediately thinking about what foods to serve with the Lynch-Bages, it's more helpful to decide on the wines that come before it. To show the Lynch-Bages at its best, the wines that precede it should establish a context within which the Lynch-Bages will shine. They should also be similar enough that when guests finally arrive at the Lynch-Bages, its flavors don't catch everyone off guard. In other words, I would serve a similar but less distinguished wine, perhaps a Pauillac (or at least a Médoc) from a younger vintage, perhaps even a younger Lynch-Bages. Such a wine establishes a context of flavors (in this case, of Bordeaux), a jumping-off point, and gives the diners the opportunity to sharpen their sensitivity to this particular palette of flavors. (Many of us have noticed how a wine seems to grow more complex and begins to reveal nuances of flavor after it has sat in the glasses for ten or fifteen minutes. Although much of this is due to the wine having had a chance to breath, it still happens when a wine has been decanted well before dinner and has had plenty of time for its flavors to open. My own theory is that our noses fatigue to the broader, more obvious flavors and aromas in the wine and allow more subtle qualities to emerge. The result is a kind of layered effect, when as our senses fatigue to one aroma, another emerges.) In this way, as the diners have begun to appreciate the wine leading up to the Lynch-Bages, the Lynch-Bages, when finally tasted, will be that much more dramatic because the groundwork has been laid for its greater depth and complexity. Obviously, if the order of these two wines were to be reversed, the lesser wine would be eclipsed and leave everyone craving more of the 1970 Lynch-Bages. Also keep in mind that the relationship between the two wines is relative; in another context, in which, for example, a 1959 Château Latour were the star wine, then the 1970 Lynch-Bages could function as the lead-up wine. This method, of course, doesn't need to be limited to Bordeaux but can be used for virtually any red wine. While there's still some of the first red in everyone's glasses, I like to pour the second red (in another glass of course!) so the wines overlap and allow everyone to compare.

After establishing the two red wines that will lead to and become part of the meal's crescendo, beginning and ending wine(s) need to be thought out. In addition to the principles that hold true when pairing two reds, any wine served before them must be appropriate for the context of the meal and mustn't interfere or eclipse any wine that follows. If I'm serving an "important" wine, I avoid serving strong cocktails before dinner and instead serve a light white wine, an aperitif wine, or Champagne. When serving a white wine as an aperitif, I like to serve something light and distinctive and often with a trace of sweetness. Gewürztraminer, German Rieslings (Kabinett or Spätlese) are often a pleasant surprise and won't upstage wines that follow. Aperitif wines such as red vermouth, Dubonnet, Suze, Lillet, and Italian Amari are gentle and sweet but can wreak havoc on any wines that follow. A dry fino sherry also makes an excellent aperitif (and it's marvelous with olives). When I do serve aperitif wines or sherry, I make sure that a modest dry white or light red is served at the table before I introduce the two crescendo reds.

Champagne is the aperitif *par excellence,* and if it weren't for its expense, I would serve it more often—it puts everyone in a marvelous humor and almost guarantees a successful dinner party. The one disadvantage of Champagne is that it tends to make white wine that follows it seem a bit flat tasting. There are a couple of ways out of this. Serve a fairly full-bodied white, a light red, or more Champagne during the start of the meal. The Champagne served at the table can be the same as the aperitif Champagne, or a lighter Champagne (perhaps a blanc de blanc) can be served as the aperitif and a fuller-bodied or more complex Champagne such as Krug, Salon, Gosset, or Bollinger R.D. served at the table.

The first wine of the meal should act as a bridge between aperitifs and the main reds. It should set the tone of the meal but be understated enough that it doesn't compete with the reds. This notion of competition applies not only to the actual flavors of the wine (rarely do the flavors of a white overshadow those of a red that follows) but psychologically as well, relative to the prestige and reputation of all the wines being served. The finesse of the opening white must also be considered. A fine Chablis should not be followed by a simple red, because the red, although fuller bodied than the Chablis, will seem coarse and clumsy. When choosing the first wine at a dinner, it's always better to err in the direction of simplicity and understatement.

I always feel that an elaborate dinner is somehow incomplete if the last wine of the evening is one of the reds served with the meat or cheese. For this reason a sweet wine is often a welcome conclusion to a long meal, but many make the mistake of trying to accompany an already sweet dessert with a sweet dessert wine. Sweet sauces such as crème anglaise or sour sauces such as unsweetened fruit coulis will detract from a sweet wine, and are best served after the wines are finished. But sweet wines are marvelous as desserts or very simply accompanied by a few nuts or a fresh ripe pear. They are also surprisingly good with cheese. Port has long been a classic accompaniment to Stilton cheese, but various combinations of Sauternes with other blue-veined cheeses and other firm cheeses can be almost unbelievably delicious. Sweet sherries such as Pedro Ximenez and Muscatel are also marvelous accompaniments to cheese and can be used to provide a conclusive note of sweetness to help bring the meal to a close.

But remember, it's less important to worry about fine-tuning the architecture of a meal than it is simply to make sure everyone has a good time. One approach to establishing an appetizing relationship of wines to each other and to the food is to base the wines and foods on a particular country or region. Burgundy and Bordeaux and, to a lesser extent, California Cabernet Sauvignon and Merlot have become universal special-occasion wines that are drunk all over the world to accompany fine meals, but it's often more fun to drink wines that are grown in the place where the dishes originated. Thus an Italian dinner would be accompanied by Italian wines, a Spanish dinner by Spanish wines, and so on. It's also worthwhile to explore lesser-known regional wines and to use them to accompany a meal of regional dishes. A Gascon dinner, for example, would be accompanied by Gascon wines such as Madiran, Jurançon, and so on, and the whole thing perhaps finished with a good Armagnac.

Pairing Wines and Sauces

White Sauces and Butter Sauces

Because white sauces are usually served with seafood or poultry (blanquette of veal and sauce soubise on veal Orloff being two obvious exceptions), we most often think of accompanying them with white wine. But because of the cream and/or milk these sauces contain, they shouldn't be served with wines that are too fruity or that have too much residual sweetness. The flavors of fruit and milk don't go well together and may end up leaving a slightly bitter impression in the mouth. In other words, avoid Gewürztraminer, Chenin Blanc, and some of the more fruity California Chardonnays. Neither should you choose a wine that is too austere (such as Muscadet, Chablis, or some of the Pinot Grigios from the Veneto), or the white sauce will overwhelm the wine. A Meursault would probably be the best, but a good St. Véran, Pouilly-Fuissé, or Mâcon Villages make good and less-expensive second choices. California Sauvignon Blanc has just the right forthrightness, but without the austerity of a Sancerre, which could be overwhelmed by a cream sauce. A Pouilly-Fumé, softer than a Sancerre, is another good choice.

Although, strictly speaking, butter sauces such as beurre blanc are considered white sauces, butter sauces are often made relatively acidic to counteract the richness of the butter and may require a correspondingly more acidic wine. Muscadet is the natural choice for beurre blanc not only because it has the necessary acidity but it comes from the same region and, at least until recently, was often the wine that went into the sauce. The acidity of Chablis or Sancerre or a Côte Chalonnaise is also welcome next to seafood served with beurre blanc.

Sauces based on crustacean butter and sauces derived from crustacean cooking liquids are among the most complex-tasting of seafood butter and "white" sauces and are best accompanied by a fairly complex white wine. Meursault, or a Puligny- or Chassagne-Montrachet are ideal, but a complex although not overwhelmingly woody or fruity California Chardonnay, or a mature white Graves, would also fit the bill.

Brown Sauces

Because brown sauces almost inevitably function as foils for meat, they're usually served with red wines. The wine should be chosen according to both the depth of flavor of the sauce and in accordance with its luxuriousness and regional traditions, if any. A simple steak topped with a dollop of marchand de vin butter could easily be accompanied with any red wine full enough to keep up with the flavors of the sauce (in this case, the melting compound butter). A Beaujolais Villages, a simple Bordeaux (perhaps a Côtes de Blaye or a Fronsac), a Zinfandel or a regional red wine (Cahors comes to mind) would all make sense, especially if the steak is being served in a relaxed and informal setting.

In terms of flavor alone, those wines served with a steak à la marchand de vin could just as well accompany a steak served with a bordelaise sauce. But again, depending on the formality of the setting and the occasion, slightly more luxurious wines might make better sense. A cru bourgeois Bordeaux or even a classified growth might replace the Côtes de Blaye, a full-bodied commune Beaujolais (perhaps a Morgon), the Beaujolais Villages, and maybe a California Cabernet, or Merlot, the Zinfandel.

Perhaps because it is made without stock and is traditionally served with poached eggs, a meurette sauce is a red wine sauce usually served in relatively informal settings. Yet because meurette sauce is from Burgundy, it's only natural to think of serving Burgundy to drink. But not all Burgundy need be old, rare, or expensive. Strictly speaking, Beaujolais counts as Burgundy, but most of us associate Burgundy with the expensive wines of the Côte d'Or. Wines from the Côte Chalonnaise (south of the Côte d'Or), such as Mercury or Givry, made from Pinot Noir, make good compromises. American Pinot Noir, especially those that are more Burgundy-like from Oregon and Santa Barbara, also make a natural accompaniment.

Because a sauce rouennaise (a bordelaise sauce finished with puréed duck livers or sometimes foie gras) is richer and more deeply flavored than a bordelaise sauce, it requires a relatively complex wine. And because rouennaise sauce hardly constitutes everyday fare, it will do well served with a rather special bottle or two. The gaminess of the liver makes Burgundy the natural choice—in an ideal world, a fine commune or vineyard wine from the Côte d'Or—but a softer Bordeaux, perhaps a Saint-Émilion or a Pomerol, would also work magic. Less luxurious but by-no-means-shabby possibilities might be a mature Rhône (Châteauneuf du Pape, Hermitage, Cornas, St. Joseph, or even a good Côtes du Rhône), a red Loire (a mature Chinon or Bourgeuil), or a Cahors.

Because brown sauces based on fortified wines are often slightly sweet, avoid accompanying them with wines containing large amounts of tannin or youthful acidity, or the wine will taste harsh. California Merlot, Cabernet Sauvignon, and Zinfandel, because of their softness, richness, and relatively low acidity, and Spanish red wines (such as Rioja and Ribera del Duero), because of their softness and full body, also work well.

Poivrade sauces, so wonderfully complex, make natural foils for deep and complex wines. Because of their peppery flavor, Rhône wines, or Rhône-style California wines (such as Bonny Doon's Cigare Volant) and Australian wines (wines labeled Shiraz are made from the Rhône grape, Syrah) come naturally to mind. If the poivrade sauce (or grand veneur or Diane) is being served with game, consider a Burgundy or California Pinot Noir.

Lastly, sauces containing truffles should provide occasions for serving our best wines. The aroma and flavor of truffles have a magical affinity for the bouquet of old wines, and although I hesitate to make overly specific wine recommendations, I can't help but remember an old Château La Mission Haut-Brion, its earthy aroma a suave tangle of berries and truffle, served with a well-truffled sauce Périgueux.

Integral Meat Sauces

The principles used for pairing wines with classic brown sauces and integral meat sauces are much the same, except that integral sauces (other than the jus from a luxurious roast), are often the result of simple homespun cooking versus the more complex classic brown sauces, which are more common to restaurant cooking. Integral sauces derived from stews, slow braises, and deglazed pans, often suggest simpler wines with more emphasis on how and where the dish is being served. When food is being served in a wine-making region, it seems natural to cook with and serve the local wines. On the other hand, there may be meals at which it is desirable to evoke the flavors and rituals of another place in a kind of gustatory armchair traveling. If we live in California, we'll probably drink mostly California wines and use them in our cooking, but on occasion serving wines from other places will evoke memories of past meals and travel and provide a welcome break from our everyday drinking habits. It's also interesting and fun to mix wines up—perhaps serving an Italian wine at the same time, or at least at the same meal, as a California wine made in a similar style.

It's also possible to adapt some integral sauces to the wines and the style of the meal and to point the diner to a regional or national culinary tradition with a simple garniture or deviation in the dish itself. For example, when serving a coq au vin in the Napa valley, the dish itself can be altered to give it a California character (such as making it a coq au Zinfandel and finishing the sauce with California brandy) and to make it seem more in keeping with California wines. The coq au vin can also be adapted to the setting and given a local character by changing the traditional Burgundian garniture of pearl onions, bacon lardoons, and mushrooms, to something such as spring California vegetables, or the local wild mushrooms.

Pasta Sauces

Because pasta dishes incorporate such a wide range of flavors and ingredients, it's impossible to generalize about which wine to serve. The natural inclination is to serve Italian wines with pasta, but this is more out of habit and in memory of past meals than it is for any absolute combination of flavors. Still, it is often true that wines and dishes from the same regions have an almost magical synergy. With this in mind, it's often best to serve a traditional pasta dish with a wine from the same region—for example, Chianti with dishes from Tuscany and wines such as Barbera, Barbaresco, or Barolo with dishes from the north. In many cases, however, an Italian wine region will produce only white or red wine, so it may be difficult to have both from the same region.

When pairing wine with pasta, many of the same principles apply as when matching wines with other foods: The flavors of the dish, the formality of the meal, and the succession of wines should all be considered. When serving a pasta course, Italian style, as a first or second course (following antipasti), a single wine—a simple Chianti perhaps—might well accompany the whole thing. At a more formal dinner, an Italian white wine (if not a regional white wine, then one of Italy's better-known whites, such as Orvieto or Soave Classico or a Pinot Grigio from the Veneto or Friuli-Venezia Giulia regions) might accompany the pasta and then be followed nicely by a red with the main course. Serving a light red with the pasta and a fuller red with the main course is also possible. (This succession of pasta to main course is an opportunity to pair two reds in ascending order of complexity: for example, a lighter-style Chianti followed by a more mature riserva or perhaps a Brunello, or a Barbera followed by a Barbaresco, and so on).

Asian Sauces

Deciding what wines to serve with Asian dishes can stump even the most experienced wine drinkers. Most give up and serve Gewürztraminer, which for some reason (the translation of its name, perhaps?) is considered spicy. Because of its delicate, floral fruitiness, Gewürztraminer is one of the worst wines to serve with assertive and full-flavored dishes. Not that all Asian dishes are assertive: A Chinese chicken dish, for example, may be as delicate and subtle as a chicken fricassée and may require the very same wine.

Admittedly, some Asian dishes—Thai curries come to mind—are impossible to accompany with delicate or complex wines. One solution is to think of the wine as just a simple refreshing beverage and serve an inexpensive well-chilled white wine with plenty of acidity and not too much alcohol—a light Pinot Grigio or QBA German Riesling perhaps (anything with too much finesse will be wasted). But when it comes to more delicate dishes—Japanese seafood dishes served in a dashi-based sauce, Peking duck, or simple stir-fries—it's worth giving serious attention to the wines. Although most of the basic foods in Asian cooking are similar to or the same as those used in Western cooking, Asian cooks do rely heavily on certain problematic ingredients. Ginger, cilantro, chiles, and sweet sauces (such as hoisin sauce) can easily dominate or at least interfere with delicately flavored wines. Hot chiles are hopeless, but dishes containing cilantro can be well accompanied by a full-bodied Sauvignon Blanc. Sweet sauces—or sweet-and-sour sauces—can be a problem in both Asian and Western cooking (for example, duck à l'orange) and can easily make an accompanying white wine taste acidic and fruitless. If the sauce isn't too sweet, a moderately sweet wine—perhaps one based on Chenin Blanc such as a Vouvray demi-sec or even moëlleux, Savennières, Bonnezeau, or Coteaux du Layon—provides enough matching sweetness without seeming cloyingly sweet in the middle of a meal. Sherry is another surprisingly delicious accompaniment to dishes that have a slight sweetness or have been flavored with ginger. A cool manzanilla-style sherry can be drunk like any wine (in wine glasses—not those depressing little sherry glasses) and doesn't have quite as much alcohol content as a fino. Richer sherries, such as dry olorosos, palo cortados, and amontillados, are probably all worth experimenting with.

Rhône wines, because of their full body and spicy aromas, are often good accompaniments to dishes that are peppery or redolent of ginger and garlic. If experimenting with a particular dish, a Côtes du Rhône from a good maker may be a good place to start.

Dessert Sauces

Dessert wines are more popular than ever and in many restaurants are offered by the glass. Perhaps because of the name "dessert" wines, many people assume that these sweet wines are designed to accompany dessert. But because a sweet dessert wreaks havoc on any wine, sweet or otherwise, it's safer to think of dessert wines *as* dessert.

It is possible to accompany a dessert wine with fruit (such as fresh pears, figs, apricots, and peaches) or undersweetened tarts or desserts made from these fruits. But it's also important to remember that the dessert must always be kept less sweet than the wine. Fruit coulis, provided they are neither too tart nor too sweet, are the only dessert sauces that won't wreck sweet wines. And although some claim that port is wonderful with chocolate, it's much better with cheese. I also think that chocolate desserts are best left to themselves (chocolate truffles and petits fours, however, are surprisingly good with after-dinner drinks).

Some people try to eliminate the "dessert-wine problem" by serving Champagne. Champagne is certainly a cool and welcome refreshment after a long dinner, but its delicate austere fruit is destroyed next to an even slightly sweet dessert. I prefer to heed Raymond Oliver's advice, in his book *La Cuisine,* to serve Champagne an hour or so after the end of the meal, when its fresh liveliness can be better appreciated.

GLOSSARY

ASPIC (GELÉE)

Meat or fish stock clarified with additional meat or fish or egg whites. Sometimes a gelatinous element, such as a calf's foot or commercial gelatin, is added. Aspic is virtually the same as cold consommé, except that it contains more gelatin (natural or otherwise).

BARD

To wrap in barding fat.

BARDING FAT

A thin sheet of fatback used to wrap meats to be roasted or braised, to keep them moist and prevent certain parts (such as the breasts of poultry) from overcooking.

BEURRE MANIÉ

A paste made of equal parts butter and flour, used to thicken sauces and braising liquids. The ingredients for beurre manié are the same as those for a roux. The only difference between the two is that beurre manié is not cooked before it is added.

BLANQUETTE

Traditionally, a French veal stew made by poaching the veal in stock or water, binding the poaching liquid with roux, and finishing it with a liaison of egg yolks and cream. The term sometimes appears on contemporary menus to mean any stew of meat, fish, or vegetables that is presented in a white sauce containing cream.

BOUQUET GARNI

A bundle of herbs, tied up with string, used for flavoring stocks and other flavorful liquids. A classic bouquet garni contains varying amounts of fresh parsley, thyme, and bay leaf. Some recipes include a stalk of celery or leek greens, but these are usually superfluous, especially if the liquid has been flavored with mirepoix. The contents of a bouquet garni can also be changed to give ethnic or regional nuances to a cooking liquid.

BRAISE

When applied to meat: to cook gently in a relatively small amount of liquid. Although there are many approaches to braising, most braises fall into one of two categories: (1) *brown braising*, wherein meat is browned and cooked for a prolonged period, until the fiber breaks down and the meat becomes tender; (2) *white braising*, wherein the meat is not browned and is cooked only long enough to heat it to the appropriate internal temperature, in the same way as roasts. *See also* Casserole-braising; *Cuillère*, à la; *Étuver*; Poêler; Pot-roasting. When applied to fish: to cook whole fish gently in enough liquid to come halfway up the sides. Braised fish is usually started on the stove and finished in the oven. Fish fillets cooked in this way are referred to in French as having been cooked *en sauce*.

BRAISIÈRE

A vessel for braising meats. Also, brown beef stock; the term is rarely used in this sense in modern kitchens.

BROTH

A flavorful liquid made by simmering meat or seafood in water. Broths and stocks are virtually the same thing. The word "stock" simply implies that it is being saved (stocked) for another preparation, such as a sauce or soup. *See also* Stock.

BROWN STOCK

A broth made by browning the main ingredients (usually meat, meat bones, or poultry) on the stove or in the oven, before adding liquid.

CASSEROLE-BRAISING

A method for cooking poultry and meats in a close-fitting covered casserole; also known as *en cocotte*.

Casserole-braising can be carried out with fat alone (*poêlage*) or with a small amount of liquid (*étuver*).

CHAUD-FROID
Aspic that is made opaque by adding ingredients such as cream, egg yolks, or béchamel. There are both brown and white chauds-froids.

CHIFFONADE
A style of cutting, into thin shreds. To cut leafy greens into a chiffonade, the leaf is usually rolled up on itself and cut with a chef's knife.

CIVET
A stew, usually containing red wine, that is finished and thickened at the end with blood.

COULIS
Originally in pre-classic French cooking, a concentrated stock made by repeatedly moistening meats with stock, double stock, and so on. When well made, it has a natural demi-glace consistency and intense flavor. It was the predecessor to classic demi-glace, which contains roux. Also, a purée or stewed mixture, usually of tomatoes or fruit, that has been strained to eliminate seeds, peels, and other solids.

CUILLÈRE, À LA
A method of brown-braising meats for a long period, until they are so soft they can be served with a spoon.

DEGLAZE
To add liquid to a sauté or roasting pan to dissolve the sucs; an important stage in making integral sauces and stews.

DEGREASE
To remove fat from the top of a sauce or from a sauté or roasting pan before deglazing.

DEMI-GLACE
Reduced stock having the consistency of a light syrup. In classic French cooking (circa 1900), demi-glace was prepared by reducing espagnole to a lightly syrupy consistency. The term is used here to refer both to the classic method and to any stock, braising liquid, or poaching liquid that has been reduced to a lightly syrupy consistency. Natural demi-glace obtained by repeated moistenings of meat with more stock or by reduction alone and containing no liaison is sometimes referred to as "natural" demi-glace or coulis.

EMULSION
A mixture of two mutually insoluble liquids, such as oil and water. Emulsions are stabilized by certain ingredients, such as egg yolks and mustard. Almost all sauces contain some kind of emulsion.

EN COCOTTE
See Casserole-braising.

EN SAUCE
Method of braising fish fillets and converting the braising liquid into a sauce, using a variety of methods.

ESPAGNOLE
Originally, highly concentrated meat stock lightly bound with roux. Until recently, this sauce was the cornerstone of French sauce making. Recipes vary over the centuries, but the use of roux, originally introduced as an alternative to the extravagant coulis of pre-classic French cooking, is common to all of them. Escoffier's espagnole contains tomatoes (a later addition) and an enormous quantity of meat. Over time, espagnole has been so continuously bastardized and cheapened—a typical version consists of boiled burned bones colored with tomato paste and thickened with roux—that chefs have completely abandoned it as a brown sauce base.

ESSENCE
A concentrated stock or extract of a flavorful ingredient such as mushrooms, truffles, celery, or leeks. In nineteenth-century French cooking, essences were used as flavorings for classic sauces. Today they are sometimes used as light sauces in themselves, perhaps lightly bound by whisking in a small cube of butter before serving or emulsified with other ingredients for contemporary vinaigrettes.

ESTOUFFADE
A stew in which the pieces of meat are first browned in fat before moistening, usually with white or red wine. Also, a concentrated brown stock made with both beef and veal; the term is rarely used in this sense in modern kitchens.

ÉTUVER
In the strictest and simplest sense, to cook in a covered container. In most recipes, étuver implies cooking covered with a very small amount of liquid. Sometimes spelled *étouffer*. Dishes cooked *à l'étuver* are called *étouf-*

fades (not to be confused with *estouffade*, a type of stew).

FAIRE TOMBER À GLACE

The process of reducing a liquid, such as a stock or a sauce, until the sucs caramelize and separate from any fat contained in the liquid. This is a useful technique for eliminating fat from liquids and enhancing the flavor of a sauce base by caramelizing the juices. The process can be repeated several times by adding additional stock after each caramelization. *See also* Pincer.

FRICASSÉE

A dish of either chicken or veal that is cut into small pieces, gently sweated in butter without coloring, sprinkled with flour, moistened with stock, and finished with a cream and egg yolk liaison. The term is used herein in a wider, more generic sense, to distinguish this cooking method from sautés and simple poaching (*see* Blanquette).

FUMET

Today, a fish stock. In nineteenth-century cooking, the term referred to small amounts of concentrated stock made from game or poultry and used to finish mother sauces, such as espagnole or velouté.

GARNITURE

In English, a decoration, such as a sprig of parsley, usually superfluous, placed on the side of a plate or platter. In French, the entire accompaniment to a preparation of meat or fish. Much of the vocabulary of classic French cuisine exists only to describe variations in garniture.

GLACE (GLACE DE VIANDE, GLACE DE POISSON)

Stock or poaching liquid that has been reduced (usually by about 90 percent) to the consistency of a syrup when hot and the texture of hard rubber when cold.

GRAVY

A jus that has been thickened with flour, either by adding flour to the roasting pan before deglazing or thickening in a saucepan with roux.

HURE

Meat, fish, or vegetables presented in aspic in a terrine. A typical *hure* is served in slices, but it can also be prepared in individual molds, which makes it possible to use a more fragile and hence more appealing jelly. In classical French cooking, an *hure* presented in individual molds would be called an aspic.

INFUSE

To soak or steep an ingredient in a liquid, to flavor a sauce or cooking liquid. Tea is a common infusion.

INTEGRAL SAUCES

Sauces derived directly from the juices released during the cooking of the main ingredients. The liquid from stews and braises, the "jus" or gravy from a roast, the reduced or bound poaching liquid for seafood or meat are all integral sauces. *See also* Nonintegral sauces and Simple sauce.

JUS

The natural juices released by meat during roasting. In some instances a jus remains in the bottom of the roasting or dripping pan and is simply degreased and served. In other instances, the drippings are caramelized, the fat poured off, and the pan deglazed.

LARD

To insert strips of fat into meats to keep them moist. The French recognize two methods: larding proper (*larder*), which consists of inserting strips of fatback into the pieces of meats to be braised with a larding needle (*lardoire*); and interlarding (*piquer aux lardons*), which consists of sewing tiny strips of fatback into the surface of meats with a second type of larding needle (*aiguille à piquer*).

LARDOON

Strip of pork breast. Lardoons cut from smoked bacon should be blanched for 10 minutes to eliminate their smoky taste when they are used as a garniture for stews, braises, and sautés. When taken from lean salt pork, lardoons are sometimes rendered or used along with vegetables in a mirepoix. Strips of fatback cut into lardoons are used to lard meats to be braised. Also spelled *lardon*.

MARINATE

To surround meats and fish with aromatic liquids (marinades) before cooking. In certain sauces (such as poivrades), the marinade is later used as the flavor base.

MATIGNON

An old term used to designate a coarsely chopped mirepoix containing ham.

MINESTRA

In Italian cooking, this is simply a broth lightly garnished with vegetables or pasta. Surrounding stuffed pasta with broth is a light and elegant alternative to tossing the pasta with a thicker sauce.

MIREPOIX

A mixture of chopped onions, carrots, and celery, used as a flavor base for sauces, braises, and roasts. Older recipes also include cubes of lean salt pork or ham.

MONTER AU BEURRE

To swirl butter into a sauce as a final liaison.

NAGE, À LA

Method of poaching and presenting foods, usually fish and seafood, in a court-bouillon surrounded by the aromatic vegetables used in its preparation. The term *nage* is sometimes used in contemporary kitchens to mean a court-bouillon.

NAP (NAPPER)

To coat. Sauces are said to nap when they leave an opaque coating on the back of a spoon. Until twenty years ago, all sauces were required to nap. The use of sauce spoons now allows the saucier to make thinner sauces.

NAVARIN

A stew of young lamb garnished with pearl onions and potatoes, or a spring version, *à la printanière*, served with carrots, turnips, peas, new potatoes, and pearl onions. The term has recently been used to describe any stew (including fish or shellfish) served with a garniture of spring vegetables.

NONINTEGRAL SAUCES

Sauces that are not derived directly from the cooking juices of the main ingredient. Nonintegral sauces may be based on a stock or its derivatives such as demi-glace or meat glace (stock-based sauces are designed to emulate integral sauces), or on completely unrelated ingredients, as in salsa. *See also* Integral sauces.

PINCER

To heat meats and vegetables to be braised in order to release and caramelize their juices before they are moistened. This preliminary caramelization enhances the flavor of braised meats and certain stews but must be carried out carefully to avoid burning the juices. Nowadays, ingredients for stocks and braised dishes

are usually browned separately or in stages, so there is less risk of over- or undercooking.

POACH

To cook foods gently, completely covered in barely simmering liquid. Poaching differs from braising only in the amount of liquid used.

POÊLER

To "roast" in a covered pot with butter and sometimes aromatic vegetables. The closest English translation of this very specific French culinary term is "pot roasting," although many people add liquid to a pot roast, which turns it into a braise. The term *en cocotte* is also sometimes used to describe this method.

POT AU FEU

A French country dish of poached beef. Traditionally, it is served in two courses: the first, a bowl of broth; the second, the poached meat itself. In recent years, chefs and menu writers have used the term more liberally to mean an assortment of meat or fish served surrounded by an unbound broth or poaching liquid.

POT ROASTING

This confusing term is used to describe a range of often conflicting techniques. In some cases it describes *poêlage*, which is the most legitimate because the technique can at least be construed as a kind of roasting. Most of the time, however, the term is used to describe braising in a covered pot.

PURÉE

Solid ingredients that have been worked with a blender, food processor, or mortar and pestle until they have a smooth, even texture or consistency. Some purées require straining to eliminate any remaining solids. Strained purées are sometimes called coulis.

REDUCE

The process of simmering a liquid to evaporate water and concentrate its flavor.

ROUX

Equal parts flour and butter cooked to varying degrees; the most traditional liaison for sauces.

SABAYON

A dessert sauce made by whisking egg yolks, wine, and sugar over heat. Also, the preliminary stage in preparing hot emulsified egg yolk sauces, such as hollandaise. This sabayon is made by whisking eggs and liquid over heat.

SALMIS

Usually applied to game and poultry, a salmis combines two cooking methods, roasting and braising. The bird is partially roasted before the meat is removed and finished in a sauce made at the last minute from the carcass.

SAUTÉ

To cook meat, fish, or vegetables in a pan over high heat so the surface lightly browns and caramelizes. A small amount of oil or other fat is usually used. Not to be confused with frying, in which the food is completely or partially submerged in hot oil. Also, a method, mostly used for poultry, veal, or rabbit, in which the meat is cut into pieces and cooked completely in butter or another fat on top of the stove or in the oven. The meat is then removed and the pan deglazed for the sauce base. The pieces of poultry should not come in contact with liquid until they are napped with the sauce when served. *See also* Fricassée and Stir-fry.

SIMMER

To bring a liquid to a temperature just below a boil. The surface of a simmering liquid should barely move. Most recipes referring to boiled foods really mean simmered foods.

SIMPLE SAUCE

A sauce made of ingredients that are neither derived from stocks nor from the foods with which they are being served is called a "simple" sauce. Salsa, chutney, and pesto are examples of simple sauces. *See also* Integral sauces and Nonintegral sauces.

SINGER

To add flour to the pan used for browning meat before liquid is added. This method is often used for thickening meat stews.

SOFFRITTO

The Italian version of mirepoix, soffritto may also contain garlic, pancetta, and herbs such as parsley, sage, or rosemary. *See also* Mirepoix.

STEW

Meat, fish, or vegetables cut into pieces and cooked in a small amount of liquid. The only difference between a stew and a braise is that the ingredients for a stew are cut into smaller pieces.

STIR-FRY

Virtually the same as sautéing except that the ingredients are stirred instead of tossed. Many cooks assume that stir-frying must be done in a wok, but an iron skillet works just as well. *See also* Sauté.

STOCK

More or less gelatinous and aromatic liquid, prepared by poaching meat, fish, or bones in water or more stock. Virtually the same as a broth or bouillon, except these terms imply that the liquid will be served as is, whereas stock implies eventual use in another preparation. *See* Broth, Brown stock, White stock.

SUCS

The savory juices released by meats and fish during cooking. In most cases the term refers to the caramelized juices left on the bottom of a sauté or roasting pan before deglazing.

SWEAT

To cook slowly in butter, usually covered, without browning; usually applied to vegetables.

WHITE STOCK

A stock made by adding liquid directly to meat, seafood, or vegetables without browning the ingredients first. White stocks are used when a clear, very pale liquid is required. *See also* Brown stock.

SOURCES

Most of the ingredients, cooking supplies, and equipment I've discussed in this book are available in local supermarkets and specialty kitchen and food shops. However, some of them may be harder to find than others, and the Internet and mail-order sources can often provide them.

What follows here is a list of some of the more frequently sought items. The numbers following each item on the list correspond to specific purveyors that can supply them for you (see "Purveyors," page 589). When multiple numbers follow an ingredient or tool, it means that the item is available from several sources.

Anchovies 8, 32, 38, 40

Artichokes 9, 15

Asian ingredients 16, 19, 20, 22, 27

Beans 14, 29, 31

Benriner vegetable slicer 2, 19, 20, 27

Chiles, dried and powdered 3, 4, 7, 9, 10, 11, 21, 29, 31

Chiles, fresh 3, 11, 21, 29

Chinese ingredients 19, 27

Dairy products, organic 9

Demi-glace (concentrated broths) 5, 6, 8, 23

Duck confit 6

Duck and goose fat 6

Foie gras 6, 8

General pantry, including ethnic 5, 8, 9, 18, 40

Herbs, dried 5, 9, 21, 28, 31, 40

Herbs, fresh 9, 12, 21

Indian ingredients 11, 18

Japanese ingredients 20, 22

Kitchen equipment 2, 30, 36

Korean ingredients 16, 27

Mandoline 2, 30, 36

Meats 6, 8, 9, 26

Mexican ingredients 3, 13, 21, 31

Middle Eastern ingredients 18

Mushrooms, dried 6, 21, 32, 38

Mushrooms, fresh 21

Nut oils 8, 32, 40

Olive oils, unfiltered 32, 38

Onions, Vidalia 1

Pasta, dried 8, 38, 40

Potatoes 21, 25

Preserved pork products 6, 8, 26, 33

Produce, specialty and organic 9, 13, 21, 39

Rice 8, 11, 18, 19, 20, 22, 29, 38, 40

Seeds, bean and vegetable 17, 24, 34, 35, 37

Spices 5, 11, 18, 28

Thai ingredients 5, 19, 22, 27

Truffles 6, 8

Vinegars 8, 32, 38

PURVEYORS

1. Bland Farms
   PO Box 506-622
   Glennville, GA 30427
   (800) 843-2542
   www.blandfarms.com

2. Bridge Kitchenware
   711 Third Avenue
   New York, NY 10017
   (212) 688-4220
   www.bridgekitchenware.com

3. Bueno Foods
   2001 Fourth Street S.W.
   PO Box 293
   Albuquerque, NM 87103
   (505) 243-2722
   www.buenofoods.com

4. The Chile Shop
   109 East Water Street
   Santa Fe, NM 87501
   (505) 983-6080
   www.thechileshop.com

5. The CMC Company
   PO Box 322
   Avalon, NJ 08202
   (800) CMC-2780
   www.thecmccompany.com

6. D'Artagnan
   280 Wilson Avenue
   Newark, NJ 07105
   (800) 327-8246
   www.dartagnan.com

7. Dave's Gourmet
   2000 McKinnon Avenue
   Bldg 428, #5
   San Francisco, CA 94124
   (800) 758-0372
   www.davesgourmet.com

8. Dean & DeLuca
   560 Broadway
   New York, NY 10012
   (800) 221-7714
   (212) 431-1691
   www.deandeluca.com

9. Diamond Organics
   PO Box 2159
   Freedom, CA 95019
   (888) 674-2642
   www.diamondorganics.com

10. The El Paso Chile Company
    909 Texas Avenue
    El Paso, TX 79901
    (915) 544-3434

11. Foods of India
    (Sinha Trading Co.)
    121 Lexington Avenue
    New York, NY 10016
    (212) 683-4419

12. Fox Hill Farm
    443 West Michigan Avenue
    Parma, MI 49269
    (517) 531-3179
    www.foxhillfarm.us

13. Frieda's Incorporated
    4465 Corporate Center Drive
    Los Alamitos, CA 90720
    (800) 421-9477
    www.friedas.com

14. Gallina Canyon Ranch
    144 Camino Escondido
    Santa Fe, NM 87501
    (505) 982-4149

15. Grant Artichoke
    11241 Merritt Street
    Castroville, CA 95012
    (408) 633-2778

16. Han Ah Rheum Market
    25 West 32nd Street
    New York, NY 10016
    (212) 695-3283
    Also in New Jersey, Georgia,
    and Washington, DC area

17. Johnny's Selected Seeds
    Foss Hill Road
    Albion, ME 04910
    (207) 437-4301
    (877) 564-6697
    www.johnnyseeds.com

18. Kalustyan's
    123 Lexington Avenue
    New York, NY 10016
    (212) 685-3451
    www.kalustyans.com

19. Kam Man Food Corp.
    200 Canal Street
    New York, NY 10013
    (212) 571-0330

20. Katagiri
    224 East 59th Street
    New York, NY 10022
    (212) 755-3566
    www.katagiri.com

21. Melissa's Brand World
    Variety Produce
    PO Box 21127
    Los Angeles, CA 90021

(800) 468-7111
(213) 588-0151
www.melissas.com

22. Mitsuwa
595 River Road
Edgewater, NJ 07020
(201) 941-9113
shop.mitsuwa.com/eng/
eindex.php
Also in Chicago area and
California

23. More Than Gourmet
115 West Barges Street
Akron, OH 44311
(800) 860-9392
www.morethangourmet.com

24. Native Seeds Search
2509 North Campbell Avenue,
#325
Tucson, AZ 85719
(520) 327-9123
www.nativeseeds.org

25. New Penny Farms
PO Box 448
Presque Isle, ME 04769
(800) 827-7551

26. Niman Ranch
www.nimanranch.com

27. Oriental Food Market
2801 West Howard Street
Chicago, IL 60645
(312) 274-2826

28. Penzey's Spices
PO Box 1448
Waukesha, WI 53187

(414) 574-0277
www.penzeys.com

29. Phipps Country Store
and Farm
2700 Pescadero Road
Pescadero, CA 94060
(650) 879-0787
www.phippscountry.com

30. J. B. Prince Co., Inc.
36 East 31st Street
New York, NY 10016
(212) 683-3553
www.jbprince.com

31. Rancho Gordo
1755 Industrial Way, #26
Napa, CA 94558
(707) 259-1935
www.ranchogordo.com

32. Rosenthal Wine
Merchant Ltd.
PO Box 658
Pine Plains, NY 12567
(518) 398-1800
www.madrose.com

33. Salumi Artisan Cured Meats
309 Third Avenue South
Seattle, WA 98104
(206) 621-8772
www.salumicuredmeats.com

34. Seeds of Change
PO Box 15700
3209 Richard's Lane
Santa Fe, NM 87506
(505) 438-6500
www.seedsofchange.com

35. Shepherd's Garden Seeds
30 Irene Street
Torrington, CT 06790
(860) 482-3628
www.whiteflowerfarm.com

36. Sur La Table
84 Pine Street
Seattle, WA 98102
(800) 243-0852
www.surlatable.com

37. Vermont Bean Seed Company
6 Garden Lane
Fairhaven, VT 05743
(802) 273-3400

38. Vivande Porta Via
2125 Fillmore Street
San Francisco, CA 94115
(415) 346-4430
www.vivande.com

39. Walnut Acres
PO Box 8
Walnut Acres Road
Penns Creek, PA 17862
(800) 433-3998
www.walnutacres.com

40. Zingerman's
422 Detroit Street
Ann Arbor, MI 48104
(313) 769-1625
www.zingermans.com

BIBLIOGRAPHY

Ali-Bab. *Gastronomie Pratique*. Flammarion, 1928

Anderson, Burton. *The Wine Atlas of Italy*. Simon and Schuster, 1990

Andoh, Elizabeth. *An American Taste of Japan*. William Morrow, 1983

Andrews, Colman. *Catalan Cuisine*. Atheneum, 1988

Apicius. *L'Art Culinaire*. Translated by Jacques André. Société d'Edition "Les Belles Lettres," 1987

Aron, Jean-Paul. *Le Mangeur du XIXe Siècle*. Robert Laffont, 1973

Artusi, Pellegrino. *The Art of Eating Well*. Translated by Kyle Phillips III. Random House, 1996

Asher, Gerald. *On Wine*. Random House, 1982

———. *Vineyard Tales*. Chronicle Books, 1996

Bayless, Rick. *Authentic Mexican*. William Morrow, 1987

———. *Mexican Kitchen*. Scribner, 1996

Beauvilliers, A. *L'Art du Cuisinier*. 2 volumes. Paris, 1814

Beef and Veal. Time-Life Books, 1979

Beeston, Fiona. *Mes Hommes du Vin*. Plon, 1989

Bertolli, Paul, with Alice Waters. *Chez Panisse Cooking*. Random House, 1988

Bhumichitr, Vatcharin. *The Taste of Thailand*. Pavillion Books Ltd., 1988

Bisson, Marie-Claude. *La Bonne Cuisine Française*. Solar, 1988

Blanc, George. *Ma Cuisine des Saisons*. Robert Laffont, 1984

Bocuse, Paul. *La Cuisine du Marché*. Flammarion, 1976

Boni, Ada. *Italian Regional Cooking*. Dutton, 1969

Bonnefons, Nicholas de. *Les Delices de la Campagne*. Paris, 1679

Bourin, Jeanne. *Les Recettes de Mathilde Brunel*. Flammarion, 1983

Boussel, Patrice. *Les Restaurants dans la Comédie Humaine*. Editions de la Tournelle, 1950

Bremzen, Anya Von, and John Welchman. *Terrific Pacific Cookbook*. Workman, 1995

Brennan, Jennifer. *The Original Thai Cookbook*. Putnam, 1981

———. *The Cuisines of Asia*. St. Martin's Press, 1984

———. *One-Dish Meals of Asia*. Times Books, 1985

Brillat-Savarin, Jean Anthèlme. *Physiologie du Goût*. Julliard, 1965

———. *The Philosopher in the Kitchen*. Translated by Anne Drayton. Penguin, 1970

Brown, James. *Fictional Meals and Their Function in the French Novel*. University of Toronto Press, 1984

Bugialli, Giuliano. *Classic Techniques of Italian Cooking*. Simon and Schuster, 1982

———. *Foods of Italy*. Stewart, Tabori and Chang, 1984

Carême, Antonin. *L'Art de La Cuisine Française au XIXe Siècle*. 5 volumes. Paris, 1843–1847

Casas, Penelope. *The Foods and Wines of Spain*. Knopf, 1988

Chang, Wonona W., Helen W. Irving, and Austin Kutscher. *An Encyclopedia of Chinese Food and Cooking*. Crown, 1970

Chiarello, Michael. *Flavored Oils*. Chronicle Books, 1995

Claiborne, Craig, and Virginia Lee. *The Chinese Cookbook*. Lippincott, 1972

———, and Pierre Franey. *Classic French Cooking*. Time-Life International, 1978

Cost, Bruce. *Bruce Cost's Asian Ingredients*. William Morrow, 1988

Courtine, Robert. *Balzac à Table*. Robert Laffont, 1976

———. *Feasts of a Militant Gastronome*. William Morrow, 1974

———. *Zola à Table*. Robert Laffont, 1978

———. *Mon Bouquet de Recettes*. Marabout, 1977

————. *The Hundred Glories of French Cooking*. Translated by Derek Coltman. Farrar, Straus and Giroux, 1973

————, and Céline Vence. Translated and adapted by Philip Hyman and Mary Hyman. *The Grand Masters of French Cuisine: Five Centuries of Great Cooking*. G. P. Putnam's Sons, 1978

Le Cuisinier Gascon. Amsterdam, 1740

David, Elizabeth. *French Provincial Cooking*. Penguin, 1968

————. *An Omelette and a Glass of Wine*. Viking, 1985

————. *Italian Food*. Harper and Row, 1954

Davidson, Alan. *Fish and Fish Dishes of Laos*. Tuttle, 1975

De Croze, Austin. *Les Plats Régionaux de France*. Paris. Reprint, Daniel Morcrette, n.d.

De Groot, Roy Andries. *Revolutionizing French Cooking*. McGraw Hill, 1975

De la Reynière, Grimod. *L'Almanach des Gourmands 1803*. Paris, 1803

Del Conte, Anna. *Gastronomy of Italy*. Prentice Hall, 1987

Delfs, Robert A. *The Good Food of Szechwan*. Kodansha International, 1974

De Rabaudy, Nicolas. *Léonel, Cuisinier des Grands*. Presses de la Renaissance, 1978

Diat, Louis. *Sauces French and Famous*. Dover, 1951

Dictionnaire des Vins. Larousse, 1969

Le Dictionnaire portatif de cuisine. . . . Paris, 1767

Dion, Roger. *Histoire de la Vigne et du Vin en France*. Flammarion, 1977

Dried Beans and Grains. Time-Life Books, 1982

Dubois, Urbain. *Cuisine Artistique*. 2 volumes. Paris, 1988

Dumas, Alexandre. *Grand dictionnaire de cuisine*. Paris, 1873

Duong, Binh, and Marcia Kiesel. *Simple Art of Vietnamese Cooking*. Prentice Hall, 1991

Fisher, Mary Frances Kennedy. *The Art of Eating*. World Publishing, 1954

Foo, Susanna. *Chinese Cuisine*. Chapters Publishing Ltd, 1995

The Food of China. Periplus Editions, 1995

————. *The Cooking of Provincial France*. Time-Life Books, 1968

Franklin, Alfred. *La Vie Privée d'Autrefois: Modes, Moeurs, Usages des Parisiens*. Plon, 1889

Freson, Robert. *The Taste of France*. Stewart, Tabori and Chang, 1983

Gilbert, Philéas. *L'Alimentation et la Technique Culinaire à Travers les Siècles*. Société des Cuisiniers de Paris, 1928

Gouffé, Jules. *Le Livre des Soupes et des Potages*. Hachette, 1875

Gringoire, Th., and L. Saulnier. *Le Répertoire de la Cuisine*. Dupont et Malgat, 1914

Guérard, Michel. *Cuisine Minceur*. Translated by Narcisse Chamberlain. William Morrow, 1976

————. *La Cuisine Gourmande*. Robert Laffont, 1978

Guillot, André. *La Grande Cuisine Bourgeoise*. Flammarion, 1976

————. *La Vrai Cuisine Légère*. Flammarion, 1981

Guy, Christian. *Almanach Historique de la Gastronomie Française*. Hachette, 1981

Haeberlin, Paul et Jean-Pierre. *Les Recettes de L'Auberge de L'Ill*. Flammarion, 1981

Hahn, Emily. *The Cooking of China*. Time-Life International, 1969

Hanson, Anthony. *Burgundy*. Faber and Faber, 1982

Hazan, Marcella. *The Classic Italian Cookbook*. Random House, 1973

————. *More Classic Italian Cooking*. Random House, 1984

Hyman, Philip, and Mary Hyman. "La Chapelle and Massialot: An 18th Century Feud." *Petits Propos Culinaires 2*, 1979

————. "Long Pepper: A Short History." *Petits Propos Culinaires 6*, 1980

————. "Vincent La Chapelle." *Petits Propos Culinaires 8*, 1981

I Secondi con il Pesce. Editoriale Del Drago, 1993

Jaffrey, Madhur. *Flavors of India*. Crown, 1995

————. *A Taste of India*. Atheneum, 1988

Jeffs, Julian. *Sherry*. Faber and Faber, 1961

Kasper, Lynne Rosetto. *The Splendid Table*. William Morrow, 1992

Kennedy, Diana. *The Cuisines of Mexico*. Harper and Row, 1972

————. *The Art of Mexican Cooking*. Bantam, 1989

King, Shirley. *Dining with Marcel Proust*. Thames and Hudson, 1979

La Chapelle, Vincent. *Le Cuisinier moderne. . . .* The Hague, 1742

Lamb. Time-Life Books, 1981

La Varenne, François Pierre de. *Le Cuisinier francois . . . .* Paris, 1651

———. *Le Parfaict confiturier.* . . . Paris, 1667

Le Divellec, Jacques, and Celine Vence. *La Cuisine de la Mer.* Robert Laffont, 1982

Le Manuel des officier de bouche. . . . Paris, 1759

Le Ricette Regionali Italiane. Solares, 1967

Lichine, Alexis. *New Encyclopedia of Wines and Spirits.* Knopf, 1974

Livingstone, John, and Melvin Master. *The Wines of the Rhône.* Faber and Faber, 1978

L.S.R. *L'Art de bien traiter.* . . . Paris, 1674

Lune, Pierre de. *Le Cuisinier ou il est tratté de la véritable méthode de apprester toutes sortes de viandes, gibbier, volatiles poissons tant de mer que d'eau douce.* . . . Paris, 1656

Maffioli, Giuseppe. *La Cucinia Veneziana.* Franco Muzzio, 1982

Manjon, Maite. *The Gastronomy of Spain and Portugal.* Prentice Hall, 1990

Marin, François. *Les Dons de Comus ou les délices de la table.* Paris, 1739

Marks, Copeland, and Aung Thein. *The Burmese Kitchen.* M. Evans and Company, 1987

———. *The Exotic Kitchens of Indonesia.* M. Evans and Company, 1989

Massialot, François. *Le Cuisinier roïal et bourgeois.* . . . Paris, 1691

May, Tony. *Italian Cuisine.* Italian Wine and Food Institute, 1990

Menon. *La Cuisinière bourgeoise.* Paris, 1756

———. *La Science du Maître-d'Hôtel Cuisinier.* Paris, 1739

———. *La Science du Maître d'Hôtel, Confiseur.* Paris, 1749

———. *Les Soupers de la Cour.* . . . Paris, 1755

Miller, Gloria Bley. *The Thousand Recipe Chinese Cookbook.* Simon and Schuster, 1966

Millon, Marc and Kim. *Flavours of Korea.* André Deutsch, 1991

Minchelli, Jean and Paul. *Le Duc: Toute la Cuisine de la Mer.* Olivier Orban, 1986

Montagné, Prosper, and Alfred Gottschalk, eds. *Larousse Gastronomique.* Paris: Larousse, 1938

———. *Larousse Gastronomique.* Translated by Nina Froud, Patience Gray, Maud Mordoch, and Barbara Macrae Taylor. Crown, 1961

Nignon, Eduard. *Eloges de la Cuisine Française.* Piazza, 1933

Nostradamus, Michel de. *Excellent et moult utile opuscule à touts necessaire.* . . . Lyons, 1555

Oliver, Raymond. *Gastronomy of France.* Translated by Claude Durrell. World Publishing, 1967

Olney, Richard. *The French Menu Cookbook.* William Collins Sons, 1975

———. *Simple French Food.* Atheneum, 1974

———. *Yquem.* Flammarion, 1985

———. *Ten Vineyard Lunches.* Interlink Books, 1988

———. *Romanée-Conti.* Flammarion, 1991

———. *Lulu's Provençal Table.* HarperCollins, 1994

Owen, Sri. *Indonesian Food and Cookery.* Prospect Books, 1976

Panjabi, Camellia. *The Great Curries of India.* Simon and Schuster, 1995

Parienté, Henriette, and Geneviève De Ternant. *La Fabuleuse Histoire de La Cuisine Française.* O.D.I.L., 1981

Le Pâtissier françois. Lyons, 1695

Pennin-Rowsell, Edmund. *The Wines of Bordeaux.* Allen Lane and Penguin Books, 1979

Pepin, Jacques. *La Technique.* Simon and Schuster, 1976

———. *La Méthode.* Times Books, 1979

Peterson, James. *Splendid Soups.* Bantam, 1993

Pichon, Jérôme, ed. *Le Ménagier de Paris.* . . . 2 volumes. Paris, 1846

———. and Georges Vicaire, eds. *Le Viandier de Guillaume Tirel, dit Taillevent.* Paris, 1892. Reprint, Edgar Soete, n.d.

Planche, Jean, Jacques Sylvestre, and Jean-Paul Champenier. *Les "Nouvelles" Bases de la Cuisine.* Lanore, 1988

Platina, Barolomeo. *Platine en françoys tresutile et necessaire pour le corps humain qui tract de hôneste volupté* . . . . Translated by Didier Christol. Lyons, 1505

Poulain, René. *Vignes et Vins de France.* Flammarion, 1960

Poultry. Time-Life Books, 1979

Read, Jan. *The Wines of Spain.* Faber and Faber, 1982

Reboul, J. B. *La Cuisinière Provençale.* Tacussel, 1988

Revel, Jean-François. *Un Festin en Paroles.* Pauvert, 1979

Reynière, Grimod de. *Manuel des Amphitryons.* Paris, 1808

Richie, Donald. *A Taste of Japan.* Kodansha International, 1982

Riley, Gilian. *Painters and Food: Renaissance Recipes.* Pomegranate Artbooks, 1993

Robertson, George. *Port.* Faber and Faber, 1978

Robinson, Jancis. *Vines, Grapes, and Wines.* Knopf, 1986

Robuchon, Joël. *Ma Cuisine Pour Vous.* Robert Laffon, 1986

Roden, Claudia. "Early Arab Cooking and Cookery Manuscripts." *Petits Propos Culinaires 6,* 1980

Rojas-Lombardi, Felipe. *The Art of South American Cooking.* Harper Collins, 1991

Root, Waverley. *The Food of France.* Knopf, 1958

———. *Food.* Simon and Schuster, 1980

———. *The Food of Italy.* Random House, 1972

Rouff, Marcel. *La Vie et la Passion de Dodin-Bouffant, Gourmet.* Librairie Stock, 1925

Routier, Nicole. *The Foods of Vietnam.* Stewart, Tabori and Chang, 1989

Roux, Michel. *Sauces.* Rizzoli, 1996

Sahni, Julie. *Classic Indian Cooking.* William Morrow, 1980

———. *Moghul Microwave: Cooking Indian Food the Modern Way.* William Morrow, 1990

———. *Classic Indian Vegetarian and Grain Cooking.* William Morrow, 1985

Sailland, Maurice Edmond (Curnonsky). *Cuisines et Vins de France.* Larousse, 1974

Saint-Ange, E. *La Cuisine de Madame Saint-Ange.* Editions Chaix, Grenoble

Salads. Time-Life Books, 1980

Sauces. Time-Life Books, 1983

Schmitz, Puangkram C., and Michael J. Worman. *Practical Thai Cooking.* Kodansha International, 1985

Seed, Diane. *The Top One Hundred Pasta Sauces.* Ten Speed Press, 1987

Sichel, Peter. *The Wines of Germany.* Hastings House, 1956

Simeti, Mary Taylor. *Pomp and Sustenance.* Knopf, 1989

Simon, Andre L. *The History of Champagne.* Octopus Books, 1971

Sodsook, Victor. *True Thai: The Modern Art of Thai Cooking.* William Morrow, 1995

Sokolov, Raymond. *The Saucier's Apprentice.* Knopf, 1987

Spoerlian, Margeurite. *La Cuisinière du Haut-Rhin.* Mulhouse, 1842. Reprint, Daniel Morcrette, n.d.

Steinberg, Rafael. *The Cooking of Japan.* Time-Life International, 1970

Tannahill, Reay. *Food in History.* Stein and Day, 1973

Tendret, Lucien. *La Table au Pays de Brillat-Savarin.* Librairie Dardel, 1934

Tower, Jeremiah. *New American Classics.* Harper and Row, 1986

Trama, Michel. *La Cuisine en Liberté.* Olivier Orban, 1987

Tridi, Vanna. *Cucina Regionale.* Demetra, 1993

Troisgros, Jean and Pierre. *Cuisiniers à Roanne.* Robert Laffont, 1977

Troisgros, Pierre and Michel. *Les Petits Plats des Troisgros.* Robert Laffont, 1985

Tropp, Barbara. *The Modern Art of Chinese Cooking.* William Morrow, 1982

———. *China Moon Cookbook.* Workman, 1992

Tsuji, Kaichi. *Kaiseki: Zen Tastes in Japanese Cooking.* Kodansha International, 1972

Tsuji, Shizuo. *Japanese Cooking: A Simple Art.* Kodansha International, 1980

Vence, Céline. *Les Recettes du Terroir.* Robert Laffont, 1984

Vergé, Roger. *Ma Cuisine de Soleil.* Robert Laffont, 1977

Viazzi, Alfredo. *Cucina e Nostalgia.* Random House, 1979

Vicaire, George. *Bibliographie Gastronomique.* Paris, 1890. Reprint, Slatkine Reprints, 1983

Walden, Hilaire. *French Provincial Cooking.* HP Books, 1995

Wheaton, Barbara Ketcham. *Savoring the Past.* University of Pennsylvania Press, 1983

———. *L'office et la bouche.* Translated by Béatrice Vierne. Calmann-Lévy, 1984

Willan, Anne. *French Regional Cooking.* William Morrow, 1981

Wilson, C. Anne. "The French Connection: Part I." *Petits Propos Culinaires 2,* 1979

———. "The French Connection: Part II." *Petits Propos Culinaires 4,* 1980

———. "The Saracen Connection: Part I." *Petits Propos Culinaires 7,* 1981

———. "The Saracen Connection: Part II." *Petits Propos Culinaires 8,* 1981

Wolfert Paula. *Couscous and Other Good Foods from Morocco.* Harper and Row, 1973

———. *Mediterranean Cooking.* Ecco Press, 1977

———. *The Cooking of South-West France.* Dial Press, 1983

———. *The World of Food.* Harper and Row, 1988

Young, Wandee, and Byron Ayanoglu. *The Young Thailand Cookbook.* Random House of Canada, 1995

Zaslavsky, Nancy. *A Cook's Tour of Mexico.* St. Martin's Press, 199

INDEX